Essentials of

Biostatistics

For Paramedical and Allied Health Sciences

Anju Dhir

PhD (Micro), MSc (Micro), BSc (Med)

Ex Lecturer (Microbiology & Biostatics)
Shivalik Institute of Nursing
Shimla, Himachal Pradesh

CBS Publishers & Distributors Pvt Ltd

• New Delhi • Bengaluru • Chennai • Kochi • Kolkata • Lucknow • Mumbai
• Hyderabad • Jharkhand • Nagpur • Patna • Pune • Uttarakhand

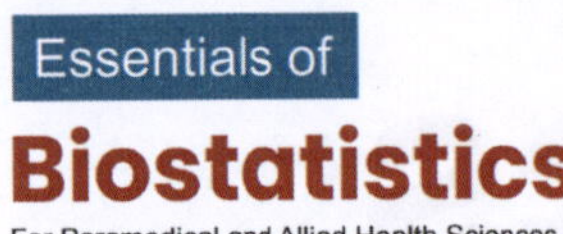

Essentials of
Biostatistics

For Paramedical and Allied Health Sciences

ISBN: 978-81-977500-5-2

Copyright © Author & Publishers

First Edition: 2025

Published by **Satish Kumar Jain** and produced by **Varun Jain** for

CBS Publishers and Distributors Pvt Ltd

4819/XI Prahlad Street, 24 Ansari Road, Daryaganj, New Delhi 110 002, India.
Ph: +91-11-23289259, 23266861, 23266867   Website: www.cbspd.com
Fax: 011-23243014
e-mail: delhi@cbspd.com; cbspubs@airtelmail.in.

Corporate Office: 204 FIE, Industrial Area, Patparganj, Delhi 110 092
Ph: +91-11-4934 4934   Fax: 4934 4935
e-mail: feedback@cbspd.com; bhupesharora@cbspd.com

Branches

- **Bengaluru:** Seema House 2975, 17th Cross, K.R. Road, Banasankari 2nd Stage, Bengaluru-560 070, Karnataka
  Ph: +91-80-26771678/79   Fax: +91-80-26771680   e-mail: bangalore@cbspd.com

- **Chennai:** 7, Subbaraya Street, Shenoy Nagar, Chennai-600 030, Tamil Nadu
  Ph: +91-44-26680620, 26681266   Fax: +91-44-42032115   e-mail: chennai@cbspd.com

- **Kochi:** 68/1534, 35, 36-Power House Road, Opp. KSEB, Cochin-682018, Kochi, Kerala
  Ph: +91-484-4059061-65   Fax: +91-484-4059065   e-mail: kochi@cbspd.com

- **Kolkata:** Hind Ceramics Compound, 1st Floor, 147, Nilganj Road, Belghoria, Kolkata-700056, West Bengal
  Ph: +91-033-2563-3055/56   e-mail: kolkata@cbspd.com

- **Lucknow:** Basement, Khushnuma Complex, 7-Meerabai Marg (Behind Jawahar Bhawan), Lucknow-226001, Uttar Pradesh
  Ph: +0522-4000032   e-mail: tiwari.lucknow@cbspd.com

- **Mumbai:** PWD Shed, Gala No. 25/26, Ramchandra Bhatt Marg, Next to J.J. Hospital Gate No. 2, Opp. Union Bank of India, Noor Baug, Mumbai-400009, Maharashtra
  Ph: +91-22-66661880/89   Fax: +91-22-24902342   e-mail: mumbai@cbspd.com

Representatives

- **Hyderabad**   +91-9885175004
- **Nagpur**   +91-9421945513
- **Pune**   +91-9623451994
- **Jharkhand**   +91-9811541605
- **Patna**   +91-9334159340
- **Uttarakhand**   +91-9716462459

Printed at : Goyal Offset Works Pvt. Ltd. Haryana

About the Author

Anju Dhir, *PhD Microbiology*, is a Former Lecturer, Department of Microbiology at Shivalik Institute of Nursing Shimla, HP. She is a Gold Medallist in Microbiology. She has been in teaching profession for the last 25 years. Her thesis and research papers are published in national and international journals. She is working as Senior Product Manager and Developmental Editor in Health Sciences, CBS Publishers, Delhi.

The author possesses vast knowledge in multiple fields. She has written chapters in book on "Women Writers"; an online book on Indian common krait"; "Applied Microbiology for BSC Nursing students" and "Textbook of Microbiology for Physiotherapy Students". This book on Biostatistics is another milestone in her career as an author. The author's simplified yet practical way of presenting a dry subject like Biostatistics will certainly help the students and researchers.

Preface

This book, **Essentials of Biostatistics for Paramedical and Allied Health Sciences** is designed for professional students in public health, dentistry, nursing, and medicine undergraduate and postgraduate students in nursing, and other biomedical sciences.

The book is arranged in the form of a user-friendly text so as to provide motivation to learn a subject that is perceived to be difficult and dry.

Statistics is not just a series of formulas that students need to know but it is a way to gather the data, to present it, and analyze it in a meaningful manner. The book contains examples and exercises as aids to learn how to use statistical procedures, which are the nuts and bolts of elementary applied statistics.

Unit I is written for professionals and undergraduate students in human health disciplines who need to know about basic biostatistics requirements to benefit from it and get through the exams.

Units II to VII have complete discussion on the way to analyze and interpret the data. The text is supported with examples related to health science. There is an attempt to let the reader be friendly with the statistical analysis with the help of computers as this is need of the hour.

Units VIII and IX are focused on the uses and applications of statistical methods in health sciences.

Unit X discusses various statistical tools and their applications in the health sciences.

"Takeaway boxes" will help the readers to imbibe the summarized points, whereas the "Practical Tips" boxes include tips that will help while analyzing and interpretation of data. "Must Know" boxes include knowledge that is necessary for a reader to know according to the topic under discussion.

The students will be benefited by the supplementary Key Terminology related to Biostatistics.

The Appendices contain many useful tips for a researcher.

The Course coverage ideas (For professional students in public health, dentistry, and medicine; undergraduate and postgraduate students in nursing, and other biomedical sciences)

Course	Chapters																	
	1	2	3	4	5	6	7	8	9	10	11	12	13	14	15	16	17	18
UG courses for health sciences	Yes	Yes	Yes	Yes	Yes	Yes	Yes	Yes	Yes	Yes	Yes	Yes	Yes	Yes			Yes	
PG courses for health sciences	Yes	Yes	Yes	Yes	Yes	Yes	Yes	Yes	Yes	Yes	Yes	Yes	Yes	Yes	Yes	Yes	Yes	Yes

Anju Dhir

Acknowledgments

I thank God for giving me vision and skills to write this book on a subject which is otherwise thought as a dry subject. Without His Blessings, I am nothing.

All the suggestions and critical evaluation by readers and academicians are highly appreciated who took pain to evaluate the content.

I extend my special thanks to **Mr Satish Kumar Jain** (Chairman) and **Mr Varun Jain** (Managing Director), M/s CBS Publishers and Distributors Pvt Ltd for their wholehearted support in publication of this book. I have no words to describe the role, efforts, inputs and initiatives undertaken by **Mr Bhupesh Aarora** [Sr. Vice President – Publishing & Marketing (Health Sciences Division)] for helping and motivating me.

In particular, I would like to thank Mr Shubham Tripathi and Mr Chander Mani for their help in proofreading and typesetting the content, respectively.

Last but not the least, I sincerely thank the entire CBS team for bringing out the book with utmost care and attractive presentation. I would like to thank Ms Nitasha Arora (Assistant General Manager Publishing – Medical and Nursing), Ms Daljeet Kaur (Assistant Publishing Manager) for their publishing support. I would also extend my thanks to Mr Shivendu Bhushan Pandey (Sr. Manager and Team Lead), Ms Surbhi Gupta (Sr. English Editor), Mr Ashutosh Pathak (Sr. Proofreader cum Team Coordinator) and all the production team members for devoting laborious hours in designing and typesetting the book.

Special Features of the Book

Learning Objectives enlist what the students will learn after studying the entire chapter.

Chapter Outline provides a quick glance of the entire chapter in one go.

Illustrations are used to make learning easy for students.

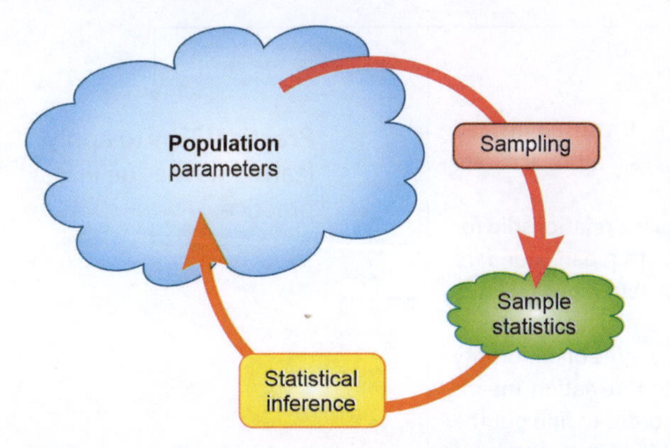

Figure 2.1: The wholesome picture of statistic and parameter

Table 2.1: Comparison of statistic and parameter

Characteristics	Statistic	Parameter
Definition	A characteristic of a small part of the population, i.e., sample.	A fixed measure that describes the target population.
Nature	A variable and known number that depend on the sample of the population.	Parameter is fixed and unknown numerical value.
Meaning	Statistic is a measure that describes a fraction of population.	Parameter refers to a measure that describes population.
Numerical value	Variable and known	Fixed and unknown

Tables provide necessary data in a concise way.

Must Know boxes covering valuable facts are strategically placed to highlight critical information, ensuring readers are well-informed of key concepts and important details.

Must Know

Modifying a distribution by dumping scores or by addition of new scores will generally change the value of the mean and it will affect: Number of scores; Sum of the scores. If a constant value is added to every score in a distribution, then the same constant value is added to the mean. Also, if every score is multiplied by a constant value, then the mean is also multiplied by the same constant value.

Practical Tips

- In both the above given formulae '$n - 1$' is used instead of n in the denominator, because it gives a more accurate estimate of population SD.
- Range and standard deviation may show a relationship for some frequency distributions. Along with mean, standard deviation can describe a frequency distribution in a unique way.
- Small standard deviation means a high degree of uniformity in observations whereas large standard deviation means that the items are widely scattered. In order to find out the dispersion, the order of reliability of different methods is:
  - Interquartile range < mean deviation < standard deviation

Practical Tips to apply learnt knowledge in practice.

Takeaway

$$\text{Mean} = \frac{\text{Sum of all values}}{\text{Total number of values}}$$

Median = Middle value (when the data are arranged in order)

Mode = Most common value

- Central tendency: A score which indicates a position where the center of a distribution tends to be located
- Mean is sum of all scores divided by the number of items
- Median is a score in the middle of arranged data, when the scores are ordered
- Mode is the most frequently occurring score.

Important and summarized facts of respective topic are covered under **Takeaway boxes**.

Detailed **Student Assignment** in the form of exercises in each and every chapter will facilitate structured learning and revision of the material provided in the respective chapters.

STUDENT ASSIGNMENT

LONG ANSWER QUESTIONS

1. What is the significance and scope of statistics?
2. How does statistics help in epidemiological studies?

SHORT ANSWER QUESTIONS

1. Write a short note on variables.
2. What are the applications of statistics in medical field?

MULTIPLE CHOICE QUESTIONS

1. **Branches of statistics include:**
   a. Applied statistics
   b. Mathematical statistics
   c. Industry statistics
   d. Both a and b

2. **Procedures of descriptive statistics and control charts which are used to improve process are classified as:**
   a. Statistical tools
   b. Parallel tools
   c. Serial tools
   d. Behavioral tools

Contents

UNIT I INTRODUCTION

UNIT II MEASURES OF CENTRAL TENDENCY

UNIT III MEASURES OF VARIABILITY

UNIT IV STANDARD NORMAL DISTRIBUTION

UNIT V MEASURES OF RELATIONSHIP

UNIT VI RESEARCH DESIGNS AND THEIR MEANINGS

Contents

UNIT X USE OF COMPUTERS FOR DATA ANALYSIS

Chapter 18 Computers in Data Analysis 349–398

Extra Multiple Choice Questions 399–405

Appendices 407–417

Glossary 419–426

Statistical Tables 427–444

Index 445–451

Unit I

Introduction

UNIT OUTLINE

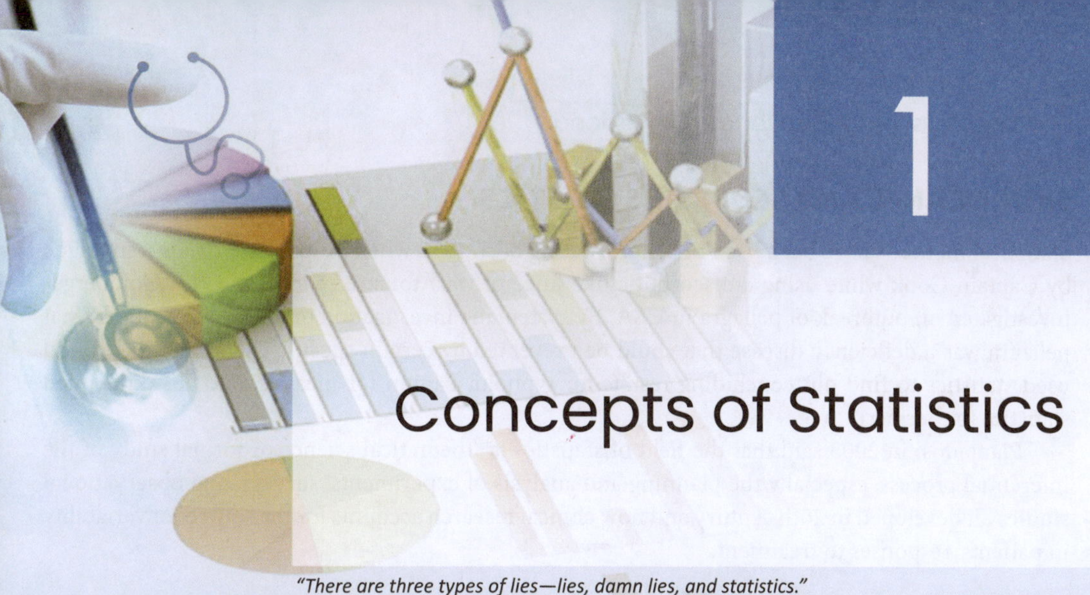

1

Concepts of Statistics

"There are three types of lies—lies, damn lies, and statistics."
—Benjamin Disraeli

LEARNING OBJECTIVES

After the completion of the chapter, the readers will be able to:
- Understand the concepts of data.
- Explain the scope of statistics.
- Know about the significance of data.

CHAPTER OUTLINE

- Introduction
- Types of Statistical Data
- Significance and Scope of Statistics

INTRODUCTION

We are living in the age of information and technology and the statistics is about how the information obtained from various sources, is analyzed and interpreted so as to draw meaningful inferences.

Statistics is a word which is derived from Latin word, 'status' or 'statista'. This word was used in context to political status which indicated toward size of a population and various aspects related to it like marital status, sources of income, etc. Nowadays this word is used to indicate facts and figures of any kind related to health, clinics, businesses, politics or trade. It includes:
- Statistical methods.
- Technique used to collect, analyze and draw inferences from the data.

Calculated values of a data are also known as statistics. Data is obtained when a specific investigation of a problem is taken up and it could be related to any field of study. Mostly two methods generate data:
1. **Counting,** for example, numbers of heart beats.
2. **Measurement,** for example, weight or height of a child.

TYPES OF STATISTICAL DATA

Please note that the types of data and data analysis are discussed in detail in Chapter 3.

SIGNIFICANCE AND SCOPE OF STATISTICS

Statistical methods have been used in history, dating back 1772 when prophylactic trials were made by Captain Cook while using antiscorbutic like juice of wart to cure scurvy. In 1913, Goldberger investigated on outbreak of pellagra in USA. By systematic investigation on diet, he concluded that pellagra was a deficiency disease that could be prevented by certain specific changes in diet. Budd used statistics to find out concluding results for typhoid, Panum for measles, and Takaki applied statistics for beriberi.

Piantadosi in 2005 said that the field of statistics is "theoretical science or formal study of the inferential process, especially the planning and analysis of experiments, surveys, and observational studies". It developed in 20th century and now clinical research accounts for the sources of variability in patients' responses to treatment.

Statistics Helps in Reasonable Decision-Making

The use of statistics allows clinical researchers and others to draw reasonable and accurate inferences from collected information and to make firm decisions in the presence of uncertainty. The expertise in statistical concepts can prevent numerous errors and biases in medical research because statistics:

- Is a science that deals with observational data to obtain reliable results.
- Helps to answer important research questions in a study.
- Enables to understand specified statistical concepts and procedures that could be applied on a particular type of research.
- Based on mathematics are used to analyze data arising from investigations.
- Forms basis for research in almost every field of medical care or research.

Statistics in Research

Data is either qualitative or quantitative and in any case the data is in numbers or it is converted to numbers before drawing a result form this data. A huge amount of numerical data collected from an experiment will have no meaning if it could not give inference. For this purpose, statistical methods are applied. These statistical methods make the data meaningful and an end result is obtained from which a researcher can predict or interpret results with confidence in either answering a present question of research or to predict future strategies.

Statistical Reasoning

It is characterized by the following:

- Forming an objective background for conducting an investigation.
- Placing data and theory on scientific equilibrium.
- Designing data production methods through experimentation.
- Enumerating the effects of chance.
- Estimating systematic and random things.
- Integration of theory and data using formal methods.

Statistics in Medical and Healthcare

- The science of statistics has been used to recognize and describe a particular disease or syndromes.

- It is applied in clinical trials to observe the effectiveness of a particular medicine.
- Many new methods and equipment are introduced from time-to-time. Their uses and efficacy is weighed by using statistics.
- The procedures and interventions used by medical healthcare professional are tested by applying experiments and then analyzed with statistical tools. It helps to take them decision to encourage a procedure; or to withdraw an old intervention.
- The emergence of diseases is a topic of concern and to find out the cause is based on research. Hence, the obtained data is again worked upon by applying statistical methods so as to interpret the results on the basis of statistics.
- The modern methods of statistics like Bayesian approach, Gibbs sampler of Bootstrap and the Cox proportional hazards regression model are applied in field of medicine to get satisfactory answers.

Statistics in Epidemiological Studies

The epidemiological research generates huge data. The geographical distribution of incidence and prevalence of a disease and its relationship with patients' risk factors all comes in the form of data. The interpretations are made by applying statistical methods to make policies in the field of public health and for forecasting the results.

In a nutshell, we can say that:

- Statistics plays a vital rate in processing data related to various fields such as health science, medical science, nursing and clinical trials in pharmacology—used extensively.
- It provides methods when we can define 'normal' or 'abnormal pathological' characters of a body.
- It helps in documentation of medical history of diseases, causes progression and variation among the patients.
- The etiology of health events and determination of related risks are carried out in clinical epidemiology with the help of statistics.
- It measures the accuracy of a diagnostic procedures or clinical approaches commonly used in medical field.

STUDENT ASSIGNMENT

LONG ANSWER QUESTIONS

1. What is the significance and scope of statistics?
2. How does statistics help in epidemiological studies?

SHORT ANSWER QUESTIONS

1. Write a short note on variables.
2. What are the applications of statistics in medical field?

MULTIPLE CHOICE QUESTIONS

1. **Branches of statistics include:**
   a. Applied statistics
   b. Mathematical statistics
   c. Industry statistics
   d. Both a and b

2. **Procedures of descriptive statistics and control charts which are used to improve process are classified as:**
   a. Statistical tools
   b. Parallel tools
   c. Serial tools
   d. Behavioral tools

3. **Scale used in statistics which provides difference of proportions as well as magnitude of differences is considered:**
   a. Satisfactory scale
   b. Ratio scale
   c. Goodness scale
   d. Exponential scale

4. **The stages of a malignant disease (cancer) are recorded using the symbols 0, I, II, III, IV. We say that the scale used is:**
   a. Alphanumeric
   b. Numerical
   c. Ordinal
   d. Nominal

2

Sample and Parameter

"I can prove anything by statistics except the truth."
—George Canning

LEARNING OBJECTIVES

After the completion of the chapter, the readers will be able to:
- Understand sample.
- Discuss the parameter.

CHAPTER OUTLINE

- Introduction
- Statistic and Parameter
- Sample and Parameter

INTRODUCTION

In statistic, we often deal with the terms sample and parameter, which play a vital role in the determination of the sample size. When the results are obtained from the population, the numerical value is attached to it, known as the parameter. On the other hand, if the result is obtained from the sample, the numerical value is called statistic.

STATISTIC AND PARAMETER

When information about a particular population characteristic (for example, the mean) is to be determined, a random sample from that population is taken because it is impossible to measure the entire population. Using that sample, the corresponding sample characteristic can be calculated, which is further used to summarize information about the unknown population characteristic(s).

The population characteristic of concern is called a parameter and the equivalent sample characteristic is the sample statistic or parameter estimate. As statistic is a summary of information about a parameter obtained from the sample, the value of a statistic depends on the particular sample drawn from the population. The statistic is a random quantity (variable) and its values change randomly from one random sample to the next one. The probability distribution of this random variable is called sampling distribution. The sampling distribution of a (sample) statistic is important as it enables a researcher to conclude about the corresponding population parameter that is based on a random sample.

For example, when a random sample is drawn from a normally distributed population, the sample mean is a statistic. The value of the sample mean based on the chosen sample is an estimate of the population mean. Randomly,

> **Must Know**
>
> - The parameter is fixed.
> - The statistic is random (depends on the sample).
> - The interval is random (depends on the statistic).

this estimated value will change if a different sample is taken from same normal population. The probability distribution, which describes those changes, is sampling distribution of the sample mean. The sampling distribution of a statistic states all the possible values of a statistic and tells that how often some range of values of the statistic occurs.

Therefore, a parameter is a number that describes some aspect of a population and a statistic is a number that is computed from data in a sample. Generally, we have a sample statistic and to make inferences about the population parameter under study (Fig. 2.1).

Statistical notations are different for population parameters and sample statistic which are given in Table 2.1.

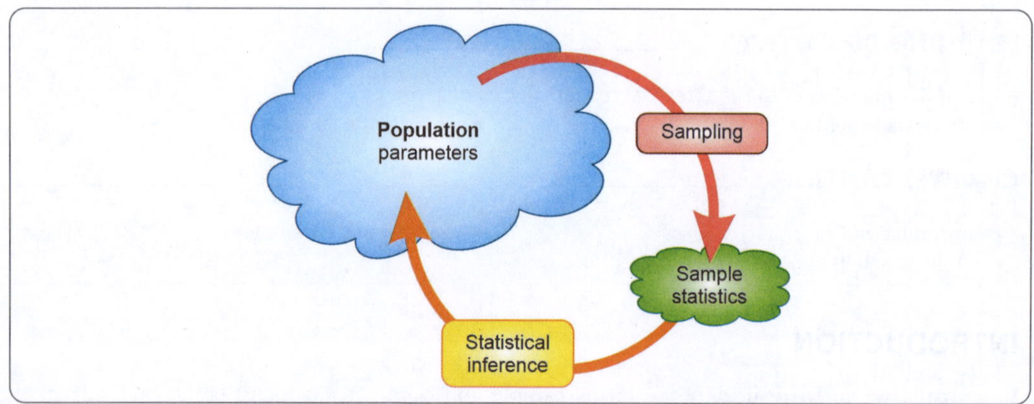

Figure 2.1: The wholesome picture of statistic and parameter

TABLE 2.1: Comparison of statistic and parameter

Characteristics	Statistic	Parameter
Definition	A characteristic of a small part of the population, i.e., sample.	A fixed measure that describes the target population.
Nature	A variable and known number that depend on the sample of the population.	Parameter is fixed and unknown numerical value.
Meaning	Statistic is a measure that describes a fraction of population.	Parameter refers to a measure that describes population.
Numerical value	Variable and known	Fixed and unknown
Statistical notation	$\bar{x}$ = Sample mean	μ = Population mean
	s = Sample standard deviation	σ = Population standard deviation
	$\hat{p}$ = Sample proportion	P = Population proportion
	x = Data elements	X = Data elements
	n = Size of sample	N = Size of population
	r = Correlation coefficient	ρ = Correlation coefficient

> **Practical Tips**
>
> **Question:** In a given sample statistic, what are reasonable values for the population parameter? How much uncertainty surrounds the sample statistics?
>
> **Answer:** It depends on how much the statistics varies from sample to sample.

SAMPLE AND PARAMETER

Sample

Sample can be defined as a small group chosen for study whereas the large group on which this study is generalized is known as population.

Sampling: It is a choosing sample from a population. The field of inferential statistics empowers a researcher to make intelligent guesses about the characteristics of large groups. The sampling gives a way to test assumptions about such groups by using only a small portion of its fellows. Sampling makes a study feasible in limited resources, if a sample is carefully selected. Here, careful selection implies that the group of individuals in a sample has all the selected characteristic under study. These characteristics are known as parameters.

Example: If one wants to know the effects of a new procedure/drug in the treatment of cancer, one cannot implement it straightly on all patients suffering from breast cancer. For this, one has to explore the effects in selected group of patients who are suffering from breast cancer. The patients of breast cancer compose population and the selected group of patients on whom the effect of procedure/drug is observed, constitute a sample.

Sample must be random: To use statistics, and to learn certain things under observations about the population, the sample has to be random. The sample represents a population because it has the characteristics which are common among them. Random word implies that every member of a population has an equal chance of being selected. The most commonly collected sample is simple random sample. The sample, population, and parameter are given in Figure 2.2.

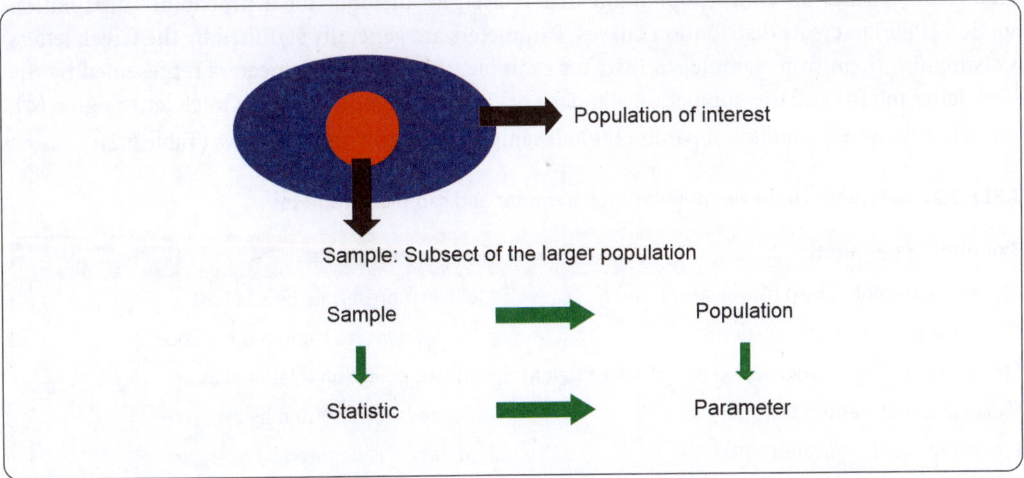

Figure 2.2: Sample, population and parameter

Parameter

The word parameter comes from the Greek, here para means "beside" or "subsidiary," and metron means "measure". Generally, it is any characteristic that can help in defining or classifying a particular arrangement like an event, project, object, situation, etc. Parameter is any measurable quantity, which characterizes a population under observation. This implies that the parameter speaks something about the whole population. Therefore, a parameter is an element of a system that is useful and critical, when a system is identified, or when its performance, status, condition is being evaluated.

> **Must Know**
>
> Sample size is important because as the sample size increases, the variability of the sample statistics tends to decrease and the sample statistics tend to be closer to the true value of the population parameter. For larger sample sizes, we get less variability in the statistics, so less uncertainty in the estimates.

Characteristics of a Parameter

A parameter is a characteristic of a population. In statistic, parameter is an important component of any statistical analysis under study. It is any characteristic which helps in defining or classifying a particular event or a situation. It means that parameter is an important element of a system to identify it or for evaluating other criteria like performance, condition, and status, etc.

Example: When we want to know the mean age of the pregnant women, who delivered on the same day, it is a parameter of a population. For this, a random sample of pregnant women will be taken and age of the pregnant women, who delivered on the same day can be found.

> **Practical Tips**
>
> In order to create a plausible range of values for a parameter:
> 1. Take many random samples from the population, and compute the sample statistic for each sample.
> 2. Compute the standard error as the standard deviation of all these statistics.
> 3. Use statistic $\pm\, 2 \times$ SE.

Parameter is a Descriptive Measure

Parameter describes an entire population that is used as an input for a probability distribution function (PDF) to create distribution curves. Parameters are generally signified by the Greek letters to distinguish them from sample statistic, for example, the population mean is represented by the Greek letter mu (μ) and the population standard deviation is signified by the Greek letter sigma (σ). Differences between population parameter and sample parameter are as follows (Table 2.2):

TABLE 2.2: Differences between population parameter and sample parameter

Population parameter	Sample parameter
Mean is represented by μ (Greek letter mu)	Mean is represented by $\bar{x}$ (x-bar)
P denotes population proportion	$\hat{p}$ (p-hat) denotes sample proportion
Standard deviation is labeled as σ (Greek letter sigma)	Standard deviation is labeled as s
Variance is represented by σ^2	Variance is represented by s^2
Population size is indicated by N	Sample size is denoted by n

Contd...

Population parameter	Sample parameter
Standard error of mean is represented by $\sigma_{\bar{x}}$	Standard error of mean is represented by $s_{\bar{x}}$
Standard error of proportion is labeled as σ_p	Standard error of proportion is labeled as s_p
Standardized variate (z) is represented by $X - \mu)/\sigma$	Standardized variate (z) is represented by $(x - \bar{x})/s$
Coefficient of variation is denoted by σ/μ	Coefficient of variation is denoted by $s/(\bar{x})$

Parameter is a Fixed Constant

Being fixed is a characteristic of a parameter, it does not vary like variables. Whereas, its value is usually unknown because it is not possible to measure an entire population. Statistically, in a normal distribution, there are two parameters which can be characterized—the mean and standard deviation. By changing these two parameters, one can obtain different types of normal distributions. Here, population refers to a summative entity of all units under consideration, which shares common characteristics. It is a numerical value that remains unchanged because every member of the population is gauged to know the parameter. It indicates true value, which is obtained after the census is conducted. The statistical parameters are tabulated as follows:

The values of parameter determine the location and shape of the curve when the plot of distribution is made, and each unique combination of parameter values produces a unique distribution curve. Several specific parameters are needed to define each distribution (usually between one and three). The table given here provides examples of the parameters required for three distributions.

Distribution	Parameter 1	Parameter 2	Parameter 3
Chi-square	Degrees of freedom		
Normal	Mean	Standard deviation	
3-Parameter Gamma	Shape	Scale	Threshold

Further when we take an example of a normal distribution, it is defined by two parameters, the mean and standard deviation. If these are specified, the entire distribution is precisely known (**Fig. 2.3**).

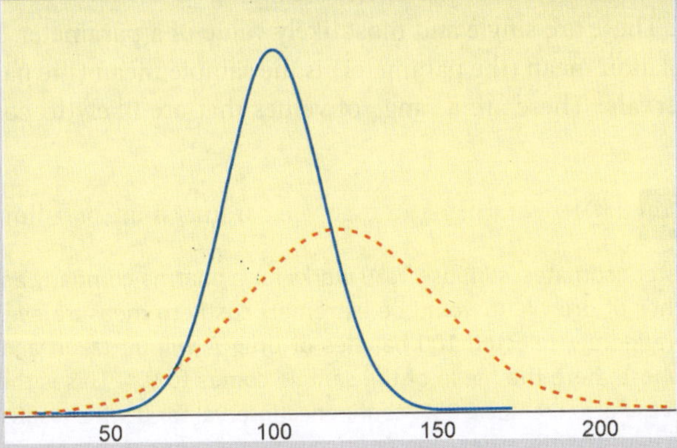

Figure 2.3: Normal distribution curve. The solid line represents a normal distribution with a mean of 100 and a standard deviation of 15. The dashed line is also a normal distribution, but it has a mean of 120 and a standard deviation of 30

TABLE 2.3. Statistical parameters

Statistic	Parameter	Pronounced
$\bar{X}$	μ	mu
p	π	pi
SD or s	σ	sigma
s^2	σ^2	sigma-squared
r	ρ	rho

Different statistical studies need different kinds of parameters in order to characterize data. Mostly, the mean or median remains a good parameter of the data (Table 2.3). For example, if a researcher wants to determine the performance of students in a test, the median score will be enough.

Uses of Parameters

The most common statistical parameters are the measures of central tendency that is mean, median and mode, which tells how the data behaves on an average parameter. It gives an idea about position of concentration of data. Standard deviation speaks about how the data is spread from the central tendency—whether the distribution of data is narrow or wide. These parameters are very useful in statistical analysis.

Parameter Estimates

Parameter estimates are also called sample statistic. As already said that parameters are descriptive measures of an entire population. Whereas, their values are generally unknown because it is impossible to measure an entire population. Because of this reason, we take a random sample from the population to obtain parameter estimates. The goal of statistical analyses is to obtain estimates of the population parameters along with the errors associated with these estimates that are known as sample statistic. Following are types of parameter estimates:

- **Point estimates:** These are single and most likely value of a parameter. For example, the point estimate of population mean (the parameter) is the sample mean (the parameter estimate).
- **Confidence intervals:** These are a range of values that are likely to comprise the population parameter.

Practical Tips

To understand parameter estimates, suppose Vasu works for a pharma company and is studying a problem in consistency in batches of drug A. It would be extremely costly to measure every single batch of drug. Instead, a sample of randomly selected 100 batches of drug A will be taken and change in consistency will be measured. Suppose, here the mean of the sample comes to 9.4. This is the point estimate for the population mean (μ). Vasu also creates a 95% confidence interval for μ which is (8.8, 9.6). This means that Vasu can be 95% confident that the true value of the average gap in consistency of all batches of drug A is between 8.5 and 9.7.

Question: A researcher wants to know the average weight of females aged 24 years or older in India. The researcher obtains the average weight of 64 kg, from a random sample of 40 females.

Solution: In the given situation, the statistics are the average weight of 64 kg, calculated from a simple random sample of 40 females in India, while the parameter is the mean weight of all females aged 24 years or older.

Variables are not parameters. Variables are quantities which can be transformed by the researcher. For example, the number of diabetic patients to study is a variable. A researcher can choose a population of 100 patients or 150 patients, totally depending on the statistical requirements. This would count as a variable. Whereas a parameter is independent of the variable as the parameters fixes the distribution irrespective of the total number of cases under study.

Must Know

Census is not recommended

The research may be conducted on whole population and this method is called as census method. But it is not recommended because more time, money and resources are required. For example, when the presence of some metabolite is to be known in blood, whole blood is not tested but only a few drops are enough for this. The results of blood tests are applied on whole blood of that particular individual.

STUDENT ASSIGNMENT

LONG ANSWER QUESTIONS

1. What is a sample? How is it different from a population? Explain.
2. Describe the differences between variable and parameter.

SHORT ANSWER QUESTIONS

1. Write a short note on the variables are not parameters.
2. What are the differences between statistic and parameter?
3. Define parameter estimates.

MULTIPLE CHOICE QUESTIONS

1. **Parameters of population are denoted by the:**
   a. Roman letters
   b. Lowercase Greek letter
   c. Uppercase Greek letter
   d. Associated roman alphabets

2. **Unknown or exact value that represents whole population is classified as:**
   a. Parameters
   b. Estimators
   c. Absolute statistics
   d. Coverage estimator

3. **Methods in statistics that use sample statistics to estimate parameters of population are considered:**
   a. Inferential statistics
   b. Absolute statistics
   c. Coverage statistics
   d. Random sample statistics

4. **Measures in sampling that are results of sample analyses are called:**
   a. Absolute statistics parameter
   b. Coverage estimators
   c. Population statistics
   d. Sample statistic

5. **In sampling, measures such as variance, mean, standard deviation are considered:**
   a. Absolute statistics
   b. Coverage estimator
   c. Parameters
   d. Estimators

3

Types and Levels of Data and their Measurements

"You use data to shape and remain informed about all decisions."

INTRODUCTION

With increase in research in the field of medicine and clinical science, evidence-based research has also increased. The clinical trials of drugs, the use of a new interventions in a hospital, getting benefits of a new medical devices, all are based on statistical results. Before implementing any new technology or drug, data from appropriate sample is collected. By data, we mean a set of observations or measurements which are collected with specific characteristics from individual subjects under study.

These characteristics are known as variables like weight, height, type of blood group or clinical stage of a disease and they will have different values in different individuals and also at different times in the same individual.

A data can be collected in many ways like using medical instruments, e.g., thermometer; observing cardinal signs and symptoms; through interviews via telephone or face to face interaction, e.g., noting history of an illness; through special psychological tools like Thematic apperception test (TAT) or Rorschach inkblot tests, etc.

Must Know

Why is it necessary to know types of data?
It is necessary to know types of data because a certain type of statistical method can only be used with particular data type. It is necessary to avoid any wrong method used to deal with a data. One has to analyse continuous data differently than categorical data otherwise, it would result in a wrong analysis.

TYPES OF DATA

Data is a group of information which is used during research.

Statistical Data Based on the Source

Based on the source of data—it can be primary or secondary (Table 3.1).

TABLE 3.1: Differences between primary and secondary data

Features	Primary data	Secondary data
Meaning	Data collected by researcher himself	Data collected by other people
Originality	Original or unique information	Not original or unique information
Adjustment	Does not need adjustment, is focused	Needs adjustment to suit actual aim
Sources	Surveys, observations, experiments	Internal records, government published data, etc.
Types of data	Qualitative data	Quantitative data
Methods	Observation, experiment, interview	Desk research method, searching online, etc.
Reliability	More reliable	Less reliable
Time consumed	More time consuming	Less time consuming
Need of investigators	Need team of trained investigators	Does not need team of investigators
Cost effectiveness	Costly	Economical
Collected when	Secondary data is inadequate	Before primary data is collected
Capability	More capable to solve a problem	Less capable to solve a problem
Suitability	Most suitable to achieve objective	May or may not be suitable
Bias	Possibility of bias exist	Somewhat safe from bias
Collected by	Researcher or his agents	People other than who collects primary data
Precaution to use	Not necessary	Quite necessary

Primary Data

Primary data is a data collected by a researcher from primary source. It is original and collected by direct interaction or investigation.

Secondary Data

Secondary data is a data collected from other sources like journals, internet, from in database of a hospital, etc.

Statistical Data Based on the Nature

The data is classified into quantitative and qualitative based upon its nature (Fig. 3.1).

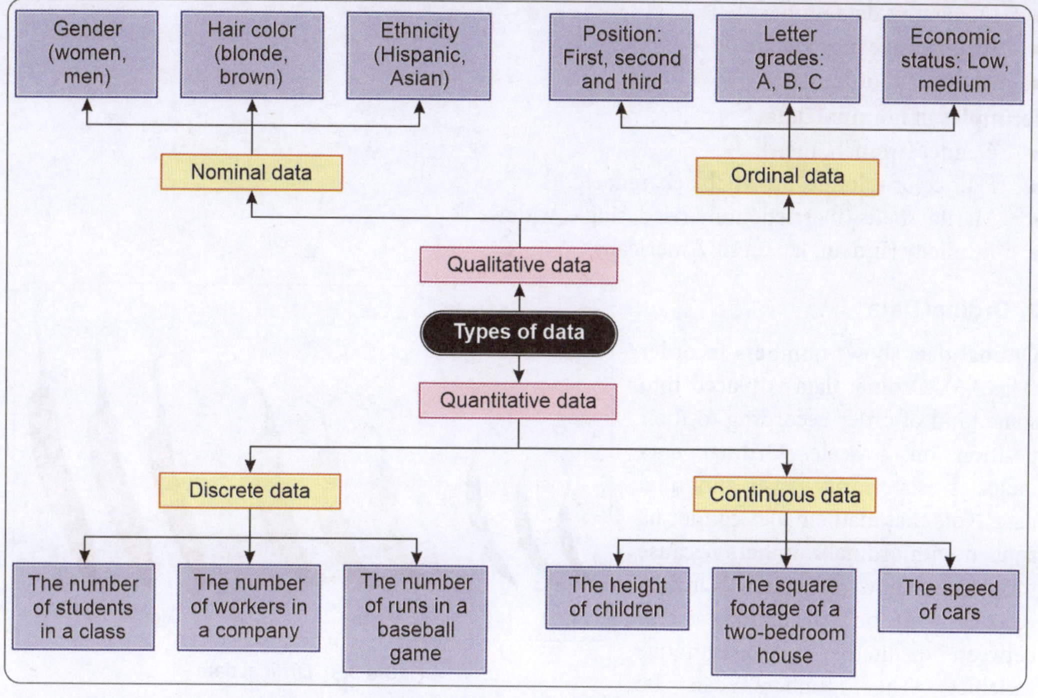

Figure 3.1: Types of data—qualitative and quantitative

Qualitative Data

Qualitative data can neither be expressed as a number nor be measured—consist of words, pictures, and symbols, but not numbers. It is called qualitative data because the information can be sorted by category, therefore it is also known as categorical data. Qualitative data can answer questions like "why this has happened" or "how this has happened", etc.

There are two general types of qualitative data:

1. Nominal Data

The name 'nominal' comes from the Latin word "nomen" which means 'name'. It is used for labeling variables, without any type of quantitative value or an order. Actually, the nominal data could just be called "labels". The characteristics of nominal data (Fig. 3.2) are as follows:

- Conclusive mode
- Alphabetical
- Not quantifiable

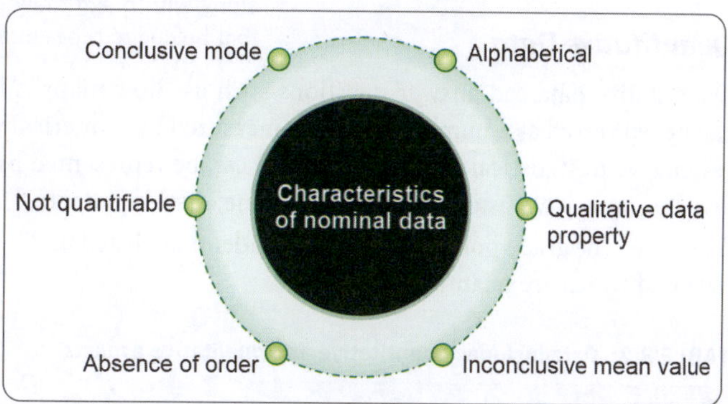

Figure 3.2: Characteristics of nominal data

- Qualitative data property
- Inconclusive mean value
- Absence of order

Examples of nominal data:

- Gender (women, men)
- Hair color (blonde, brown, black, red, etc.)
- Marital status (married, unmarried, single, widowed)
- Ethnicity (Indian, Japanese, American)

2. Ordinal Data

Ordinal data shows numbers in order (Fig. 3.3). Ordinal data is placed into some kind of order according to their position on a scale. Ordinal data indicates superiority over nominal data. Note that mathematics cannot be applied with ordinal numbers because they only show sequence. Ordinal variables can be considered as "in between" qualitative and quantitative variables. The numbers can be assigned to ordinal data to show their relative position but without applying mathematics.

Examples of ordinal data:

- **Position:** First, second and third place in a competition
- **Grades:** A, B, C, etc.
- **Rating:** To rate the experience on a scale of 1–10
- **Economic status:** Low, medium and high

Quantitative Data

Figure 3.3: Ordinal data

> ### Must Know
>
> The qualitative data generates information about physically observable characters like, color of hair or skin of employees in a hospital or the healthiness of skin, etc., which could be important in statistical analysis, especially when both quantitative and qualitative features of data are to be studied together. Moreover, qualitative data allows researcher to have parameters through which one can observe large sets of data. For example, a hospital wants to determine the diversity of its healthcare team and for this he will like to look at qualitative data like religion, age, residential background of its employees along with quantitative data of the frequency of employees that belong to those qualitative parameters.

Quantitative data can answer questions such as "how many", "how much" and "how often", etc. It can be expressed as a number. It can be measured by numerical variables. Quantitative data is easily responsive to statistical manipulation and can be represented by a wide variety of statistical graphs and charts such as histogram, bar graph, line, scatter plot, etc.

Example: The grade point averages of 5 students are listed in the Table 3.2. Which data are qualitative data and which are quantitative data?

TABLE 3.2: Data includes quantitative and qualitative aspects

Student	Sakshi	Bobby	Kamini	Mohan	Kalpana	Qualitative data
GPA	3.22	3.98	2.75	2.24	3.84	Quantitative data

Examples of quantitative data:

- **Scores:** In tests and exams like 85, 67, 90, etc.
- **Weight:** Weight of a person or a subject.
- **Size:** Shoe size or size of clothes.
- **Temperature:** Temperature of water or in a room.

Quantitative data is also known as numerical data. This type of data is used during experiments concerned with measurement. For example, measuring a person's weight, height, IQ and blood pressure, etc. Numerical data can further be divided into two types: (1) Discrete and (2) Continuous (Table 3.3).

1. Discrete Data

Discrete data is referred to as frequencies which can be counted. The values obtained here are fixed or infinite, for example number of needle punctures, number of pregnancies, etc. It has values that are distinct. It is a count that involves only integers. The discrete values cannot be subdivided into parts. For example, the number of children in a class is discrete data. One can count whole individuals and cannot count as 1.5 boys. Discrete data can take only certain values and data variables cannot be divided into smaller parts. It has a limited number of possible values such as days of a week or month. This type of data basically represents information and can be categorized into classes.

TABLE 3.3: Numerical data—discrete and continuous

Parameters	Discrete data	Continuous data
Meaning	Discrete data has clear spaces between values	Continuous data falls on a continuous sequence
Can you count the data?	Yes, data is usually units counted in whole numbers	Generally, NO
Values	It has a finite number of possible values. The values cannot be divided into smaller pieces and add additional meaning	It has an infinite number of possible values within an interval. The values can be subdivided into smaller and smaller pieces
Graphical representation	Bar chart	Histogram
Examples	<ul><li>The number of students in a class.</li><li>The number of workers in a company.</li><li>The number of parts damaged during transportation.</li><li>Shoe sizes.</li><li>Number of languages an individual speaks.</li><li>The number of homes runs in a baseball game.</li><li>The number of test questions you answered correctly.</li></ul>	<ul><li>The amount of time required to complete a project.</li><li>The height of children.</li><li>The amount of time it takes to sell shoes.</li><li>The amount of rain, in inches, that falls in a storm</li><li>The square footage of a two-bedroom house.</li><li>The weight of a truck.</li><li>The speed of cars.</li><li>Time to wake up.</li></ul>

Examples of discrete data:
- Number of students in a class.
- Number of workers in a company.
- Number of test questions answered correctly.

2. Continuous Data

Continuous data is the data which cannot be counted but can only be measured. It is an information, which is meaningfully divided into finer levels. This type of data is often described using intervals on the real number line. It can be recorded at many different levels of measurements like width, temperature, time, etc. It can be measured on a scale having numeric values, for example, height of a person, weight, age, arm length, blood pressure, temperature, glucose level.

Examples of continuous data:
- Height of children
- Amount of time required to complete a project
- Speed of cars

Practical Tips

A good rule for defining whether a data is continuous or discrete is that if the point of measurement can be reduced in half but it still makes sense, the data is continuous.

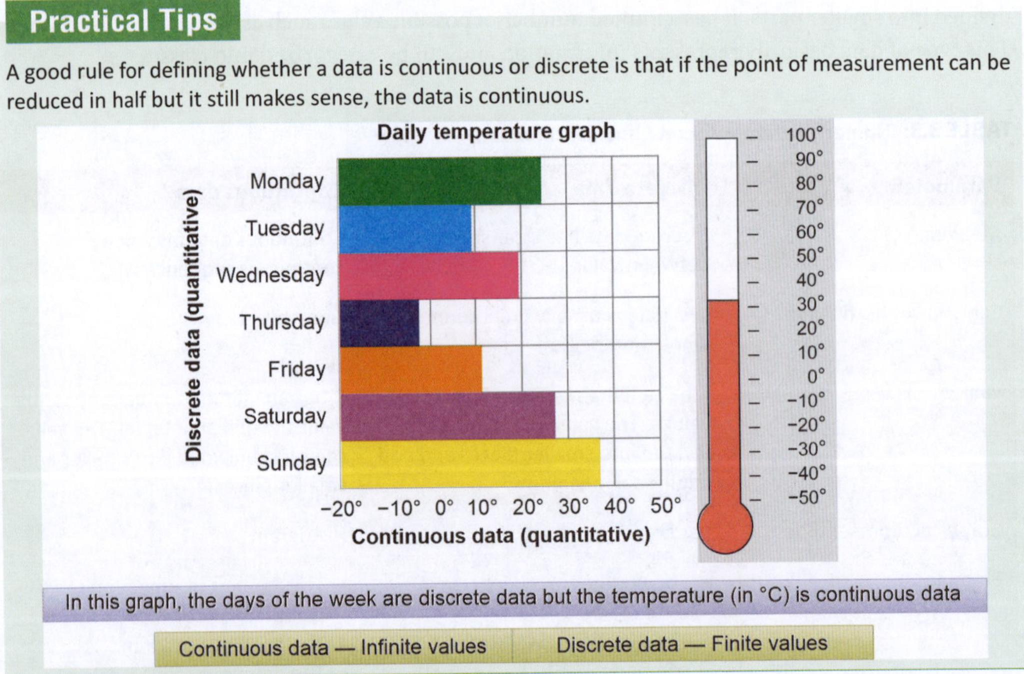

In this graph, the days of the week are discrete data but the temperature (in °C) is continuous data

Continuous data — Infinite values   Discrete data — Finite values

TYPES OF DATA ANALYSIS

Following are types of data analysis:
- **Descriptive data analysis:** It is used to describe some basic features of data under the study. It is simple summaries of sample or the measures.
- **Exploratory data analysis:** It is an approach to analyze sets of data by visual methods.
- **Inferential data analysis:** It is conclusion based and some inference is drawn after working on a data.

- **Predicative data analysis:** It turns data into a valuable as well as actionable information. The data is utilized to determine the probable future outcome of events.
- **Causal data analysis:** When two events exist in a way that occurrence of the first causes the other, it is called causal relationship. Here, a controlled study is carried out so as to see the effect of a cause between different variables.

Practical Tips

Visualizing Continuous Data

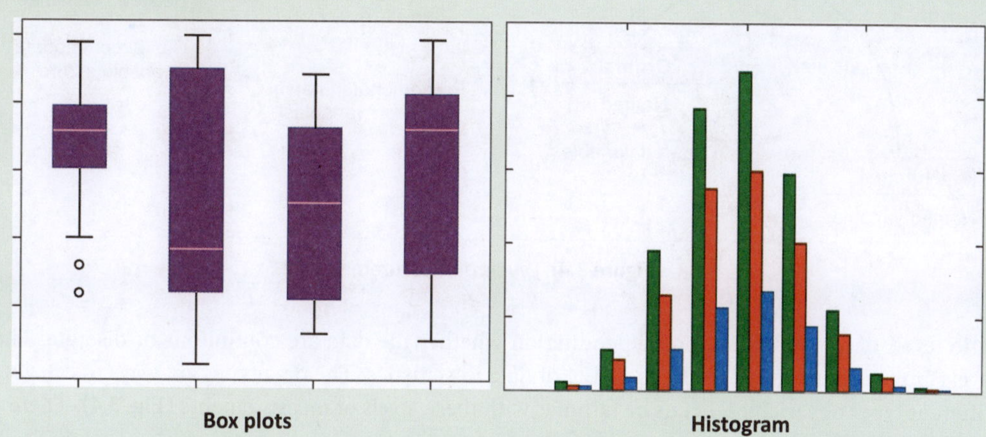

- To deal with continuous data, one can utilize mean, mode, median, range, interquartile range, standard deviation, and percentiles.
- To visualize continuous data, histogram or a box plots can be used. With a histogram, the central tendency, variability, and kurtosis of a distribution can be checked.
- Histogram cannot show you, if you have any outliers. An outlier is a single data point that goes far outside the average value of a group of statistics. This is why we also use box plots.
- **Outlier:** By outlier we mean that it is an observation which lies outside the overall pattern of a distribution or an outlier is a point that lies >1.5 times in the interquartile range, above the third quartile or below the first quartile.
- **Box plot:** It is a simple way of representing statistical data. Here, a rectangle is drawn which represents the second and third quartiles, mostly with a vertical line inside it to indicate the median value of data. The lower and upper quartiles are shown as horizontal lines which are on either side of the rectangle. Box plots are often used in explanatory data analysis. They are used to show the shape of the distribution, the central value, and variability of data.

SCALES OR LEVELS OF MEASUREMENT

Four levels of measurement of data were described by SS Stevens in 1946. According to this, quantities or attributes of sample under observation can be measured and calculated and these sets of data do not always involve numbers which can be calculated. These are determined by level of measurements for each set of data.

The word 'measurement' can be defined as assigning a number to objects or events according to a set of rules. For this, we must be familiar with various measurement scales which were originally developed by psychologist Stanley Smith. The data can be subjected to analysis according to the level of measurement which were involved in data collection that is nominal, ordinal, interval, and

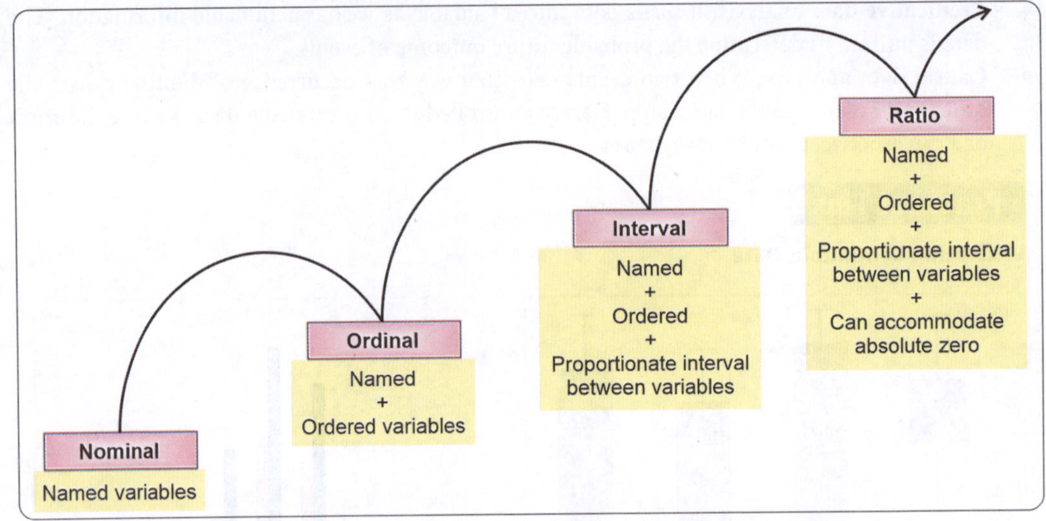

Figure 3.4: Levels of measurement

ratio levels of measurement, not depending on whether the data are continuous or discrete. These levels of measurement tell us the meaning of data in statistics. The data types are ways to categorize different types of variables. Let us be familiar with these levels of measurements **(Fig. 3.4)**. There are four levels of measurement in science as follows:

Having a good understanding of the different data types, or measurement scales, is a decisive prerequisite for doing further data analysis as statistical tests are suited for either one or another type of data. Moreover, it is again necessary to know about it because to choose right analyzing method one must be sure of data type.

Nominal Scale

Nominal scale is the lowest level of scale of measurement. The name itself suggests that it consists of naming the observation into various categories which may be exclusive or exhaustive. Nominal variables are used to give name, or label to a series of values. Nominal scale is the crudest among all measurement scales but it is also the simplest scale. In this scale, the different scores of measurements simply indicate different categories. The nominal scale does not express any values or relationships between variables. The nominal scale is often referred to as a categorical scale. The assigned numbers have no arithmetic properties and act only as labels. The only statistical operation that can be performed on nominal scales is a frequency count. We cannot determine an average except mode (Fig. 3.5).

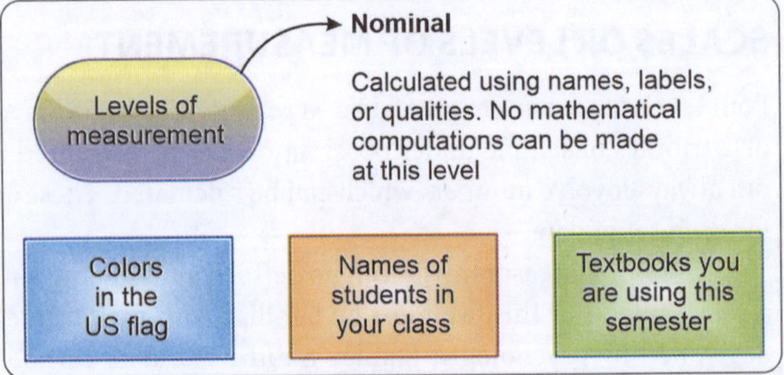

Figure 3.5: Nominal level of measurement

For example: Labeling men as '1' and women as '2' which is the most common way of labeling gender for data recording purpose does not mean women are 'twice something or other' than men. Nor it suggests that men are somehow 'better' than women.

Nominal variables may have categories but without any kind of natural order. Observations are placed in broad categories that could be labeled, symbolized or categorized. For example, observation is categories when the data can be bifurcated as male or female, old or young, dead or alive and married or unmarried, etc. These are also termed dichotomous categorization.

The variables in nominal data have no numeric values, for example occupation of different employees at different levels or categories in a hospital or ID numbers of nurses in a hospital. There is no need to calculate such types of numbers, because statistics has no meaning here. Nominal data has only a mode. Data at the nominal level of measurement is qualitative only. Nominal values are simple labels and are used to represent discrete units to mark variables, which have no quantitative value. They are only labels. The nominal data does not have any order. Therefore, even if we change the order of its values, the meaning of data remains unchanged, e.g.:

> **Practical Tip**
>
> The presence of a character can be assigned code I and absence of a character can be assigned code 0.

What is your gender?	What languages do you speak?
• Female • Male	• English • French • German • Spanish

When we talk about nominal data, the information is obtained through:

- **Frequencies** which are the rates at which something occurs over a period of time or within a data set.
- **Proportions** which are calculated by dividing the frequency by the total number of events.
- **Percentages**

> **Must Know**
>
> To transform nominal data into a numeric data there is a process called as 'one hot encoding' in data science.

To visualize nominal data, a pie chart or a bar chart can be used as shown in **Figures 3.6A and B**.

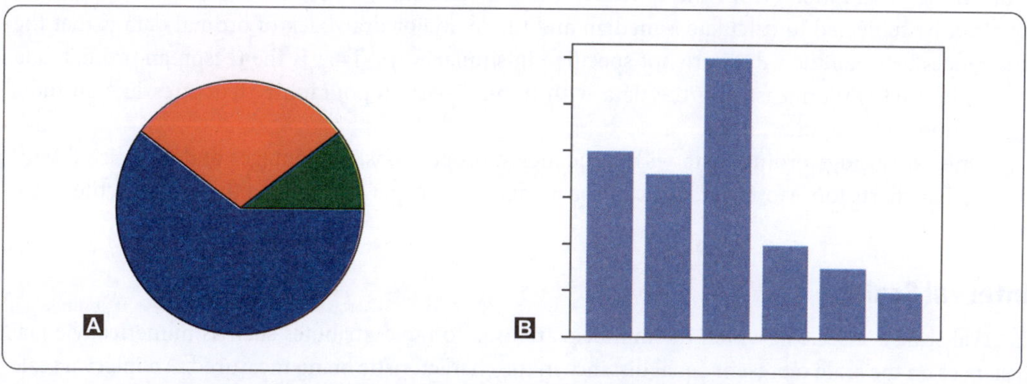

Figures 3.6A and B: **A.** Pie chart; **B.** Bar chart

Ordinal Scale

Ordinal scale involves the ranking of items along the continuum of the characteristic being scaled. In this scale, the items are classified according to whether they possess more or less of a characteristic. The main characteristic of the ordinal scale is that the categories have a logical or ordered relationship. This type of scale permits the measurement of degrees of difference, (i.e., 'more' or 'less') but not the specific number of differences (i.e., how much 'more' or 'less'). This scale is very common in satisfaction, marketing, and attitudinal research. Using ordinal scale data, we can perform statistical analysis like median and mode, but not the mean.

For example, a researcher may ask patients: How would you rate the service of our staff?

a.   Excellent

b.   Very good

c.   Good

d.   Poor

e.   Worst

It is a mixture of numerical data and qualitative or categorical data. Here, the data can be denoted in categories, and the numerical number assigned to these categories gives meaning to them. As an example, the rating the attitude on scale of 0 (least) to 10 (highest) is a form of an ordinal data. Whole information gathered can be ordered in the form of graphs and charts—a property of quantitative data. The statistical data has natural, ordered categories but the distances between the different categories are not known (Fig. 3.7) Likert scale is an example of it.

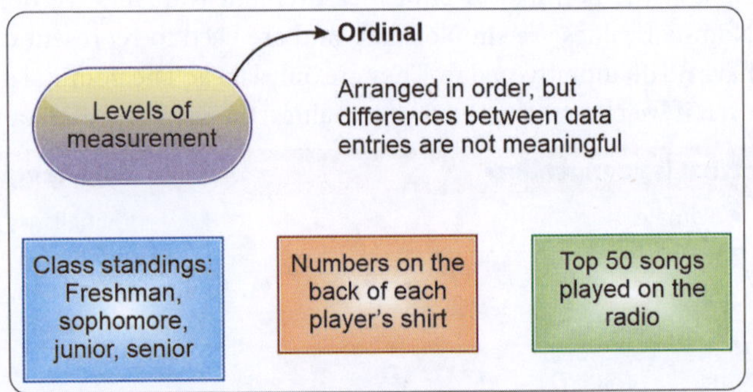

Figure 3.7: Ordinal level of measurement

When the observations are different from one category to another category, we can assign ranks according to some criteria measured on an ordinal scale. For example, the degree of pain can further be assigned as no pain, mild pain and severe pain. Researcher can further give code to these criteria as no pain–0, mild pain–1, moderate pain–2, severe–3. It suggests the degree of pain but the actual magnitude of pain cannot be measured. The purpose of assigning numbers to ordinal data are to order these observations from the lowest to highest rank-wise, hence it is ordinal scale. Ordinal data can be subjected to calculate a median and mode. Major drawback of ordinal data is that the differences between the values are not specified in similar ways. That is the reason an ordinal data is mostly used while measuring the data with non-numeric topographic structures like attitude, satisfaction and happiness, etc.

One can abridge ordinal data with frequencies, proportions, percentages and visualize it with pie and bar charts too. Moreover, one can use median, mode, percentiles and the interquartile range for this data.

Interval Scale

Interval scale is a scale in which the numbers are used to rank attributes such as numerically equal distances on the scale represent equal distance in the characteristic being measured. An interval scale contains all the information of an ordinal scale, but it also allows to compare the difference or distance between attributes. Interval scales may be either in numeric or semantic formats. The interval scales allow the calculation of averages like mean, median and mode and dispersion like range and standard deviation. For example, the difference between '1' and '2' is equal to the difference between '3' and '4'. Further, the difference between '2' and '4' is twice the difference between '1' and '2'. Measuring temperature is an example of interval scale. But, we cannot say 40°C is twice as hot as 20°C.

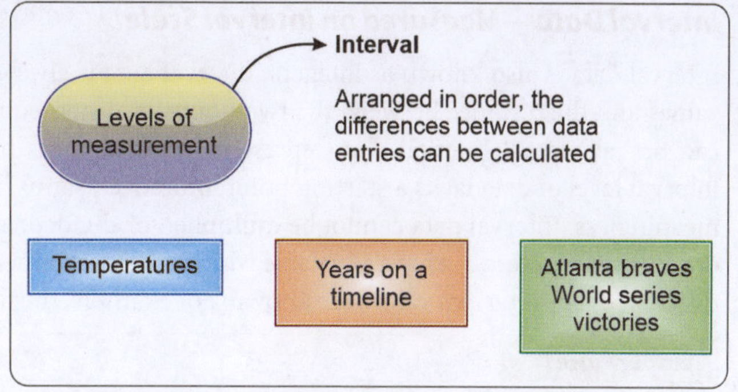

Figure: 3.8: Interval level of measurement

It is more sophisticated scale as compared to nominal or ordinal because here it is possible to have ordered measurements with known distance between any two measurements. It has two main features which make interval scale more useful—equal units of measurement (equal intervals) and a zero point which is taken arbitrarily. The selected zero point indicates a total absence of a quantity under observation (Fig. 3.8). This scale is a quantitative scale. Measurement of temperature is in degrees Celsius like 24°C or 4°C, indicating the exact heat or rise in temperature at a particular point of time. A zero entry simply represents a position on a scale.

Example: Interval scale in numeric format

Food supplied is:						Indicate the score on the concerned blank and circle the appropriate number on each line.
Fresh	1	2	3	4	5	
Tastes good	1	2	3	4	5	
Value for money	1	2	3	4	5	
Attractive packaging	1	2	3	4	5	
Prompt time delivery	1	2	3	4	5	

Example: Interval scale in semantic format

Indicate the views on the food supplied in a hospital by scoring them on a 5 points scale from 1–5. Here 1 = excellent; 2 = very good; 3 = good; 4 = poor; 5 = worst. Indicate the response by ticking the appropriate response.

Food supplied is:	Excellent	Very good	Good	Poor	Worst
Fresh					
Tastes good					
Value for money					
Attractive packaging					
Prompt time delivery					

Here, each score indicates an actual amount with equal units of measurement separating any two scores, for example, the measurement of difference between 20 and 30 is the same as 40 and 50. Interval scale is truly a quantitative scale contrary to nominal or ordinal scale.

Interval Data—Measured on Interval Scale

Interval data is also known as integers. Interval data is always in the form of numbers or numerical values and the distance between the two points is always equal and standardized. These differences can be calculated. Interval data represents ordered units having the same differences. However, interval level of data lacks a starting point, moreover, ratios between the obtained values of data are meaningless. Interval data cannot be multiplied or divided, although it can be subjected to addition or subtraction. Here, we have a variable which contains numeric values which are in order, with exact differences between two values are known. For example, the temperature of a place at different times:

Temperature?	−10	−5	0	+5	+10	+15

Limitations

The problem with interval data is that it has no true zero value. In the example given above, there is no value which can signify 'no temperature'. Moreover, because of absence of true zero value, a lot of descriptive or inferential statistics can not be applied. In calculation of interval data, one can add and subtract, but cannot multiply, divide or calculate ratios.

Ratio Scale

Ratio values are ordered units with similar differences. They are the same as interval values, with a difference that they have an absolute zero. In other words, there can be no negative numerical value in ratio data, e.g., area or distance, etc. It is the highest level of measurement because of its precision and it has a true zero point indicating the absence of a particular trait. Ratio scale is the highest level of measurement scales. It has the properties of an interval scale together with a fixed (absolute) zero point. The absolute zero point allows a researcher to construct a meaningful ratio. Ratio scales permit the researcher to compare both-differences in scores and relative magnitude of scores. Examples of ratio scales include weights, lengths and times. For example, the number of patients visiting a hospital in the last three months is a ratio scale. This is because one can compare this with previous three months **(Fig. 3.9)**.

As an example, the difference between 10 and 15 minutes is the same as the difference between 25 and 30 minutes and 30 minutes is twice as long as 15 minutes **(Fig. 3.9)**.

Ratio level of data has variables with a meaningful zero-point, which tells that a variable with zero has no property that is under observation like, 0 kg/pound means that the object has no weight. This zero point is called absolute zero point.

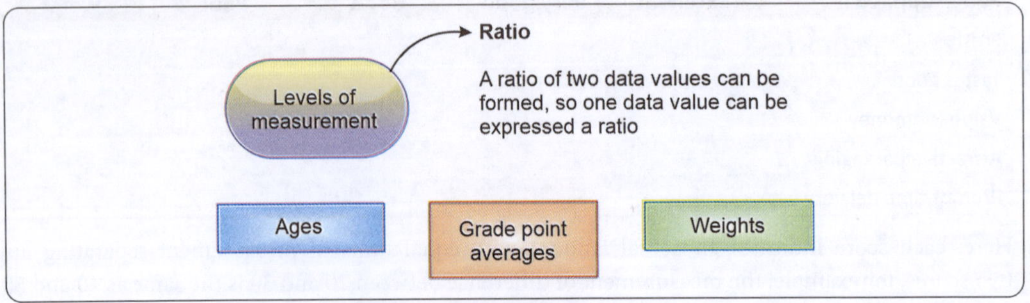

Figure 3.9: Ratio level measurement

Ratio data possesses all characteristics of interval data like, but in contrast to interval data where zero has no meaning and is arbitrary, in ratio data, zero is absolute. An example of ratio data is the measurement of weight or height. Data at this level (ratio level) can not only be ordered and subtracted, but it can be divided too because this data has a zero value or starting point. The temperature scale (Kelvin) does have a zero point or starting point. For example, a man has 90 kg body weight and woman has 60 kg body weight—here it implies that man is 1.5 times heavier as compared to a woman. The unit kilogram or kg is a constant unit. Absence of weight is measurable and allows mathematical calculations.

Here scores indicate true amount of a variable and measures actual amount. The calculation provides fractional numbers and they are converted into decimal, which are meaningful.

Properties of Levels of Measurement

Levels of measurement define the relationship among the values assigned to the characteristics of an object (Fig. 3.10). We can say that what properties of an object, the scale is measuring or not measuring, is denoted by the levels of measurement.

- **Description:** The description means a particular unique label and descriptor which is used to designate the values of the scale. For example, we have the descriptors 1. Male, 2. Female. Here, male and female are unique descriptors denoting values 1 and 2 on gender scale. All scales have unique descriptors or labels which are used to define the values of the scale and the response options.
- **Order:** The order means the relative size and position of the descriptor. Here, the order is associated with only relative values and no absolute values. Thus, the order is denoted by descriptors like "less than", "greater than", "equal to". For example, optician's preference for three brands of lenses is shown in the order given below with the most preferred brand listed first and the least preferred on the last.

1. Essilor 360 DS   2.   Bausch and Lomb
3   Soflens 59

This shows that the preference for Essilor 360 DS is greater than the preference for Bausch and Lomb and likewise, the preference for Soflens 59 is less than the preference for Bausch and Lomb.

It is important to note that all the scales do not possess order characteristics. Such as gender scale (1. Female; 2. Male) does not possess order as one cannot determine whether a female is greater than or lesser than a male.

- **Distance:** Distance means that the absolute differences between the descriptors on a scale are known and can be expressed in units. For example, a 5-person room has one patient more than a 4-person room and likewise a 4-person room has one patient more than the 3-person room. It is to be noted that, the scale that has the distance characteristic and also has the order. As we

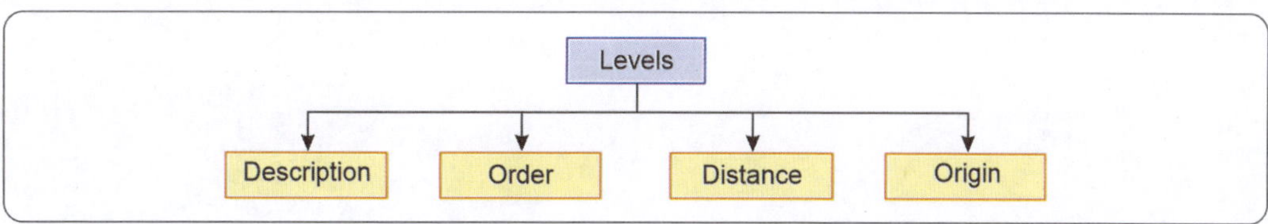

Figure 3.10: Properties of levels of measurement

know that 5-person classroom is greater than the 4-person classroom in terms of a number of persons in the class. Thus, we can say that distance implies order, but the reverse is not true, i.e., order does not necessarily imply distance.

- **Origin:** The origin shows that scale has a unique or fixed starting or true zero point. A scale having origin characteristic also has the distance, order, and description. Many scales used in the marketing research do not have any fixed origin.

For example, in case of unfavorable-favorable scale,

1 = extremely unfavorable	2 = unfavorable
3 = neither unfavorable nor favorable	4 = favorable
5 = extremely favorable	

Here, 1 is an arbitrary origin or starting point. This scale could have started with 0 = extremely unfavorable and 4 = extremely favorable. Likewise, it can also be started with −2, where −2 = extremely unfavorable and 2 = extremely favorable. Thus, this scale does not have any fixed origin and hence does not possess the origin characteristic.

You must have observed that description, order, distance, and origin depict successively higher level characteristics. Origin being the highest level characteristic while the description being the most basic characteristic. If the scale has order characteristic, it will also have the description, and likewise the scale with distance characteristic has both the description and order. The scale with origin characteristic has all that is distance, order and description.

It means that the higher level characteristics possess the lower level characteristics, however the lower level characteristics may not necessarily possess the higher level characteristics.

Must Know

Ratio scale is the highest level of measurement.
Comparative Summary of Levels of Measurements

Level of measurement	Put data in category	Arrange data in order	Subtract data values	Determine if one data value is a multiple of another
Nominal	Yes	No	No	No
Ordinal	Yes	Yes	No	No
Interval	Yes	Yes	Yes	No
Ratio	Yes	Yes	Yes	Yes

These tools for measurement need standardization and must have high degree of reliable consistency, repeatability or reproducibility, accuracy or validity as without it the data cannot be interpreted accurately.

STUDENT ASSIGNMENT

LONG ANSWER QUESTIONS

1. Discuss the data types. Elaborate.
2. What are levels of measurements? Why are they important?

SHORT ANSWER QUESTIONS

1. Write a short note on the differences between qualitative and quantitative data.
2. What is the ratio level of measurement?

MULTIPLE CHOICE QUESTIONS

1. **The nominal level of measurement is represented in which variable below:**
   a. Fear of crime
   b. Temperature
   c. Income
   d. Gender
2. **The ordinal level of measurement is represented in which variable below:**
   a. Fear of crime
   b. Temperature
   c. Income
   d. Gender
3. **Ratio level of measurement is the only level to have:**
   a. An indicator of magnitude
   b. Arithmetic manipulation
   c. Exhaustive categorization
   d. Absolute zero
4. **Levels of measurement refers to:**
   a. The stair-like process involved in measuring
   b. The essence of what numbers mean
   c. The use of variance to determine error in numbers
   d. The difficulty involved in measuring
5. **Ordinal scales have the property of:**
   a. Absolution
   b. Metricity
   c. Ranking
   d. Variability
6. **Measurement is:**
   a. Any time numbers are used
   b. The use of numbers to represent concepts
   c. The primary concern of statistical power
   d. All of the above
7. **The meaning of a number is a product of:**
   a. Its use in a statistic
   b. The level of measurement
   c. Its relationship to some condition
   d. Both b and c

ANSWER KEY

1. d	2. a	3. d	4. a	5. c	6. d	7. d

4

Organization and Presentation of Data—Tabulation

"Clutter is nothing more than postponed decisions."
—Barbara Hemphill

LEARNING OBJECTIVES

After the completion of the chapter, the readers will be able to:
- Understand classification of data and objectives of classification.
- Know about tabulation of data.

CHAPTER OUTLINE

- Introduction
- Purposes of Data Presentation
- Classification of Data
- Scientific Way to Collect Data
- Presentation of Data—Tabulation

INTRODUCTION

A researcher collects data in relation to the objectives of a research. When a sample is small and parameters are limited, it is a simple matter to process it, especially when questionnaires and tools of research have been formulated properly. Although when the sample size is large, parameters are more or number of correlations are to be studied then it becomes a hard task without a proper plan for efficient data processing.

The processing of data must start as early as possible so as to keep a check on inconsistency, errors or any other flaw. It will further help in quality control of data and in visualizing final data analysis. For this data collected must be organized/classified and presented in concise and precise manner.

PURPOSES OF DATA PRESENTATION

- Reporting of results is very important part of any research because it is first means of communication with the onlookers.
- Appropriate sampling methods/techniques increase the chances to obtain better results.
- The data has to be collected by scientific methods before it is subjected to further statistical analysis.

CLASSIFICATION OF DATA

The data can be classified into different types based on some common characteristics into different classes:

- **Geographical** that is area wise, for example, total population of Himachal Pradesh, infant deaths in Haryana, number of deaths due to cholera in Punjab, Haryana or Odisha.
- **Chronological or temporal**, based on time, for example, yearwise data of deaths due to lightening (Table 4.1).

TABLE 4.1: Deaths due to lightening from 1990 to 2002

Chronological or temporal (i.e., on the basis of time)													
Year	1990	1991	1992	1993	1994	1995	1996	1997	1998	1999	2000	2001	2002	Total
No.	10	5	12	6	9	3	3	5	12	12	8	7	8	100

- **Qualitative** that is based on some attribute, for example, classification of people by place of residence, sex and literacy (Table 4.2).

TABLE 4.2: Classification of people based on literacy rate

Place of residence			
Rural (Punjab)	Urban (Punjab)	Rural (Delhi)	Urban (Delhi)
Male	Female	Male	Female
Literate Illiterate	Literate Illiterate	Literate Illiterate	Literate Illiterate

- **Quantitative** that is based on quantitative class interval, for example, classification of students according to their weights (Table 4.3).

TABLE 4.3: Weights of students in a class

Wt. in (LBS)	90–100	100–110	110–120	120–130	130–140	140–150	Total
No. of students	50	200	260	360	90	40	1000

Objectives of Classification

- It helps in condensing huge mass of data according to similarities and dissimilarities which can be easily distinguished.
- It facilitates comparison between different attributes.
- The data can be presented at one place and is available at a glance. It further facilitates statistical treatment of data:
  - The averages can be calculated.
  - Variations can be revealed.
  - Associations can be studied.
  - Prediction/forecasting can be made.
  - Hypothesis can be formulated and tested.

Principles of Classification

- Generally, it depends on:
  - Knowledge of data.
  - Lowest and highest values of a set of data.
- Use of class interval for meaningful comparison and interpretation.
- Classification is exclusive when class intervals are so fixed that the upper limit of one class is the lower limit of next class and the upper limit is not included in the class (Table 4.4).
- Classification is inclusive when the upper and lower limit of one class are included in the class itself (Table 4.5).

TABLE 4.4: Exclusive class intervals

Income (₹)	No. of families
1000–1100 = (1000 but under 1100)	15
1100–1200 = (1100 but under 1200)	25
1200–1300 = (1200 but under 1300)	10
Total	**50**

TABLE 4.5: Inclusive class intervals

Income (₹)	No. of persons
1000–1099 = (1000 but ≤1099)	50
1100–1199 = (1100 but ≤1199)	100
1200–1299 = (1200 but ≤1299)	200
Total	**350**

Practical Tips

- Classes must be collectively nonoverlapping and exhaustive that is mutually exclusive.
- Number of classes should not be too large otherwise purpose of classes to summarize data will not be served.
- Number of classes should not be too small either as it will affect the nature of distribution.
- Classes should be of equal length (preferably) to avoid laborious calculations.
- More specifically, sturge's formula can be used to decide the number of class intervals:
  - $K = 1 + 3.322 (\log_{10} n)$
    Where k = no. of classes, n = no. of observation
  - The width of the class interval may be determined by dividing the range by k

$$w = \frac{R}{k}$$

    Where R = difference between the highest and the lowest observation.
      W = width of the class interval.
- When the nature of data makes them appropriate, class interval width of 5 or 10 units or width which is a multiple of 10 tends to make the summarization more comprehensible.

SCIENTIFIC WAY TO COLLECT DATA

In order to tabulate, a data has to be collected according to set norms, scientifically.

Scientific method is a technique where some scientific information is obtained, presented and analyzed so as to produce unbiased replicable inference. It is recognized universally and is an acceptable method based on the empirical approach because the decision to be taken depends on the outcomes of the statistical data analysis. The scientific steps that are followed to observe and summarize a research data have been mentioned as follows:

- **First step: To focus on a research problem:** A result is based on the observations on a question that arise in a researcher's mind, for example, it is observed by researcher that menstrual hygiene affects the health of a female or the knowledge of various birth control measures among people have direct relation for keeping a gap between birth of two babies or the body weight can be reduced by changing food habits and regular exercise.
- **Second step: To formulate a hypothesis:** Hypothesis is formulated, to make out some quantitative prediction. Hypothesis is formed after extensive background studies of similar research and reviews of literature and it helps in forming a firm research hypothesis or statistical hypothesis. The hypothesis is formed in such a way that a valid conclusion could be drawn at the end of a research study analysis.
- **Third step: Design of experiment:** Improperly designed experiments lead to inaccurate results and wrong conclusions. Whether a research study is appropriate or not decided on the base of a research design. In order to make a research design proper, two things are to be considered:
  1. **Validity or accuracy:** It is observations or measurements that are made accurately. The tools used are valid, which means they not only serve the purpose of a research but are also formulated according to need of the study.
  2. **Precision or reliability:** It is the measurement made in precise to produce reliable results. For example, while measuring weight of a jogger to observe effect of exercise on weight reduction, the measurement difference of +0.5 will produce effect on the result because of some fault in weighing machine.
- **Fourth step: Summarizing the data:** After collecting a large number of data, a researcher has to summarize it by grouping and this forms the frequency distribution (Table 4.6).

Example: The live births by 50 females have been collected and the data is:

1, 2, 0, 1, 0, 2, 4, 1, 1, 1, 1, 2, 0, 1, 2, 3, 0, 0, 1, 2, 2, 3, 2, 2, 4, 0, 0, 0, 0, 1, 1, 2, 4, 2, 2, 2, 2, 1, 1, 1, 1, 1, 3, 0, 1, 1, 1, 1, 1, 2

Solution: Now as we can see that the data is discrete and the lowest value is 0 and highest is 4 that is it ranges from 0 to 4. This data has to be presented in a frequency distribution so, that it could serve the purpose of statistical analysis. Otherwise such a huge set of data will not be meaningful. We need to make it concise, manageable and feasible for further calculations.

The table given here is giving a precise as well as concise view of 50 females' parity, which is easy to understand. It is labeled and is showing what each column is about whereas the data in question given above was not easy to understand.

After making the frequency table (Table 4.6), it can be subjected to statistical tests that are discussed later in this book.

TABLE 4.6: Frequency distribution table

Live birth	Tally marks	Frequency
0	||||, ||||	10
1	||||, ||||, ||||, ||||	20
2	||||, ||||, ||||	14
3					3
4					3
		Total = 50

PRESENTATION OF DATA—TABULATION

Presenting the huge data from a research is essential part to complicated vast sets of data in a meaningful and concise way. The other ways to represent data are through graphs, diagrams and charts, etc. Here we will discuss tables in detail as it is one of the practical need of any research presentation.

Tables

Definition of Table

- According to professor LR Connor, "Table involves the orderly and systematic presentation of numerical data in a form designed to elucidate the problem under consideration".
- According to professor MM Blaire, "Table in its broadest sense is an orderly arrangement of data in columns and rows".
- In the light of above definitions we can say that table is systematic organization and presentation of data in the form of columns (vertical) and rows (horizontal). It compresses the data and simplifies a complex data. It gives identity to data and reveals a certain pattern.

Characteristics of a Good Table

- Title is compatible with the objective of study.
- It facilitates comparison.
- Ideal size with stubs and headings.
- Uses zero, abbreviations, footnote, total and source of data.

Classification of Table

The tables (Fig. 4.1) can be classified according to:

- Purpose
- Originality
- Construction
- **According to purpose:** Such tables are published by governments like statistical abstract of India or census reports.
  - **General purpose table:** It does not serve specificity to a problem under consideration.
  - **Special purpose table:** It is prepared with some specific purpose in mind.
- **According to originality:**
  - **Original table:** Here data is presented in same form and manner in which the data was collected, to maintain its originality.

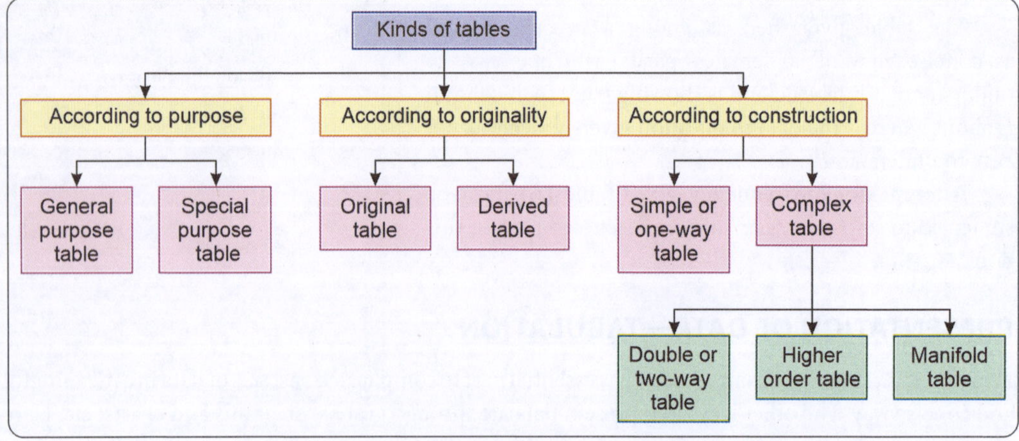

Figure 4.1: Different types of tables

- ▪ **Derived table:** The data can be presented in table after calculating their ratios, percentages, etc, and such tables are known as derived table.
- ● **According to construction:** Table can be simple ad complex according to construction.
  - ▪ **Simple table:** These are based on only one characteristic. It is also known as one-way table because it contains data of one characteristic only. It is simple to prepare and can be easily understood (Table 4.7).
  - ▪ **Complex table:** They show more than one characteristics and is formed when more attributes are considered under experiment.
    - ◆ **Two-way table:** When two characteristics are shown either in stub or the caption is divided into two coordinate parts (Table 4.8).
    - ◆ **Higher order table:** When it shows three characteristics in same table (Table 4.9).
    - ◆ **Manifold or multivariate table:** This type of table has more than two characteristics and is complex but provides complete information with facts based on the research. It is not used much and mostly one-way and the two-way tables are used (Table 4.10).

TABLE 4.7: Simple or one-way table showing frequency distribution of weight of school children

Age	14 years	15 years	16 years	17 years	Total
Frequency	92	71	58	19	**240**

TABLE 4.8: Two-way table—average number of patients in a PHC grouped according to age

OPD patients			
Age (in years)	Male	Female	Total
Below 25	25	5	30
25–35	30	4	34
35–45	25	5	30
45–55	22	3	25
Above 55	15	1	16
Total	**117**	**18**	**135**

TABLE 4.9: Higher order table showing number of patients in a PHC grouped according to age, religion, rank and sex

Religion	Age (in years)	Rank											
		Supervisor			Assistant			Clerks			Total		
		F	M	T	F	M	T	F	M	T	F	M	T
Hindu	Below 25												
	25–35												
	35–45												
	45–55												
	55 and above												

Contd...

Religion	Age (in years)	Rank											
		Supervisor			Assistant			Clerks			Total		
		F	M	T	F	M	T	F	M	T	F	M	T
Muslim	Below 25												
	25–35												
	35–45												
	45–55												
	55 and above												
	Total												

TABLE 4.10: Multivariate/manifold table

	OR (95% CI)[a]	P (two-tailed)
Sufficiency of equipment and personnel for Pap examination		
None to insufficient	3.1 (0.9–11.2)	0.09
Sufficient or better (Ref)	1.0	
Cancer fatality beliefs		
High to invariable fatality	1.9 (0.9–4.4)	0.12
Low to average fatality (Ref)	1.0	
Fear or embarrassment of Pap examination		
Above average to very high	16.2 (5.1, 51.5)	<0.01
None to average (Ref)	1.0	
Spousal/partner acceptance of Pap examination		
None to low	5.8 (1.3, 25.3)	0.02
Average to very high (Ref)	1.0	

[a]Adjusted for age at initiation of sexual activity, civil status, level of education, previous or current use of family planning/birth control, and income.
Abbreviations: CI, confidence interval; OR, odds ratio; Ref, reference group

Purposes of Tables

- To present data in concise form to provide information from a large number of observations. For example, census reports—such tables are accompanied with footnote, symbols, scales of measurements, etc.
- Tables form part of reports to be presented along with text, graphs and figures, etc.
- In any case, a table should be wisely designed so as to give a clear picture of a set of observations.
- For reducing huge volumes of data and to give it a meaningful look. It conserves space too and saves the labor of saving large data.
- They facilitate comparative analysis easily.
- It helps in detecting errors, which we come across while tabulating.
- The data is more presentable to the readers when it is tabulated.

Elements of a Table

- **Title:** An indicative title which should tell about the data contained in the table, along with number of table. The title should be short, precise and simple.
- **Head note:** It is placed below the title to provide extra information.
- **Column headings:** It should be concise and self-explanatory. It can have subheadings.
- **Stubs:** These are descriptions of characteristics in horizontal rows.
- **Interpretative aids:** These are totals, % of totals, carry forward figures or % difference, used in tables.
- **Body of table:** It has all numerical information of frequencies of observations in the columns and rows.
- **Unit of measurement:** These are given in stubs or columns to give it universal approach.
- **Dividers or lines:** Marks the different parts of a table.
- **Foot note:** It is given at the foot of table to indicate any fact or information which is presented through it. They give explanation of the data in precise and concise manner.
- **Source note:** It is at the bottom of table which indicates primary or secondary source of data if it has been collected from various sources.

Process of Table Making

- The data represents observations of some attributes. For statistical calculations these have to be on a numerical scale.
- The numerical scale may be discrete like in case of RBC count or continuous like hemoglobin measurement.
- The data is divided into suitable range having smaller division known as class intervals. The number of observation falling in each interval is counted and recorded.

Practical Tips

To determine class interval following guidelines can be kept in mind:
- The number of class intervals should be enough to condense the observed data, so as to bring out the significant features. Mostly 10–30 class intervals are sufficient for a long series.
- Uniform sized class intervals are more preferred (unless some important details are lost by this arrangement). Uniformity makes the interpretation easy and complications can be avoided in calculations and graph making.

Protein intake of 180 families from the urban population

Protein intake in g/consumption/day	15–25	25–35	35–45	45–55	55–65	65–75	Total
Number of families	40	30	40	20	30	20	180

- At times open end class intervals as given in the following table are also used, though these should be avoided.

Distribution of live birth of babies according to weight

Weight	<1200	1200–1699	1700–2199	2200 and above	Total
Number of babies	20	50	400	4000	4470

- Class limits must be precise and clear to understand.

Midpoints of intervals. For calculations the midpoint of each interval is used as a representative of each item in that interval. Here a few points must be kept in mind:
- Any tendency of an item to concentrate at a certain point should be recognized
- Intervals must be selected in a way that each class interval includes the items in that range.
- As much as possible, the midpoint and limits must be in whole numbers.

STUDENT ASSIGNMENT

LONG ANSWER QUESTIONS

1. What do you understand by classification of data? Discuss it.
2. What is tabulation? How does it help in presentation of data?

SHORT ANSWER QUESTIONS

1. Write a short note on tabulation of data.
2. Write different parts of table.

MULTIPLE CHOICE QUESTIONS

1. **Classification of data by attributes is called:**
   a. Quantitative classification
   b. Chronological classification
   c. Qualitative classification
   d. Geographical classification

2. **Classification of data according to location or areas is called:**
   a. Qualitative classification
   b. Quantitative classification
   c. Geographical classification
   d. Chronological classification

3. **Classification is applicable in case of:**
   a. Normal characters
   b. Quantitative characters
   c. Qualitative characters
   d. Both b and c

4. **The number of tally sheet count for each value or a group is called:**
   a. Class limit
   b. Class width
   c. Class boundary
   d. Frequency

5. **The frequency distribution according to individual variate values is called:**
   a. Discrete frequency distribution
   b. Cumulative frequency distribution
   c. Percentage frequency distribution
   d. Continuous frequency distribution

6. **The number of classes in a frequency distribution is obtained by dividing the range of variable by the:**
   a. Total frequency
   b. Class interval
   c. Mid-point
   d. Relative frequency

7. **The largest and the smallest values of any given class of a frequency distribution are called:**
   a. Class intervals
   b. Class marks
   c. Class boundaries
   d. Class limits

8. If in a frequency table, either the lower limit of first class or the upper limit of last class is not a fixed number, then classes are called:
   a. One-way classes
   b. Two-way classes
   c. Discrete classes
   d. Open-end classes

9. Total angle of the pie-chart is:
   a. 45°
   b. 90°
   c. 180°
   d. 360°

5

Frequency Distribution

"Clutter is nothing more than postponed decisions."
—Barbara Hemphill

LEARNING OBJECTIVES

After the completion of the chapter, the readers will be able to:
- Understand frequency distribution.
- Make frequency distribution table.
- Make cumulative frequency distribution table.
- Make relative frequency percentage table.

CHAPTER OUTLINE

- Introduction
- Practical Importance of Frequency Distribution
- Frequency Distribution Table

INTRODUCTION

Frequency distribution is a tabular/graphical representation of a data. The counts or frequencies of various outcomes in a sample are presented within a particular interval. Therefore, frequency distribution is a summary of values obtained from a sample data. Frequency distribution shows a compiled view of the entire data in an organized way.

- **Univariate:** The frequency distribution can be univariate when single variable is depicted.
- **Multivariate**: It can be multivariate when more than one variable is depicted.

Let us understand what frequency is?

Frequency: Suppose, we have data of marks obtained by 10 students from a class in a test as given here: 23, 26, 11, 18, 9, 21, 23, 11, 22, 11

This form of data is known as raw data. When we look at the data, it is clear that some digits are repeating. For example, 23 is repeating for 2 times, 11 is repeating for 3 times, whereas other digits are occurring only once. It means the frequency of 23 is 2, and of 11 is 3, whereas for other digits it is 1.

> **Must Know**
>
> - Frequency distribution is used in both qualitative as well as quantitative data.
> - Histograms, bar charts, pie charts and line charts are used as frequency distribution charts.

Therefore, we can say that the frequency of a particular data value is the number of times the data value occurs in that particular set of data. The frequency of a data value is represented by 'f'.

PRACTICAL IMPORTANCE OF FREQUENCY DISTRIBUTION

- A well-constructed frequency distribution table makes it possible to analyze the structure of population with respect to a given characteristic.
- The groups into which a population can be broken down, are easily determined by looking at the frequency distribution.
- The nature of distribution of the members of a population with respect to a given characteristic can be ascertained—whether the distribution is symmetric or asymmetric; or the degree of concentration of a particular value.
- Calculation of statistics becomes comfortable like calculation of range of a character or average value, etc.
- We can calculate the degree of skewness, and the measure of kurtosis (the degree of closeness of a cluster of values of characteristics around an average value).
- For easy understanding, a frequency distribution can be represented graphically such as histogram, polygon, etc.

FREQUENCY DISTRIBUTION TABLE

A large data is very difficult to understand and interpret unless it is 'organized'. Here, we have used a term interpret which means 'statistical interpretation' to get the results and to forecast some strategy. To do so, we have to organize data into a concise form so that interpretation and analysis becomes easy. A frequency distribution table talks about the grouping of data of a population with respect to quantitative characteristics. Sometimes, we arrange the values in increasing or decreasing values of magnitude and then it is called 'ranked'. The frequency table is based on some continuously varying characteristic like age, or height, or weight and so on.

- **Ungrouped data:** Here, we calculate the frequency for each observation one by one.

  Example: The test scores of 20 students are as follows (Table 5.1):

  23, 26, 11, 18, 9, 21, 23, 30, 22, 11, 21, 20, 11, 13, 23, 11, 29, 25, 26, 26

  Solution: Some values are appearing more than once in this data that is frequency of few values is more. The table here can help in understanding frequency as:
  In the above example, the frequency of 21 is 2, frequency of 26 and 23 is 3 and the frequency of 11 is 4.

TABLE 5.1: Frequency table for the students marks obtained in the test

Marks obtained in the test	9	11	13	18	20	21	22	23	25	26	29	30	Total
No. of students (frequency)	1	4	1	1	1	2	1	3	1	3	1	1	20

- **Grouped data:** Now consider a situation where we have to collect data for the test scores of 100 students. We will have 100 observations and now it will become difficult to tally for each and every score of all 100 observations. Moreover, the table obtained will be very large in length, will occupy more space and will not be easy to understand. Here, we use a grouped frequency

Practical Tip

The total frequency must always be total of the number of observations after tallying. In the example given above, the total is 20 which is the total number of observations too.

distribution table. Most of the data that we come across in real life is in the form of grouped data. Generally, the amount of data is large and associated with corresponding frequencies of each value and we may divide data items into class intervals to further condense our data. For example, we have a data about hypertension patients of varying age groups in a hospital. The data here can be displayed in classes associated with their corresponding frequencies depending on the number of patients falling in each class interval. Grouped data can be further classified into two types:

1. **Discrete frequency distribution:** Frequency distributions can be grouped like for a discrete characteristic if the range of this particular characteristic is fairly large. Here, the individual data entry is accompanied by its corresponding frequency. There are two columns and in one column we write the individual data items, denoted by **X,** and in other column we write frequencies, denoted by **f.** For example, the distribution of primary health centers in a state with respect to number of patients visiting it.

2. **Continuous frequency distribution:** Here, the data entries are grouped into various class intervals and their corresponding frequencies. There is one column for class intervals and another column for frequencies.

Process of Making Frequency Distribution Table

To make a frequency distribution, several steps are followed:

- **First step is to decide the number of classes:** Neither too less classes nor too many classes are good, as in either case the data will not be presented justifiably. The maximum number of classes can be determined by formula:

Number of classes (C) = 1 + 3 − 3 log (n)

Or C = $\sqrt{n}$ (approximately); where n is total number of observations in a data.

- **Second step is to calculate the range of data:** By looking carefully on the values collected in a data.

Range: It is defined as the difference between the maximum (L) and minimum value (S) of a data. Therefore, range can be calculated as:

Range = L–S

- **Third step is to calculate the width (h) of a class:**

h = range/number of classes

Third step will give class interval or width to condense our huge data.

Practical Tips

- Keep the width of the class interval uniform in all the classes.
- The first class must cover the lowest value of data and the last class must contain the highest value of the data.
- The starting point of first class is arbitrary and may be less than or equal to the minimum value obtained from the data. The midpoint or the average of lower- and upper-class limits of the first-class limits must be perfectly included.
- Keep running tally till the last observation, to keep a check that no observation is missed.

Let us understand with examples:

Example: A survey was taken of 20 families, to find out how many kids they have and the results were recorded as follows:

1, 2, 1, 0, 3, 4, 0, 1, 1, 1, 2, 2, 3, 2, 3, 2, 1, 4, 0, 0

Solution:

- Divide the results (x) into intervals, and then count the number of results in each interval. In this case, the intervals would be the number of households with no child (0), one child (1), and two children (2) and so on.
- Make a table with separate columns for the interval numbers (the number of children per families), the tallied results, and the frequency of results in each interval. Label these columns as—number of children, tally and frequency (Table 5.2).
- Read the list of data from left to right and place a tally mark in the appropriate row. For example, the first result is 1, so place a tally mark in the row beside where 1 appears in the interval column (number of children). The next result is 2, so place a tally mark in the row beside the 2, and so on. When you reach your fifth tally mark, draw a tally line through the preceding four marks to make your final frequency calculations easier to read. Now it will look like a stack.

TABLE 5.2: Frequency table for the number of children in each family

Number of children (x)	Tally	Frequency (f)
0	IIII	4
1	JHT, I	6
2	JHT	5
3	III	3
4	II	2
		Total = 20

- Add up the number of tally marks in each row and record them in the final column entitled Frequency.

  By looking at this frequency distribution table we can quickly see that out of 20 families surveyed, 4 families had no children, 6 families had 1 and so on (Table 5.2).

Constructing a Cumulative Frequency Distribution Table

A cumulative frequency distribution table is more detailed table. It looks almost like a frequency distribution table, but it has a column with added values and it contains the cumulative frequency and there may be a column for cumulative percentage of the results, as well.

Class intervals:
- If a variable takes a large number of values, then it is comfortable to present and handle the data by grouping the values into class intervals. Continuous variables are presented in class intervals, while for discrete variables they can be grouped into class intervals or not. For example, we have set out age ranges for a study of young people, while allowing for the possibility that some older people may also fall into the scope of our study.
- The frequency of a class interval is the number of observations that occur in a particular predefined interval. For example, if 20 people aged 5–9 appear in our study data, the frequency in class 5–9 intervals will be 20.
- The endpoints of a class interval are the lowest and highest values that a variable can take.
- If we have data showing following class intervals—0–4 years, 5–9 years, 10–14 years, 15–19 years, 20– 24 years, and 25 years and over, then the endpoints of the first interval are 0 and 4 if the variables are discrete, and 0 and 4.999 if the variable is continuous. It means the values from 0–4 will fall under 0–4 years and so on.

Contd...

Class interval width:
- Class interval width is the difference between the lower endpoint of an interval and the lower endpoint of the next interval. Therefore, if our data has continuous intervals like 0–4, 5–9, etc., then the width of the first 5 intervals is 5, and the last interval is open, because no higher endpoint is assigned to it. The intervals could also be written as $0 - <5$, $5 - <10$, $10 - <15$, $15 - <20$, $20 - <25$, and 25 and >25.
- For deciding on the width of the class intervals, you have to decide between having intervals short enough so that most of the observations fall in the same interval, but they should be long enough so that you do not end up with only one observation per interval. It is equally important to make sure that the class intervals are mutually exclusive.

Example: The ages of the participants in a survey were recorded as follows:

36, 48, 54, 92, 57, 63, 66, 76, 66, 80

Solution:

- Divide the results into intervals, and then count the number of results in each interval. Here, intervals of 10 will be appropriate. Again, 36 is the lowest age and 92 is the highest age, so start the intervals at 35–44 and end the intervals with 85–94.
- Make a table similar to the earlier frequency distribution table but with 3 extra columns.
    - **Lower value column:** Write the lower values of the result intervals in the first column. For example, in the first row, you will write the number 35.
    - **Upper value column:** Write the upper values of the result in the second column. For example, in the second row, you will write the number 44.
    - **Frequency:** Note down the number of times a result in the third column—a particular digit appears between the lower and upper values. For example, in the third row, you will write the number 1.
    - **Cumulative frequency:** Here, you will add the cumulative frequency. Because it is the first row, the cumulative frequency will remain the same. Whereas, in the second row, the frequency for the 35–44 interval (i.e., 1) is added to the frequency for the 45–54 interval (i.e., 2). Thus, the cumulative frequency will be 3 here, meaning we have 3 participants in the age group of 34–54.
    - **Percentage:** In this column, write the percentage of the frequency. To do so, divide each frequency by the total number of results and multiply by 100. Here, the frequency of the first row is 1 and the total number of results is 10 which will be equal to 10%.

$$10 \ (1 \div 10) \times 100 = 10$$

    - **Cumulative percentage:** In this column, divide the cumulative frequency by the total number of results, then to make a percentage, multiply by 100. Note that the last number in this column should be equal to 100.

    Now the cumulative frequency distribution table will look like this (Table 5.3):

TABLE 5.3: Ages of participants

Lower value	Upper value	Frequency (f)	Cumulative frequency	Percentage	Cumulative percentage
35	44	1	1	10	10
45	54	2	(2+1) = 3	20	30
55	64	2	(3+2) = 5	20	50
65	74	2	(5+2) = 7	20	70
75	84	2	(7+2) = 9	20	90
85	94	1	(9+1) = 10	10	100

Example: Construct a frequency distribution table for the large numbers of observations of diabetic patients.

423, 369, 387, 411, 393, 394, 371, 377, 389, 409, 392, 408, 431, 401, 363, 391, 405, 382, 400, 381, 399, 415, 428, 422, 396, 372, 410, 419, 386, 390

Solution:

After observing the data, we find that here the lowest value is 363 and the highest is 431. We will take a class interval of 10, the interval for the first class is 360–369 and includes 363 (the lowest value). Remember, there should always be enough class intervals so that the highest value is included. The completed frequency distribution table will look like this (Table 5.4):

TABLE 5.4: Sugar levels in diabetic patients

Classes (x)	360–369	370–379	380–389	390–399	400–409	410–419	420–429	430–439	Total
Tally marks	II	III	IIII	IIII II	IIII	IIII	III	I	
Frequency (f)	2	3	5	7	5	4	3	1	30

Practical Tips

Rules for data sets that contain very large number of observations

In short follow these basic rules while constructing a frequency distribution table for a data set which contains a large number of observations:

1. Find the lowest and highest values of the variables.
2. Decide on the width of the class intervals.
3. Include all possible values of the variable.

Relative Frequency and Percentage Frequency

Relative frequency and percentage frequency may also be required by a researcher, as he/she may like to know what proportion of the values falls into each class interval.

The relative frequency of a particular observation or class interval is calculated by dividing the frequency (**f**) by the number of observations (**n**): that is, (**f ÷ n**). Thus:

$$\text{Relative frequency} = \frac{\text{Frequency}}{\text{Number of observations}}$$

Further the percentage frequency is calculated by multiplying each relative frequency value by 100.

Thus:

$$\text{Percentage frequency} = \text{relative frequency} \times 100$$

Example: Constructing relative frequency and percentage frequency in a table.

Solution:

Using the data of example 4, here is table of relative frequency and percent frequency:

After looking at the above data we can conclude that:

- 7% of values fall in the class 360–369 (in the first class for example).
- And the probability of any randomly selected observation in this range is approximately 0.07.
- The first column in the table here represents the marks obtained in class interval form. The lowest number in a class interval is called the **lower limit** and the highest number is called the **upper limit**. This example is the case of continuous class intervals as the upper limit of one class is the lower limit of the following class (Table 5.5).

TABLE 5.5: Relative frequency and percentage frequency table

Classes (x)	Frequency (f)	Relative frequency	Percent frequency
360–369	2	0.07	7
370–379	3	0.10	10
380–389	5	0.17	17
390–399	7	0.23	23
400–409	5	0.17	17
410–419	4	0.13	13
420–429	3	0.10	10
430–439	1	0.03	3
Total	**30**	**1.00**	**100**

Practical Tips

In continuous cases, any observation corresponding to the extreme values of a class is always included in that class where it is the lower limit. For example, if we had a student who has scored 5 marks in the test, his marks would be included in the class interval 5–10 and not 0–5. Here, we have assumed that a representative sample has been drawn but in the real world, researcher has to refer to an estimate of variability, in order to complete the analysis.

Example: The following is the distribution for the age of the students in a school:

Age	0–5	5–10	10–15	15–20
Number of students	35	45	50	30

Calculate the following:
- The lower limit of the first-class interval.
- The class limits of the third class.
- The class mark for the interval 5–10.
- The class size.

Solution:
- The lower limit of the first class interval, i.e., 0–5 is '0'.
- The class limits of the third class, i.e., 10–15 are 10 (lower limit) and 15 (upper limit).
- The class mark is defined as the average of the upper and the lower limits of a class. For 5–10, the class mark is $\frac{5+10}{2} = 7.5$.
- The class size is the difference between the lower and the upper class-limits. Here, we have a uniform class size, which is equal to 5 (5–0, 10–5, 15–10, 20–15, all are equal to 5).

STUDENT ASSIGNMENT

LONG ANSWER QUESTIONS

1. What is frequency distribution table? Discuss in detail.
2. Explain the relative frequency and percentage frequency with an example.

SHORT ANSWER QUESTIONS

1. What is a relative frequency?
2. Define frequency.
3. Define range.
4. Write a short note about the class interval.
5. What is an ungrouped data?
6. Define grouped data.

MULTIPLE CHOICE QUESTIONS

1. **Type of cumulative frequency distribution in which class intervals are added in top to bottom order is classified as:**
   a. Variation distribution
   b. Less than type distribution
   c. More than type distribution
   d. Marginal distribution

2. **Type of cumulative frequency distribution in which class intervals are added in bottom to top order is classified as:**
   a. More than type distribution
   b. Marginal distribution
   c. Variation distribution
   d. Less than type distribution

3. **'Less than type distribution' and 'more than type distribution' are types of:**
   a. Class distribution
   b. Cumulative class distribution
   c. Cumulative frequency distribution
   d. Upper limit distribution

4. **Distribution which shows cumulative figure of all observations placed below upper limit of classes in distribution is considered:**
   a. Cumulative frequency distribution
   b. Upper limit distribution
   c. Class distribution
   d. Cumulative class distribution

5. **Class frequency is divided by number of observations in frequency distribution to convert it into:**
   a. Relative margin distribution
   b. Relative variable distribution
   c. Relative frequency distribution
   d. Relative width distribution

6

Diagrammatic or Graphical Presentation

"You have to write your own story so draw your own graph and follow your own rhythm"
—Anju Dhir

LEARNING OBJECTIVES

After the completion of the chapter, the readers will be able to:
- Understand practical importance of diagrammatic or graphical presentation of data contrast both therapy and fluidotherapy.
- Make diagrams and graphs by following the rules and knowledge that are given in the chapter.

CHAPTER OUTLINE

- Introduction
- Practical Importance of the Diagrammatical/ Graphical Presentation
- Rules to be Followed While Diagrammatical/ Graphical Presentation
- Types of Diagrams and Graphs
- Graphical Presentation

INTRODUCTION

Figures or diagrams and tables make a text presentation livelier. They are used to represent a data in attractive visual way. Even a layman can understand the data presented in a figure or diagram or in a graph. It is a known fact that the visual presentation makes a more lasting impression as compared to detailed numbers or the messages. They help us to have a real grasp of the overall picture of the data.

PRACTICAL IMPORTANCE OF THE DIAGRAMMATICAL/GRAPHICAL PRESENTATION

- The data is condensed in the form of a diagram and it can be retained in memory for long period of time.
- It saves space, time and energy.
- It makes the comparison of data much easier, without calculations.
- They are more attractive and convey information that can be understood even without the knowledge of statistics.
- They are widely used in all fields of science, technologies and information.

RULES TO BE FOLLOWED WHILE DIAGRAMMATICAL/GRAPHICAL PRESENTATION

- Diagram or graph must be chosen appropriately based on the data and need of study.
- It should be neatly, properly drawn by using various symbols, colors and appropriate scales.
- Size of the graph or diagram depends on the available space.
- The proportions of x- and y-axis must be maintained so as to give accurate picture of the data.
- Diagram/graph must have clearly indicative parameters on x- and y-axis so as to know which variable each of these is represented.
- The caption below the diagram/graph should be clear enough so as to suggest about in data it represents.
- Any symbol, abbreviation, digit or statistical calculation must be shown along the side.

TYPES OF DIAGRAMS AND GRAPHS

Line Diagram/Graph

Line diagram is one of the simplest ways of presenting data. Here, line is drawn to present data by taking two corresponding variables on x- and y-axis. It can be vertical or horizontal. The variables are presented on two axes (Fig. 6.1).

Practice question: The scores of 15 students in an examination are given here. Draw a line graph for it.

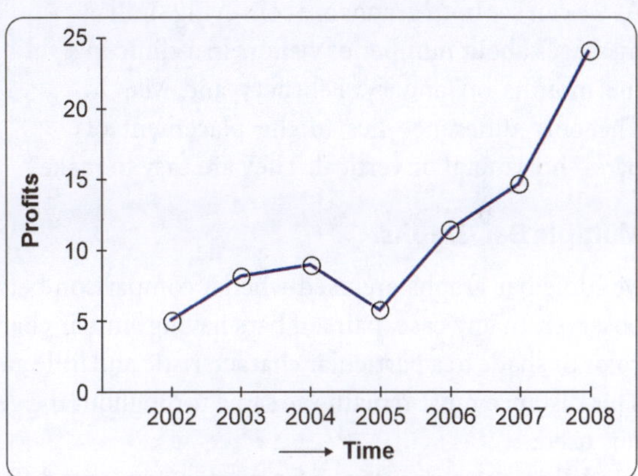

Figure 6.1: Line graph

Students	1	2	3	4	5	6	7	8	9	10	11	13	13	14	15
Scores	20	30	90	85	89	30	60	45	80	48	52	75	57	52	70

Bar Diagram/Graph

As the name suggests, when data is presented in form of bars or rectangles, it is termed to be a bar diagram. Discrete variables like number of relapses of a particular disease in a hospital or number of patients can be presented graphically with the help of bar graphs. Each value is represented by a bars, and the height of bar indicates the frequency of occurrence of that particular value.

Features of a Bar Graph

- The rectangular box in a bar diagram is known as a bar. It represents the value of a variable.
- These bars can be arranged either vertically or horizontally.
- Bars are equidistant from each other.
- Each bar originates from a common baseline or axis.
- The width of bars remains the same but the height changes, depending on the values of a variable, to denote the difference between their values.
- Unless they are in a specific order, conventionally bars can be arranged in an ascending or descending order.

Types of Bar Graphs

They serve different purposes with a little modification as follows:

Simple Bar Graphs/Diagrams

Simple bar graphs explain one variable and are constructed on x-axis with heights which reflect the occurrence of a particular value on y-axis. A little space is kept between two bars to show them distinctly. They are of two types:

1. Horizontal bar graph (Fig. 6.2A).
2. Vertical bar graph (Fig. 6.2B).

As we can see both graphs are conveying similar messages about number of visitors in a clinic in the months of January, February and March. The only difference lies in the placement of bars—horizontal or vertical. They are easy to make.

> ### Practical Tips
>
> - Simple vertical bar graph is the finest, when one has to compare between two or more independent variables. Each variable on either axis will tell a fixed value.
> - If data has negative and positive values, but it is to be represented as a comparison between two or more fixed independent variables, horizontal bar graph is the answer. Vertical axis can be oriented in the middle of horizontal axis so as to present negative and positive.

Multiple Bar Graphs

Multiple bar graphs are used when a comparison between two or more variables is required by an observer. In any case, pairs of bars having similar characteristics are drawn on x-axis with the same color or shade to a particular characteristic and little gap is left between two consecutive pairs of bars. This distance must remain the same throughout the graph.

It is used:

- When the observations from categories have different components.
- When the comparison between component parts is required.

Example: The scores of a class in coeducational nursing institute have been presented in the form of a multiple bar graph. The class was divided into groups based on the ages of the male and female students into groups 1, 2, 3, 4 and 5. The average can be calculated directly from the graph as is depicted in the **Figure 6.3**.

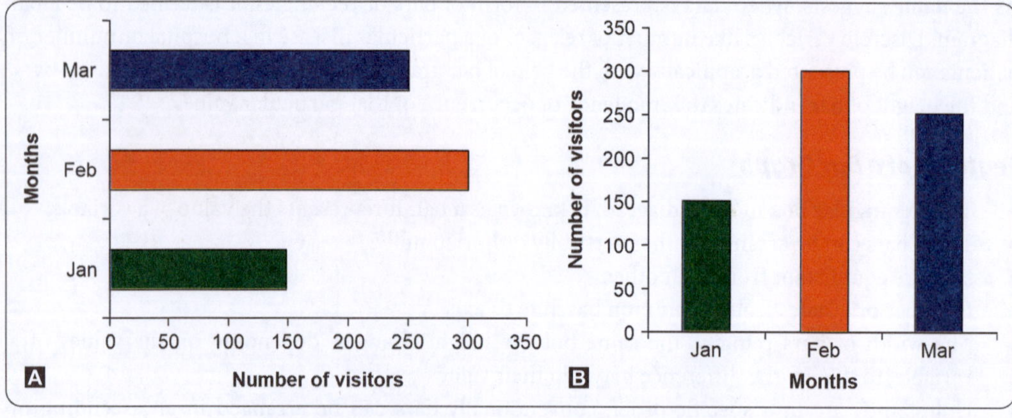

Figures 6.2A and B: **A.** Horizontal bar; **B.** Vertical bar

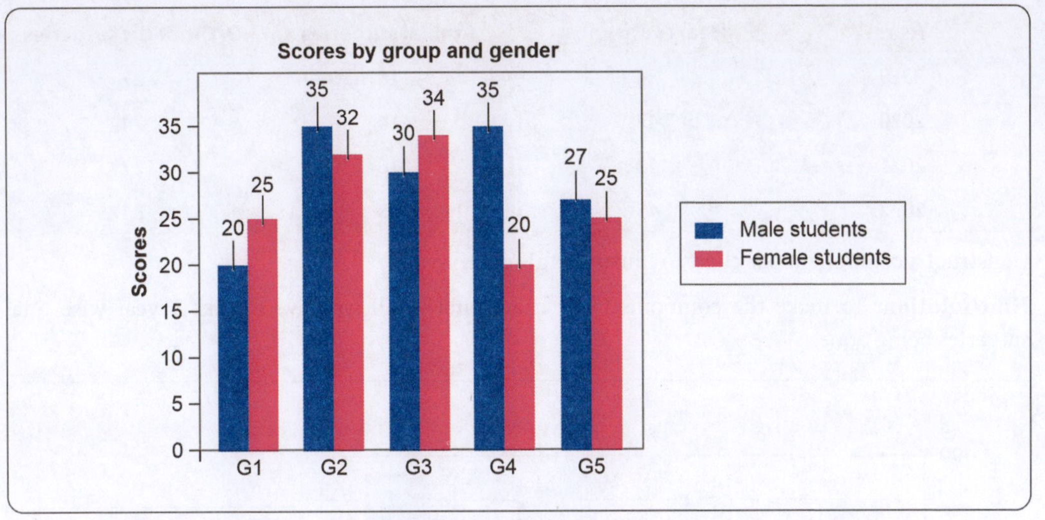

Figure 6.3: Multiple bar graph

Group 1 has averages as male – 20 and female – 25,

Group 2 has averages as male – 35 and female – 32,

Group 3 has averages as male – 30 and female – 34,

Group 4 has averages as male – 35 and female – 20,

Group 5 has averages as male – 27 and female – 25,

Practice question: In a particular hospital, the number of deliveries is given for the last 6 months. Draw a bar graph to depict following data.

Months	Normal delivery	Assisted delivery	Cesarean
January	70	20	40
February	20	10	25
March	50	18	45
April	80	15	50
May	60	10	35

Component or Subdivided Bar Graphs

Subdivided bar graphs are also known as component graphs, as each bar is broken into more than one complements. It is a modification of multiple bar diagram and requires less space as compared to multiple bar graph. It gives good results when the number of components is less, like 3 or 5. The space occupied by a particular character in bar remains uniform in all the bar segments with similar colors.

Example: The table given here shows the heart surgeries, cranial surgeries and orthopedic surgeries done in a hospital during the years 2019–2022 (Fig. 6.4).

Years	Heart surgeries	Cranial surgeries	Orthopedic surgeries
2019	34	18	27
2020	43	14	24
2021	43	16	27
2022	45	13	34

Construct a component bar chart to illustrate this data.

Hint/solution: To make the component bar chart, first of all we have to take a year-wise total surgeries being done.

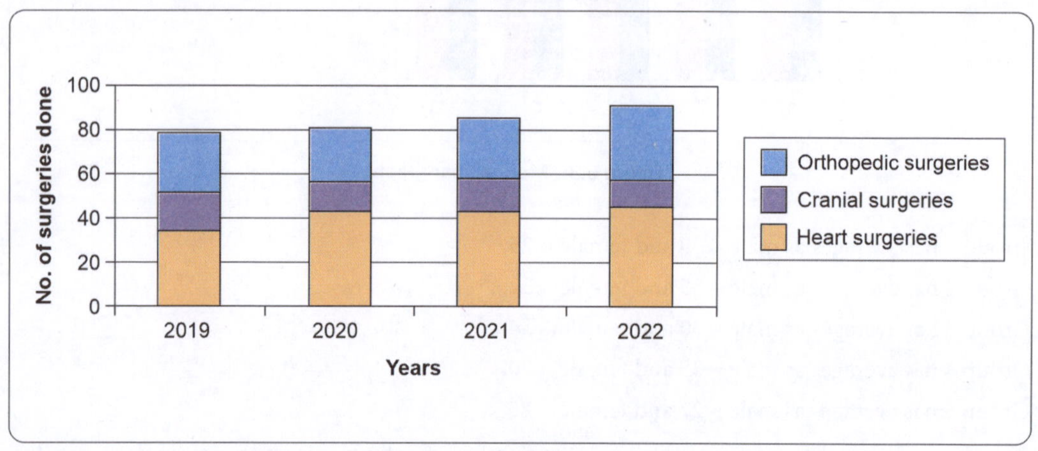

Figure 6.4: Component bar graph

Percentage Bar Graph

Percentage bar graph is variation of subdivided bar graph and here quantities are first transformed into percentages in such a way that all components in one graph equals to 100%. It is used when comparison of different items is important.

Example: The percentage of expenditure on various items by 3 families has been shown in **Figure 6.5**. The data is given in table.

Hint/solution: The expenditure by each family for every component is first converted into percentage and a table is made as shown here in below:

Components	Family 1	Family 2	Family 3
Food	57.3	53.5	58.0
Clothing	10.7	11.0	12.0
Rent	13.3	13.5	8.2
Others	18.7	22.0	21.8

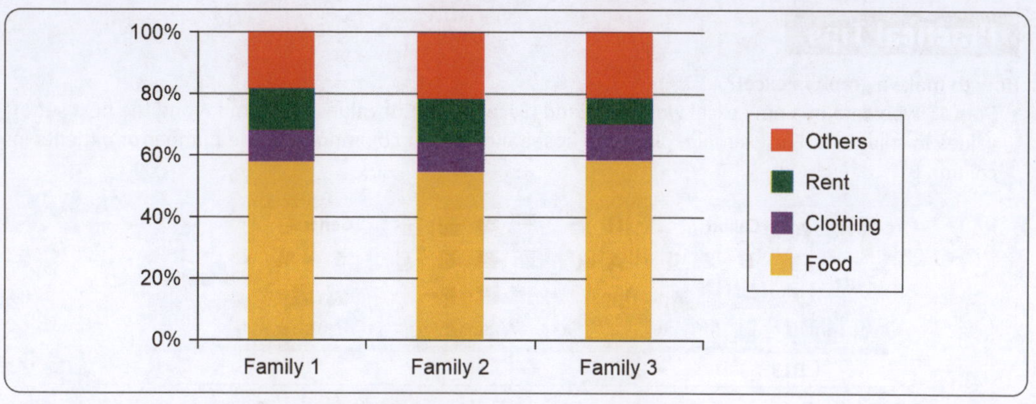

Figure 6.5: Percentage bar graph

Broken Bar Graphs

Broken bar graphs are used to show a value which is very high or low as compared to others. The higher value bars are broken as they are having abnormal high values. The data displayed in the table here, contains high value at one place and if we have to show it in graph along with other values, the graph will be very abnormal looking. So, to represent this data broken graph is used.

As we can observe that most of the data is below 1,000 units. Data at 4th place above 35,000 units. Therefore, we break the data here and the graph looks as shown in Figure 6.6.

Data	Patients admitted in various specialities
ENT	899
Cardiac	543
Neuro	787
General ward	35323
Ortho	121
Pediatric	234

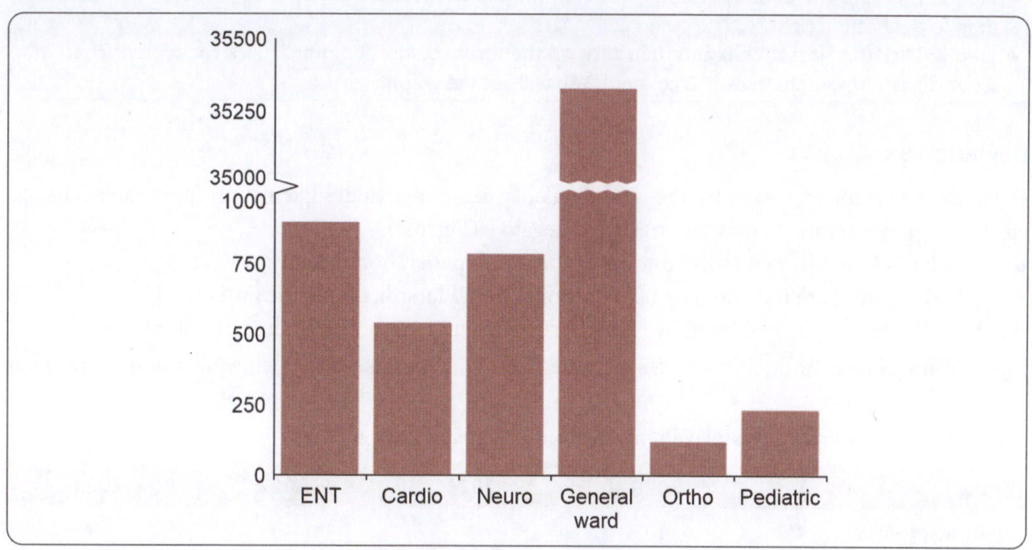

Figure 6.6: Broken bar graph

Practical Tips

How to make a graph in excel?

- **Step 1:** Type data in a new excel worksheet and place one set of values in column A and the next set of values in column B. For example, place the hospital names in column A and the number of patients in column B.

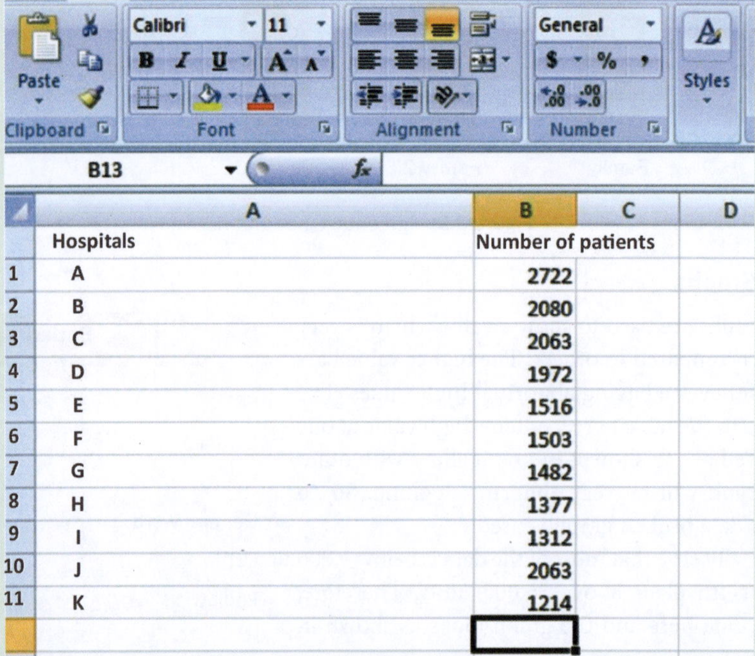

- **Step 2:** Highlight the data by selecting. Click in the top left (cell A1 in this example) and then hold and drag to the bottom right.
- **Step 3:** Click the "insert" tab and then click on the arrow below "Column." Click the type of chart you would like (for example, click "2D column). You will get the graph.

Deviation Bar Graphs

Deviation bar graphs are used to represent data obtained as net values like net profit, payable balance, etc. Here, the observations may be positive or negative (Fig. 6.7).

- The basic line is drawn in the middle of the graph paper, horizontally.
- Positive values are indicated by bars of proportional length, above the horizontal line.
- Negative values are indicated by bars of proportional length, below the horizontal line.

The graph will be as shown in following figure. Example: Represent the below data in deviation bar graph.

Profit and loss statement of a private multispeciality hospital for 4 years

Years	2020	2021	2022	2023
Profit/loss (millions of ₹)	10	3	−5	−8

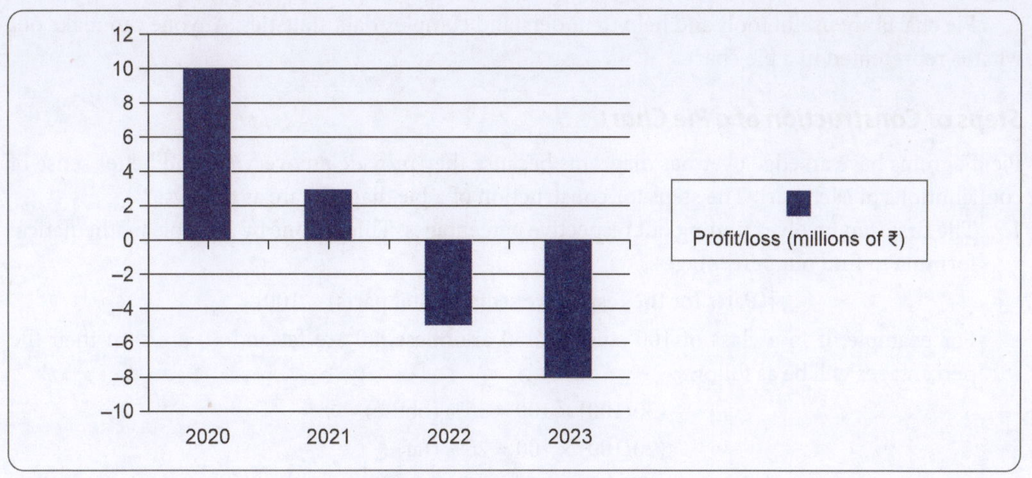

Figure 6.7: Deviation bar graph

Stacked Bar Graphs

Stacked bar graphs are similar to grouped bar graphs in a way that they are used to display information about the sub-groups which are in different categories. The bars represent the sub-groups and are placed on top of each other so as to make a single column (Fig. 6.8).

They can also be placed side by side to make a single bar. The total height or length of the bar represents the total size of each category whereas different colors or shadings are utilized to indicate the relative contribution of different sub-groups.

Example: Draw a stacked bar graphs to show the adults and children visiting patients in a clinic in the months of April, May and June.

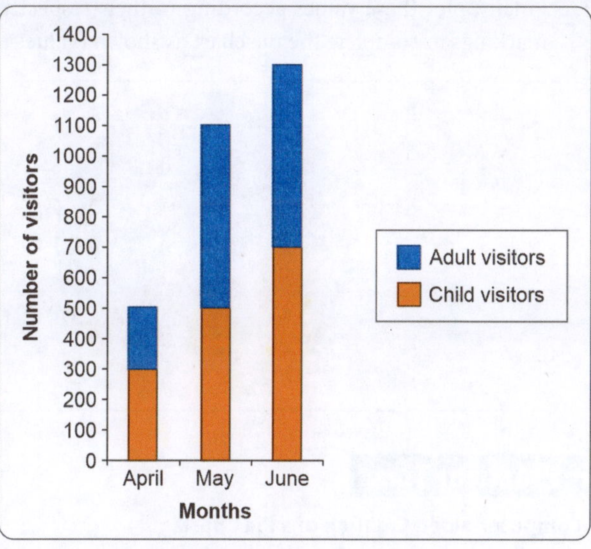

Figure 6.8: Stacked bar graph

Stacked bar graphs are also used to present the percentage contribution of different sub-groups within each category. The same information can be presented in a series of pie charts.

Pie Chart/Diagrams

The variables which are nominal in nature, are represented by pie charts. These are circular diagrams with divided sectors, where each sector is proportional to the percentage of the category it represents. The total area of circle represents the total value and the different parts of it indicate toward different values. The total sum of all angles in all sectors taken together is 360°. Pie chart is used widely as it depicts whole data in one condensed picture. They are easy to understand with a quick look.

Pie charts are useful tools and help to understand complex data statistics. Anyone can make out what is represented in a pie chart.

Steps of Construction of a Pie Chart

Pie diagrams have an edge over bar diagrams because they provide an overview and better sense of contributions of each part. The steps for construction of a pie diagram are as follows:

1. The first step involves finding out respective percentages. This is done by a simple mathematical formula to find out percentages:

$$[(\text{Parts for the respective sector})/\text{total parts}) \times 100]$$

    For example, if in a class of 100 students, 30 are obese, 20 are fat and 50 are slim then the percentages will be as follows:

$$(30/100) \times 100 = 30\% \text{ (obese)}$$
$$(20/100) \times 100 = 20\% \text{ (fat)}$$
$$(50/100) \times 100 = 50\% \text{ (slim)}$$

2. A circle is comprised of 360°. The angles that each sector will have across the circle is decided by:

$$(\text{Percentage value}/100) \times 360°$$

3. Finally, plot these values according to their respective angles on a circle and give appropriate markings to complete the pie chart as shown (values are arbitrary here).

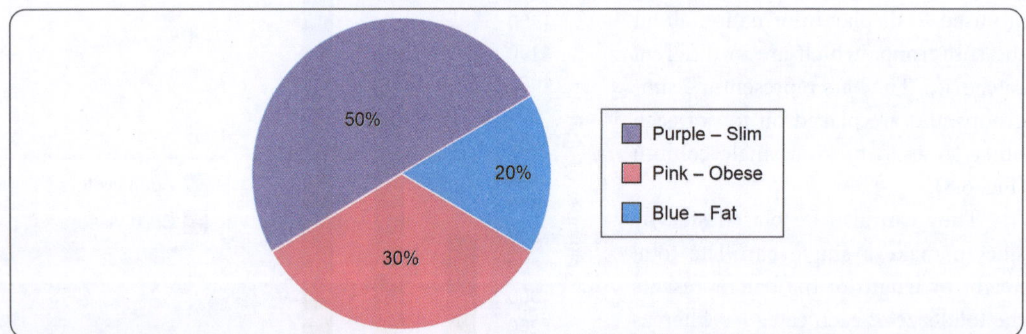

Practical Tips

Computer-aided Creation of a Pie Chart

- Getting the data ready for a pie chart is simple.
- Just make sure that the **categories and associated values are each on separate lines**.
- Once the data is formatted, making a pie chart only takes a couple of clicks.
- First, **highlight the data** you want in the chart.
- Then click to the **Insert** tab on the Ribbon. In the **Charts** group, click on **Insert Pie or Doughnut Chart**.

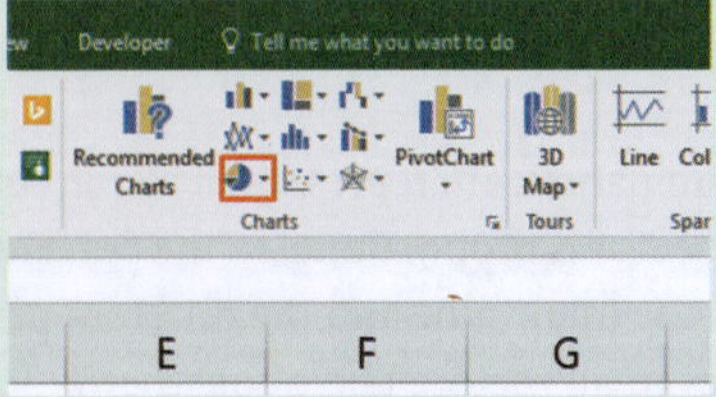

Contd...

- In the resulting menu, click on **2D Pie**:

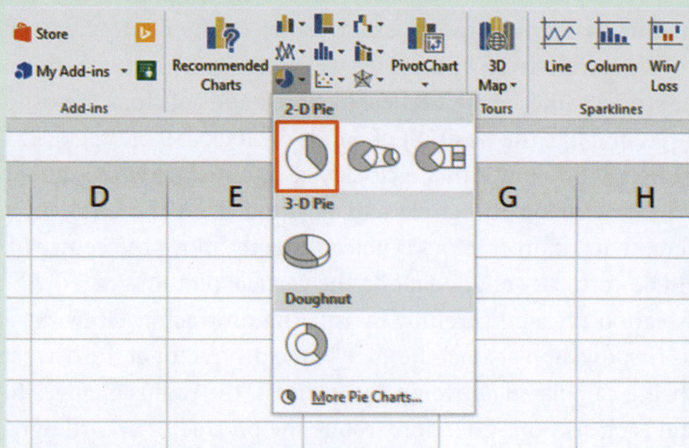

- After this, pie chart will appear.

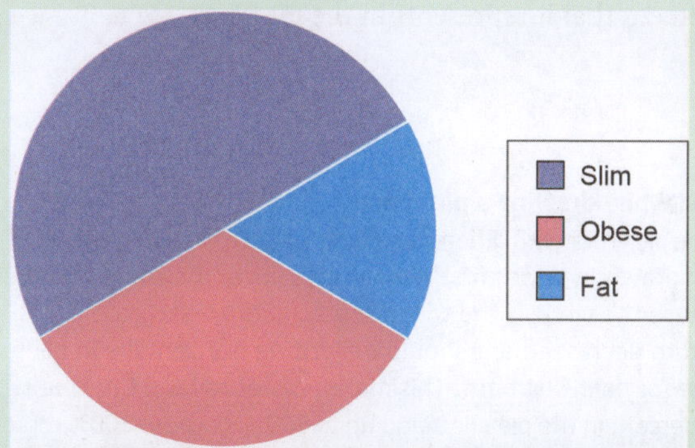

- To give an entirely new look to pie chart go to **chart styles**.
- From **Design** portion of the Ribbon, a number of different styles will be displayed in a row. Move the mouse over them to see a preview and select according to the liking.

Manually Making a Pie Chart

- **Step 1**
  - Gather the numerical data and label information, write it down in descending order.
  - Add this data to calculate the total (denominator).
  - Calculate the proportion of the total for each data point by dividing each data in a category one by one (numerator/denominator or total that has been calculated above). Here you will get a percentage value.

- **Step 2:** Calculate the angle between the two sectors of each pie slice. In order to do this, multiply each percentage (still in decimal form) by 360°. It is done because there are 360° in a circle. For example, 30% of 360° is 108°.

- **Step 3:** Check again your calculations because after adding the number of degrees you have calculated for each data value, the sum must be 360°. If this is not so then double-check your work because something has been missed.

- **Step 4:** The pie chart can be drawn accurately with the help of a compass and a protractor to measure the angles. In case, a compass is not available, fetch a circle template like a lid or a CD or a bangle.
  - Draw the radius by starting in the exact center of the circle. Draw a straight line to the periphery of the circle from the center. (First make a dot with the compass to find the center). The straight line can be vertical like the hands of clock at position 12 or 6 o'clock or it can be horizontal like the position of hands of clock at 9 or 3 o'clock. The segments which are to be created will follow either a clockwise or anticlockwise sequence.
  - Place your protractor on the circle and position it on the circle in such a way that the 90° mark (crosshair of protractor) is placed exactly above the center of the circle. The zero point should be vertically aligned along the vertical plot line.
  - Draw each section division carefully by rotating protractor. Draw the sections carefully by marking the first division against the edge of the protractor at the correct angle, and by using the angles being calculated above. In this process, the radius changes to the line just drawn when we add each section. Therefore, rotate the protractor accordingly. When marking the angle lines, make sure that they are sharp and fine, so that it looks clear and easy to visualize.
- **Step 5:** Color each segment differently depending on the requirement and likings. Name the sections and the percent that it represents in the pie chart.

Takeaway

Points to be kept in mind while drawing a pie chart:
- Color each section of the pie chart with different color or pattern so as to make each section easily visualizable.
- If everything has been drawn in pencil first then always ink in the circle first, before starting to color any of the segments. Because the circle is the trickiest part to draw accurately.
- Labels or words added to each segment should be written horizontally in centered with the same visual distance from the edge for each segment. This makes easier to read the labels.
- Make sure that all the percent in the pie chart add up to 100%, because 100% represents the entire pie chart.
- Separate each sector on a pie chart from others by using different designs or colors to make it easy to understand.
- Double check that all angles are measured accurately.
- Add title and labels.
- Double check the calculations, as with wrong calculations naturally, pie chart will be incorrect.
- Add a key to indicate colors or symbols so that others can understand well.
- To calculate the angle, divide each frequency by the total frequency multiplied by 360°.
- Use a protractor and a ruler when making your chart after making sure that all equations are correct.

For example: Here is a figure showing different age groups of patients in a hospital ward. Key has been given aside to indicate the meaning of colors.

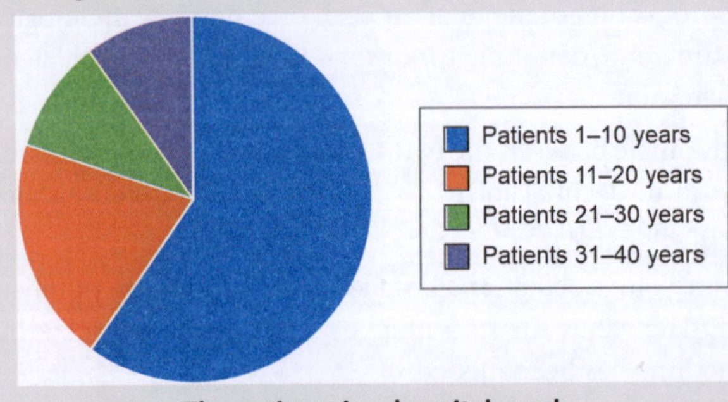

The patients in a hospital ward

Practice question: Make a pie chart to show the following data:

Diseases	TB	Diabetes	Cancer	UTI	Influenza	Arthritis
Percentages	18	14	8	24	18	8

Solution:

Disease	Percentages	Degree of angle (18/5 × %)
TB	18	$\frac{18}{5} \times 18 = 64.8°$
Diabetes	14	$\frac{18}{5} \times 14 = 50.4°$
Cancer	8	$\frac{18}{5} \times 8 = 28.8°$
UTI	24	$\frac{18}{5} \times 24 = 86.4°$
Influenza	18	$\frac{18}{5} \times 18 = 64.8°$
Arthritis	8	$\frac{18}{5} \times 8 = 28.8°$

Note: 360/100 = 18/5

Now with the help of a ruler, protractor and a compass or round object you can easily draw the pie chart manually.

Pictogram

The statistical data is presented in pictures. The pictograms are attractive and easy to understand. Mostly private and government organizations use it. In the figure given here, the types of blood group possessed by people have been shown with the help of picture. (Fig. 6.9).

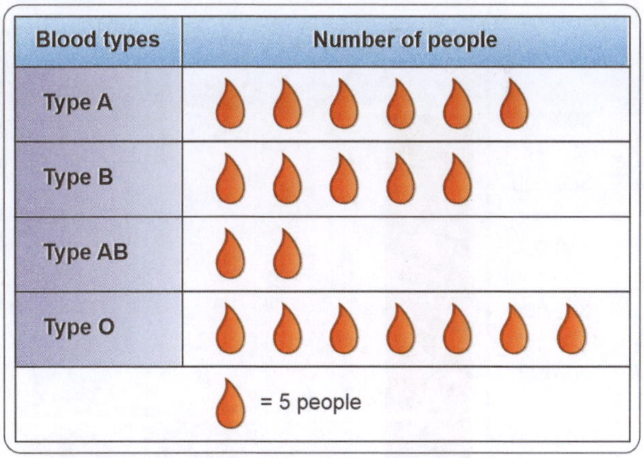

Limitations of Above Mentioned Methods

The above mentioned methods are easy to construct and to understand the data. Their utility is limited as magnitude is not understood. Wrong conclusions could be made for a situation by different people.

Figure 6.9: Pictogram

GRAPHICAL PRESENTATION

With regard to frequency distribution, important types of graphs are discussed further.

Histogram

First introduced by Karl Pearson, it is a special type of bar diagram which is used to represent frequency distribution of a character being measured on a continuous scale. The area of each rectangle indicates the frequency of corresponding class interval.

The histogram (Fig. 6.10) here shows the patients with a particular disease being admitted in a government hospital in a particular year.

> The width of each bar represents the size of the class interval on x-axis and the frequency of each class interval is represented by height of the bar on y-axis. The total area of histogram reflects total frequency. The areas of bars or rectangles are proportional to the frequencies.

Must Know

Difference between a histogram and a bar chart

Both look the same, though they have one important differences that is they are used to plot different types of data.

- For discrete data a bar chart is used, and for continuous data a histogram is used.
- Again, bar graph is used when the data is in categories like, types of procedures used in a clinic, different types of feeds for pets, etc. It is a good choice when a comparison is required.
- Bar graph can also be used when a significant change is to be tracked, for example, changing medical practices or nursing skills in decades or centuries.
- If we have continuous data, like people's weights or IQ scores, then histograms are best.

Practice question: The data is given here in tables. Draw histograms for each series.

a.   In continuous (exclusive) series

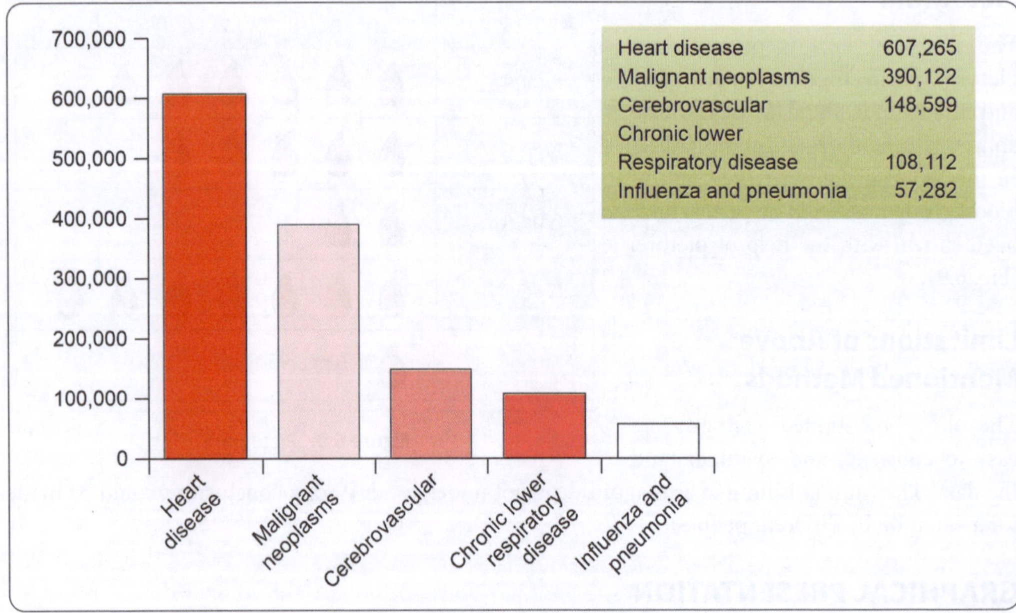

Figure 6.10: Histogram

Class intervals	0–10	10–20	20–30	30–40	40–50
Frequency	5	6.5	7	8	2

b. In discontinuous (inclusive) series

Class intervals	16–20	21–25	26–30	31–35	36–40
Frequency	15	10	30	20	25

Note: In order to remove gaps between subsequent class intervals, we have to adjust the data by adjustment factor that is [½ (lower limit of next class – upper limit of previous class)].

For example, ½(21 – 20) = 0.5.

New class intervals will be:

Class intervals	15.5–20.5	20.5–25.5	25.5–30.5	30.5–35.5	35.5–40.5
Frequency	15	10	30	20	25

Now, you can draw the histogram easily with ruler, rubber and pencil (with sharp tip).

Frequency Polygon

Frequency polygon is a modification of histogram. After constructing rectangles in histograms, the mid-points are marked at the tops of each rectangle and the points are joint by straight lines. These lines touch the x-axis on either end.

Another way is to not to construct rectangles and plot points by taking mid-points of class intervals on x-axis and later join them with a straight line in similar way as is done earlier by constructing histograms first. The class intervals are taken on x-axis and frequency on y-axis. In any case, a polygon will be obtained (Fig. 6.11). The frequency polygon can be drawn with two or more sets of data like birth and death rate of a chosen sample, normal and cesarean deliveries in a hospital, etc.

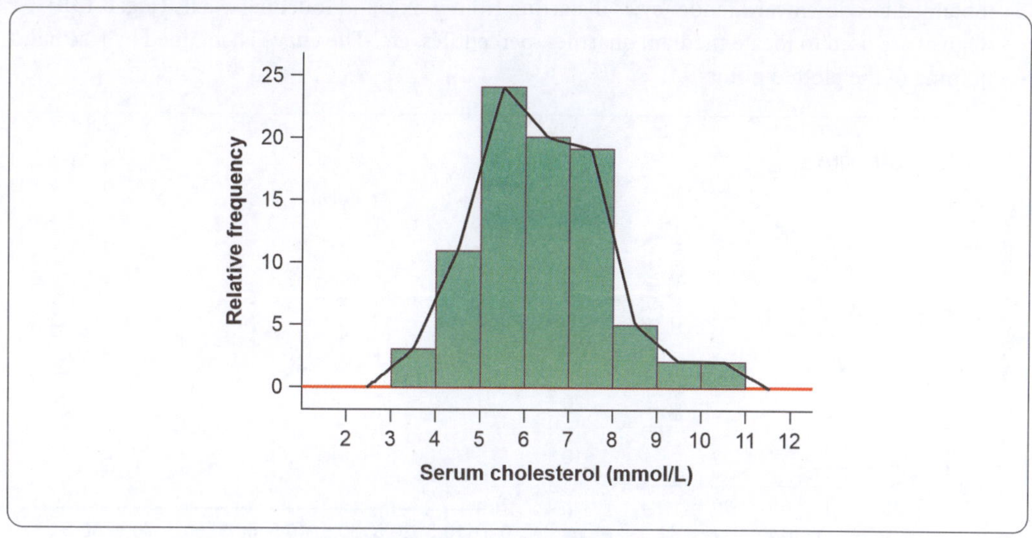

Figure 6.11: Frequency polygon

Practice question: Following data represents total births in Punjab and Maharashtra among the different age groups of females. Construct a frequency polygon:

Age of females	15–20	20–25	25–30	30–35	35–40	40–45
Frequency in Punjab	7	26	31	24	15	5
Frequency in Maharashtra	8	30	29	25	18	2

Frequency Curve

When a large data is present, the frequency polygon gives a smooth look like a curve. This is known as frequency curve. Here, the points are taken on x-axis corresponding with y-axis and are joined by free hand drawn lines and not by straight lines. The corners and angles are smoothed with free hand lines (Fig. 6.12).

Ogive or Cumulative Frequency Polygon

Ogive or cumulative frequency polygon is plotted by taking cumulative frequencies on y-axis and variable on x-axis. Total values are displayed at a given particular time. It is of two types:

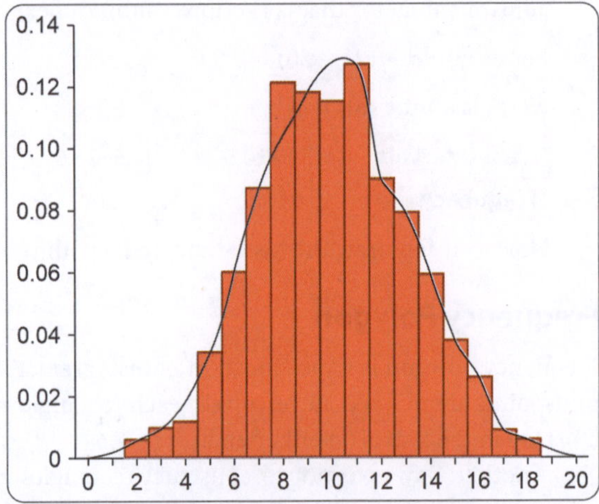

Figure 6.12: Frequency curve

1. **Less than ogive:** When cumulative frequencies are plotted from higher values. The curve obtained from this goes upward from x-axis (Fig. 6.13A).
2. **More than ogive:** When cumulative frequencies are plotted starting from lower values. The curve obtained has downward tendency as if starting from y-axis and touching x-axis (Fig. 6.13B). Ogives are used to locate median, quartiles, percentiles, etc. The curve is obtained by free hand joining of the plotted points.

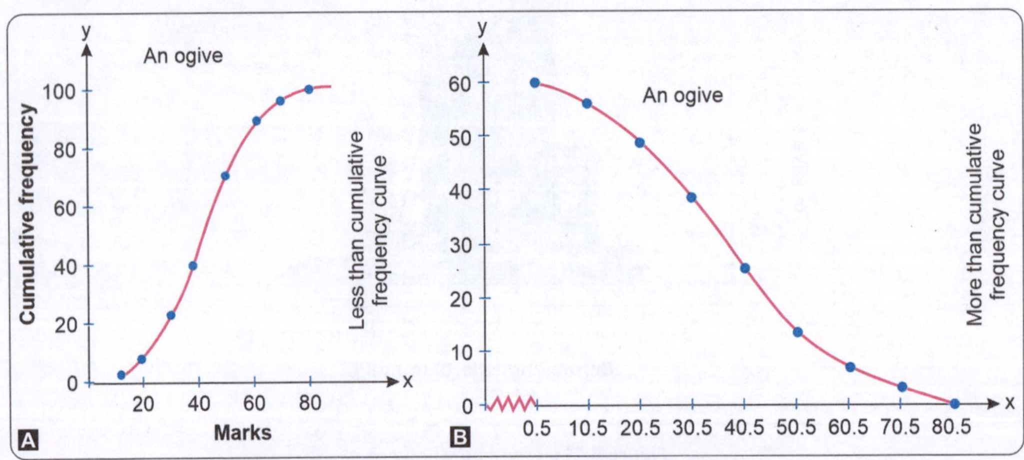

Figures 6.13A and B: A. Less than ogive; **B.** More than ogive

STUDENT ASSIGNMENT

LONG ANSWER QUESTIONS

1. Discuss the graphical presentation of data.
2. Explain the different types of diagrams and graphs in detail.

SHORT ANSWER QUESTIONS

1. What is a graphical presentation of data?
2. Define the frequency polygon.
3. Write short note on histogram.
4. Define pie charts.

MULTIPLE CHOICE QUESTIONS

1. **Diagrams are another form of:**
   a. Classification
   b. Tabulation
   c. Angle
   d. Percentage

2. **A sector diagram is also called:**
   a. Bar diagram
   b. Histogram
   c. Historigram
   d. Pie diagram

3. **Histogram can be drawn only for:**
   a. Discrete frequency distribution
   b. Continuous frequency distribution
   c. Cumulative frequency distribution
   d. Relative frequency distribution

4. **The graph of the cumulative frequency distribution is called:**
   a. Histogram
   b. Frequency polygon
   c. Pictogram
   d. Ogive

5. **Cumulative frequency polygon can be used for the calculation of:**
   a. Mean
   b. Median
   c. Mode
   d. Geometric mean

6. **Which among the following is not a feature of a bar in the bar diagram?**
   a. The width is the same but the heights are generally different
   b. They are rectangular in shape
   c. Bars should not be equidistant
   d. Each bar originates from a common baseline

ANSWER KEY

1. b   **2.** d   **3.** b   **4.** d   **5.** b   **6.** c

Note

Unit II

Measures of Central Tendency

7

Central Tendencies

"Anyone can be average, but not you. You have the ambition, talent, persistence, and motivation to be the best."
—Anonymous

LEARNING OBJECTIVES

After the completion of the chapter, the readers will be able to:
- Understand concepts of central tendencies.
- Know about the relation between the measures of central tendencies.
- Implement the knowledge in calculating the central tendencies like mean, mode and median.

CHAPTER OUTLINE

- Introduction
- Central Tendency
- Mean
- Mode
- Median
- Relation between the Measures of Central Tendency

INTRODUCTION

The degree of certainty with which we observe an average depends on our knowledge of the variation among observations in given population. The words by Sherlock Holmes have led us to two most important statistical concepts, that are average and variation. For example, we can never foretell what an individual will do in a particular situation, but we can say with precision what an average individual will be doing in a certain situation. Therefore, average values are important in statistics as well as in day-to-day life.

CENTRAL TENDENCY

- The measures of central tendency describe a set of data by identifying the central position in it, as a single value. We can say that it is a score which indicates a position where the center of a distribution tends to be located.
- Again, it tells us about the shape and nature of the distribution. Therefore, first arrange the data so as to reduce the volume and later interpret a result from it by using measures of central tendency. We have dealt with reduction of the volume of data in first unit now, we will move on to the next part that is measures of central tendency.

- It is a common feature of research data to get clustered around a central value. This central value suggests a point where the items of data tend to be clustered. For example, we say that the average price of gold is ₹4,200/ ounce or the car average is 30 km/L of petrol. Here, one is describing a feature about the entire population, which is known as an average.
- Measures of central tendency are used in a variety of settings. There are many ways to compute averages, but we will study only three of the major ones and these are: mean, mode and median. In different situations, some measure of central tendency become more appropriate to use than others. Mode is the easiest average to compute among these.

MEAN

The mean of a set of values or measurements is the sum of all the measurements divided by the number of measurements in the set. Mean is the most popular measure of central tendency and is widely used average. It is sometimes called the arithmetic mean. Computation of the mean requires scores that are numerical values measured on an interval or ratio scale.

Definitions

Conceptually, the mean can also be defined in the following ways:
- The mean is the amount that each individual receives when the total (ΣX) is divided equally among all N individuals.
- The mean is a balance point of the distribution because the sum of the distances below the mean is exactly equal to the sum of the distances above the mean.

When to Use the Mean

- Sampling stability is desired.
- Other measures are to be computed such as standard deviation, coefficient of variation and skewness.

When we compute the mean, we sum up the given data (notation to indicate the sum is Σ—sigma). If 'x' represents any value in the data, then ΣX is the sum of all given x values in that data. When we divide ΣX by n (total number of observations), mean is obtained which is denoted by (x bar).

$$\overline{X} = x_1 + x_2 + \ldots\ldots\ldots x_n/n$$

$$\text{Mean } (\overline{X}) = \Sigma X/n$$

Characteristics of Mean

- Mean measures stability. It is the most stable and reliable among other measures of central tendency because every score contributes to the value of the mean.
- The sum of each score's distance from the mean is zero.
- It may not be an actual score in the distribution.
- It is very easy to compute.
- Mean can be calculated for any set of numerical data, so it always exists.
- A set of numerical data has one and only one mean.
- It is greatly affected by extreme or deviant values (outliers).
- It is used only if the data is interval or ratio.

Advantages of Mean

- Easy to understand and compute.
- Formula is rigidly defined.
- Unique and relatively stable average.
- Based on all the given items in a series.
- It can be subjected to algebraic treatment.

Disadvantages of Mean

- Affected by extreme values in a data which may lead to wrong interpretations. For example, when a distribution contains a few extreme scores (or is much skewed), the mean will be shifted toward the extremes (displaced toward the tail of probability curve).
- When the data is from a nominal scale, it is impossible to compute a mean, and when data is measured on an ordinal scale (ranks), it is again inappropriate to compute a mean.
- Graphical representation cannot be done.
- Cannot be applied to qualitative data.

Mean for Ungrouped Data

- **Sample mean:** Mean of the sample denoted by ("x bar").

$$\text{Sample mean} = \frac{\text{Sum of all the values in the sample}}{\text{Number of values in the sample}}$$

- **Population mean:** Mean of the population—the parametric or population mean, denoted by μ (read "mu").

$$\text{Population mean} = \frac{\text{Sum of all the values in the population}}{\text{Number of values in the population}}$$

Example: Rina needs B Grade in science. She could not perform well in her first 3 sessional tests; though she scored well in the quarterly exams. Her scores are 58, 67, 60, 84, 93, 98, 100. Compute the mean and see, if Rina could get B Grade that is 80–89 or C that is 70–79.

Solution:

When we sum up the given scores, we get: $58 + 67 + 60 + 84 + 93 + 98 + 100 = 560$

Number of observations = 7

$$\overline{X} = \frac{\Sigma X}{N} = \frac{560}{7} = 80$$

Interpretation: Because the mean is 80, Rina will get Grade B (80–89).

Example: Calculate the mean for serum albumin values given in g% of 24 patients.

2.90	3.43	3.62
3.75	3.55	3.43
3.66	3.84	2.98
3.57	3.69	3.76
3.45	3.72	3.68
3.76	3.30	3.61
3.73	3.77	3.38
3.71	3.88	3.76

Solution:

$$\text{Mean } (\overline{X}) = \Sigma X / n$$

Sum up the given scores $\Sigma X = 85.93$

Number of observations $= 24$

$$(\overline{X}) = \frac{85.93}{24}$$

$$= 3.58 \text{ in g\%}$$

> **Must Know**
>
> Modifying a distribution by dumping scores or by addition of new scores will generally change the value of the mean and it will affect: Number of scores; Sum of the scores. If a constant value is added to every score in a distribution, then the same constant value is added to the mean. Also, if every score is multiplied by a constant value, then the mean is also multiplied by the same constant value.

Mean for Grouped Data

Calculating arithmetic mean (AM) for grouped data: Here, following methods are used.

- Direct method: $$\overline{X} = \frac{\Sigma fx}{N}$$

- Shortcut method: $$\overline{X} = A + \frac{\Sigma fd}{N}$$

- Step deviation method: $$\overline{X} = A + \frac{\Sigma fd}{N} \times i$$

Midpoint method: The formula to solve mean here, is known as midpoint method, and is given as:

$$\overline{X} = \frac{\Sigma f X_m}{N}$$

Where,

$\overline{X}$ = mean value

X_m = midpoint of each class or category

f = frequency in each class or category

$\Sigma f X_m$ = summation of the product of $f X_m$

Steps

1. Find the midpoint or class mark (X_m) of each class or category.

   Using the formula:

   $$X_m = \frac{LL + UL}{2}$$

2. Multiply the frequency and the corresponding class mark $f X_m$.
3. Find the sum of the results in step 2.
4. Solve the mean using the formula:

$$\overline{X} = \frac{\Sigma f X_m}{N}$$

Example: The data of 40 students in a class is tabulated below.

X	f	X_m	fX_m
10–14	5	12	60
15–19	2	17	34
20–24	3	22	66
25–29	5	27	135
30–34	2	32	64
35–39	9	37	333
40–44	6	42	252
45–49	3	47	141
50–54	5	52	260
	$n = 40$		$\Sigma fX_m = 1345$

$$\overline{X} = \frac{\Sigma fX_m}{n} = \frac{1345}{40} = 33.63$$

Interpretation: The mean performance of 40 students in science quiz is 33.63. Those students who got scores below 33.63 did not perform well in the same examination while those students who got scores above 33.63 performed well.

Example: Calculate the mean for 400 families for protein intake as was observed in a survey on malnutrition.

Protein intake/day (in g)	Number of families (f)	Midpoint of class interval (x)	Number of families × midpoint (fx)
15–25	110	20	2200
25–35	80	30	2400
35–45	30	40	1200
45–55	10	50	500
55–65	30	60	1800
65–75	40	70	2800
75–85	100	80	8000
Total	400		18900

Mean

$$\overline{X} = \frac{\Sigma fX}{N}$$

$$= \frac{18900}{400} = 47.25$$

Unit II   Measures of Central Tendency

Weighted Mean

Weighted mean is the mean of a set of values where each value or measurement has a different weight or degree of importance. The formula is:

$$\bar{X} = \frac{\Sigma xw}{\Sigma w}$$

Where, $\bar{X}$ = mean

x = measurement or value

w = number of measurements

Must Know

The mean does not help in situations mentioned as follows:
- A distribution contains a few extreme scores (or is much skewed), the mean will be shifted toward the extremes (displaced toward the tail of the probability curve). In this case, the mean will not provide a central value.
- When the data are from a nominal scale it is impossible to compute a mean, and when data are measured on an ordinal scale (ranks), it is again inappropriate to compute a mean.

Therefore, the mean does not always work as a measure of central tendency and it is necessary to have alternative procedures available.

Example: Following are data of a student. The marks obtained and the units have been given in the table. Calculate the weighted mean.

Subjects	A	B	C	D	E	F	G
Marks	86	85	88	87	86	83	87
Units	0.9	1.5	1.5	1.8	0.9	1.2	1.2

Solution:

Marks (X)	Units (W)	X W
86	0.9	86 × 0.9 = 77.4
85	1.5	85 × 1.5 = 127.5
88	1.5	88 × 1.5 = 132
87	1.8	87 × 1.8 = 156.6
86	0.9	86 × 0.9 = 77.4
83	1.2	83 × 1.2 = 99.6
87	1.2	87 × 1.2 = 104.4
	$\Sigma w = 9$	$\Sigma xw = 774.9$

$$\bar{X} = \frac{\Sigma xw}{\Sigma w} = \frac{774.9}{9} = 86.1$$

Interpretation: The average performance of the student is 86.1

Harmonic Mean

Harmonic mean is quotient of number of the given values and sum of the reciprocals of the given values. It is calculated as:

For ungrouped data:

$$\text{HM of X} = \bar{X} = \frac{n}{\Sigma\left(\dfrac{1}{x}\right)}$$

For grouped data:

$$\text{HM of X} = \bar{X} = \frac{\Sigma f}{\Sigma\left(\dfrac{f}{x}\right)}$$

Example: Calculate the harmonic mean of the numbers: 13.2, 14.2, 14.8, 15.2 and 16.1

Solution:

X	13.2	14.2	14.8	15.2	16.1	
$\dfrac{1}{X}$	0.0758	0.0704	0.0676	0.0658	0.0621	**Total** $\sum \dfrac{1}{x} = 0.3417$

$$\text{HM of } X = \bar{X} = \frac{n}{S\left(\dfrac{1}{x}\right)}$$

$$\text{HM of } X = \bar{X} = \frac{5}{0.3417} = 14.63$$

Example: Calculate the harmonic mean for the data given as follows:

Marks	30–39	40–49	50–59	60–69	70–79	80–89	90–99
Frequency	2	3	11	20	32	25	7

Solution:

Marks	x	f	$\dfrac{f}{x}$
30–39	34.5	2	0.0580
40–49	44.5	3	0.0674
50–59	54.5	11	0.2018
60–69	64.5	20	0.3101
70–79	74.5	32	0.4295
80–89	84.5	25	0.2959
90–99	94.5	7	0.0741
Total		**100**	**1.4368**

Harmonic mean is:

$$\bar{X} = \frac{\sum f}{\sum \left(\dfrac{f}{x}\right)} = \frac{100}{1.4368} = 69.60$$

Geometric Mean

The geometric mean is well-defined only for sets of positive real numbers. This is calculated by multiplying all the numbers (that is the number of numbers 'n'), and taking the nth root of the total. A common example of where the geometric mean is the correct choice is when averaging growth rates. The geometric mean is NOT the arithmetic mean and it is NOT a simple average.

Mathematically, we can define it as the nth root of the product of n numbers.

For ungrouped data: $\qquad GM = Antilog \dfrac{\Sigma log\ x}{N}$

For grouped data: $\qquad GM = Antilog \dfrac{\Sigma f\ log\ x}{N}$

Example: Find the geometric mean of the following values: 15, 12, 13, 19 and 10

Solution:

x	15	12	13	19	10	Total
Log x	1.1761	1.0792	1.1139	1.2788	1.0000	**5.648**

$$N = 5, \Sigma \log x = 5.648$$

$$\text{As GM} = Antilog \left(\frac{\Sigma \log x}{N} \right)$$

$$= Antilog \left(\frac{5.648}{5} \right)$$

$$= Antilog \,(1.1296)$$

MODE

Mode is the most frequently occurring score. It is the most popular value in a given set. It is frequently used to describe a central value without calculation. Mode typically describes central tendency when the scores reflect a nominal scale of measurement. The mode or the modal score is a score or scores that occurred most in the distribution. It is not necessary to have mode for all data sets. For example, if a professor gives equal numbers of A's or B's, or C's, then there will be no modal grade. Moreover, mode is not very stable as changing just one number in a data set can change the mode radically. Still the mode is a useful average when we want to know the most frequently occurring value in a set of data, for example the most frequently ordered garment size on Amazon.

Croxton and Cowden defined it as, "the mode of a distribution is the value at the point armed with the item tend to most heavily concentrated. It may be regarded as the most typical of a series of value."

While there is just one value for the mean and one value for the median, there may be more than one value for the mode of a data set. It is classified as unimodal, bimodal, trimodal or multimodal.

- Unimodal is a distribution of scores that consists of only one mode.
- Bimodal is a distribution of scores that consists of two modes.
- Trimodal is a distribution of scores that consists of three modes or multimodal is a distribution of scores that consists of >2 modes.

Mode for Ungrouped Data

Example: Find the mode for: 2, 6, 3, 9, 5, 6, 2, 6

Solution: When one observes the data, it can be easily seen that the most frequently occurring value is 6. (It is repeated here 3 times). Therefore, the mode is 3.

Example: "Count the letters in each word of this sentence and give the mode". (Read and count the letters in this sentence)

Solution: When we count the numbers of letters in the words of the above written sentence "count the ---------- the mode", we have a data set: 5, 3, 7, 2, 4, 4, 2, 4, 8, 3, 4, 3, 4 When we observe the data, we find that 4 is repeated 5 times. Therefore, the mode is 4.

Example: Find the mode for the data given as follows:

Scores of section A	25	24	24	20	20	20	16	12	10	7
Scores of section B	25	24	24	20	18	18	17	10	9	7
Scores of section C	25	25	25	22	21	21	21	18	18	18

Solution:

- The score that appeared most in section A is 20, therefore, the mode of section A is 20. As there is only one mode, it is unimodal.
- The score that appeared most in section B are 18 and 24. Both 18 and 24 are appearing twice so there are two modes in section B, therefore, it is bimodal.
- Section C has three modes 18, 21 and 25 so it is trimodal or multimodal.

Mode for Grouped Data

The formula to solve mode in grouped series is:

$$\text{Mode} = L + \left(\frac{f - f1}{(f - f1) + (f - f2)}\right) \times h$$

- L is the lower class limit of the modal class.
- f is the frequency of the modal class.
- $f1$ is the frequency of the class before the modal class in the frequency table.
- $f2$ is the frequency of the class after the modal class in the frequency table.
- h is the size of class interval of the modal class.

Example: Find out the modal class and mode for given set of data.

Number	1–3	4–6	7–9	10–12	13–15	16–18	19–21	22–24	25–27	28–30
Frequency	7	6	4	9	2	8	1	2	3	2

Solution:

Modal class is 10–12, as it has highest frequency.

Here model class = 10–12

$$L = 10, f = 9, f1 = 4, f2 = 2, h = 3$$

$$\text{Mode} = L + \left(\frac{f - f1}{f - f1) + (f - f2)}\right) \times h$$

$$= 10 + \left(\frac{9 - 4}{(9 - 4) + (9 - 2)}\right) \times 3$$

$$= 10 + \left(\frac{5}{5 + 7}\right) \times 3$$

$$= 10 + 1.26$$

$$\text{Mode} = 11.26$$

The mode of the scores that consists of 11.26.

Characteristics of Mode

- It can be used when the data are qualitative and quantitative.
- It may not exist.
- It may not be unique.
- It is affected by extreme values.
- It is used when you want to find the value which occurs most often.
- It is a quick approximation of the average.
- It is an inspection average.
- It is the most unreliable among the three measures of central tendency because its value is undefined in some observations.

When to Use the Mode

- When the "typical" value is desired.
- When the data set is measured on a nominal scale, then the mean or median cannot be used.
- In interval, ordinal, or ratio data, it is used with mean and median.

Advantages of Mode

- Mode is readily comprehensible and easily calculated.
- It is the best representative of data.
- It is not at all affected by extreme value.
- The value of mode can also be determined graphically.
- It is usually an actual value of an important part of the series.

Disadvantages of Mode

- It is not based on all observations.
- It is not capable of further mathematical manipulation.
- Mode is affected to a great extent by sampling fluctuations.
- Choice of grouping has great influence on the value of mode.

Problems while Using Mode

- It gives the limited information about a distribution that may be misleading. For example, if we have to calculate mode in a data such as: 7, 7, 7, 20, 20, 20, 21, 22, 22, 23, 23, 23, 24.
- It is not possible to find mode as 7, 20, and 23 are repeating 3 times each. Hence, it is not possible to calculate mode in this data set. Therefore, we have to find average with some other method.

Practical Tips

Where to use and which average:

Measurement scale	Average can be used	Best average used
Nominal scale	Mode	Mode
Ordinal scale	Mode, median	Median
Interval scale	Mode, median, mode	Symmetrical data—mean Skewed data—median
Ratio scale	Mode, median, mode	Symmetrical data—mean Skewed data—median

MEDIAN

The median is a middle value of a given set of data. These are arranged in ascending or descending order. Median is used in ordinal or ratio interval. Connor has defined median as a value of the variables, which divides the group into two equal parts. One-part comprising all values greater and other part having all values less than median. For this, the data has to be arranged in the numerical order first, from the highest to the lowest score. It can be called score at the 50th percentile that is in the middle of data.

Characteristics of Median

- It may not be an actual observation in the data set.
- It is not affected by extreme values because median is a positional measure.
- It can be applied in ordinal level.

When to use the Median

- The exact midpoint of the score distribution is desired.
- There are extreme scores in the distribution.

For ungrouped data median is calculated as:

$$\text{Median } (M) = \text{size of } \left(\frac{N+1}{2}\right)\text{th item}$$

For grouped data median is calculated as:

$$\text{Median } (M) = L + \frac{\frac{N}{2} - cf}{f} \times i$$

Practical Tips

- If the data is having an odd number of scores, the median is middle position score.
- If the data is having an even number of scores, the median is an average of the two middle scores.

Example: Find the median of 19, 5, 2, 17, 10, 15, and 16.

Solution:

- Here, we have odd number of scores in discrete series. Ordering the data will get: 19, 17, 16, 15, 10, 5, 2.
- On looking at this arranged data we can find out that the middle value is 15, which is median and it is a positional average.

Median for Ungrouped Data

For an odd number of scores

Median = value of $\frac{N+1}{2}$. N is number of observations. For above example no. 13, N = 7.

Therefore, $\frac{7+1}{2} = 4$ or the fourth item in the data.

For even number of scores like 1, 2, 3, 3, 4, 7, 9, 10, 11, 6. Ordering the data will give 1, 2, 3, 3, 4, 6, 7, 9, 10, 11

The median is between 2 values that is 4 and 6. Hence, median will be sum of these two values + 1, divided by 2 that is 5.5. Or, 5th and 6th items in the data which are again as,

$$\frac{4+6}{2} = \frac{10}{2} = 5$$

Median for Grouped Data

Marks	0–4	5–9	10–14	15–19	20–24	Total
Number of students	2	8	14	17	9	50
Cf	2	10	24	41	50	

Solution:

As median

$$= L + \left(\frac{n/2 - cf}{f} \times h \right)$$

$$n = 50;\ h = 4;\ L = 15$$
$$f = 17 \text{ and } cf = 24$$

Median

$$= 15 + \left[\frac{\frac{50}{2} - 24}{17} \times 4 \right]$$

$$= 15 + \left[\frac{25 - 24}{17} \times 4 \right]$$

$$= 15 + \left[\frac{1}{17} \times 4 \right]$$

$$= 15 + \frac{4}{17}$$

$$= 15 + 0.235$$

$$= 15.235$$

Example: Calculate median value for data given in table here:

Sl. no.	Data	Sl. no.	Data	Sl. no.	Data
1.	2.90	9.	3.55	17.	3.72
2.	2.98	10.	3.57	18.	3.43
3.	3.30	11.	3.61	19.	3.73
4.	3.38	12.	3.62	20.	3.75
5.	3.43	13.	3.66	21.	3.76
6.	3.43	14.	3.68	22.	3.77
7	3.43	15.	3.69	23.	3.84
8.	3.45	16.	3.71	24.	3.88

Solution: Here, I have used arranged data or, you can arrange the data in increasing order.

Here,   12th observation = 3.62

13th observation = 3.66

Median

$$= \frac{1}{2}\left[\left(\frac{n}{2}\right)^{th} + \left(\frac{n}{2}+1\right)^{th}\right]$$

$$= \frac{1}{2}\left[\left(\frac{24}{2}\right) + \left(\frac{24}{2}+1\right)\right]$$

$$= \frac{1}{2}(12+13)$$

$$= \frac{1}{2}(3.62+3.66)$$

$$= \frac{1}{2}(7.28)$$

$$= 3.64$$

Example: Calculate median value for data given in table as follows:

Class interval	Frequency	Cumulative frequency
15–25	30	30
25–35	40	30 + 40 = 70
35–45	100	70 + 100 = 170
45–55	110	170 + 110 = 280
55–65	80	280 + 80 = 360
65–75	30	360 + 30 = 390
75–85	10	390 + 10 = 400

(I have highlighted cells here because it will help you to choose the values to be put in the formula of median). To understand it further:

Total frequency or N = 400 and N/2 = 200 which lies between the values in (cf column) between 170 and 280. Hence, we choose the 'f' just lower to 200 and the class will be 45–55 with frequency as 110, i.e., (highlighted in green color).

Median

$$= l + \frac{\left(\frac{n}{2} - c\right)}{f} \times h$$

Therefore, median value lies in class 45 – 55

Hence, l or lower limit of class $= 45$

$$n = 400; \; cf = 170; \; f = 110$$

$$= 45 + \left(\frac{200 - 170}{110} \right) \times 10$$

$$= 45 + 2.72$$

$$= 47.72$$

> ### Practical Tips
>
> In a data with classes, such as: 21–30, 31–40, 41–50, 51–60.., we must arrange it like: 20.5-30.5 (decreasing 0.5 from the lower value of class and increasing 0.5 in the upper limit of class).

Advantages of Median

- It is better measure of central tendency and is rigidly defined.
- Only one value can be median, and it will always be at a place where most scores are situated.
- Extreme items do not affect it.
- Median can be calculated in all distributions.
- Median can be understood even by the common people.
- Median can be ascertained even with the extreme items.
- It can be located graphically.
- It is most useful dealing with qualitative data.

Disadvantages of Median

- It is not based on all the values.
- It is not capable of further mathematical treatment.
- It is affected by fluctuation of sampling.
- The data has to be arranged and it is generally cumbersome in large data.
- It is a positional average and may be misleading at times, when all values are not given importance.

RELATION BETWEEN THE MEASURES OF CENTRAL TENDENCY

- In symmetric distribution the median and mean are equal.
- For normal distribution mean = median = mode.
- In positively skewed distribution mean is greater than median.

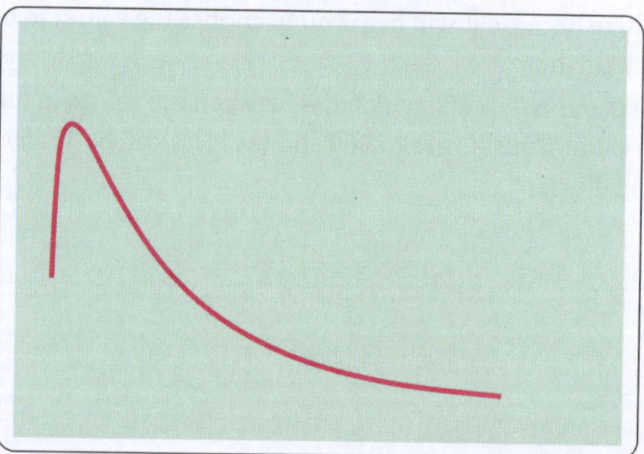

- In negatively skewed distribution mean is smaller than median.

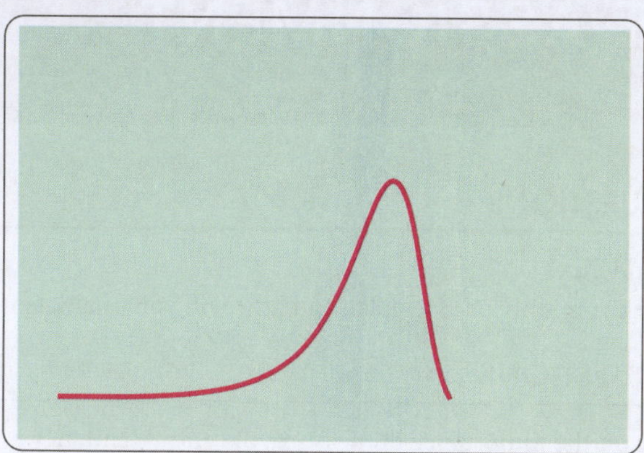

Takeaway

$$Mean = \frac{Sum\ of\ all\ values}{Total\ number\ of\ values}$$

Median = Middle value (when the data are arranged in order)
Mode = Most common value

- Central tendency: A score which indicates a position where the center of a distribution tends to be located
- Mean is sum of all scores divided by the number of items
- Median is a score in the middle of arranged data, when the scores are ordered
- Mode is the most frequently occurring score.

STUDENT ASSIGNMENT

LONG ANSWER QUESTIONS

1. What is central tendency?
2. Which is the most commonly used average and how will you calculate it?

SHORT ANSWER QUESTIONS

1. Write a short note on the importance of measures of central tendency.
2. Write about the advantages and disadvantages of various averages.
3. Define mean.
4. Define median.
5. What is mode?
6. Find mean, median and mode of the data given below.

Class interval	21–30	31–40	41–50	51–60	61–70	71–80
Frequency	8	5	10	4	28	1

MULTIPLE CHOICE QUESTIONS

1. **Which measure of central tendency is calculated by adding all the values and then dividing the sum by the number of items?**
   a. Mean
   b. Median
   c. Mode
   d. None of these

2. **Which of the following measures can be determined for quantitative data?**
   a. Mean
   b. Median
   c. Mode
   d. All of these

3. **Which of the following measures can be calculated for qualitative data?**
   a. Mean
   b. Median
   c. Mode
   d. None of these

4. **Method used to compute average or central value of collected data is considered:**
   a. Measures of positive variation
   b. Measures of central tendency
   c. Measures of negative skewness
   d. Measures of negative variation

5. **Mean or average used to measure central tendency is called:**
   a. Sample mean
   b. Arithmetic mean
   c. Negative mean
   d. Population mean

6. **The observation which occurs the most frequently in a sample is the:**
   a. Median
   b. Mean deviation
   c. Standard deviation
   d. Mode

7. What is the median of the sample 5, 5, 11, 9, 8, 5, 8?
    a. 5   b. 6
    c. 8   d. 9

8. The following scores were obtained by eleven footballers in a goal-shoot competition:
    5 3 6 8 7 8 3 11 6 3 2 4.
    A. The modal score was:
    a. 3   b. 6
    c. 8   d. 11
    B. The median score was:
    a. 3   b. 6
    c. 8   d. 11

9. The mean of 10 numbers is 58. If one of the numbers is 40, what is the mean of the other nine?
    a. 18   b. 60
    c. 162   d. 540

10. The mean of 11 numbers is 7. One of the numbers, 13, is deleted. What is the mean of the
    remaining 10 numbers?
    a. 7.7   b. 6.4
    c. 6.0   d. 5.8

11. The sum of values divided by their number is called:
    a. Median   b. Harmonic mean
    c. Mean   d. Mode
    e. None of the above

12. _______________ is based on all observations of data.
    a. Median   b. Mode
    c. Mean   d. None of these

13. The calculation of mean and variance is based on:
    a. Small values only   b. Large values only
    c. Extreme values only   d. All values

14. Arithmetic mean is _______________ affected by extreme values.
    a. Not   b. Highly
    c. Less   d. None of these

15. Arithmetic mean of two positive numbers "X" and "Y" is:

    a. $\dfrac{ab}{2}$ b. $\dfrac{2a}{2}$

    c. $\dfrac{a+b}{2}$ d. $\dfrac{a-b}{2}$

    e. $\dfrac{2}{a+b}$

16. The mean of 10 numbers is 9, then sum of these numbers will be:
    a. 9   b. 0.9
    c. 70   d. 90

17. For a certain distribution, if $\Sigma(x - 2) = 18$, $\Sigma(x - 24) = 0$, $\Sigma(x - 28) = -24)$, then arithmetic mean is:

a. 21
b. 24
c. 28
d. 0

18. If $C = A - B$, then C is:

a. $A - A$
b. $A + A$
c. $X \times Y$
d. 0

19. Sum of deviations will be zero, if it is taken from:

a. Median
b. Mode
c. Median
d. Standard deviation

20. The sum of squared deviation is least from:

a. Median
b. Mean
c. Mode
d. Standard deviation

21. If "X" is a constant, then $\sum_{i=1}^{2} a = \underline{\hspace{1cm}}$

a. X
b. $2X$
c. nX
d. 0

22. The mean of a constant "b" is:

a. Zero
b. b
c. None
d. Cannot say

23. Which of the following is least, if $X = 14$:

a. $\Sigma(X - 10)^2$
b. $\Sigma(X - 12)^2$
c. $\Sigma(X - 14)^2$
d. $\Sigma(X - 15)^2$

24. The average of first n natural numbers is:

a. $\dfrac{n + 1}{2}$
b. $\dfrac{n}{2}$
c. None of these
d. 0

25. The combined arithmetic mean is calculated as:

a. $\dfrac{\overline{X}_1 + \overline{X}_2}{n_1 + n_2}$
b. $\dfrac{n_1 + n_2}{2}$
c. $\dfrac{n_1\overline{X}_1 + n_2\overline{X}_2}{n_1 + n_2}$
d. $\dfrac{n_1 X_1 + n_2 X_2}{n_1 + n_2}$

Measures of Variability

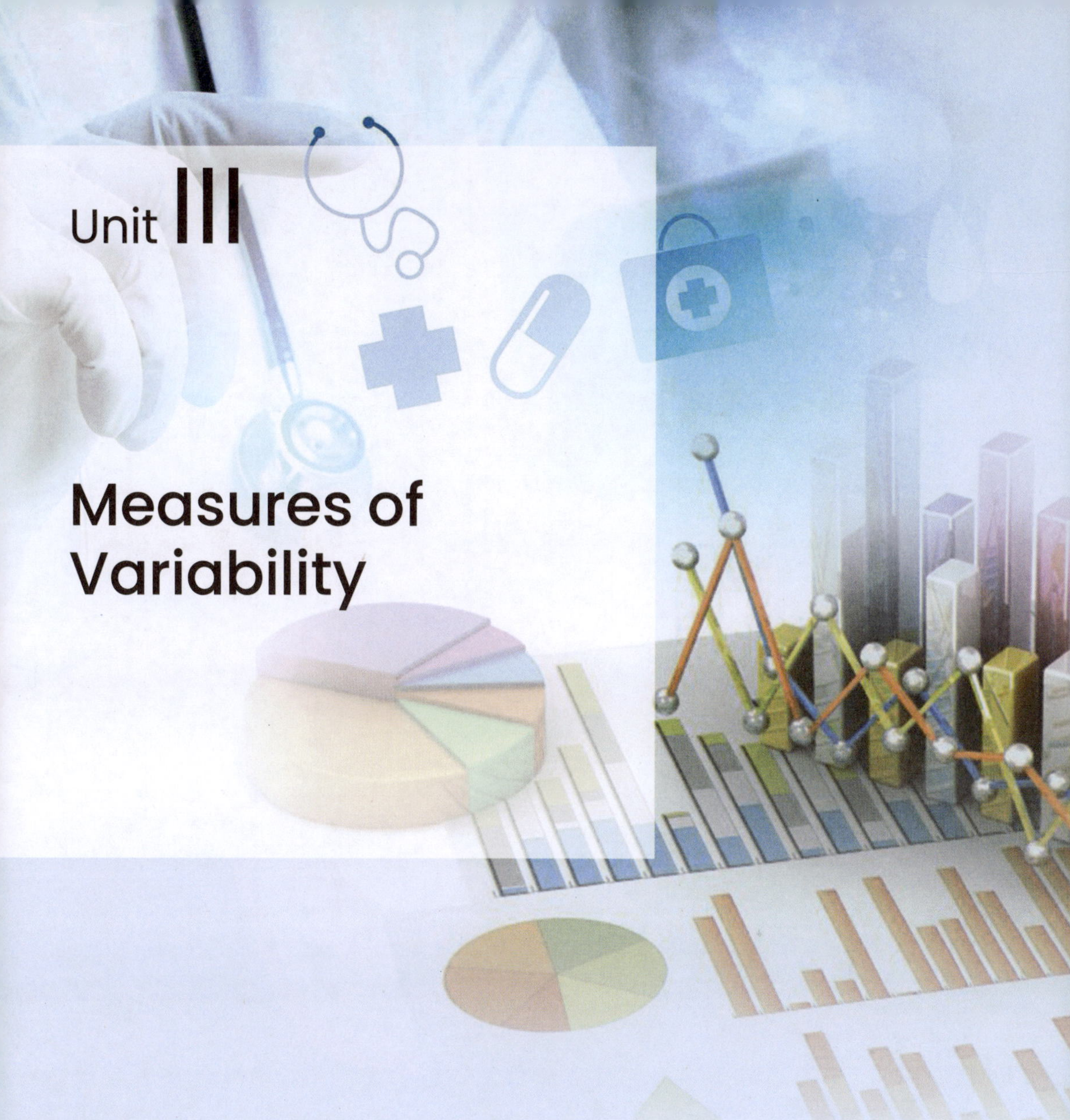

8

Variabilities in Biostatistics

"Comfort makes you weaker. We need some variability, some stressors. Not too much, but just enough."
—Nassim Nicholas Taleb

LEARNING OBJECTIVES

After the completion of the chapter, the readers will be able to:
- Understand variability.
- Apply the concepts learnt to calculate measures of variability.

CHAPTER OUTLINE

- Introduction
- Variability or Dispersion

INTRODUCTION

In previous unit we discussed about averages which are central values but this concept further indicates that there must be variability in a data. The data from research contains variety which means dissimilar values and it can be measured in terms of variability. The average alone has little significance but with variability measurement, it becomes meaningful and useful.

VARIABILITY OR DISPERSION

The measures of variability talks about the amount of dispersion in a data. Dispersion or variability or scatter may be small when the observed values are close enough. The averages must be based on all observations and the extreme values must not unduly affect the measures of variability. But when there is variation between values and we have data with very large or very small values—scattered values, then the variability will be large. In fact, variability or spread or dispersion explores the spread out of data. It gives a way to describe variation and facilitates comparison of the data with other sets of similar data which may be available.

Uses of Variability

- It compares two or more sets of data to talk about uniformity.
- It tests the significance of an average because an average alone is meaningless. By using measures of variability average becomes meaningful and it indicates the significance of central tendencies.

- It helps in controlling the variation. It is affected by extreme values and has impact on deviations. In order to control variation, avoid extreme values in a set of observations to have homogenous data.
- The measures of variability are necessary for further computation of statistical analysis.

We already know that:

- When the graph of the scores is a normal curve, the mode, median, and mean are equal
- The mean is the most common measure of central tendency.
- When the scores are quite skewed or the data is ordinal lacking a common interval, the median is a better measure of central tendency.
- The mode is used only when the mean or median cannot be calculated (e.g., nominal data) or when the only information wanted is the most frequent score (e.g., most uniform size or injury site).

> In order to have a good measure of variability it must be easy to compute, based on all the observations, extreme values must not unduly affect and simple to understand. The measure of variability is best when they do not fluctuate and are rigidly defined and they must be available for further mathematical treatment.

Measures of Variability

The measures of variability describes the set of scores in terms of their spread, or heterogeneity. Consider two groups of scores:

$$\text{Group } 1 = 9, 5, 1; \text{Group } 2 = 5, 6, 4$$

Both groups have a mean and median of 5 but group 2 has much more homogeneous or similar scores than group 1.

A deviation or difference between an observed value and the true value of a quantity of interest (such as a population mean) is an error and a deviation or difference between the observed value and an estimate of the true value (such an estimate may be a sample mean) is a residual. These concepts are applicable for data at the interval and ratio levels of measurements.

Statisticians use some measures to define the amount of variability or spread in a given set of data discussed as follows:

The most common measures of variability are:

- Range
- Interquartile range (IQR)
- Average or mean deviation
- Percentile
- Standard deviation
- Variance

Range

Range is a simplest measure of variability. It is simply the difference between the highest and lowest scores. It is defined as an interval between the smallest and highest observation in a given set of observations. Here, only highest and lowest values of a data are considered whereas other observations are neglected. For example, consider the numbers: 1, 3, 4, 5, 5, 6, 7, 11. For this set of numbers, the range would be 11 – 1 or 10.

Range = highest score – lowest score

Example: The hemoglobin values of 25 children are given as follows. What does it represent?

11.8	11.6	10.5	12.2	13.2
12.4	12.9	11.2	11.6	14.2
10.4	12.3	12.4	12.4	13.5
12.2	10.8	11.7	13.3	13.8
10.8	12.0	12.7	12.9	12.2

Solution: After observing the data, we can find out that the highest value is 14.2 and lowest value is 10.4 Therefore, we conclude that hemoglobin value of 25 children lies in the range of 10.4–14.2 g%. Moreover, the range is 14.2 − 10.4 = 3.8.

Advantages

- Range is easy to calculate and understand.
- It produces a single value.
- An idea of variability is obtained quickly.
- If extreme values are present in a set of data, it will not affect the range.
- It is the easiest measure of variability to calculate.
- It is used when the measure of central tendency is the mode (nominal data or when the most frequent score is of interest) or median (ordinal data or skewed data).

Disadvantages

Use is limited because it takes into consideration only two values that is the highest and the lowest, so it is good to have some other measure of variability.

Interquartile Range

In descriptive statistics, the interquartile range (IQR) is the range of the middle 50% of the scores in a distribution. It is a strong measure of variability. It is also called the mid spread or middle 50%, or technically H-spread. It is a measure of statistical dispersion.

Interquartile range is defined as the difference between the 25th and 75th percentile (which are also called the first and third quartile, respectively) or between upper and lower quartiles.

The IQR is computed as follows:

$$IQR = 75\text{th percentile} - 25\text{th percentile}$$

Or,
$$IQR = Q_3 - Q_1.$$

The IQR is based on dividing a data set into quartiles. Quartiles divide ordinal data set into four equal parts and the values that divide each part are called the first, second, and third quartiles; and they are denoted by Q_1, Q_2, and Q_3, respectively.

- Q_1 is the middle value in the first half of the ordinal data
- Q_2 is the median value
- Q_3 is the middle value in the second half of the ordered data set.

The interquartile range is equal to $Q_3 - Q_1$. For example, observe the numbers: 1, 2, 3, 4, 5, 6, 7, 8.

$$
\begin{array}{ccc}
Q_1 & Q_2 & Q_3 \\
\downarrow & \downarrow & \downarrow \\
\end{array}
$$

1 2 3 4 5 6 7 8

Here, we can see that Q_2 is the median of the entire data set—middle value. In this example, we have an even number of data points, so the median is equal to the average of the two middle values. Thus,

$$Q_2 = (4 + 5)/2 \text{ or } Q_2 = 4.5$$

Q_1 is the middle value in the first half of the data set. Since there are again even number of data points in the first half of the data set, the middle value is the average of the two middle values; that is,

$$Q_1 = (2 + 3)/2 \text{ or } Q_1 = 2.5$$

Q_3 is the middle value in the second half of the data set. Again, since the second half of the data set has an even number of observations, the middle value is the average of the two middle values; that is,

$$Q_3 = (6 + 7)/2 \text{ or } Q_3 = 6.5$$

The interquartile range is Q_3 minus Q_1,

or $\hspace{4cm}$ IQR = 6.5 − 2.5 = 4

This process has divided the data set into four equal parts of equal sizes. The first part consists of 1 and 2; the second part, 3 and 4; the third part, 5 and 6; and the fourth part, 7 and 8. Therefore, the interquartile range designates the middle 50% of observations. If the interquartile range is more, it means that the middle 50% of observations are spread out wide apart.

Example: We have a data set of observations as: 6, 1, 3, 12, 15, 19, 2, 5, 27, 18, 7. Calculate the interquartile deviation.

Solution:

Step 1: Put the numbers in order as 1, 2, 5, 6, 7, 9, 12, 15, 18, 19, 27.

Step 2: Find the median value 1, 2, 5, 6, 7, 9, 12, 15, 18, 19, 27.

Step 3: Group the numbers above and below the median by placing parentheses around them.

Note: It is not necessary statistically, but it makes Q_1 and Q_3 easier to spot. (1, 2, 5, 6, 7), 9, (12, 15, 18, 19, 27).

Step 4: Find Q_1 and Q_3

Assume Q_1 as a median in the lower half of the data and Q_3 as a median for the upper half of the data.

(1, 2, 5, 6, 7), **9**, (12, 15, 18, 19, 27).

$Q_1 = 5$ and $Q_3 = 18$.

Step 5: Subtract Q_1 from Q_3 to find the interquartile range.

18 − 5 = 13.

Advantages of Interquartile Range

- It can be used as a measure of variability even when the extreme values are not being recorded accurately (like in case of open-ended class intervals in a frequency distribution).
- It is not affected by extreme values.

Disadvantage of Interquartile Range

It cannot be subjected to mathematical operations.

Average or Mean Deviation

The average or mean deviation is defined as the mean of the absolute values obtained after getting the differences of each observation from its mean. It is an average distance of any observed value from its mean. It can be obtained by calculating the absolute distance of every observation from the mean, i.e., $(X-\mu)$

In order to calculate the average deviation of a set of values, it is mandatory to calculate their mean. The distance between each score and the calculated mean or the difference between each observation and mean is specified, ignoring positive or negative signs. It further means that difference is calculated without regard to whether the score is above or below the mean.

Mathematically, average deviation is given as follows:

Height (in Inches) 54, 77, 67, 68, 46, 64, 62, 56, 38

$\mu = 59.11$

$$\text{Average deviation} = \frac{\Sigma|X-\mu|}{N}$$

$$\text{For these data} = \frac{\Sigma|X-\mu|}{N}$$

$$= \frac{\begin{array}{c}|54-59.11|+|77-59.11|+|67-59.11|+|68-59.11|+|46-59.11|+\\|64-59.11|+|62-59.11|+|56-59.11|+|38-59.11|\end{array}}{9}$$

$$= \frac{(5.11) + (17.89) + (7.89) + (8.89) + (13.11) + (4.89) + (2.89) + (3.11) + (21.11)}{9}$$

$$= 9.43$$

Our data here is of measurements of heights (in inches): 54, 77, 67, 68, 46, 64, 62, 56, and 38. Where $|x_i - \mu|$ indicates the difference between the value of the observation and the arithmetic mean, ignoring the sign of the difference.

> **Must Know**
>
> $$\text{Coefficient of mean} = \frac{\text{Mean deviation}}{\text{Average deviation}} \times 100\,/\text{Average}$$

Here, X is value of data and μ is the mean of the data calculated as usual. N is total number of observations.

Example: Calculate the average deviation for 2, 5, 7, 10, 12, 14.

Solution:

1. Calculate the average of these values by adding them and dividing them by the number of values.
   $2 + 5 + 7 + 10 + 12 + 14 = 50$, which is divided by $6 = 8.3$
   Here, the average comes as 8.3

2. Find the difference between each value and the average, separately
   Here, the differences are: $2 - 8.3 = 6.3$, $5 - 8.3 = 3.3$, $7 - 8.3 = 1.3$, $10 - 8.3 = 1.7$, $12 - 8.3 = 3.7$, $14 - 8.3 = 5.7$ (as it is modulus, so negative sign is ignored)

3. Add these values and divide by the number of observations
   $$6.3 + 3.3 + 1.3 + 1.7 + 3.7 + 5.7 \div 6 = 3.66$$

Advantages of Average Deviation

- It is least affected by extreme values in contrary to standard deviation.
- It is easy to compute and understand.
- It is based on all items of series and can be calculated from any average of central tendency.
- It is a better way of calculating dispersion as compared to range.

Disadvantages of Average Deviation

As the positive and negative signs are ignored, it cannot be subjected to algebraic treatment.

Percentiles

Percentiles are used regularly without universal definition. The most common definition of a percentile is that it indicates a number where a certain percentage (say 40 or 30 or any other number) of scores fall below that number. With percentiles, there are two items of interest:
1. The position of the percentile (found using the formula)
2. The value of the percentile (for example, P_{50} = 139, means the 50th percentile has a value)

Percentiles are positional measures used mainly in education and healthcare, to indicate the position of an individual value in a group. For example, the graphs and tables show the percentiles for various measures such as test scores, height or weight.
- The 25th percentile is also called the first quartile.
- The 50th percentile is generally the median of the test series.
- The 75th percentile is also called the third quartile.
  The difference between the third and first quartiles is the interquartile range.

Must Know

Difference between percent and percentile

Percentile is in everyday use. Percentiles are normally used to report scores in tests, like the CAT, MAT, etc. Percentiles (denoted Px) divide a set of data into 100 equal parts. They are used as positional measures to indicate what percent of the data set have a value less than a specified value.

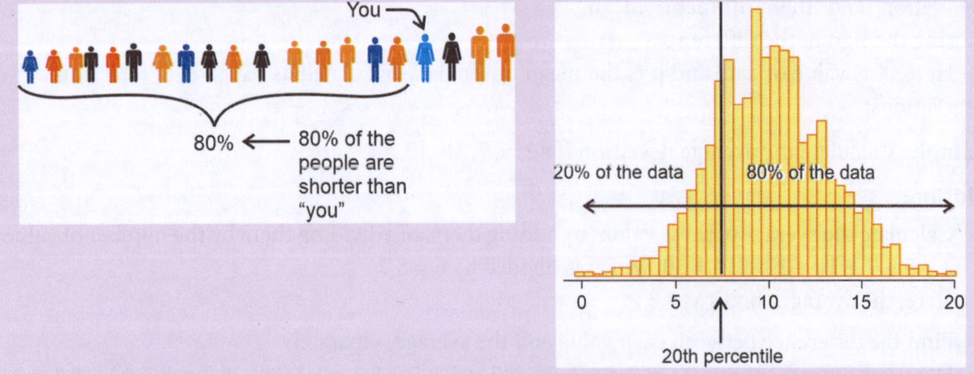

On observing the **Figure**, we can say that 80% of the people are shorter than "you", although percentiles are not the same as percentages. For example, one says that the 70th percentile in a test this year was 156 in a particular test. That means his score is better than 70% of all participants in the test. If a student gets 72 correct answers out of 100 in a test, they earn 72%. If a score of 72 correct answers corresponds to the 64th percentile, then they did better than 64% of the students in the class, but still received a score of 72%. It is clear from the figure given here that 20th percentile means that 20% of data is below it and 80% is above.

Some frequently used percentiles have specific names:

- The median is the value that is in the halfway position of a data set. Median = P_{50}.
- The quartiles are the values that are in the quarter positions of a data set.
  First quartile $= (Q_1) = P_{25}$
  Third quartile $= (Q_2) = P_{75}$
- The deciles are the values that are in the positions that divided the data into 10 pieces.
  $D_1 = P_{10}$
  $D_2 = P_{20} \dots D_{10} = P_{100}$

Comparative view of quartile, median and decile is given as follows:

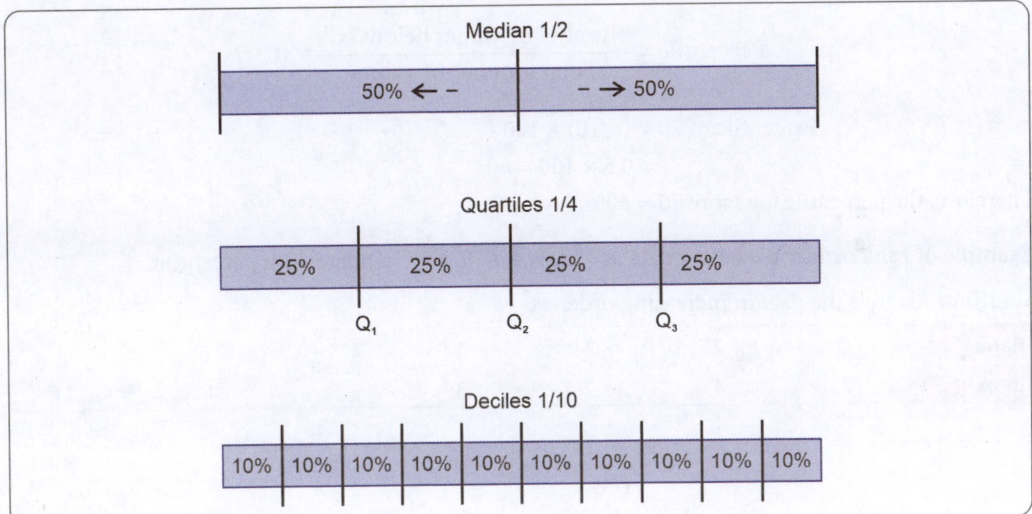

Calculation of Percentile

The percentile formula is:

$$P = (n/N) \times 100$$

Where,

- n = ordinal rank of the given value or value below the number
- N = number of values in the data set
- P = percentile

The percentile of x is the ratio of the number of values below x to the total number of values multiplied by 100. i.e., the percentile formula is:

$$\text{Percentile} = \frac{\text{Number of values below "}x\text{"}}{\text{Total number of values}} \times 10$$

Step 1: Collect the data set

Step 2: Arrange the data set in ascending order

Step 3: Determine the total number of observations

Step 4: Identify the data value for which you are interested to find the percentile

Step 5: Count the number of data values that are less than the above value

Step 6: Divide the number from Step 5 by the number from Step 3 to find the percentile of the given data value

Example: The scores obtained by 10 students are 38, 47, 49, 58, 60, 65, 70, 79, 80, 92. Using the percentile formula, calculate the percentile for score 70?

Solution:

Scores obtained by students are 38, 47, 49, 58, 60, 65, 70, 79, 80, 92.

Number of scores below 70 = 6

Using the percentile formula,

$$\text{Percentile} = \frac{\text{Number of values below "}x\text{"}}{\text{Total number of values}} \times 10$$

$$\text{Percentile of } 70 = (6/10) \times 100$$
$$= 0.6 \times 100 = 60$$

Therefore, the percentile for score 70 = 60%

Example of rank order: We have a data as 7, 2, 9, 1, 4, 8, 13. Calculate 40th percentile.

Solution: Arrange the data in increasing order as:

Rank	1	2	3	4	5	6	7
Item	2	4	7	8	9	11	13

$$R = \frac{P}{100} \times (N+1)$$

$$R = \frac{40}{100} \times (N+1)$$

$$R = 0.40 \times 8$$

$$R = 3.2$$

Formula generally used to find percentile: Provided data is ordered in increasing order, the position number of the percentiles can be calculated using the formula:

$$\text{Position number of } P_x = \frac{n+1}{100}(x)$$

Example: Here is a data set of 22 patients with diabetes.

111	131	147	151	151	179
182	190	197	201	209	234
286	294	295	310	319	337
353	377	377	439		

Determine:

a. The median

b. The first quartile

c. The third quartile

d. The fourth decile

Solution:

a. The median

111	131	147	151	151	179
182	190	197	201	**209**	**234**
286	294	295	310	319	337
353	377	377	439		

11th and 12th positions

$$\text{Position number of } P_{50} = \frac{22+1}{100}(50)$$

$$= 11.5$$

$$P_{50} = \text{11th value} + 0.5\,(\text{12th value} - \text{11th value})$$
$$= 209 + 0.5\,(234 - 209)$$
$$= 221.5$$

b. The first quartile

111	131	147	151	**151**	**179**
182	190	197	201	209	234
286	294	295	310	319	337
352	377	377	439		

5th and 6th positions

$$\text{Position number of } P_{25} = \frac{22+1}{100}(25)$$

$$= 5.75$$

$$P_{25} = \text{5th value} + 0.75\,(\text{6th value} - \text{5th value})$$
$$= 151 + 0.75\,(179 - 151)$$
$$= 172$$

c. The third quartile

111	131	147	151	151	179
182	190	197	201	209	234
286	294	295	310	**319**	**337**
353	377	377	439		

17th and 18th positions

$$\text{Position number of } P_{75} = \frac{22+1}{100}(75)$$

$$= 17.25$$

$$P_{75} = \text{17th value} + 0.25\,(\text{18th value} - \text{17th value})$$
$$= 319 + 0.25\,(337 - 319)$$
$$= 323.5$$

d. The fourth decile

111	131	147	151	151	179
182	190	**197**	**201**	209	234
286	294	295	310	319	337
353	377	377	439		

9th and 10th positions

$$\text{Position number of } P_{40} = \frac{22+1}{100}(40)$$

$$= 9.2$$

$$P_{40} = \text{9th value} + 0.2\,(\text{10th value} - \text{9th value})$$
$$= 197 + 0.2\,(201 - 197)$$
$$= 197.8$$

Percentile Rank

Commonly we use percentile to indicate that a certain percentage falls below that percentile. For example, if Ruby scored 25th percentile, then only 25% of test takers are below her score. The "25" is the **percentile rank**. In statistics, we use following definitions of percentile based on an arbitrary value as 25th percentile:

- **Definition 1:** The nth percentile is the lowest score that is greater than a certain percentage (n) of the scores. Here, n is 25, so we are looking for the lowest score which is greater than 25%.
- **Definition 2:** The nth percentile is the smallest score that is greater than or equal to a certain percentage of the scores. In other words, it is the percentage of data which falls at or below a certain observation. Here, in the example, the 25th percentile is the score which is greater than or equal to 25% of the scores.

Practical Tips

These definitions of percentile rank may seem very similar, but they can lead to big differences in results although they are both taking the 25th percentile rank (in our example).

Example: Find out where the 25th percentile is in the list given as follows that is arranged by ranks

Score	30	33	43	53	56	67	68	72
Rank	1	2	3	4	5	6	7	8

Solution:

- **Step 1:** Calculate what rank is at the 25th percentile by using the following formula:
  Here we have number of items as 8 and percentile to be calculated is 25. Therefore:
  $$\text{Rank} = \text{Percentile}/100 \times (\text{number of items} + 1)$$
  $$\text{Rank} = 25/100 \times (8 + 1) = 0.25 \times 9 = 2.25$$
  It means that a rank of 2.25 is at the 25th percentile. However, there a rank of 2.25 does not indicate much so we have to either round up, or round down. Now, 2.25 is closer to 2 than 3 therefore we can round down our results to a rank of 2.
- **Step 2:** Choose either definition 1 or 2 to interpret the results:
  - According to definition 1 the lowest score which is **greater than** 25% of the scores equals a score of 43 on the list given in example (indicating a rank of 3).
  - According to definition 2 the smallest score which is greater than **or equal to** 25% of the scores is a score of 33 on this list (indicating a rank of 2).
  - One can see that there is a lot of difference when we apply definition 1 or 2 to interpret our result. Here, the 25th percentile could be reported at 33 or 43 which is confusing.
  - A third approach tries to correct this possible misinterpretation:
    - A weighed mean of the percentiles is used from the first two definitions. For above example, the percentile will be calculated by using the formula of weighted mean:
      - Multiply the difference between the scores by 0.25 (the fraction of the rank calculated in the example above).
      - The scores were 43 and 33, and difference will be 10.
        $$(0.25)(43 - 33) = 2.5$$
      - Add the result to the lower score as $2.5 + 33 = 35.5$

In this case, the 25th percentile score is 35.5, which makes more sense because it is in the middle of 43 and 33. In most cases, the percentile is usually described by Definition 1. Although it will be wise to double check percentiles calculated by using first definition.

Percentile Range

A percentile range is the difference between two specified percentiles (theoretically, any two percentiles), but mostly 10–90 percentile range is common. To find the 10–90 percentile range:
- Calculate the 10th percentile using the steps given in example above.
- Similarly, calculate the 90th percentile.
- Subtract result of step 1 (the 10th percentile) from step 2 (the 90th percentile).

- SD is used as a measure of dispersion when mean is used as measure of central tendency like for symmetrical numerical data.
- Whereas for ordinal data or skewed numerical data, median is used as measure of central tendency and interquartile range is used as a measure of dispersion.

Standard Deviation

Standard deviation is the measure of variability used with the mean (normally distributed interval or ratio data). Standard deviation (SD) is the most commonly used measure of variability or dispersion. It is a measure of spread of data about its mean. To find out variability standard deviation is widely used and it is simplest measure of dispersion. It indicates the amount that all scores differ or deviate from the mean. More the scores differ from the mean, higher is the standard deviation (s). Sum of the deviations of scores from the mean is always is 0. It is denoted by σ.

Standard deviation is the square root of the average of the squared deviations of the signs of +ve or –ve are not ignored here.

$$SD = \sqrt{\frac{\Sigma\,(x-\bar{x})^2}{n-1}}$$

This formula is according to definition but for calculations, easier formula is used. This computational formula avoids the rounding errors that we obtain during calculations.

$$SD = \sqrt{\frac{\Sigma x^2 - \dfrac{\left(\Sigma x\right)^2}{n}}{n-1}}$$

Practical Tips

- In both the above given formulae '$n-1$' is used instead of n in the denominator, because it gives a more accurate estimate of population SD.
- Range and standard deviation may show a relationship for some frequency distributions. Along with mean, standard deviation can describe a frequency distribution in a unique way.
- Small standard deviation means a high degree of uniformity in observations whereas large standard deviation means that the items are widely scattered. In order to find out the dispersion, the order of reliability of different methods is:
  - Interquartile range < mean deviation < standard deviation

Calculation of SD

Example: During a survey, 6 students were asked how many hours per day they study on an average? Their answers were as follows: 2, 6, 5, 3, 2, 3. Evaluate the standard deviation.

Solution:

Find the mean of the data: $X = \dfrac{(2 + 6 + 5 + 3 + 2 + 3)}{6} = \dfrac{21}{6} = 3.5$

Construct the table:

X	$(X-\overline{X})$	$(X-\overline{X})^2$
2	−1.5	2.25
6	2.5	6.25
5	1.5	2.25
3	−0.5	0.25
2	−1.5	2.25
3	−0.5	0.25
21		= 13.5

Now standard deviation

$$SD = \sqrt{\dfrac{\Sigma(X - \overline{X})^2}{n-1}}$$

$$= \sqrt{\dfrac{(13.5)}{5}}$$

$$= \sqrt{2.7}$$

$$= 1.643$$

$$SD = \sqrt{\dfrac{\Sigma X^2}{n} - \dfrac{(\Sigma X)^2}{n^2}} \qquad \dots (1)$$

ΣX^2 is sum of squared scores
ΣX is sum of scores
n is number of scores
When we use $n - 1$, the formula is:

$$SD = \sqrt{\dfrac{\Sigma X^2 - (\Sigma X)^2 / n}{n-1}} \qquad \dots (2)$$

Here, X = scores; n = number of scores

Formula (2) should be used if the group tested is viewed as a representative part of the population; considered then as a sample. Here, standard deviation calculated on the sample is used as an estimate of the population standard deviation.

X = scores; n = number of scores

Formula is typically used for manual calculation.

Calculation of SD using formulas (1) and (2) of test scores 7, 2, 7, 6, 5, 6 and 2.

X	X²
7	49
2	4
7	49
6	36
5	25
6	36
2	4
$\sum x = 35$	$\sum x^2 = 203$

Where $\sum X$ is 35, $\sum X^2$ is 203, and n is 7, the standard deviation is 2:

Using formula (1):

$$s = \sqrt{\frac{203}{7} - \frac{35^2}{7^2}} = \sqrt{\frac{203}{7} - \frac{1225}{49}}$$

$$= \sqrt{29 - 25} = \sqrt{4} = 2$$

Using formula (2):

$$SD = \sqrt{\frac{203 - 35^2 / 7}{7 - 1}} = \sqrt{\frac{203 - 1225 / 7}{6}}$$

$$= \sqrt{\frac{203 - 175}{6}} = \sqrt{4.67} = 2.2$$

Advantages of SD

The reason why SD is a so useful measure of dispersion is that, if the observations are obtained from a normal distribution, then 68% of observations will lie between mean ±1 SD and 95% of observations lie between mean ±2 SD and 99.7% of observations lie between mean ±3 SD

Disadvantage of SD

The disadvantage of SD is that it is not appropriate measure of dispersion for skewed data.

Variance

Variance is the average squared deviation from the mean of a set of data. It can be used to find the standard deviation (by taking square root of SD). It is average squared distance of an observed value from its mean. It is a useful statistics in certain high level statistical procedures like regression analysis and analysis of variance (ANOVA).

- Variance is calculated by squaring the standard deviation (s^2)
- Standard deviation (SD) or $s = 4$
- Variance = $s^2 = 4^2 = 16$

Sample variance (S^2)

$$S^2 = \frac{\Sigma (X_1 - \bar{X})^2}{n-1}$$

S^2 = variance

X_1 = term in data set

$\bar{X}$ = sample mean

Σ = sum

n = sample size

Must Know

It is used to measure the distance between mean and any given value of x

- 68% of values fall within ±1 standard deviation from mean.
- 95% values lie within ±2 standard deviation from mean
- 99% values lie within ±3% standard deviation from mean.

Steps to calculate variance are as follows:

1. Find the mean of the data.
2. Mean is the average so add up the values and divide by the number of items.
3. Subtract the mean from each value—the result is called the deviation from the mean.
4. Square each deviation of the mean.
5. Find the sum of the squares.
6. Divide the total by the number of items.

The formula to calculate variance is:

$$= \frac{\Sigma (x - \mu)^2}{n}$$

Mean is represented by μ and n is the number of items.

It gives variability in squared distance when calculated from mean deviation and interpretation becomes complex. This problem is overcome by calculating variance from standard deviation.

- Variance is used to measure the distance between mean and any given value of x.
- 68% of values fall within ±1 standard deviation from mean.
- 95% values lie within ±2 standard deviation from mean.
- 99% values lie within ±3% standard deviation from mean.

Calculating SD from Variance

1. Find the **variance**.
   - Find the **mean** of the data.
   - Subtract the mean from each value.
   - Square each deviation of the mean.
   - Find the sum of the squares.
   - Divide the total by the number of items.
2. Take the square root of the variance.

Advantages of Variance

- It is based on all observations and is widely used.
- Signs are not ignored.
- It can be subjected to further algebraic treatment.
- Least affected by fluctuations in sampling.
- It provides unit measurement for normal distribution.

Practical Tips

When we have mean and standard deviation we can calculate Z (standardized score) from formula:

Standard Score, $\underline{Z} = \dfrac{X - \mu}{\sigma}$

here,

μ = mean (pronounced 'mu')

X = score

σ = standard deviation (pronounced 'sigma')

From $\underline{Z}$ we can compute the comparison of individual items which may be from different destitution.

Disadvantage of Variance

Difficult to compute.

Example: Calculate standard deviation and variance for following data.

Students	Age (X)	(X–$\overline{X}$)	(X–$\overline{X}$)^2
1	26	1.4	1.96
2	22	−2.6	6.76
3	25	0.4	0.16
4	33	8.4	70.56
5	19	−5.6	31.36
6	24	−0.6	0.36
7	29	4.4	19.36
8	31	6.4	40.96
9	20	−4.6	21.16
10	17	−7.6	57.76
11	25	0.4	0.16
	$\sum X = 271$	$\sum(X - \overline{X}) = 0$	$\sum(X–\overline{X})^2 = 250.56$

$$X = 24.6$$

$$SD = \sqrt{\frac{\sum (X - \overline{X})^2}{N - 1}}$$

$$= \sqrt{\frac{250.76}{10}}$$

$$SD = \sqrt{25.056}$$

$$\text{Variance} = (\sigma)^2$$
$$\text{or } (SD)^2$$
$$= \left(\sqrt{25.056}\right)^2$$
$$= 25.056$$

Coefficient of Variation

The coefficient of variation is the standard deviation expressed as a percentage of the arithmetic mean. It is used when the observations are in different units of measurement or to facilitate comparison of relative variability in different groups or different measurements.

$$\text{Coefficient of variation (\%) or CV} = \frac{\text{Standard deviation}}{\text{Mean}} \times 100$$

Example: Calculate coefficient of variation of following data:

	Sample 1	Sample 2
Age	25 years	11 years
Mean weight	145 pounds	80 pounds
SD	10 pounds	10 pounds

Which sample is more variable shown above?

Solution:

CV of sample 1 = 10/145 × 100 = 6.9%

CV of sample 2 = 10/80 × 100 = 12.5%

On comparing we can see that variation is more in sample 2.

Must Know

Variability and Deviations
- Variability summarizes deviations from the Mean.
- Variability describes how spread out the data is.
- For any given value in a data set, the deviation from the mean is the value minus the mean.
- The greater the variability (spread) of the distribution, the greater is the deviations from the mean (ignoring the signs of the deviation).

STUDENT ASSIGNMENT

LONG ANSWER QUESTIONS

1. What do you understand by measures of dispersion?
2. What is percentile? What are the uses of percentile? How is percentile different from percent?

SHORT ANSWER QUESTIONS

Write short notes on:
1. Standard deviation
2. Range
3. Interquartile range
4. Variance
5. Average deviation

MULTIPLE CHOICE QUESTIONS

1. **The standard deviation of ungrouped data can be calculated by:**
   a. Taking the square root of the variance
   b. $\Sigma i{-}1 n(Xi{-}\overline{X})n$
   c. Both a and b
   d. None of the above

2. **A measure of relative dispersion is given by the:**
   a. Coefficient of variance   b. Standard deviation
   c. Quartile deviation   d. Variance

3. **The _____ is the easiest measure of dispersion to calculate.**
   a. Standard deviation   b. Range
   c. Mean absolute deviation   d. Variance

4. **If arithmetic mean is multiplied to coefficient of variation then resulting value is classified as:**
   a. Coefficient of deviation   b. Coefficient of mean
   c. Standard deviation   d. Variance

5. **For recorded observation, ratios measured by absolute variation are considered:**
   a. Nonrelative measures   b. Relative measures
   c. High uniform measures   d. Low uniform measures

6. **The scatter in a series of values about the average is called:**
   a. Central tendency   b. Dispersion
   c. Skewness   d. Symmetry

7. The measurements of spread or scatter of the individual values around the central point is called:
   a. Measures of dispersion
   b. Measures of central tendency
   c. Measures of skewness
   d. Measures of kurtosis

8. The measures used to calculate the variation present among the observations in the unit of the variable is called:
   a. Relative measures of dispersion
   b. Coefficient of skewness
   c. Absolute measures of dispersion
   d. Coefficient of variation

9. The measures used to calculate the variation present among the observations relative to their average is called:
   a. Coefficient of Kurtosis
   b. Absolute measures of dispersion
   c. Quartile deviation
   d. Relative measures of dispersion

10. The degree to which numerical data tend to spread about an average value called:
    a. Constant
    b. Flatness
    c. Variation
    d. Skewness

11. The measures of dispersion can never be:
    a. Positive
    b. Zero
    c. Negative
    d. Equal to 2

12. If all the scores on examination cluster around the mean, the dispersion is said to be:
    a. Small
    b. Large
    c. Normal
    d. Symmetrical

13. If there are many extreme scores on all examination, the dispersion is:
    a. Large
    b. Small
    c. Normal
    d. Symmetric

14. Problem with solution: A population consists of four observations: 1, 3, 5, 7. What is the variance?
    a. 2
    b. 4
    c. 5
    d. 6

Unit IV

Standard Normal Distribution

9

Normal Distribution

"Most people are average. Founders are not. Founders' traits seem to have an inverse normal distribution to them."
—Peter Thiel

LEARNING OBJECTIVES

After the completion of the chapter, the readers will be able to:

- Understand normal distribution.
- Explain skewness and kurtosis.
- Discuss the applications of normal probability curve.

CHAPTER OUTLINE

- Introduction
- Normal Distribution
- Properties of the Normal Probability Curve
- Standard Normal Distribution (Z) and Standard Scores (Z-score)
- Skewness and Kurtosis

INTRODUCTION

In statistic we have many different classifications of probability distributions—the normal distribution, binomial distribution, chi square distribution and Poisson distribution. The different types of probability distributions have different purposes and they represent processes of different data generation. For example, binomial distribution evaluates the probability of occurring of an event in a trial such as tossing a coin to figure out the probability of that coin coming up with heads in 10 flips. Here either there will be head or tail. A binomial distribution is discrete, as opposed to continuous, because only valid response is head or tail; 1 or 0 and so on.

Most frequently used distribution is the normal distribution that is used very often in science, finance, and engineering. Unlike the binomial distribution, the normal distribution is continuous which means that all possible values are signified (in contrast to just 0 and 1 with nothing in between, in case of binomial distribution).

NORMAL DISTRIBUTION

Normal distribution that is also known as the Gaussian distribution is a probability distribution which is symmetric about the mean. It shows that the data near the mean are more repeated than data which is far from the mean. In graphical form, normal distribution will appear as a bell-shaped curve.

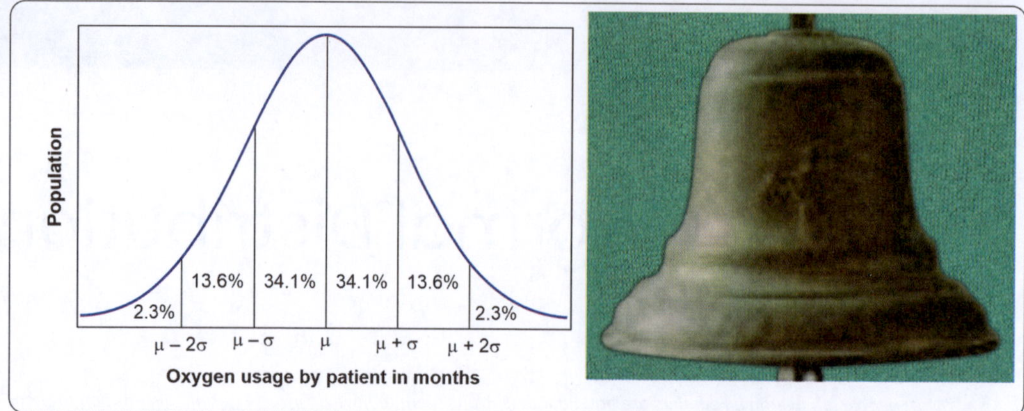

Figure 9.1: Bell-shaped curve of normal distribution

Bell-shaped curve: It is defined as a continuous frequency distribution of infinite range which describes the real world situations. A function that tells the probability of a number in some context falling between any two real numbers is called normal distribution. The term bell-shaped curve is used to describe the mathematical concept called normal distribution, and it also sometimes referred to as Gaussian distribution (Fig. 9.1).

Characteristics of a variable described as normally distributed are as follows:

A variable whose values can be described as normally distributed should have the following characteristics:

- If graphed in a frequency polygon, the polygon will be essentially bell-shaped and symmetrical.
- When computed, the mean, median, and mode will be similar.
- Most values will fall between 1 standard deviations from the mean; a few values may fall below or above three standard deviations from the mean.

The important things to note about a normal distribution is that the curve is concentrated in the center and decreases on either side. This is significant in that the data has less tendency to produce unusually extreme values, called outliers, as compared to other distributions.

A bell-shaped curve graph depends on two factors, the mean and the standard deviation. The mean identifies the position of the center and the standard deviation determines the height and width of the bell.

Many things closely follow a normal distribution:
- Heights of people
- Size of things produced by machines
- Errors in measurements
- Blood pressure

Probability distribution describes all the possible values and likelihoods that any random variable can take within a given range. This range is bounded between the minimum and maximum values although exactly where the possible value is likely to be plotted on the probability distribution depends on a number of factors. These factors include the distributions mean or average, standard deviation, skewness and kurtosis.

Characteristics

- Normal distributions are symmetric around their mean.
- The mean, median, and mode of a normal distribution are equal.
- The area under the normal curve is equal to 1.
- Normal distributions are denser in the center and less dense in the tails.
- Normal distributions are defined by two parameters, the mean (μ) and the standard deviation (σ).
- 68% of the area of a normal distribution is within one standard deviation of the mean.
- Approximately 95% of the area of a normal distribution is within two standard deviations of the mean.

Importance

- Many dependent variables are commonly assumed to be normally distributed in the population so it can precisely tell about any population distribution.
- If a variable is normally distributed then we can infer its values.
- It is most important probability distribution in statistics because it fits in many natural phenomena like, heights, blood pressure and IQ scores, etc.
- The normal distribution is a probability function which indicates about the distribution of values of a variable.

Example: Heights measured in a class is an example of normally distributed data. The data obtained from measurements of heights are normally distributed. (Fig. 9.2).

We can see that the distribution of heights follows a typical pattern for all normal distributions. Most girls have heights close to the average which is 1.512 m. There are small differences between an individual girl's height and the mean which occurs more repeatedly as compared to any significant deviations from the mean. The standard deviation is 0.0741 m that indicates the typical distance which height of an individual girl tends to fall from mean.

The distribution is symmetric. The number of girls shorter than average is equal to the number of girls taller than average. On both tail ends of the distribution, extremely short girls occur equally infrequently as extremely tall girls.

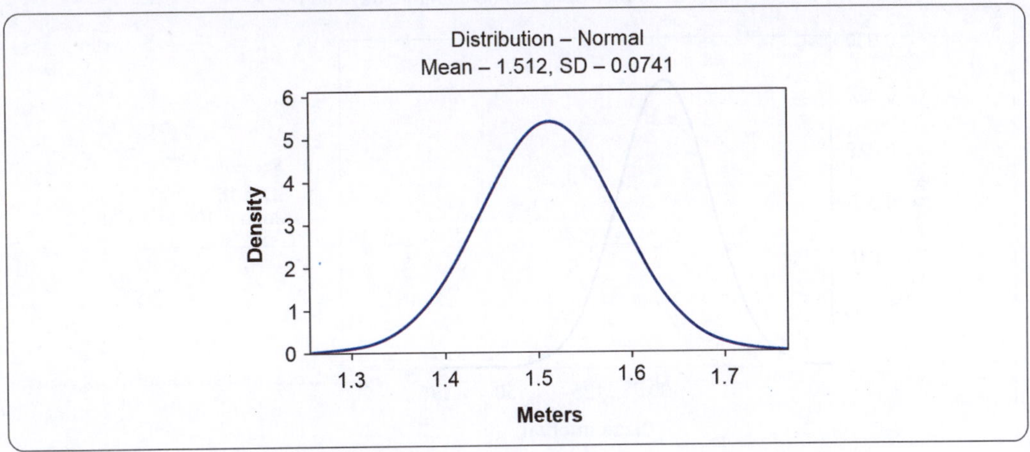

Figure 9.2: Heights of girls showing normal probability curve

- Many statistical tests for testing of hypothesis assume that the data under observation is following a normal distribution.
- Linear and nonlinear regression assume that the observations follow a normal distribution.
- With increase in sample size, the sampling distribution of the mean follows a normal distribution in spite of the fact that the underlying distribution of the original variable is not normal.
- A probability distribution shows an expected outcome of possible values for a given data under process.
- Probability distributions come in different shapes with different characteristics, like: defined by mean or standard deviation or skewness or kurtosis, etc.
- Investors apply probability distributions to foretell returns on assets like stocks and to hedge their risk.

Parameters of the Normal Distribution

Like any probability distribution, the shape and probabilities of normal distribution are defined by the parameters. The normal distribution has two parameters: (1) **The mean** (2) **Standard deviation**. It means that the normal distribution does not have only a single form instead the shape of curve changes based upon the parameters as is shown ahead in the graphs (**Figs 9.3A and B**).

Effect of Mean on Normal Distribution

The mean defines the location of the peak of bell-shaped curve in a normal distribution. Most values are clustered around the mean. On a graph, when we plot the mean, the entire curve may shift to left or right on the x-axis (Fig. 9.3A).

Effect of Standard Deviation on Normal Distribution

Standard deviation talks about the width of the normal distribution. The standard deviation decides how far away the values will tend to fall from the mean. It signifies the typical distance between the observations and the average for a particular data (Fig. 9.3B).

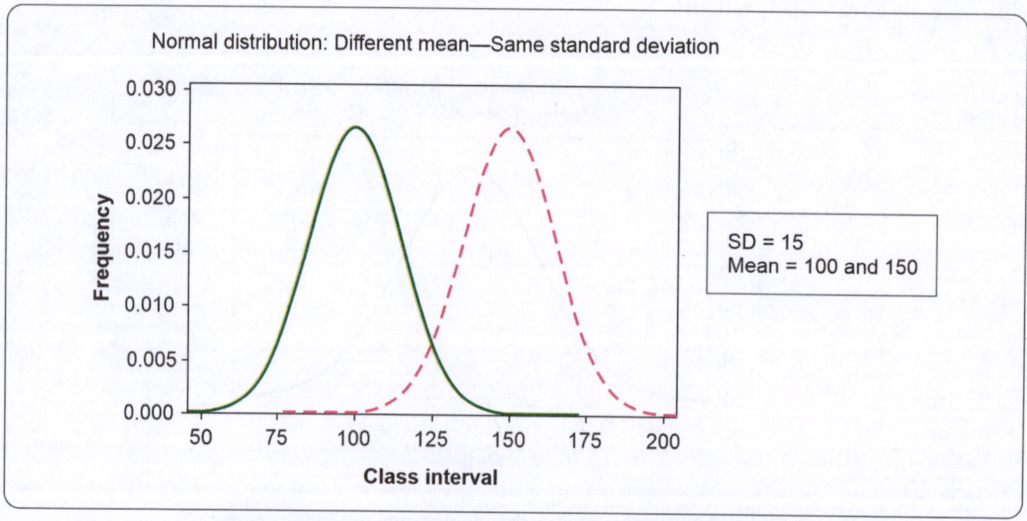

Figure 9.3A: Effect of mean on a normal distribution curve

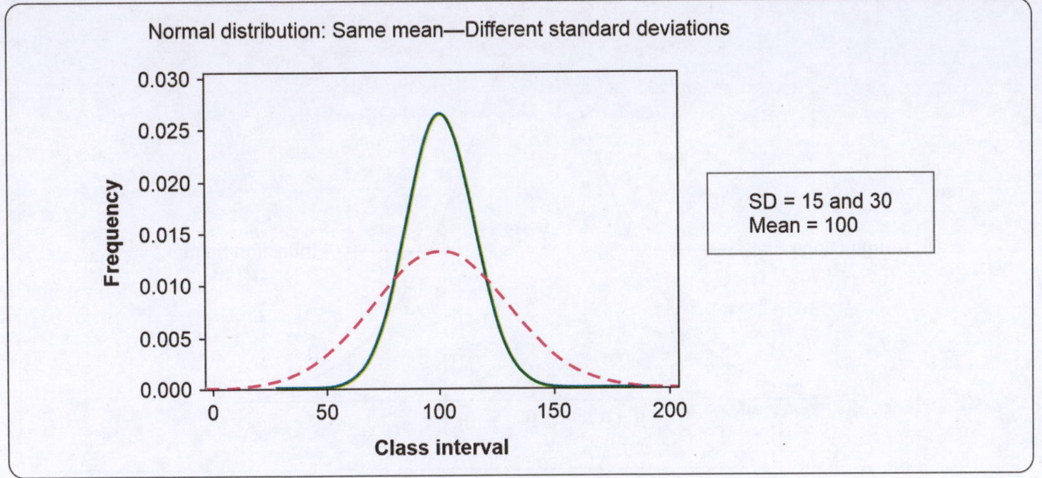

Figure 9.3B: Effect of SD on a normal distribution

When the standard deviation is changed on a graph, either it tightens the curve or spreads out the width of the distribution along the x-axis. Larger standard deviations produce distributions that are more spread out.

PROPERTIES OF THE NORMAL PROBABILITY CURVE

- The highest point occurs at x = μ.
- It is symmetric about the mean, μ. The curve is smooth and bell shaped.
- One half of the curve is a mirror image of the other half, i.e., the area under the curve to the right of μ is equal to the area under the curve to the left of μ equals to ½.
- The curve is asymptotic to the horizontal axis at the extremes. It does not meet the baseline at the ends, as it is based on an infinite range of data.
- It is bilaterally symmetrical.
- It is unimodal, and has only one peak.
- Mean, mode and median coincide.
- It has two inflections. The central part is convex while at the points of inflection, the curve changes from convexity to concavity (Fig. 9.4).
  Mean = Mode = Median (Fig. 9.5).

Empirical Rule

In normal distributions:
- 68% of observations fall within the first standard deviation (μ ± σ) of the mean.
- 95% of observations fall within the first 2 standard deviations (μ ± 2σ) of the mean.
- 99.7% of observations fall within the first 3 standard deviations (μ ± 3σ) of the mean.

When we have narrow distributions (with small differences), the probabilities are higher, and all values will not fall far from the mean. As we increase the spread of the distribution, the observations will move away from the mean.

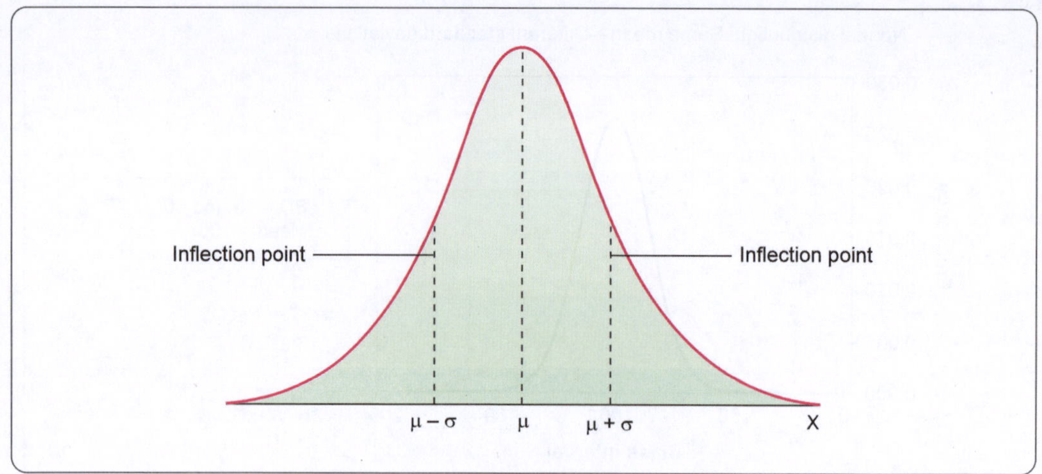

Figure 9.4: Normal curve showing inflection points

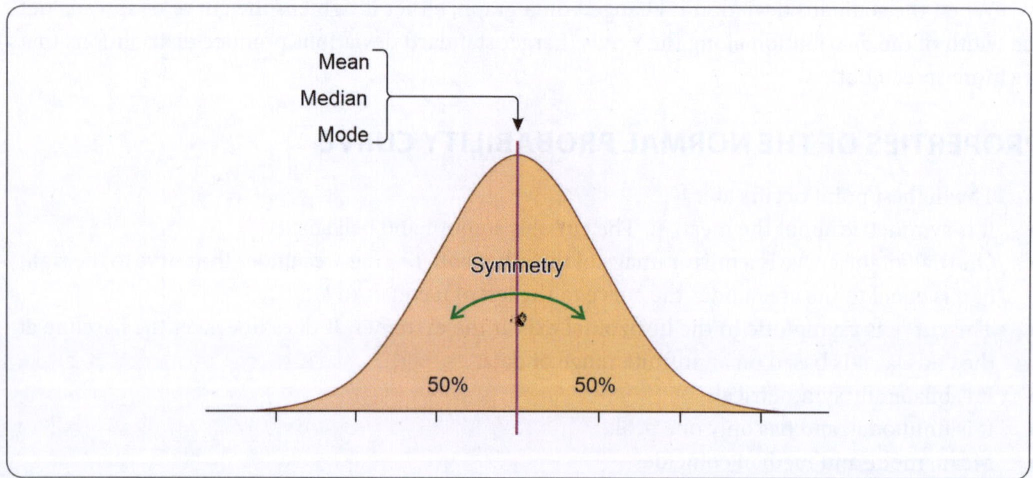

Figure 9.5: Mean, median and mode are equal in normal distribution curve

Central Limit Theorem (CLT)

According to CLT, distribution of sample means will approach normal or Gaussian distribution as the sample size increases. CLT describes fluctuations around the center/mean/average. CLT is used to get an estimate of the population value from the sample value.

Empirical Rules of CLT

- The date must be random.
- Samples must be independent of each other,
- Sample size must be large enough but must not exceed 10% of the total population.

Note that a sample size of 30 and >30 is considered as a large sample size.

Practical Tips

While the normal distribution is essential in statistics, it is just one of many probability distributions which may not fit in cases of all populations. To know about what type of data is obtained from our experiment, one has to graph the raw data. Here is a histogram plotted for the data obtained in an experiment (Fig. 9.6).

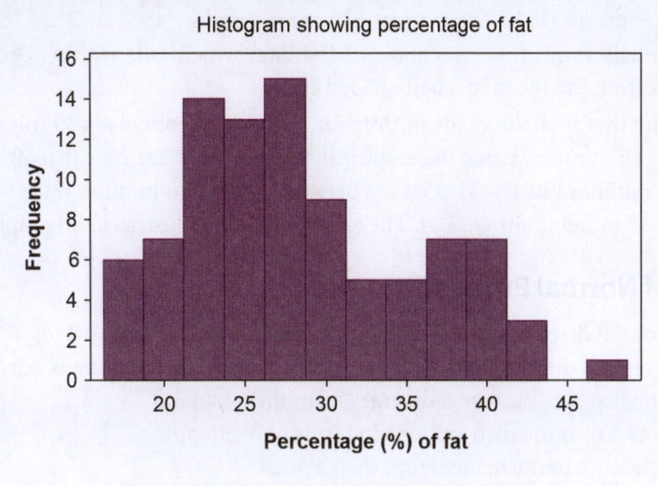

Figure 9.6: Histogram of raw data

The histogram gives a decent overview of the obtained data. In one glance, we can see that these data which we have plotted are not normally distributed. They are skewed on right end. The peak is around 27%, and the distribution is extending into the higher values than to the lower values. These data are not normal.

The empirical rule for the normal distribution (Fig. 9.7) allows us to determine the proportion of values which are falling within certain distances from the mean value.

- Normal distribution is the appropriate term for a probability bell-shaped curve.
- It is symmetrical in distribution, but all symmetrical distributions are not normal.
- Actually, most distributions are not perfectly normal.

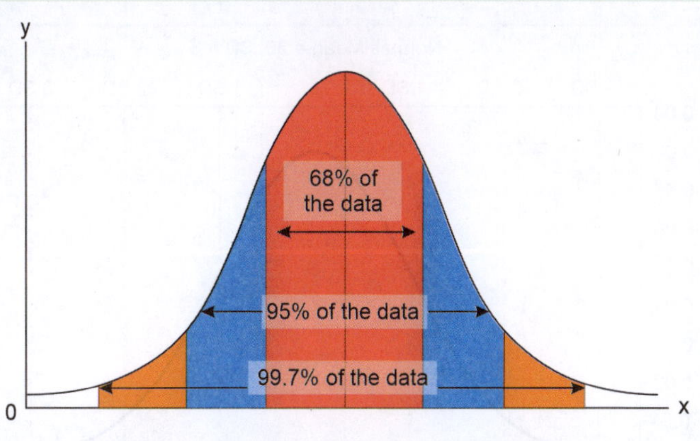

Figure 9.7: Empirical rule of normal distribution

When we have normally distributed data, the standard deviation is particularly valuable. It can be used to determine the proportion of the values that fall within a specified number of standard deviations from the mean. For example, in a normal distribution, 68% of the observations fall within +/− 1 standard deviation from the mean. This characteristic is part of the empirical rule that tells about the percentage of the data which falls within specific numbers of standard deviations from the mean in a bell-shaped curve.

+/– Standard deviations	Percentage of data contained
1	68%
2	95%
3	99.7%

For example, assume that in a clinic, mean time for the visit of patients is 30 minutes and it has a standard deviation of 5 minutes. Using the empirical rule, we can determine that 68% of the visits are between 25 and 35 minutes (30 +/− 5), 95% are between 20 and 40 minutes (30 +/−2.5), and 99.7% are between 15 and 45 minutes (30 +/−3.5). The following figure illustrates this graphically (Fig. 9.8).

Applications of Normal Probability Curve

- **Represents a model distribution:** Normal curve can be used as a model to:
  - Compare various distributions with it, i.e., whether the distribution is normal or not and if not then in what specific way it diverges from the normal.
  - Compares two or more distributions in terms of overlapping.
  - Evaluate student's performance from their scores.
  - It is used for computing percentiles and percentile ranks in a given normal distribution.
- **Ability of grouping:** A group of individuals may be conveniently grouped into categories (assumed to be normally distributed) like A, B, C, D and E or very good, good, average, poor and very poor in terms of some traits with the help of a normal curve.
- **Converting raw scores into comparable standard normalized scores:** With the help of a normal curve, we can convert the raw scores which belong to different tests into a standard normal scores like sigma scores and Z-scores, etc. A standard Z-score clearly indicates how many standard deviation units a raw score is above or below the mean therefore it provides a standard scale for the purpose of valuable comparison.

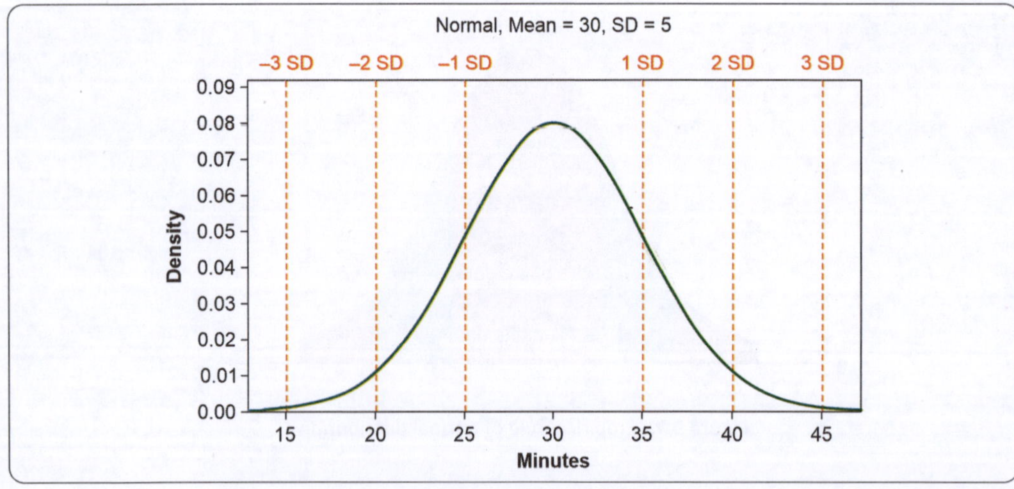

Figure 9.8: Patients visiting a clinic

- **Determining the relative difficulty of test items:** Normal curve offers the simplest rational method of scaling test items for difficulty and therefore, may be suitably employed for determining the related difficulty of questions, problems and other test items under observations.

STANDARD NORMAL DISTRIBUTION (Z) AND STANDARD SCORES (Z-SCORE)

The normal distribution has many different shapes that depend on the values of parameters. Whereas the standard normal distribution is a distinct case of normal distribution where the mean is 0 and the standard deviation is 1. This type of distribution is known as the Z-distribution.

Standard Score

The values of standard normal distribution are known as standard scores (Z-score). The number of SDs from the mean is also called as "standard score", "Sigma" or "Z-score" (Fig. 9.9). A standard score signifies the deviation of a specific observation that falls above or below the mean in terms of standard deviations. As an example, a standard score of 1.5 signifies that the observation is 1.5 standard deviation above the mean. Whereas a negative score represents a value below the average. The mean has a Z-score of 0.

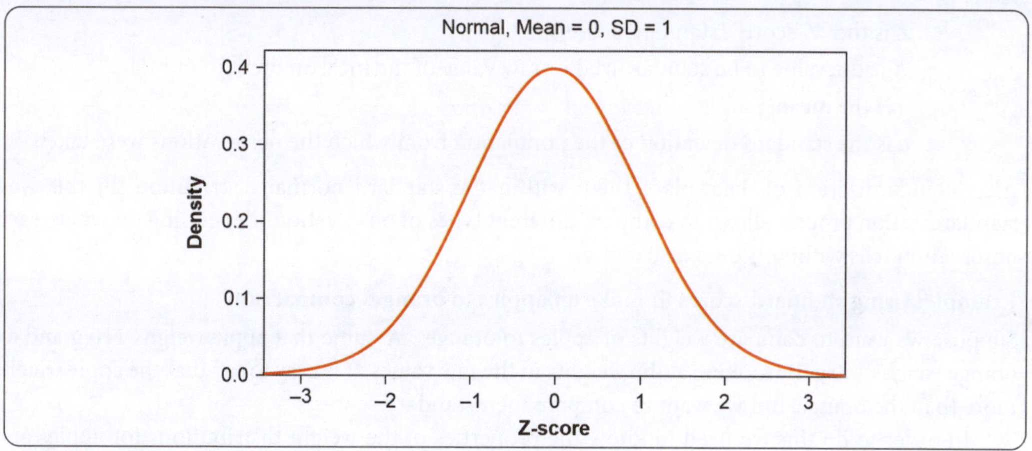

Figure 9.9: Z and Z-score

Practical Tips

Standardization: How to Calculate Z-scores

- In statistics, standardization is a way of putting different variables on the same scale. The process allows to compare scores between various types of variables. Generally, in order to standardize variables, one can calculate the mean and standard deviation for a variable. Then, for each observed value of that variable, subtract the mean and then divide by the standard deviation.
- This process gives standard scores which represent the number of standard deviations above or below the mean that a particular observation falls. For example, a standardized value of 2 tells that the observation falls 2 standard deviations above the mean. This interpretation of a variable is perfect regardless of the type of variable that is standardized.
- Suppose we weigh an apple and its weight comes out as 125 g. We want to compare it with other apples but there is no way to tell from the weight alone how this apple which we weighed compares to other apples. However, with the help of its Z-score, we can tell where it falls relative to other apples.

Converting a Value to a Standard Score (Z-score)

First subtract the mean, then divide by the standard deviation and doing this is called "Standardizing."

The standard scores are a great way to understand about the position of a specific observation where it falls relative to the entire distribution. They also permit to take observations from normally distributed populations having different means and standard deviations and to place them on a standard scale. This standard scale enables to compare observations which would otherwise be tough. This process is known as standardization and it permits to compare observations and calculation of probabilities across different populations. In other words, it permits to compare heights to lengths. Statistics is great! In order to standardize a data, we need to convert the raw measurements into Z-scores (Fig. 9.10).

Convert the values to Z-scores (standard scores)

To calculate the standard score for an observation, select the raw measurement then subtract the mean, and divide the outcome by the standard deviation.

$$Z = \frac{X - \mu}{\sigma}$$

Here,

Z is the "Z-score" (standard score).

X is the value to be standardized or raw value of the measurement in our data.

μ is the mean.

σ is the standard deviation of the population from which the observations were taken.

After standardization of data, place them within the standard normal distribution. In this way, standardization process allows to compare different types of observations depending on where each observation falls within its own distribution.

Example: Using standard scores to make an apples to oranges comparison

Suppose we want to compare weights of apples to oranges. Assume that apple weighs 110 g and an orange weighs 140 g. By looking at the weights in the raw values, it is easy to say that the apple weighs more than the orange. But we want to compare their standard scores.

In order to do this we need to know the properties of the weight distributions for apples and oranges. Now suppose that the weights of apples and oranges have a normal distribution with assumed mean as 100 and following parameter values:

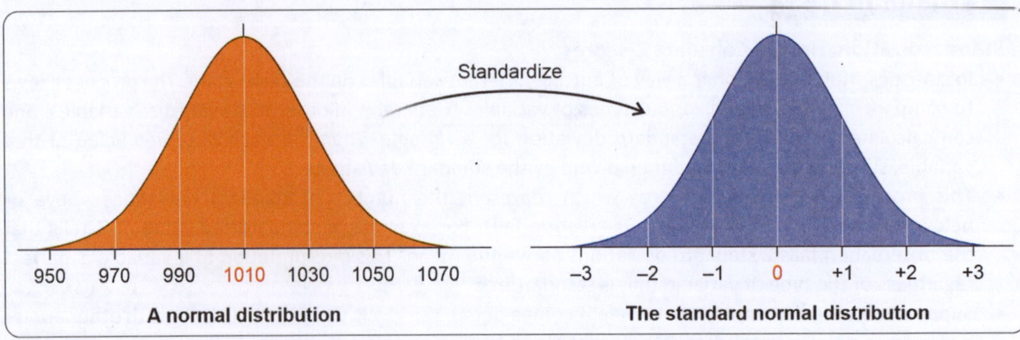

Figure 9.10: Standardization of normal distribution

	Apple	Orange
Mean weight (grams)	110	140
Standard Deviation	15	25

Now calculate the Z-scores, separately, as:

- Apple = $(110 - 100)/15 = 0.667$

- Orange = $(100 - 140)/25 = \dfrac{-40}{25} = -1.6$

The Z-score for the apple (0.667) is positive and it means that apple weighs more than any other average apple. It is not an extreme value, but it is above average for apples. The orange has negative Z-score (−1.6). It is far below the mean weight for oranges. These Z-values have been put in the standard normal distribution as in the Figure 9.11.

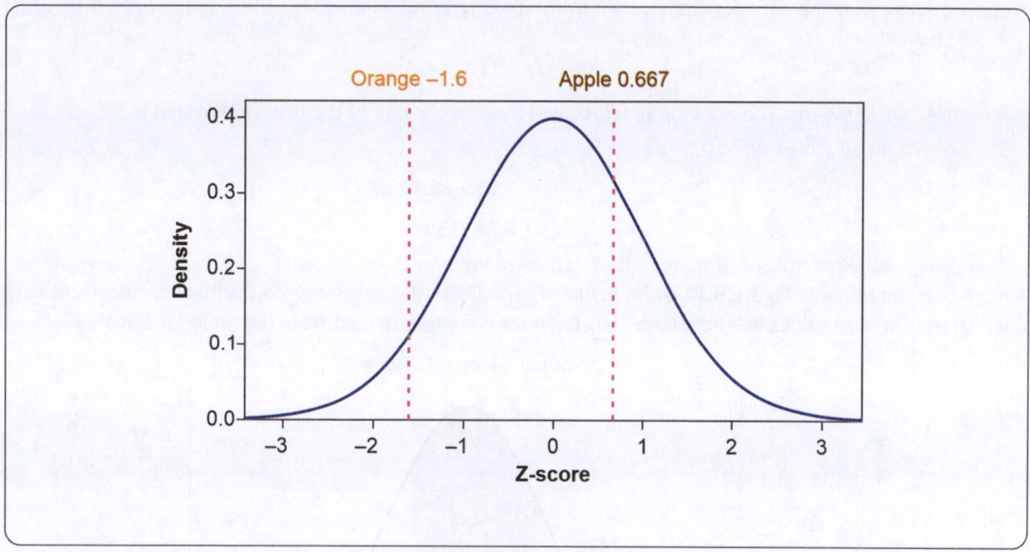

Figure 9.11: Comparison of apples with oranges by using Z-score

Practical Tips

Finding Areas Under the Curve of Normal Distribution

While converting values to standard scores, one can calculate areas by looking at Z-scores provided in a standard normal distribution table. Because we have an infinite number of different normal distributions, it will be difficult to print a table for all distributions. Although one can convert the values from any normal distribution into Z-scores, and after this a table of standard scores can be used to calculate probabilities.

Using a Table of Z-scores

Suppose we have Z-score for apple as 0.667. We can use Z-score to determine its weight as percentile. We know that percentile is the proportion of a population which falls below a specific value. Therefore, to determine the percentile, we need to find the area which matches with the range of Z-scores which are <0.667. In the segment of the following table, the closest Z-score to 0.667 is 0.65, which will be used further.

Contd...

A portion of Z-score table

Z	0.00	0.05	0.10	0.15	0.20	0.25	0.30	0.35	0.40	0.45	0.50	0.55	0.60	0.65	0.70
Height	39.89	39.84	39.69	39.45	39.10	38.67	38.14	37.52	36.83	36.05	35.21	34.29	33.32	32.30	31.23
Area	0	3.99	7.97	11.92	15.85	19.74	23.58	27.37	31.08	34.73	38.29	41.77	45.15	**48.43**	51.61

Now we have to use this table in combination with the properties of the normal distribution so as to find out the probability which we need. Here, the table value indicates an area of the curve between −0.65 and +0.65 as 48.43%. But that is not what we want to know. We are interested in finding out the area which is less than a Z-score of 0.65.

The two halves of the normal distribution with positive and negative values are mirror images of each other and we know that the area for the interval from −0.65 to +0.65 is 48.43%, so the range from 0 to +0.65 should be half of it, as:

$$48.43/2 = 24.215\%.$$

Moreover, we know that the area for all scores less than zero is half of the distribution that is 50%.

So, the area for all scores up to 0.65 is:

$$= 50\% + 24.215\%$$

$$= 74.215\%$$

Therefore, apple under our observation is at 74th percentile.

Note that the curve in **Figure 9.12** is the result of probability distribution produced by statistical software which uses precise values like here 0.667 has been used in place of 0.65 from the table for Z-score.

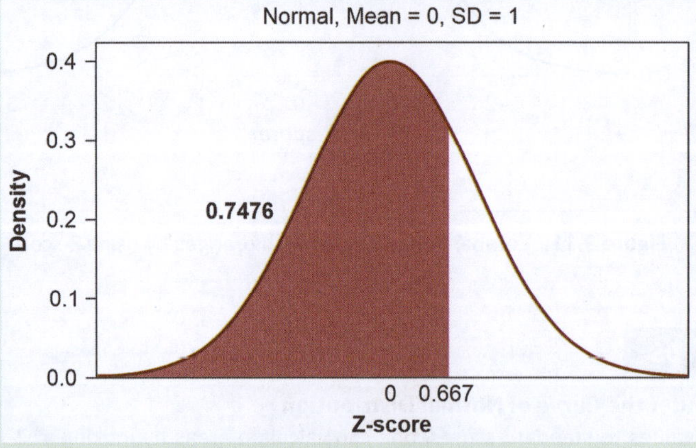

Figure 9.12: Percentile for apple weight using Z-score

SKEWNESS AND KURTOSIS

Data in real life rarely follow a perfect normal distribution. The coefficients like skewness and kurtosis measure the amount of difference for a given data distribution from a normal distribution. The skewness measures the evenness of a distribution. The normal distribution is symmetric without skewness.

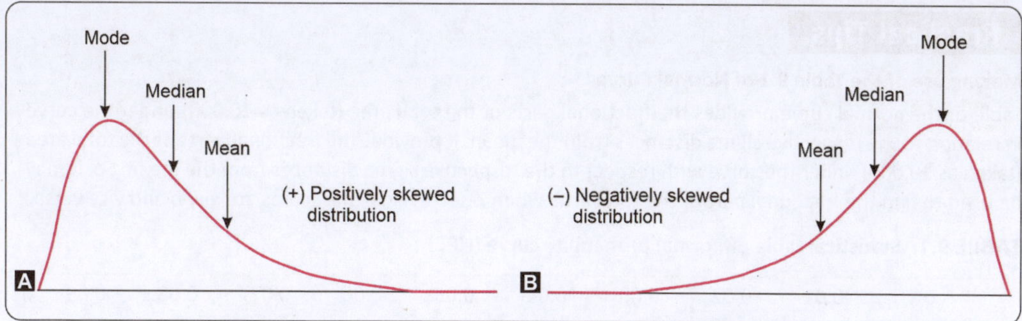

Figures 9.13A and B: A. Positive skewness; **B.** Negative skewness

- If the distribution of a data set has a skewness less than zero that is negative skewness, then it trails toward the left side (Fig. 9.13B). The tail of the distribution is longer than the right tail in case of negative skewness.
- In case of positive skewness, the right tail of the distribution is longer than the left (Fig. 9.13A). The kurtosis measures the thickness of the tail ends of a distribution with respect to the tails of the normal distribution.

Distributions with large kurtosis show tail data which exceed the tails of the normal distribution (e.g., five or more standard deviations from the mean).

Distributions with low kurtosis show tail data which is mostly less extreme as compared to the tails of the normal distribution. The normal distribution has a kurtosis of 3, which means that the distribution has neither fat nor thin tails. It means if an observed distribution has a kurtosis >3, the distribution is said to have heavy tails with comparison to the normal distribution. If the distribution has a kurtosis <3, it is said to have thin tails with respect to the normal distribution.

Types of Kurtosis

Platykurtic: A frequency distribution is said to be platykurtic when the curve is flatter than the normal curve. It happens with small number of individuals having scores near to the average scores (Fig. 9.14A). On other side, when there are too many cases in the central area, the distribution curve becomes too 'peaked' in the middle as compared to the normal curve. Both these characteristics of being flat or peaked are used to describe the term kurtosis.

Leptokurtic: A frequency distribution that is more peaked than the normal curve (Fig 9.14B).

Mesokurtic: A frequency distribution which resembles normal curve (Fig. 9.14C).

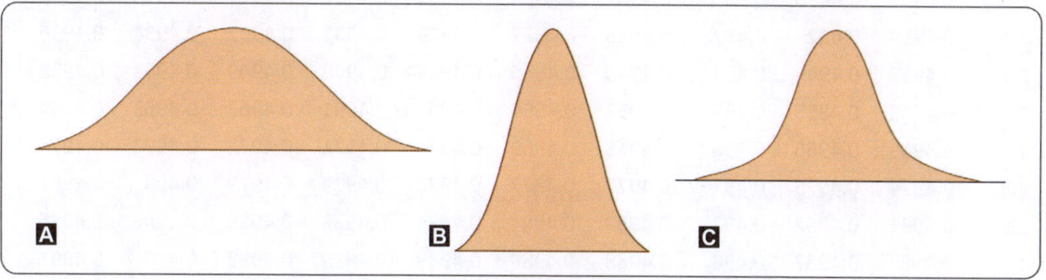

Figures 9.14A to C: A. Platykurtic; **B.** Leptokurtic; **C.** Mesokurtic

Practical Tips

Making use of the Table 9.1 of Normal Curve

Table of the normal curve provides the fractional parts of the total area (taken as 10,000) under the curve in relation to the respective sigma distances from the mean. It provides the fractional parts of the total area (taken as 10,000) under the curve with respect to the respective sigma distances from the mean. So, it may be used to find the fractional part of the total area when Z-scores or sigma scores are given and vice versa.

TABLE 9.1: Statistical table of normal probability curve (NPC)

	0	0.01	0.02	0.03	0.04	0.05	0.06	0.07	0.08	0.09
0	0	0.004	0.008	0.012	0.016	0.0199	0.0239	0.0279	0.0319	0.0359
0.1	0.0398	0.0438	0.0478	0.0517	0.0557	0.0596	0.0636	0.0675	0.0714	0.0753
0.2	0.0793	0.0832	0.0871	0.091	0.0948	0.0987	0.1026	0.1064	0.1103	0.1141
0.3	0.1179	0.1217	0.1255	0.1299	0.1331	0.1368	0.1406	0.1443	0.148	0.1517
0.4	0.1554	0.1591	0.1628	0.1664	0.17	0.1736	0.1772	0.1808	0.1844	0.1879
0.5	0.1915	0.195	0.1985	0.2019	0.2054	0.2088	0.2123	0.2157	0.219	0.2224
0.6	0.2257	0.2291	0.2324	0.2357	0.2389	0.2422	0.2454	0.2486	0.2517	0.2549
0.7	0.258	0.2611	0.2642	0.2673	0.2704	0.2734	0.2764	0.2794	0.2823	0.2852
0.8	0.2881	0.291	0.2939	0.2967	0.2995	0.3023	0.3051	0.3078	0.3106	0.3133
0.9	0.3159	0.3186	0.3212	0.3238	0.3264	0.3289	0.3315	0.334	0.3365	0.3389
1	0.3413	0.3438	0.3461	0.3485	0.3508	0.3531	0.3554	0.3577	0.3599	0.3621
1.1	0.3643	0.3665	0.3686	0.3708	0.3729	0.3749	0.377	0.379	0.381	0.383
1.2	0.3849	0.3869	0.3888	0.3907	0.3925	0.3944	0.3962	0.398	0.3997	0.4015
1.3	0.4032	0.4049	0.4066	0.4082	0.4099	0.4115	0.4131	0.4147	0.4162	0.4177
1.4	0.4192	0.4207	0.4222	0.4236	0.4251	0.4265	0.4279	0.4292	0.4306	0.4319
1.5	0.4332	0.4345	0.4357	0.437	0.4382	0.4394	0.4406	0.4418	0.4429	0.4441
1.6	0.4452	0.4463	0.4474	0.4484	0.4495	0.4505	0.4515	0.4525	0.4535	0.4545
1.7	0.4554	0.4564	0.4573	0.4582	0.4591	0.4599	0.4608	0.4616	0.4625	0.4633
1.8	0.4641	0.4649	0.4656	0.4664	0.4671	0.4678	0.4686	0.4693	0.4699	0.4786
1.9	0.4713	0.4719	0.4726	0.4732	0.4738	0.4744	0.475	0.4756	0.4761	0.4767
2	0.4772	0.4778	0.4783	0.4788	0.4793	0.4798	0.4803	0.4808	0.4812	0.4817
2.1	0.4821	0.4826	0.483	0.4834	0.4838	0.4842	0.4846	0.485	0.4854	0.4857
2.2	0.4861	0.4864	0.4868	0.4871	0.4875	0.4878	0.4881	0.4884	0.4887	0.489
2.3	0.4893	0.4896	0.4898	0.4901	0.4904	0.4906	0.4909	0.4911	0.4913	0.4916
2.4	0.4918	0.492	0.4922	0.4925	0.4927	0.4929	0.4931	0.4932	0.4934	0.4936
2.5	0.4938	0.494	0.4941	0.4943	0.4945	0.4946	0.4948	0.4949	0.4951	0.4952
2.6	0.4953	0.4855	0.4956	0.4957	0.4959	0.496	0.4961	0.4962	0.4963	0.4964
2.7	0.4965	0.4966	0.4967	0.4968	0.4969	0.497	0.4971	0.4972	0.4973	0.4974
2.8	0.4974	0.4975	0.4976	0.4977	0.4977	0.4978	0.4979	0.4979	0.498	0.4981
2.9	0.4981	0.4982	0.4982	0.4983	0.4984	0.4984	0.4985	0.4985	0.4986	0.4986
3	0.4987	0.4987	0.4987	0.4988	0.4988	0.4989	0.4989	0.4989	0.499	0.499

Contd...

Application 1: To determine the percentage of cases in a normal distribution within given limits. There can be situations under this:

a. To find the percentage of cases below a given score point.
b. To find the percentage of cases above a given score point.
c. To find the percentage of cases lying between two given score points.

Example: Given a normal distribution, N = 1,000; Mean = 80 and SD = 16. Find the percentage of individuals whose scores lie below the score point 40.

Solution: First the raw scores will be converted into Z-scores by using the formula $Z = \dfrac{X - \mu}{\sigma}$

or

$$Z = \frac{40 - 80}{16}$$

$$= -2.5\sigma$$

Table value of σ score 2.5 is 0.4938. This value is further converted into percentage by dividing it with 10,000 and then multiplying it with 100. We get the value as 49.38% that means 49.38% cases lie between mean and −2.5σ.

In all, 50 − 49.38 = 0.62% cases lie below the score point 40 and out of 1000, 6 individuals achieve below the score point 40 which is also the percentile rank.

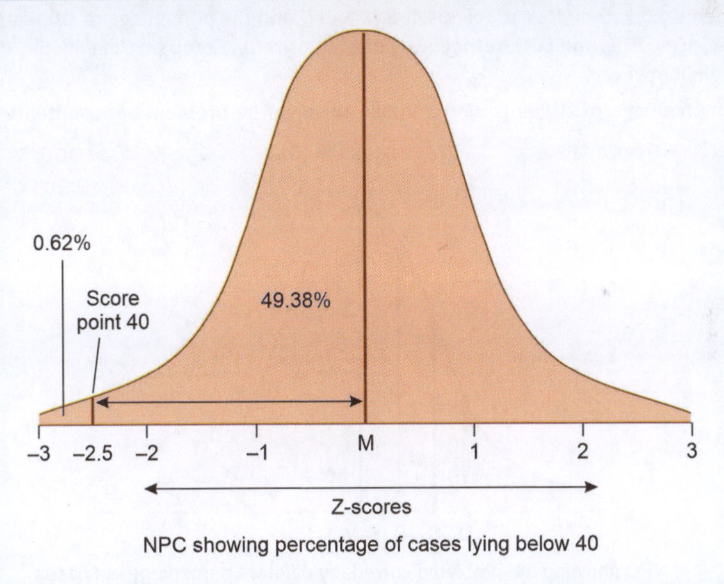

NPC showing percentage of cases lying below 40

Application 2: To determine the limits of the scores between which a certain percentage of cases lie.

Example: If a distribution is normal with Mean = 100, SD = 20, find out the two points between which the middle 60% of cases lie.

Solution: The middle 60% means that 30% of the cases fall to the left and the rest 30% (3000 out of 10,000) to right of the mean.
Referring to statistical table of normal curve, corresponding sigma distance for 3,000 fractional parts of total area will be calculated that comes out to be 0.84σ and −0.84σ for the cases falling to the left of mean. The standard Z-scores will be converted to raw scores with the help of same formula as [X − μ/σ]. Here value of raw scores comes out to be 117 and 83 (rounding the figures) which includes the middle 60% of cases.

Contd...

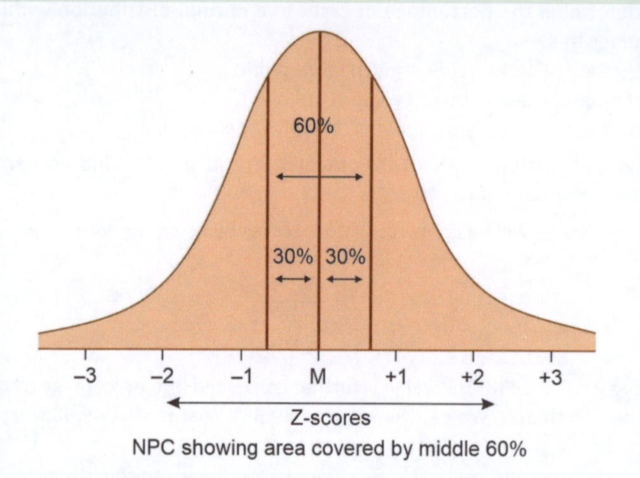

NPC showing area covered by middle 60%

Application 3: To determine the relative difficulty value of the test items.

Example: Students worked on four problems A, B, C and D and the percentage of students who solved the problem is 50%, 60%, 70%, and 80%, respectively of a large group. Compare the difficulty between A and B, with the difficulty between C and D.

Solution: The percentage of students who are able to solve the problem are counted from the extreme right.

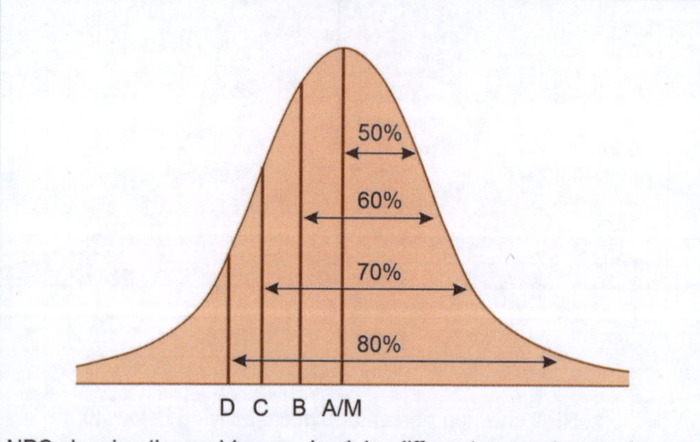

NPC showing the problems solved by different percentages of cases

- Problem A was solved by 50% of the group, also, it means that 50% of the group was not been able to solve it. It further means that it was an average problem having 0 difficulty level.
- Problem B was solved by 60% of the group, also, it means that comparative to A, and 10% more individuals were able to solve it.
- Problem C was solved by 70% of the group, also, it means that 20% more individuals were able to solve it as compared with the average.
- Problem D was passed by 80% of the group, also, it means that 30% more individuals were able to solve it than the average.

Contd...

Problem	Solved by (%)	Difficulty value	Relative difficulty
A	50	0	
B	60	−0.253 σ	−0.253 σ
C	70	−0.252 σ	
D	80	−0.840 σ	−0.315 σ

Problem B is simpler than problem A by having 0.253 σ less difficulty value and problem D is simpler than problem C by having 0.315 σ less difficulty value.

Application 4: To divide a given group into categories according to an ability or trait assumed to be distributed normally.

Example: There is a group of 200 students to be classified into 5 categories: A, B, C, D and E according to their abilities, the range of abilities being equal in each category. If trait under ability is normally distributed, how many students should be placed in each category?

Solution: Base line of curve that extends from −3 σ to +3 σ, i.e., over a range of 6 σ, may be divided into 5 equal parts. It gives 1.2 σ to be allotted to each category.

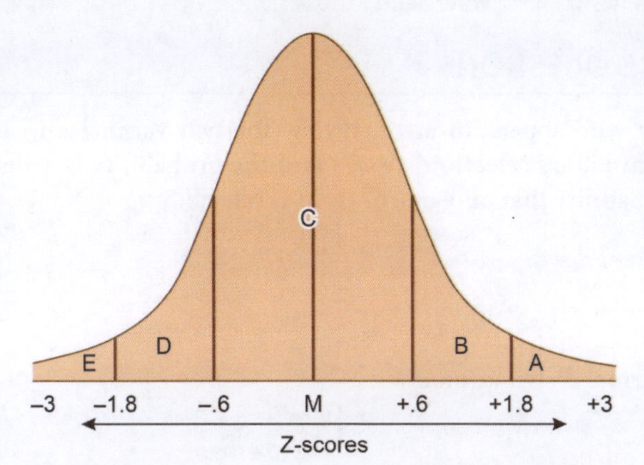

NPC showing division of the area into five equal categories

Now we have to calculate the percentage of cases which lie within each of these areas.

- Area under A extends from 1.8 σ to 3 σ, therefore group A may be comprised of 3.5% of the whole group.
- B will cover the cases lying between 0.6 σ and 1.8 σ, so group B may be comprised of 23.84% of the entire group.
- Group C may be comprised of 45.14% of the entire group.
- Similarly group D and E are said to be comprised of 23.8% and 3.5% respectively in the whole group.

	A	B	C	D	E
Percentage of whole group in each category	3.5	23.84	45.4	23.8	3.5
No. of students in each category out of 200	7.0	47.68	90.28	47.6	7.0
No. of students in whole	7	48	90	48	7

[Hint: 3.5% of 200 students = 7 and so on]

LONG ANSWER QUESTIONS

1. What is normal probability curve? Enumerate the characteristics and application of normal probability curve.
2. What is skewness and kurtosis? Write about different types of kurtosis.

SHORT ANSWER QUESTIONS

1. What is Z-score?
2. Write about bell-shaped curve.
3. Write differences between skewness and kurtosis.

MULTIPLE CHOICE QUESTIONS

1. **A man and his wife appear in an interview for two vacancies in the same post. The probability of husband's selection is (1/7) and the probability of wife's selection is (1/5). What is the probability that only one of them is selected?**

   a. $\dfrac{2}{7}$

   b. $\dfrac{1}{7}$

   c. $\dfrac{3}{4}$

   d. $\dfrac{4}{5}$

2. **The range of normal distribution is:**
   a. 0 to n
   b. 0 to ∞
   c. -1 to $+1$
   d. $-\infty$ to $+\infty$

3. **In normal distribution:**
   a. Mean = Median = Mode
   b. Mean < Median < Mode
   c. Mean > Median > Mode
   d. Mean $\neq$ Median $\neq$ Mode

4. **Which of the following is true for the normal curve?**
   a. Symmetrical
   b. Unimodal
   c. Bell-shaped
   d. All of these

5. **In a normal curve, the ordinate is highest at:**
   a. Mean
   b. Variance
   c. Standard deviation
   d. Q_1

6. **The parameters of the normal distribution are:**
   a. μ and σ^2
   b. μ and σ
   c. np and nq
   d. n and p

7. The shape of the normal curve depends upon the value of:

   a. Standard deviation
   b. Q_1
   c. Mean deviation
   d. Quartile deviation

8. The normal distribution is a proper probability distribution of a continuous random variable, the total area under the curve $f(x)$ is:

   a. Equal to 1
   b. <1
   c. >1
   d. Between -1 and $+1$

9. In a normal probability distribution of a continuous random variable, the value of standard deviation is:

   a. 0
   b. <0
   c. >0
   d. None of these

10. In a normal curve, the highest point on the curve occurs at the mean, μ, which is also the:

    a. Median and mode
    b. Geometric mean and harmonic mean
    c. Lower and upper quartiles
    d. Variance and standard deviation

11. The normal curve is symmetrical and for symmetrical distribution, the values of all odd order moments about mean will always be:

    a. 1
    b. 0.5
    c. 0.25
    d. 0

12. If $X \sim N(\mu, \sigma^2)$, the points of inflection of normal distribution are:

    a. $\pm\sigma$
    b. $\pm\mu$
    c. $\sigma \pm \mu$
    d. $\mu \pm \sigma$

13. In normal probability distribution for a continuous random variable, the value of a mean deviation is approximately equal to:

    a. 2/3
    b. $2/3\,\sigma$
    c. 4/5
    d. $4/5\,\sigma$

10

Sample and Sampling Errors

"A single death is a tragedy; a million death is a statistic."
—Joseph Stalin

LEARNING OBJECTIVES

After the completion of the chapter, the readers will be able to:
- Understand sample and its characteristics.
- Know how to choose null hypothesis.
- Discuss sampling and nonsampling errors.

CHAPTER OUTLINE

- Introduction
- Sample
- Parameters
- Sampling
- Sampling Methods
- Choosing Null Hypothesis
- Errors of Sampling

INTRODUCTION

It is not practical and is even impossible to contact every patient in a setting like hospital to do research on a certain intervention used on them. Therefore, a researcher selects a sample from the population. A sample is a small group of members units of a population which represents the entire population. A sample must be random as it gives opportunity to every member units of a population, of being selected. A good sample is the one which has all characteristics of a population. A good sample is free from biasness and measurement errors.

SAMPLE

Sample is a unit selected from population and it is chosen in a way that it represents the population and the process to take out sample for a research study is called sampling. We need a sample because:
- It is difficult to study each and every unit of a population when the units are heterogeneous in nature.
- Time constraints may be there.
- Financial aspects may be faced during a research process.

Characteristics of a Good Sample

- It should be representative of population.
- It must be easily accessible.
- The cost of sampling should be less.

PARAMETERS

The parameter is a characteristic of a population under study. In inferential statistics an educated guess about a population parameter is made, based on a statistic that was computed from a randomly drawn sample (Fig. 10.1).

Suppose, the mean cholesterol of the patients in a particular hospital is a parameter of the population. We draw a random sample of 100 patients and determine their mean cholesterol value. Researcher concludes that the population mean cholesterol (μ), is likely to be close to sample mean. This example is one of the statistical inferences. Various symbols used to denote parameters are tabulated as follows (Table 10.1):

It is easy and convenient to draw the sample from homogenous population. But in case of heterogeneous population, having significant variations, one needs to find out multiple individuals with possible characteristics (Fig. 10. 2).

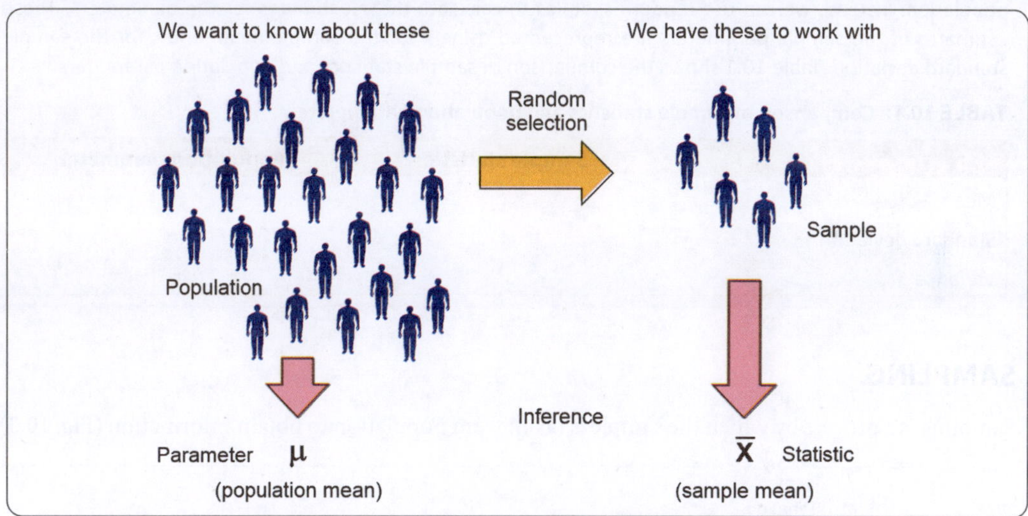

Figure 10.1: Parameter: Populations and samples mean

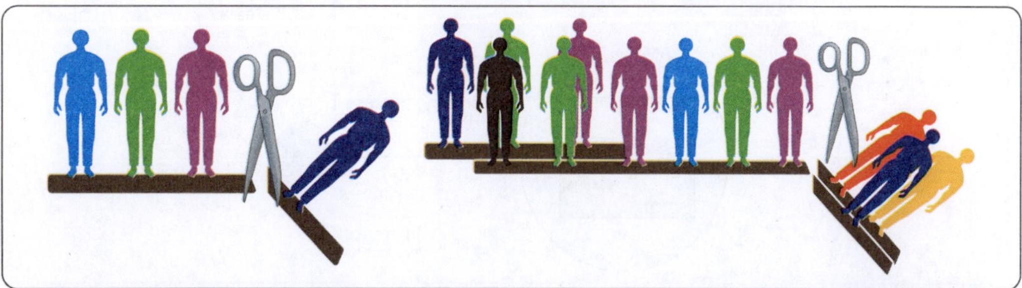

Figure 10.2: Sample from—homogenous population (left) and heterogeneous population (right)

Must Know

Population parameters versus sample estimates

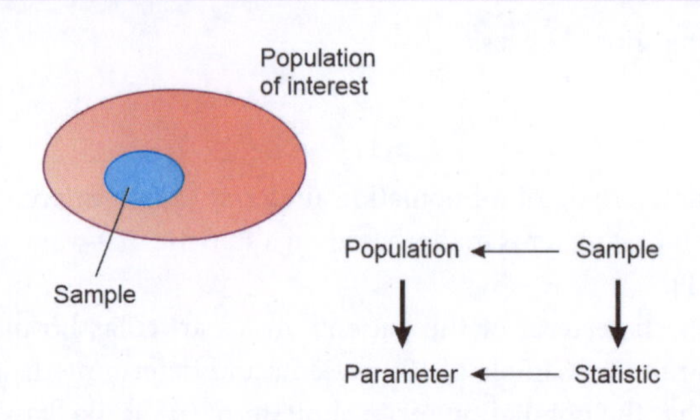

Population versus sample

The mean and standard deviation are parameter values that are applicable to entire population. For a normal distribution, the parameters are denoted as—for population mean the Greek symbol μ (mu) is used and for the population standard deviation σ (sigma) is used.

Population parameters are generally unknown because it is mostly impossible to measure an entire population. Instead, we can use random samples to calculate these estimates for the parameters. These estimates of the sample parameters are represented using $\bar{x}$ for the sample mean and s for the sample standard deviation. Table 10.1 shows the comparison of sample statistics and population parameters.

TABLE 10.1: Comparison of sample statistics and population parameters

	Sample statistic	Population parameter
Mean	$\bar{x}$	μ
Standard deviation	s	σ
Variance	s^2	σ^2

SAMPLING

Sampling is a process by which the sample is taken from population to obtain information (Fig. 10.3).

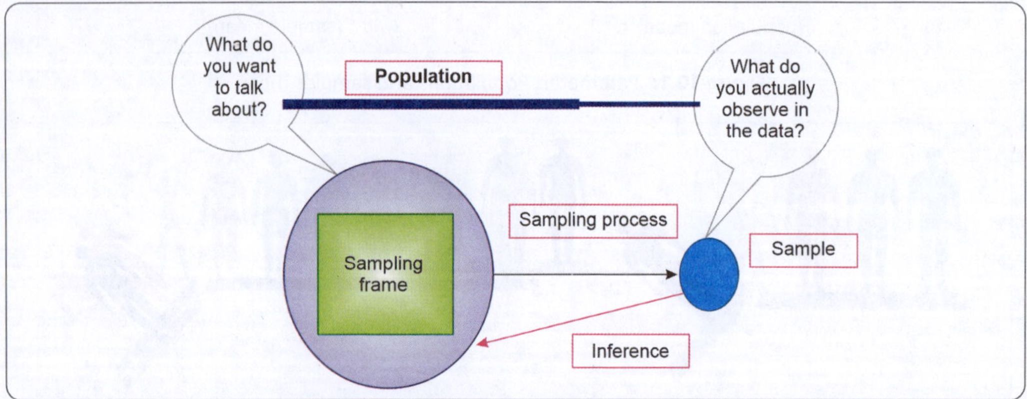

Figure 10.3: Sampling

Advantages of Sample

- Sample can provide reliable information at less cost and less time.
- Sample saves labor.
- Because sample is small in size, a researcher pays more attention to the chosen characteristics. A quality data is obtained with elaborated information.

Steps in Sampling

The five steps followed in sampling process (Fig. 10.4) are:

1. Define the population.
2. Identify the sampling frame.
3. Select a sampling design or procedure.
4. Determine the sample size.
5. Draw the sample.

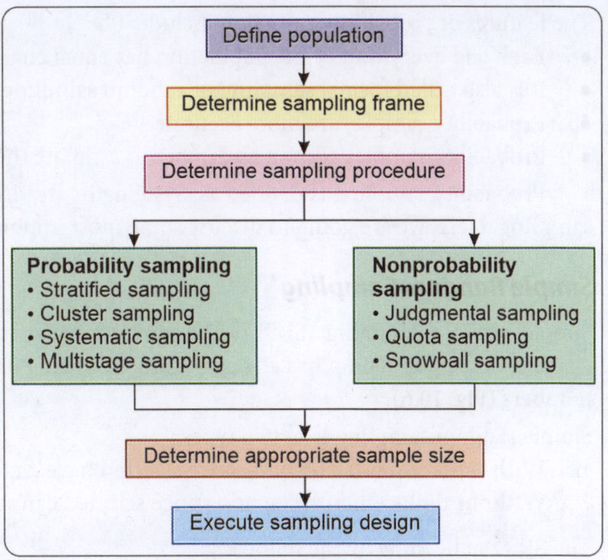

Figure 10.4: Sampling process

SAMPLING METHODS

The sampling methods can be classified broadly in two categories as probability sampling and nonprobability sampling methods **(Fig. 10.5)**. In random sampling (probability) each member in the population has chance to be selected. These are systematic, cluster, simple random, stratified and multistage sampling methods. Nonprobability sampling is further classified as convenience, judgment, quota and snowball sampling.

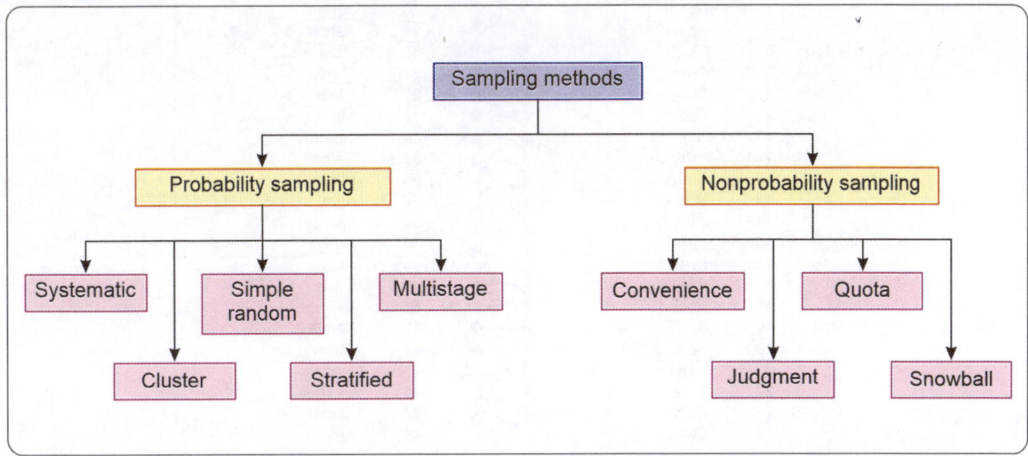

Figure 10.5: Classification of sampling methods

Probability Sampling

The features of probability sampling include:

- Each and every unit of the population has equal chance of selection as a sampling unit.
- It is also called formal sampling or random sampling.
- Probability samples are more accurate.
- Probability samples allow a researcher to estimate the accuracy of the sample.

Probability sampling is divided as: Systematic, stratified, cluster, simple random and multistage sampling. Here, we are going to discuss some most important used methods and important points.

Simple Random Sampling

Simple random sampling (SRS) is the purest form of probability sampling. It assures that each element in the population has an equal chance of being included in the sample. It generates random numbers (Fig. 10.6).

Simple random sampling is of two types:

1. **With replacement:** The units once selected have chances of selection again.
2. **Without replacement:** The units once selected cannot be selected again.

The SRS can be done by the following:

- **Tippet method:** This method was evolved by LHC Tippet, hence the method name. A lottery is drawn by writing numbers or names of various units and then putting them in a container. This is shaken thoroughly to mix and then certain numbers are picked up from the container. Those picked are taken up for the sampling.
- **Lottery method:** A researcher randomly picks the numbers, and each number corresponds to a subject or item, to create the sample.

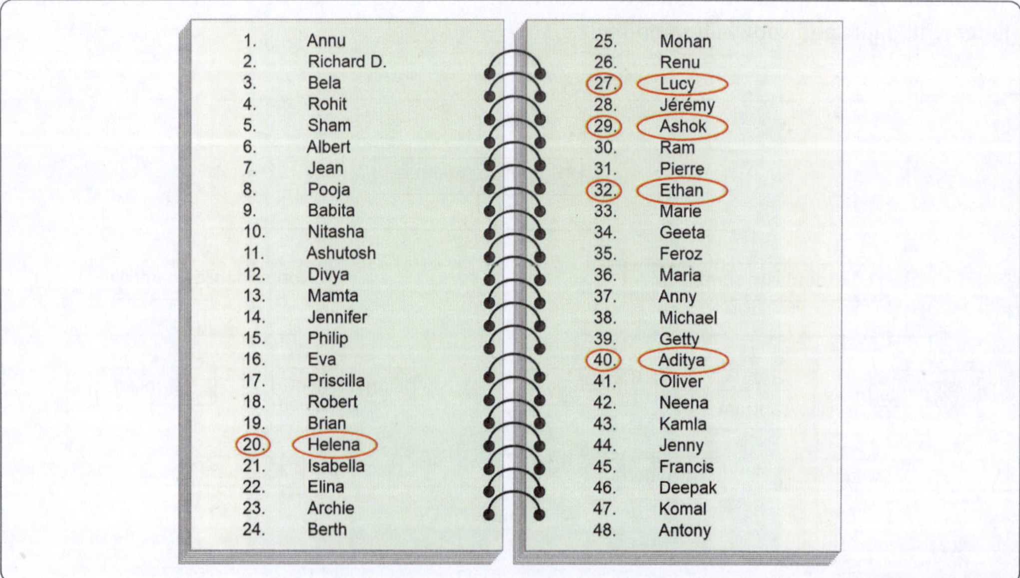

Figure 10.6: Simple random sampling

- **Random number tables:** These are a series of digits (0–9) arranged randomly in form of rows and columns, as shown in **Figure 10.7**. Generally, the table contains 5-digit numbers, arranged in rows and columns, for ease of reading. A full table may extend to four or more pages.

```
6 8 4 2 5 7 9 5 4 1 2 5 6 3 2 1
                1 0
5 8 2 0 3 2 1 5 4 7 8 5 9 6 2 0
                2 4
3 6 2 3 3 3 2 5 4 7 8 9 1 2 0 3
                2 5
9 8 5 2 6 3 0 1 7 4 2 4 5 0 3 6
```

Figure 10.7: Random number tables

Advantages of Simple Random Sampling

- Minimum knowledge of population is required.
- External and internal validity is high.
- Statistical estimation of error can be done.
- Easy to analyze the data.

Disadvantages of Simple Random Sampling

- High cost.
- Low frequency of usage.
- Require sampling frame.
- Do not use expertise of researcher.
- A larger risk of error compared to stratified sampling.

Stratified Random Sampling

In this method, the population is divided into two or more groups called strata based on some criteria such as grade level, geographical location, age, income, etc. The subsamples are randomly selected from each strata. The elements in strata are homogeneous but they are heterogeneous across data. (Fig. 10.8).

The stratified random sampling is of two types:

1. **Proportionate:** A proportion of samples is selected from each strata.
2. **Disproportionate:** The sample units are allocated according to analysis. It is also known as equal allocation technique.

Advantages of Stratified Random Sampling

- Assure representation of all groups in the sample population.
- The characteristics of stratum can be estimated and comparisons can be made.
- Reduce variability.

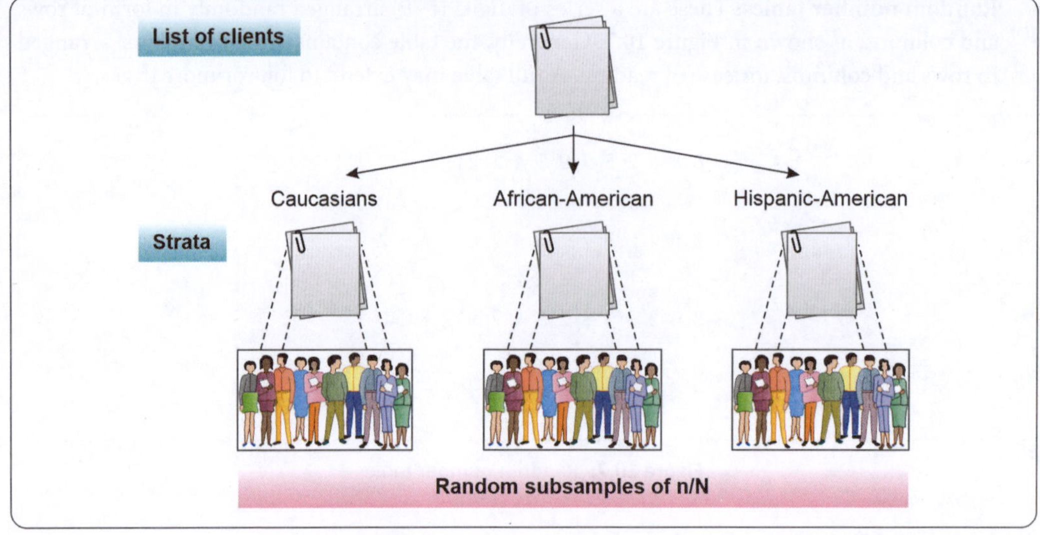

Figure 10.8: Stratified random sampling

Disadvantages of Stratified Random Sampling

- Requires accurate information on proportions of each stratum.
- The method is costly.

Cluster Sampling

The population is divided into clusters or subgroups like families. A simple random sample is taken from each subgroup and then all the units are studied (Fig. 10.9).

Advantages of Cluster Sampling

- Low cost and high frequency of use.
- Require list of all clusters but only of individuals or sample units, chosen in clusters.
- Can estimate characteristics of both cluster and population.
- Researchers lack a good sampling frame for a dispersed population.

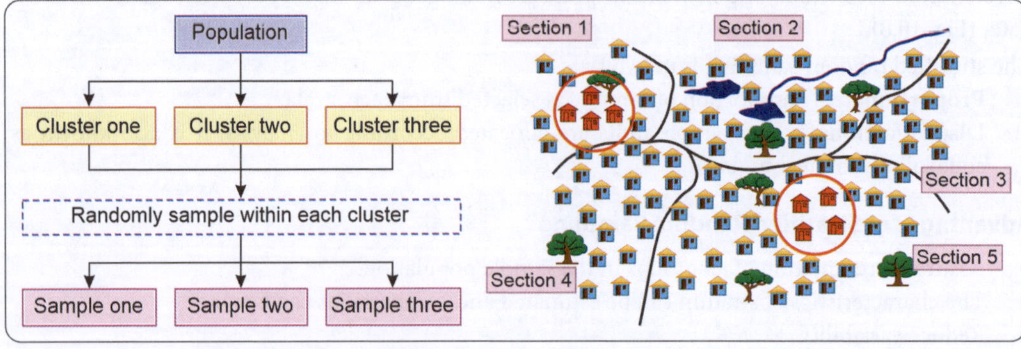

Figure 10.9: Cluster sampling

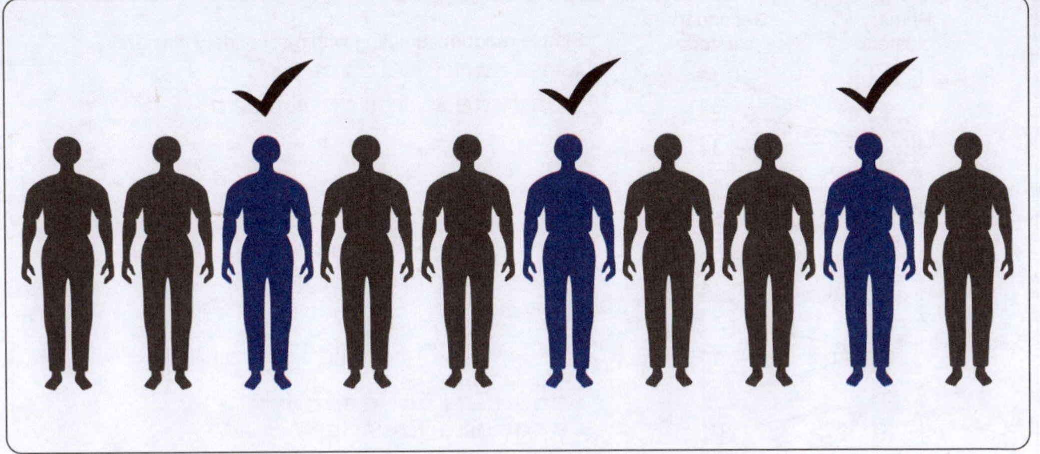

Figure 10.10: Systematic random sampling

Disadvantages of Cluster Sampling

- The cost is very high.
- It is less expensive than SRS but not as accurate as SRS.
- At each stage, there is sampling error—the more are the stages, the more error there tends to be.

Systematic Random Sampling

Order all the units in a sample based on some variables, then every nth number on the list is selected. Here, gaps between elements are equal and constant giving a periodicity (Fig. 10.10).
N = Sampling interval

Advantages of Systematic Random Sampling

- Its cost is moderate with moderate usage.
- External and internal validity are high.
- It is simple to draw sample and is easy to verify the results.

Disadvantages of Systematic Random Sampling

- To carry out this method, the sample has to be ordered periodically.
- Require the sample frame.

Multistage Random Sampling

Multistage random sampling is a sampling method where sampling is carried out in stages using smaller and smaller sampling units at each stage. It is useful in geographically dispersed area (Fig. 10.11).
To carry out the process:
- Select all schools and sample within the schools.
- Sample schools and then measure all students.
- Sample schools and then sample students.

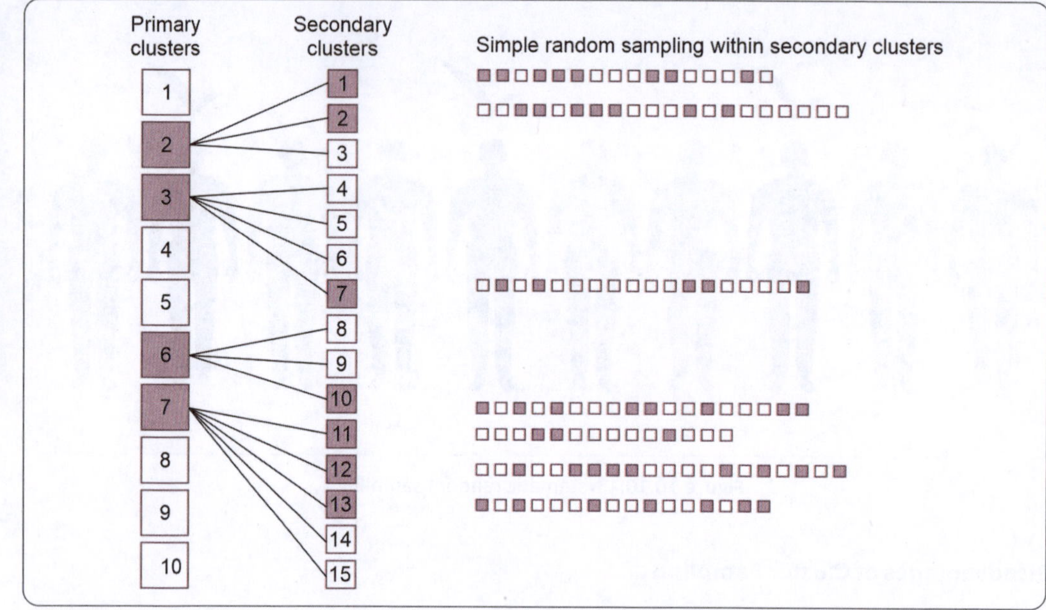

Figure 10.11: Multistage random sampling

Nonprobability Sampling

The probability of each case selected from the total population is not known. Units of sample are chosen on the basis of personal judgment or convenience. There are no techniques for measuring random sampling error in a non-probability sample. Therefore, generalization is not possible. It involves nonrandom methods in selection of the sample. All elements do not have chance of being selected. The selection depends on situation. The method is less expensive. The method is convenient and the sample can be chosen in many ways.

Purposive Sampling

- Purposive sampling is also known as judgment sampling.
- It should be started with a purpose in mind.
- The sampling procedure involves experienced researcher who selects a sample based on some appropriate characteristic of the sample members to serve the purpose (Fig. 10.12).
- People or elements who do not fit in the sample are rejected during sampling.

Advantages of Purposive Sampling

- The sample is chosen based on some set criteria.
- There is an assurance of quality response.
- The method meets the specific objective of research.

Disadvantages of Purposive Sampling

- The process is biased.
- It is time consuming.

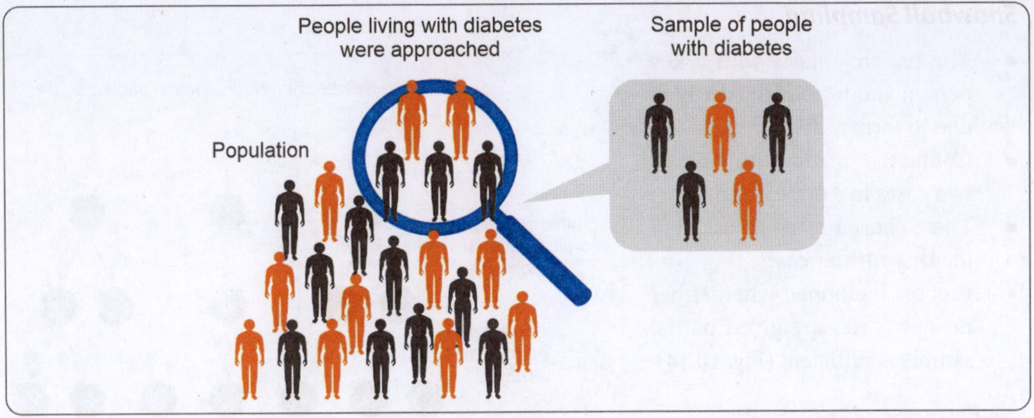

Figure 10.12: Purposive sampling

Quota Sampling

The population is divided into cells on the basis of relevant control characteristics (Fig. 10.13). A quota of sample units is established for each cell. A convenient sample is drawn for each cell. It is entirely nonrandom and is mostly used for interview surveys.

Advantages of Quota Sampling

- It is used when research budget is limited.
- It is extensively used and well understood.
- There is no need of population elements.
- It introduces some elements of stratification.

Disadvantages of Quota Sampling

- Variability and biasedness cannot be controlled or measured.
- It is time consuming.

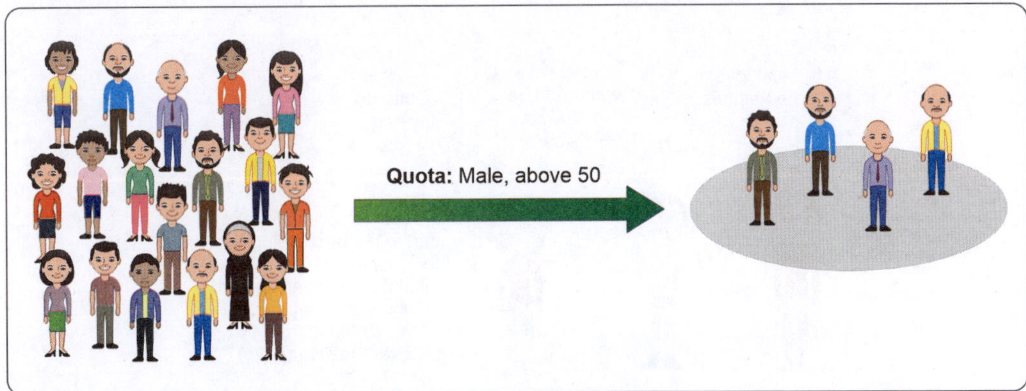

Figure 10.13: Quota sampling

Snowball Sampling

- The research starts with a key person and introduces the next one to form a chain.
- Contact is made with one or two cases in a population.
- These chosen cases are asked to identify further cases.
- Process is stopped when either no new cases are given or the sample is sufficient (Fig. 10.14).

Researchers recruit initial subjects

Initial subjects recruit additional subjects...

...who recruit additional subjects

Figure 10.14: Snowball sampling

Advantages of Snowball Sampling

- Cost is low.
- Useful in specific circumstances.
- Useful for locating rare populations.

Disadvantages of Snowball Sampling

- Biased because the sampling units are not independent.
- Projecting data beyond sample is not justified.

Self-selection Sampling

Self-selection sampling occurs when researcher allows each case (usually) individuals to identify their desire to take part in the research. The researcher publicizes the need of research through appropriate sources like media to take part in the sampling. The data is collected from those who respond (Fig. 10.15).

Advantages of Self-selection Sampling

- More accurate.
- Useful in specific circumstances to serve the purpose.

Figure 10.15: Self-selection sampling

Disadvantages of Self-selection Sampling

- Costly because of advertisement.
- Masses are left.

Convenience Sampling

Convenience sampling is done at the convenience of researcher. It is also known as accidental or incidental sampling. The process involves selecting haphazardly those cases which are easily available. Most easily available samples are chosen (Fig. 10.16).

Figure 10.16: Convenience sampling

Advantages of Convenience Sampling

- Cost is very low.
- Widely used and understood.
- No need for list of population elements.

Disadvantages of Convenience Sampling

- Neither variability nor biasedness can be controlled.
- Projecting data beyond sample is not justified.
  Simple random sampling will give a closer estimate of the population than the convenience sample.

CHOOSING NULL HYPOTHESIS

You use probability to decide whether a statistical test provides evidence for or against the predictions. If the likelihood of obtaining a given test statistic from the population is very small, you reject the null hypothesis and say that you have supported the hunch/idea that the sample you are testing is different from the population.

But it could be wrong!

Even if you choose a probability level of 5% that means there is a 5% chance, or 1 in 20, that you rejected the null hypothesis when it was, in fact, correct. You can be wrong in the opposite way too; you might fail to reject the null hypothesis when it is in fact, incorrect. These two errors are called Type I and Type II, respectively. Table 10.2 presents the possible outcomes of any hypothesis test based on:

- Whether the null hypothesis was accepted or rejected.
- Whether the null hypothesis was true in reality.

TABLE 10.2: Types of statistical errors

	H_0 is Actually:	
	True	**False**
Reject H_0	Type I error	Correct
Accept H_0	Correct	Type II error

Practical Tips

Determination of a Sample Size

The sample size computation must be done appropriately because the inference drawn from the sample must be authentic to help in drawing right conclusions. A sample with the smallest sampling error will always be considered a good representative of the population. Generally, bigger samples have less sampling errors. When the sample survey becomes the census survey, the sampling error becomes zero.

There are two measures that affect the accuracy of the data:

1. **Confidence interval:** First of all, there is the margin of error (or confidence intervals). This is the positive and negative deviation that is allowed by researcher in survey results for the sample. (In other words, the deviation between the opinions of respondents and the opinion of the entire population).

   Example: Suppose the margin of error is 5%. If 90% of the survey respondents have responded positively to an intervention, a 5% margin of error means that you can be 'sure' that between 85% (90% − 5%) and 95% (90% + 5%) of the entire population actually will respond positively to the survey on that particular intervention.

2. **Confidence level:** Secondly, this tells, how often the percentage of the population responded positively to an intervention, actually lies within the boundaries of the margin of error. Or, it tells you how sure you can be that between 85% and 95% of the population responded positively to an intervention. Suppose, you chose the 95% confidence level then in 95% of the time between 85% and 95% of the population responded positively to an intervention.

   - Decide about the number of respondents you require. Once decision is made about how accurate you want your sample data to be, you can start calculating how many respondents you actually need.
   - An indicative table on how to calculate the number of samples is given as follows.

| Population size | Confidence level = 95% | | | Confidence level = 99% | | |
	Margin of error			Margin of error		
	5%	2.5%	1%	5%	2.5%	1%
100	80	94	99	87	96	99
500	217	377	475	285	421	485
1.000	278	606	906	399	727	943
10.000	370	1.332	4.899	622	2.098	6.239
100.000	383	1.513	8.762	659	2.585	14.227
500.000	384	1.532	9.423	663	2.640	16.055
1.000.000	384	1.534	9.512	663	2.647	16.317

   - Suppose population consists of approximately 400 million adults. As a consequence, the appropriate number will be found on the last row of the table as given. Depending on the confidence level and the margin of error, the number will vary. When we chose a margin of error of 5% and a confidence level of 95% for our survey, approximately 400 samples will be required (it is advisable to round to the nearest hundred) for the survey.

ERRORS OF SAMPLING

The main objective of any research project is to obtain accurate and error free results. For this, total errors have to be minimized (Fig. 10.17).

$$\text{Total error} = \text{Sampling error} + \text{nonsampling error}$$

Sampling Errors

Error caused by the act of taking a sample. They cause sample results to be different from the results of census. Statistical errors are sample errors. We have no control over these but the sampling

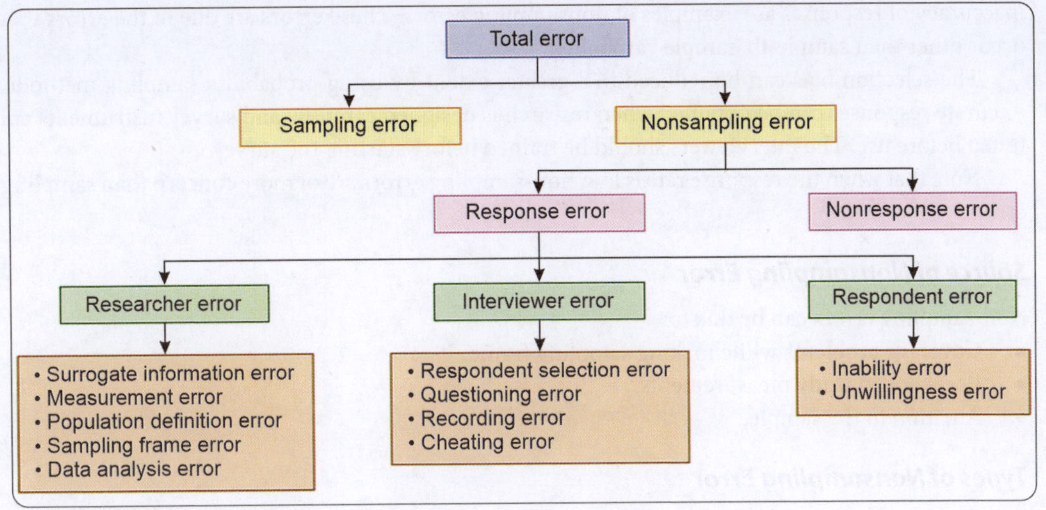

Figure 10.17: Potential sources of errors in research

technique chosen will influence the extent of error. The sampling error occurs when probability sampling method used to collect a sample is not representative of population concerned. For example, a random sample of 400 people composed of only people falling in the age group of 35–50 years are not representative of adult population. In research, measuring sample errors is not easy in the case of a large population. By increasing the size of sample, this type of sampling error can be reduced.

The sampling errors refer to the difference between the sample and the population that exists only because of the observations that happened to be selected for the sample. Theoretically, it means the difference between survey answer and the true value that a researcher wants to measure. For example, selecting different random samples of similar size from the same population will give different estimates. This is termed sample-to-sample variability.

Errors can arise at all stages of sampling—from problem formulation to report presentation. A research is rarely free of sampling errors. For some factual questions, one can cross check survey answers with reliable records like respondent's age or numbers of visits to a clinic but in practice such checks are not possible. For problems based on feelings, emotions, behavior, etc., that are qualitative in nature, such checks are not possible.

Sampling error is affected by the homogeneity of the population under study. In general, more homogeneous the population, less is the sampling error. In fact, sampling error falls to zero in the case of a census study.

The margin of error given in a survey is an expression of sampling error, the error that results from taking one sample instead of examining the whole population. For large sample surveys, the margin of error of an estimate is half-width of the confidence interval, i.e., $1.96 \times$ SE of estimate.

Nonsampling Errors

Nonsampling errors consist of all other errors which are related to the research under study. These errors are diverse in nature. They occur due to biasedness which means a systematic error. The biasedness enters the project due to preconceptions of a researcher or uncalibrated instruments. In fact, the nonsampling errors are composed of totally random components. Selection bias and inaccuracy of responses are examples of nonsampling errors. These errors are due to the errors that occur other than sample-to-sample variability.

The selection bias can be reduced to a greater extent by using probability sampling methods. Accurate responses can be obtained when research is designed carefully and survey instruments are tested before use. The interviewers should be trained before starting the survey.

Note that when the response rate is low, non-sampling errors are of more concern than sampling errors.

Source of Nonsampling Error

Non-sampling errors can be due to:
- Coverage problems while making sampling frame.
- Problems in study measurements.
- Attrition in the sample.

Types of Nonsampling Error

Nonresponse Error

Nonresponse error occurs when the obtained sample differs from the original selected sample. It occurs in two ways:

1. **Noncontact** that is the when the respondent member of the sample was not contacted due to some reason. The reason may be inaccessibility of a respondent, respondent is not at home (NAH) or may have moved away from the area either permanently or for certain period in which survey was conducted.

   Noncontact errors can be reduced by carefully analyzing the selected sample.

2. **Refusal** that is some members have not given any response. It arises when the respondent does not respond to a particular item or to multiple items of the questionnaire like, religion, sex, monthly income, and politics etc.,—refused items. Sometimes the respondent is aware of the answers but is unable to provide adequate answer—cannot say, do not know.
   - Time constraints, bad experience or bad health may be the reason of refusal in a survey.
   - The refusal can be brought down by giving training to the interviewers and continuously monitoring the process of investigation.

Response Error

Response error occurs when the respondent provides inaccurate answers, the answers are not recorded correctly or are incorrectly analysis. Types of response errors are given as follows:

Researcher Error

- **Population specific error:** It occurs when some inappropriate population is selected by researcher to obtain data. For example, a company who produces packed food may conduct a survey by selecting housewives as in their opinion housewives are the end users of their products. This may affect the true result of the survey because children and husband may also affect the buying decisions in a house.
- **Sample frame error:** It implies to all the elements of a population. It is mostly a listing of all the elements which identifies a population. A good sampling frame identifies the elements once and there is no overlapping of them from other population. For example, in a survey on oral care

products, a researcher may miss the people who are using babool or neem sticks, homemade powders and toothpastes. This will lead to frame errors in defining a population.

- **Surrogate information error:** Here the information is collected from substitute place of the original sample. Such need in a research, may arise due to inability or unwillingness of the respondent to provide the required information. Attitude, beliefs, etc., are the examples of surrogate information as on that basis a researcher tries to predict the future behavior of the respondents.
- **Measurement error in the collection of data:** This can be defined as the noncorrespondence of information obtained by the measurement process in case of information sought by a researcher. It arises by the measurement process itself and represents the difference between information generated and information sought by a researcher. This type of error could arise at any phase of the measurement.

Respondent Error

- **Inability error:** The inability of the respondent to answer a question because of no understanding or misunderstanding of the questions.
- **Unwillingness error:** The respondent may like to skip some questions as that might be very personal or he may be short of time and answer hurriedly without understanding.

Experimental Errors

During the research process, there may be errors from the development of instruments till the analysis of findings. The errors may also occur at the stage when an interviewer is questioning the respondent. Faulty wording of questions, non-preparation of nonverbal clues, behavior of the interviewer, etc., may together contribute to these. For example, in a study on cancer a sample that was selected may help in concluding that eating bread is responsible for cancer because all the sample members are consuming it. It will lead to faulty predictions.

Data Analysis Errors

In the analysis phase where errors could arise due to incorrect editing, coding and/or descriptive summarization and inferences contribute substantially to the measurement errors. These are called data analysis errors or measurement errors too.

Interviewer Errors

- **Respondent selection error:** That means selection of respondent was wrong.
- **Questioning error:** The method of asking question is not correct.
- **Recording error:** The data is not recorded correctly.
- **Cheating error:** The data is compromised for the sake of convenience so as to save time, money and hard work.
- **Biasedness:** Different interviewers administer a survey in different ways
    - Differences occur in reactions of respondents to different interviewers, e.g., to interviewers of their own sex or own ethnic group.
    - Inadequate training of interviewers.
    - Inadequate attention to the selection of interviewers.
    - There is too high a workload for the respondent.

LONG ANSWER QUESTIONS

1. What do you understand by a sample? What are the advantages of studying a sample over a population?
2. What are sampling errors? Discuss in detail.
3. What are types of sampling errors. Elaborate it.

SHORT ANSWER QUESTIONS

1. Define sample.
2. What are non-sampling errors?
3. Write briefly about experimental error.

MULTIPLE CHOICE QUESTIONS

1. **Sample is a subset of:**
   a. Population
   b. Data
   c. Set
   d. Distribution

2. **Any population constant is called a:**
   a. Statistic
   b. Parameter
   c. Estimate
   d. Estimator

3. **List of all the units of the population is called:**
   a. Random sampling
   b. Bias
   c. Sampling frame
   d. Probability sampling

4. **Any calculation on the sampling data is called:**
   a. Parameter
   b. Static
   c. X
   d. Error

5. **Any measure of the population is called:**
   a. Finite
   b. Parameter
   c. Without replacement
   d. Random

6. **Probability distribution of a statistics is called:**
   a. Sampling
   b. Parameter
   c. Data
   d. Sampling distribution

7. **The difference between a statistic and the parameter is called:**
   a. Probability
   b. Sampling error
   c. Random
   d. Nonrandom

8. **Which of the following statement is true?**
    a. Standard error is always one
    b. Standard error is always zero
    c. Standard error is always negative
    d. Standard error is always positive

9. **Non-random sampling is also called:**
    a. Biased sampling
    b. Nonprobability sampling
    c. Random sampling
    d. Representative sample

10. **Sampling error can be reducing by:**
    a. Nonprobability sampling
    b. Increasing the population
    c. Decreasing the sample size
    d. Increasing the sample size

Note

Unit V

Measures of Relationship

11

Correlation and Regression Analysis

"Relationships are like glass. Sometimes it's better to leave them broken than try to hurt yourself putting them back together".
—Anonymous

LEARNING OBJECTIVES

After the completion of the chapter, the readers will be able to:

- Understand correlation and its importance in statistics.
- Compute and interpret coefficient of correlation.
- Compute regression line.

CHAPTER OUTLINE

- Introduction
- Correlation
- Coefficient of Correlation
- Simple Linear Regression Analysis

INTRODUCTION

Croxton and Cowden said that when the relationship is of a quantitative nature, the approximate statistical tool is covering and measuring the relationship and expressing it in a brief formula, known as correlation.

CORRELATION

According to A M Tuttle, correlation is an analysis of the covariation between two or more variables. When a change in one variable is accompanied by a change in another variable then the two variables are said to be in correlation or covariation. The two variables vary simultaneously, for example, study and good marks in examinations, height and weight of students, etc. Therefore, it can be said that when two variables are varying together, they are in correlation. It indicates the relationship of one variable with the other and in statistics, correlation is a method of determining the correlation or proportionality between two variables (or scores).

Importance of Correlation

- It measures the degree of association or relationship between two variables quantitatively, and is an index of relationship which is used in nursing and other healthcare studies as coefficient of correlation.

- Coefficient of correlation is a numerical index which shows the extent of relationship between two variables.
- In field of medical healthcare, researcher tries to find out the relationship between the variables and these are often manipulated to see whether the change in one variable, changes the other or not?
- The sampling error which we have discussed in detail in Chapter 10, can be calculated with the help of correlation coefficient.
- The relation between two variables under study is statistically significant or not can be observed with its help.
- It reduces the level of uncertainty in our prediction to make out some decisions based on strategy.
- It forms the basis of concept of regression and ratio of variation.
- Correlation gives meaning to research results. Correlational analysis is essential for basic psycho educational research. In fact, most of the basic and applied psychological researches are correlation in nature.
- It helps in finding characteristics of educational and psychological tests like reliability, validity or item analysis, etc.
- It makes consistency testing of certain data with hypothesis.
- One variable can be predicted on the basis of the knowledge of the other variable(s).
- The psychological educational models and theories can be built with its help.
- The variables/measures are used here for parsimonious (It is a principle according to which an explanation of a thing or event is made with the fewest possible assumptions) interpretation of data which is otherwise not feasible.
- It helps to carry out multivariate statistical tests like MANCOVA, MANOVA, factor analysis and discriminant analysis, correlation is helpful.
- It is used for isolating influence of variables on a research data, statistically.

Meaning of Negative and Positive Signs in Correlation

When we interpret the results, '1' indicates that the two variables are moving in unison. They rise and fall together and have perfect correlation. '–1' means that the two variables are moving in opposite directions. When one goes up the other one goes down, in a negative way. Any two variables under study can be calculated for correlation value. Even when they are not correlated, the correlation value can be computed as '0'.

The correlation value always lies between –1 and 1 (where '0' means that there is no correlation at all). Correlation can be comfortably explained for simple linear regression as there are only two variables x and y. For multiple variables, the computation of correlation is a little difficult. Therefore, instead of 'r', 'r^2' is a better term as it can explain both simple linear regressions and also multiple linear regressions.

The coefficient of correlation is symbolized by r or ρ (Rho). It is also known as product moment correlation coefficient or Karl Pearson's coefficient of correlation, rank difference correlation coefficient or spearman's rank correlation coefficient.

The size of 'r' indicates the degree or extent of correlation between two variables. If the correlation value of 'r' is +ve it is positive and if the value of 'r' is –ve the correlation is negative. Thus, the signs of the coefficient indicate the kind of relationship.

> **Must Know**
>
> The coefficient of correlation is a percentage. The value of r is generally rounded up to two decimal places.

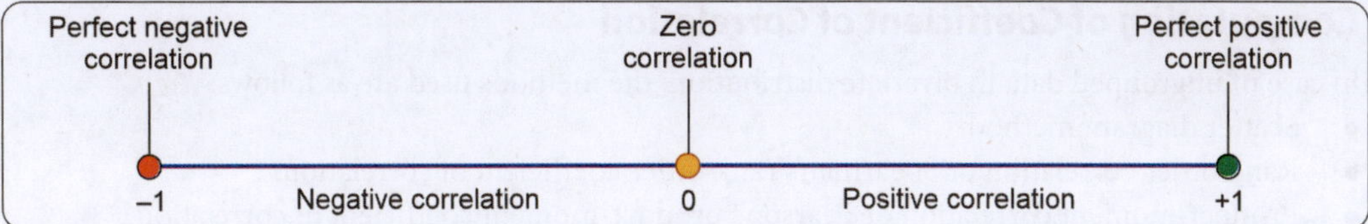

Figure 11.1: Types of correlation

Types of Correlation

The types of correlation (Fig. 11.1) is based on the number of variables, therefore in a bivariate distribution, the correlation may be:

Positive Correlation

When an increase in one variable (x) is followed by a simultaneous increase in the other variable (y); the correlation is said to be positive. The positive correlation ranges from 0 to +1 and has an upper limit as +1 is the perfect positive coefficient of correlation. It specifies that, for every unit increase in one variable, another is proportionally increasing for example increase in heat and increases temperature as these two variables have a perfect positive correlation.

Negative Correlation

On the other hand, if increase in one variable (x) results in a simultaneous decrease in other variable (y), the correlation is said to be negative. It ranges from 0 to − 1 and its lower limit indicates a negative correlation. The negative correlation indicates that for every unit increase in one variable, there is proportional unit decrease in the other variable.

Zero Correlation

Zero correlation means that there is no relationship between two variables 'x' and 'y' that is the change in one variable 'x' is not associated with the change in the other variable 'y'. For example, intelligence and body weight no correlation. Similarly, shoe size and monthly salary have no correlation. The '0' correlation is the mid-point of the range −1 to +1.

Linear or Curvilinear Correlation

The linear correlation is a ratio of change between two variables, either in the same direction or in opposite direction. The graphical representation of one variable with respect to other variable gives a straight line.

Here, first with increase of one variable say 'x' the second variable 'y' increases proportionately up to some point and after that with an increase in the first variable 'x' the second variable 'y' starts decreasing. The graphical representation of these two variables gives a curved line and this type of relationship between the two variables is called the curvilinear correlation.

COEFFICIENT OF CORRELATION

In statistics, the correlation coefficient 'r' measures the strength and direction of a linear relationship between two variables when we plot a scatter diagram. The value of 'r' always lies between +1 and −1. It shows the degree of relationship between two variables say x and y.

Computation of Coefficient of Correlation

In case of ungrouped data in bivariate distribution, the methods used are as follows:

- Scatter diagram method.
- Rank order correlation or Spearman's rank order coefficient of correlation.
- Product-moment correlation or Pearson's product-moment coefficient of correlation.

Scatter Diagram Method

Scatter diagram also known as 'dot diagram' is a graphic method that is used for drawing certain conclusions about the correlation between two variables under study. In order to make a scatter diagram, the observed pairs of observations are plotted in the form of dots on a graph paper by taking convenient scales for the two variables. X variable is taken on the horizontal axis and Y variable is on the vertical axis. The position of these dots on the graph tells about the change in the variables that is whether they are changing in the same direction or in the opposite directions. This method is very easy, simple but raw way of computing correlation **(Fig. 11.2)**.

The plotted points will tend to concentrate in a group more or less of similar width on graph paper. Now 'The line of best fit' is drawn with a free hand. The direction of this line indicates the nature of correlation between variables under study **(Fig. 11.3)**.

The line going upward from left to right will show positive correlation. The lines moving downward from left to right will show negative correlation. If the plotted points are scattered widely it shows absence of correlation between two variables under study.

The degree of slope of the line indicates the degree of correlation. This method simply tells about the correlation being positive or negative.

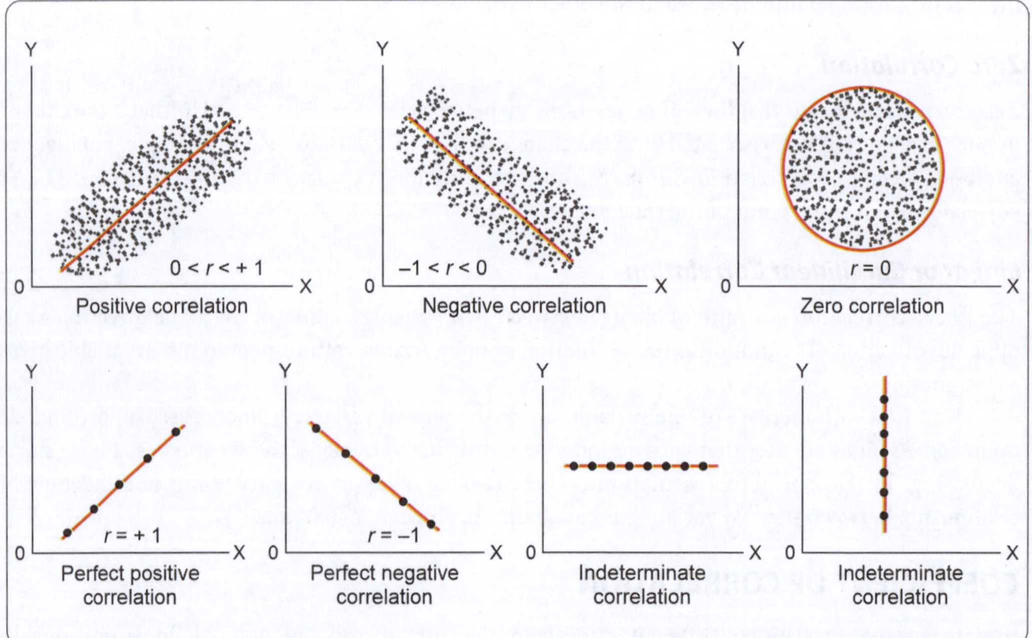

Figure 11.2: Scatter diagrams showing varying degree of relationship between X and Y

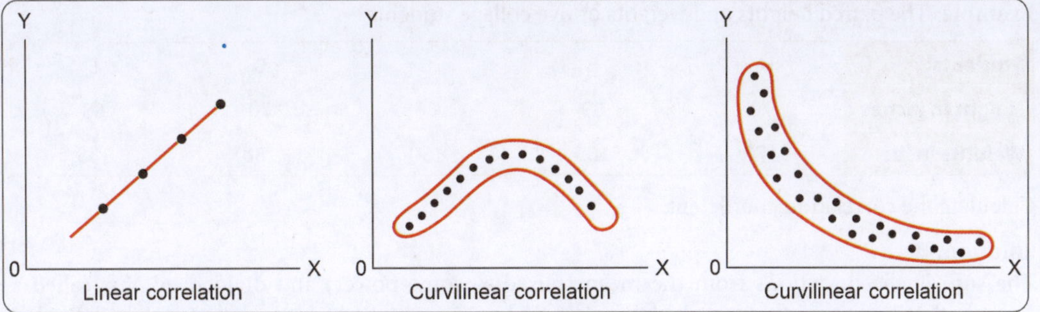

Figure 11.3: Scatter diagram illustrating linear and curvilinear relationships

Pearson's Product-Moment Coefficient of Correlation

The coefficient of correlation 'r', is known as the "Pearson r" as it was developed by Professor Karl Pearson, in continuation of the work of Gallon and Bravais. The product-moment coefficient of correlation is considered ratio which shows the extent to which change(s) in one variable is dependent on changes in second variable.

Practical Tips

Difference between R^2 and r

r is coefficient of correlation. R^2 is coefficient of determination. To get R^2, multiply r times r. Or it can be said that coefficient of determination is the square of coefficient of correlation.

R^2 shows percentage variation in Y that can be explained by all the X variables together. Higher the R^2, better for us. Its value always lies between 0 and 1. It can never be negative because it is a squared value. R^2 can be explained easily in terms of regression but it is not so easy to explain the R in terms of regression.

Uses of Product Moment 'r'

Correlation coefficient is one of the most widely used analytical techniques in the field of education and psychological measurement and evaluation. It is helpful in:

- Describing the degree of relationship or correspondence between two variables
- Prediction of one variable whether it is dependent on the independent variable or not
- For validating a test for example a group intelligence test
- Determining the degree of objectivity (fairness) of a test
- For educational and occupational directions in a neutral way for decision-making.
- Determining the reliability and validity of a test.
- Determining the role of various correlates (aptitude).

Characteristics of Product-Moment 'r'

- **Normal distribution:** The variables from which we want to calculate the correlation must be normally distributed—obtained by taking a random sample.
- **Linearity:** The product-moment correlation can be shown as a straight line, known as linear correlation.
- **Continuous series:** Measurement of variables in a continuous series.
- **Homoscedasticity:** It must satisfy the condition of equal variability (homoscedasticity).

Example: The paired heights and weights of five college students:

Students	A	B	C	D	E
Height in inches	72	69	66	70	68
Weights in lbs	170	165	150	180	185

Calculate the correlation coefficient.

Solution:

The sum of the deviations from the mean (raised to some power) and divided by N is called a "moment". When corresponding deviation in x and y are multiplied together. summed, and divided by N $\left(\text{to give } \dfrac{\Sigma xy}{N}\right)$ the term "product moment" is used.

$\Sigma x.y/N$ will not give appropriate measure of relationship between x and y because it is not a stable measure and it is not independent of the units in which weight and height have been expressed. In order to avoid this difficulty, it is better to express each deviation or mean as a 'σ score' or 'standard score or Z-score' which is obtained by dividing each x and y by its own σ. Then each x and y deviation is expressed as a ratio and it will now be a pure number independent of the test units.

- The sum of the products of the σ scores divided by N will give a ratio which is a stable expression of relationship between two variables. This ratio is called the 'product-moment' coefficient of correlation. In the example given above, the value was calculated as 0.36, which signifies a fairly high positive correlation between weight and height in the sample under observation.

Characteristics of Correlation Coefficient 'r_{xy}'

- r_{xy} is a product moment r $\left(r_{xy} = \dfrac{\Sigma ZxZy}{N}\right)$

- It can be positive or negative bounded by limits -1.00 to $+1.00$.
- It can be regarded as an arithmetic mean because r_{xy} is the mean of standard score products.
- r_{xy} is not affected by any linear transformation of scores on either X, or Y, or both.
- It is equal to $\sqrt{b_{yx} \, b_{xy}}$ here b_{yx} is the regression coefficient of Y on X, b_{xy} is the regression coefficient of X on Y. Hence, r_{xy} is square root of the slopes of the regression lines.
- When variables under study are in standard score forms, r offers a degree of the average amount of change in one variable which is associated with the change of the other variable.
- r_{xy} is not affected by the magnitude of means as scores are always relative.
- It cannot be computed if one of the variables has no variance (S^2x) or S^2y is 0 (because either of the two must be 0).
- r_{xy} of 60 means a magnitude of relationship like $r_{xy} = -0.60$. The sign ($+/-$) tells about the magnitude, direction and strength of relationship.
- Here, df for r_{xy} is $N = 2$, that has been used for testing significance of r_{xy}. Indirectly, the testing of significance of r implies testing the significance of regression. As 2 df is lost due to slope and intercept of the regression line. Therefore when $N = 2$, it means that r_{xy} is either $+1$ or -1 as there is no freedom for sampling variation in the numerical value of r.

Computation of 'r' for Ungrouped Data

It depends on 'where from the deviations are taken' like deviations can be taken according to different situations, can be taken from either actual mean or from zero or from arithmetic mean. Therefore type of formula that could conveniently be applied for the calculation of 'r' depends upon mean value which may be either in fraction or whole number.

1. **The formula of 'r', when deviations are taken from means:**

$$r_{xy} = \frac{\Sigma xy}{N\sigma_x\sigma_y}$$

Here, r_{xy} = Correlation between X and Y

x = deviation of any X score from the mean in the test X

y = deviation of Y score from the mean in test Y

Σxy = Sum of all the products of deviations that is X and Y

σ_x and σ_y = standard deviations of the distribution of X and Y score in which x and y are deviations from the actual means

> **Practical Tips**
>
> 0 = agreement equivalent to chance
> 0.10–0.20 = slight agreement
> 0.21–0.40 = fair agreement
> 0.41–0.60 = moderate agreement
> 0.61–0.80 = substantial agreement
> 0.81–0.99 = near perfect agreement
> 1 = perfect agreement

If we write $\sqrt{\dfrac{\Sigma x^2}{N}}$ for σx and $\sqrt{\dfrac{\Sigma y^2}{N}}$ for σ_y the N is cancelled and formula becomes:

$$r_{xy} = \frac{\Sigma xy}{\Sigma x^2 \times \Sigma y^2}$$

Σx^2 and Σy^2 are the sums of squared deviations in x and y taken from the two means.

This formula is preferred to calculate the value of 'r' when,

- Mean values of both the variables are not in fraction.
- We have to find out correlation between short, ungrouped series (like, 25 cases).
- Deviations are to be taken from actual means of the two distributions.

Steps of Calculating 'r'

The steps to calculate 'r' are enumerated here:

Step 1: Write in parallel columns the paired X and Y scores, carefully so that corresponding scores are together.

Step 2: Determine the two means—Mean$_x$ and Mean$_y$. In Table 11.1 given here, these are 7.5 and 8.0, respectively.

Step 3: Determine the two deviations x and y for every pair of scores (check them by finding algebraic sums, which should be zero).

Step 4: Square all the deviations and write in separate two columns. This is for the purpose of computing σ_x and σ_y.

Step 5: Sum up the squares of the deviations to find Σx^2 and Σy^2. Find the product of 'x' and 'y' as '$x.y$' and sum up these to get Σxy.

Step 6: Now from these values compute σ_x and σ_y.

Step 7: Calculate the value of 'r' by applying formula.

TABLE 11.1: Computation of r when deviations are taken from means

X	Y	x	y	x^2	y^2	xy
13	11	5.5	3	30.25	9	16.5
12	14	4.5	6	20.25	36	27.0
10	11	2.5	3	6.25	9	7.5
10	7	2.5	-1	6.25	1	-2.5
8	9	0.5	1	0.25	1	0.5
6	11	-1.5	3	2.25	9	-4.5
6	3	-1.5	-5	2.25	25	7.5
5	7	-2.5	-1	6.25	1	2.5
3	6	-4.5	-2	20.25	4	9.0
2	1	-5.5	-7	30.25	49	38.5
$\Sigma X = 75$	$\Sigma Y = 80$	$\Sigma x = 0$	$\Sigma y = 0$	$\Sigma x^2 = 124.5$	$\Sigma y^2 = 144$	$\Sigma xy = 102$
$M_x = 7.5$	$M_y = 8$					

$$\sigma_x = \sqrt{\frac{\Sigma x^2}{N}} = \sqrt{\frac{124.50}{10}} = \sqrt{12.45} = 3.528$$

$$\sigma_y = \sqrt{\frac{\Sigma y^2}{N}} = \sqrt{\frac{144}{10}} = \sqrt{14.4} = 3.795$$

$$r_{xy} = \frac{\Sigma xy}{N\sigma_x\sigma_y} = \frac{102}{(10)(3.528)(3.795)} = \frac{102}{133.88} = 0.76$$

An alternative and shorter solution to find out 'r':

$$r_{xy} = \frac{\Sigma xy}{\sqrt{(\Sigma x^2)(\Sigma y^2)}} \quad \text{(Alternative formula for a Pearson } r)$$

$$= \frac{102}{\sqrt{124.5)(144)}} = \frac{102}{\sqrt{17.928}} \quad \frac{102}{133.9} = 0.76$$

It is an alternative and shorter way to find out 'r' where computation of σ_x and σ_y is omitted.

Calculation of r_{xy} from Raw Scores Original Scores

It is another method for ungrouped data, where the use of deviations is not needed. It deals entirely with original raw scores. The formula looks cumbersome but can be easily applied.

$$r_{xy} = \frac{N\Sigma XY - (\Sigma X)(\Sigma Y)}{\sqrt{[N\Sigma X^2 - (\Sigma X)^2][N\Sigma Y^2 - (\Sigma Y)^2]}}$$

Above formula is preferred in situations like:

- When researcher needs to compute 'r' from direct raw scores.
- When mean values are in fractions.

- When a good calculating machine is available.
  (X and Y are original scores in variables X and Y in the Table 11.2).

TABLE 11.2: Computation of 'r' from original scores

X	Y	X²	Y²	XY
13	7	169	49	91
12	11	144	121	132
10	3	100	9	30
8	7	64	49	56
7	2	49	4	14
6	12	36	144	72
6	6	36	36	36
4	2	16	4	8
3	9	9	81	27
1	6	1	36	6
$\Sigma X = 70$	$\Sigma X = 65$	$\Sigma X^2 = 624$	$\Sigma Y^2 = 533$	$\Sigma XY = 472$

Step 1: Square all X and Y scores

Step 2: Find the product of XY for every pair of scores

Step 3: Sum up—the X's, the Y's, the X², the Y² and the XY.

Step 4: Apply formula to calculate the value of 'r'

$$\gamma_{xy} = \frac{N\Sigma XY - [(\Sigma X)(\Sigma Y)]}{\sqrt{[N\Sigma X^2 - (\Sigma X)^2][N\Sigma Y^2 - (\Sigma Y)^2]}}$$

$$= \frac{(10 \times 472) - (70 \times 65)}{\sqrt{(10 \times 624 - 4,900)(10 \times 533 - 4,225)}}$$

$$= \frac{170}{\sqrt{1,340 \times 1,105}}$$

$$= \frac{170}{\sqrt{1,480,700}}$$

$$= \frac{170}{1216.84}$$

$$= 0.14 \text{ (Round off)}$$

Computation of r_{xy} when Deviations are Taken from Assumed Mean

The formula given above in the example is useful in calculating 'r' directly from two ungrouped series of scores, but the disadvantage is that it needs lots of calculations like means and standard deviations. The deviations x and y are mostly in decimals when these are taken from actual means and the multiplication and squaring of these values turn into a tedious task.

For this reason, even when working with short ungrouped series, it is often easier to do the calculations from assumed means after calculating deviations from their corresponding assumed means before applying the following formula.

$$r_{xy} = \frac{\dfrac{\Sigma x'y'}{N} - C_x C_y}{\sigma'_x \sigma'_y}$$

This formula is preferred in situations when:

- Actual means are in decimals and the multiplication and squaring of the values are tedious tasks.
- Deviations are taken from arithmetic means.
- We want to avoid fractions.

The steps followed here to compute 'r' are as follows:

Step 1: Find the mean of X and the mean of Y (scores in Test 1 and Test 2). In Table. 11. 3 these means are Mean$_X$ = 62.5 and Mean$_Y$ = 30.4, respectively.

Step 2: Choose assumed means of both X and Y. Here in the table these are arithmetic mean (AM) of X and Y: (AM)$_X$ = 60, (AM)$_Y$ = 30.

Step 3: Find the deviation of each score in Test1 from its arithmetic mean which is = 60.0, and write these values in column x'. Similarly find the deviation of each score in Test 2 from its arithmetic mean which is = 30, and write these values in column y'.

Step 4: Square all of the x' and all of the y' and note these squares in columns of x'^2 and y'^2, respectively. Total these columns to get the sum as $\Sigma x'^2$ and $\Sigma y'^2$.

Step 5: Multiply x' and y', and enter these products carefully along with their respective signs, in the $x'y'$ column. Sum up the $x'y'$ column considering their signs, to get $\Sigma x'y'$.

Step 6: The corrections are found by subtracting arithmetic mean of 'x' from M_x and arithmetic mean of 'y' from M_y to obtain C_x and C_y. In the following example C_x = 2.5 (62.5 – 60) and C_y = 0.4 (30.4 – 30).

Step 7: Apply the formula to calculate 'r_{xy}' and here

$$\Sigma x'y' = 334, \text{ for } \Sigma x'^2 = 670 \text{ and for } \Sigma y'^2 = 285$$

TABLE 11.3: Computation of r_{xy} when deviations are from assumed mean

Subjects	X	Y	x'	y'	x'²	y'²	x'y'
A	50	22	−10	−8	100	64	80
B	54	25	−6	−5	36	25	30
C	56	34	−4	4	16	16	−16
D	59	28	−1	−2	1	4	2
E	60	26	0	−4	0	16	0
F	62	30	2	0	4	0	0
G	61	32	1	2	1	4	2
H	65	30	5	0	25	0	0
I	67	28	7	−2	49	4	−14
J	71	34	11	4	121	16	44
K	71	36	11	6	121	36	66
L	74	40	14	10	196	100	140
	ΣX = 750	ΣY = 365			$\Sigma x'^2$ = 670	$\Sigma y'^2$ = 285	$\Sigma x'y'$ = 334

$$AM_X = 60.0 \quad AM_Y = 30.0 \quad \sigma_x' = 7.04$$
$$M_x = 62.5 \quad M_Y = 30.4 \quad \sigma_y' = 4.86$$
$$C_x = 2.5 \quad C_y = .4$$
$$C_x^2 = 6.25 \quad C_y^2 = .16$$

By using formula:

$$r_{xy} = \frac{\Sigma x'y'}{\sigma_x' \sigma_y'}$$

$$= \frac{\dfrac{334}{12} - 1}{7.04 \times 4.86}$$

$$= \frac{27.83 - 1}{34.21}$$

$$= \frac{26.83}{34.21}$$

$$= 0.78$$

$$\sigma_x' = \sqrt{\frac{\Sigma x^2}{N} - C_x^2}$$

$$= \sqrt{\frac{670}{12} - 6.25}$$

$$= \sqrt{55.85 - 6.25}$$

$$= 7.04$$

$$\sigma_y' = \sqrt{\frac{\Sigma y'^2}{N} - C_y^2}$$

$$= \frac{285}{12} - 0.16$$

$$= \sqrt{23.59}$$

$$= 4.86$$

Coefficient of Correlation in Grouped Data

In the absence of a calculating machine and a large set of paired data (on two variables X and Y), the procedure is:

1. To group data in both X and Y.
2. To make a scatter diagram or correlation diagram which is also known as bivariate frequency distribution or two-way frequency distribution.

The rules remain same for drawing the diagram as given before. Here, as an example, consider a bivariate data which is concerned with the scores earned by a class of 20 students in Mathematics and Physics examination.

Scatter Diagram Method

To set up a group of data, a table is prepared with columns and rows. The example is taken as written above. Here, we classify each pair of score in Physics (X) and the other in Mathematics (Y) as shown in data in the following table:

Student no.	Scores in Physics (X)	Scores in Mathematics (Y)	Student no.	Scores in Physics (X)	Scores in Mathematics (Y)
1	32	25	11	31	10
2	34	41	12	42	25
3	48	53	13	57	44

Contd...

Student no.	Scores in Physics (X)	Scores in Mathematics (Y)	Student no.	Scores in Physics (X)	Scores in Mathematics (Y)
4	35	12	14	48	32
5	52	26	15	63	42
6	45	28	16	53	45
7	57	51	17	48	31
8	62	54	18	43	23
9	67	50	19	71	28
10	73	48	20	52	22

Now the scores of 20 students in both Physics (X) and Mathematics (Y) are arranged in following bivariate frequency Table 11.4 by putting tallies for each pair of scores:

TABLE 11.4: Bivariate frequency table

Y- Variate (Scores in Mathematics)

X- Variate (Scores in Physics)

Class intervals	10–19	20–29	30–39	40–49	50–59	f_x
70–79		1 /		1 /		2
60–69				1 /	2 //	3
50–59		2 //		2 //	1 /	5
40–49		3 ///	2 //		1 /	6
30–39	2 //	1 /		1 /		4
f_y	2	7	2	5	4	N = 20

- After this, the scatter diagram is made. The class intervals of X-distribution are arranged from bottom to top in ascending order on the left hand.
- The class intervals of Y-distribution are arranged from left to right in ascending order along the top of the table.
- Each pair of scores that is both of X and Y, is represented with the help of a tally in their respective cells. For example, if No. 1 student has secured 32 marks in Physics (X) and 25 in Mathematics (Y). His score of 32 in (X) will be written in the last row and 25 in (Y) will be in the second column. Therefore, for a pair of scores (32, 25) a tally will be marked in the second column of 5th row.
- Similarly, for scores (34, 41), a tally will be added in the 4th column of the 5th row. Likewise, all tallies will be placed in the respective rows and columns. The rows are representing X-scores and the columns are representing Y-scores.
- On the right-hand margin the f_x column that is the number of cases in each class interval of X-distribution is tabulated and on the bottom of the diagram in the f_y row the number of each class interval of Y-distribution are tabulated.

The total f_x column = 20 and the total f_y row = 20. That means it is a bivariate distribution as it represents the dual distribution of two variables. So this type of scatter diagram is a "correlation table."

Calculation of 'r' from a Correlation Table

In continuation with Table 11.6, here are outlines of the steps which are followed in calculating 'r' and these will be best understood if the student will constantly refer to Table 11.5 as one reads through each steps:

Step 1: Construct a scatter diagram for the two variables that are to be correlated, and from it make a correlation table.

Step 2: Count the frequencies of each class interval of distribution – X and write in the f_x column. Count the frequencies for each class interval of distribution – Y and them in f_y row.

TABLE 11.5: Computation of coefficient of correlation

Y-variables–Score on mathematics

X-variable–Score on physics

Class intervals	10–19	20–29	30–39	40–49	50–59	f_x	d_x	fd_x	fd_x^2	d_y	d_x,d_y
70–79		1		1		2	3	6	18	2	6
60–69				1	2	3	2	6	12	8	16
50–59		2		2	1	5	1	5	5	7	7
40–49		3	2		1	6	0	0	0	5	0
30–39	2	1		1		4	−1	−4	4	0	0
f_y	2	7	2	5	4	20		$\Sigma fd_x = 13$	$\Sigma fd_x^2 = 39$	$\Sigma d_y = 22$	$\Sigma d_x,d_y = 29$
d_y	−1	0	1	2	3						
fd_y	−2	0	2	10	12	$\Sigma fd_y = 22$					
fd_y^2	2	0	2	20	36	$\Sigma fd_y^2 = 60$					
d_x	−2	4	0	6	5	$\Sigma d_x = 13$					
d_x,d_y	2	0	0	12	15	$\Sigma d_x,d_y = 29$					

Step 3: Assume a mean for the X-distribution and mark the class intervals in double lines. For the given correlation table, assume the mean in the class interval 40–49 and put double lines as is shown in the table. The deviations above the line of AM will be (+ve) and the deviations below it will be (−ve), totally depending on position of the assumed mean which is 3 here.

- Next, we take out the deviations from assumed mean (column 8). The deviation against the line of assumed mean—against the class interval where we assumed mean has been marked is zero and above it the deviations are +1, +2; and below it the deviation is −1. After filling d_x column, multiply f_x and d_x of each row to get fd_x (column 9).
- Square the d_x and multiply with f to get fd_x^2 (column 10).

(The process is similar to calculating the SD in the assumed mean method)

Step 4: By following similar procedure as in step 3 calculate dy, fd_y and fd_y^2. For the distribution—Y, assumed mean has been taken in the class interval 20–29 and double lines have been marked off as is shown in the table.

Step 5: (The whole procedure for y has been shown in the lower left side of the table which is similar to the calculations done for x variable). Calculate $d_x.d_y$ (column 12).

Step 6: Now, take the algebraic sum of the values of the columns containing fd_x, fd_x^2, dx; fd_y, fd_y^2, d_y and $d_x.d_y$ (for distributions of x and y).

Step 7: (These results have been marked with arrows to show the calculations). The student can observe that:

$$\Sigma d_x.d_y \text{ of X-distribution} = \Sigma d_x.d_y \text{ of Y-distribution} = 22$$

$$\Sigma fd_x = \text{total of } fd_x \text{ row} = 13, \text{ and } \Sigma fd^2{}_x = 39$$

$$\Sigma fd_y = \text{total of } fd_y \text{ column} = 22, \text{ and } \Sigma fd^2{}_y = 60$$

$$\Sigma d_x.d_y = 29 \text{ and N} = 20.$$

Step 8: To compute coefficient of correlation:

$$r = \frac{\dfrac{\Sigma d_x.d_y}{N} - C_x.C_y}{\sigma_x.\sigma_y}$$

$$C = \frac{\Sigma fd}{N}$$

Thus, for $\dfrac{\Sigma fd_x}{N}$ we can write C_x and for $\dfrac{\Sigma fd_y}{N}$ we can write C_y,

Again while calculating SD by assumed mean method we know that

$$\sigma = i \times \sqrt{\frac{\Sigma fd^2}{N} - \left(\frac{\Sigma fd}{N}\right)^2}$$

Therefore,

$$C_x = \frac{\Sigma fd_x}{N} = \frac{13}{20} = .65, \quad C_y = \frac{\Sigma fd_y}{N} = \frac{22}{20} = 1.1$$

$$\sigma_x = \sqrt{\frac{\Sigma fd^2{}_x}{N} - \left(\frac{\Sigma fd_x}{N}\right)^2} = \sqrt{\frac{39}{20} - \left(\frac{13}{20}\right)^2} = \sqrt{1.95 - (.65)^2}$$

$$= \sqrt{1.95 - .4225} = \sqrt{1.5275} = 1.24$$

$$= \sqrt{\frac{\Sigma fd^2{}_y}{N} - \left(\frac{\Sigma fd_y}{N}\right)^2} = \sqrt{\frac{60}{20} - \left(\frac{22}{20}\right)^2} = \sqrt{3 - (1.1)^2}$$

$$= \sqrt{3 - 1.21} = \sqrt{1.79} = 1.34$$

So, σ_y (ignoring 'i') = 1.34

Applying formula:

$$r = \frac{\dfrac{\Sigma d_x.d_y}{N} - C_x.C_y}{\sigma_x.\sigma_y} = \frac{\dfrac{29}{20} - 0.65 \times 1.1}{1.24 \times 1.34} = \frac{0.735}{1.66} = 0.44$$

Practical Tips

Interpretation of the Coefficient of Correlation:
- We must *determine how large 'r' should be in order to be significant*, and *what does 'r' tells us about the data*?
- Also, what is *the meaning of the obtained value of coefficient of correlation?* This has been given in the following table.

Size of correlation	Interpretation
± 1	Perfect positive/negative correlation
± 0.90 to ± 0.99	Very high positive/negative correlation
± 0.70 to ± 0.90	High positive/negative correlation
± 0.50 to ± 0.70	Moderate positive/negative correlation
± 0.30 to ± 0.50	Low positive/negative correlation
± 0.10 to ± 0.30	Very low positive/negative correlation
± 0.00 to ± 0.10	Markedly low and negligible positive/negative correlation

Must Know

Misinterpretation of 'r':

Sometimes, *student may misinterpret the values 'r' and find the cause and effect relationship*, i.e., one variable causing the variation in the other variable—a *sound logical base is required* for this.

One must note that 'r' gives us a quantitative determination of the degree of relationship between two variables and not an information about the nature of association between them (two variables). Causation suggests an invariable sequence that is A always leads to B, whereas correlation coefficient suggests a measure of mutual association between two variables only.

*For example, there may be a high correlation between maladjustment and anxie*ty, but on the basis of high correlation we cannot say that maladjustment is cause of anxiety. Though high anxiety may be the cause of maladjustment but 'r' indicates that anxiety and maladjustment are mutually associated variables. Let's take another example of finding a high correlation between aptitude and achievement in the subject, in a school. But at the end of the school examinations will this reveal causal relationship? It may or may not.

Aptitude in the study of a subject causes variation in the achievement of that subject, but high success of the student in a particular subject is not the result of high aptitude only; it may be due to the other variables like types of questions in an examination, the study hours that the student has devoted to that particular subject throughout the year, etc.

Therefore, when we are interpreting the size of 'r' in terms of cause and effect, it is appropriate only when the variables under investigation provide a logical base for such interpretation.

Factors Influencing the Size of the Correlation Coefficient

Following factors influence the size of the coefficient of correlation and may lead to misinterpretation:
- The size of 'r' depends on the variability of measured values in the correlated sample. More is the variability, the higher will be the correlation (everything else being equal).
- The size of 'r' gets altered, when a researcher selects an extreme group of subjects in order to compare. In such cases 'r' will be large as compared to 'r' from a random sample of the same group.

- Addition of/or dropping the extreme cases from the group may also lead to change in the size of 'r'. Addition of the extreme cases will increase the size of correlation coefficient and dropping of the extreme cases lowers the value of 'r'.

Spearman's Rank Correlation Coefficient

Many times the results are ranked and arranged in order of merit or proficiency on two variables when we study problems in the field of Education and Psychology. When such a situation arises that the objects are ranked, or when these two sets of ranks covary or they have agreement between them, we measure the degrees of relationship by Spearman's rank correlation. It is applied in situations when there is problem to decide the relationship among the measurements made which are non-linear in nature. In such situations correlation cannot be described by the product-moment 'r'.

We take an example of the evaluation of a group of students on the basis of leadership abilities or assessment of females in a beauty contest or students' evaluation or order of preference in a case of food choice or ranking of pictures according to their visual values or ranking of employees by supervisors according to job performance. In such cases the results will be in ranks. Here, correlation coefficient will be calculated by Spearman's Rank Correlation Coefficient to find out relation between 2 sets of ranks.

This coefficient of correlation is denoted by Greek letter ρ (called Rho) and is given as:

$$\rho = 1 - \frac{6 \times \Sigma D^2}{N(N^2 - 1)}$$

where, ρ = rho is Spearman's Rank Correlation Coefficient

N = Total number of items/individuals ranked

D = Difference between paired ranks (in each case)

Characteristics of 'ρ'

- Here, the observations or measurements of the bivariate variable are based on the ordinal scale (in the form of ranks).
- The size of the coefficient is affected by the size of the differences in ranks. That means:
  - If the ranks are same for both tests, the rank difference will be zero and as a result D^2 will be zero. It will give a result telling that the correlation is perfect, i.e., 1.
  - If the rank differences are very large (and the fraction is greater than one) then the correlation will be negative.

Assumptions of 'ρ'

- **N is small or may be the data is badly skewed:** The data is free or independent of some features of the population distribution. These are described as nonparametric tests. In many situations quantitative measurements are not available so we use ranking methods. The quantitative measurements may be available but they have been substituted by ranks to reduce arithmetical labor.
- The data is comprised of groups of ordinal numbers like 1st, 2nd, 3rd ….Nth. Later on these are substituted by the cardinal numbers 1, 2, 3,………, N for calculation. This always assumes equality of intervals.

Calculating 'ρ' from Test Scores

Example: The following data gives the scores of 5 students in General Science and Mathematics and respectively. Compute the correlation between the two series of test scores by Spearman's rank difference method (Table. 11.6).

TABLE 11.6: Computation of 'ρ'

Student	Scores in Mathematics	Scores in General Science	Rank in Test 1 R_1	Rank in Test 2 R_2	Diff. in ranks $D = R_1 - R_2$	D^2
A	8	10	2	1	1	1
B	7	8	3	2	1	1
C	9	7	1	3	−2	4
D	5	4	4	5	−1	1
E	1	5	5	4	1	1
$N = 5$					$\Sigma D = 0$	$\Sigma D^2 = 8$

$$\rho = 1 - \frac{6 \times \Sigma D^2}{N\,(N^2 - 1)} = 1 - \frac{6 \times 8}{5\,(5^2 - 1)} = 1 - \frac{48}{120} = 1 - 0.40 = 0.60$$

The value of coefficient of correlation between scores (0.60) in General Science and Mathematics is positive and moderate.

Steps of Calculation of Spearman's Coefficient of Correlation

Step 1: List the names or serial numbers of students in column 1.

Step 2: In column 2 and 3 enter the scores of each student obtained in test I and II.

Step 3: Consider one set of scores in column 2 and assign rank 1 to the highest score (here, it is 9), then a rank of 2 will be given to the next highest score (which is 8, here) and so on till the last score.

Step 4: Take the 2nd set of scores in column 3 and give rank 1 to highest score (highest score is 10 here). Follow the same process as given in step 3.

Step 5: Now calculate the difference of ranks for each student and write down (column 6).

Step 6: Check the sum of the differences recorded in column 6. It is always zero.

Step 7: Now square each difference of ranks obtained in column 6 and record in column 7. Sum it up and note it as ΣD^2.

Step 8: Put the values in the formula of Spearman's coefficient of correlation.

Calculating 'ρ' from Ranked Data

Example: In a speech contest Prof. Mehta and Prof. Sharma, judged 10 contestants. They gave judgments in ranks, as given in Table. 11.7. Determine the level up to which their judgments are in agreement.

TABLE 11.7: Computation of ρ (Rho)

Contestants	Prof. Mehta Ranks (R_1)	Prof. Sharma Ranks (R_2)	Difference $D = (R_1 - R_2)$	D^2
A	1	1	0	0
B	3	2	1	1
C	4	5	−1	1
D	7	9	−2	4
E	6	6	0	0
F	9	8	1	1
G	8	10	−2	4
H	10	7	3	9
I	2	4	−2	4
J	5	3	2	4
$N = 10$			$\sum D = 0$	$\sum D^2 = 28$

$$\rho = 1 - \frac{6 \times \sum D^2}{N(N^2 - 1)} = 1 - \frac{6 \times 28}{10(10^2 - 1)} = 1 - \frac{6 \times 28}{990} = 1 - 0.17 = 0.83$$

The value of coefficient of correlation is 0.83 and shows a high degree of agreement between the judgments of two judges.

Calculating 'ρ' for tied Ranks

Example: The following data is of scores of 10 students in two test trials with a gap of 2 weeks. Compute the correlation between the scores of two trials by rank difference method (Table. 11.8).

TABLE 11.8: Computation of 'ρ'

Student	Trial-1 (X)	Trial-2 (Y)	Rank on Trial I (R_1)	Rank on Trial II (R_2)	Diff. $D = R_1 - R_2$	D^2
A	10	16	6.5	5.5	1.0	1.00
B	15	16	3	5.5	−2.5	6.25
C	11	24	5	1.5	3.5	12.25
D	14	18	4	4	0	0
E	16	22	2	3	−1.0	1.00
F	20	24	1	1.5	−0.5	0.25
G	10	14	6.5	7.5	−1.0	1.00
H	8	10	9	10	−1.0	1.00
I	7	12	10	9	1.0	1.00
J	9	14	8	7.5	0.5	0.25
$N = 10$					$\sum D = 0$	$\sum D^2 = 24$

$$\rho = 1 - \frac{6 \times \sum D^2}{N(N^2 - 1)} = 1 - \frac{6 \times 24}{10(10^2 - 1)} = 1 - \frac{6 \times 24}{10 \times 99} = 1 - 0.145$$

$$\rho = 0.855$$

The correlation coefficient calculated as 0.885 here indicates positive and very high degree of correlation.

The students must note down that there are scores which have been repeated in the above example. Such type of repetitive scores are known as tied ranks. So in the above table in column 2 (A and G are getting the same score viz. 10) and in column 3 too there is repetition of scores.

Definitely such pairs will have same ranks or 'Tied Ranks'. Therefore, the procedure of assigning ranks to the repeated scores is a little different from the nonrepeated scores.

On observing column 4 we can see that student A and G have similar scores of 10 so they will possess 6th and 7th rank in the group. But here we take an average of 6th and 7th rank which is 6.5 (6 + 7/2 = 13/2) and assign it to each of them.

The same procedure will be followed for scores of Trial II. Here, we have ties at three places. Students C and F (average of their ranks is 1 + 2/2 = 1.5). Student A and B (average of their ranks is 5 + 6/2). Similarly, student G and J (average of their ranks is 7 + 8/2).

If the values are repeated more than twice, the same process is followed, for example, if three students have a score of 10, at 5th, 6th and 7th ranks, then average will be taken as 5 + 6 + 7/3 = 6.

The calculation steps of ρ (rho) are the same as explained earlier.

Interpretation

The value of ρ is interpreted in similar way as Karl Pearson's coefficient of correlation. The value varies from -1 to $+1$. The value $+1$ indicates a perfect positive agreement or relationship between two sets of ranks and -1 indicates a perfect negative relationship. If the value of $\rho = 0$, then there is no relationship or agreement between ranks.

Advantages

- The computation is quicker and easier than 'r' computed by the Pearson's product-moment method.
- It is an agreeable method when data is available only in ordinal form/or number of paired variables is >5 but not greater than 30 having minimum/or a few ties in the ranks.

Limitations

- When the interval data is converted into rank-order data, the information about the size of the score differences is lost, for example in the above example, if D in Trial II got scores in class interval of 18 up to 21, his rank will remain only 4.
- If the number of participants is more, assigning ranks to them is a tedious job.

SIMPLE LINEAR REGRESSION ANALYSIS

The change in some variables may tell about or may cause changes in other variables. The two types of variables are termed:

1. Explanatory variables or the independent variables.
2. Dependent variables, the variables which are to be explained.

The regression model evaluates the nature of the relationship between independent and dependent variables. A change in dependent variables which results from change in independent variables is known as size of the relationship.

In simple linear regression, we predict scores of one variable from the scores of a second variable. The variable that we are predicting in the process is called the criterion variable and is referred to as Y. The variable on which our predictions are based on is called the predictor variable and is referred to as X.

When there is only one predictor variable, the prediction method is called simple regression. Here, the predictions of Y when plotted as a function of X give a straight line.

The data in Table 11.9 is plotted in Figures 11.4A and B. One can see that there is a positive relationship between X and Y. If one has to predict Y from X, the higher the value of X, the higher is prediction of Y.

TABLE 11.9: Example data of two variables

X	1.00	2.00	3.00	4.00	5.00
Y	1.00	2.00	1.30	3.75	2.25

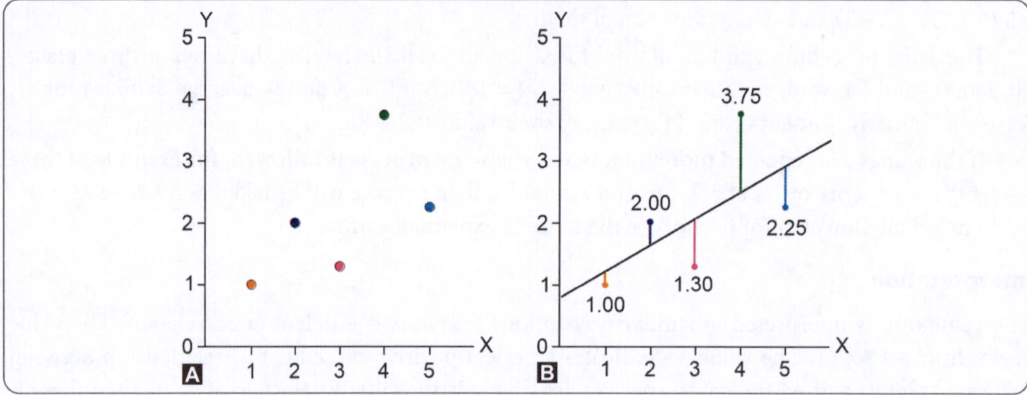

Figures 11.4A and B: A scatter plot of the example data

The points are the actual data, black line consists of the predictions, and the vertical lines between the points and the black line signify errors of prediction.

Example: The data are given as:

X	72	73	75	76	77	78	79	80	80	81	82	83	84	85	86	88
Y	45	38	41	35	31	40	25	32	36	29	34	38	26	32	28	27

a. Sketch a scatterplot, and **b.** Compute the correlation coefficient 'r'.

Hint:

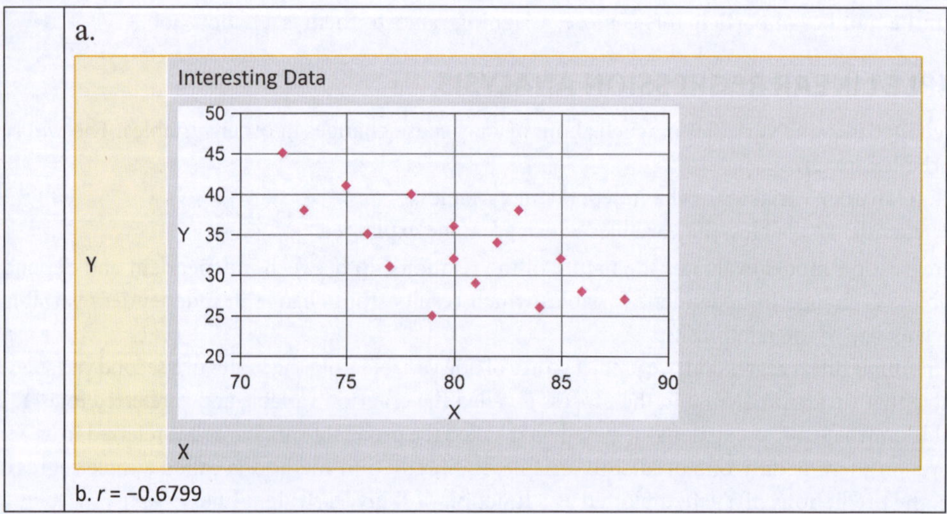

b. r = −0.6799

Linear regression involves finding the best-fitting straight line through the plotted points. This "best-fitting line" is called a regression line. The black line marked diagonally in right side figure is the regression line and it consists of the predicted scores on Y for each possible value of X.

Interpretation: The vertical lines which are falling from the points to the regression line represent the errors of prediction. As one can see, the red point is very near to the regression line therefore its error of prediction is small. Whereas, the yellow point which is much higher than the regression line has larger error of prediction. As such, a prediction error signifies a deviation of the current state with respect to what is predicted based on the existing prototype in the world. We can define the error of prediction for a point as the value of the point minus the predicted value (that is value on the line).

Table 11.10 displays the predicted values (Y') and the errors of prediction ($Y-Y'$). For example, the first point has a Y of 1.00 and a predicted Y (called Y') of 1.21. Therefore, its error of prediction is -0.21.

TABLE 11.10: **Example data of error of prediction**

X	Y	Y'	Y–Y'	(Y–Y')²
1.00	1.00	1.210	−0.210	0.044
2.00	2.00	1.635	0.365	0.133
3.00	1.30	2.060	−0.760	0.578
4.00	3.75	2.485	1.265	1.600
5.00	2.25	2.910	−0.660	0.436

Here, the meaning of "best-fitting line" is the line that minimizes the sum of the squared errors of prediction. It is the criterion that was used to find the line in **Figure 11.4B**.

The last column in **Table 11.10** displays the squared errors of prediction. The sum of the squared errors of prediction shown in **Table 11.10** is lower than it would be for any other regression line. The formula for a regression line is:

$$Y' = bX + A$$

where, 'Y' is the predicted score, b is the slope of the line, and A is the Y intercept. The equation for the line in **Figure 11.4B** is:

$$Y = 0.425X + 0.785$$

For

$$X = 1$$

$$Y' = (0.425)(1) + 0.785 = 1.21$$

For

$$X = 2$$

$$Y = (0.425)(2) + 0.785 = 1.64$$

Computing the regression line

In the age of computers, the regression line is computed with the help of statistical software. However, the calculations are relatively easy, and are given here.

The calculations are based on the statistics shown in **Table 11.11**. M_X is the mean of X, M_Y is the mean of Y, S_X is the standard deviation of X, S_Y is the standard deviation of Y, and r is the correlation between X and Y.

TABLE 11.11: **Statistical values for computing the regression line.**

M_X	M_Y	S_X	S_Y	r
3	2.06	1.581	1.072	0.627

The slope (b) can be calculated as follows:

$$b = r\, S_Y/S_X$$

and the intercept (A) can be calculated as

$$A = M_Y - bM_X.$$

Here the calculations have been shown in terms of sample statistics not in terms of population parameters. The formulas are same. Simply use the parameter values for means, standard deviations, and the correlation.

For the data given here,

$$b = (0.627)(1.072)/1.581 = 0.425$$
$$A = 2.06 - (0.425)(3) = 0.785$$

Significance of errors of prediction

The significance of errors of prediction lies in the fact that how much the current results are deviating from the existing results on the similar study in the world. In fact, there are three major areas of questions that the regression analysis answers:

1. Causal analysis
2. Forecasting an effect
3. Trend forecasting

1. **A causal relationship** between two variables where the dependent variable is continuous and the predictor is either categorical (dummy coded), dichotomous or continuous. Unlike correlation analysis which does not indicate direction of effects, the regression analysis is based on assumption that the independent variable has an effect on the dependent variable.

    For examples: Does the body weight have an influence on the blood cholesterol level?

    Answer: The researcher has to measure body weight and blood cholesterol level in various subjects under study. The linear regression analysis can then show whether the body weight taken as independent variable has an effect on the dependent variable that is blood cholesterol level.

    For example: Is anxiety influenced by personality traits?

    Answer: The team of researchers would measure anxiety (e.g., Brain interview questions or BAI) and one personality trait like consciousness. Linear regression analysis would then be used to test whether there is a causal link between both variables. However, it does not prove that the causal direction is from anxiety to personality or vice versa.

2. **To forecast values:**

    For example: With X cigarettes smoked per day, the life expectancy is Y years.

    Answer: The research team can observe smoking habits and age reached at the death of a few participants. The regression coefficient is estimated with a linear regression equation $y = a + b.x$. It can then tell the researchers about the life expectancy (y) when smoking x cigarettes/day.

3. **To predict trends in data:**

    For example: By how many years does the life expectancy decrease for every additional overweight (in pounds)?

    Answer: The researchers observe overweight and the age at death, linear regression analysis can be used to predict trends. This is especially useful when the regression analysis finds no significant reason. So here the regression coefficient can at least predict a trend, if the coefficient is significant.

STUDENT ASSIGNMENT

LONG ANSWER QUESTIONS

1. What is correlation? How is it measured and interpreted?
2. What is regression line? What are its uses?

SHORT ANSWER QUESTIONS

1. Write a short note on scatter diagram.
2. Write about rank order correlation.
3. What is product moment correlation?
4. Write a short note on needs of correlation.

MULTIPLE CHOICE QUESTIONS

1. **To test linear relationship of y (dependent) and x (independent) continuous variables, which of the following plot best suited?**
   a. Scatter plot
   b. Bar chart
   c. Histogram
   d. None of these

2. **Which of the following indicates a fairly strong relationship between X and Y?**
   a. Correlation coefficient = 0.9
   b. The p-value for the null hypothesis Beta coefficient = 0 is 0.0001
   c. The t-statistic for the null hypothesis Beta coefficient = 0 is 30
   d. None of these

3. **A correlation between age and health of a person is found to be −1.09. On the basis of this you would tell the doctors that:**
   a. The age is good predictor of health
   b. The age is poor predictor of health
   c. None of these
   d. All of these

Note

Unit VI

Research Designs and their Meanings

12

Research Designs

"Good design is like a refrigerator—when it works, no one notices, but when it doesn't, it sure stinks."
—Irene Au

LEARNING OBJECTIVES

After the completion of the chapter, the readers will be able to:
- Understand designs of experiment.
- Explain the principles and classification of research designs.
- Discuss nonexperimental research designs.

CHAPTER OUTLINE

- Introduction
- Research Design
- Matched-Pairs Design
- Completely Randomized Design
- Block Design
- Randomized Block Design
- Latin Square Design

INTRODUCTION

One of the main objectives of designing an experiment is to verify the hypothesis in an economical and efficient way. When a researcher has to verify the null hypothesis of equality of several means of normal populations with same variances, the analysis of variance technique can be used. Such techniques are based on certain statistical assumptions, if these assumptions are violated, the outcome of the test of hypothesis will also be faulty and the analysis of data becomes meaningless. Therefore, the main demand is how to obtain the data so that the assumptions are met and the data is readily available for the application of statistical tools like analysis of variance.

Design of experiment offers a method by which the treatments are allocated randomly on the experimental units in a way that the responses could be assessed with the precision.

RESEARCH DESIGN

A research design is a rudimentary plan that directs the data collection and analysis, the two important phases of the research. It provides the outline which stipulates the type of information to be collected, its sources and the collection procedure.

Research design is like a blueprint. Before starting an experiment, a researcher plans:
- How the study will be conducted?
- How the data will be collected?
- What means are to be used to obtain this data, after the variables are identified and quantified?
- What is the purpose of research?

Considerations to Minimize Errors in Research Design

One of the important considerations is to minimize errors and maximize the reliability and validity of data.

- **Reliability** refers to the consistency, stability or dependability of the data. A research method must give out same/similar results even if carried out for any number of times.
- **Validity** refers to data that are not only reliable but also true and accurate. It denotes to which extent an instrument is able to actually measure what it is supposed to measure.
- **Threats to validity:** There are some threats to validity which needs to be mentioned here:
  - **History:** It denotes the events that may occur during the time frame of study which are not actually part of the study. In fact, they influence the study by either decreasing or increasing the expected outcomes of a research.
  - **Selection:** It occurs when the respondents for a study are chosen as a group and not individually.
  - **Testing:** It refers to the pretest carried out that results in an improved performance in the post-test. In order to avoid this threat, a pretest may not be required. Although in case pretest is given, then in order to control this threat, it is recommended to use an alternative form of instrument.
  - **Instrumentation:** It denotes the unreliability in measuring the instruments which may result to provide invalid measurement of performance under a research experiment. Changing the instrument between pretest and post-test may also result in an unwanted effect on the results which is not caused by treatment introduced.
  - **Maturation:** It denotes to the psychological and physiological changes that could occur to the respondents of the study during the period of study. For example, if the time frame of a data collection is very long and rigid, the participants may feel some psychological discomforts because of tiredness, boredom and time constraints (on behalf of respondents).
  - **Mortality:** It denotes loss of participant/participants during the post-test stage or while implementing the time frame of the study. If a researcher has chosen some study with participants in the age group of 21–75 years, then some kind of mortality is unavoidable during the time period of test. The respondent may also decide to opt out or bluntly refuse to participate further in study.

Characteristics of a Research Design

- **Setting:** The setting in which the research occurs is an important factor for outcomes of a study. The study is carried out in laboratory or in the field.
- **Laboratory studies:** The study is carried out in a laboratory when a high degree of control is required in regard to the environment and to regulate the extraneous and intervening variables.
- **Field study:** It occurs outside the laboratory settings in natural surroundings or backgrounds and uses a variety of methods like:
  - Field experiments

- Questionnaires
- Observation of participants in village or hospital or any other chosen place of study
- Interviews in office, homes or parks, etc.
- **Timing of data collection:** According to time of the research the collection of data is affected as:
  - **Retrospective studies:** These are also called historical or ex post facto study. Here the events have already occurred in the past.
  - **Prospective studies:** These are also known as longitudinal study. Here the events have not occurred and they are expected or are underway to happen in future.
  - **Cross sectional studies:** Here the data collection is strictly in the present time.
    - The participants or subjects to be included in the research—this factor directly or indirectly affects the data as the sample size or number of subjects in the study.
    - The method used to collect a research data.
    - The plan of researcher for communication the research findings.

Categories of Research Designs

There are many frameworks of research design and these can be broadly classified into two major categories:

1. Exploratory (qualitative study)
2. Conclusive (quantitative study)

Exploratory research is concerned with qualitative study whereas conclusive research is concerned with quantitative study. The qualitative research gives vision and understanding of the problem, while quantitative research searches for quantifying the data and is typically applied in one or other form of statistical analysis.

While solving a research problem, both research methods work in unison and quantitative research is preceded by appropriate qualitative research. A researcher has to decide the research design to undertake the research problems and this decision is based on the pros and cons of the research designs and the type of problem under study.

While studying the various research designs, the readers are expected to be familiar with some of the symbols which are originally given by Campbell and Stanley (1963) are as follows:

R: Random selection of subject or random assignment of treatment to experimental groups.

X: Treatment or the experimental variable or the independent variable. More than one treatment condition is labeled as X_1, X_2, X_3 and so on.

O: Observation: O_1, O_2, O_3 represent subsequent observations.

Classification of Research Designs

The research design is classified into different types (Fig. 12.1) based on the method adopted. Mainly two types of research designs are used – experimental and nonexperimental, depending on the need of study.

Descriptive Research Design

Descriptive research design is the most commonly used method in research. It is used when the purpose of study is to know about the predominant conditions of events, people or objects. This design describes about "what is there" in regard to the variables under consideration. The characteristics of descriptive research are as follows:

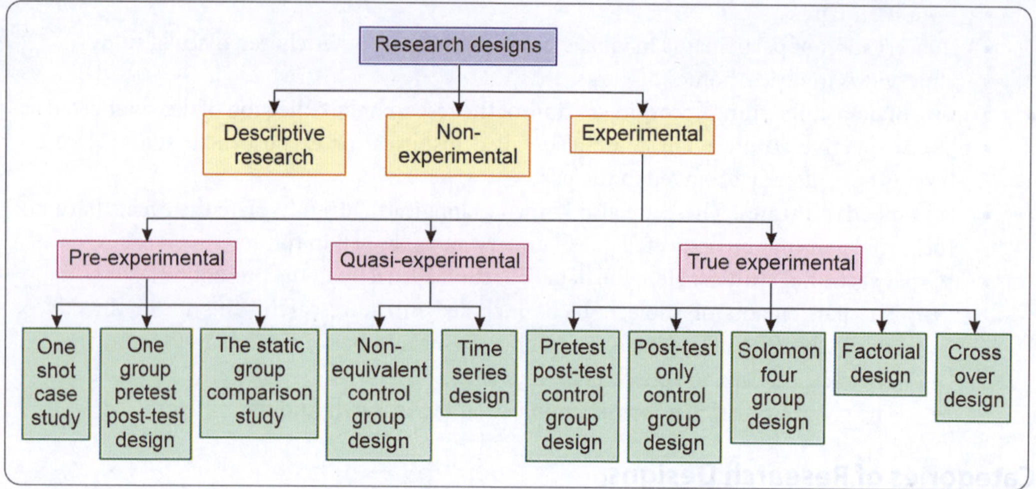

Figure 12.1: Classification of research designs

- It provides either a qualitative or quantitative or both types of description about the general characteristics of the case or group under study.
- It determines the prevailing conditions of facts in a case study or group.
- The cause of prevailing conditions is not emphasized.
- Comparison characteristics of two groups may be made in order to determine the similarities and dissimilarities.
- The study of conditions at different periods of time may be made and the changes that took place between the periods may be evaluated for the value generated.
- The variables involved in study are generally controlled.
- The study on prevailing conditions may be or can be repeated for comparison and verification.

Types of Descriptive Research

The descriptive research is of following types:

Exploratory descriptive design

- Exploratory word itself denotes that nothing much is known about the topic under study.
- It provides an in-depth exploration of a single variable, concept or a process.
- It further indicates that a survey of the literature failed to reveal any significant research in the field of study under question.

Descriptive survey design

- This is used to measure existing phenomenon without inquiring about its cause.
- This method is used when researcher wants to collect a relatively limited data from a relatively large number of subjects.

Correlational research design

- It helps to study the relationship of two or more variables.
- It is based on concepts and looks for cause and effect relationship in the study results.
- Although it can not specify the direction of the relationship at the start of study.

Comparative research design

- It examines and describes differences in variables in two or more groups that occur naturally in a research setting.
- It further specifies cause and effect at the start of a study which is based on theoretical framework.

Case study

Here research is carried out by extensive exploration of a single unit of study, for example:

- Persons.
- Family groups.
- Communities or institutions.
- Very small number of subjects who are extensively examined.

Feasibility study

This type of study tries to determine the viability of an undertaking or a business venture, for example, establishing an institution or constructing an infrastructure.

Experimental Research Design

Principles of Experimental Design

There are three basic principles of research design which were developed by Sir Ronald A Fisher and these have been discussed as follows:

1. **Randomization:** The principle of randomization involves the appointment of treatment to experimental units at random so as to avoid any bias in the experiment which may result from the influence of some inessential unknown factor/factors. For example, in the development of analysis of variance, researcher assumes that the errors are random and independent. Automatically the observations also become random. The principle of randomization confirms it. The random assignment of experimental units to treatments facilitates following:
   - Elimination of the systematic bias.
   - It is required to obtain a representative sample from the population.
   - It helps in distributing the unknown variation due to variables throughout the experiment and breaks the influence of unknown variables.

   If the randomization process is such that each experimental unit has equal chance of receiving each treatment, then it is called complete randomization.

2. **Replication:** The replication principle involves any treatment to be repeated for a number of times to obtain valid and reliable estimate than could have been possible with one treatment only. Replication is an efficient way to increase the precision of an experiment. The precision increases with the increase in the number of observations. Replication gives more observations when the same treatment is used and increases precision. Therefore, as observations increase variance decrease.

3. **Local control (error control):** The replication is carried out with local control to reduce the experimental error. For example, if the experimental units are divided into different groups in a way that they are homogeneous within the blocks, than the variations among the blocks are eliminated. Ideally the error component will enclose the variations because of the treatments only. This will further increase the efficiency of research design.
   - **Controlling variables:** Attempt to control all other variables except dependent variables—known as control. The methods used for experimental control are as follows:

- ◆ **Physical control:** All subjects are given an equal chance of exposure to the independent variable. It controls the effects of nonexperimental variables that may affect the dependent variable.
- ◆ **Selective control:** Manipulates indirectly by selecting in or out variables that cannot be controlled.
- ◆ **Statistical control:** Variables not conducive to physical or selective manipulation may be controlled by statistical techniques (example: Covariance).
- ◆ **Observation:** The observation of effects on independent variables.

Validity of Experimental Design

The validity of experimental research design depends on internal and external validity.

Internal validity

Asks the questions like—did the experimental treatment make some difference in this particular situation as compared to other extraneous variables?

Factors threatening internal validity:

- **History:** It means events occurring between the first and second measurements in addition to the experimental variable which might affect the measurement. For example, researcher collects data before and after a 5 day of an intervention. During this gap a fire broke and resulted in disturbing the study, not the intervention.
- **Maturation:** The natural process of maturation that takes place in an individual during the duration of the experiment, not as a result of specific events but because of simply growing older and more tired. For example, subjects become tired after completing a training session, and it affects their responses on the post-test.
- **Pretesting:** The effect created on the second measurement by having a measurement before the experiment. For example, subjects take a Pretest and remember some of the items. In the post-test they shift to more acceptable answers. Experimental group learns from the pretest.
- **Measuring instruments:** Changes in instruments, calibration of instruments, observers or scorers may cause changes in the measurements. For example, interviewers are very careful with their first two or three interviews but on the 4th, 5th or 6th interviews they get fatigued and less careful which leads to errors.
- **Statistical regression:** Groups may have extreme scores of measurements and these scores or measurements tend to move toward the mean with repeated measurements even without an experimental variable. For example, hospital managers performing poorly are selected for training. Their average post-test scores will be higher than their pretest scores because of statistical regression, even if no training was given.
- **Differential selection:** Different individuals or groups will have different previous knowledge or ability which would affect the final measurement. For example, A group who has watched a video on intervention is compared with a group which has not. There is no way of comparing these two groups as they cannot be equivalent because they were not randomly assigned to watch the intervention's video.
- **Experimental mortality:** The loss of subjects from comparison groups can greatly affect the comparisons because of unique characteristics of those subjects. Groups to be compared need to be the same after and before the experiment. For example, over a 6 months experiment that was aimed to change nursing practices, 12 nurses dropped out of the experimental group but none

dropped out of the control group. Not only is there differential loss in the two groups, but the 12 dropouts may be very different from those who remained in the experimental group.

External validity

It discusses about the effect of experiment that can be generalized.

Factors threatening external validity/generalizability:

- **Pretesting:** Individuals who were pretested might become less or more sensitive to the experimental variable or might have "learnt" from the pretest making them unsuitable of the population who had not been pretested. For example, prior to viewing a film on Environmental Effects of Chemicals, a group of subjects is given a 60-item questionnaire test. Taking the pretest may increase the effect of the film. The results may vary for the group who have not watched the movie.

- **Differential selection:** The selection of the subjects further determines how the findings can be generalized. Subjects selected from a small group or one with particular characteristics would limit generalizability. Randomly chosen subjects from the entire population can be generalized to the entire population. For example, a researcher, seeking permission to conduct experiment, is turned down by 7 hospitals, but the 8th hospital gives permission. The 8th hospital is obviously different than the others because they accepted on some worthy grounds. Thus, subjects in the 8th hospital may be more sensitive to the experimental treatment.

- **Experimental procedures:** The experimental procedures and arrangements have a certain amount of effect on the subjects in the experimental settings. Generalization to persons not in the experimental setting may be precluded. For example, department heads in a hospital realize they are being studied, tries to guess what the researcher wants and responds accordingly rather than responding to the treatment.

- **Multiple treatment interference:** If the subjects are exposed to more than one treatment then the findings could only be generalized to individuals exposed to same treatments in the same order of presentation. For example, a group of medical students is given training with managers followed by training in working with nurses. Since training effects learnt cannot be deleted, the first training will affect the second.

Tools of experimental design used to control factors threatening validity:

- **Pretest:** The pretest, or measurement before the start of an experiment, can help to control differential selection by determining the presence/knowledge of the experimental variables before the experiment begins. It can help to control experimental mortality because the subjects can be removed from the entire comparison by removing their pretests.

  However, pretests cause problems by their effect on the second measurement and cause problems in generalizability, to a population which has not undergone pretest.

- **Control group:** The use of a matched or similar group which is not exposed to the experimental variable can help reduce the effect of history, maturation, instrumentation, and interaction of factors. The control group is exposed to all conditions of the experiment except the experimental variable.

- **Randomization:** Use of random selection procedures for subjects can help to control differential selection, and the interaction of factors and statistical regression. It helps to increase generalizability by making the groups representative of the populations.

- **Additional groups:** The effects of pretests and experimental procedures can be partially controlled by the use of groups which were not pretested or exposed to experimental arrangements.

TABLE 12.1: Change in dependent and independent variables in experimental and control groups

Groups	Independent variable	Dependent variable
Experimental group	Changed	Measured
Control group	Unchanged	Measure

They are used simultaneously with other pretested groups or other factors that may be threatening validity. It has one main characteristic that it manipulates the independent variable and measures the effects of dependent variables. Classic examples are experimental group and control group (Table 12.1).

- **Experimental group:** The independent variable can be manipulated here.
- **Control group:** The dependent variable is measured without any manipulation to experimental group. The control is achieved by:
  - Allowing for no variables.
  - Specifying the variations to be allowed.
  - Distributing the variations equally.

Types of Experimental Research Design

Pre-experimental

Pre-experimental research design is called one shot case study and involves one group that is exposed to treatment (X) and then post-test (Y). Here, none of the threats to validity are controlled (Fig 12.2).

- **One shot case study design:** In this type of research design, subjects are presented with some type of treatment, like 6 months of college work experience and then the outcome measure is applied, like effect on college grades. The goal is to determine whether the treatment had any effect on the outcome.
- **One group pretest-post-test study design:** It is a research design which is mostly used by behavioral science researchers to determine the effect of a particular treatment or intervention on a given sample. It has two characters:
  1. **Use of a single group of participants,** i.e., one-group design which denotes that all participants are part of a single situation and all participants will be given same treatments and assessments.
  2. **Linear ordering,** which requires assessment of a dependent variable before and after a treatment is implemented (i.e., a pretest–post-test design).
- **Static group comparison:** Here, a group that has experienced some treatment is compared with other group that has not met the treatment. The observed differences between the two groups are assumed as the result of treatment.

Quasi-experimental

It can be:

- Nonequivalent control group design (Fig. 12.3)

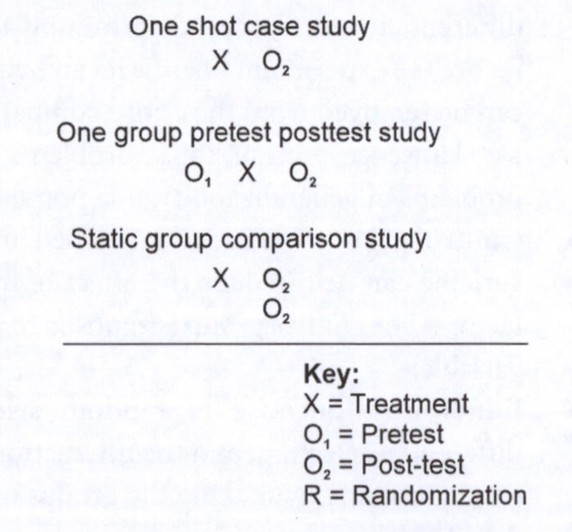

Figure 12.2: Pre-experimental research design

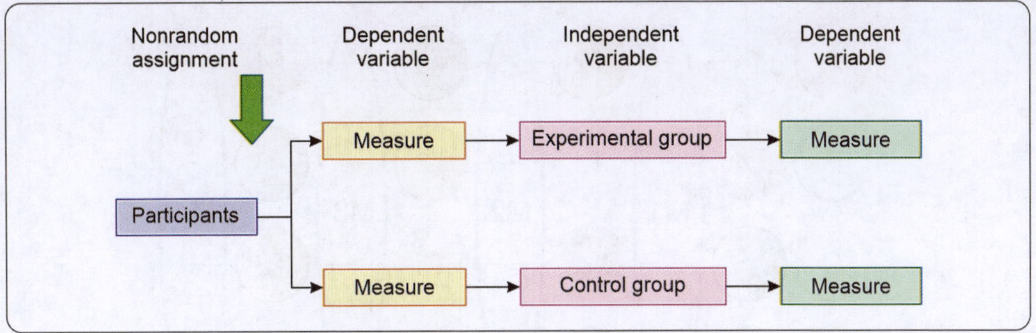

Figure 12.3: Nonequivalent control group design

- A nonequivalent control group post-test-only is quasi-experimental in which a dependent variable is measured following a treatment in one group and also in a nonequivalent control group that does not receive the treatment. It is similar to the pretest post-test control group design and does not involve random assignments.
- Remember that the results may be compromised due to the nonequivalent control group which may be threat to validity.
- The lack of random assignments adds a source of invalidity that is not associated with the pretest post-test control group design.

- **Time series research design (Fig. 12.4):** It is an elaboration of the one-group pretest post-test design in which one group is:
  - Repeatedly pretested
  - Then exposed to a treatment
  - Repeatedly post-tested
- **Advantages of time series research design:**
  - It is one of the most practical and feasible research designs.
  - Less time consuming.
  - Feasible with less resources.
  - Comparison with other groups is possible.
- **Disadvantage of time series research design:** Unexpected factors might affect the results.
- **Counterbalance design (Fig. 12.5):** It is another quasi-experimental design. The counterbalanced design is often useful when several interventions are being tested simultaneously. After random selection from the population, the study subjects are divided into independent groups.

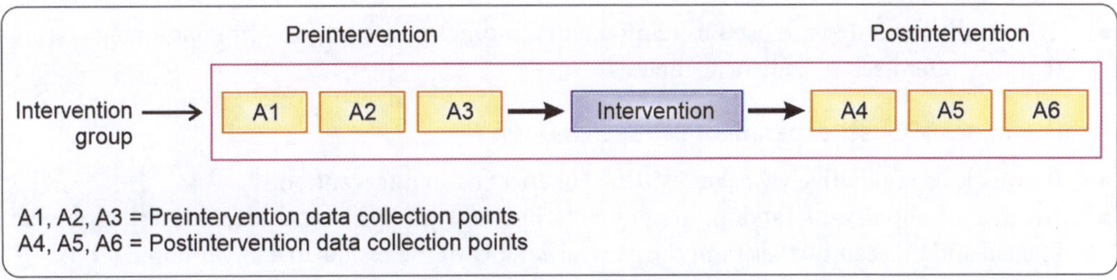

Figure 12.4: Time series research design

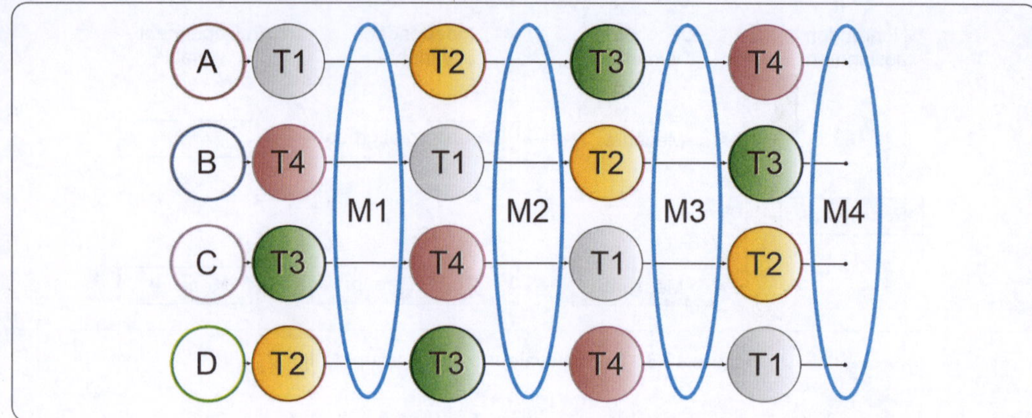

Figure 12.5: Counter balance design

- Each group receives each intervention, but in a different order from the other respective groups.
- An observation of the outcome is taken after each series of interventions.
- The counterbalance design is a powerful design because each participant serves as their own control and multiple interventions can be tested at the same time.
- The restrictions or the conditions remain that the number of test groups should be equal to the number of control groups.

Advantages of Quasi-experimental Research Design

- It is very practical as well as possible research design especially in medical field and healthcare.
- Less time is taken and it is economical too.
- True experimental designs are sometimes impractical or impossible because the research can only be carried out effectively in natural set-tings. An artificial situation is created that may not always represent real-life situations because all other variables are tightly controlled. For this reason, external validity is more in quasi-experimental research where real situations are present.
- Reactions of test subjects are genuine because quasi-experimental research is not an artificial research environment.
- It is very useful in identifying general trends from the results, especially in case of social sciences.
- It reduces the troubles and ethical concerns that are associated with the preselection and random assignment of test subjects.
- Matching procedures can be used to create a reasonable control group, making generalization more achievable.
- The results generated are used to reinforce the findings of case studies by conducting research that may offer itself to statistical analysis.

Disadvantages of Quasi-experimental Research Design

- It provides comparatively weaker evidence of effect of an intervention.
- Because of absence of random assignments into test groups, nonequivalent test groups are formed and this can further limit the generalizability of the results to a larger population.
- Moreover, the lack of randomization reduces internal validity and conclusions about causality in quasi-experimental designs.

TABLE 12.2: Pretest post-test control group design

Group	Pretest	Treatment	8th week post-test
RE	1	X	2
RC	3	—	4

Abbreviations: R, randomization; RC, control group; RE, experimental group; X, treatment; O, observation

- Due to the lack of randomization and the threats to internal validity, statistical analyzes may not be meaningful.
- Unexpected factors might affect the results. Pre-existing factors and other influences are not taken into account as the variables are less controlled in quasi-experimental research.
- Human error also plays a key role in the validity.

True-experimental research designs

These are the research designs where researcher has control over the extraneous variables and can predict confidently that the observed effect on the dependable variable is only due to the manipulation of the independent variable. They can be further divided as:

- **One group pretest post-test design:** It involves one group that is pretested (x) and then post-tested (y). It controls the threats to validity but several other factors which may also cause relevant effects are not controlled. Further these are as follows:
  - **Pretest post-test control group design (Table 12.2).**
    - ◆ It involves at least two groups which are formed by random assignments.
    - ◆ Both groups have a pretest of the independent variables.
    - ◆ One group receives a new or unusual treatment and both groups are post-tested.
  - **Post-test only control group design (Fig. 12.6).**
  - It is also called after only control group research design.
  - It is similar to the pretest control group design except that there is no pretest.
  - The subjects are randomly assigned to the groups and exposed to the independent variables.
  - Neither of the groups is pretested or premeasures.
  - The post-test is carried out on them.
- **Solomon four-group design (Fig. 12.7).**
  - It was first proposed by Solomon in 1949.
  - It is identical to the pretest post-test control group design having two groups with addition of two more groups.
  - Main advantage of additional two groups is that validity is increased.
  - It involves random assignment of subjects to one of the four groups.
  - Two groups are pretested and the other two are not.
  - One group of the pre0tested groups and one of the unpretested groups receives the experimental treatment.

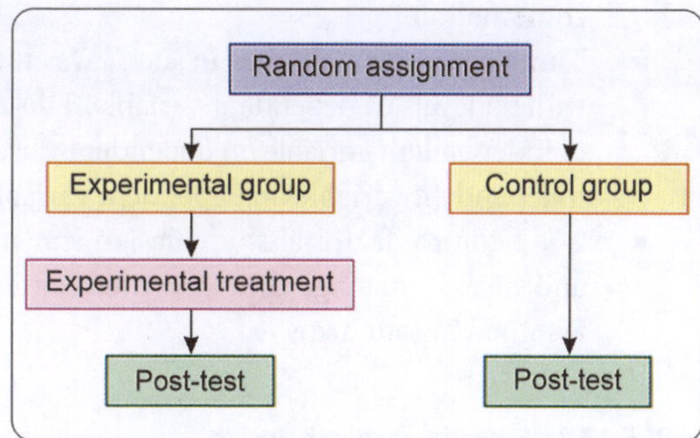

Figure 12.6: Post-test only control group design

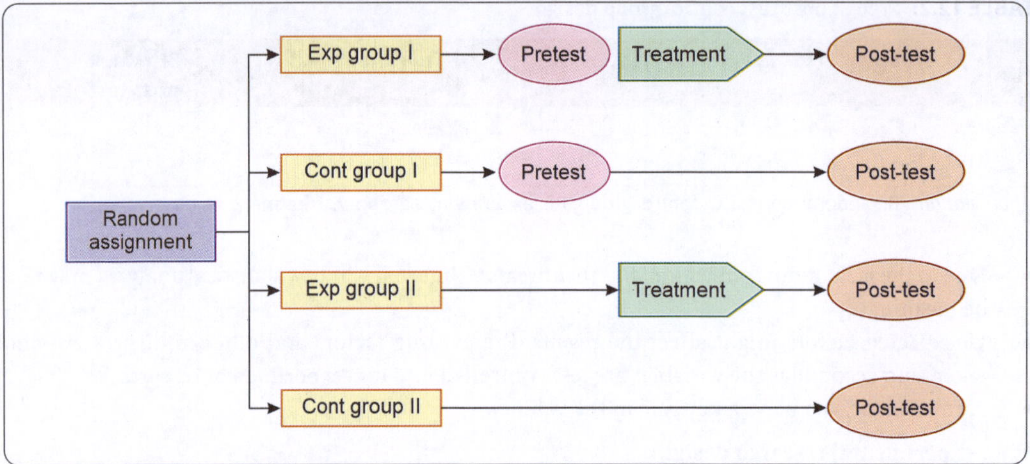

Figure 12.7: Solomon four-group research design

Abbreviations: Cont group, control group; Exp group, experimental group

- **Factorial research design (Table 12.3):**
  - The researcher manipulates two or more independent variables simultaneously to observe their effects on the dependent variables.
  - This is useful when more than two independent variables called factors are to be tested. For instance, a researcher wants to observe the effect of two different protocols of mouth care on prevention of VAP when performed at different frequencies in a day.
  - This design facilitates testing of several hypothesis at a single time.
  - A typical factorial design incorporates 2×2 or 3×3 factorial, although it can be in any combination.
  - The experiment is planned in such a way that all levels of independent variables are combined with all levels of dependent variable. This enables the researcher to observe the direct effect of independent variable on dependent variable. The interactive effects of the various levels of independent variable on dependent variable are also observed.
  - 2×2 control factorial study design shown here is on malaria in relation to vector control and disease management and interventions. The population of six villages is randomly assigned in four arms.

TABLE 12.3: Factorial research design

		Disease Management Intervention	
		No early detection and treatment	**Early detection and treatment**
Vector control intervention	**No larviciding**		
	Larviciding	**Arm 1** (6 villages, ~240 households total)	**Arm 2** (6 villages, ~240 households total)
		Arm 3 (6 villages, ~240 households total)	**Arm 4** (6 villages, ~240 households total)

- First arm has control/no intervention.
- Second arm has early detection and treatment.
- Third arm has larviciding intervention (vector control).
- Fourth arm has both early detection and treatment and larviciding interventions.

- **Cross over design (Fig. 12.8):** These designs are a mixture of within and between group designs. To understand this design let's take an example.

Example 1: Recruit a cohort (group) of epilepsy patients, who have been followed-up for a baseline period of approximately 8 weeks before randomization. Participants are randomized in 1:1 ratio to active drug or placebo, over a period of 2–6 weeks. It is followed by an evaluation period generally of 8–12 weeks. After this, initial treatment is tapered off. After a period of around 2–4 weeks (washout), the patients are switched on to the alternative treatment (active drug or placebo). Again, after second evaluation period, the participants are either withdrawn from the study or given another opportunity to enter a long-term extension phase.

Advantages:

- Each subject acts as his/her own control.
- A smaller number of patients are required as compared to parallel-group studies.

Disadvantages:

- The cross-over studies are generally of longer duration as compared to parallel-group studies.
- There may be difficulty in incorporating multiple dosages in groups and there may be drop-outs.
- The patients who have completed first evaluation phase do not contribute much to the analysis.
- There is also possibility of unblinding as the information of drug and placebo may be leaked.
- Moreover, the drugs with carry-over effects may also hinder the results due to long elimination half-lives.

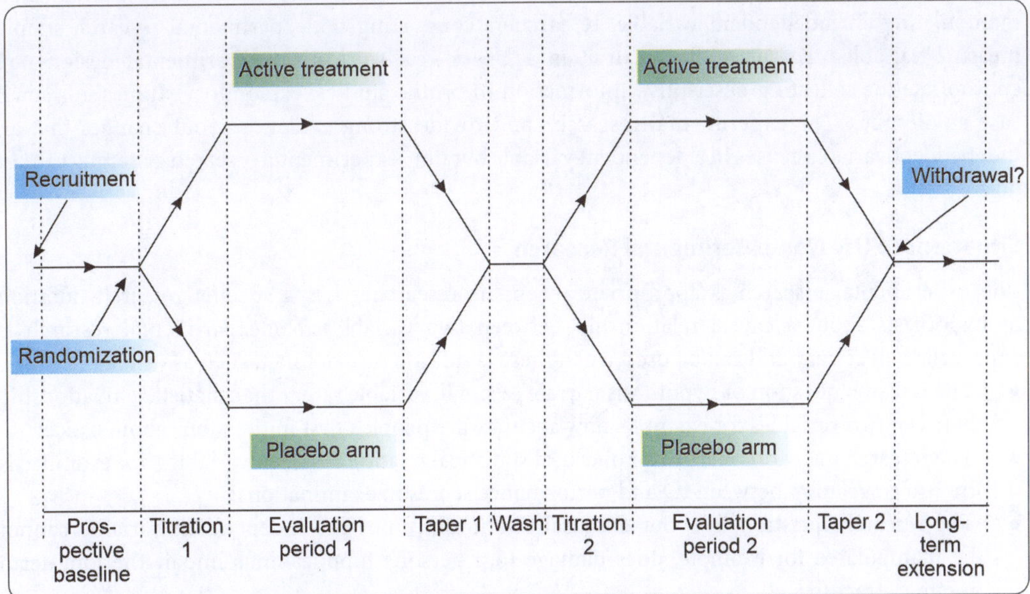

Figure 12.8: Cross over design

Advantages of true-experimental research designs

It is very basic, straightforward, efficient type of research that can be applied in wide variety of disciplines:

- Experimental research designs are repeatable therefore results can be checked as well as verified.
- Due to the controlled environment of experimental research, generally bet-ter results are achieved.
- Artificial situations not found in natural setting can be created that allows for greater control of extraneous variables.
- Conditions that may take longer time to occur in a natural environment may occur more quickly in an experimental setting.
- The manipulation of variables allows a researcher to be able to look at different cause-and-effect relationships.
- It can be combined with other research methods. It further allows experimental research to be able to provide the scientific precision that may be required for the results to be authentic.

Disadvantages of true-experimental research designs

Human error plays a key role in the validity of the project. Any error, whether it is systemic or random, can result in distorting the information about the other variables and it would eliminate the validity of the experiment and research under study.

- This process is lengthy most of the times and requires a large amount of financial and personnel resources.
- It may not be possible to control all extraneous variables.
- The health, mood and life experiences of the subjects may influence their reactions and such variables may not even be known to a researcher.

Nonexperimental Research Designs

Nonexperimental research lacks the manipulation of an independent variable. Rather than manipulating an independent variable, researchers conducting nonexperimental research simply measure variables that naturally occur it in a lab or real world. Nonexperimental designs are appropriate for collecting descriptive information in profile studies, exploratory studies, for small case studies, etc. The experimental research can provide strong evidence about changes that an independent variable causes in a dependent variable but non-experimental research generally cannot do so.

Situations to Use Nonexperimental Research

The experimental research is appropriate when the researcher has a specific research question or hypothesis about a causal relationship between two variables. Nonexperimental research is appropriate, necessary and can be used when these conditions are not met, such as when:

- The research question or hypothesis narrates a single variable rather than statistical relationship between two variables for example, how accurate are people's first impressions about cancer?
- The research question refers to a noncausal statistical relation between variables, for example, is there a correlation between IQ and performance scores in examinations?
- The research question is about a causal relationship, but the independent variable cannot be manipulated for example, does damage to a person's hippocampus impair the long-term memory traces?
- The research question is broad and exploratory and is about what it is like to have a particular experience, for example, what is it like to be a working mother diagnosed with depression?

Practical Tips

Selection of design

Choice between the experimental and nonexperimental approaches is generally made by the nature of the research question. As we know that the three goals of science are to describe, to predict, and to explain. If the goal is to explain a situation and the research question needs to establish causal relationships, then the experimental approach is typically preferred.

If the goal is to describe or to predict—a nonexperimental approach will suffice. The two approaches can also be used simultaneously to address the same research question in complementary ways. For example, after completing original research about obedience, a researcher conducts experiments to explore the factors that affect obedience. Here, several independent variables can be manipulated, like the distance between the experimenter and the participant, the participant and the confederate, and the location of the study, etc.

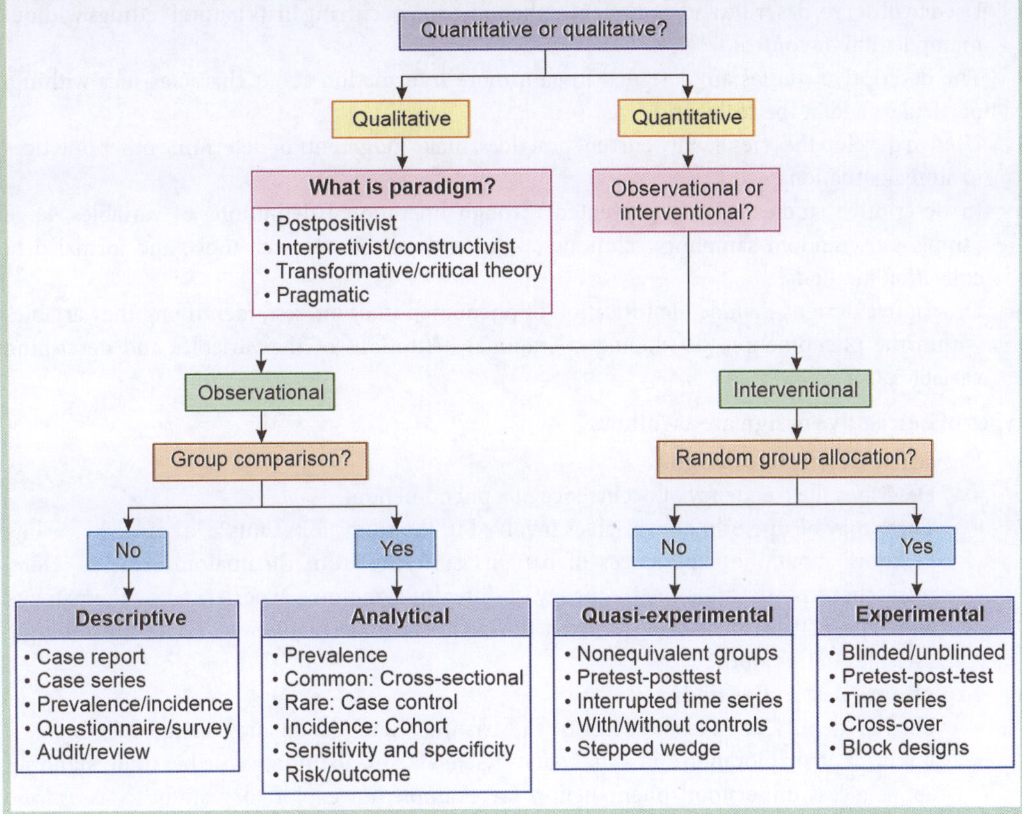

Types of Nonexperimental Research Designs

- **Descriptive research designs**
  - Univariate descriptive designs
  - Exploratory descriptive designs
  - Comparative descriptive designs
- **Correlational research designs**
  - Prospective design
  - Retrospective design

- **Developmental research design**
  - Cross-sectional design
  - Longitudinal design
- **Epidemiological research design**
  - Case control studies
  - Cohort studies

Descriptive Research Designs

The purpose of descriptive studies is to observe, describe and document aspects of a situation as it naturally occurs and sometimes to serve as a starting point for hypothesis generation or development of theory.

Main features are as follows:

- Used to observe, describe and document a phenomenon occurring in its natural settings without manipulation or control.
- The descriptive studies are designed to gain more information about characteristics within a particular field in the real world.
- Used to develop theories, justify current practices, make judgments or determine other practices in similar situations.
- In descriptive studies, bias is prevented through operational definitions of variables, large sample size, random sampling techniques, valid and reliable research tools, and formal data collection methods.
- Descriptive designs include identification of phenomenon of interest, identifying the variables within the phenomenon, developing operational definitions of the variables and describing variables.

Types of descriptive design are as follows:

- **Univariate descriptive designs:**
  - Describes the frequency of occurrence of a phenomenon.
  - There may be one or more variables involved in the study, for example, a researcher wants to know about the experiences of patients suffering from rheumatoid arthritis. Here, researcher may describe the frequency of different symptoms experienced by the patients and type of treatment they received during the course of disease. There are multiple variables in this study.
- **Exploratory descriptive designs:**
  - Used to identify, explore and describe the existing phenomenon and its related factors.
  - It is in-depth exploration and a study of its related factors to improve further understanding about a less-understood phenomenon for example, an exploratory study to assess the incidences of fall among elderly and home safety measures in a city.
- **Comparative descriptive designs:**
  - It involves comparing and contrasting two or more samples on study subjects, often at a single point of time (on one or more variables).
  - Used to compare two distinct groups based on selected attributes like physical or psychological symptoms, knowledge level, etc. For example, a comparative study on health problems among rural and urban towns in Himachal.

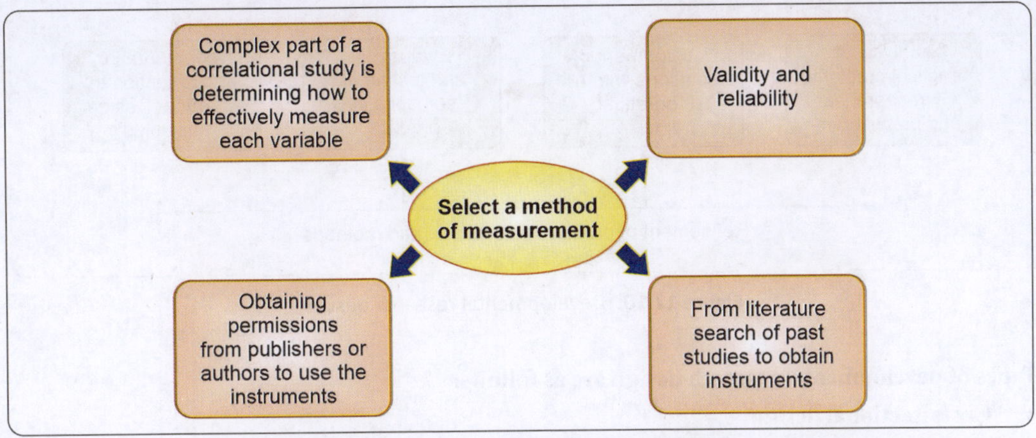

Figure 12.9: Correlational research design

Correlational Research Design

In this design (Fig. 12.9), researcher examines the relationship between two or more variables in a natural setting without manipulation or control. There is no intervention. For example, a study on effects of smoking on lung cancer.

Main features are as follows:

- Researcher examines the strength of relationship between variables by observing how a change in one variable can affect the other.
- Effect of independent variable is observed without manipulating dependent variable.

Types of correlational research design are as follows:

- **Prospective design:**
  - Researcher relates the present to the future.
  - Starts with presumption of cause and then goes to presumed effects.
  - Often longitudinal but may be cross-sectional. For example, in a study on effect of maternal infection during pregnancy—effects on fetal development and pregnancy outcome, the data are collected from pregnant women regarding history of infection during pregnancies. Then fetal development and pregnancy outcomes are observed. Analyze the relationship of maternal infection during pregnancies and fetal development and pregnancy outcome.

- **Retrospective design:**
  - A design in which researcher studies the current phenomenon by seeking information from past.
  - Researcher links the present phenomenon with past events (backward approach). For example, a retrospective correlational study on substance abuse related high-risk factors among traumatic head injury patients admitted in neurosurgery ICU in X hospital.
  - The researcher here first approached head injury patients and then tried to identify the number of head injuries that occurred under the influence of substance abuse.

Developmental Research Design

It examines the phenomenon with reference to time (Fig. 12.10). Generally used as adjunct with other research designs like cross-sectional descriptive or longitudinal correlational research designs.

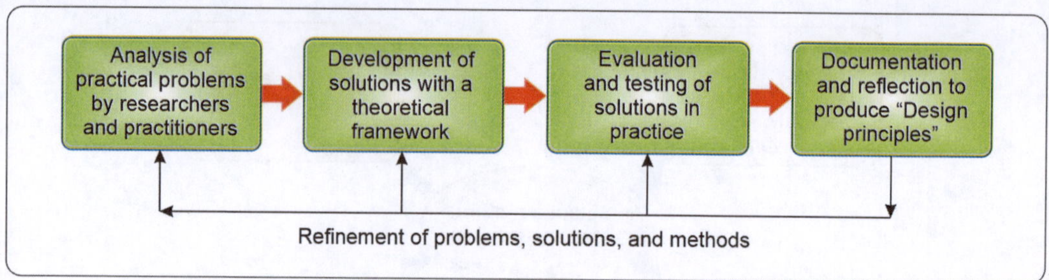

Figure 12.10: Developmental research design

Types of developmental research design are as follows:

- **Cross-sectional design:**
  - Researcher collects data at a particular point of time (period of data collection).
  - Easier and more convenient to carry out.
  - For example, a researcher is interested in assessing the awareness on AIDS among people of an area. The researcher will interact only once to collect awareness- related data from respondents.
- **Longitudinal designs:**
  - Used to collect data over an extended period of time (long period of time).
  - It evaluates the change in chosen period of time.
  - For example, a researcher studies the perception of nursing students toward the nursing profession from start till the end. Here longitudinal studies will be appropriate by using: trend studies; panel studies and follow-up studies.
    - **Trend studies** help to investigate a sample from general population over a time with respect to another phenomenon. These permit a researcher to study patterns and rate of change. It makes the researcher to make predictions based on identified patterns and rate of change.
    - **Panel studies** involve same people and over a period of time they become more informative on the phenomenon than subjects involved in trend studies. Here, the researcher can find out the reason of change also. The same people are contacted for two or more times to collect data.
    - **Follow-up studies** are undertaken to know the subsequent states of subjects with a specific condition or those who have received a specific intervention.

Epidemiological Research Design

Epidemiology is study that investigates the distribution and causes of the diseases in a population. The study is conducted to investigate causes of different diseases in either prospective (cohort) or retrospective (case-control) studies **(Fig. 12.11)**.

Types of epidemiological research design are as follows:

- **Cohort studies**

  A longitudinal approach is used to investigate the occurrence of a disease in existing presumed causes. For example, a researcher longitudinally observes the smokers for development of lung cancer.

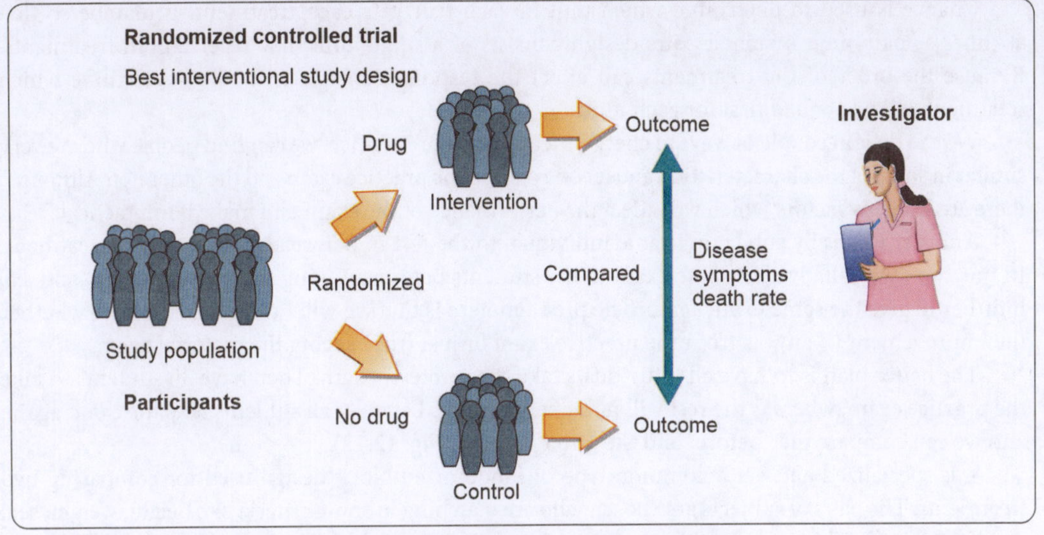

Figure 12.11: Epidemiological design

- **Case-control studies**

  The causes of disease are investigated after its occurrence. For example, a researcher investigates the history of smoking in patients with lung cancer.

Advantages of epidemiological design
- Tends to be closest to real life situation.
- Most suitable for nursing and medical research.
- Characteristics which can not be subjected to experimental manipulations are studied here like blood pressure, blood type, etc.
- Manipulating variables is forbidden on ethical grounds.

Disadvantages epidemiological design
- The results obtained and relationships between dependent and independent variables are never error free.
- As comparative studies are conducted using nonrandomized selected groups, which are not homogeneous. This tends to be dissimilar in different traits or characteristics which may affect the authenticity of study results.

MATCHED-PAIRS DESIGN

A matched-pairs design is a special case of a randomized block design. It is common type of randomized block design for comparing two treatments. When the experimental units are paired up and each of the pair is assigned to a different treatment, it is known as a matched-pair design. It can be used when:
- The experiment has only two treatment conditions.
- The subjects can be grouped into pairs, based on some blocking variable.

Further within each pair the subjects are randomly assigned to subject them to different treatments. The idea is to create blocks by matching pairs of similar experimental units.

Chance is used to determine which unit in each pair gets each treatment. It may be so that at times a "pair" in a matched-pairs design consists of a single unit may receive both treatments. Because the order of the treatments can affect the response, chance is used to determine which treatment will be applied first for each unit.

We can do it in couple of ways to check its feasibility. For instance, we can find people who are very similar in some of the characteristics, and let one pair do the practice exam and the other not. Although, there are so many factors which will affect the performance of the exam and make it impractical.

Another way is by subjecting same individual to the test in before and after type of treatment. In this case, we will give the same exam to the students before studying the practice exam, and ask him/her to give the same exam again. The problem here is that we will not be able to know whether the improvement (if any) is from the practice exam or just from seeing the material again.

The better plan is to have all individuals take the "pretest" exam. Then have 30 students to take the practice exam, whereas the rest will not take the exam. Later, let all students take the exam again, and we can compare the "before" and the "after" results (Fig. 12.12).

It is specialized and yet a common type of randomized block design used for comparing two treatments. The pairs of subjects are chosen who are matching in some criteria like height, weight, sex, age or income. Within each pair the treatment is randomly assigned. The purpose of this design is to compare the responses in more efficient way. Again, we can say that a matched-pairs design is when we have different participants in two different conditions, but we match them according to certain variables, such as age, personality, gender, IQ, etc. For example, in the Table 12.4 we have taken pairs of participants in age group 24, both are males and subjected each to experimental or control conditions. Second pair is taken from age group 46 and so on to ensure that both groups are pretty similar.

The control group is the group that is not subjected to the experimental condition. For example, if we are testing to see if vitamin tablets help to recall in exams, the experimental group would be given a vitamin tablet; the control group might be given a sweet tablet or placebo, but would be told that it was a vitamin tablet. This allows the researcher to compare the two groups.

This method can be used when an experiment has only two treatment conditions; and the subjects can be grouped in the form of pairs, based on some characteristic variable. Further, within each pair, the subjects are randomly assigned to different treatments.

Take another example of a medical experiment, in which 1000 subjects have been taken and grouped into 500 matched pairs. Each pair is matched on the basis of gender and age. For example, Pair 1 includes two women, both having age 21. Pair 2 includes two men, both age 21. Pair 3 might

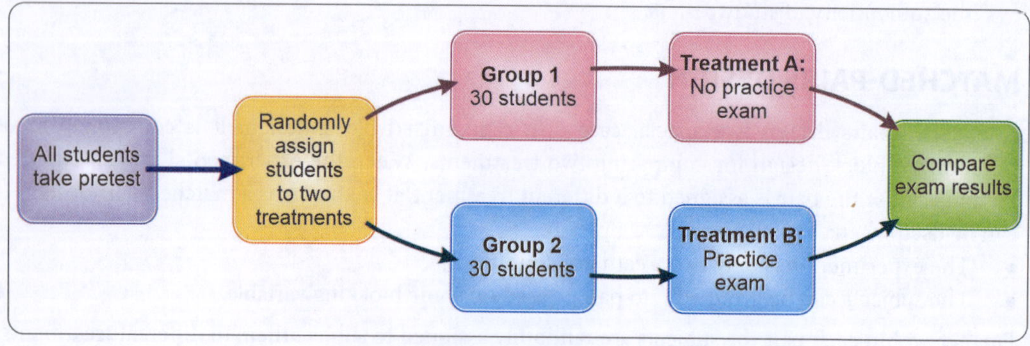

Figure 12.12: Matched-pairs design

TABLE 12.4: Matched-pairs design

Experimental condition	Control condition
Participant 1 – Age 24, Male	Participant 2 – Age 24, Male
Participant 3 – Age 46, Male	Participant 4 – Age 46, Male

TABLE 12.5: Matched-pairs design—vaccine versus placebo

Pair	Treatment	
	Placebo	Vaccine
1	1	1
2	1	1
...	...	...
499	1	1
500	1	1

be two women, both age 22; and so on. Each one receives one of the two treatments, either a placebo or a vaccine. The Table 12.5 shows a matched-pairs design.

We can see that the matched pairs design is an improvement over completely randomized design. Like the completely randomized design, the matched pairs design uses randomization to control for confounding.

Advantages of Matched-Pairs Design

- Reduces participant variables because the researcher has tried to pair up the participants so that each condition has people with similar abilities and characteristics.
- Avoids order effects, so counterbalancing is not necessary. There are no order effects as there may be repeated measures, since there are different people in both groups.

Disadvantages of Matched-Pairs Design

- It is quite time consuming and difficult to find closely matched pairs. Generally, it is impossible to match people exactly, unless they are identical twins.
- We need twice as many participants as a repeated measures design.
- If one participant drops out in a pair, we lose two persons' data.

Practical Tips

Order Effects

It refers to differences in responses of research participants' which result from the order (e.g., first, second, third) in which the experimental materials are made accessible to them.

Order effects can occur in any kind of research. In a survey, people may answer questions differently depending on the order in which the questions are asked. Order effects are important in 'within-subject' designs that is, when the same participants are included in all conditions and the researcher wants to compare responses between conditions. The order in which the conditions are presented to participants may affect the outcome of the study.

Contd...

Types of Order Effects
- **Practice effects** occur when participants improve their performance over time. For example, participants usually respond faster as a result of prepractice of the task.
- **Fatigue effects** are more likely when the procedure is lengthy and the task is repetitive or uninteresting. For example, the participants may also perform differently at the end of an experiment or survey because they are bored or tired.
- **Carryover effects** occur when the effect of an experimental condition is carried over which might influence performance in a successive condition. This effect is more likely to occur when the experimental conditions follow each other quickly.
- **Interference effects** occur when previous responses interfere the performance of a subsequent task. It happens more often when the second task quickly follows the first and the response required in the second task clashes with the response required in the first task.

Ways to Control Order Effects
The choice of method depends on the type of effect that is expected to be controlled.
- Practice effects can be reduced by providing a warm-up exercise before starting an experiment.
- Fatigue effects can be reduced by making the task more interesting and making the procedures short.
- Carryover and interference effects can be reduced by increasing the time between different conditions.
- **Counterbalancing:** Order effects can also be reduced by systematically varying the order of conditions so that each condition is present equally in each ordinal position. This procedure is known as counterbalancing. For example, with two conditions, half of the participants will receive treatment A first followed by condition B; the other half will receive treatment B first followed by condition A. Counterbalancing is a technique that is used to deal with order effects while using a repeated measures design. With the help of counterbalancing, the participant sample is divided in two halves. One half completes the two conditions in one order and the other half completes the conditions in the reverse order.

COMPLETELY RANDOMIZED DESIGN

When each experimental unit is assigned to a treatment completely at random, it is known as completely randomized design. In a way, it is similar to simple random sampling.

For example, we select 60 students randomly and further split them into two groups with 30 each, randomly. One group does not take the practice exam, whereas the other does. Then we compare results (Fig. 12.13).

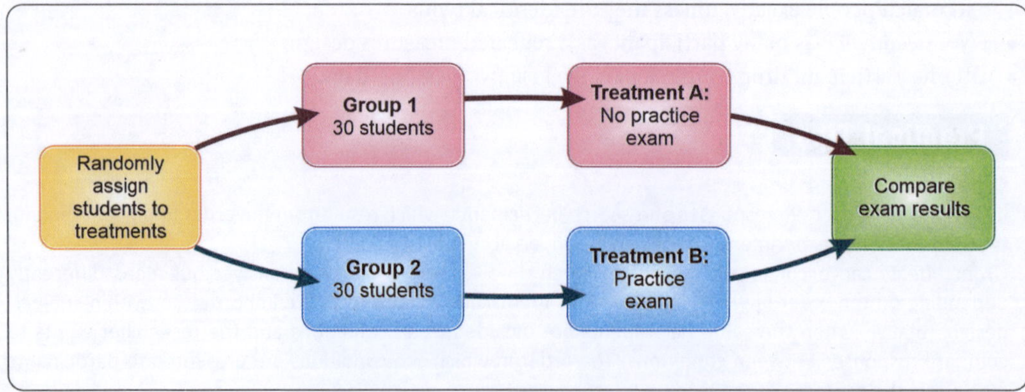

Figure 12.13: Completely randomized design

Must Know

Lurking Variable

A lurking variable is a variable which is not included as an explanatory or response variable in the analysis but it can affect the interpretation of relationships between variables. A lurking variable can identify a strong relationship between variables on false basis or it can hide the true relationship. Statistically, the error term explains lurking variables which affects the process. To discover lurking variables, one has to take time to understand him/her data. The varying characteristics of the experimental units can also behave as lurking variables. Lurking variables can distort the process. To find out lurking variable one can create a plot of the data and by looking at the nonlinear trends one can identify the presence of lurking variables. A bad design of experiment can also distort the results due to the lurking variables.

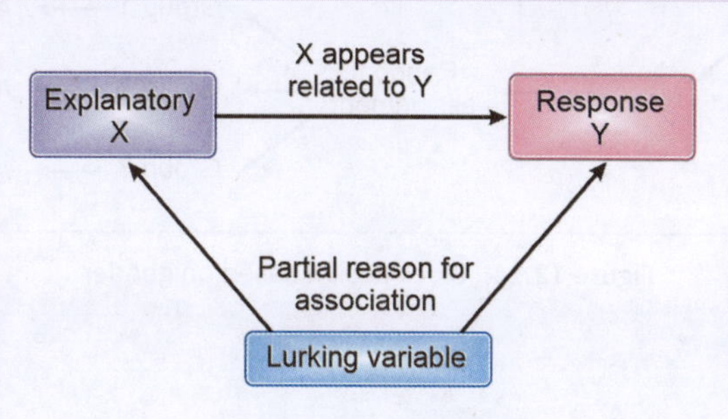

Effect of Lurking variables

Because variability in the experimental units is generally unavoidable, the effect of lurking variables on the response cannot be prevented. Although, it is possible in an experiment, to allocate treatments to the experimental units in such a way which either eliminates, or at least reduces, the relationship between the treatment X, and characteristics of the experimental units.

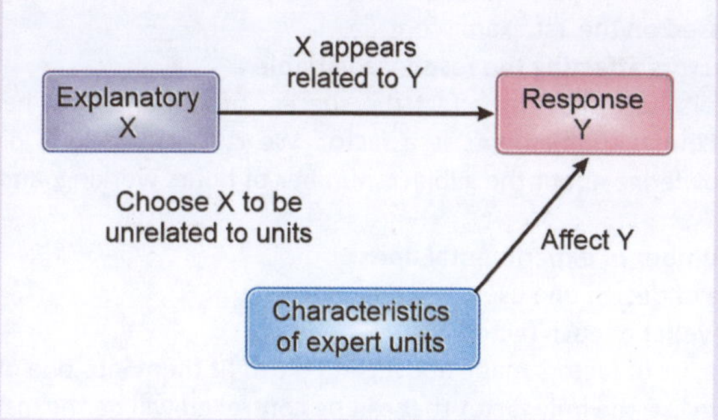

Avoiding lurking variable

Good experimental design can avoid the potential effect of lurking variables.

BLOCK DESIGN

In a block or stratified design, subjects are divided into groups or blocks before starting an experiment to test a hypothesis about differences between groups (**Fig. 12.14**).

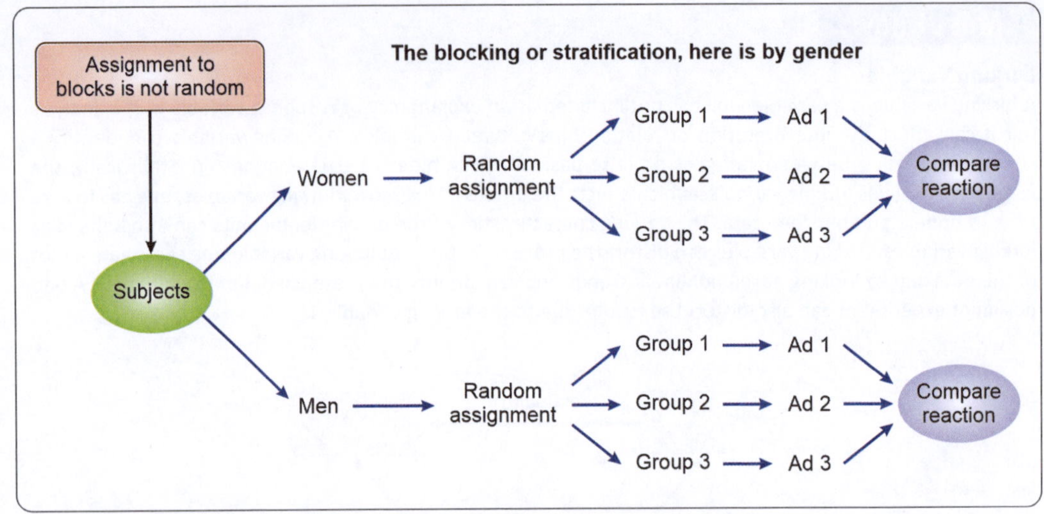

Figure 12.14: Block design based on gender

Practical Tips

Let's find out how a research design is selected with the help of an example.

Example: Determine the effect of using the course supplements on scores of students' exam.

Solution. In a survey on this problem, we may not really understand whether the practice exams are making a difference on scores or not. For this, we must have a design process.

Step 1: Identify the problem to be studied.

Here, we want to study the effectiveness of course supplements on success of students. For the purpose of this study, we will specify our population as all 120 students in a class, in college X. In addition, we will characterize "success" based on the 1st exam score.

Step 2: Determine the factors affecting the response variable.

There are plenty of factors here that can affect the success of students, but here we are listing a few. Apparently, the use of course supplements is a factor. We can also include diet, study habits, sleep, intelligence, previous knowledge about the subject, number of hours working, and the instructor. One can add more factors to it.

Step 3: Determine the number of experimental units.

This depends on the type of design one uses.

Step 4: Determine the level(s) of each factor.

Now, we will consider the list of factors made above, and try to fit them into one of the groups.

1. **Control:** Looking at the list, the only factor that can be controlled will be the instructor. Therefore, make sure that all the students involved have same instructor.

2. **Manipulate:** This is the treatment that is supplements (Video Lecture Series) used. We can have two levels here—Students studying without the video and students using the Video Lecture Series.

3. **Randomize:** This is everything else—intelligence, previous knowledge, study habits, sleep, diet, and number of hours working.

RANDOMIZED BLOCK DESIGN

When the experimental units are divided into homogeneous groups called blocks and are subjected to treatments, it is known as randomized block design. It is similar to stratified sampling. A block is a group of experimental units which are similar in some way and are expected to affect the response to the treatments. We can say that they are homogeneous. In a randomized block design, treatments of the experimental units are carried out separately but randomly.

By taking the same example as in Figure 12.15, student maturity is a huge factor in success in examinations. We can split our sample based on academic year—those in their first year versus those in their second. Then randomly split the groups into two groups. Give treatment A to one group and treatment B to another one. Here, we have stratified the sample, and then a completely randomized design is applied on each of the "strata". The blocks are formed based on some most important and unavoidable sources of variability (known as lurking variables) among the experimental units. The randomization process will average out the effects of the remaining lurking variables and permits an unbiased comparison of the treatments.

The principle followed here is:

Control what you can **block** on what you cannot control **randomize** to create comparable groups.

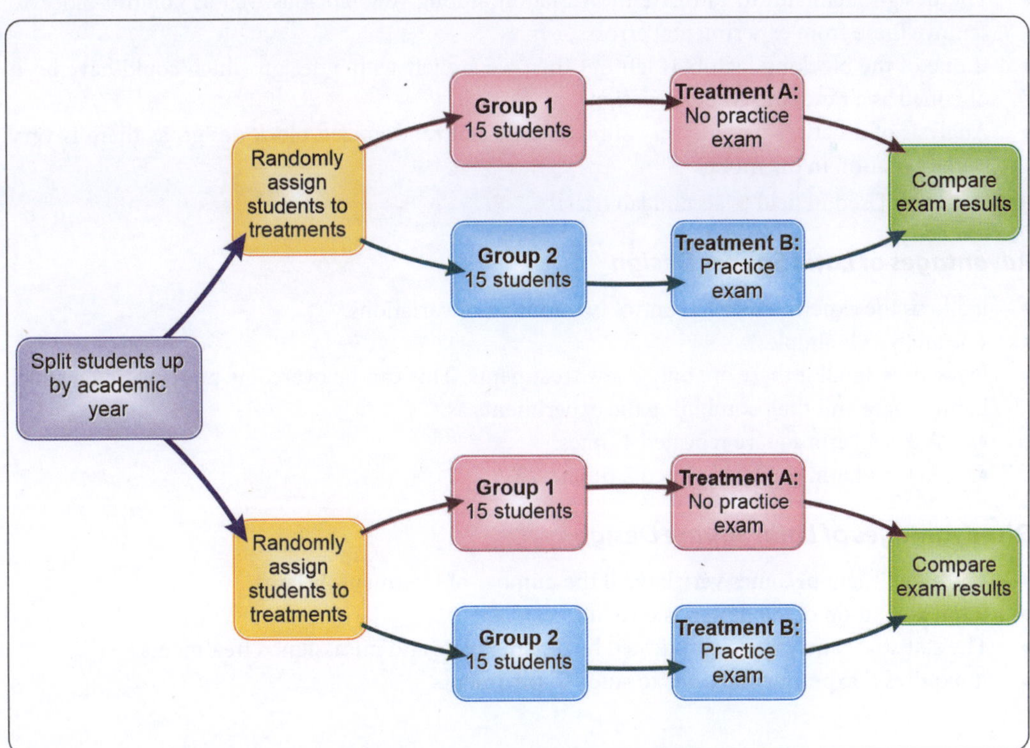

Figure 12.15: Randomized block design

LATIN SQUARE DESIGN

A Latin Square design is an arrangement of 't' treatments in which each one is repeated 't' times, in a way that each treatment appears exactly one time in each row and each column in the design. Roman characters are used to denote the treatments. This kind of design is used to reduce systematic error due to rows (treatments) and columns. Latin square design has three main factors as rows, columns and treatments. It is assumed that there is no interaction between rows, columns and treatments. The degrees of freedom for the interactions is used to estimate error. The example is—A veterinary researcher wants to study weight gain in piglets but knows that both—initial weights and race of animal significantly affect the response.

In random block design, whole experimental area is divided into homogeneous blocks and randomization is kept restricted within the block but in Latin square design the experimental rows and columns are equal and each treatment occurs only once in a row and a column.

Main features are as follows:

- It is a classical experimental design which allows two sources of blocking. It is also known as row-blocking and column-blocking.
- It has capacity to simultaneously handle two known sources among experimental units.
- It is accompanied by ensuring that every treatment occurs only once in each row-block and only once in each column-block.
- It can be constructed for any number of treatments but the cost increases. If there are more 't' treatments then 't^n' experimental units will be required.
- The design facilitates to estimate the variation among row-block as well as column-block to remove these from experimental errors.
- If one of the blocking factors is left out then we are left with a design which could have been obtained as a randomized block design.
- Analysis of a Latin square is very similar to that of randomized block design as there is very slight variation in the model.

Applications: Used in field trials and lab trials.

Advantages of Latin Square Design

- It allows the experimenter to control two sources of variations.
- The analysis is simple. .
- Error df is small if there are only a few treatments. This can be overcome by repeating a small Latin square and then combining the experiments as:
  - A 3 × 3 Latin square repeated 4 times.
  - A 4 × 4 Latin square repeated 2 times.

Disadvantages of Latin Square Design

- The experiment becomes very large if the number of treatments is large.
- Implementation of the design is difficult.
- The statistical analysis is complicated by missing plots and misassigned treatments.
- It requires t^2 experimental units to study 't' treatments.

STUDENT ASSIGNMENT

LONG ANSWER QUESTIONS

1. Define experimental research design. What are the characteristics of experimental research?
2. What are the threats to validity? How can you control them?
3. Discuss randomized block design.

SHORT ANSWER QUESTIONS

1. Write a short note on Latin Square design.
2. Write a short note on Solomon design.
3. Write a short note on Quasi-experimental research design.

MULTIPLE CHOICE QUESTIONS

1. **Which of the following is not a type of purposive sampling?**
   a. Probability sampling
   b. Deviant case sampling
   c. Theoretical sampling
   d. Snowball sampling

2. **The minimum sample size for qualitative interviewing is:**
   a. 30
   b. 31
   c. 60
   d. It is hard to say

3. **What is a research design?**
   a. A way of conducting research that is not grounded in theory
   b. The choice between using qualitative or quantitative methods
   c. The style in which you present your research findings, e.g., a graph
   d. A framework for every stage of the collection and analysis of data

4. **Facts, figures and other relevant materials serving as bases for a study is called:**
   a. Sample
   b. Method
   c. Data
   d. Theory

5. **"A systematic step-by-step Procedure following logical process of reasoning" called:**
   a. Experiment
   b. Observation
   c. Deduction
   d. Scientific method

ANSWER KEY

1. a   **2.** d   **3.** d   **4.** c   **5.** d

Note

Unit **VII**

Significance of Statistics and Testing Hypothesis

13

Testing Hypothesis

"If your experiment needs a statistician, you need a better experiment."
—Ernest Rutherford

INTRODUCTION

Statistically significant is a phrase packed with both meaning, and syllables. It represents the results of a rational exercise with numbers at the same time it has a way of arousing emotions like confusion, bewilderment, hatred, and even arrogance. Let's understand its most important concepts now.

STATISTICALLY SIGNIFICANT

Principally, a statistically significant result (generally a difference) is a result which is not credited to chance. Technically, it means that if the null hypothesis is true (which means that there is no difference), there is a low probability of getting a good result. Two factors specify the phrase 'statistically significant':

1. **Sampling error:** There is always a possibility that the differences observed while measuring a sample of users is just the result of random selection, chance fluctuations and coincidence.
2. **Probability:** It means never certainty. Statistics is about probability. There is never a 100% certainty. It manages risk.
   - If we want to be sure of certainty of our result then what is the probability that it may have 10% likelihood that decision is wrong.
   - The answer also depends on situation that is what is the cost of increasing the probability of making the right choice; and what will be the consequences (or potential consequences) of making the wrong choice?

Mostly a probability of 5% is said to be okay, which means to be wrong (by randomness) 1 time out of 20. It is a reasonably high standard. Although it could expose a researcher to far more risk than he/she can afford.

Detect Statistical Significance

To detect statistical significance, the choice of test depends on our data type and on the fact whether we are comparing within subjects (the same users) or between subjects (different users). It depends on type of data we have.

- The primary need is to know whether the data is binary or not.
  - **Binary** (yes/no, pass/fail) and coded as 1 or 0.
  - **Continuous:** If the data is not coded as 1's or 0's then we treat it as continuous or metric.

After establishing whether data is binary or continuous, start with the appropriate decision map. It will help you to decide the statistical test to be done.

Data Decision Map to Find Type of Data

Shown in Figures 13.1A and B.

Here examples have been given to make you understand the working of decision maps.

Example: A rating scale question in a survey was presented that went from strongly disagree to strongly agree and was coded from 1 to 5 for each level of agreement. The average score was a 3.9 (SD was 1.2) from 36 people. Which test would you use to find out how much that sample mean would fluctuate?

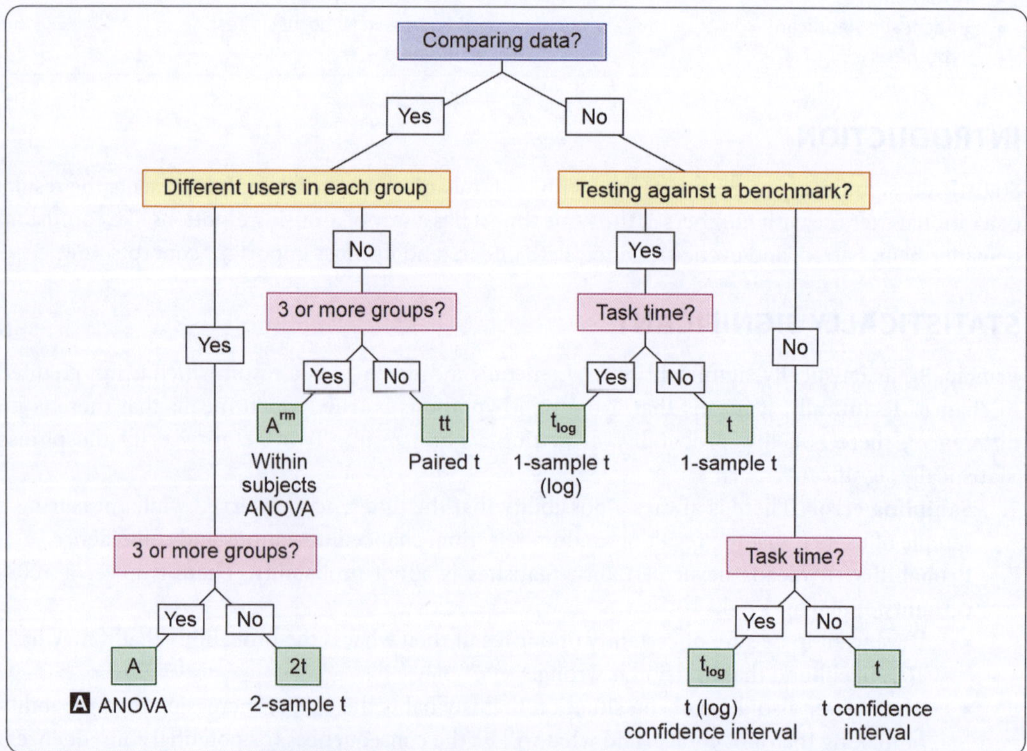

Figure 13.1A: Data decision map: **A.** Continuous

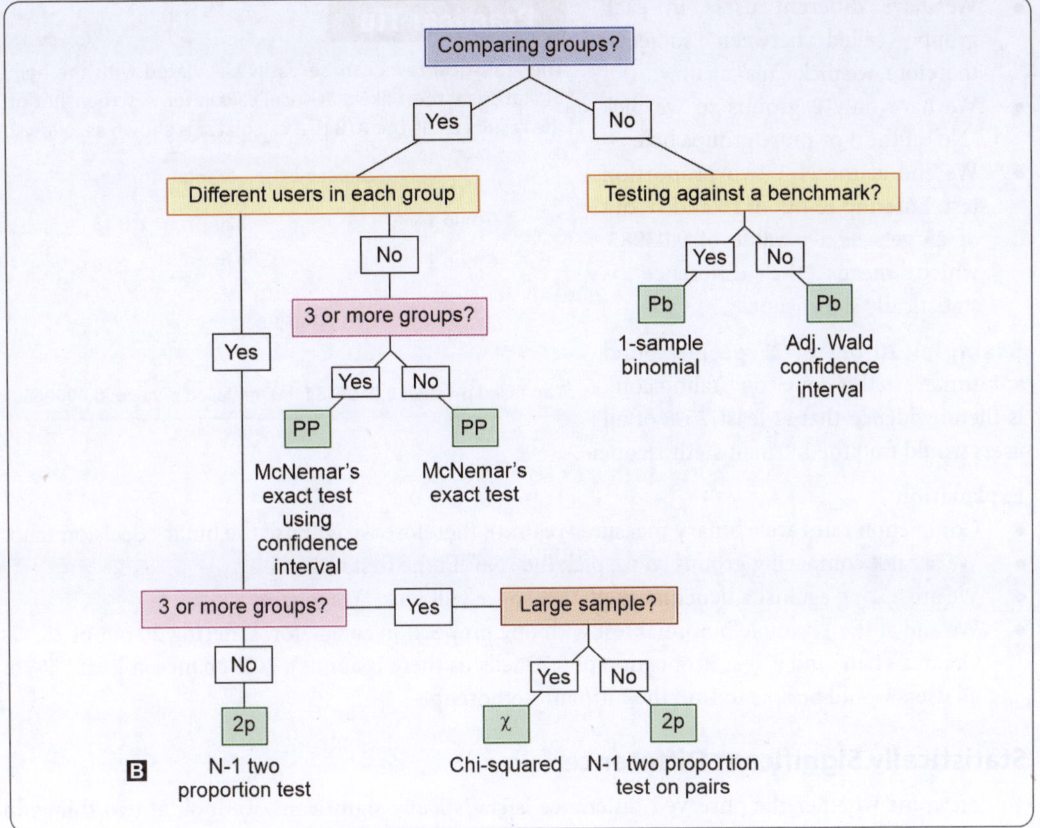

Figure 13.1B: Data decision map: **B. Binary**

Explanation (Figure 13.1A):
- It is not a binary measure, therefore we have to use the continuous decision map.
- We are not comparing data; we only want to know how precise our estimate is therefore we pick "No" in the first branch.
- We do not have a benchmark and we are going to test such as testing whether the average exceeds 3.5 therefore, we again pick "No".
- The data is not task time so we pick "No" and end up at the 't confidence' interval line. Entering in the mean, standard deviation and sample size as summary data gets us a 95% confidence interval.

Example: You had two different groups of users who attempted to locate the nearest location of cardio care hospital. In one group 14 out of 14 users found the correct location on website. In another group, 18 out of 25 found the correct location on another website. Is there a statistically significant difference between these websites?

Explanation (Figure 13.1B):
- Completion rates are a binary measure (pass/fail) so we will use the binary decision map.
- We are comparing groups and we want to know if users on different websites will have different completion rates when searching a location, therefore we pick the "Yes" in the first branch.

- We have different users in each group (called between subjects) therefore, we pick "Yes" again.
- We have only 2 groups so we pick "No" at the 3 or more groups box.
- We end at the N-1 two proportion test. Entering 13 out of 13 and 18 out of 25 gets us a p-value of 0.03985, which means the difference is statistically significant.

Example: 20 out of 25 people found a Littman stethoscope on Yahoo.com. Is there evidence that at least 75% of all users would find the Littman stethoscope?

> ## Practical Tip
>
> The statistical tests can be easily calculated with the help of statistical tools like statistical calculator. A screenshot of the results using the A/B test calculator is shown as follows:
>
> | | Successes | Total | % |
> |---|---|---|---|
> | Group 1 | 18 | 220 | 8.18 |
> | Group 2 | 6 | 215 | 2.79 |
>
> Compute
>
> Two tailed p-value: **0.0139171**   One tailed p-value: **0.0069586**

Explanation:

- Completion rates are a binary measure (yes/no), therefore we will use the binary decision map.
- We are not comparing groups so we pick the "No" in the first branch.
- We are testing against a benchmark of 75% so we will pick "Yes" again.
- We end at the 1-sample binomial test with one proportion calculator. Entering 20 out of 25, "Is Greater Than" and a Test Proportion of 0.75 tells us there is about a 70% chance at least 75% of all users would be able to find the Littman stethoscope.

Statistically Significant Difference

To determine whether the observed difference is statistically significant, we look at two things in statistical test:

1. **P-value:** The primary output of statistical tests is the p-value (probability value). It tells about the probability of observing the difference, if no difference exists. For example, p-value 0.014, indicates that we expect to see a meaningless (random) difference of 5% or more only about 14 times in 1000.

   If we are comfortable with that level of chance (which we should consider before starting the test) then we declare the observed difference to be statistically significant. In most cases, this would be declared a statistically significant result.

   > ## Must Know
   >
   > **Level of chance** is the accuracy that will be reached when repeatedly forecasting for majority class of classes.

2. **Confidence interval (CI) around difference:** A confidence interval around a difference that does not cross zero indicates statistical significance. For example, in the graph (Fig. 13.2) ahead there is 95% confidence interval around the difference between the proportions. The observed difference was 5% (8%–3%) but we can expect that difference itself will fluctuate. The CI around the difference indicates that it will most likely fluctuate between nearly 1% and 10% in favor of survey. But as the difference is >0%, we can conclude that the difference is statistically significant and is not due to chance. If the interval crossed zero that is if it goes from 2% to 7%—we could not be 95% confident that the difference is nonzero, and it will not be in favor of survey (Fig. 13.2).

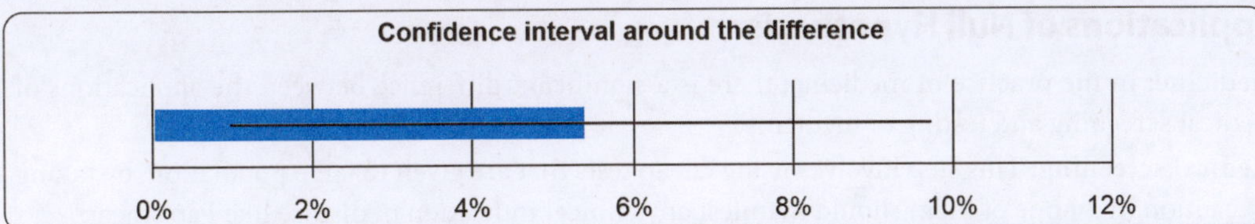

Figure 13.2: The blue bar shows 5% difference. The black line shows the boundaries of the 95% confidence interval around the difference. Because the lower boundary is above 0%, we can also be 95% confident that the difference is at least 0 – another indication of statistical significance.

HYPOTHESIS

Statistics provides an approach to decision-making under uncertainty. It helps to sort in decision-making by choosing in similar way a person bets. It also maximizes expected utility (subjective value). Statistics is helpful in decision-making. Because of uncertainty (have to estimate things), we will be wrong sometimes. Statistics allows us to calculate probabilities and to base our decisions on these. We choose (at least partially) the amount and kind of error.

- The hypothesis actually tested is called the null hypothesis, H_0
- Other hypothesis assumed true (if the null is false), is the alternative hypothesis, H_1

Researchers conduct tests in order to determine whether or not a set hypothesis concerning the observed phenomena of the population can be supported. Whether the results agree or not with the speculated hypothesis.

Null and Alternate Hypotheses

Conventionally it is always assumed that the speculated hypothesis is wrong. Here, the null hypothesis is set that says that the observed phenomena simply occur by chance and as a consequence, the speculated agent has no effect. The test will now determine whether this hypothesis is right or wrong. It is called null hypothesis, because it is this hypothesis that is to be either nullified or not nullified, by the test. When the null hypothesis is nullified, it is concluded that data supports the alternative hypothesis which is the original speculation.

The statisticians Neyman and Pearson always represented the hypothesis to be nullified with the expression H_0 and it led to mean it as nil hypothesis. Although as per Fisher (1966), "the null hypothesis must be exact, that is free from vagueness and ambiguity, because it must supply the basis of the 'problem of distribution,' of which the test of significance is the solution."

As a result, in experimental science the null hypothesis is a statement saying that a particular treatment has no effect; or it has no difference between the values of a particular variable being measured, and that of an experimental prediction.

Statistical Significance of Null Hypothesis

If the probability (of obtaining a result is as extreme as the one obtained, assuming that the null hypothesis was true) is lower than a prespecified probability (for example, 5%), then the result is said to be statistically significant and the null hypothesis is rejected.

British statistician Fischer said that 'the null hypothesis is never proved or established, but is possibly disproved, in the course of experimentation. Every experiment may be said to exist only in order to give the facts a chance of disproving the null hypothesis.'   **—Fisher, 1935**

Applications of Null Hypothesis

Medicine: In the practice of medicine, there is a significant difference between the applications of medical screening and testing of medicine.

Medical screening: This step involves using cheap tests that are given to large population, by taking precaution that none of them should manifest any clinical indication of disease like Pap smear.

Medical testing: It involves far more expensive, usually invasive procedures which are given to selected people who manifest clinical symptoms or indications of disease. These tests are generally applied to confirm a suspected diagnosis. For example, in USA, newborns are screened for hypothyroidism: Here, the hypothesis will be: "The newborns have hypothyroidism."

- **Null hypothesis (H_0):** "The newborns do not have hypothyroidism."
- **Type I error (false positive):** The true fact is that the newborns do not have hypothyroidism but we are considering that they have the disorders rendering the data.
- **Type II error (false negative):** The true fact is that the newborns have hypothyroidism but we consider that they do not have the disorder rendering the data.

Although medical testing gives a high rate of false positive results, the screening tests are valuable as they increase the likelihood of detecting these disorders at a very early stage.

Hypothesis Testing

Hypothesis testing (also called significance testing) uses a quasi-deductive procedure to judge the claims about parameters. Before testing a statistical hypothesis, it is important to clearly state the nature of the claim to be tested. We are going to use a four-step procedure (as outlined in the last bullet) to test the claim.

- The first step in the procedure is to state the hypotheses null and alternative forms. The null hypothesis (abbreviate "H naught") is a statement of no difference. The alternative hypothesis ("H sub a") is a statement of difference. Seek evidence against the claim of H_0 as a way of supporting H_a.
- Convert the research question to null and alternative hypotheses
  - The null hypothesis (H_0) is a claim of "no difference in the population."
  - The alternative hypothesis (H_a) claims "H_0 is false."
- Collect data and seek evidence against H_0 as a way of endorsing H_a (deduction).

Example: In an experiment, it was found that the weight of men between 20 and 29 years of age had a log-normal distribution with a mean of 170 pounds and standard deviation of 40 pounds. The overweight and obese conditions seem to be more prevalent today, constituting a major public health problem.

Explanation: To illustrate the hypothesis testing procedure, we ask if body weight in this group has increased since 2020.

- **Null hypothesis H_0:** $\mu = 170$ ("no difference")
- The **alternative hypothesis** can be either:
  H_a: $\mu > 170$ (**one–sided test**) or H_a: $\mu \neq 170$ (**two-sided test**)
- Under the null hypothesis, there is no difference in the mean body weight between then and now, in which case μ would still equal 170 pounds.
- Under the alternative hypothesis, the mean weight has increased. Therefore, H_a: $\mu > 170$. This statement of the alternative hypothesis is one-sided. That is, it looks only for values larger than stated under the null hypothesis.

- There is another way to state the alternative hypothesis. We could state it in a "two-sided" manner, looking for values that are either higher- or lower-than expected. For the current illustrative example, the two-sided alternative is $H_a: \mu \neq 170$. Although for the current illustrative example, this seems unnecessary, two-sided alternative offers several advantages and are much more common in practice.

Steps of Testing Statistical Hypothesis

The steps are as follows:

1. State the null and alternative hypotheses.
2. Assume the required values to specify the (e.g., SD, normal distribution, etc.) sampling distribution of the statistic.
3. Find rejection region of sampling distribution—that place which is not likely if null is true.
4. Collect sample data. Find whether statistic falls inside or outside the rejection region. If statistic falls in the rejection region, result is said to be statistically significant.

Example:

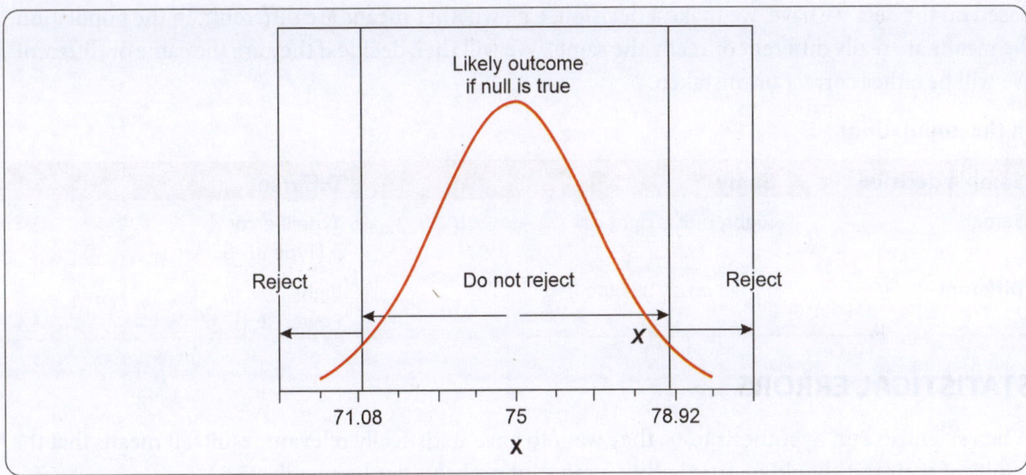

Suppose $H_0: \mu = 75$; $H_1: \mu \neq 75$

- Assume $\sigma = 10$ and population is normal, so sampling distribution of means is known (to be normal).
- Rejection region:

$$\text{Region (N}-25) = 75 \pm 1.96 \, \frac{10}{\sqrt{25}} = 71.08 \leftrightarrow 78.92$$

- We get data $N = 25$; $\overline{X} = 79$
- Conclusion: Reject null
  - Rejection region in z (unit normal)
  - Sample result (79) just over the line

    $Z = (79 - 75)/2$

    $Z = 2$

    $(2 > 1.96)$

Calculated value is more then tabulated value so, we reject the null hypothesis.

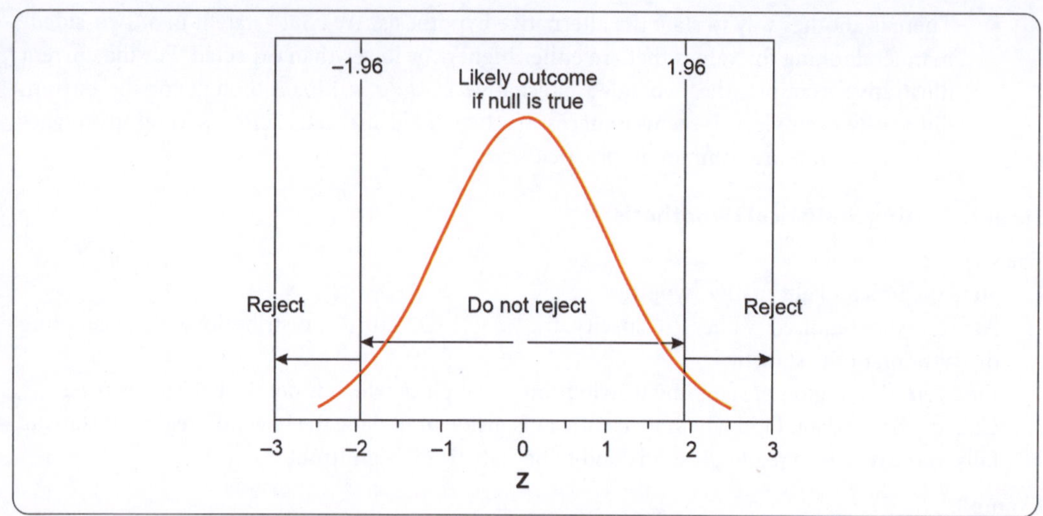

Based on the data we have, we make a decision, e.g., whether means are different. In the population, the means are really different or really the same. We will then decide if they are the same or different. We will be either correct or mistaken.

In the population:

Sample decision	Same	Different
Same	Right, null is right	Type II error p (Type II)–β
Different	Type I error, p (Type I)–α	Right Power–1–β

STATISTICAL ERRORS

When scientists run hypothesis tests, they want to have statistically relevant results. It means that the results of their test should be true within a range of probabilities (generally 95%).

In statistical hypothesis testing, type I error is the rejection of a true null hypothesis that is also known as "false positive" finding, or conclusion, whereas, type II error is the nonrejection of a false null hypothesis that is also known as "false negative" finding, or conclusion. The knowledge of type I and type II error is widely used in medical field resulting in the importance of distinguishing and controlling of these two types of errors. Choice of hypothesis and types of errors are interdependent (Fig. 13.3). While making the decision, two types of errors could occur:

Type I Errors

The first kind of error is the rejection of a true null hypothesis as the result of a test procedure. This kind of error is called a type I error and is sometimes called an error of the first kind. In terms of the courtroom example, a type I error corresponds to convicting an innocent defendant.

- Type 1 errors are often assimilated with false positives—happens in hypothesis testing when the null hypothesis is true but rejected. The null hypothesis is a general statement or default position that there is no relationship between two measured phenomena.

- Simply, type 1 errors are "false positives"—they happen when the tester validates a statistically significant difference even though there is not one.
- Type 1 errors have a probability of "α" correlated to the level of confidence that you set. A test with a 95% confidence level means that there is a 5% chance of getting a type 1 error.

Consequences of a Type 1 Error

Type 1 errors can happen due to bad luck (the 5% chance has played against you) or because you did not respect the test duration and sample size initially set for your experiment. Consequently, a type 1 error will bring in a false positive. This means that you will wrongfully assume that your hypothesis testing has worked even though it has not **(Fig. 13.3)**.

Type II Errors

The second kind of error is the failure to reject a false null hypothesis as the result of a test procedure. This sort of error is called a type II error and is also referred to as an error of the second kind. In terms of the courtroom example, a type II error corresponds to acquitting a criminal. Thus, a type I error is equivalent to a false positive, and a type II error is equivalent to a false negative **(Fig. 13.4)**.

Understanding Type II Errors

If type I errors are commonly referred to as "false positives", type II errors are referred to as "false negatives". Type II errors happen when you inaccurately assume that no winner has been declared between a control version and a variation although there actually is a winner.

In more statistically accurate terms, type II errors happen when the null hypothesis is false and you subsequently fail to reject it.

If the probability of making a type I error is determined by "α", the probability of a type II error is "β". Beta depends on the power of the test (i.e., the probability of not committing a type II error, which is equal to $1-\beta$). There are three parameters that can affect a test:

1. Sample size (n)
2. The significance level of test (α)
3. The "true" value of tested parameter

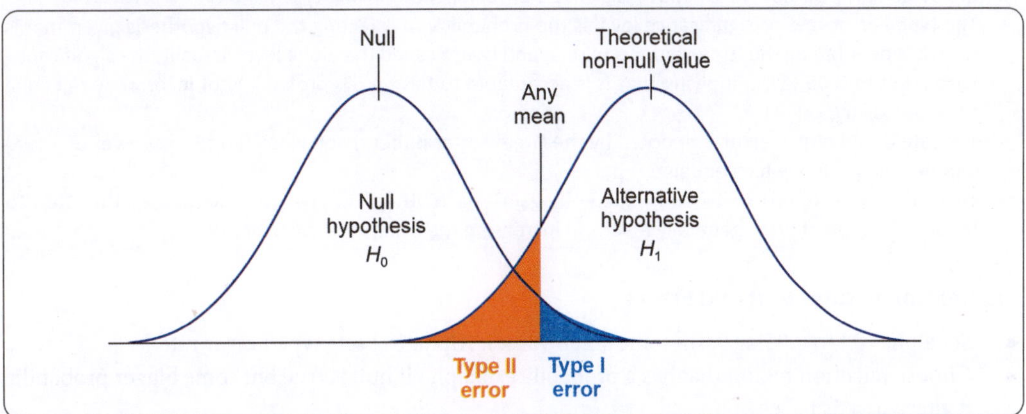

Figure 13.3: Relation of hypotheses and types of errors

Must Know

Relations between truthfulness or falseness of the null hypothesis and outcomes of the test

Error types		Null hypothesis (H_0) is	
		True	**False**
Decision about null hypothesis (H_0)	**Do not reject**	Correct inference (true negative) (probability = $1 - \alpha$)	Type II error (false negative) (probability = β)
	Reject	Type I error (false positive) (probability = α)	Correct inference (true positive) (probability = $1 - \beta$)

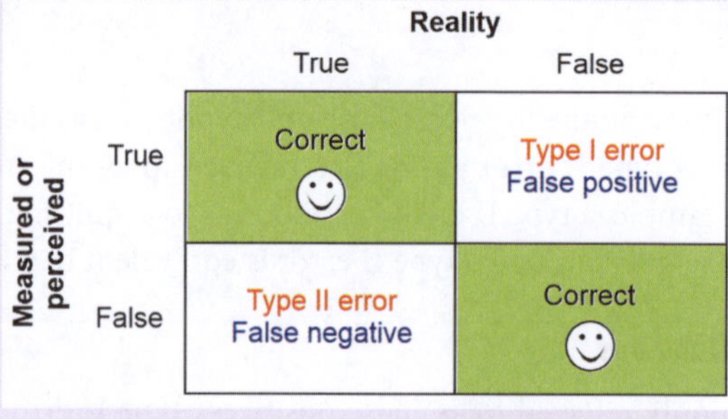

Figure 13.4: Reality versus perceived errors

Consequences of a Type II Error

Similar to type I errors, type II errors can lead to false assumptions and poor decision-making that can result in indecisions and wrong inferences in medical field.

Must Know

Error Rate

A perfect test would have zero false positives and zero false negatives. However, statistics is a game of probability. Whenever, there is uncertainty, there is the possibility of making an error. Considering this nature of statistics, all statistical hypothesis have a probability of making type I and type II errors.

- The type I error rate or significance level is the probability of rejecting the null hypothesis given that is true. It is denoted by the Greek letter α (alpha) and is also called the alpha level. Usually, the significance level is set to 0.05 (5%), implying that it is acceptable to have a 5% probability of incorrectly rejecting the true null hypothesis.
- The rate of the type II error is denoted by the Greek letter β (beta) and is related to the power of a test, denoted as p-value, which equals $1 - \beta$.
- These two types of error rates are traded off against each other: For any given sample set, the effort to reduce one type of error generally results in increasing the other type of error.

Conventional Rules to Avoid Errors

- Set alpha (α) to 0.05 or 0.01 (some small value). Alpha (α) sets type I error rate.
- Choose rejection region that has a probability of alpha if null is true but some bigger probability if alternative is true.
- Call the result significant beyond the alpha level (e.g., $p < 0.05$) if the statistics falls in the rejection region.

Practical Tips

Type I error = erroneous rejection of true H_0
Type II error = erroneous retention of false H_0

Decision	Truth	
	H_0 true	H_0 false
Retain H_0	Correct retention	Type II error
Reject H_0	Type I error	Correct rejection

$\alpha \equiv$ Probability of a type I error
$\beta \equiv$ Probability of a type II error

Preventing type II error
These could be avoided by:

- $\beta \equiv$ Probability of a type II error
  $\beta \equiv$ Probability (retain H_0 | H_0 false)
  (the "|" is read as "given")

- $1 - \beta =$ "Power" $\equiv$ probability of avoiding a Type II error
  $1 - \beta =$ Probability (reject H_0 | H_0 false)

POWERS IN HYPOTHESIS TESTING

- Alpha (α) sets type I error rate. We say different, but it means same.
- There could also be type II errors. We say same, but it means different. Power is 1 or 1-p (Type II).
- It is permissible to have both a small alpha (few type I errors) and good power (few type II errors).
- To figure out power we need a specific H_1.

Factors Affecting Power

Four factors affecting power are as follows:

1. H_1, the alternative hypothesis
2. The value and placement of rejection region
3. Sample size
4. Population variance

The larger the difference in means, the greater the power. This indicates choosing H_1.

Sample size and population variability both affect the size of the standard error of the mean. Sample size is controlled directly. The standard deviation is influenced by experimental control and reliability of measurement.

Rejection Regions in Hypothesis Testing

1-tailed versus 2-tailed tests

- The alternative hypothesis tells the tale (determines the tails)
- If H_0: $\mu = 100$
  H_1: $\mu \neq 100$ Nondirectional; 2-tail
  H_1: $\mu > 100$ H_1: $\mu < 100$ Directional; 1 tail (need to adjust null for these)

In practice most tests are two-tailed.

- 1-tailed tests have better power on the hypothesized size.
- 1-tailed tests have worse power on the nonhypothesized side.
- When in doubt, use the 2-tailed test.

Reasoning Behind Power

- Competing sampling distributions (Figs 13.5A and B).
- Figure 13.5A curve assumes H_0 is true.
- Figure 13.5B Bottom curve assumes H_a is true.
- α is set to 0.05 (two-sided).
  - We will reject H_0 when a sample mean exceeds 189.6 (right tail, top curve) Figure 13.5A.
  - The probability of getting a value greater than 189.6 on the bottom curve (Figure 13.5B) is 0.5160, corresponding to the power of the test.

Practical Tips

H_o	H_a
When the test is done between two samples	
$\mu_1 - \mu_2 = 0$	$\mu_1 - \mu_2 \neq 0$
When sample mean with a known standard	
$\mu - \mu_0$	$\mu \neq \mu_0$

P-VALUE

- P is the probability of being wrong when H_0 rejected.

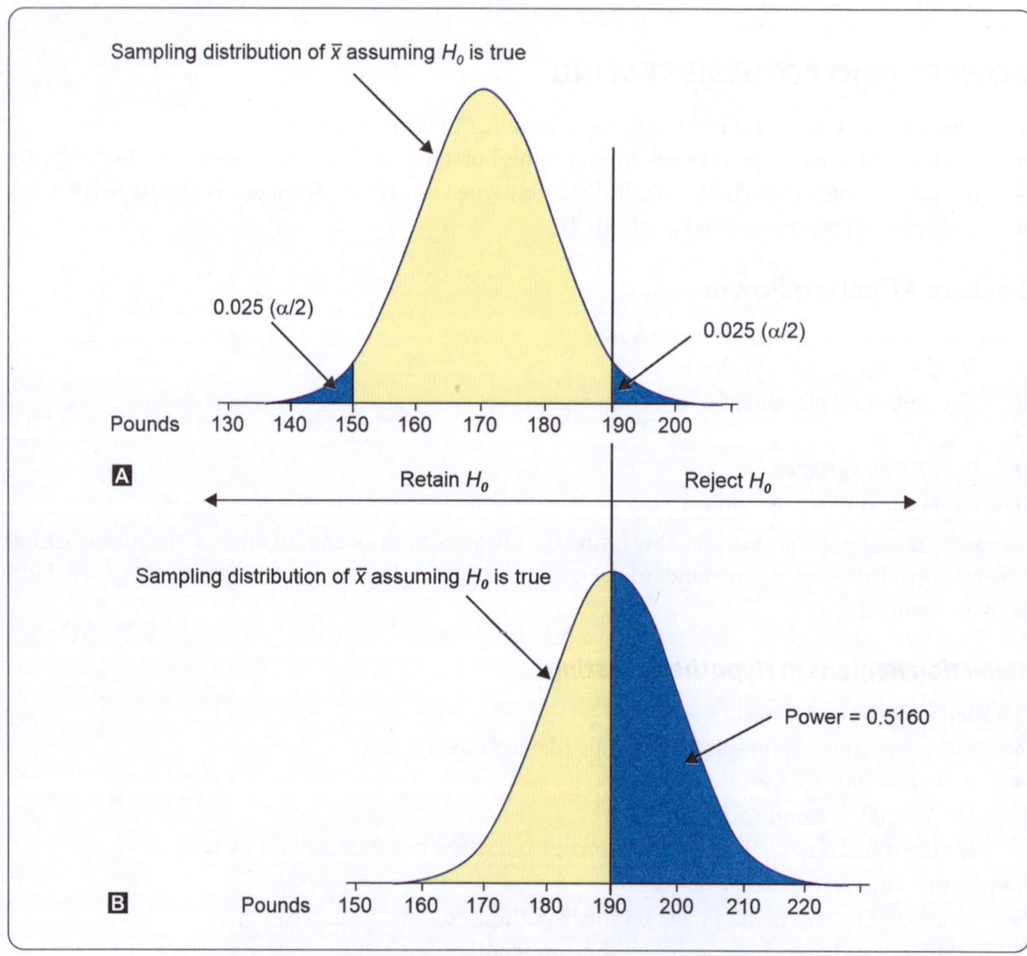

Figures 13.5A and B: Competing sampling distributions - H_o/H_a

- When the level of Significance is set at 5% and the test statistics fall in the region of rejection, then the p value must be <5% <(p <0.05).
- P-value is when we will accept H_0 (p >0.05).
- It is a number that tells us how unusual our sample results are, given that the null hypothesis is true. A P-value indicating that the sample results are not likely to have occurred, if the null hypothesis is true.
- The P-value can be one-sided or two-sided (Figs 13.6A and B).

One-sided P-value (Fig. 13.6)

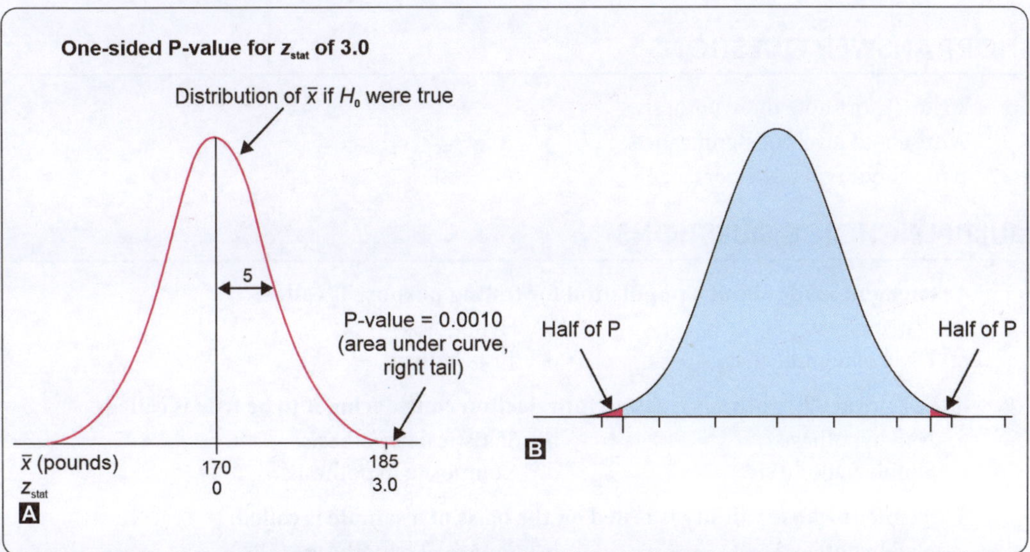

Figures 13.6A and B: A. One-sided P-value; **B.** Two-sided P-value

Practical Tips

Interpretation of P-value
- P-value answers the question: What is the probability of the observed test statistic when H_0 is true?
- Smaller and smaller P-values provide stronger and stronger evidence against H_0
- $P >0.10 \Rightarrow$ nonsignificant evidence against H_0
- $0.05 < P \leq 0.10 \Rightarrow$ marginally significant evidence
- $0.01 < P \leq 0.05 \Rightarrow$ significant evidence against H_0
- $P \leq 0.01 \Rightarrow$ highly significant evidence against H_0

For examples
- $P = 0.27 \Rightarrow$ nonsignificant evidence against H_0
- $P = 0.01 \Rightarrow$ highly significant evidence against H_0

It is unwise to draw firm borders for "significance"

STUDENT ASSIGNMENT

LONG ANSWER QUESTIONS

1. What do you mean by significance of statistics? Discuss in detail.
2. How do you find significance of difference between two statistics.

SHORT ANSWER QUESTIONS

1. Write a short note on hypothesis.
2. Write about levels of significance.
3. Write about types of errors.

MULTIPLE CHOICE QUESTIONS

1. **A statement made about a population for testing purpose is called:**
   a. Statistic
   b. Hypothesis
   c. Level of Significance
   d. Test-Statistic

2. **If the assumed hypothesis is tested for rejection considering it to be true is called:**
   a. Null hypothesis
   b. Statistical hypothesis
   c. Simple hypothesis
   d. Composite hypothesis

3. **A statement whose validity is tested on the basis of a sample is called:**
   a. Null hypothesis
   b. Statistical hypothesis
   c. Simple hypothesis
   d. Composite hypothesis

4. **A hypothesis which defines the population distribution is called:**
   a. Null hypothesis
   b. Statistical hypothesis
   c. Simple hypothesis
   d. Composite hypothesis

5. **If the null hypothesis is false then which of the following is accepted:**
   a. Null hypothesis
   b. Positive hypothesis
   c. Negative hypothesis
   d. Alternative hypothesis

6. **The rejection probability of null hypothesis when it is true is called:**
   a. Level of confidence
   b. Level of significance
   c. Level of margin
   d. Level of rejection

7. **The point where the null hypothesis gets rejected is called:**
   a. Significant value
   b. Rejection value
   c. Acceptance value
   d. Critical value

8. **If the critical region is evenly distributed then the test is referred to:**
   a. Two-tailed
   b. One-tailed
   c. Three-tailed
   d. Zero-tailed

9. **The type of test is defined by which of the following:**
   a. Null hypothesis
   b. Simple hypothesis
   c. Alternative hypothesis
   d. Composite hypothesis

10. **Which of the following is defined as the rule or formula to test a null hypothesis?**
    a. Test statistic
    b. Population statistic
    c. Variance statistic
    d. Null statistic

14

Parametric Tests

"You cannot feed the hungry on statistics."
—Heinrich Heine

LEARNING OBJECTIVES

After the completion of the chapter, the readers will be able to:
- Understand steps followed for statistical analysis.
- Compute parametric tests.
- Calculate ANOVA, ANCOVA and MANOVA tests.

CHAPTER OUTLINE

- Introduction
- Parametric versus Nonparametric Tests
- Parametric Tests
- Types of Parametric Tests

INTRODUCTION

The tests of significance play an important role in interpreting the results of any research; therefore, the choice of an appropriate statistical test is very crucial because it decides the fate of outcome of the study. They are tools for analyzing data and should never be used as a substitute for knowledgeable interpretation of outcomes. In statistics, we use two types of tests: (1) Parametric and (2) Nonparametric.

Steps followed for statistical analysis

Steps followed for statistical analysis by either of the above-mentioned tests are as follows:
1. State the research hypothesis.
2. State the level of significance.
3. Calculate the test statistic.
4. Compare the calculated test statistic with the tabulated values.
5. Decision.
6. Statement of result.

PARAMETRIC VERSUS NONPARAMETRIC TESTS

Characteristics	Parametric	Nonparametric
Assumed distribution	Normal	Any
Assumed variance	Homogeneous	Any
Typical data	Ratio or interval	Ordinal or nominal
Data set relationships	Independent	Any
Usual central measure	Mean	Median
Benefits	Can draw more conclusions	Simplicity; less affected by outliers
Choosing parametric or nonparametric test		
Test	Choosing parametric test	Choosing a nonparametric test
Correlation test	Pearson	Spearman
Independent measures, 2 groups	Independent-measures t-test	Mann-Whitney test
Independent measures, >2 groups	One-way, independent-measures ANOVA	Kruskal-Wallis test
Repeated measures, 2 conditions	Matched-pair t-test	Wilcoxon test
Repeated measures, >2 conditions	One-way, repeated measures ANOVA	Friedman's test

PARAMETRIC TESTS

The parametric tests are hypothesis testing procedures based on the assumption that observed data is distributed according to some distributions of well-known form. For example, the population mean is a parameter, while the sample mean is a statistic. Parametric tests are used:

- For quantitative data.
- For continuous variables.
- When data are measured on approximate interval or ratio scales of measurement.

A parametric statistical test makes an assumption about the population parameters and the distributions that the data came from.

Applications of Parametric Tests

The parametric tests, test the statistical significance of the:

- Difference in sample and population means.
- Difference in two sample means.
- Several population's means.
- Difference in proportions between sample and population.
- Difference in proportions between two independent populations.
- Significance of association between two variables.

Advantages of Parametric Tests

- Parametric tests are preferred because nonparametric tests are less sensitive in analyzing differences between samples or an effect of the independent variable on the dependent variable.
  - When the data set is large, e.g., $n > 100$, the central limit theorem can be applied, therefore it makes little sense to use nonparametric tests.

- Another assumption that is homogeneity of variance is need of statistical tests. When the data under analysis meet the assumptions for parametric tests, we must go for parametric tests as they are more powerful when compared with nonparametric tests.

Limitations of Parametric Tests

- If the data do not meet the criteria of assumptions for parametric test, and a researcher still choses the parametric tests, it will lead to incorrect conclusions.
- When sample size is small like $n < 30$, the parametric assumption of normality is critical. In such cases the nonparametric tests are a good option.

Practical Tips

How to choose the test to be applied in our research when we have one sample and two sample:

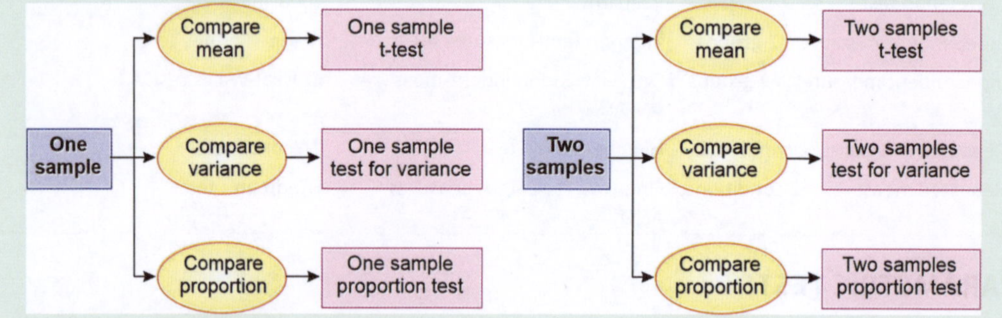

TYPES OF PARAMETRIC TESTS

Parametric tests include Pearson's coefficient of correlation, Z-test, Student's t-test and ANOVA, which assume that data is from normal distribution.

Student's t-Test

This test was developed by Prof WS Gossett in 1908, who published statistical papers under the pen name of 'Student'. Thus, the test is known as Student's 't'-test. The indications for the test are as follows:

- When samples are small.
- Population variance is not known.

Assumptions Made in the Use of 't' Test

- Samples are randomly selected.
- Samples are small, mostly <30.
- Variable follows normal distribution.
- Data utilized in the test is quantitative.
- Sample variances are mostly same in both the groups under the study.

Uses of t-test

The t-test compares the difference between two means of different groups and determines the difference as statistically significant (Fig. 14.1).

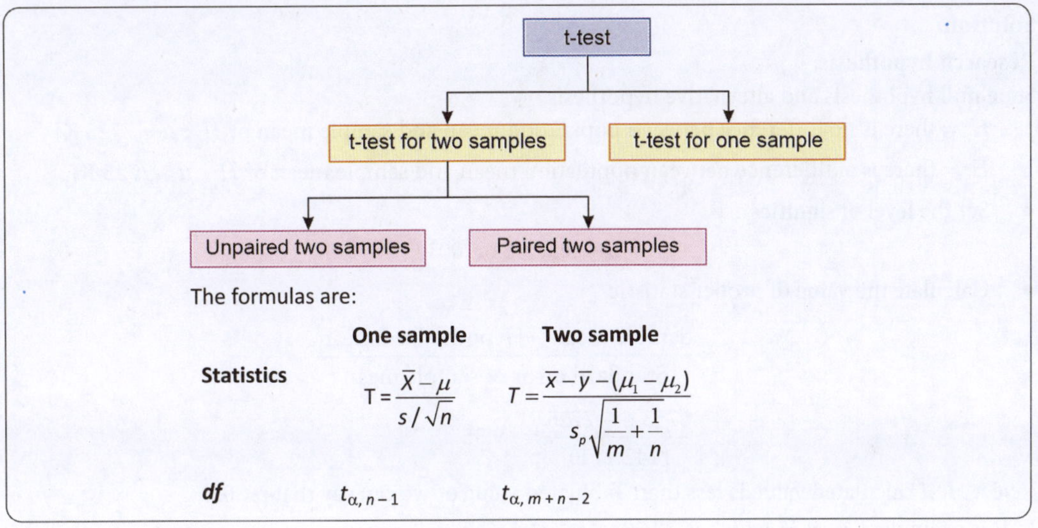

Figure 14.1: t-test

One-Sample t-Test

This test is used when we want to compare the mean of a single group of observations with a specified value. In this test, we know the population mean. A random sample from the population is drawn and comparison of the sample mean with the population mean is made. Then we make statistical decision whether or not the sample mean is different from the population. The formula is:

$$t = \frac{\bar{x} - \mu}{S/\sqrt{\eta}}$$

Where, $\bar{x}$ = sample mean, μ = population mean $S/\sqrt{n}$ = standard error

$$S^2 = \frac{\sum(x - \bar{x})^2}{n - 1}$$

Where, x = element of sample, = $\bar{x}$ sample mean $n - 1$ = degrees of freedom

Now we compare calculated value with table value at certain level of significance (generally 5% or 1%). If absolute value of 't' obtained is greater than table value then reject the null hypothesis and if it is less than table value, the null hypothesis is accepted.

Example: Compare mean dietary intake of a particular group of individuals with the recommended daily intake. When we say that the energy intake of these women in relation to a recommended daily intake is 7725 KJ.

The mean average daily energy intake (ADEI) = 6753.6
SD of ADEI   = 1142.1

Data: Average daily energy intake (ADEI) over 10 days of 11 healthy women

Sub	1	2	3	4	5	6	7	8	9	10	11
ADEI (KJ)	5260	5470	5640	6180	6390	6515	6805	7515	7515	8230	8770

Solution:

Research hypothesis:

State null hypothesis and alternative hypothesis

H_0 = there is no difference between population mean and sample mean or $H_0 : \mu = 7725$ KJ

H_1 = there is a difference between population mean and sample mean or $H_1 : \mu \neq 7725$ KJ

- Set the level of significance

$$\alpha = .05, .01 \text{ or } .001$$

- Calculate the value of proper statistic

$$t = \frac{\text{Sample mean} - \text{Hypothesized mean}}{\text{Standard error of sample mean}}$$

$$= \frac{6753.6 - 7725}{1142.1 / 11} = -9.35$$

Reject H_0 if calculated value is less than Tabulated value or we can say that p<.05.

In this example, $t = -9.35$ which is <2.23.

P-value suggests that the dietary intake of these women was significantly less than the recommended level of 7725 KJ.

Two-Sample 't' Test

Unpaired Two-Sample 't'-Test:

- Unpaired t-test is used when we wish to compare two means.
- It is used when the two independent random samples come from the normal populations having unknown or same variance.
- We test the null hypothesis—that the two-population means are same, i.e., $\mu_1 = \mu_2$ against an appropriate one sided or two-sided alternative hypotheses.

Assumptions

- The distribution of dependent variable is normal.
- The samples are random and independent of each other.
- The variances are equal in both the groups.

Test statistic is given by

$$t = \frac{\text{Mean1} - \text{Mean2}}{SE \ (\text{Mean1} - \text{Mean2})}$$

SE (Mean1 – Mean2) $= S \sqrt{[1/n_1 + 1/n_2]}$

$$S = \frac{(n_1 - 1)S_1^2 + (n_2 - 1)S_2^2}{(n_1 + n_2 - 2)}$$

Where S_1^2 and S_2^2 are respectively called SD's of first and second group.

Example: A study was conducted to compare the birth weights of children born to 15 nonsmoking females with those of children born to 14 heavy smoking mothers (Table. 14.1).

TABLE 14.1: Birth weight of babies

Nonsmoking mothers ($n = 15$)	3.99	3.79	3.60	3.73	3.21	3.60	4.08	3.61	3.83	3.31	4.13	3.26	3.54	3.51	2.71
Heavy smoking mothers ($n = 14$)	3.18	2.84	2.90	3.27	3.85	3.52	3.23	2.76	3.60	3.75	3.59	3.63	2.38	2.34	

Solution:

- **Research hypothesis:** State null hypothesis and alternative hypothesis
  - H_0 = there is no difference between the birth weights of children born to nonsmoking and smoking mothers.
  - H_1 = there is a difference between the birth weights of children born to nonsmoking and smoking mothers.
- Set the level of significance $\alpha = 0.05$, 0.01 or 0.00128
- Calculate the value of proper statistic with the help of formula given before.
- State the rule for rejecting the null hypothesis.
- If $t_{cal} > t_{tab}$ we can say that P <0.05 then we reject the null hypothesis and accept the alternative hypothesis.

Inference: If we reject the null hypothesis, we can say that weight of children born to nonsmoker females are more than children born to heavy smokers.

Paired Two-Sample t-Test:

When we have paired data of observations from one sample only and when each individual gives a pair of observations, this method is used. Same individuals are studied more than once in different circumstances and measurements are made on the same people before and after interventions and we get a pair of observations for same individuals.

Assumptions

- The outcome variable should be continuous.
- The difference between pre and post measurements should be normally distributed.

$$t = \frac{\bar{d}}{SD/\sqrt{n}}$$

Where,

d = difference between x_1 and x_2, $\bar{d}$ = Average of d

SD = Standard deviation for the difference, n = sample size

Example: A study was carried to evaluate the effect of the new diet on weight loss. The study population is consist of 12 people who have used the diet for 2 months. Their weights before and after the diet are given as:

Patient no.		1	2	3	4	5	6	7	8	9	10	11	12
Weight (kg)	Before diet	75	60	68	98	83	89	65	78	95	80	100	108
	After diet	70	54	58	93	78	84	60	77	90	76	94	100

Solutions:

Research hypothesis: State null hypothesis and alternative hypothesis

H_0 = there is no reduction in weight after diet.

H_1 = there is reduction in weight after diet.

- Further analysis can be done manually or through Statistical software SPSS and it remains same as previous example.
- Same formula is used to reject or accept the null hypothesis as used in previous example.

Inference: If we reject the null hypothesis then there is a statistically significant reduction in weight.

Analysis of Variance—ANOVA

Treatment is given to A, B, C and D and we have to check the response level of BP. Here, t-test cannot be used here. Therefore, instead of using a series of individual comparisons, we check the differences among the groups through an analysis that considers the variation among all groups at once, i.e., Analysis of Variance or ANOVA.

The test was given by Sir Ronald Fisher in 1920. It was developed for situations when the number of samples is more than two, neither Z-test nor t-test can be used. The principal aim of statistical tests is to explain the variations. The statistical test involving a test of significance of the difference in mean values of the variable between two groups is the student's, 't' test. When there are more than two groups, the appropriate statistical test is Analysis of Variance (ANOVA).

Example: A study was conducted on men of age group 18–25 years in community to assess effect of Socioeconomic status (SES) on BMI

Lower SES	Middle SES	Higher SES
18, 17, 18, 19, 19	22, 25, 24, 26, 24, 21	25, 26, 24, 28, 29
$N_1 = 5$	$N_2 = 6$	$N_3 = 5$
Mean = 18.2	Mean = 23.6	Mean = 26.4

- This method is used to test differences between two or more means. The technique is called "Analysis of Variance" rather than "Analysis of Means" because inferences about means are made by analyzing variance.
- The variance analysis studies the significance of the difference in means by analyzing variance and it should be noted that the variances would differ only when the means are significantly different.

F-statistics in ANOVA

It measures two sources of variations in the data and compares their relative sizes:

1. **Variation between groups:** For each data value look at the difference between its group mean and the overall mean.
2. **Variation within groups:** For each data value we look at the difference between that value and the mean of its group.
- The ANOVA F-statistic is a ratio of the between group variation divided by the within group variation:

$$F = \frac{Variance\ between\ the\ samples}{Variance\ within\ the\ samples}$$

$$= \frac{MSC}{MSE}$$

- A large F is evidence against H_0, since it indicates that there is more difference between groups than within groups.
- The technique of analyzing the variance in case of a single variable and in case of two variables is similar. In both cases, a comparison is made between the variance of sample means with the residual variance.
    - **For a single variable:** In case of a single variable, the total variance is divided in two parts only
        1. Variance between the samples.
        2. Variance within the samples. The latter variance is the residual variance.
    - **For two variables:** In this case, total variance is divided in three parts, which are as follows:
        1. Variance due to variable number 1
        2. Variance due to variable number 2
        3. Residual variance.

Practical Tips

Key Points to Remember in Analysis of Variance
1. **Design of experiments**
    - ANOVA is typically used for analyzing the findings of experiments.
    - It can be one-way ANOVA, repeated measures ANOVA, multi-factorial ANOVA (two or more factor analysis of variance).
2. **Calculating differences and sum of squares**
    - Differences between group means, individual values and grand mean are squared and summed up. This leads to the fundamental equation of ANOVA.
    - Test statistics for significance test is calculated from the means of the sums of squares.
3. **Verification of the model and the factors**
    - Is the overall model significant? (F-test)? Are the factors significant?
    - Are prerequisites met?
4. **Checking measures**
    - Adjusted R squared/partial Eta squared.

ANOVA compares variance by means of a simple ratio, called F-ratio.

$$F = \frac{Variance\ between\ groups}{Variance\ within\ groups}$$

The resulting F statistics is then compared with critical value of F (critic), obtained from F tables in much the same way as is done with 't'.

If the calculated value exceeds the critical value for the appropriate level of α, the null hypothesis will be rejected. F-test is therefore a test of the Ratio of Variances.

F-test can also be used on their own, independently of the ANOVA technique, to test hypothesis about variances. In ANOVA, the F-test is used to establish whether a statistically significant difference exists in the data being tested.

Assumptions for ANOVA

- Sample population can be easily approximated to normal distribution.
- All populations have same standard deviation.
- Individuals in population are selected randomly.
- Independent samples.

Prerequisites of ANOVA

- **Robustness:** ANOVA is relatively robust against violations of prerequisites.
- **Sampling:** Random sample, no treatment effects a well-designed study avoids violation of this assumption.
- **Distribution of residuals:** Residuals (= error) are normally distributed.
  Correction → transformation
- **Homogeneity of variances:** Residuals (= error) have constant variance.
  Correction → weight variances
- **Balanced design:** Same sample size in all groups
  Correction → weight mean

> **Must Know**
>
> SPSS automatically corrects unbalanced designs by Sum of Squares "Type III" Syntax: /METHOD = SSTYPE(3)

Classification of ANOVA

Classification of ANOVA is shown in **Figure 14.2**

One-Way ANOVA

If the various experimental groups differ in terms of only one factor at a time—a one-way ANOVA is used, e.g., a study to assess the effectiveness of four different antibiotics on *S. sanguis*.

In one-way classification we take into account only one variable—say, the effect of different types of drugs on tuberculosis. Other factors like difference in diet, environment, individual immunity, etc., are not considered. For one-way classification we may conduct the experiment through a number of sample studies. The one-way ANOVA:

- Determines means of ≥3 independent groups significantly different from one another.
- Only 1 independent variable (factor/grouping variable) with ≥3 levels.
- Grouping variable nominal.
- Outcome variable interval or ratio.

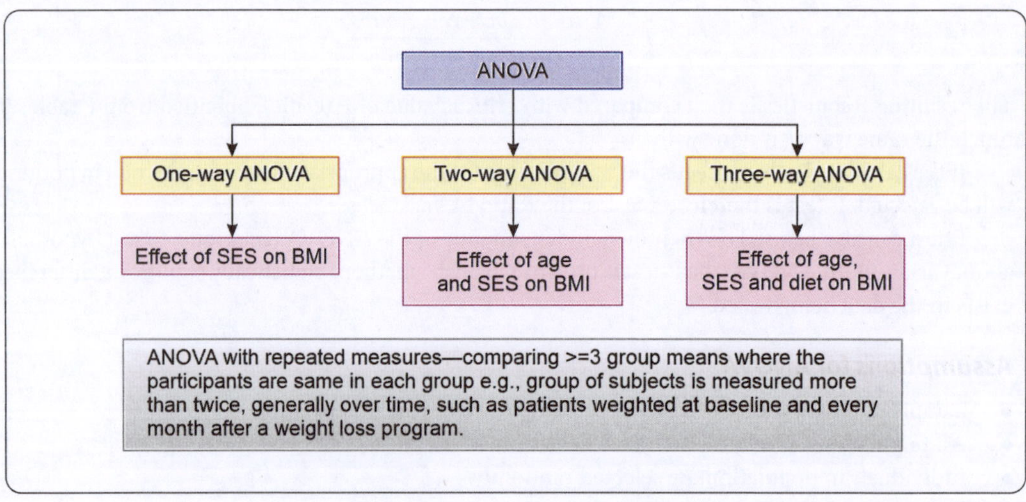

Figure 14.2: Classification of ANOVA

Steps of calculations

1. State null and alternative hypotheses.
2. State alpha, i.e., 0.05.
3. Calculate degrees of freedom ($k - 1$ and $n - 1$) k = number of Samples, n = Total number of observations
4. State decision rule. If calculated value of F >table value of F, reject H_0
5. Calculate test statistic

Calculate variance between samples

i. Calculate the mean of each sample.
ii. Calculate the grand average.
iii. Take the difference between means of various samples and grand average.
iv. Square these deviations and obtain total which will give sum of squares between samples (SSC).
v. Divide the total obtained in step 4 by the degrees of freedom to calculate the mean sum of square between samples (MSC).

$$MSC = \frac{SSC}{k-1}$$

Calculate variance within the samples

i. Calculate mean value of each sample.
ii. Take the deviations of the various items in a sample from the mean values of the respective samples.
iii. Square these deviations and obtain total which gives the sum of square within the samples (SSE).
iv. Divide the total obtained in 3rd step by the degrees of freedom to calculate the mean sum of squares within samples (MSE).

$$MSE = \frac{SSE}{n-k}$$

k = number of samples, n = total number of observations

Calculate F-statistics

$$F\text{-}statistics = \frac{MSC}{MSE}$$

$$F = \frac{Variability\ between\ groups}{Variability\ within\ groups}$$

Inference: Compare the F-statistics value with F (critical) value which is obtained by looking for it in F distribution tables against degrees of freedom. When calculated value, of F > table value H_0 is rejected.

State results and conclusion (Figs 14.3A and B):

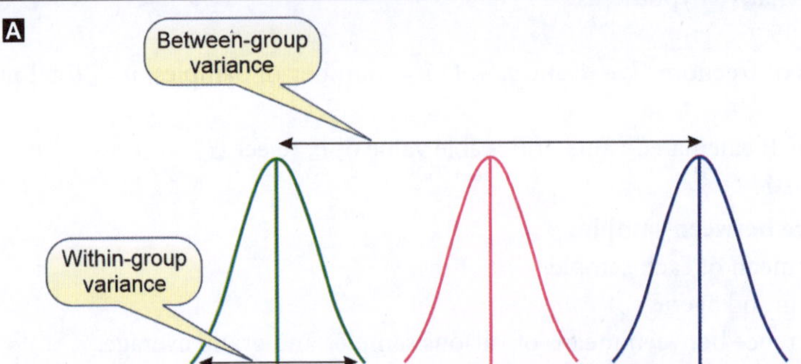

Results: Between-group variance is large relative to the within-group variance, so F-statistic will be larger and > critical value, therefore statistically significant

Conclusion:
• At least one of group means is significantly different from other group means
• Between-group variance is large relative to the within-group variance, so F-statistic will be larger and > critical value, therefore statistically significant

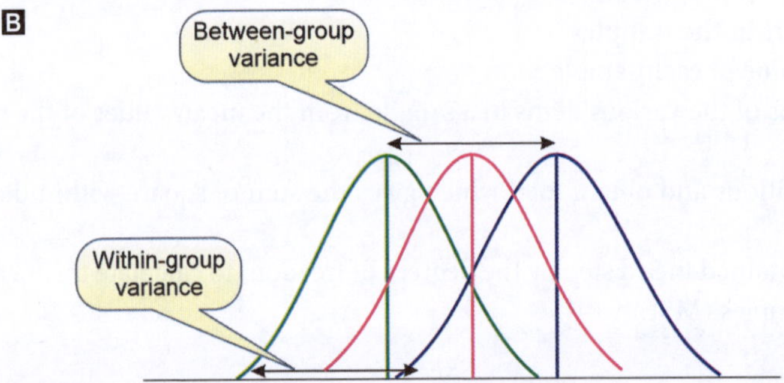

Results: Within-group variance is larger, and the between-group variance smaller, so F will be smaller

Conclusion:
• Reflecting the likely-hood of no significant differences between these 3 sample means
• Within-group variance is larger, and the between-group variance smaller, so F will be smaller (it reflects the likelihood of no significant differences between these three sample means)

Figures 14.3A and B: A. Between group variance; **B.** Within group variance

Example: The data of three samples obtained from normal populations with equal variances are given as follows. Test the hypothesis that sample means are equal.

Sample 1	Sample 2	Sample 3
8	7	12
10	5	9
7	10	13
14	9	12
11	9	14

Solution:

Steps followed are as follows:

1. Null hypothesis—no significant difference in the means of three samples
2. Set alpha as 0.05.
3. Calculate degrees of freedom $k - 1$ and $n - k$: 2
4. State decision rule (table value of F at 5% level of significance for df 2 and 12 is 3.88).
5. The calculated value of $F > 3.88$, H_0 will be rejected.
6. Calculate test statistic.

X_1	X_2	X_3
8	7	12
10	5	9
7	10	13
14	9	12
11	9	14
Total 50	**40**	**60**
$M_1 = 10$	$M_2 = 8$	$M_3 = 12$

$$\text{Grand average} = \frac{10 + 8 + 12}{3} = 10$$

Variance between samples ($M_1 = 10, M_2 = 8, M_3 = 12$)

- Sum of squares between samples (SSC) =

$$n_1 (M_1 - \text{grand avg})^2 + n_2 (M_2 - \text{grand avg})^2 + n_3(M_3 - \text{Grand avg})^2$$

$$5(10 - 10)^2 + 5(8 - 10)^2 + 5(12 - 10)^2 = 40$$

- Calculation of mean sum of squares between samples **(MSC)**

$$MSC = \frac{SSC}{k-1} = \frac{40}{2} = 20$$

Here k = No. of samples and n = Total no. of observations

X_1	$(X_1 - M_1)^2$	X_2	$(X_2 - M_2)^2$	X_3	$(X_3 - M_3)^2$
8	4	7	1	12	0
10	0	5	9	9	9
7	9	10	4	13	1
14	16	9	1	12	0
11	1	9	1	14	4
	30		16		14

- Sum of squares within samples (SSE) = 30 + 16 + 14 = 60
- Calculation of Mean Sum of squares within samples (MSE)

$$MSE = \frac{SSE}{n - k} = \frac{60}{12} = 5$$

Calculation of F ratio

$$F = \frac{Variability\ between\ groups}{Variability\ within\ groups}$$

$$F\text{-}statistics = \frac{MSC}{MSE} = \frac{20}{5} = 4$$

Interpretation:

The table value of F at 5% level of significance for df 2 and 12 is 3.88.

The calculated value of F > table value.

H_0 is rejected. Hence, there is significant difference in sample means.

Practical Tips

Short-way to Calculate ANOVA by using Correction Factor

X_1	$(X_1)^2$	X_2	$(X_2)^2$	X_3	$(X_3)^2$
8	64	7	49	12	144
10	100	5	25	9	81
7	49	10	100	13	169
14	196	9	81	12	144
11	121	9	81	14	196
Total 50	**530**	**40**	**336**	**60**	**734**

Total sum of all observations = 50 + 40 + 60 = 150

Correction factor = T^2/N = $(150)^2/15$ = 22500/15 = 1500

Total sum of squares = 530 + 336 + 734 − 1500 = 100

Sum of square between samples = $(50)^2/5 + (40)^2/5 + (60)^2/5 − 1500$ = 40

Sum of squares within samples = 100 − 40 = 60

To violate assumptions:

- **In case of normality:** Choose the nonparametric Kruskal-Wallis H-test which does not require the assumption of normality.
- **In case of homogencity of variances:** Choose Welsch test or Brown and Forsythe test or Kruskal-Wallis H-test.

Must Know

Both the one-way ANOVA and the Independent Samples t Test can compare the means for two groups. Although only the one-way ANOVA can compare the means across three or more groups.

Two-Way ANOVA

When two independent variables (nominal/categorical) have an effect on one dependent variable (ordinal or ratio measurement scale), two-way ANOVA is applied. The test:

- Compares relative influences on dependent variables.
- Examines interactions between independent variables.

Just as we had sum of squares and mean squares in one-way ANOVA, we have the same in two-way ANOVA.

Advantages of two-way ANOVA

- It is more efficient to study two factors simultaneously rather than separately.
- We can reduce the residual variation in a model by including a second factor thought to influence the response.
- We can investigate interactions between factors.

Example: We have test score of boys and girls in the age group of 10 years, 11 years and 12 years. Study the effect of gender and age on score.

Two independent factors: Gender, age

Dependent factor: Test score

Solution:

H_o—Gender will have no significant effect on student score.

H_a—Gender will have significant effect on student score.

H_o—Age will have no significant effect on student score.

H_a—Age will have significant effect on student score.

H_o—Gender and age interaction will have no significant effect on student score.

H_a—Gender and age interaction will have significant effect on student score.

> **Must Know**
>
> Two-way ANOVA includes tests of three null hypotheses:
> 1. Means of observations grouped by one factor are same.
> 2. Means of observations grouped by the other factor are the same.
> 3. There is no interaction between the two factors. The interaction test tells whether the effects of one factor depend on the other factor.

The two-way ANOVA table is as follows:

Source of variation	Degrees of freedom	Sum of squares	Mean square	F-ratio	P-value
Factor A	$r-1$	SS_A	MS_A	$F_A = MS_A/MS_E$	Tail area
Factor B	$c-1$	SS_B	MS_B	$F_B = MS_B/MS_E$	Tail area
Interaction	$(r-1)(c-1)$	SS_{AB}	MS_{AB}	$F_{AB} = MSA_B/MS_E$	Tail area
Error (within)	$rc(n-1)$	SS_E	MS_E		
Total	$rcn-1$	SS_r			

Main effects are as follows:

The direct effect of an independent variable on the dependent variable is called main effect (Figs 14.4A and B). In the example:

- **Experience effect:** The main effect of experience reveals that the nurses' salaries depend on their level of professional experience.
- The main effect of position reveals that the nurses' salaries depend on whether they work in the office or the hospital. Profile plots are used as visualization:
- If the profile plot shows a (nearly) horizontal line, the main effect in question is presumably not significant. (***Note*** that SPSS cuts off lower area of graph, y-axis often does not start at 0!)

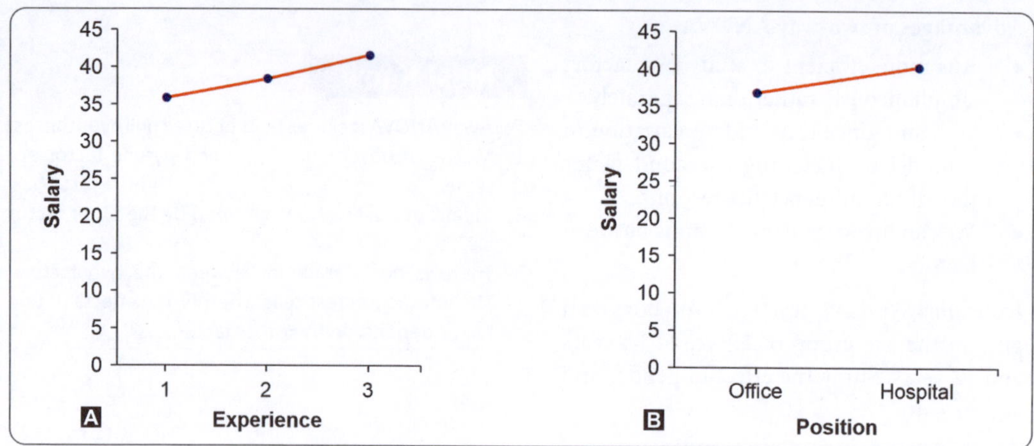

Figures 14.4A and B: Main effects: **A.** Experience; **B.** Position

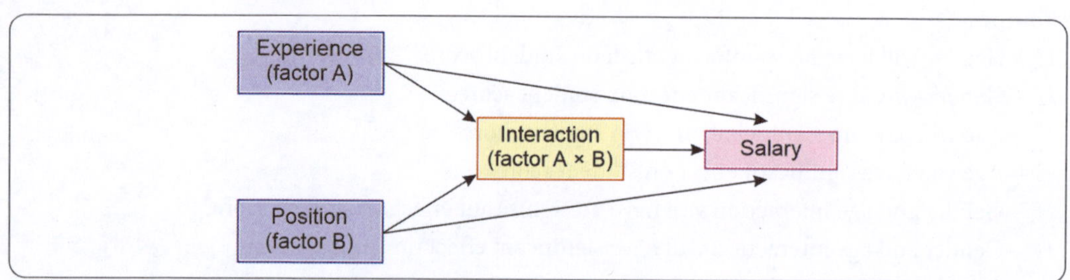

Figure 14.5: Interaction effect

Interaction effects: An interaction between experience and position means there is dependency between the two variables. The independent variables have a complex influence on the dependent variable. The factors do not just function additively but act together in a different manner. An interaction means that the effect of one factor depends on the value of another factor (Fig. 14.5).

Experience and position: The interaction between experience and position means:

- That the effect of work experience on salary is not the same for healthcare workers who work in offices and for healthcare workers who work in the hospital.
- That the difference in salary between various healthcare workers working in the hospital and healthcare workers working in the office depends on the level of experience.

Profile plots are shown in **Figures 14.6A and B:**

If there is an interaction, the lines are not parallel. The more the lines deviate from being parallel, the more likely is an interaction. If there is no interaction, the lines are parallel.

Now do the calculations either manually or by using SPSS.

Note that in this chapter, we have not discussed three way ANOVA due to complexity.

Takeaway

If the grouping variable has only two groups, then the results of a one-way ANOVA and the independent samples t test will be equivalent. In fact, if you run both an independent samples t-test and a one-way ANOVA in this situation, you should be able to confirm that $t^2 = F$.

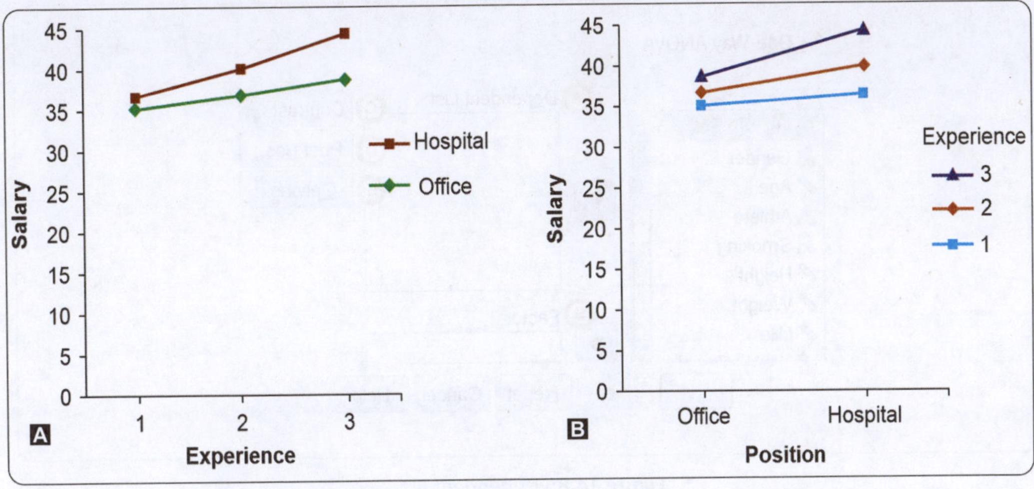

Figures 14.6A and B: Separate lines: **A.** For position; **B.** For experience

Calculations of ANOVA by Using SPSS

Step 1: In order to run a one-way ANOVA in SPSS, click **Analyze > Compare Means > One-way ANOVA (Fig. 14.7)**.

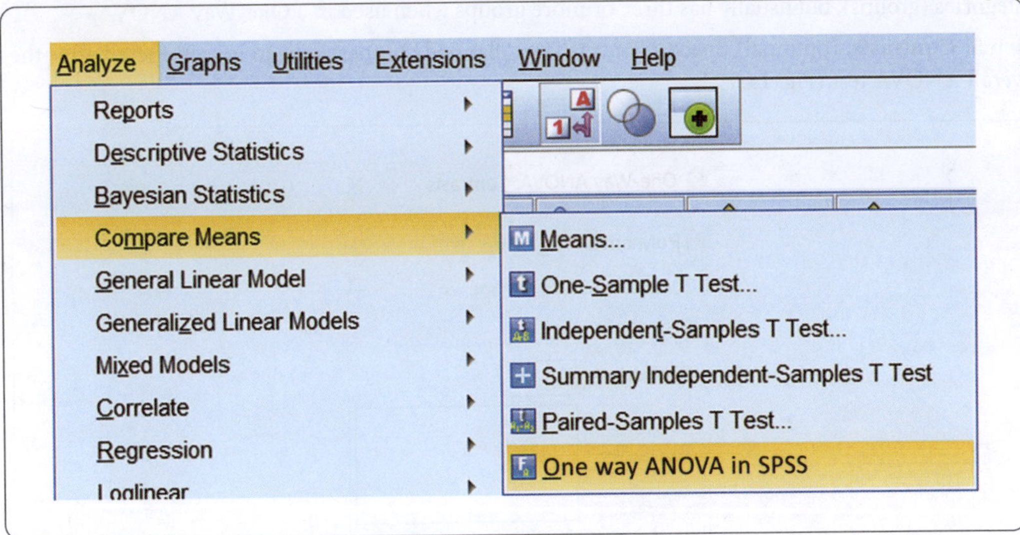

Figure 14.7: One-way ANOVA in SPSS

Step 2: The One-Way ANOVA window opens, specify the variables to be used in the analysis. All variables in dataset appear in the list on the left side. Move variables to the right by selecting them in the list and clicking the blue arrow buttons. You can move a variable(s) to either of two areas: **Dependent list** or **Factor**.

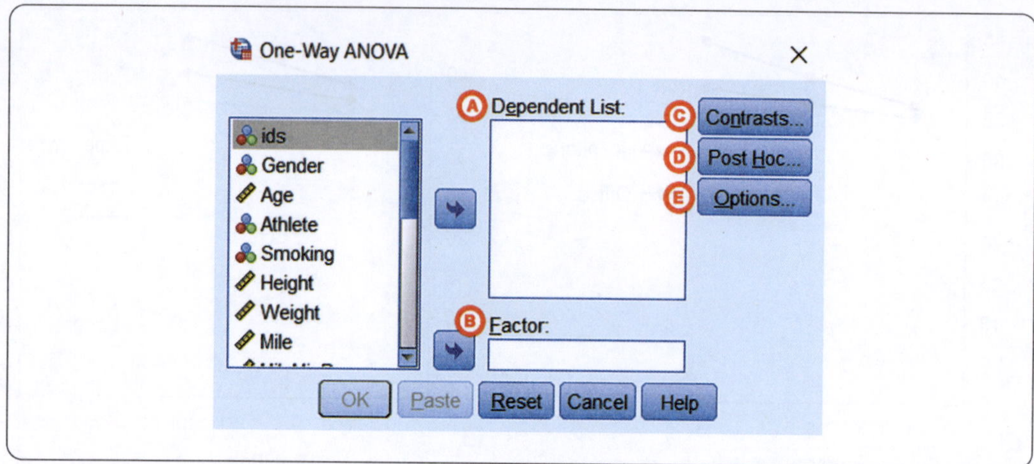

Figure 14.8: Dependent list

Step 3: Dependent list will contain the dependent variable(s) (Fig. 14.8). This is the variable whose means will be compared between the samples (groups). One can run comparisons of multiple means, simultaneously, by selecting more than one dependent variable.

Step 4: Factor will contain the independent variable. The categories (or groups) of the independent variable will define which samples will be compared. The independent variable must have at least two categories (groups), but usually has three or more groups when used in a One-Way ANOVA.

Step 5: Contrasts: (optional) Specify contrasts, or planned comparisons, to be conducted after the overall ANOVA test (Fig. 14.9).

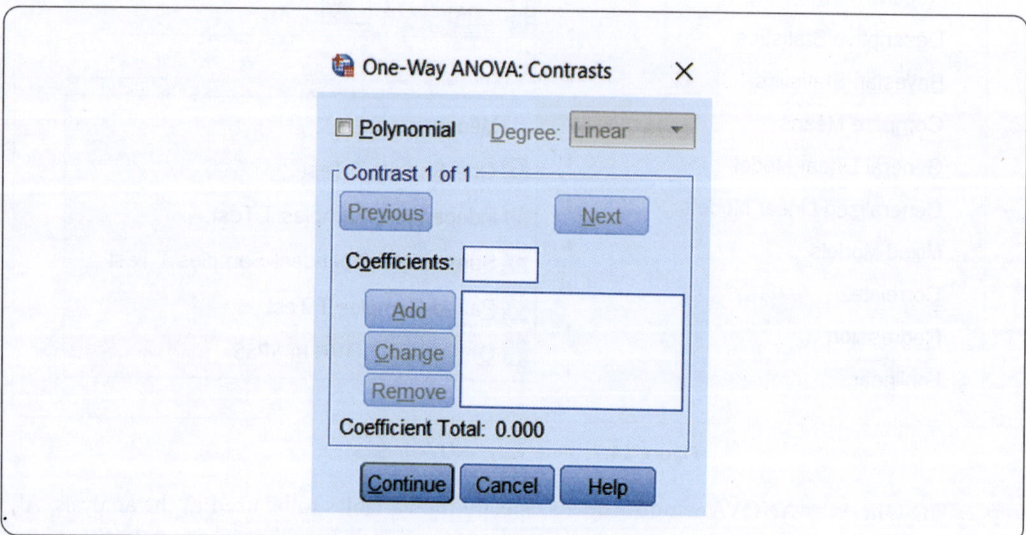

Figure 14.9: One-way ANOVA contrast

Step 6: When the initial *F*-test indicates that significant differences exist between groups means, contrasts are helpful for determining which specific means are significantly different when you have specific hypotheses that you wish to test. Contrasts are decided **before** analyzing the data (i.e., a priori). Contrasts break down the variance into component parts. They may involve using weights, nonorthogonal comparisons, standard contrasts, and polynomial contrasts (trend analysis).

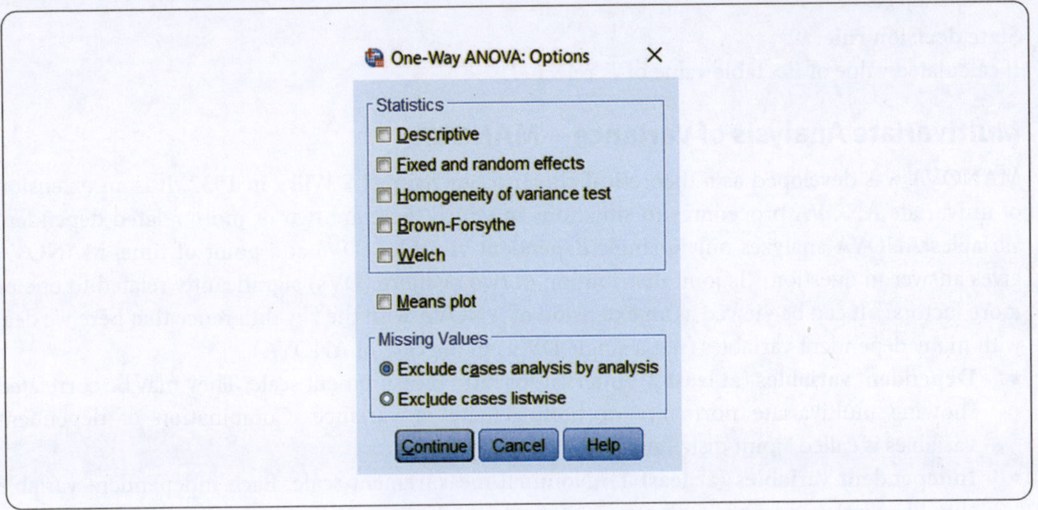

Step 7: After this, Click **OK** to run the One-Way ANOVA.

ANOVA with Repeated Measures

- Determines whether means of three or more measures from same person or matched controls are similar or different.
- Measures dependent variables (DV) for various levels of one or more independent variables (IV).
- Used when we repeatedly measure the same subject multiple times.

Assumptions

- Dependent variable is interval/ratio (continuous).
- Dependent variable is approximately normally distributed.
- One independent variable where participants are tested on the same dependent variable at least 2 times.

Steps to Calculate ANOVA with Repeated Measures

1. Define null and alternative hypotheses.
2. State alpha.
3. Calculate degrees of freedom
4. State decision rule
5. Calculate test statistic.
    - Calculate variance between samples
    - Calculate variance within the samples
    - Calculate ratio F
    - If F is significant, perform post hoc test
6. State results and conclusion

Calculate degrees of freedom (*df*) for:

- *df* between samples = $k - 1$
- *df* within samples = $n - k$
- *df* subjects = $r - 1$
- *df* error = *df* within-*df* subjects
- *df* total = $n - 1$

State decision rule:

If calculated value of F > table value of F, reject H_0

Multivariate Analysis of Variance—MANOVA

MANOVA was developed as a theoretical construct by Samuel S Wilks in 1932. It is an extension of univariate ANOVA procedures to situations in which there are two or more related dependent variables ANOVA analyzes only a single dependent variables (DV) at a point of time. MANOVA gives answer to question: "Is joint distribution of two or more (DVs) significantly related to one or more factors?" It can be viewed as an extension of ANOVA with the key difference that here we deal with many dependent variables (not a single DV as in the case of ANOVA).

- **Dependent variables (at least 2):** Interval /or ratio measurement scale. They may be correlated showing multivariate normality or homogeneity of variance. Combination of dependent variables is called "joint distribution".
- **Independent variables (at least 1):** Nominal measurement scale. Each independent variable should be independent of each other.

Uses of MANOVA

The MANOVA identifies inferentially whether:

- There are interactions between the IVs and a linear combination of DVs.
- Different levels of IVs have a significant effect on a linear combination of each of the DVs.
- There are significant univariate effects for each of the DVs separately.

Precautions

- It is more complicated than ANOVA, and therefore there can be some ambiguity about which independent variable affects each dependent variable. Therefore, the observer must make many potentially subjective assumptions.
- Moreover, one degree of freedom is lost for each dependent variable that is added. The dependent variables should be largely uncorrelated. If the dependent variables are highly correlated, use of a single ANOVA test would be preferable.
- Because of the increase in complexity and ambiguity of results with MANOVA, one of the best recommendations is "Avoid it, if you can".

Assumptions of MANOVA

- **Sample size**
  - Rule of thumb is that in each cell should be more than the number of DVs.
  - Larger samples make the procedure more robust to violation.
- **Normality**
  - MANOVA tests assume multivariate normality, however when cell size is more than or equal to 20–30, the procedure is more robust violating this assumption. Note that univariate normality is not a guarantee of multivariate normality.

- ■ We can check univariate normality via histogram, normal probability plots, skewness, kurtosis, etc.
- **Linearity**
  - ■ Linear relationships among all parts of DVs.
  - ■ Assessed by scatter plots and bivariate correlations (checked for each level of IVs)
- **Homogeneity of regression:** It is important when we are using step-down analysis that means there is reason for ordering the DVs.
- **Homogeneity of variance-covariance matrix:** MANOVA is fairly robust to this assumption where there are equal sample sizes for each cell.
- **Multicollinearity and singularity:** MANOVA works best when the DVs are only moderately correlated.
  - ■ When correlations are low, consider running separate ANOVA.

Must Know

ANOVA versus MANOVA

Parameter	ANOVA	MANOVA
Stands for	Analysis of Variance	Multivariate Analysis of Variance
Meaning	It determines the difference between three or more group mean values on the basis of a single dependent variable.	It determines the difference between multiple groups' mean values on the basis of multiple dependent variables.
Purpose	The main idea behind conducting ANOVA is to find the difference between the mean values of different groups.	The purpose of using MANOVA is to know how independent variables affect dependent variables and what possible interactions they have with each other.
Type of test	It is a parametric test.	MANOVA test is nonparametric test.
Number of variables	One single dependent variable	More than two dependent variable
Sample size	Minimum sample size required is 128.	The larger the sample size it will have, the better performance it will give.
Models	It uses three different models to find the difference in mean values.	It does not use any model.
Results	It gives the result in the form of the F-statistics.	It gives the result in the form of Wilks' Lambda.
Relationship	It uses a relationship of a single dependent variable with an independent variable.	It uses the relationship between variance and covariance.

- **Outliers**
  - ■ MANOVA is sensitive to the effect of outliers (they impact on the type 1 error rate).
  - ■ If there are too many outliers, consider deleting or these cases or transforming the variables involved.

Practical Tips

Decision-making in MANOVA

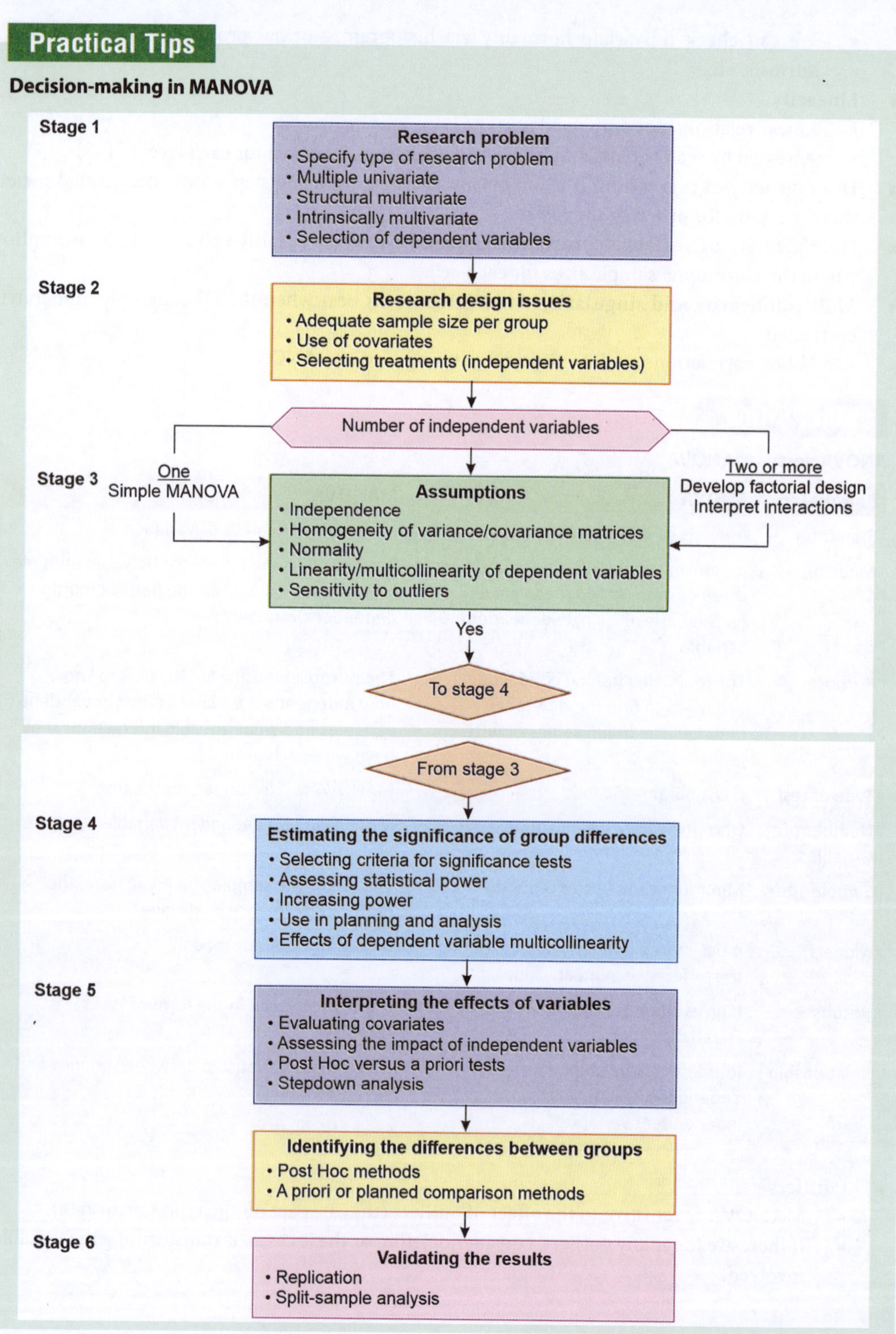

Contd...

Various tests used in MANOVA are as follows:

- **Wilks' lambda:**
  - Widely used; good balance between power and assumptions.
  - It is used to test whether there are differences between the means of identified groups of subjects on a combination of dependent variables.
  - Most commonly used for overall significance.
  - Considers differences over all the characteristic roots.
  - The smaller the value of Wilks' lambda, the larger is the between-groups dispersion.
- **Pillai's trace:**
  - Test is useful when sample sizes are small, cell sizes are unequal, or covariances are not homogeneous.
  - Considers differences over all the characteristic roots.
  - More robust than Wilks'. It should be used when sample size decreases, unequal cell sizes or homogeneity of covariances is violated.
- **Hotelling's (Lawley-Hotelling) trace:**
  - Test is useful when examining differences between two groups.
  - Considers differences over all the characteristic roots.
- **Roy's greatest characteristic root**
  - Tests for differences on only the first discriminant function.
  - Most appropriate when DVS are strongly interrelated on a single dimension.
  - Highly sensitive to violation of assumptions–most powerful when all assumptions are met.

Advantages of MANOVA

- It tests the effects of several independent variables and several outcome (dependent) variables within a single analysis.
- It has the power of convergence (no single operationally defined dependent variable is likely to capture perfectly the conceptual variable of interest).
- Independent variables of interest are likely to affect a number of different conceptual variables. For example: An organization's nonsmoking policy will affect satisfaction, production, absenteeism, health insurance claims, etc.
- It can provide a more powerful test of significance than available when using univariate tests.
- It reduces error rate compared with performing a series of univariate tests.
- It provides interpretive advantages over a series of univariate ANOVAs.
- Since only 'one' dependent variable is tested, the researcher is protected against inflating the type 1 error due to multiple comparisons.

Disadvantages of MANOVA

- Discriminant functions are not always easy to interpret—they are designed to separate groups, not to make conceptual sense. In MANOVA, each effect evaluated for significance uses different discriminant functions (factor A may be found to influence a combination of dependent variables totally different from the combination most affected by factor B or the interaction between factors A and B).
- Like discriminant analysis, the assumptions on which it is based are numerous and difficult to assess and meet.

Limitations of MANOVA

- The number of people (N) in the smallest cell should be larger than the total number of dependent variables.

- It can be very sensitive to outliers, (for small N).
- It assumes a linear relationship (some sort of correlation) between the dependent variables.
- MANOVA will not give you the interaction effects between the main effect and the repeated factor.

Avoiding MANOVA

- Combine or eliminate dependent variables so that only one dependent variable need to be analyzed.
- Use factor analysis to find orthogonal factors that make up the dependent variables, then use univariate ANOVAs on each factor (because the factors are orthogonal each univariate ANOVAs on each factor (because the factors are orthogonal each univariate analysis should be unrelated).

Practical Tips

Use SPSS to do MANOVA

Step 1: Click **Analyze > General Linear Model > Multivariate...** on the top menu as shown in the following image:

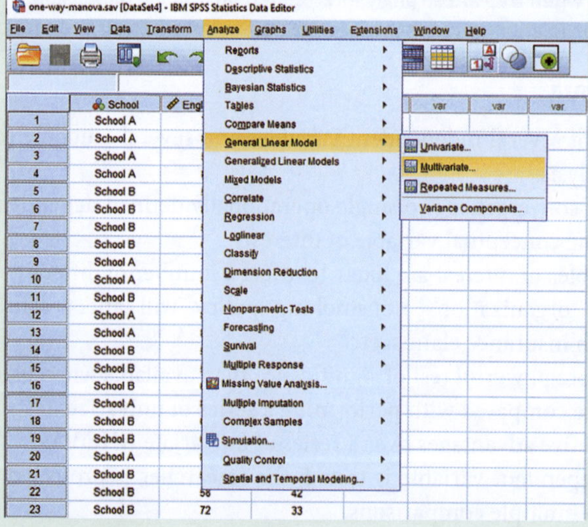

Step 2: Multivariate dialogue box will open:

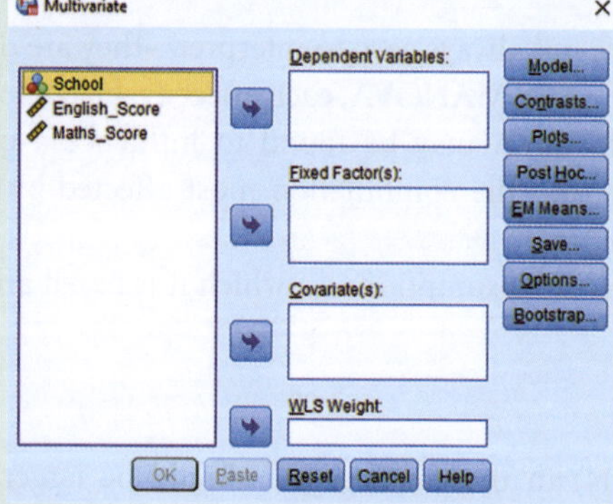

Contd...

Step 3: Transfer the independent variable like nursing school into the **Fixed factor's** box and transfer the dependent variables like Scores in English or Maths into the **Dependent variable box**. One can do this by drag-and-dropping the variables into their respective boxes or by using the ➡ button. The result is shown follows:

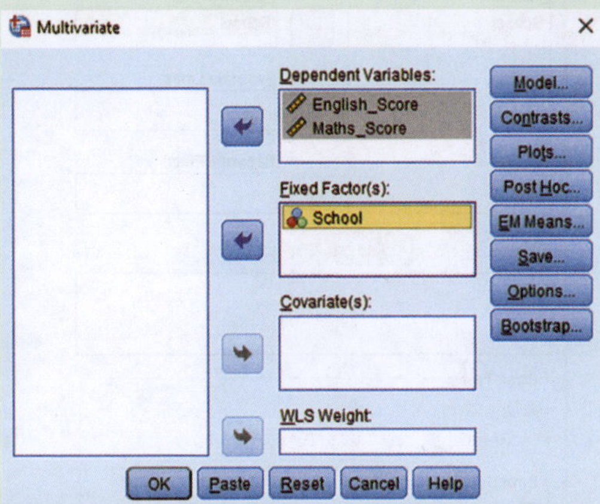

Note: For this analysis, you will not need to use the Covariate(s) box (used for MANCOVA) or the WLS Weight box.

Step 4: Click on the Plots… button. The **Multivariate: Profile Plots** dialogue box will open.

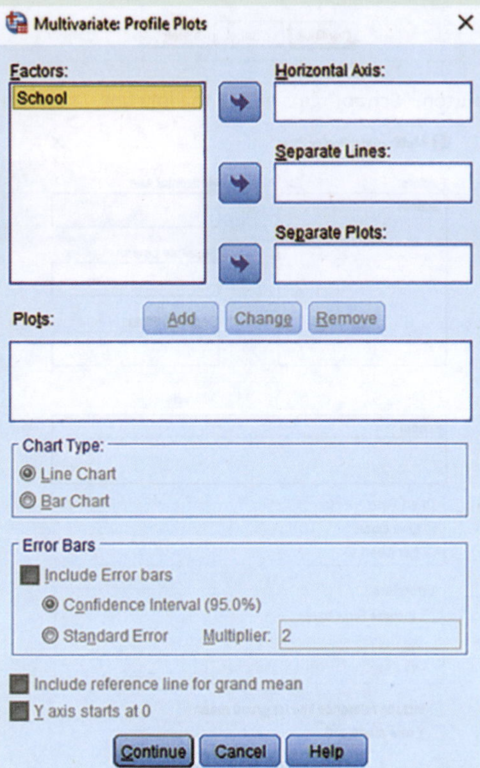

Contd...

Step 5: Transfer the independent variable that is school into the Horizontal axis box as:

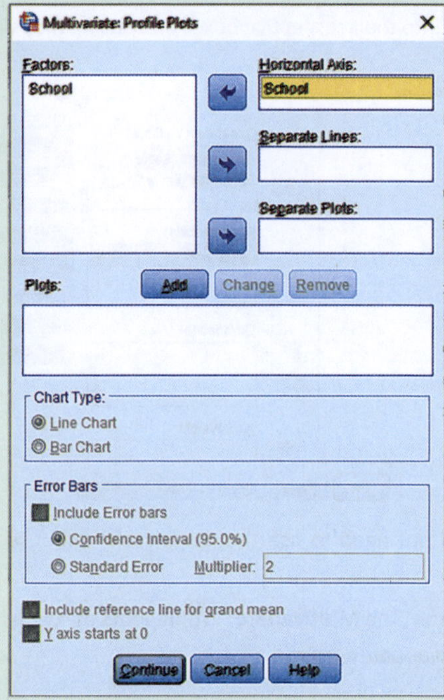

Step 6: Click on the Add button. "**School**" gets added to Plots box, as shown.

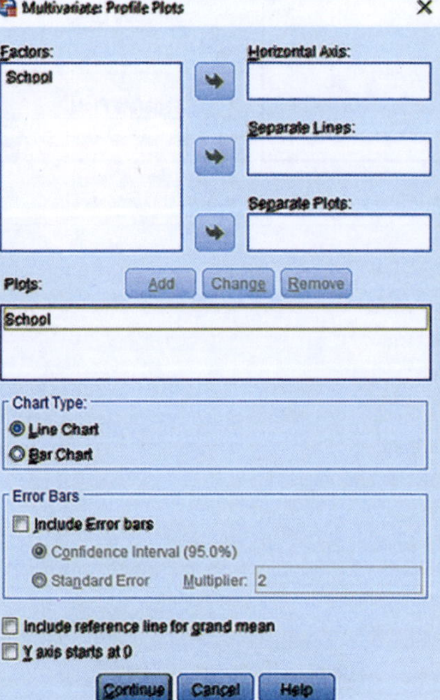

Contd...

Step 7: Click on the Continue button and this will be take you to the **Multivariate** dialogue box.

Step 8: Click on the Post Hoc… button. The **Multivariate: Post Hoc Multiple Comparisons for Observed Means** dialogue box, will open

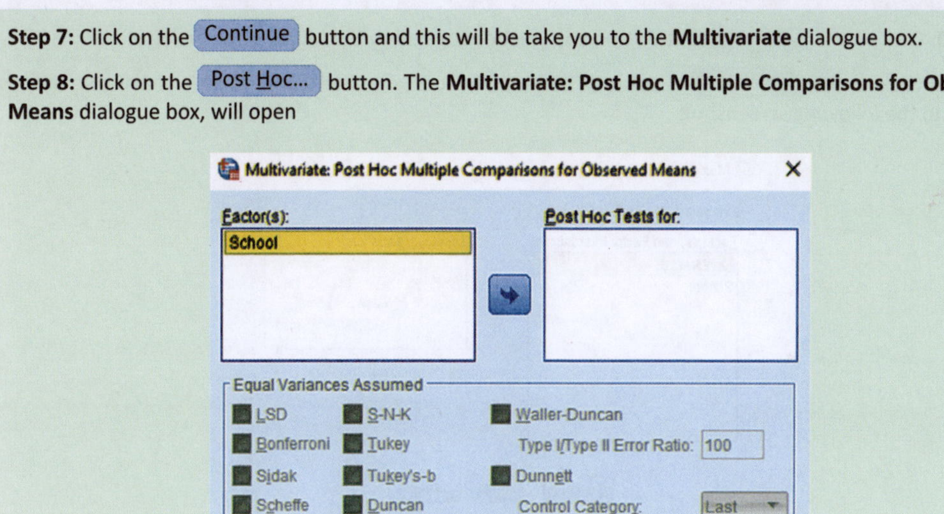

Step 9: Transfer the independent variable, that is School into the box for Post Hoc test and select the *Tukey* checkbox *in Equal variances assumed area* is as shown:

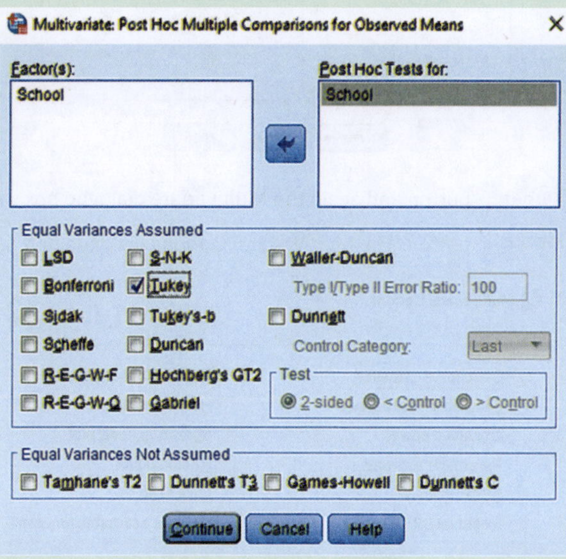

Note: You can select other Post Hoc Tests depending on your data and study design. If your independent variable has only two levels/categories, you do not need to complete this post hoc section.

Contd...

Step 10: Click on the `Continue` button and you will be returned to the Multivariate dialogue box.

Step 11: Click on the `EM Means...` button. The Multivariate: Estimated Marginal Means dialogue box, as shown in the following screenshot:

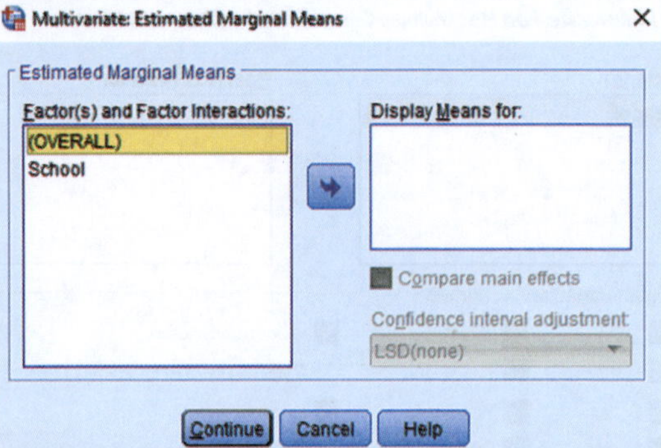

Step 12: Transfer the independent variable, "**School**", from the Factors and Factor Interactions box into the Display Means box. The following screen appears:

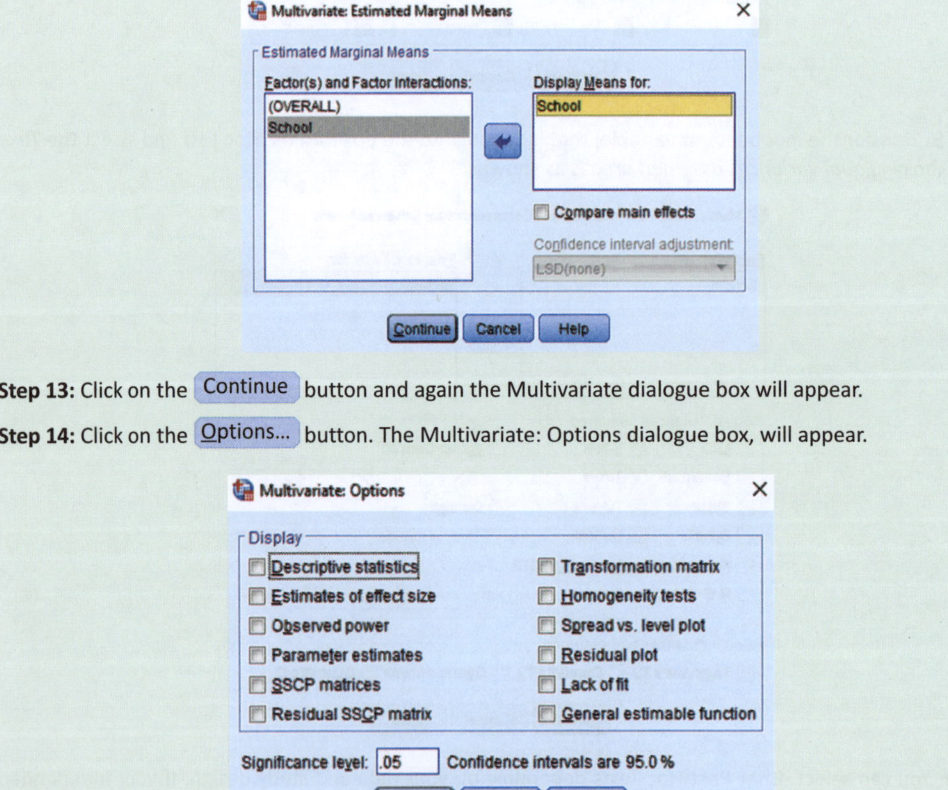

Step 13: Click on the `Continue` button and again the Multivariate dialogue box will appear.

Step 14: Click on the `Options...` button. The Multivariate: Options dialogue box, will appear.

Contd...

Step 15: Select the Descriptive statistics and Estimates of check size checkboxes in Display area. The following screen will appear.

Step 16: Click on the Continue button and this will take you to the Multivariate dialogue box.

Step 17: Click on the OK button to generate the output.

ANCOVA

ANCOVA is known as Analysis of Covariance. It is a statistical test related to ANOVA. It tests whether there is a significant difference between groups after controlling for variance explained by a covariate. A covariate is a continuous variable that correlates with the dependent variable. It means that one can, in effect, "partial out" a continuous variable and run an ANOVA on the results. This is one-way that a statistical test can be done with both categorical and continuous independent variables.

Hypotheses for ANCOVA

H_0 and H_1 need to be stated slightly differently for an ANCOVA than a regular ANOVA.
- H_0: the group means are equal after controlling for the covariate.
- H_1: the group means are not equal after controlling for the covariate.

Assumptions for ANCOVA

ANCOVA assumptions are followed here too:
- Variance is normally distributed.
- Variance is equal between groups.
- All measurements are independent for ANCOVA:
  - Relationship between DV and covariate is linear.
  - The relationship between the DV and covariate is the same for all groups.

ANCOVA works by adjusting the total SS, group SS, and error SS of the independent variable to remove the influence of the covariate. However, the sum of squares must also be calculated for the covariate. For this reason, SSdv (sum of the squared deviations) will be used for SS scores for the dependent variable, and SScv (sum of the squared covariance) will be used for the covariate.

Sum of squares

$$SS_x\,total = \Sigma\Sigma\,(xi_j - \overline{x})^2$$

$$SS_x\,group = \Sigma_{nj}\,(\overline{x} - \overline{x})^2$$

$$SS_x \, error = \Sigma\Sigma \, (xi_j - \overline{x}_j)^2$$

$$SS_x \, error = SS_x total - SS_x group$$

Sum of products: To control for the covariate, the sum of products (SP) for the DV and covariate must also be used. This is the sum of the products of the residuals for both the DV and the covariate

Total sum of products: This is just the sum of the multiplied residuals for all data points.

$$SP_{xy} \, total = \sum_j \sum_i (xi_j - \overline{x})(yi_j - \overline{y})$$

Here, x is the covariate, and y is the DV, i is individual subject, and j is the group.

Group sum of products: This is the sum of the products of the group means minus the grand means times the group size.

$$SP_{xy} \, group = \sum_j nj(\overline{xj} - \overline{x})(\overline{yi} - \overline{y})$$

Adjusting the sum of squares: Using the SS's for the covariate and the DV, and the SP's, we can adjust the SS's for the DV.

Sum of squares

$$SS_y \, adjusted \, total = SS_y \, total - \frac{(SP_{xy} \, total)^2}{SS_x \, total}$$

$$SS_y \, adjusted \, group = SS_y group + \frac{(SP_{xy} \, error)^2}{SS_x \, error} - \frac{(SP_{xy} \, total)^2}{SS_x \, total}$$

$$SS_y \, adjusted \, error = SS_y group - \frac{(SP_{xy} \, error)^2}{SS_x \, error}$$

Now, using the adjusted SS's, we can run an ANOVA to see if there is a difference between the groups. Note that this is exactly same as a regular ANOVA, but here we use the adjusted SS's instead of the original ones. Degrees of freedom are not affected.

Error sum of products

$$SP_{xy} error = \sum_j \sum_i (xii - \overline{xj})(yij - \overline{yi})$$

$$SP_{xy} \, error = SP_{xy} \, total - SP_{xy} \, group$$

- This is the sum of the products of the DV and residual minus the group means of the DV and residual
- This just happens to be the same as the difference between the other two sum of products.

Post Hocs for ANCOVA

Post-Hoc tests can be done using the adjusted means for ANCOVA, including LSD and Bonferroni.

We can also determine whether the covariate is significant by getting a F score, as:

$$F(1, N-2) = \frac{\left(\frac{(SP_{xy} \, total)^2}{SS_x \, total}\right)(N-2)}{SS_y \, adj \, total}$$

The group means can also be adjusted to estimate the effect of the covariate:

$$adj \, \overline{y}_j = \overline{yj} - \left(\frac{SP_{xy} \, error}{SS_x \, error}\right)(\overline{xj} - \overline{x})$$

Example of ANCOVA: Subjects (individuals) were given a self-esteem test, with scores of 1–10. Then we primed subjects with either positive or negative emotions. We asked them to spend a few minutes writing about themselves. Our dependent measure is the number of positive emotion words they used (e.g., happy, good).

- The null hypothesis is that the priming does not make a difference after controlling for self-esteem.
- The alternative hypothesis is that the priming does make a difference after controlling for self-esteem

Data			
Subject #	Priming	Self-esteem	Positive words
1	Positive	1	7
2	Positive	5	10
3	Positive	7	11
4	Negative	8	7
5	Negative	3	4
6	Negative	6	5

Practical Tips

ANCOVA in SPSS

To do ANCOVA in SPSS, all one needs to do is to add the covariate to the "covariate" box in the "univariate" menu. Everything else is the exactly same as it is for ANOVA.

Summary table of statistical tests

Level of measurement	Sample characteristics					Correlation
	1 sample	2 sample		K sample (i.e., >2)		
		Independent	Dependent	Independent	Dependent	
Categorical or Nominal	χ^2 or binominal	χ^2	McNemar's χ^2	χ^2	Cochran's Q	
Rank or Ordinal	χ^2	Mann-Whitney U	Wilcoxon Matched-pairs signed ranks	Kruskal-Wallis H	Friedman's ANOVA	Spearman's rho
Parametric (Interval and ratio)	Z-test or t-test	t-test between groups	t-test within groups	One-way ANOVA between groups	One-way ANOVA (within or repeated measure)	Pearson's
		Factorial (two-way) ANOVA				

STUDENT ASSIGNMENT

LONG ANSWER QUESTIONS

1. What are parametric tests? Discuss.
2. What are the different types of parametric tests? Discuss t-test.

SHORT ANSWER QUESTIONS

1. Write about assumptions of ANOVA.
2. Write characteristics of t-test.

MULTIPLE CHOICE QUESTIONS

1. **A researcher measured the same group of people's physiological reactions while watching horror films and compared them to when watching erotic films, and a documentary about wildlife. The resulting data were skewed. What test should be used to analyze the data?**
   a. Independent analysis of variance
   b. Repeated-measures analysis of variance
   c. Friedman's ANOVA
   d. Kruskal-Wallis test

2. **If the assumptions of parametric tests are met, nonparametric tests compared to their parametric counterparts:**
   a. Have less statistical power
   b. Are more conservative
   c. Are less likely to accept the alternative hypothesis
   d. All of the above

3. **Analysis of variance is a statistical method of comparing _______ of several populations.**
   a. Means
   b. Variances
   c. Standard deviations
   d. None of these

4. **The _________ sum of squares measures the variability of the observed values around their respective treatment means.**
   a. Error
   b. Total
   c. Treatment
   d. Interaction

5. **In a study, subjects are randomly assigned to one of three groups: control, experimental A, or experimental B. After treatment, the mean scores for the three groups are compared. The appropriate statistical test for comparing these means is:**
   a. Analysis of variance
   b. Correlation coefficient
   c. Chi Square
   d. t-Test

6. **What would happen if instead of using an ANOVA to compare 10 groups, you performed multiple t- tests?**
   a. Making multiple comparisons with a t-test increases the probability of making a Type I error
   b. Sir Ronald Fischer would be turning over in his grave; he put all that work into developing ANOVA, and you use multiple t-tests

c. Nothing serious, except that making multiple comparisons with a t-test requires more computation than doing a single ANOVA

d. Nothing, there is no difference between using an ANOVA and using a t-test

7. **What is the function of a post-test in ANOVA?**
   a. Describe those groups that have reliable differences between group means
   b. Set the critical value for the F test (or chi-square)
   c. Determine if any statistically significant group differences have occurred
   d. None of the above

8. **If the MSE of an ANOVA for six treatment groups is known, you can compute:**
   a. The pooled standard deviation
   b. The standard deviation of each treatment group
   c. df1
   d. All answers are correct

9. **In one-way ANOVA, which of the following is used within the F-ratio as a measurement of the variance of individual observations?**
   a. SSE
   b. MSE
   c. MSTR
   d. None of these

10. **A numerical value used as a summary measure for a sample, such as sample mean, is known as a:**
    a. Population parameter
    b. Sample parameter
    c. Sample statistic
    d. Population mean

11. **Since the population size is always larger than the sample size, then the sample statistic:**
    a. Can never be larger than the population parameter
    b. Can never be equal to the population parameter
    c. Can never be zero
    d. None of the answers is correct.

12. **The mean of a sample is:**
    a. Always equal to the mean of the population
    b. Always smaller than the mean of the population
    c. Computed by summing the data values and dividing the sum by $(n-1)$
    d. Computed by summing all the data values and dividing the sum by the number of items

13. **The sum of the percent frequencies for all classes will always equal to:**
    a. One
    b. The number of classes
    c. The number of items in the study
    d. 100

14. **In a-5-number summary, which of the following is not used for data summarization?**
    a. The smallest value
    b. The largest value
    c. The median
    d. The 25th percentile

15. **Since the mode is the most frequently occurring data value, it:**
    a. Can never be larger than the mean
    b. Is always larger than the median
    c. Is always larger than the mean
    d. None of the given answers is correct

15

Nonparametric Tests

"Statistics are no substitute for judgment."
—Henry Clay

LEARNING OBJECTIVES

After the completion of the chapter, the readers will be able to:
- Understand nonparametric tests.
- Calculate parametric tests by manually and using SPSS.

CHAPTER OUTLINE

- Introduction
- Uses of Nonparametric Tests
- Advantages of Nonparametric Tests
- Disadvantages of Nonparametric Tests
- Chi-square Test
- Sign Test
- Median Test
- Mann-Whitney U test
- McNemar's Test
- Kruskal-Wallis One-way Analysis-of-Variance

INTRODUCTION

Nonparametric statistics is the branch of statistics that is not based solely on parameters of probability distributions. Nonparametric statistics is based on either being distribution-free or having a specified distribution but with the distribution's parameters unspecified.

Nonparametric tests are used when data is not normal. Therefore, the key is to figure out if you have normally distributed data. For example, one looks at the distribution of data and if this data is approximately normal, then parametric statistical tests are more preferred.

USES OF NONPARAMETRIC TESTS

We use nonparametric test when:
- There is no constant of a population.
- The data do not follow any specific distribution and no assumptions are made, e.g., to classify good, better and best and we just allocate arbitrary numbers or marks to each category.

Practical Tips

There is no graph to know the normality of data, first check skewness and kurtosis using software like Excel. A normal distribution has no skew. If distribution is not normal, one can use a nonparametric test like chi square test.

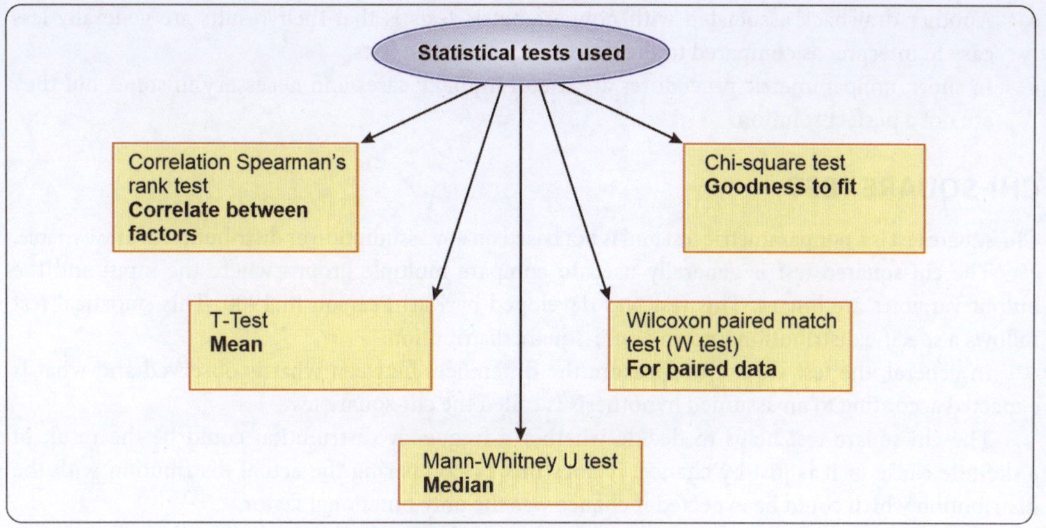

Figure 15.1: Nonparametric tests

ADVANTAGES OF NONPARAMETRIC TESTS

- In nonparametric tests, (Fig. 15.1) data are not normally distributed. Most psychological data are measured in ordinal and interval levels of measurement. Parametric tests are influenced by the character of normal distribution.
- Nonparametric tests are "distribution free statistics" and they can describe some or other attribute of a population. The relationship or differences among other attributes in populations where no assumptions are required can be tested by these tests.
- It can test hypotheses about particular attribute. The nonparametric tests are used when testing ordinal or nominal variables or when the assumptions of parametric tests are not fulfilled.
- A nonparametric statistical test does not specify conditions about the parameters of the population.
- Nonparametric tests need very small samples like N = 6.
- These tests can treat samples that are drawn from several different populations and these can treat data which are characteristically in ranks or their numerical scores have the strength in ranks.
- Nonparametric tests are available to treat data which are arranged in orders.
- They are easier to learn and apply than parametric tests.

DISADVANTAGES OF NONPARAMETRIC TESTS

- Nonparametric tests are less precise and somehow lead to wastefulness of data.
- There are no softwares for quick and large scale analysis.
- They have low power and false sense of security.
- Nonparametric tests are used for testing distributions only and higher-ordered interactions not dealt with.
- They are generally statistically less powerful compared to analog parametric.
- Nonparametric test will require a slightly larger sample size to have the same power as the corresponding parametric test.

- Another drawback associated with nonparametric tests is that their results are generally less easy to interpret as compared to the results of parametric tests.
- In short, nonparametric procedures are useful in many cases and necessary in some, but they are not a perfect solution.

CHI-SQUARE TEST

Chi-square test is a nonparametric test and is not based on any assumption or distribution of any variable.

The chi-squared test is generally used to compare multiple groups where the input and the output variables are binary. This test was developed by Karl Pearson in 1900. This statistical test follows a specific distribution known as chi-square distribution.

In general, the test we use to measure the differences between what is observed and what is expected according to an assumed hypothesis is called the chi-square test.

The chi-square test helps to decide whether a frequency distribution could be the result of a definite cause or it is just by chance. It does this by comparing the actual distribution with the distribution which could be expected if chance was the only functional factor.

If the difference between the observed results and the expected results is small, then chance is the only factor. On the other hand, if the difference between observed and expected results is large, then the difference is said to be significant and we expect that something is causing it.

Characteristics of a Chi-square Test

- This test as a nonparametric test is based on frequencies and not on the parameters such as mean and standard deviation.
- The test is used for testing the hypothesis and is not useful for estimation.
- This test can also be applied to a complex contingency table with several classes, as such is a very useful test in research work.
- This test is an important nonparametric test because no rigid assumptions are necessary in regard to the type of population, no need of parameter values and relatively less mathematical details are involved.

Chi-square Distribution

If $\chi_1, \chi_2,....\chi_n$ are independent normal variants and each is distributed normally with mean zero and standard deviation unity, then $\chi_1^2 + \chi_2^2 + ... + \chi_n^2 = \Sigma\chi_i^2$ is distributed as chi-square (χ^2) with n degrees of freedom (df), where n is large. The chi-square curve (Fig. 15.2) for df, $N = 1, 5$ and 9 is as follows:
- If degree of freedom > 2: Distribution is bell-shaped.
- If degree of freedom = 2: Distribution is L-shaped with maximum ordinate at zero.
- If degree of freedom <2 (>0): Distribution is L-shaped with infinite ordinate at the origin.

Applications of a Chi-square Test

Test of Goodness of Fit of Distributions

This test enables us to see how well does the assumed theoretical distribution such as Binomial distribution, Poisson distribution or Normal distribution, fit to the observed data. The chi-square test formula for goodness of fit is:

$$\chi^2 = \Sigma\frac{(O - E)^2}{E}$$

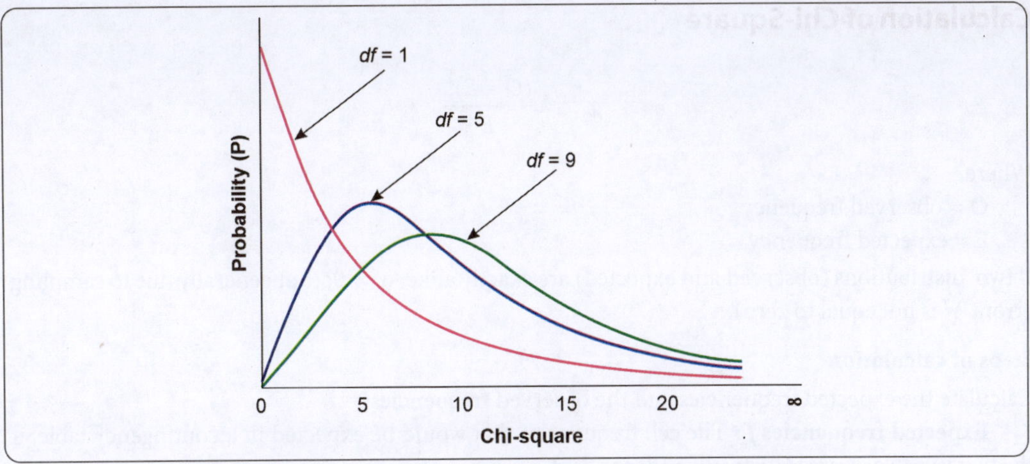

Figure 15.2: Chi-square distributions for 1, 5, 9 degrees of freedom

Where,

$\quad$ O = observed frequency

$\quad$ E = expected frequency

- If χ^2 (calculated) $>\chi^2$ (tabulated), with $(n - 1)$ *df*, the null hypothesis is rejected, otherwise accepted.
- And if null hypothesis is accepted, then it can be concluded the given distribution follows theoretical distribution.

Test of Independence of Attributes

This test enables us to explain whether or not two attributes are associated. For instance, we may be interested in knowing whether a new medicine is effective in controlling fever or not, here chi-square test is useful. In such a situation, we proceed with the null hypothesis that the two attributes—new medicine and control of fever are independent which means that new medicine is not effective in controlling fever.

χ^2 (calculated) $> \chi^2$ (tabulated) at a certain level of significance for given degrees of freedom, the null hypothesis is rejected, i.e., two variables are dependent, (i.e., the new medicine is effective in controlling the fever) and if, χ^2 (calculated) $<\chi^2$ (tabulated), the null hypothesis is accepted, i.e., Two variables are independent, (i.e., the new medicine is not effective in controlling the fever).

When null hypothesis is rejected, it can be concluded that there is a significant association between two attributes.

Test of Homogeneity

This test can also be used to test whether the occurrence of events follow uniformity or not, e.g., the admission of patients in government hospital in all days of week is uniform or not can be tested with the help of chi-square test.

If χ^2 (calculated) $<\chi^2$ (tabulated), then null hypothesis is accepted, and it can be concluded that there is a uniformity in the occurrence of the events, uniformity in the admission of patients throughout the week.

Calculation of Chi-Square

$$\chi^2 = \Sigma \frac{(O - E)^2}{E}$$

Where,

O = observed frequency

E = expected frequency

If two distributions (observed and expected) are exactly alike, $\chi^2 = 0$; (but generally due to sampling errors, χ^2 is not equal to zero).

Steps of calculation

Calculate the expected frequencies and the observed frequencies:

Expected frequencies f_e: The cell frequencies that would be expected in a contingency table, if the two variables were statistically independent.

Observed frequencies f_o: The cell frequencies actually observed in a contingency table.

$$f_e = \frac{(\text{column total}) \ (\text{row total})}{N}$$

To obtain the expected frequencies for any cell in any cross-tabulation in which the two variables are assumed independent, multiply the row and column totals for that cell and divide the product by the total number of cases in the table.

$$\chi^2 = \Sigma \frac{\left(f_e - f_o\right)^2}{f_e}$$

Conditions for the Application of Chi-Square Test

The following conditions should be satisfied before chi-square test can be applied:

- The data must be in the form of frequencies.
- The frequency data must have a precise numerical value and must be organized into categories or groups.
- Observations recorded and used are collected on a random basis.
- All the items in the sample must be independent.
- No group should contain very few items, say <10. In case, where the frequencies are <10, regrouping is done by combining the frequencies of adjoining groups so that the new frequencies become >10. Some statisticians take this number as 5, but 10 is regarded as better by most of the statisticians.
- The overall number of items must also be reasonably large. It should normally be at least 50.

Example: A nurse wants to discover whether there is a correlation or relationship between fever and person exposed to the cold. The expected outcome is that 90 patients out of 100 will develop a fever from being exposed to the cold.

Solution:

- Decide on a hypothesis that should be tested such as, Gather data. Out of 100 patients, 75 experience a fever when exposed to the cold, while 25 experience a fever without being exposed to the cold. These are the aspects of the experiment that have been observed.

- Calculate: The number of patients observed with a fever from the cold, 75. Subtract the number of expected patients with fever, 90.
  75 – 90 = 15, multiply by 2 or square, 30, ignore the negative.
- Divide 30 against the expected number of cases.
- Determine the degrees of freedom (*df*). The *df* are calculated by dividing the number of cases compared with the number of cases compared.
  In this case, the equation would be 100/100 = 1.
  This determine whether or not the probability is significant.
  In this case, p = 0.05, p is found on the chi-square probability table.
- Find 0.01 under p = 0.05 on the chi-square distribution table. In this case, chi-square equals, 47.4. It means that the null hypothesis is true or exposure to the cold causes a fever 47% of the time.

> **Practical Tips**
>
> Chi-square must be computed carefully. It is easy to miss a step and receive a false negative or false positive.

Yate's Correction

If in the 2 × 2 contingency table, the expected frequencies are small say <5, then chi-square test cannot be used. In that case, the direct formula of the chi-square test is modified and given by:

$$\chi^2 \text{(corrected)} = \frac{N\,(|ad - bc| - 0.5\,N)^2}{R_1 R_2 C_1 C_2}$$

Limitations of a Chi-Square Test

- The data is from a random sample.
- This test applied in a fourfold table, will not give a reliable result with one degree of freedom, if the expected value in any cell is <5. In such case, Yate's correction is necessary, i.e., reduction of the mode of (O – E) by half.
- Even if Yate's correction, the test may be misleading if any expected frequency is much below 5. In that case another appropriate test should be applied.
- If contingency tables are larger than 2 × 2, Yate's correction cannot be applied.
- Interpret this test with caution if sample total or total of values in all the cells is <50.
- This test tells the presence or absence of an association between the events but does not measure the strength of association.
- This test does not indicate the cause and effect, it only tells the probability of occurrence of association by chance.
- The test is to be applied only when the individual observations of sample are independent which means that the occurrence of one individual observation (event) has no effect upon the occurrence of any other observation (event) in the sample under consideration.

SIGN TEST

The sign test is a statistical test used to compare the sizes of two groups. It is "distribution free" test and does not assume that the data is from normal distribution. The sign test is an alternative to unpaired or paired t test. It can also be used for ordered or ranked categorical data. The null hypothesis for sign test is that the difference between medians is zero. The sign test is used to determine if there is a significant difference between the mean characteristics of two populations (like A and B).

Responses for each pair of A and B are compared. The number of times A exceeded B is used as the test statistic. It is denoted as the letter X. The test is called the sign test because X is the number of positive (or negative) signs associated with the difference between the pairs in population A and B. In such cases, the implied null hypothesis is that the two population distributions are identical or there is no significant difference between the two population distributions A and B. For any given pair, the probability that A exceeds B is p = 0.5, when the null hypothesis is true.

Steps of Calculation of Sign Test

The following are the steps for doing the sign test:

- State the null hypothesis (H_0): There is no significant difference between the two populations being compared.
- State the alternative hypothesis (H_a): There is a significant difference between the two populations being compared.
- Test the null hypothesis using the following procedure:
  - Examine each pair (A and B) of observations. If A > B, assign a plus (+) sign, if A, <B, assign a minus (−) sign, if A = B, the pair must be discarded.
  - Count the number of pairs remaining and denote it by n.
  - Count the number of times the less frequent sign occurs and denote this by r.
- To test the null hypothesis, compare r with the critical values tabulated n the table for critical values of r for the sign test in the Appendix.
- Make decision. If r is less than or equal to the tabulated value for the chosen significance level, reject the null hypothesis.

Example: Apply sign test for the given data.

Solution: This set of data represents test scores before the beginning of a procedure and after ending it. The hypothesis is that the procedure produces a significant difference in both scores.

- H_0: No difference in medians of the signed differences.
- H_1: Median of the signed differences is less than zero.

Step 1: Subtract set 2 from set 1 and put the result in the third column.

Sl. no.	Set 1	Set 2	Set 1 – Set 2	Sign
1	443	57	386	+
2	421	352	69	+
3	436	587	−151	−
4	376	415	−39	−
5	458	458	0	Not applicable
6	408	424	−16	−
7	422	463	−41	−
8	431	583	−152	−
9	459	432	27	+
10	369	379	−10	−
11	360	370	−10	−
12	431	584	−153	−

Contd...

Sl. no.	Set 1	Set 2	Set 1 – Set 2	Sign
13	403	422	−19	−
14	436	587	−151	−
15	376	415	−39	−
16	370	419	−49	−
17	443	57	386	+

Step 2: Add a fourth column indicating the sign of the numbers mentioned in column 3.

Step 3: Count the positive and negative.

- 4 positives.
- 12 negatives.
- 12 negatives seem like a lot, but we cannot say for sure that it is significant, i.e., it did not happen by chance, until we did the sign test.

Step 4: Add up the number of items in the sample and subtract if a difference of zero is there (in column 3). The sample was of 17 subjects in this question and we subtract one $(n-1) = 16$.

Step 5: Use tables of the binomial distribution to find the probability of observing a value of r or higher assuming $p = 1/2$ and $n = n'$. If the test is one-sided, this is our p-value.

Find the *p*-value using a table. Probability is 0.5 here. If the test is a two-sided test, double the probability obtained in (2) to obtain the p-value.

Interpretation: Now, the null hypothesis was that there is an equal number of signs (i.e., 50/50). Therefore, the test is a simple binomial experiment with 0.5 chance of the sign being negative and 0.5 of it being positive when the null hypothesis is true.

- 16 is the number of trials.
- 4 is the number of successes. Here, successes means the smaller of either the positive or negative signs from Step 2.

The p-value in the table is 0.038, which is smaller than the alpha level of 0.05. We can reject the null hypothesis and say there is a significant difference.

Example: The data in the table shows the hours of relief provided by two analgesic drugs in 12 patients suffering from arthritis. Is there any evidence that one drug provides longer relief than the other?

Case	Drug A	Drug B	Case	Drug A	Drug B
1	2.0	3.5	7	14.9	16.7
2	3.6	5.7	8	6.6	6.0
3	2.6	2.9	9	2.3	3.8
4	2.6	2.4	10	2.0	4.0
5	7.3	9.9	11	6.8	9.1
6	3.4	3.3	12	8.5	20.9

Solution: In this case, our null hypothesis is that the median difference is zero. Our actual differences (Drug B – Drug A) are:

$$+1.5, +2.1, +0.3, -0.2, +2.6, -0.1, +1.8, -0.6, +1.5, +2.0, +2.3, +12.4$$

Our actual median difference is 1.65 hours.

We have $r+ = 9$, $r- = 3$, $n = 12$, $r = \max(r-, r+) = 9$.

Therefore, our two-sided *p*-value (from binomial tables) is $p = 0.146$.

Interpretation: We would conclude that there is no evidence for a difference between the two treatments.

Carrying Out the Sign Test in SPSS

Case 1: Paired data (Figs 15.3 and 15.4).

- Choose Analyze.
- Select Nonparametric Tests.
- Select two Related Samples.
- Specify which two variables comprise the pairs of observation by clicking on them both and then clicking on the arrow to put them under Test Pair(s) List.
- Under Test Type select Sign.
- Click on OK button.

The output will look like this:

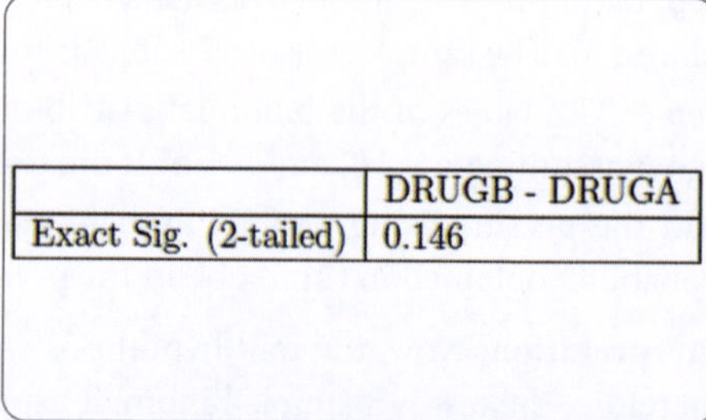

		N
Drug B - Drug A	Negative Differences^a	3
	Positive Differences^b	9
	Ties^c	0
	Total	12

a. DRUGB < DRUGA
b. DRUGB > DRUGA
c. DRUGA = DRUGB

	DRUGB - DRUGA
Exact Sig. (2-tailed)	0.146

Figure 15.3: Output on SPSS for paired data   **Figure 15.4:** Test statistics

If you are carrying out a one-sided test, you require to divide the p-value by 2.

Case 2: Single set of observations

Note that in this case, SPSS includes values that are exactly equal to the median and it takes $r+$ = the number of observations that are greater than M; and $r-$ = the number of observations that is less than or equal to M. Any ties should therefore be excluded manually as follows:

- Choose "Data then Select Cases"
- Choose "If" condition is satisfied and click on "If" in the box type in variable name (M is not equal), where M is the median value specified in the null hypothesis.
- Click on "Continue, then OK" and proceed as:
  - Choose "Analyze."
  - Select "Nonparametric Tests."
  - Select "Binomial."
  - Choose the relevant variable as the "Test Variable."
  - Under "Define Dichotomy" in the lower left hand corner of the pop-up screen, choose "Cut Point" and specify the null value (i.e., 0 in the case of paired data, etc.).
  - Click on "OK button."

The output will look like this:

Binomial Test

		Category	N	Observed Prop.	Test Prop.	Exact Sig. (2-tailed)
Drug B - Drug A	Group 1	≤ 0	3	0.25	0.50	0.146
	Group 2	> 0	9	0.75		
	Total		12	1		

If you were carrying out a one-sided test, you would need to divide the p-value by 2.

MEDIAN TEST

The median test is a nonparametric test used to test whether two (or more) independent groups differ in central tendency—specifically whether the groups have been drawn from a population with the same median.

It gives information whether it is likely that two independent groups (not necessarily of the same size) have been drawn from populations with the same median.

- Null hypothesis: The two groups are from populations with the same median.
- Alternate hypothesis: The median of one population is different from that of the other (two-tailed test) or the median of one population is higher than that of the other (one-tailed test).

Principle of Median Test

The principle of the test is that if two samples have the same median, they should have more or less the same proportion of observations above and below that median. If any score falls at the value of the combined median that score either is dropped from the analysis, or is included with scores less than the median.

Advantages of Median Test

- It has advantage over Mann-Whitney test because it is only test for differences in the median irrespective of any differences in the shape of the distribution. But, it has much less power.
- There is no alternative to median test when one or more observations are off the scale (e.g., censored observations).
- It is more robust to outliers.

Steps of Calculation of Median Test

- Determine the combined median of the $m + n$ scores.
- Split each group's score at that combined median—those which exceed the median and those which do not. Enter the resultant frequencies into a 2 × 2 table.

	Group I	Group II	Combined
No. of scores above combined median	A	B	A + B
No. of scores below combined median	C	D	C + D

- Find the probability of the observed values by either the fisher exact test, if $m + n \leq 20$ or its Chi–square corrected for continuity, if $m + n > 20$.

$$p = \frac{(A + B)! \, (C + D)! \, (A + C)! \, (B + D)!}{N! \, A! \, B! \, C! \, D!}$$

$$x^2 = \frac{N(|AD - BC| - \frac{N}{2})^2}{(A + B)(C + D)(A + C)(B + D)}$$

Example: Perform median test for following data:

The following are observations for two independent samples:

Sample I	10	10	10	12	15	17	17	19	20	22	25	26	The combined
Sample II	6	7	8	8	12	16	19	19	22				median is 16.

	Sample I	Sample II	Combined d	
No. of scores above combined median	5	6	11	$\chi^2 = 0.48125$
No. of scores below combined median	12	9	21	

I. H_0: the two groups are from populations with the same median.

 H_1: the median of one population is different from that of the other.

II. Statistical test: Median test

III. Level of significance is at. 1% with df = 1

IV. Decision rule: if $\chi^2 \geq 6.64$, reject H_0

 if $\chi^2 < 6.64$, accept H_0

V. Computation

VI. Decision: Since 0.48125 < 6.64, accept H_0 at. 1% level

MANN-WHITNEY U TEST

Mann-Whitney U test was originally proposed by Wilcoxon in 1945, later was modified by Mann and Whitney in 1947 to allow for different sample sizes. Where the assumptions are not met for a parametric test, a Wilcoxon-Mann-Whitney test is more robust and more or less equally powerful. It is a nonparametric test. Because,

- The sum of ranks is much more sensitive to differences in location than of variance.
- Although the sum of ranks is unaffected by outlying observations, it weighs observations in place of merely counting how many ranks lie above and below the median under test. So, unless the observations are highly skewed, their sum of ranks is approximately normal for modest sample sizes.

It is analogous to the t-test for continuous variable but can be used for ordinal data. It is used to analyze the difference between the medians of different data sets. The critical values table is used to assess the degree of difference. The test compares two independent populations to determine their difference in statistics.

Uses of Mann-Whitney U Test

The Mann-Whitney U test can be used if:

- The difference between two samples of data is to be investigated.

- Data is nonparametric.
- The data is ordinal.
- There are >5 pieces of data in each sample.

Advantages of Mann-Whitney U Test

- It is valid for ordinal as well as for measurement variables, including derived variables.
- It is quite powerful. The Wilcoxon-Mann-Whitney test approaches 95.5% of power of a *t*-test for large samples under assumptions.
- It needs less assumptions than analogous parametric test, and is more robust when these assumptions are disrupted.
- It requires less computation.

Steps of Calculations of Mann-Whitney U Test

H_0: The two populations are equal versus.

H_1: The two populations are not equal.

This test is often performed as a two-sided test and, thus, the research hypothesis indicates that the populations are not equal. A one-sided research hypothesis is used if we want to detect a positive or negative shift in one population as compared to the other.

The procedure for the test involves pooling the observations from the two samples into one combined sample, (keeping track of which sample each observation comes from) and then ranking lowest to highest from 1 to $n_1 + n_2$, respectively.

Example: A Phase II clinical trial was designed to investigate the effectiveness of a new drug to reduce symptoms of asthma in children. A total of 10 participants are randomized to receive either the new drug or a placebo. Participants are asked to record the number of episodes of shortness of breath over a one week period following receipt of the assigned treatment. The data are:

Placebo	7	5	6	4	12
New drug	3	6	4	2	1

Is there a difference in the number of episodes of shortness of breath over a one week period in participants receiving the new drug as compared to those receiving the placebo? By inspection, it appears that participants receiving the placebo have more episodes of shortness of breath, but is this statistically significant?

Solution: Here, the outcome is a count and in this sample the data do not follow a normal distribution. Moreover, the sample size is small ($n_1 = n_2 = 5$), so a nonparametric test is appropriate.

We run the test at the 5% level of significance (i.e., $\alpha = 0.05$).

H_0: The two populations are equal.

H_1: The two populations are not equal.

Note: If the null hypothesis is true (i.e., the two populations are equal), we expect to see similar numbers of episodes of shortness of breath in each of the two treatment groups, and we would expect to see some participants reporting few episodes and some reporting more episodes in each group. This does not appear to be the case with the observed data. A test of hypothesis is needed to determine whether the observed data is an evidence of a statistically significant difference in populations (Fig.15.5).

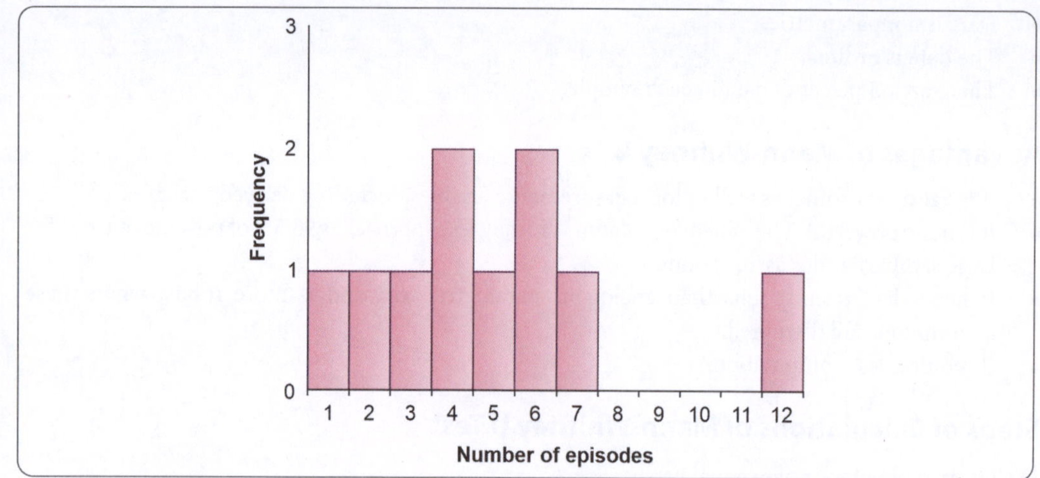

Figure 15.5: Frequency histogram of number of episodes of shortness of breath

Step 1: Assign ranks to order the data from smallest to largest values. This is done on the combined or total sample (i.e., pooling the data from the two treatment groups ($n = 10$)), and assigning ranks from 1 to 10, as follows. We also need to keep track of the group assignments in the total sample.

Placebo	New drug	Total Sample (ordered smallest to largest)		Rank	
		Placebo	New drug	Placebo	New drug
7	3		1		1
5	6		2		2
6	4		3		3
4	2	4	4	4.5	4.5
12	1	5		6	
		6	6	7.5	7.5
		7		9	
		12		10	

Note that the lower ranks (e.g., 1, 2 and 3) are assigned to responses in the new drug group while the higher ranks (e.g., 9, 10) are assigned to responses in the placebo group. Again, the goal of the test is to determine whether the observed data supports a difference in the populations of responses. We produce a test statistic based on the ranks.

Step 2: Now, we sum the ranks in each group. In the placebo group, the sum of the ranks is 37; in the new drug group, the sum of the ranks is 18. Remember, the sum of the ranks will always equal to $n(n + 1)/2$.

$$n(n + 1)/2 = \frac{10(11)}{2}$$

$$= 55 \text{ or } 37 + 18 = 55$$

Step 3: For the test, we call the placebo group 1 and the new drug group 2 (assignment of groups 1 and 2 is arbitrary). R_1 denotes the sum of the ranks in group 1 (i.e., $R_1 = 37$), and R_2 denotes the sum of the ranks in group 2 (i.e., $R_2 = 18$). If the null hypothesis is true (i.e., if the two populations are equal), we expect R_1 and R_2 to be similar.

In this example, the lower values (lower ranks) are clustered in the new drug group (group 2), while the higher values (higher ranks) are clustered in the placebo group (group 1). This indicates the effect, but is the observed difference in the sums of the ranks simply due to chance?

Test statistic

The test statistic for Mann-Whitney U test is denoted by U. U_1 and U_2, are given as:

$$U_1 = n_1 n_2 + \frac{n_1(n_1+1)}{2} - R_1$$

$$U_2 = n_1 n_2 + \frac{n_2(n_2+1)}{2} - R_2$$

R_1 = sum of the ranks for group 1
R_2 = sum of the ranks for group 2.

In this example,

$$U_1 = 5(5) + \frac{5(6)}{2} - 37 = 3$$

$$U_2 = 5(5) + \frac{5(6)}{2} - 18 = 22$$

In our example, U = 3.

Interpretation: Now, we will see whether this evidence is in support of the null or research hypothesis. First we will consider the range of the test statistic U in two different situations.

First situation: When there is complete separation of the groups and it is supporting the research hypothesis that the two populations are not equal.

If all the higher numbers of episodes of shortness of breath (thus, all of the higher ranks) are in the placebo group, and all of the lower numbers of episodes (and ranks) are in the new drug group and there are no ties, then:

$$R_1 = 6 + 7 + 8 + 9 + 10 = 40 \text{ and } R_2 = 1 + 2 + 3 + 4 + 5 = 15$$

and

$$U_1 = 5(5) + \frac{5(6)}{2} - 40 = 0 \text{ and } U_2$$

$$= 5(5) + \frac{5(6)}{2} - 15 = 25$$

Therefore, when there is clearly a difference in the populations, U = 0.

Second situation: When there are low and high scores approximately evenly distributed in the two groups it supports the null hypothesis that the groups are equal. If ranks of 2, 4, 6, 8 and 10 are assigned to the numbers of episodes of shortness of breath reported in the placebo group and ranks of 1, 3, 5, 7 and 9 are assigned to the numbers of episodes of shortness of breath reported in the new drug group, then:

$$R_1 = 2 + 4 + 6 + 8 + 10 = 30 \text{ and } R_2 = 1 + 3 + 5 + 7 + 9 = 25$$

$$U_1 = 5(5) + \frac{5(6)}{2} - 30 = 10 \text{ and } U_2 = 5(5) + \frac{5(6)}{2} - 25 = 15$$

Hence, there is clearly no difference between populations, then U = 10.

Thus, smaller values of U support the research hypothesis, and larger values of U support the null hypothesis.

Practical Tips

- For any Mann-Whitney U test, the theoretical range of U is from 0 (complete separation between groups, H_0 most likely is false and H_1 most likely true) to $n_1 \times n_2$ (little evidence in support of H_1).
- In every test, **$U_1 + U_2$ is always equal to $n_1 \times n_2$**. In the example above, U can range from 0 to 25 and smaller values of U support the research hypothesis (i.e., we reject H_0 if U is small).
- The critical value of U can be found in the table given in appendix. To determine the appropriate critical value we need sample sizes (for example: $n_1 = n_2 = 5$) and our two-sided level of significance ($\alpha = 0.05$).
- Precisely, we determine a critical value of U in a way that if the observed value of U is less than or equal to the critical value, we reject H_0 and if the observed value of U exceeds the critical value, we do not reject H_0.

In our example, the critical value is 2, and the decision rule is to reject H_0 if U $\leq$2. We do not reject H_0 because 3 >2. We do not have statistically significant evidence at $\alpha = 0.05$, to show that the two populations of numbers of episodes of shortness of breath are not equal.

Example: A new approach to prenatal care is proposed for pregnant women living in a rural community. The new program involves in-home visits during the course of pregnancy in addition to the usual or regularly scheduled visits. A pilot randomized trial with 15 pregnant women was designed to evaluate whether women who participate in the program deliver healthier babies than women receiving usual care. The outcome is the Appearance, Pulse, Grimace, Activity, and Respiration score (APGAR) measured 5 minutes after birth.

(APGAR scores ranges from 0 to 10 with scores of 7 or higher considered normal (healthy), 4–6 low and 0–3 critically low). The data are shown here:

Usual care	8	7	6	2	5	8	7	3
New program	9	9	7	8	10	9	6	

Is there statistical evidence of a difference in APGAR scores in women receiving the new and enhanced versus usual prenatal care?

Solution:

Step 1: Set up hypotheses and determine level of significance.

H_0: The two populations are equal versus.

H_1: The two populations are not equal.

$$\alpha = 0.05$$

Step 2: Select the appropriate test statistic.

Because APGAR scores are not normally distributed and the samples are small ($n_1 = 8$ and $n_2 = 7$), we will use the Mann-Whitney U test. The test statistic is U, the smaller of

$$U_1 = n_1 n_2 + \frac{n_1(n_1+1)}{2} - R_1 \quad \text{and} \quad U_2 = n_1 n_2 + \frac{n_2(n_2+1)}{2} - R_2$$

Where R_1 and R_2 are the sums of the ranks in groups 1 and 2, respectively.

Step 3: Set up decision rule.

The appropriate critical value can be found in the critical value table for U. To determine the appropriate critical value we need sample sizes ($n_1 = 8$ and $n_2 = 7$) and our two-sided level of significance ($\alpha = 0.05$). The critical value for this test with $n_1 = 8$, $n_2 = 7$ and $\alpha = 0.05$ is 10 and the decision rule is as follows: Reject H_0 if U ≤ 10.

Step 4: Compute the test statistic.

The first step is to assign ranks of 1–15 to the smallest through largest values in the total sample, as follows:

		Total sample (ordered smallest to largest)		Rank	
Usual care	New program	Usual care	New program	Usual care	New program
8	9	2		1	
7	8	3		2	
6	7	5		3	
2	8	6	6	4.5	4.5
5	10	7	7	7	7
8	9	7		7	
7	6	8	8	10.5	10.5
3		8	8	10.5	10.5
		9			13.5
		9			13.5
		10			15
				$R_1 = 45.5$	$R_2 = 74.5$

Next, we sum the ranks in each group. In the usual care group, the sum of the ranks is $R_1 = 45.5$ and in the new program group, the sum of the ranks is $R_2 = 74.5$.

(The sum of the ranks will always equal $n(n + 1)/2$).

As a check on our assignment of ranks, we have:

$n(n + 1)/2 = 15(16)/2 = 120$ which is equal to $45.5 + 74.5 = 120$

We now compute U_1 and U_2, as follows:

$$U_1 = n_1 n_2 + \frac{n_1(n_1+1)}{2} - R_1 = 8(7) + \frac{8(9)}{2} - 45.5 = 46.5$$

$$U_2 = n_1 n_2 + \frac{n_2(n_2+1)}{2} - R_2 = 8(7) + \frac{7(8)}{2} - 74.5 = 9.5$$

Thus, the test statistic is U = 9.5.

Interpretation: We reject H_0 because $9.5 \leq 10$. We have statistically significant evidence at $\alpha = 0.05$ to show that the populations of APGAR scores are not equal in women receiving usual prenatal care as compared to the new program of prenatal care.

Example: A clinical trial is run to assess the effectiveness of a new antiretroviral therapy for patients with HIV. Patients are randomized to receive a standard antiretroviral therapy (usual care) or the new antiretroviral therapy and are monitored for 3 months. The primary outcome is viral load which represents the number of HIV copies per milliliter of blood. A total of 30 participants are randomized and the data are shown here:

Standard therapy	7500	8000	2000	550	1250	1000	2250	6800	3400	6300	9100	970	1040	670	400
New therapy	400	250	800	1400	8000	7400	1020	6000	920	1420	2700	4200	5200	4100	Undetectable

Is there statistical evidence of a difference in viral load in patients receiving the standard versus the new antiretroviral therapy?

Solution:

Standard Antiretroviral	New Antiretroviral	Total sample (Ordered smallest to largest) Standard Antiretroviral	Total sample (Ordered smallest to largest) New Antiretroviral	Rank Standard Antiretroviral	Rank New Antiretroviral
7500	400		Undetectable		1
8000	250		250		2
2000	800	400	400	3.5	3.5
550	1400	550		5	
1250	8000	670		6	
1000	7400		800		7
2250	1020		920		8
6800	6000	970		9	
3400	920	1000		10	
6300	1420		1020		11
9100	2700	1040		12	
970	4200	1250		13	
1040	5200		1400		14
670	4100		1420		15
400	Undetectable	2000		16	
		2250		17	
			2700		18
		3400		19	

Contd...

Standard Antiretroviral	New Antiretroviral	Total sample (Ordered smallest to largest)		Rank	
		Standard Antiretroviral	**New Antiretroviral**	**Standard Antiretroviral**	**New Antiretroviral**
			4100		20
			4200		21
			5200		22
			6000		23
		6300		24	
		6800		25	
			7400		26
		7500		27	
		8000	8000	28.5	28.5
		9100		30	
				$R_1 = 245$	$R_2 = 220$

Step 1: Set up hypotheses and determine level of significance.

H_0: The two populations are equal versus.

H_1: The two populations are not equal.

$$\alpha = 0.05$$

Step 2: Select the appropriate test statistic.

Because viral load measures are not normally distributed (with outliers as well as limits of detection (e.g., "undetectable")), we use the Mann-Whitney U test. The test statistic is U, the smaller of:

$$U_1 = n_1 n_2 + \frac{n_1(n_1+1)}{2} - R_1 \ and \ U_2 = n_1 n_2 + \frac{n_2(n_2+1)}{2} - R_2$$

Where R_1 and R_2 are the sums of the ranks in groups 1 and 2, respectively.

Step 3: Set up the decision rule.

The critical value can be found in the table of critical values based on sample sizes ($n_1 = n_2 = 15$) and a two-sided level of significance ($\alpha = 0.05$). The critical value is 64 and the decision rule is as follows: Reject H_0 if $U \leq 64$.

Step 4: Compute the test statistic.

The first step is to assign ranks of 1 through 30 to the smallest through largest values in the total sample. In the table above, the "undetectable" measurement is listed first in the ordered values (smallest) and assigned a rank of 1.

Next, we sum the ranks in each group. In the standard antiretroviral therapy group, the sum of the ranks is $R_1 = 245$. In the new antiretroviral therapy group, the sum of the ranks is $R_2 = 220$. (The sum of the ranks will always equal $n(n + 1)/2$. We have $n(n + 1)/2 = 30(31)/2 = 465$ which is equal to $245 + 220 = 465$. We now compute U_1 and U_2, as follows:

$$U_1 = n_1 n_2 + \frac{n_1(n_1+1)}{2} - R_1 = 15(15) + \frac{15(16)}{2} - 245 = 100$$

$$U_2 = n_1 n_2 + \frac{n_2(n_2+1)}{2} - R_2 = 15(15) + \frac{15(16)}{2} - 220 = 125$$

Thus, the test statistic is U = 100.

Step 5: Conclusion: We do not reject H_0 because 100 >64. We do not have sufficient evidence to conclude that the treatment groups differ in viral load.

Calculating Mann-Whitney Value with SPSS

This data was collected from a randomized controlled trial on patients with leg ulcers. It was aimed to compare a new treatment regime in the clinic with usual care at home. One of the variables of interest was the number of weeks patients remained ulcer free (UFW).

	PATID	GROUP	UFW
1	11119	Clinic	32.0
2	11206	Home	.0
3	11212	Home	35.1
4	11214	Home	.0

Research question: Is there a difference between the mean number of ulcer free weeks for the control and intervention groups?

Dependent variables: Numerical/continuous (skewed) or ordinal

Independent variables: Nominal (binary)

Data: Leg Ulcer data

The methods for running a Mann-Whitney test in SPSS is as follows:

Step 1: To run the test, go to **Analyze > Nonparametric Tests > Independent Samples** and leave the default setting on the "Objective" tab which is "Automatically compare distributions across groups", then select the "Fields" tab (Fig. 15.6).

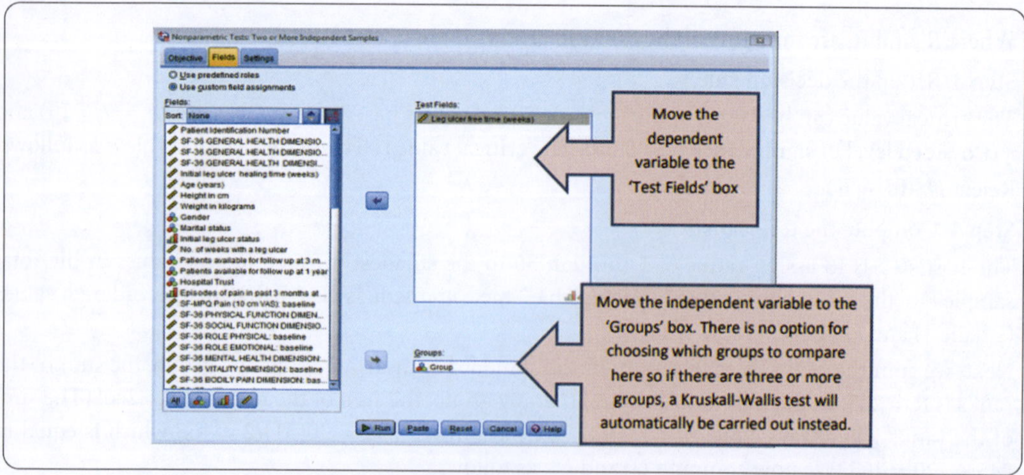

Figure 15.6: Input in SPSS for Mann-Whitney U test

Step 2: Click on "Run" to run the standard Mann-Whitney U test to get the output here (Figure 15.7):

Hypothesis Test Summary

	Null Hypothesis	Test	Sig.	Decision
1	The distribution of Leg ulcer free time (weeks) is the same across categories of Group.	Independent-Samples Mann-Whitney U Test	.017	Reject the null hypothesis.

Asymptotic significances are displayed. The significance level is .05.

Figure 15.7: Output in SPSS

Step 3: The output clearly indicates that the distributions are being compared, that the p-value is 0.017. The null hypothesis of equal distributions is rejected.

Step 4: If you double click on the results in the Output window, a new window with more information on the right hand side appears.

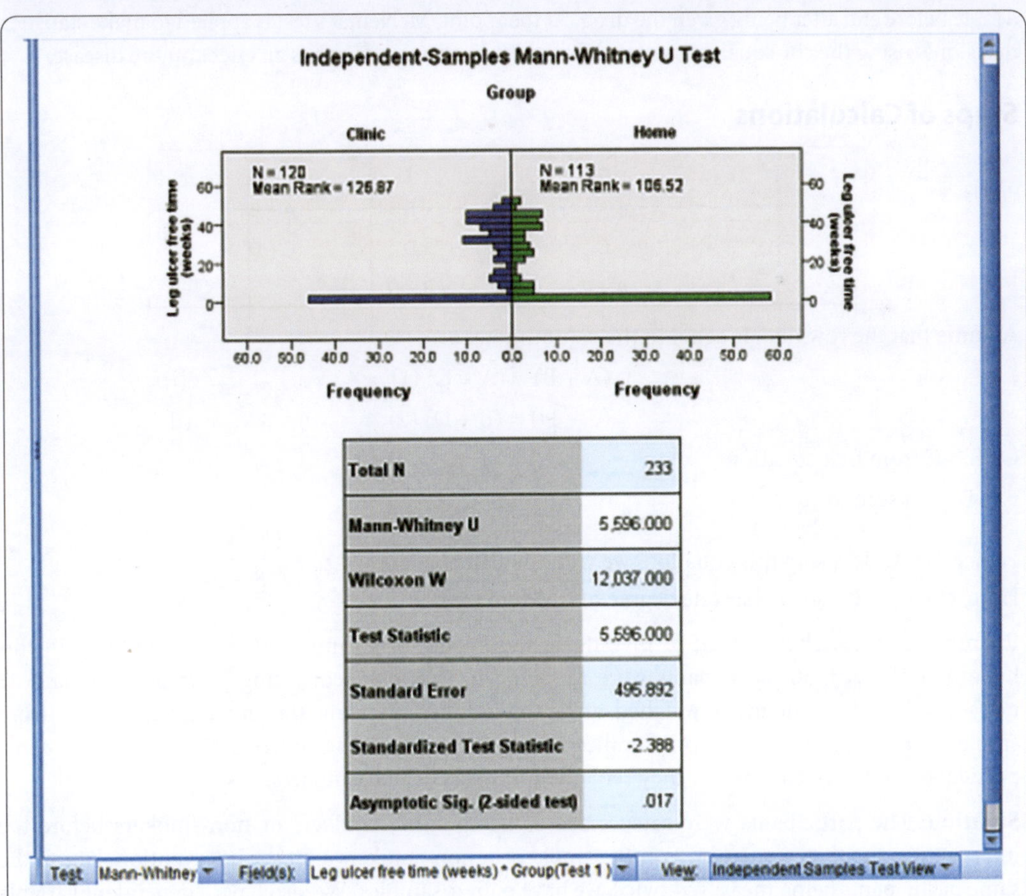

Total N	233
Mann-Whitney U	5,596.000
Wilcoxon W	12,037.000
Test Statistic	5,596.000
Standard Error	495.892
Standardized Test Statistic	-2.388
Asymptotic Sig. (2-sided test)	.017

Step 5: The chart shows the distributions of the two groups with mean ranks for each group. The "Clinic" group has higher ranks suggesting that it generally has higher values of ulcer free weeks.

There are three test statistics in the table (U, W and Z) but the Mann-Whitney U statistic is commonly reported. A Mann-Whitney U test shows that there was a significant difference (U = 5596, p = 0.017) between the leg ulcer free weeks for the "Clinic" group compared to the group receiving the standard treatment. The median ulcer free weeks was 20 weeks for the "Clinic" group compared to 3.1 weeks for those receiving the standard treatment at home suggesting that the new treatment is more effective.

McNEMAR'S TEST

McNemar's test was first published in 1947 and was created by Quinn McNemar, who was a professor in the Psychology and Statistics department at Stanford University. This is a nonparametric test that assesses a statistically significant change in proportions which could have occurred on a dichotomous trait at two time points in the same population.

It is done by using a 2 × 2 contingency table with the dichotomous variable at time 1 and time 2. In medical research, if a researcher wants to determine whether or not a particular drug has an effect on a disease like yes or no, then a number of the individuals is recorded (as + and – sign, or 0 and 1) in a table before and after being given the drug. At that point, McNemar's test is applied to make statistical decisions (using the chi-square test statistic)—whether or not a drug has an effect on the disease.

Steps of Calculations

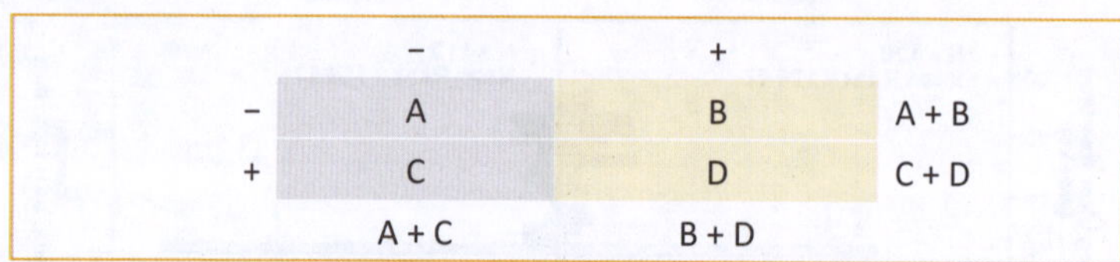

	–	+	
–	A	B	A + B
+	C	D	C + D
	A + C	B + D	

Assume that the row total is equal to the column total or:

$$(A + B) = (A + C) \quad (1) \qquad \dots (i)$$
$$(C + D) = (B + D) \quad (2) \qquad \dots (ii)$$

Or B = C from first equation

C = B from second equation

Hence, B = C. By using this equation, we will calculate the test as: $\chi^2 = \dfrac{(B - C)^2}{B + C}$

Here, chi-square statistic has one degree of freedom (*df*).

Example: A researcher wanted to investigate the impact of an intervention on smoking. In this hypothetical study, 50 participants were recruited to take part, consisting of 25 smokers and 25 nonsmokers. All participants watched an emotive video showing the impact that deaths from smoking-related cancers had on families. Two weeks after this video intervention, the same participiants were asked whether they remained smokers or non-smokers.

Solution: The participants were categorized as being either smokers or non-smokers before the intervention and then reassessed as either smokers or non-smokers after the intervention. Due to the same participants being measured twice, we have paired-samples. We also have a dependent variable that is dichotomous with two mutually exclusive categories (i.e., "Smoker" and "Non-smoker"). As a result, a McNemar's test is the appropriate choice to analyze the data.

- **Set null hypothesis:** Assume that the total rows are equal to the sum of columns. The mean of paired samples is equal and no (significant) change has occurred. In medical research—the intervention has no impact on smoking.
- **Alternative hypothesis:** Assume that the total number of rows is not equal to the total number of columns, or that the paired sample means are not equal. In medical research, alternative hypothesis is that the intervention has an impact on the smoking.

For a McNemar's test, there will be either two or three variables. These are:
- The dichotomous responses of related groups (e.g., Before, which reflects whether participants were "Non-Smokers" or "Smokers", **before** the video intervention).
- The dichotomous responses of related groups (e.g., After, which reflects whether participants were "Non-Smokers" or "Smokers", **after** the video intervention).
- The frequencies (i.e., total counts) for the four possible paired combinations:
  a. "Non-Smoker" before and after the intervention.
  b. "Non-Smoker" before the intervention, but a "Smoker" after the intervention.
  c. "Smoker" before and after the intervention.
  d. "Smoker" before the intervention, but a "Non-Smoker" after the intervention. These come under the variables.

Computing with SPSS

Step 1: Set up our data in the **"Data View"** of SPSS Statistics:

(a) The individual scores for each participant (shown in the image on the left below), where only two variables are there.

(b) Total count data, or frequencies, shown on the right side in the image (Figs 15.8A and B). having three variables.

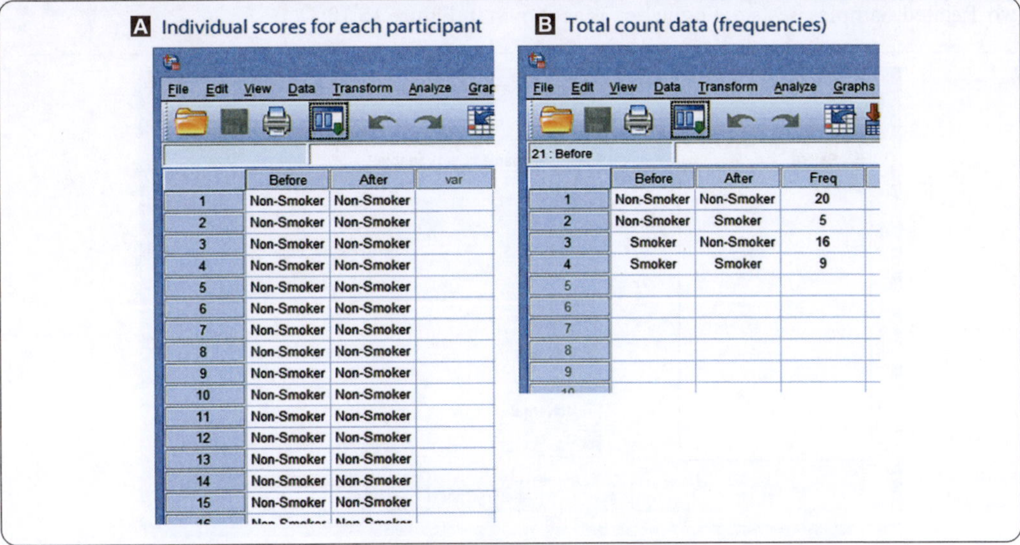

Figures 15.8A and B: Input window

Remember that if the data has been entered using total count data (i.e., frequencies), shown in the diagram on the right above, one has to **weight the cases** before analysis of data (this is an additional procedure in SPSS Statistics).

Step 2: For SPSS Statistics **versions 18 to 26** (including the **subscription version** of SPSS Statistics), click **Analyze > Nonparametric Tests > Legacy Dialogs >2 Related Samples...** on the main menu (as shown in image below) but, for **versions 17 and older** of SPSS Statistics, click **Analyze > Nonparametric Tests > 2 Related Samples...** on the main menu as shown ahead (Fig. 15.9).

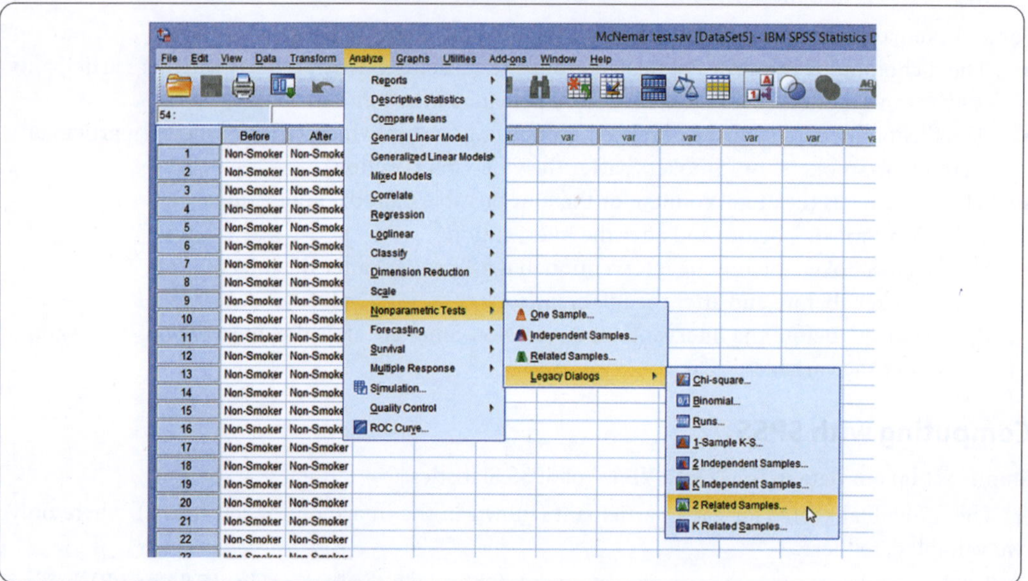

Figure 15.9: SPSS Statistics data entry

Two-Related-Samples Tests dialogue box is as shown in Figure 15.10:

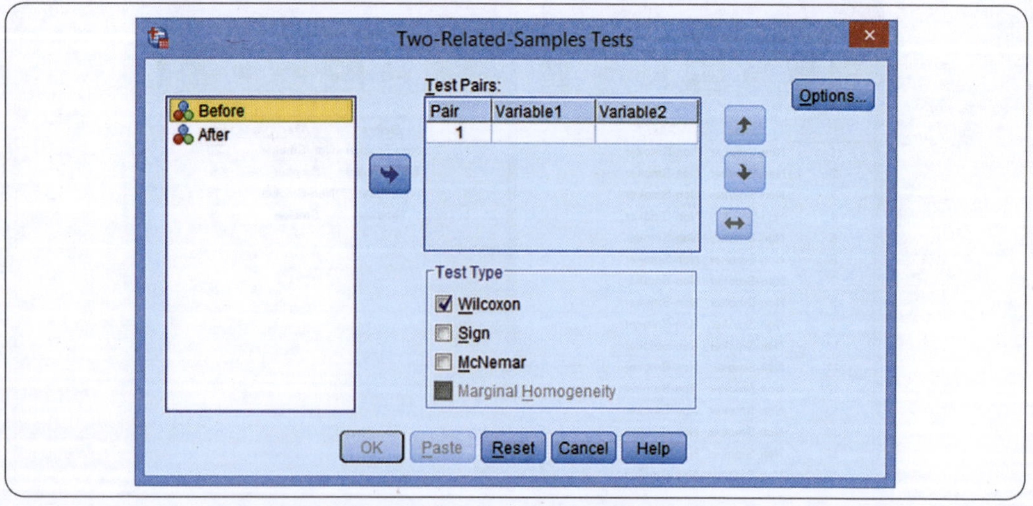

Figure 15.10: Two-Related-Samples Tests dialogue box

Step 3: Transfer the variables "before" and "after" into the "test pair" box. To do this, highlight both variables by clicking on one, for example "before" then holding down the shift-key, click the other variable, for example "after" Now, click on the ↩ button. A screen similar to the one below will appear (Fig. 15.11):

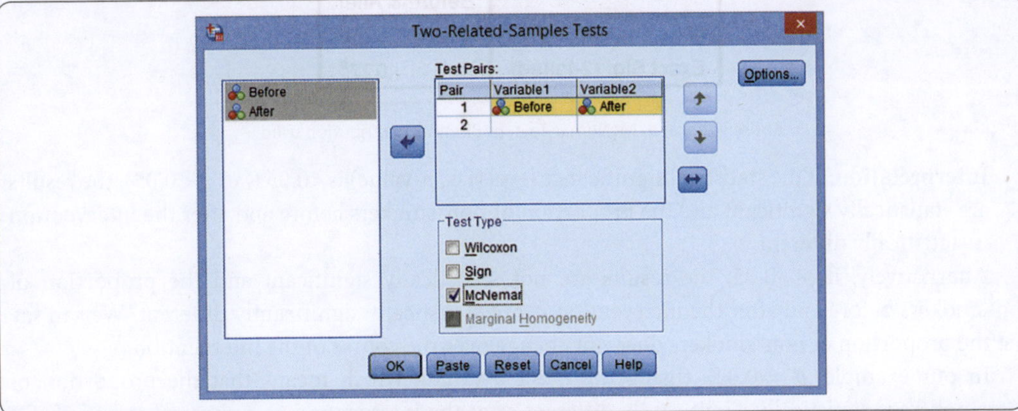

Figure 15.11: Final prompt screen

Step 4: Click on the OK button to generate the output.

Step 5: SPSS Statistics generates two main tables of output for McNemar's test when using the **legacy procedure: cross tabulation** table and **Test statistics** table.

Step 6: Cross tabulation table: The proportion of non-smokers and smokers is clear from this table.

Before & After

Before	After	
	Non-Smoker	Smoker
Non-Smoker	20	5
Smoker	16	9

- **Interpretation:** When we see the bottom-left cell there were 16 participants that were originally smokers, but following the intervention, they became non-smokers. In the sense that the intervention was designed to reduce smoking, these participants could be considered the intervention's successes. However, by seeing the top-right cell, five non-smokers actually took up smoking following the intervention. Clearly, this is not the effect you were looking for, and it is important that you note this in your report. So, overall there were more "positive" changes than "negative" changes, it can be eye-opening to know the different directions of effects that the participants took.

- **Test statistics table:** Now, we would like to know whether the above noted difference is statistically significant. To know this, we can use **Test Statistics** table as shown here:

Test Statistics[a]

	Before & After
N	50
Exact Sig. (2-tailed)	.027[b]

Abbreviations: **a.** McNemar Test; **b.** Binomial distribution used

- **Interpretation:** If the statistical significance level (i.e., *p*-value) is <0.05 (i.e., $p < 0.05$), the results are statistically significant and the proportion of non-smokers before and after the intervention is statistically different.

  Alternatively, if $p > 0.05$, the results are not statistically significant and the proportion of non-smokers before and after the intervention is not statistically significantly different. We can say that the proportion of non-smokers does not change over the course of the intervention.

  In our example, $p = 0.027$ (using the exact *p*-value), which means that the proportion of non-smokers is statistically significantly different after the intervention as compared to before. Or the change in the proportion of non-smokers following the intervention was statistically significant.

Manual Method

McNemar's test is used to compare the marginal frequencies of two factors (each with two levels) based on a 2 × 2 contingency table of n matched pairs of subjects. It is used on a nominal data with dichotomous trait as shown in table here.

	Y = 1 (Yes, present)	Y = 0 (No, absent)	Total
X = 1 (Yes, present)	A	B	A + B
X = 0 (No, absent)	C	D	C + D
Total	**A + C**	**B + D**	**N**

Thus, the null hypothesis is that B = C as already explained before.

The McNemar test statistic with a continuity correction is given by:

$$\chi^2 = (B - C - 1)^2/B + C$$

If χ^2 results are significant, the null hypothesis is rejected and the alternative hypothesis, i.e., B ≠ C is accepted, which means that the marginal proportions significantly differ from each other.

Example: Following is the data of the effectiveness of a medicine on tuberculosis of 335 subjects. The data is presented in a 2 × 2 contingency table.

	After: Yes	After: Yes	Total
Before: No	122	121	243
Before: No	48	44	92
Total	**170**	**165**	**335**

Solution:

H_0: The null hypothesis is that there is no effect of medicine on the treatment of tuberculosis.
The McNemar test statistic with a continuity correction is given by:

$$\chi^2 = (121 - 48 - 1)^2/121 - 48$$
$$= 71.013$$

When we compare the obtained χ^2 value with the table value at $df = 1$ and $p = 0.05$, the results were found to be statistically significant. Thus, the null hypothesis is rejected and it is concluded that the medicine had significant effects on the treatment of tuberculosis.

KRUSKAL-WALLIS ONE-WAY ANALYSIS-OF-VARIANCE

- Kruskal-Wallis one-way analysis-of-variance is used when data have a ranking but no clear numerical interpretation, such as when assessing preference. In terms of levels of measurement, nonparametric methods result in "ordinal" data.
- It is a nonparametric method for testing whether samples originate from the same distribution.
- It is an extension of the Mann-Whitney U test to three or more groups.
- Kruskal-Wallis is also used when the examined groups are of unequal size (different number of participants).
- **Limitations:**
  - Note that Kruskal-Wallis test is not robust. It lacks confidence intervals for marginal hypotheses.
  - It is also not suitable for two-sided hypotheses.
  - The Kruskal-Wallis test does not assume a normal distribution of the residuals, unlike the analogous one-way analysis of variance.
  - This test does not tell which group specifically differ. It only tells that at least two groups have significantly different medians.
  - The Kruskal-Wallis test is not as powerful as ANOVA.

STUDENT ASSIGNMENT

LONG ANSWER QUESTIONS

1. What are nonparametric tests? What are their advantages and limitations?
2. Why are they called nonparametric? Explain it.
3. Discuss Mann-Whitney U Test with two appropriate examples?

SHORT ANSWER QUESTIONS

1. What is chi-square test?
2. Define Mann-Whitney test.
3. Write about sign test.
4. Define median test.

MULTIPLE CHOICE QUESTIONS

1. A researcher was interested in stress levels of lecturers during lectures. She took the same group of 8 lecturers and measured their anxiety (out of 15) during a normal lecture and again in a lecture in which she had paid students to be disruptive and misbehave. The data were not normally distributed. Which test should she use to compare her experimental conditions?
   a. Paired samples t-test
   b. Mann-Whitney test
   c. Wilcoxon rank-sum test
   d. Wilcoxon signed-rank test

2. A researcher measured the same group of people's physiological reactions while watching horror films and compared them to when watching erotic films. The resulting data were skewed. What test should be used to analyze the data?
   a. Independent t-test
   b. Wilcoxon signed-rank test
   c. Dependent (related) t-test
   d. Mann-Whitney test

3. What symbol represents the test statistic for the Mann–Whitney test?
   a. W_s
   b. T
   c. U
   d. H

4. Test the hypothesis that the dice is unbiased ($c2 = 11.7$). Calculate the frequency observed for Chi-square distribution:
   a. Dice is unbiased, 11.3
   b. Dice is biased, 12.9
   c. Dice is unbiased, 10.9
   d. Dice is biased, 12.3

5. Consider a set of 18 samples from a standard normal distribution. We square each sample and sum all the squares. The number of degrees of freedom for a Chi-square distribution will be:
   a. 17
   b. 18
   c. 19
   d. 20

6.   What is the mean of a Chi-square distribution with 6 degrees of freedom?
     a. 4   b. 12
     c. 6   d. 8

7.   Which Chi-square distribution looks the most like a normal distribution?
     a. A Chi-square distribution with 4 degrees of freedom
     b. A Chi-square distribution with 5 degrees of freedom
     c. A Chi-square distribution with 6 degrees of freedom
     d. A Chi-square distribution with 16 degrees of freedom

8.   Which of these distributions is used for a testing hypothesis?
     a. Normal distribution   b. Chi-square distribution
     c. Gamma distribution   d. Poisson distribution

9.   The dividing point between the region where the null hypothesis is rejected and the region where it is not rejected is said to be:
     a. Critical region   b. Critical value
     c. Acceptance region   d. Significant region

10. If the critical region is located equally in both sides of the sampling distribution of test-statistic, the test is called:
     a. One-tailed   b. Two-tailed
     c. Right-tailed   d. Left-tailed

11. The choice of one-tailed and two-tailed tests depends upon:
     a. Null hypothesis   b. Alternative hypothesis
     c. Composite hypotheses   d. None of these

12. Test of hypothesis H_0: $\mu = 50$ against H_1: $\mu > 50$ leads to:
     a. Left-tailed test   b. Right-tailed test
     c. Two-tailed test   d. Difficult to tell

13. Test of hypothesis H_0: $\mu = 20$ against H_1: $\mu < 20$ leads to:
     a. Right one-sided test   b. Left one-sided test
     c. Two-sided test   d. All of these

14. Testing H_0: $\mu = 25$ against H_1: $\mu \neq 20$ leads to:
     a. Two-tailed test   b. Left-tailed test
     c. Right-tailed test   d. None of these

15. A rule or formula that provides a basis for testing a null hypothesis is called:
     a. Test-statistic   b. Population statistic
     c. Both a. and b.   d. None of these

16. The range of test statistic-Z is:
     a. 0 to 1   b. -1 to $+1$
     c. 0 to ∞ d. $-\infty$ to $+\infty$

17. The range of test statistic-t is:
     a. 0 to ∞ b. 0 to 1
     c. $-\infty$ to $+\infty$ d. -1 to $+1$

18. If H_0 is true and we reject it is called:
    a. Type-I error
    b. Type-II error
    c. Standard error
    d. Sampling error

19. The probability associated with committing type-I error is:
    a. β
    b. α
    c. $1 - \beta$
    d. $1 - \alpha$

20. A failing student is passed by an examiner, it is an example of:
    a. Type-I error
    b. Type-II error
    c. Unbiased decision
    d. Difficult to tell

21. A numerical value used as a summary measure for a sample, such as sample mean, is known as:
    a. Population parameter
    b. Sample parameter
    c. Sample statistic
    d. Population mean
    e. None of the above

22. Since the population size is always larger than the sample size, then the sample statistic
    a. Can never be larger than the population parameter
    b. Can never be equal to the population parameter
    c. Can never be zero
    d. Can never be smaller than the population parameter
    e. None of the above

23. The mean of a sample is:
    a. Always equal to the mean of the population
    b. Always smaller than the mean of the population
    c. Computed by summing the data values and dividing the sum by $(n - 1)$
    d. Computed by summing all the data values and dividing the sum by the number of items
    e. None of the above

24. The sum of the percent frequencies for all classes will always equal:
    a. One
    b. The number of classes
    c. The number of items in the study
    d. 100
    e. None of the above

25. In a five number summary, which of the following is not used for data summarization?
    a. The smallest value
    b. The largest value
    c. The median
    d. The 25th percentile
    e. The mean

26. Since the mode is the most frequently occurring data value, it:
    a. Can never be larger than the mean
    b. Is always larger than the median
    c. Is always larger than the mean
    d. Must have a value of at least two
    e. None of the above

ANSWER KEY

1. d	**2.** b	**3.** c	**4.** b	**5.** b	**6.** c	**7.** d	**8.** b
9. b	**10.** b	**11.** b	**12.** b	**13.** b	**14.** a	**15.** a	**16.** d
17. c	**18.** a	**19.** b	**20.** b	**21.** c	**22.** e	**23.** d	**24.** d
25. d	**26.** e						

Unit **VIII**

Use of Statistical Methods in Psychology and Education

16

Scaling to Improve Reliability and Validity

"Good design is like a refrigerator—when it works, no one notices, but when it doesn't, it sure stinks."
—Irene Au

LEARNING OBJECTIVES

After the completion of the chapter, the readers will be able to:
- Understand scaling and application of its technique.
- Know about T-score in psychology and education.
- Interpret reliability of test scores.

CHAPTER OUTLINE

- Introduction
- Statistics as a Tool
- Applications of Statistical Knowledge
- Importance of Statistics for Students of Psychology and Education
- Scaling
- Measurement
- Standard Score and T-Score
- Reliability and Validity of Test Scores

INTRODUCTION

Knowledge of statistics is important for the students of psychology and education. Reasons are as follows:
- These courses deal with theories and research studies which are based on statistical analysis.
- Students have to undertake research where they have to handle, analyze and interpret data.

STATISTICS AS A TOOL

Statistics is a useful tool for the students. It is a means of communicating knowledge which is required to read and evaluate surveys, experiments, and other practical problems in the field of psychology and education. It is used in research starting with planning a study, analyzing the data, and interpreting the results. The courses on statistics are necessary in the first and second year of the courses of psychology and education. The background of high school statistics is nil for the majority of fresh students. There is no developed problem-solving and analyzing skills in these students. Analysis revealed that students have difficulties with:
- Graphical representation

- Working on methodology based on mathematics.
- Manipulation of summation symbol Z, etc.

Most students while dealing with statistics:
- Wait until somebody tells them how to tackle the problem.
- Prefer verbal expressions to mathematical ones.
- Memorize without trying to understand.

Although the availability of statistical computer packages has changed statistics courses both in contents and in methods used. Mathematical competence is not in focus while using these softwares.

APPLICATIONS OF STATISTICAL KNOWLEDGE

Competence in Reading and Evaluating Research

- **Competence in reading:**
  - Knowing and understanding the techniques used, their area of application, and their assumptions.
  - Knowing and understanding the decisions taken concerning methodological aspects.
- **Competence in evaluating:**
  - Competence in evaluating the decisions against other competing decisions.
  - Evaluating subprocedures used during the statistical techniques.
  - Evaluating the interpretation given by the researcher versus alternative interpretations.
  - Competence to characterize features of the study.

Competence in Doing Research

Because of the availability of statistical computer softwares, the use of complex statistical techniques is not difficult. Mathematical abilities are no longer core of the matter for using statistics. But these are of little help at the planning stage of the study, while choosing the appropriate technique, and in interpreting the results. A good statistical understanding is still required which includes a certain level of mathematical and problem-solving skills.

The task of research is to establish causal relationships and to explain this relationship. Researchers in the field of psychology and education have different backgrounds and rely in general on one model that is humanistic.

IMPORTANCE OF STATISTICS FOR STUDENTS OF PSYCHOLOGY AND EDUCATION

Statistics is a process to collect and analyze the data for interpreting the results. A student deals with many questions which need to be analyzed via statistics, e.g., researcher may ask the subjects (thousands) to rate their favorite movie from 1 to 5 on a rating scale.

Issues Faced in Attitude Measurement by Psychiatry Student

When a researcher is interested in measuring the attitudes, feelings or opinions of respondents he/she should be cleared about the following:
- What is to be measured?
- Who is to be measured?
- The choices available in data collection techniques.

He/she must know which type of variables will be used like nominal, or ordinal or interval or ratio level, etc. Therefore, statistics can help a student in following ways:

- **Organize the data in a better way:** In the field of psychology and education, student will come across a large data which is not easy to handle. But by using graphs and pie charts, etc., data can be presented in an easy way.

- **Describing data gets easy:** One can easily describe the data collected during its collection. In the field of psychology, it is called descriptive statistics. For example, how many men and women are employed in an area along with other problems can be described with statistics. Researcher can make conclusions based upon the data after its collection and treatment.

- **Makes teaching and learning easy:** Statistics is important in education and psychology because of the different types of problems that are come across. Data involved is always huge. Therefore, statistics helps in making it concise. Statistics enables us to study the scores of data, objectively.

- **Helps teacher to provide exact description:** For example, the marks obtained in a class test can indicate about the effect of teaching method. The scores obtained by students show their perception toward a topic. Therefore, the data can be accurately described with the help of statistics.

- **Makes the teacher exact and precise in procedures and thinking:** It may become vague to describe a student's performance if knowledge of the statistics is lacking. With statistics methods, it becomes easy.

- **Summarization of results becomes easy with statistics:** Statistics arranges the data in an ordered manner. The data can be expressed in an understandable and meaningful way.

- **Enables a user to draw general conclusions:** It not only enables a user to draw general conclusions but helps to extract the inferences, step by step.

- **Future performance can be predicted:** Statistics enables its users to predict what will be the outcome under specific situations. Hence, the decisions can be taken accordingly. Although some margin of error is always there.

- **Statistics enables to analyze some of the causal factors underlying complex and otherwise confusing events:** Behavioral outcome is result of causal factors. Therefore, the cause of performance of a student or behavior of a patient can be studied by keeping extraneous variables as constant.

SCALING

Scaling is used to:

- Assigning numbers or other symbols to the characteristics of objects according to the certain prespecified rules.
- The measurement of physical properties is not a complex deal, whereas measurement of psychological properties requires a careful attention of a researcher.

Basic Characteristics of Scales

All scales used in scaling techniques can be explained in terms of four basic characteristics which are: description, order, distance, and origin. These characteristics collectively define the level of measurements of scale (Refer to Unit I). The level of measurement indicates that what properties of an object are measured or not measured by the scale.

Scaling is a procedure of measuring and assigning the objects to the numbers according to specified rules. In other words, the process of finding the measured objects in a range having a continuous sequence of numbers, to which the objects are assigned, is called scaling.

The data consists of quantitative variables, like height, weight, income, sales, etc., and qualitative variables like knowledge, performance, character, etc. For further analysis, the qualitative information must be converted into numerical form. This is possible through measurement and scaling techniques. Most commonly, feature of survey-based research is to have respondent's feelings, attitudes, opinions, etc. in some measurable form.

Practical Tips

Levels of measurement define the relationship among the values assigned to the characteristics of an object. We can say that what properties of an object, the scale is measuring or not measuring, is denoted by the levels of measurement.

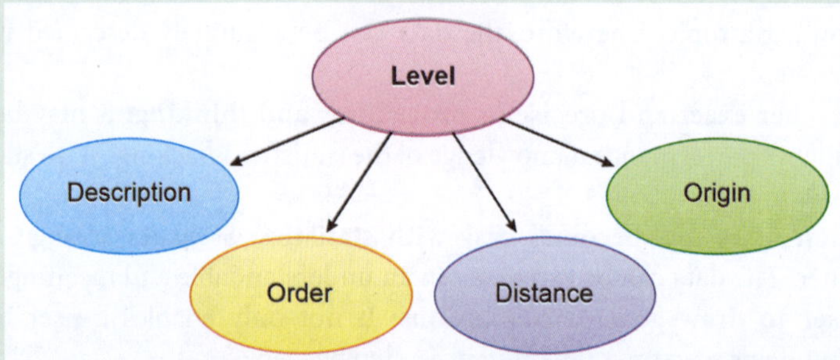

1. **Description:** The description means a particular unique label and descriptor which is used to designate the values of the scale. For example, we have the descriptors 1. Male, 2. Female. Here, male and female are unique descriptors denoting values 1 and 2 on gender scale. All scales have unique descriptors or labels which are used to define the values of the scale and the response options.

2. **Order:** The order means the relative size and position of the descriptor. Here, the order is associated with only relative values and no absolute values. Thus, the order is denoted by descriptors like "less than", "greater than", "equal to". For example, optician's preference for three brands of lenses is shown in the order given below with the most preferred brand listed first and the least preferred on the last.
    - Essilor 360 DS
    - Bosch and Lomb
    - Softens 59

    This shows that the preference for Essilor 360 DS is greater than the preference for Bosch and Lomb and likewise, the preference for Softens 59 is less than the preference for Bosch and Lomb.

    It is important to note that all the scale does not possess order characteristic. Such as gender scale (1. Female, 2. Male) does not possess order as one cannot determine whether a female is greater than or less than male.

3. **Distance:** Distance means that the absolute differences between the descriptors on a scale are known and can be expressed in units. For example, a five-person room has one patient more than a four-person room and likewise a four-person room has one patient more than the three-person room.

    It is to be noted that, the scale that has the distance characteristic also has the order. As we know that five-person classroom is greater than the four-person classroom in terms of a number of persons in class. Thus, we can say that distance implies order, but the reverse is not true, i.e. order does not necessarily imply distance.

Contd...

4. **Origin:** The origin shows that scale has a unique or fixed starting or true zero point. A scale having origin characteristic also has the distance, order, and description. Many scales used in the marketing research do not have any fixed origin.

   For example, in case of unfavorable-favorable scale,

   1 = extremely unfavorable

   2 = unfavorable

   3 = neither unfavorable nor favorable

   4 = favorable

   5 = extremely favorable

   Here, 1 is an arbitrary origin or starting point. This scale could have started with 0 = extremely unfavorable and 4 = extremely favorable. Likewise, it can also be started with –2, where –2 = extremely unfavorable and 2 = extremely favorable. Thus, this scale does not have any fixed origin and hence does not possess the origin characteristic.

   You must have observed that description, order, distance, and origin depict successively higher level characteristics. Origin being the highest level characteristic while the description being the most basic characteristic. If the scale has order characteristic, then it will also have the description, and likewise the scale with distance characteristic has both the description and order. The scale with origin characteristic has all that is distance, order and description.

   It means that the higher level characteristics possess, the lower level characteristics, however, the lower level characteristics may not necessarily possess the higher-level characteristics.

Scaling—as the Extension of Measurement

Scaling is a process of placing respondents on a continuum or range with respect to their preference for the object. Generally, in research, the numbers are assigned to the qualitative traits of the object because the quantitative data helps in statistical analysis of the data and further facilitates the communication of the measurement rules and results.

The measurement is a process of assigning numbers or symbols to the characteristics of the object as per the specified rules. The researcher assigns numbers, not to the object, but to its characteristics like perceptions, attitudes, preferences, and other relevant traits.

Measurement is a process of observing and recording the observations that are collected as part of research. It may be in terms of numbers or other symbols to characteristics of objects according to certain prescribed rules. The respondent's, characteristics are feelings, attitudes, opinions, etc. The most important aspect of measurement is the specification of rules for assigning numbers to characteristics. The rules for assigning numbers are standardized and applied uniformly. They do not change over time or objects.

Scaling is the assignment of objects to numbers or semantics according to a rule. In scaling, the objects are text statements, usually statements of attitude, opinion, or feeling.

Applications of Scaling Technique

- Explain the concepts of measurement and scaling.
- Classify and discuss different scaling techniques.
- Discuss four levels of measurement scales.
- Select an appropriate attitude measurement scale for a research problem.

Types of Scaling Techniques

The scaling techniques vary and are used as per the requirement of a researcher (Fig. 16.1).

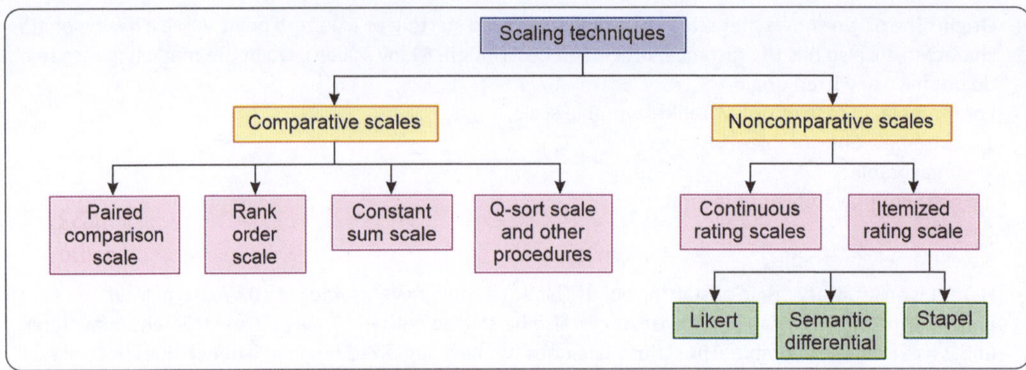

Figure 16.1: Types of scaling techniques

Comparative Scales

In comparative scaling, the respondent is asked to compare one object with another. The comparative scales can further be divided into the following four types of scaling techniques:

Paired Comparison Scale

This is a comparative scaling technique in which a respondent is presented with two objects at a time and asked to select one object according to some criterion. The data obtained are ordinal in nature. For example, there are four opticians A, B, C, and D. The respondents can prefer A to B or B to C, etc., (Table 16.1).

TABLE 16.1: Preference of optician using paired comparison scale

Preference	Optician	A	B	C	D
A–B	A	–	#	–	–
A–C	B	–	–	–	–
A–D	C	#	#	–	–
B–C	D	#	#	#	
Total		2	3	1	0

Rank Order Scale

This is another type of comparative scaling technique in which respondents are presented with several items simultaneously and asked to rank them in the order of priority. This is an ordinal scale that describes the favored and unfavored objects, but does not reveal the distance between the objects. The resultant data in rank order is ordinal data. This yields better results when direct comparison is required between the given objects. The major disadvantage of this technique is that only ordinal data can be generated.

Example: Rank the following opticians in order of preference.

Solution: Begin by picking out the optician you like most and assign it a number 1, then find second most preferred one, and assign it number 2. Continue this procedure until all opticians are marked in order of preference. Least preferred should be assigned rank 4. Also remember that no two opticians receive the same rank (Table 16.2).

TABLE 16.2: Preference of optician using rank order

Optician	A	B	C	D
Rank	3	1	2	4

Constant Sum Scale

In this scale, the respondents are asked to allocate a constant sum of units like points or rupees among a set of stimulus objects with respect to some criterion. For example, researcher wants to determine how important the attributes of price, fragrance, packaging, cleaning power, and lather of a disinfectant are to consumers. Respondents might be asked to divide a constant sum to indicate the relative importance of the attributes. The advantage of this technique is that time is saved. However, main disadvantages are as follows:

- The respondents may allocate more or fewer points than those specified.
- The second problem is respondents might be confused.

Example: Between the attributes of detergent please allocate 100 points among the attributes so that your allocation reflects the relative importance you attach to each attribute.

Solution: The more points an attribute receives, the more important attribute is. If an attribute is not important, assign it zero point. If an attribute is important, it should receive twice as many points Table. 16.3.

TABLE 16.3: Importance of disinfectant attributes using a constant sum scale

Attribute	Price	Fragrance	Packaging	Cleaning power	Lather	Total score
Points	50	5	10	30	5	**100**

Q-sort Scale and other Procedures

This is a comparative scale that uses a rank order procedure to sort objects based on similarity with respect to some criterion. The important characteristic of this methodology is that it is more important to make comparisons among different responses of a respondent than the responses between different respondents. Therefore, it is a comparative method of scaling rather than an absolute rating scale. In this method, the respondent is given statements in large number for describing the characteristics of a product or a large number of brands of a product.

Example: The packet given to you contains pictures of 90 journals. Please choose 10 journals you 'Prefer most', 20 journals you 'Like', 30 journals you 'Dislike' and 10 journals you 'Prefer least'. Please list the scored journals names in the respective columns of the form provided to you (Table. 16.4).

Solution: The data is sorted according to instructions in the Table 16.4.

Noncomparative Scales

In noncomparative scaling, respondents need only to evaluate a single object. Their evaluation is independent of the other object or objects, which the researcher is studying. The noncomparative scaling techniques can be further divided into:

TABLE 16.4: Preference of journals according to Q-sort scale

Prefer most	Like	Neutral	Dislike	Prefer least
....	....	....	....	....
....	....	....	....	....
....	....	....	....	....
....	....	....	....	....
....	....	....	....	......
10	....	....	....	....
	....	....	....	....
	....	....	....	....
	....	....	....	....
	20	....	20	....
		....		....
		....		....
		......		....
		30		10

Continuous Rating Scales

Continuous rating scale is very simple and highly useful. In continuous rating scale, the respondents rate the objects by placing a mark at the appropriate position on a continuous line that runs from one extreme of the criterion variable to the other (Fig. 16.2).

Example: How would you rate TV advertisement as a guide for buying a product?

Solution: Shown in Figure 16.2 according to continuous rating scale.

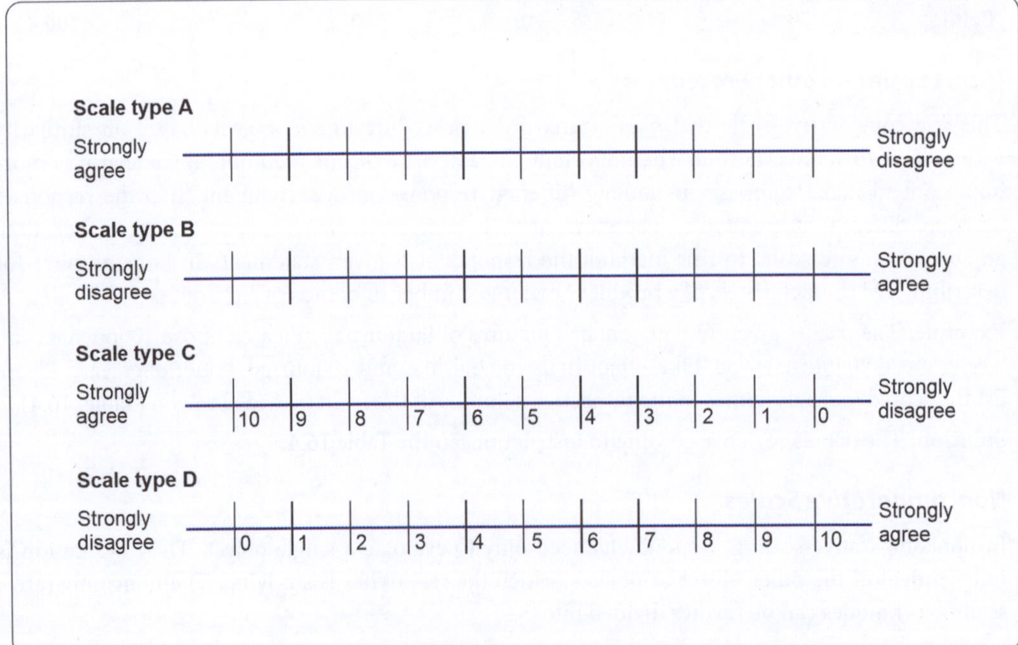

Figure 16.2: Continuous rating scale

Itemized Rating Scales

Itemized rating scale is a scale having numbers or brief descriptions associated with each category. The categories are ordered in terms of scale position and the respondents are required to select one of the limited number of categories that best describes the product, brand, company, or product attribute being rated. Itemized rating scales are widely used in marketing research. Itemized rating scales is further divided into three parts:

1. Likert scale
2. Semantic differential scale
3. Staple scale

The itemized rating scales can be graphic, verbal or numeric (Fig. 16.3):

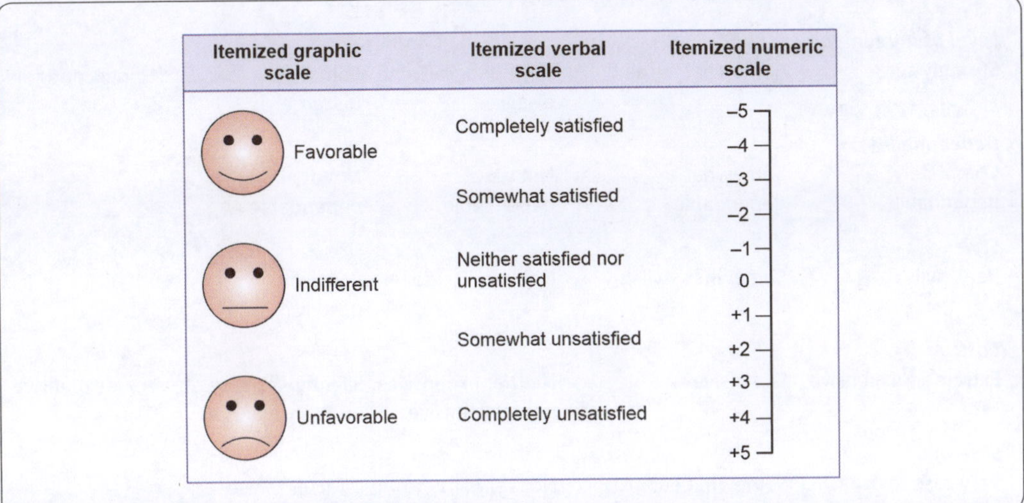

Figure 16.3: Types of itemized rating scales

Some common words for categories used in itemized rating scales are shown into Table 16.5:

TABLE 16.5: Common words for categories used in itemized rating scales

Quality:				
Excellent	Good	Not decided	Poor	Worst
Very Good	Good	Neither good nor bad	Fair	Poor
Importance:				
Very Important	Fairly important	Neutral	Not so important	Not at all important
Interest:				
Very interested	Somewhat interested	Neither interested nor disinterested	Somewhat uninterested	Not very interested

Contd...

Satisfaction: Completely satisfied	Somewhat satisfied	Neither satisfied nor unsatisfied	Somewhat unsatisfied	Completely unsatisfied
Frequency: All of the time Very often	Very often Often	Often Sometimes	Sometimes Rarely	Hardly even Never
Truth: Very true	Somewhat true	Not very true	Not at all true	
Purchase Interest: Definitely will buy	Probably will buy	Probably will not buy	Definitely will not buy	
Level of Agreement: Strongly agree	Somewhat agree	Neither agree nor disagree	Somewhat disagree	Strongly disagree
Dependability: Completely dependable	Somewhat dependable	Not very dependable	Not at all dependable	
Style: Very stylish	Somewhat stylish	Not very stylish	Completely unstylish	
Cost: Extremely expensive	Expensive	Neither expensive nor inexpensive	Slightly inexpensive	Very inexpensive
Ease of use: Very case to use	Somewhat easy to use	Not very easy to use	Difficult to use	
Modernity: Very modern	Somewhat modern	Neither modern nor old-fashioned	Somewhat old fashioned	Very old fashioned
Alert: Very alert	Alert	Not alert	Not at all alert	

Likert Scale

Likert is extremely popular for measuring attitudes, because the method is simple to administer. With the Likert scale, the respondents indicate their own attitudes by checking how strongly they agree or disagree with carefully worded statements that range from very positive to very negative toward the attitudinal object. Respondents generally choose from five alternatives (like strongly agree, agree, neither agree nor disagree, disagree, strongly disagree). A Likert scale may include a number of items or statements.

Disadvantage of Likert Scale: It takes longer time to complete than other itemized rating scales because respondents have to read each statement. Despite this disadvantage, this scale has several advantages. It is easy to construct, administer and use (Table 16.6).

TABLE 16.6: Example of Likert scale

	Strongly agree	Agree	Neither agree nor disagree	Disagree	Strongly disagree
If the price of raw materials fall, firms too should reduce the price of the food products	1	2	3	4	5
There should be uniform price through out the country for food products	1	2	3	4	5
The food companies should concentrate more on keeping hygiene while manufacturing food products	1	2	3	4	5
The expiry dates should be printed on the food products before they are delivered to consumers in the market	1	2	3	4	5
There should be government regulations on the firms in keeping acceptable quality and on the prices	1	2	3	4	5
Now-a-days most food companies are concerned only with profit making rather than taking care of quality	1	2	3	4	5

Semantic Differential Scale

This is a seven-point rating scale with end points associated with bipolar labels (such as good and bad, complex and simple) that have semantic meaning (Table 16.7).

- It has been widely used in comparing brands, products and company images.
- It has also been used to develop advertising and promotion strategies and in a new product development study.
- It can be used to find whether a respondent has a positive or negative attitude toward an object.

Example: A data of some examples semantic differential scales is given in Table 16.7. Show the trends followed by the respondents.

TABLE 16.7: Examples of semantic differential scales

Examples of semantic differential scales							
Modern	–	–	–	–	–	–	–	Old-fashioned
Good	–	–	–	–	–	–	–	Bad
Clean	–	–	–	–	–	–	–	Dirty
Important	–	–	–	–	–	–	–	Unimportant
Expensive	–	–	–	–	–	–	–	Inexpensive
Useful	–	–	–	–	–	–	–	Useless
Strong	–	–	–	–	–	–	–	Weak

Contd...

Examples of semantic differential scales								
Quick	–	–	–	–	–	–	–	Slow
	+3	+2	+1	0	–1	–2	–3	
Useful	–	–	–	–	–	–	–	Useless
Attractive	–	–	–	–	–	–	–	Unattractive
Passive	–	–	–	–	–	–	–	Active
Beneficial	–	–	–	–	–	–	–	Harmful
Interesting	–	–	–	–	–	–	–	Boring
Dull	–	–	–	–	–	–	–	Sharp
Pleasant	–	–	–	–	–	–	–	Unpleasant
Cold	–	–	–	–	–	–	–	Hot
Good	–	–	–	–	–	–	–	Bad
Likable	–	–	–	–	–	–	–	Unlikable

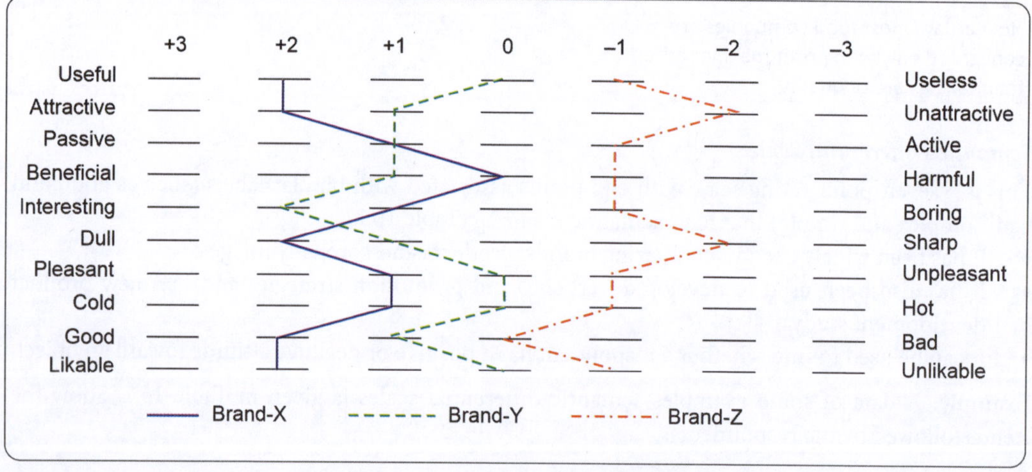

Figure 16.4: Trends followed by respondents

Solution: In example given in Table 16.7, the broken lines in the format (Fig. 16.4) clearly are showing the trends followed among the respondents toward an object.

Staple Scale

The staple scale (Fig. 16.5) was originally developed to measure the direction and intensity of an attitude simultaneously. Modern versions of the staple scale place a single adjective as a substitute for the semantic differential when it is difficult to create pairs of bipolar adjectives. The modified staple scale places a single adjective in the center of an even number of numerical values.

Example: Select a plus number for words that you think describe personnel banking of a bank accurately. The more accurately you think the word describes the bank, the larger the plus number you should choose. Select a minus number for words you think do not describe the bank accurately. The less accurately you think the word describes the bank, the larger the minus number you should choose.

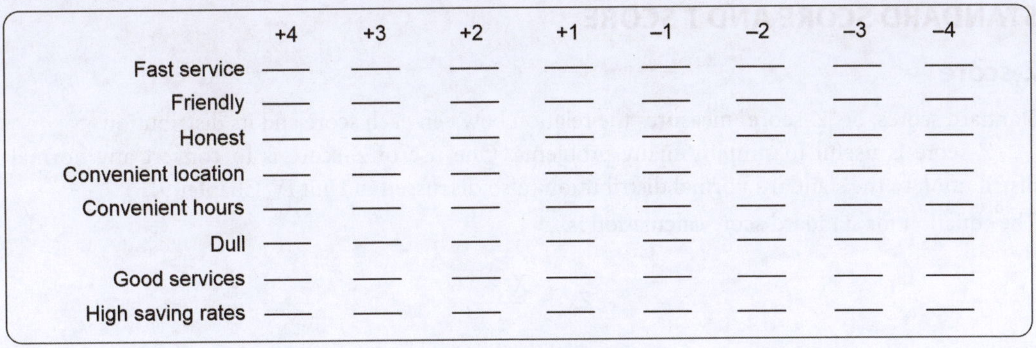

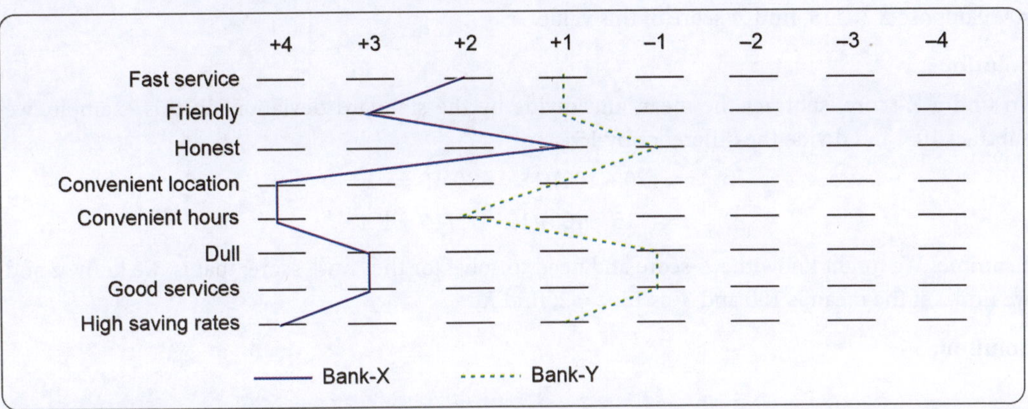

Figure 16.5: Staple scale

Solution: The response (Fig. 16.6) by respondents is recorded as follows:

Figure 16.6: Response in staple scale

Practical Tips

Selection of an appropriate scaling technique:

A number of issues decide the choice of scaling technique. Some significant issues are as follows:

- Problem definition and statistical analysis
- The choice between comparative and noncomparative scales
- Type of category labels
- Number of categories
- Balanced versus unbalanced scale
- Forced versus nonforced categories

Therefore, one can say that number of scaling techniques are available for measurement of attitudes although there is no unique way to choose a particular scaling technique for research study.

MEASUREMENT

The level of measurement refers to the relationship among the values that are assigned to the attributes, feelings or opinions for a variable. (*Refer Unit 1, Chapter 3 for details on Levels of Measurements*).

STANDARD SCORE AND T SCORE

Z-score

Standard scores, or "Z-score" measures the relation between each score and its distribution.

Z-score is useful to simplify many problems. One use of Z-score is to convert any normal distribution to the standard normal distribution (also discussed in Unit IV, Chapter 9). The equation for standard score calculation is:

$$Zx_i = \frac{X_i - \bar{X}}{s_x}$$

Example:

- Suppose the Mean is 100 and the standard deviation is 15.
- Suppose $X_i = 70$, find Z-score.
- Suppose $X_i = 115$, find Z-score of this value.

Solution:

To find a Z-score, subtract the mean and divide by the standard deviation. In this example, we subtract 100, and divide the difference by 15:

$$z = (70 - 100)/15 = -30/15 = -2$$
$$z = (115 - 100)/15 = 15/15 = 1$$

Example: We might know the Z-score and need to solve for the "raw" score; that is, we know z and we find X if the mean is 100 and S_x is 15, $z = 2$; find X_i.

Solution:

$$Z = \frac{X_i - Mean}{Sx}$$

$$2 = \frac{X_i - 100}{15}$$

$$30 = X_i - 100$$

Add 100 to both sides

$$100 + 30 = X_i - 100 + 100$$

$$X_i = 130$$

Must Know

Properties of Z-score
- Z-score always have a mean of zero.
- Z-score always have a variance *and* standard deviation of 1.
- If X is above the mean, its Z-score is positive; if X is below its mean, its Z-score is negative.
- In biostatistics, comparing scores to the mean is both useful and easy. All you have to do is calculate a **Z-score.**

Applications of Z-score

Comparing with the Z-score: The Z-score basically converts raw scores into new scores that shows how they can be compared to the mean. Once we have a Z-score for one value, it becomes easier to compare it to other values with the help of formula:

$$Z = \frac{X - \bar{X}}{SD}$$

- The numerator tells us how much the raw score differs from the mean and is sometimes called the deviant score (it is most often used for calculation of standard deviation).
- The standard deviation is in the denominator and indicates that researcher is converting the deviant score into units of standard deviations.
- Any distribution of raw scores can be converted to a distribution of Z-scores. This means that instead of the raw score units, like test percentage points, along the x-axis, we will have units of standard deviations and it is useful for measuring.

Measuring with the Z-score: A Z-score just measures how much a score deviates from the mean in terms of standard deviations. It means that we can compare two raw scores by putting them both in terms of standard deviations. So, a Z-score allows to compare raw scores, even from different distributions. This is because they are in terms of standard deviations instead of other units. Therefore, we can say that Z-scores are a strong statistical tool worth having and using.

For example, suppose the national average MAT score is 1002 with a standard deviation of 194 points. With the help of formula, the Z-score is calculated as +1.48. It means that the student's score is 1.48 standard deviations above the mean.

T-score

A T-score is a form of standardized test statistic besides the Z-score. The T-score formula enables to take an individual score and transform it into a standardized form which further helps a researcher to compare scores. For example, T-score shows how much your bone density is higher or lower than the bone density of a healthy 30-year-old adult. A healthcare provider looks at the lowest T-score to diagnosis osteoporosis. According to the World Health Organization (WHO) "T-score of −1.0 or above is normal bone density". To compare T-score with Z-score, we can say that T-score is a comparison of a person's bone density with that of a healthy 30-year-old of the same sex. Whereas, Z-score is a comparison of a person's bone density with that of an average person of the same age and sex.

Features of T-score

- Very similar to Z-scores.
  - A bunch of T-scores form a T-distribution.
  - Provides way of judging how extreme a sample mean is.
- T-test is done when SD (σ) is unknown.
- Used for hypothesis testing:

  For example: You wonder if college students really get 8 hours of sleep
  - $H_0: \mu = 8$ (College students do get eight hours of sleep)
  - $H_a: \mu \neq 8$ (College students do not get eight hours of sleep)

- T-distribution provides foundation for T-test:
  - Can be done on SPSS.
  - Can be done by hand.
- Key difference: T-test is done when σ is unknown.
- T-score is calculated as:

$$t = \frac{\bar{x} - \mu}{\frac{S}{\sqrt{n}}}$$

t = T-score

$\bar{x}$ = sample mean

μ = population mean

S = sample standard deviation

n = sample size

If you have only one item in sample, the square root in the denominator becomes $\sqrt{1}$. This means the formula becomes:

$$t = \frac{\bar{x} - \mu_0}{s}$$

Must Know

The larger the t score, the larger the difference is between the groups under test. It is influenced by many factors including:

- How many items are in your sample
- The means of your sample
- The mean of the population from which your sample is drawn
- The standard deviation of your sample

Example: A pharmaceutical institute claims its graduates earn an average of rupees 300 per hour. A sample of 15 graduates is selected and found to have a mean salary of rupees 280 with a SD of rupees 50. Assuming the claim of pharmaceutical institute true, what is the probability that the average salary of graduates will be no >₹280.

Solution:

Step 1: Put the information into the formula and solve:

$\bar{x}$ = sample mean = 280

μ_0 = population mean = 300

s = standard deviation of sample = 50

n = sample size = 15

Now,

$$t = (280 - 300)/ (50/\sqrt{15}) = -20/12.909945 = -1.549.$$

Step 2: Subtract 1 from the sample size to get the degrees of freedom as $15 - 1 = 14$. The degrees of freedom lets one to know which form of the T-distribution is to be used.

Step 3: Use an online calculator to find the probability using the obtained degrees of freedom. Here are the results (Fig. 16.7).

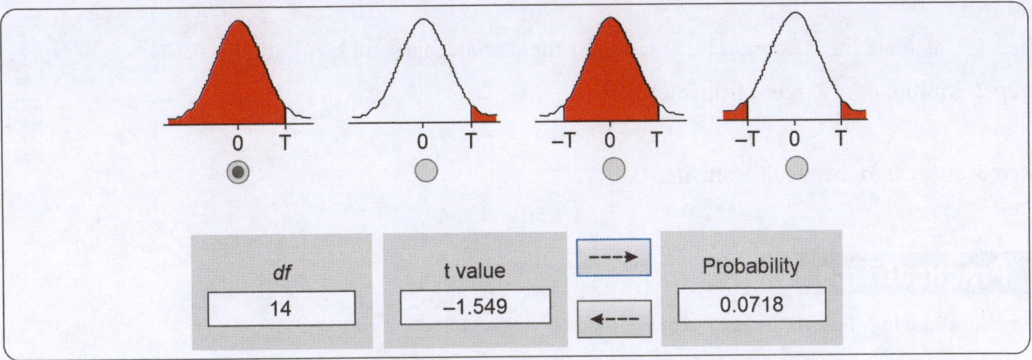

Figure 16.7: Using an online calculator to find the probability

Note that button under the left tail has been selected, as we are looking for a result that is not <₹280: The probability is 0.0718, or 7.18%.

T-score in Psychology and Education

A T-score testing is a special term, which is not the same as a T-score that we get from a T-test.

> **Practical Tip**
>
> T-scores in T-test can be positive or negative but T-scores in psychology testing are always positive, with an average of 50.

A T-score is similar to a Z-score as it represents the number of SDs **from the mean**. While the Z-score returns values between −5 and 5 (generally, scores fall between −3 and 3) standard deviations from the mean, whereas the T-score has a greater value and results return between 0 and 100 (most scores fall between 20 and 80) (Table 16.8). Many people prefer T-scores because they lack negative numbers and are easier to work with. Moreover, there is a larger range so decimals are almost eliminated. The table here shows Z-scores with their equivalent T-scores.

TABLE 16.8: Z-scores with their equivalent T-scores

Z-score	−5	−4	−3	−2	−1	0	1	2	3	4	5
T-score	0	10	20	30	40	50	60	70	80	90	100

T-score Conversion in Psychology

Calculating a T-score is just a conversion from a Z-score to a T-score, like conversion of Celsius to Fahrenheit. The formula is:

$$\text{T-score} = (Z \times 10) + 50$$

Example: A candidate takes a written test for a job where the average score is 1026 and the standard deviation is 209. The candidate scores 1100. Calculate the T-score for this candidate.

Note: If the Z-score for a question is given, jump to Step 2.

Solution:

Step 1: Calculate the Z-score. The Z-score for the data in this sample question is 0.354.

Step 2: Multiply the Z-score from Step 1 by 10:

$$10 \times 0.354 = 3.54$$

Step 3: Add 50 to the result from Step 2:

$$3.54 + 50 = 53.54$$

Practical Tips

Decision-Making: T-score Versus Z-score

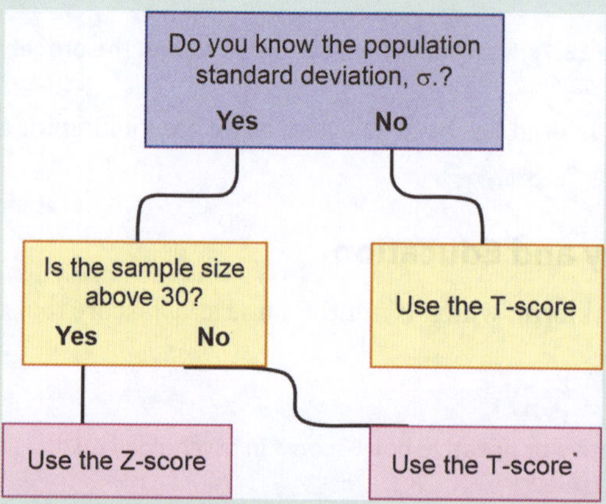

- **Note that** Z-scores and T-scores both represent standard deviations from the mean, but while "0" on a Z-score is 0 standard deviations from the mean, a "50" on a T-score represents the same thing. It is because T-scores use a mean of 50 and Z-scores use a mean of 0.
- A T-score of >50 is above average; below 50 is below average. In general, a T-score of above 60 means that the score is in the top one-sixth of the distribution; above 63, the top one-tenth. A T-score below 40 indicates a lowest one-sixth position; below 37, the bottom one-tenth.

T-score versus Z-score—WHO diagnostic

T-scores	Z-scores
• WHO diagnostic classification in postmenopausal women and men age 50 and older • WHO classification with T-score cannot be applied to healthy premenopausal women, men under age 50, and children	• For use in reporting BMD in healthy premenopausal women, men under age 50, and children • Z-score −2.0 or less is defined as "below the expected range for age" • Z-score above −2.0 is "within the expected range for age"

RELIABILITY AND VALIDITY OF TEST SCORES

Before discussing reliability, we have to know why we need it. The errors come in the research due to systemic errors or they may occur randomly.

Reliability of test is connected with validity. Accuracy followed in all the steps of research from inception till inference, gives accurate, reliable and valid results.

Validity

Validity refers to a test's accuracy. A test is valid when it measures what it is intended to measure. The intended uses for most tests fall into one of three categories, and each category is associated with a different method for establishing validity:

- **Content validity:** The test is used to obtain information about an examinee's familiarity with a particular content or behavior domain.
- **Construct validity:** The test is administered to determine the extent to which an examinee possesses a particular hypothetical trait
- **Criterion-related validity:** The test is used to estimate or predict an examinee's standing or performance on an external criterion.

Content Validity

A test has content validity (Fig. 16.8) to the extent that it adequately samples the content or behavior domain that it is designed to measure.

- If test items are not a good sample, results of testing will be misleading.
- Although content validation is sometimes used to establish the validity of personality, aptitude, and attitude tests, it is most associated with achievement-type tests that measure knowledge of one or more content domains and with tests designed to assess a well-defined behavior domain.

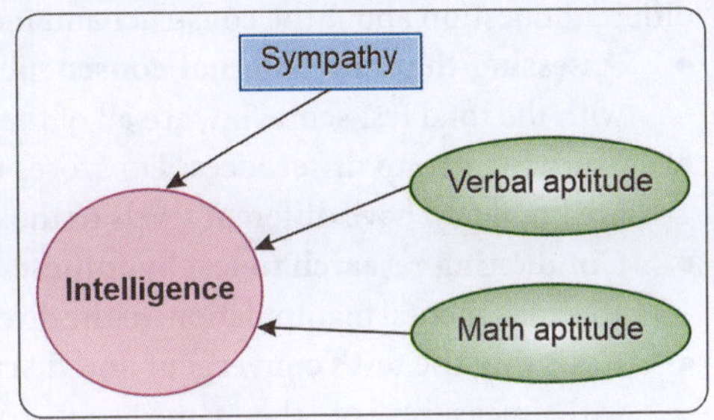

Figure 16.8: Content validity

- Adequate content validity would be important for a statistics test and for a work (job) sample test.
- The degree to which the measured variable appears to have adequately.
- Content validity is usually "built into" a test as it is constructed through a systematic, logical, and qualitative process that involves clearly identifying the content or behavior domain to be sampled and then writing or selecting items that represent that domain.
- Once a test has been developed, the establishment of content validity relies primarily on the judgment of subject matter experts.
- If experts agree that test items are an adequate and representative sample of the target domain, then the test is said to have content validity.

Although content validation depends mainly on the judgment of experts, supplemental quantitative evidence can be obtained.

Characteristics of Content Validity

If a test has adequate content validity:

- A coefficient of internal consistency will be large.
- The test will correlate highly with other tests that purport to measure the same domain; and
- Pre-/post-test evaluations of a program designed to increase familiarity with the domain will indicate appropriate changes.

Unit VIII Use of Statistical Methods in Psychology and Education

Construct Validity

When a test has been found to measure the hypothetical trait (construct) it is intended to measure, the test is said to have construct validity. A construct is an abstract characteristic that cannot be observed directly but must be inferred by observing its effects. Intelligence, mechanical aptitude, self-esteem, and neuroticism are all constructs. When a test has been found to measure the hypothetical trait (construct) it is intended to measure, the test is said to have construct validity. A construct is an abstract characteristic that cannot be observed directly but must be inferred by observing its effects.

Methods to Establish Construct Validity

There is no single way to establish a test's construct validity. Instead, construct validation entails a systematic accumulation of evidence showing that the test actually measures the construct it was designed to measure. Various methods used to establish this type of validity each answer a slightly different question about the construct and include the following:

- **Assessing the test's internal consistency:** Do scores on individual test items correlate highly with the total test score; i.e., are all of the test items measuring the same construct?
- **Studying group differences:** Do scores on the test accurately distinguish between people who are known to have different levels of the construct?
- **Conducting research to test hypotheses about the construct:** Do test scores change, following an experimental manipulation, in the direction predicted by the theory underlying the construct?
- **Assessing the test's convergent and discriminant validity:** Does the test have high correlations with measures of the same trait (convergent validity) and low correlations with measures of unrelated traits (discriminant validity)?
- **Assessing the test's factorial validity:** Does the test have the factorial composition it would be expected to have; i.e., does it have factorial validity?

Face Validity

The extent to which the measured variable appears to be an adequate measure of the conceptual variables. For example, liking for Japanese was assessed on a scale:

> Strongly disagree 1 2 3 4 5 6 7 8 Strongly agree.

The results obtained are shown in Figure 16.9 as measured variable among all the subjects that is liking for Japanese and the result was represented by conceptual variable.

> **Must Know**
>
> Construct validity is said to be the most theory-laden of the methods of test validation. The developer of a test designed to measure a construct begins with a theory about the nature of the construct, which then guides the test developer in selecting test items and in choosing the methods for establishing the test's validity.

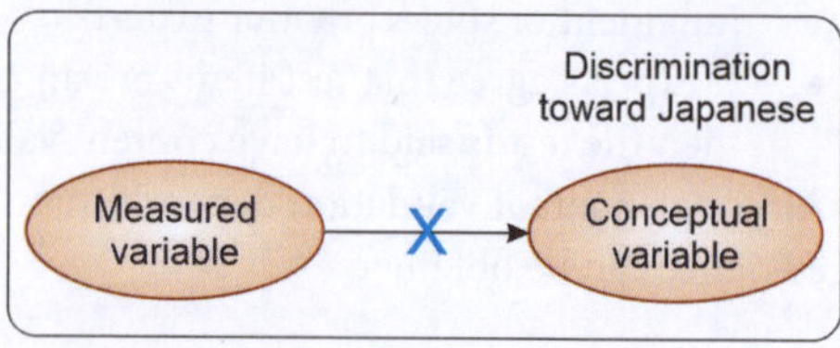

Figure 16.9: Results of liking for Japanese

> **Must Know**
>
> **Difference between Content Validity and Face Validity**
> Content validity refers to the systematic evaluation of a test by experts who determine whether or not test items adequately sample the relevant domain, while face validity refers simply to whether or not a test "looks like" it measures what it is intended to measure.
>
> Although face validity is not an actual type of validity, it is a desirable feature for many tests. If a test lacks face validity, examinees may not be motivated to respond to items in an honest or accurate manner. A high degree of face validity does not, however, indicate that a test has content validity.

Criterion-Related Validity

- **Convergent validity:** The extent to which a measured variable is found to be related to other measured variables designed to measure the same conceptual variable.
- **Discriminant validity:** The extent to which a measured variable is found to be unrelated to other measured variables designed to measure the different conceptual variables.
- **Criterion validity:** The extent to which a self-report measure correlates with a behavioral measured variable.
- **Predictive validity:** The extent to which the scores can predict the participants' future performance.
- **Concurrent validity:** The extent to which the self-report measure correlates with the behavioral measure that is assessed at the same time.

> ### Practical Tips
>
> **To improve reliability and validity of test:**
> - Conduct a pilot test, trying out a questionnaire or other research instruments on a small group.
> - Use multiple measures.
> - Ensure variability that is in your measures (that can be controlled by a researcher).
> - Write good items.
> - Request the respondents to take questions seriously
> - Make your items nonreactive.
> - Be certain to consider face and content validity by choosing reasonable terms and cover a broad range of issues reflecting the conceptual variables.
> - Use existing measures.

Reliability

Reliability is one of the important characteristics of any consistency test. It refers to the precision or accuracy of the measurement of score. Reliability means the stability consistency of a test measure or protocol (Fig. 16.10).

- Rosenthal in 1991 described reliability as a major concern when a psychological test is used to measure some attribute or behavior.
- Anastasi in 1968 said that reliability refers to the consistency of scores that are obtained by the same individuals when:
  - Re-examined with test on different occasions.
  - Or with different sets of equivalent items.
  - Or under other variable examining conditions.

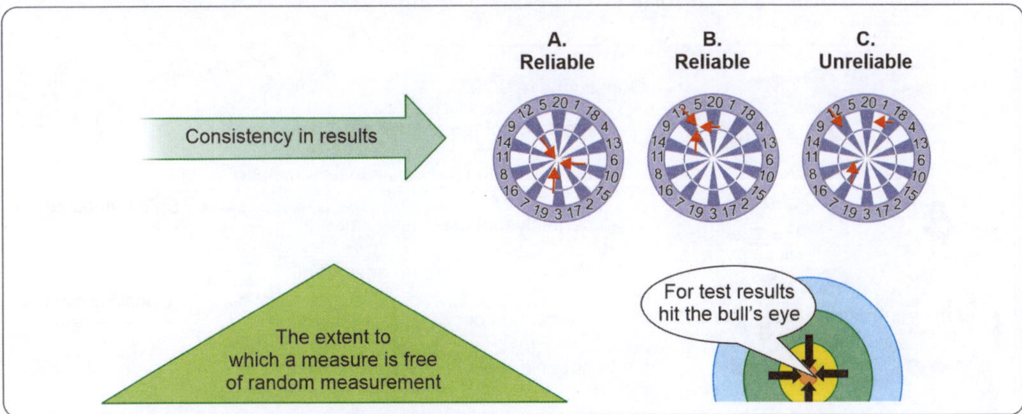

Figure 16.10: Consistency is reliability

Source of Errors in Reliability

Errors are caused by:

- **Examinee-specific factors** such as concentration, motivation, fatigue, boredom, momentary lapses of memory, carelessness in marking answers, and luck in guessing.
- **Test-specific factors** like the specific set of questions selected for a test, ambiguous or tricky items, and poor directions.
- **Scoring-specific factors** like carelessness, no uniform scoring guidelines, and counting or computational errors.

These errors are random. Therefore, it is desirable to use tests with good measures of reliability so as to ensure that the test scores reflect more than just random error.

Tests of Reliability

Test reliability means the consistency of scores that subjects will receive on alternate forms of the same. It provides a measure of the extent to which an examinee's score reflects random measurement error. When a test is reliable, it provides dependable consistent results and, for this reason, the term consistency is often given as a synonym for reliability.

Reliability is a precursor to test validity. That is, if test scores cannot be assigned consistently, it is impossible to conclude that they accurately measure the domain of interest. Validity as earlier explained means the extent to which the inferences made from a test are justified and accurate. Further, validity is the psychometric property about which we are most concerned. However, formally assessing the validity of a specific use of a test is laborious and time-consuming. Therefore, reliability analysis is often a first-step in the test validation process.

If the test is unreliable, one can stop investigating. If the test has adequate reliability, then a validation study is important.

Reliability is also internal consistency. It is the extent to which the scores on the items correlate with each other and thus are all measuring the true score rather than reflecting random error (Fig. 16.11).

Norm referenced tests:

- It is frequently used for norm referenced tests (NRTs). It is a measure of how well the items on the test measure the same construct or idea. This method has an advantage that it is capable to be conducted using a single form given in a single administration.

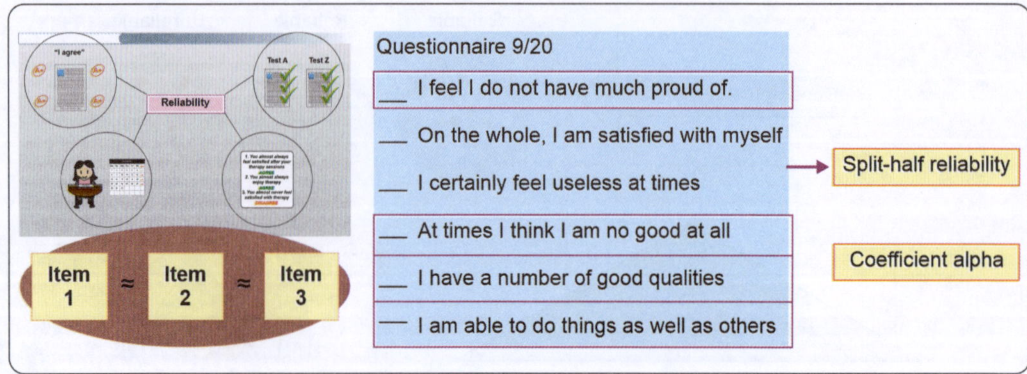

Figure 16.11: Measuring internal consistency

- The internal consistency method estimates how well the set of items on a test correlate with one another; that is, how similar the items on a test form are to one another.
- Many test analysis software programs produce this reliability estimate automatically.
- **Split-half reliability and coefficient alpha** are two methods for evaluating internal consistency. Both involve administering the test once to a single group of subjects, and both yield a reliability coefficient that is also known as the coefficient of internal consistency.

Necessity of Reliability

We need reliability to know the truth of research outcomes. We need it to have effective results. Reliability gives statistical power to the results. The relationship between variables can be assured with the help of reliability (Fig. 16.12).

Reliability Coefficient

Most methods for estimating reliability produce a reliability coefficient, which is a correlation coefficient that ranges in value from 0.0 to + 1.0. When a test's reliability coefficient is 0.0, this means that all variability in obtained test scores is due to measurement error. Conversely, when a test's reliability coefficient is +1.0, this indicates that all variability in scores reflects true score variability.

The reliability coefficient is symbolized with the letter "r" and a subscript that contains two of the same letters or numbers (e.g., "r_{xx}"). The subscript indicates that the correlation coefficient was calculated by correlating a test with itself rather than with some other measure.

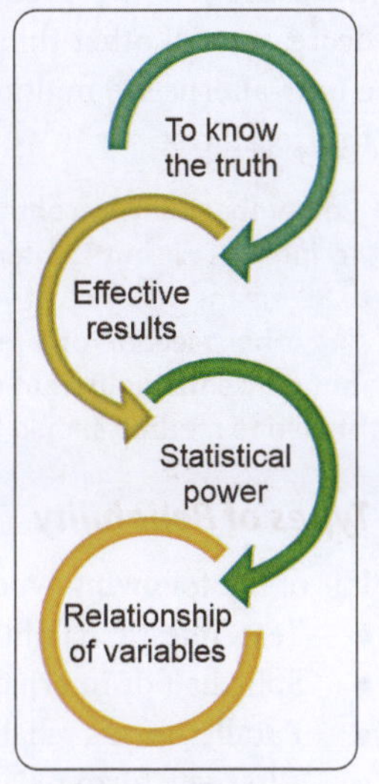

Figure 16.12: Necessity of reliability

Regardless of the method used to calculate a reliability coefficient, it is interpreted directly as the proportion of variability in obtained test scores that reflects true score variability.

For example, a reliability coefficient of 0.84 indicates that 84% of variability in scores is due to true score differences among examinees, while the remaining 16% (1.00 – 0.84) is due to measurement error.

True score variability (84%)	Error (16%)

It must be noted that a reliability coefficient does not provide any information about what is actually being measured by a test. It only indicates whether the attribute measured by the test—whatever it is being assessed in a consistent and precise way. Whether the test is actually assessing what it was designed to measure, is addressed by an analysis of the test's validity.

Factors Affecting Reliability Coefficient

The magnitude of the reliability coefficient is affected not only by the sources of error, but also by the length of the test, the range of the test scores, and the probability that the correct response to items can be selected by guessing.

- Test length
- Range of T-scores
- Guessing

Test length: The longer the test, the larger the test's reliability coefficient.

Range of test scores: The range is directly affected by the degree of similarity of subjects with regard to the attribute measured by the test. When examinees are heterogeneous, the range of scores is maximized. The range is also affected by the difficulty level of the test items. When all items are either very difficult or very easy, all examinees will obtain either low or high scores, resulting in a restricted range. Therefore, the best strategy is to choose items so that the average difficulty level is in the mid-range ($r = 0.50$).

Guessing: As the probability of correctly guessing answers increases, the reliability coefficient decreases. All other things being equal, a true/false test will have a lower reliability coefficient than a four-alternative multiple-choice test which, in turn, will have a lower reliability coefficient than a free recall test.

> Remember that in contrast to other correlation coefficients, the reliability coefficient is never squared to interpret it but is interpreted directly as a measure of true score variability. A reliability coefficient of 0.89 means that 89% of variability in obtained scores is true score variability.
>
> The selection of a method for estimating reliability depends on the nature of the test. Each method not only entails different procedures but is also affected by different sources of error. For many tests, more than one method should be used.

Types of Reliability

It is of the following types (Fig. 16.13):
- Test–retest reliability
- Split-half or internal consistency reliability
- Parallel-forms reliability or equivalent-forms
- Alternate form reliability
- Inter-rater reliability

Test-retest Reliability

The test-retest method for estimating reliability involves administering the same test to the same group of examinees on two different occasions and then correlating the two sets of scores. When using this method (Fig. 16.14), the reliability coefficient indicates the degree of stability (consistency) of examinees' scores over time and is also known as the coefficient of stability.

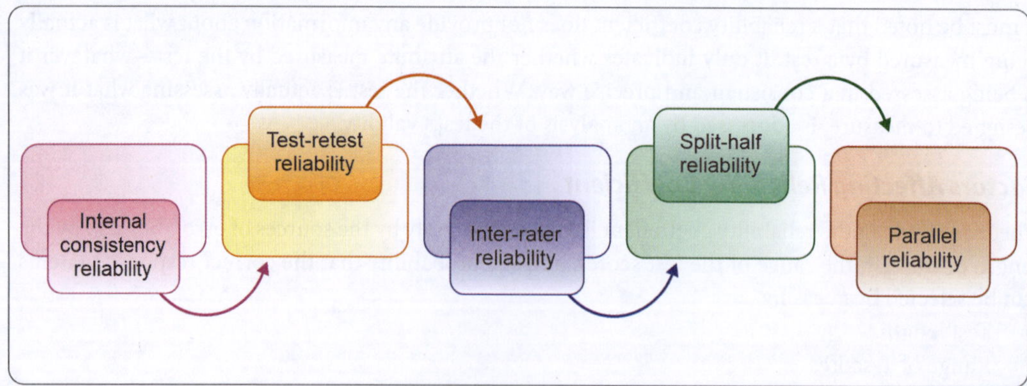

Figure 16.13: Types of reliability

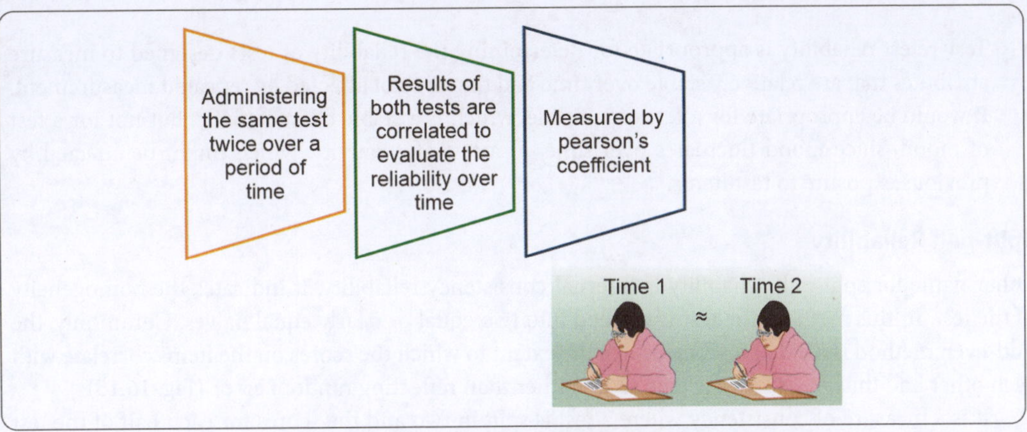

Figure 16.14: Process of test-retest reliability

The two sets, when correlated, give the value of the reliability coefficient. The test-retest reliability is an instrument that measures at two times for multiple persons. It computes correlation between the two measures. It assumes that there is no change in the underlying trait between Time 1 and Time 2. The scores from Time 1 to Time 2 can then be correlated in order to evaluate the test for stability, over time. For example, it can determine how much data a student memorizes on a test. The extent to which scores on the same measured variable correlates with each other on two different times is shown in the Table 16.9 as:

Factors contributing to test-retest reliability:
- Clear instructions for administrators, research participants, and raters.
- Unambiguously phrased tasks/questions.
- Tasks/questions in participants' first language or target language at appropriate level of difficulty.
- Reliability has subtypes that must be satisfied before a test or assessment is carried out.

Primary sources of measurement error:
- Any random factors related to the time that passes between the two administrations of the test. These time sampling factors include:
  - Random fluctuations in examinees over time (e.g., changes in anxiety or motivation) and random variations in the testing situation.
  - Memory and practice also contribute to error when they have random carryover effects; i.e., when they affect many or all examinees but not in the same way.

TABLE 16.9: Retesting effects of test-retest reliability

Score at one time	Score at another time
4 I feel I do not have much proud of	4 I feel I do not have much proud of
3 On the whole, I am satisfied with myself	4 On the whole, I am satisfied with myself
2 I certainly feel useless at times	1 I certainly feel useless at times
1 At times I think I am no good at all	1 At times I think I am no good at all
4 I have a number of good qualities	4 I have a number of good qualities
3 I am able to do things as well as others	4 I am able to do things as well as others

Use:

- Test-retest reliability is appropriate for determining the reliability of tests designed to measure attributes that are relatively stable over time and that are not affected by repeated measurement.
- It would be appropriate for a test of aptitude, which is a stable characteristic, but not for a test of mood, since mood fluctuates over time, or a test of creativity, which might be affected by previous exposure to test items.

Split-half Reliability

Other name for split-half reliability is internal consistency reliability. It indicates the homogeneity of the test. In this method, the test is divided into two equal or nearly equal halves. Commonly, the odd-even method is used here. It measures the extent to which the scores on the items correlate with each other and thus measures the true score rather than reflecting random error (Fig. 16.15).

It is a measure of consistency where a test is split in two and the scores for each half of the test are compared with one another. A test is split into two—odds and evens. If the two scores for the two tests are similar then the test is reliable. It measures internal consistency. It tells how well the test components contribute to the construct that is being measured.

In split-half reliability, a test for a single area of knowledge, is split into two parts and then both parts are given to one group of students at the same time. Then scores from both parts of the test are correlated. A reliable test will show high correlation, indicating that a student would perform equally well or poorly on both halves of the test.

It is most commonly used for multiple choice tests that one can theoretically use for any type of test—even tests with essay questions.

Steps to calculate split-half reliability:

1. Administer the test to a large group students (generally, over 30).
2. Randomly divide the test questions into two parts. For example, separate even questions from odd questions.
3. Score each half of the test for each student.
4. Find correlation coefficient for the two halves.

Drawbacks:

It only works for a large set of questions (100-point test is required), which measures the same construct/area of knowledge.

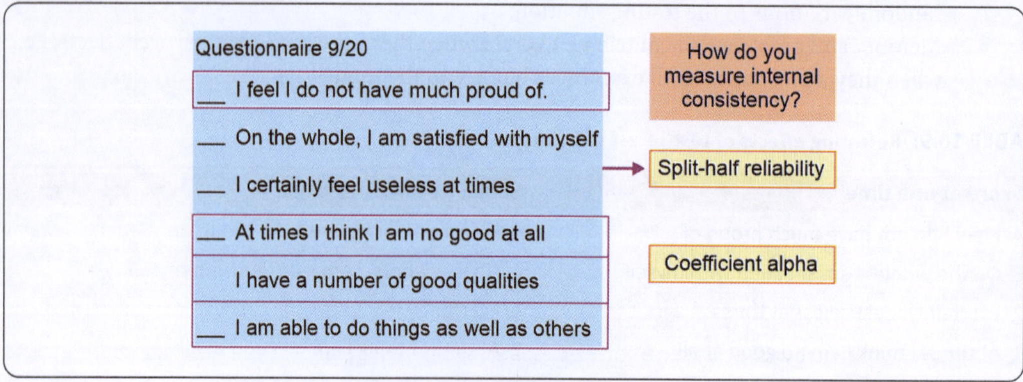

Figure 16.15: Split-half reliability

Parallel-forms Reliability

Parallel-forms reliability is a measure of reliability obtained by administering different versions of an assessment tool (both versions must contain items that probe the same construct, skill, knowledge base, etc.) to the same group of individuals. The scores from the two versions can then be correlated in order to evaluate the consistency of results across alternate versions.

Many programs develop multiple and parallel-forms of an examination to provide test security like Series A, Series B and so on. These are constructed to match the test blueprint or originality, and the parallel test forms are constructed to be similar in difficulty level of average item. In other words, it uses one set of questions divided into two sets or forms which measure the same knowledge or skill.

Parallel-forms reliability is estimated by administering both patterns of the exam to the same group of examinees. While the time between the two test administrations should be short, it does need to be long enough as it may affect the scores of examinees due to fatigue. The examinees' scores on the two test forms are correlated in order to determine how similarly the two-test pattern function. This reliability estimate is a measure of how consistent examinees' scores can be expected to be across test patterns. For example, the test patterns in GRE, SAT, GMAT, TOEFL, etc.

To assess a test's alternate forms reliability, two equivalent forms of the test are administered to the same group of examinees and the two sets of scores are correlated.

> ### Must Know
>
> **Difference between split-half and parallel-forms reliability tests:**
> - Split-half reliability is similar to parallel form reliability that uses one set of questions divided into two equivalent sets. The sets are given to the same students, usually within a fixed time frame, for example, one set of test questions is given on Monday and another set on Saturday. With split-half reliability, the two tests are given to one group of students who sit the test at the same time.
> - The two tests in parallel-forms reliability are equivalent and are independent of each other. This is not required in split-half reliability. Here, the two sets do not have to be equivalent ("parallel").

Alternate form Reliability

Indicates the consistency of responding to different item samples (the two test forms) and, when the forms are administered at different times, the consistency of responding over time.

- The alternate forms reliability coefficient is also called the coefficient of equivalence when the two forms are administered at about the same time;
- The coefficient of equivalence and stability when a relatively long period of time separates administration of the two forms.

Source of error: The primary source of measurement error for alternate forms reliability is content sampling, or error introduced by an interaction between different subjects' knowledge and the different content assessed by the items included in the two forms (e.g., Form A and Form B).

The items in Form A might be a better match of one subject's knowledge than items in Form B, while the opposite is true for another subject. In this situation, the two scores obtained by each examinee will differ, which will lower the alternate form reliability coefficient.

When administration of the two forms is separated by a period of time, time sampling factors also contribute to error.

Limitations: Like test-retest reliability, alternate form reliability is not appropriate when the attribute measured by the test is likely to fluctuate over time (and the forms will be administered at different times) or when scores are likely to be affected by repeated measurement.

- If the same strategies required to solve problems on Form A are used to solve problems on Form B, even if the problems on the two forms are not identical, there are likely to show practice effects.
- When these effects differ for different subjects (i.e., the effects are random), practice will serve as a source of measurement error.
- Although alternate form reliability is considered by some experts to be the most rigorous (and best) method for estimating reliability, it is not often assessed due to the difficulty in developing forms that are truly equivalent.

Inter-Rater Reliability

All of the methods for estimating reliability discussed are intended to be used for objective tests. When a test like performance task is there, or other items, which need to be scored by human raters, then the reliability of those raters has to be estimated. This reliability method asks the question, "If multiple raters scored a single subject or examinee's performance, would the examinee receive the same score". Inter-rater reliability measures (Figs 16.16A and B).

- The dependability or consistency of scores that might be expected across raters.

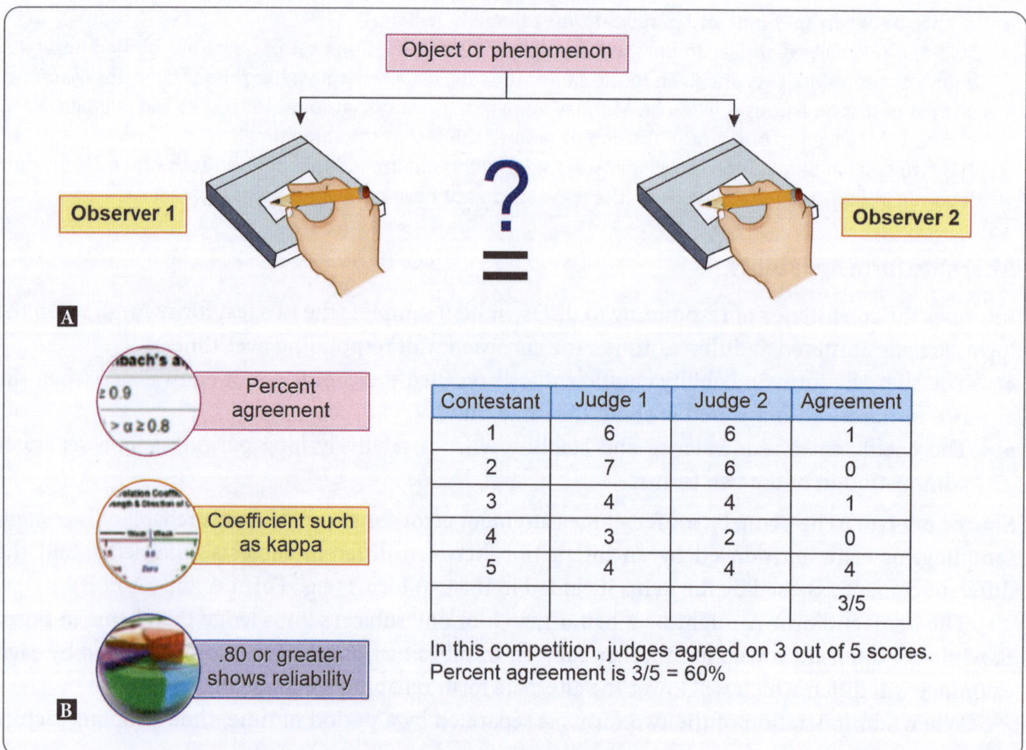

Contestant	Judge 1	Judge 2	Agreement
1	6	6	1
2	7	6	0
3	4	4	1
4	3	2	0
5	4	4	4
			3/5

In this competition, judges agreed on 3 out of 5 scores. Percent agreement is 3/5 = 60%

Figures 16.16A and B: A. Inter-rater reliability; **B.** Measurement of inter-rater reliability

- It tells about the degree of agreement between raters.
- It gives a score that tells how much similarity or consensus is there in the ratings given by judges or raters.

Inter-rater reliability is of concern whenever test scores depend on a rater's judgment.

A test constructor may want to make sure that an essay test, a behavioral observation scale, or a projective personality test have adequate inter-rater reliability. This type of reliability is assessed either by calculating a correlation coefficient (e.g., a kappa coefficient or coefficient of concordance) or by determining the percent agreement between two or more raters.

Sources of error for inter-rater reliability include factors related to the raters such as lack of motivation and rater biases and characteristics of the measuring device.

An inter-rater reliability coefficient is likely to be low, for instance, when rating categories are not exhaustive (i.e., do not include all possible responses or behaviors) and/or are not mutually exclusive.

Practical Tips

To determine a test's split-half reliability, the test is split into equal halves so that each subject has two scores (one for each half of the test).

Scores on the two halves are then correlated. Tests can be split in several ways, but probably the most common way is to divide the test on the basis of odd- versus even-numbered items.

A problem with the split-half method is that it produces a reliability coefficient that is based on test scores that were derived from one-half of the entire length of the test.
If a test contains 30 items, each score is based on 15 items. Because reliability tends to decrease as the length of a test decreases, the split-half reliability coefficient usually underestimates a test's true reliability. For this reason, the split-half reliability coefficient is ordinarily corrected using the Spearman-Brown prophecy formula, which provides an estimate of what the reliability coefficient would have been had it been based on the full length of the test.

Cronbach's coefficient alpha: *Cronbach's coefficient alpha* also involves administering the test once to a single group of subjects. However, rather than splitting the test in half, a special formula is used to determine the average degree of inter-item consistency.

One way to interpret coefficient alpha is as the average reliability that would be obtained from all possible splits of the test. Coefficient alpha tends to be conservative and can be considered the lower boundary of a test's reliability.

When test items are scored dichotomously (right or wrong), a variation of coefficient alpha known as the Kuder-Richardson Formula 20 (KR-20) can be used.
Note that content sampling is a source of error for both split-half reliability and coefficient alpha.

- For split-half reliability, content sampling refers to *the error resulting from differences between the content of the two halves of the test* (i.e., the items included in one half may better fit the knowledge of some examinees than items in the other half); for coefficient alpha, content (item) sampling refers to *differences between individual test items rather than between test halves*. Coefficient alpha also has as a source of error, *the heterogeneity of the content domain.*
- A test is heterogeneous with regard to content domain when its items measure several different domains of knowledge or behavior.
- The greater the heterogeneity of the content domain, the lower the inter-item correlations and the lower the magnitude of coefficient alpha.
- The methods for assessing internal consistency reliability are useful when a test is designed to measure a single characteristic, when the characteristic measured by the test fluctuates over time, or when scores are likely to be affected by repeated exposure to the test.
- They are not appropriate for assessing the reliability of speed tests because, for these tests, they tend to produce spuriously high coefficients. (For speed tests, alternate form reliability is usually the best choice.)

Methods to Improve Reliability and Validity

- Consensual observer drift can be eliminated by having raters work independently or by alternating raters.
- Rating accuracy is also improved when raters are told that their ratings will be checked.
- Overall, the best way to improve both inter- and intra-rater accuracy is to provide raters with training that emphasizes the distinction between observation and interpretation.

> **Must Know**
>
> Remember the Spearman-Brown formula is related to split-half reliability and KR-20 is related to the coefficient alpha. Also know that alternate form reliability is the most thorough method for estimating reliability and that internal consistency reliability is not appropriate for speed tests.

Interpretation of Reliability

The interpretation of a test's reliability entails considering its effects on the scores achieved by a group of examinees as well as the score obtained by a single examinee.

Reliability Coefficient

A reliability coefficient is interpreted directly as the proportion of variability in a set of test scores that is attributable to true score variability.

A reliability coefficient of 0.84 indicates that 84% of variability in test scores is due to true score differences among examinees, while the remaining 16% is due to measurement error.

While different types of tests can be expected to have different levels of reliability, for most tests in the social sciences, reliability coefficients of 0.80 or larger are considered acceptable.

When interpreting a reliability coefficient, it is important to keep in mind that there is no single index of reliability for a given test.

Instead, a test's reliability coefficient can vary from situation to situation and sample to sample. Ability tests, for example, typically have different reliability coefficients for groups of individuals of different ages or ability levels.

Confidence Interval

A common practice when interpreting obtained score is to construct a confidence interval around that score.

The confidence interval helps a test user estimating the range within which an examinee's true score is likely to fall given him or her obtained score.

Standard Error of Measurement

The range is calculated using the standard error of measurement, which is an index of the amount of error that can be expected in obtained scores due to the unreliability of the test. (When raw scores have been converted to percentile ranks, the confidence interval is referred to as a percentile band). The following formula is used to estimate the standard error of measurement:

Standard Error of Measurement or

$$SE_{meas} = SD_x \times (1 - r_{xx})^{1/2}$$

Where,

SE_{meas} = Standard error of measurement

SD_x = Standard deviation of test scores

r_{xx} = Reliability coefficient

The magnitude of the standard error is affected by two factors:

1. Standard deviation of the test scores (SD_x)
2. The test's reliability coefficient (r_{xx}).

The lower the test's standard deviation and the higher its reliability coefficient, the smaller the standard error of measurement (and vice versa).

Practical Tips

- The standard error is a type of standard deviation, it can be interpreted in terms of the areas under the normal curve.
- With regard to confidence intervals, this means that a 68% confidence interval is constructed by adding and subtracting one standard error to a subject's obtained score; a 95% confidence interval is constructed by adding and subtracting two standard errors; and a 99% confidence interval is constructed by adding and subtracting three standard errors.
- Due to the effects of measurement error, obtained test scores tend to be biased (inaccurate) estimates of true scores. More specifically, scores above the mean of a distribution tend to overestimate true scores, while scores below the mean tend to underestimate true scores.
- The farther are the mean and obtained score, the greater is the bias.

STUDENT ASSIGNMENT

LONG ANSWER QUESTIONS

1. What do you understand by scaling? Describe it.
2. What is Z-score and T-score?
3. What is reliability of test scores? What are its reasons and is reliability similar to validity? Discuss.

SHORT ANSWER QUESTIONS

1. Write a short note on test-retest method of reliability.
2. Write about parallel-forms
3. Write a short note on split-half method.

MULTIPLE CHOICE QUESTIONS

1. **The measurement of variability which we use as a unit of the scale of measurement in a normal distribution is:**
   a Average deviation   b Standard deviation
   c Range   d Quartile deviation

2. **The most stable index of variability is:**
   a Average deviation   b Standard deviation
   c Range   d Median

3. **When the scores are distributed symmetrically around a central point and the distribution is not badly skewed, we generally compute:**
   a Mean   b Median
   c Mode   d None of these

4. **The formula for finding out Mode from a frequency distribution is:**
   a 3 median – 2 mean   b 2 median – 3 mean
   c 2 mean – 3 median   d 3 mean – 2 median

5. **In Psychology and Education, we come across measurement data heavily dependent upon:**
   a Nominal scale   b Ordinal scale
   c Interval scale   d Ratio scale

6. **Sex, nationality, occupation, religion, marital status are examples of:**
   a Quantitative variable   b Qualitative variable
   c Discontinuous variable   d Continuous variable

7. **The numerical quantities which characterize a population are called:**
   a Parameters   b Statistics
   c Data   d Scores

8. **All the important characteristics of a population can be specified in terms of a few:**
    a Parameters   b Scores
    c Data   d Statistics

9. **Statistical inference is concerned with derivation of Scientific inference about generalization of results from:**
    a The study of a few particular cases
    b The study of population as a whole
    c The study of a random group
    d The study of the entire population of the world.

10. **The branch which deals with collection, analysis and interpretation of data obtained by conducting a survey or an experimental study is known as:**
    a Psychology   b Statistics
    c Sociology   d Mathematics

11. **A psychologist wants to make a statement about the mean IQ in the complete population of students in a particular university from a knowledge of the mean completed on the sample of 100 and to estimate the error involved in this statement. For this purpose, he will use procedures from:**
    a Mathematics   b Geometry
    c Geography   d Inferential statistics

Note

Note

Applications of Statistical Methods in Health

17

Vital Health Statistics

"Data is not information, information is not knowledge, knowledge is not understanding, understanding is not wisdom".
—Clifford Stoll

LEARNING OBJECTIVES

After the completion of the chapter, the readers will be able to:
- Understand the role of biostatistics in medical field.
- Discuss the concepts of vital health statistics.

CHAPTER OUTLINE

- Introduction
- Origin and Development of Biostatistics in Medical Research
- Role of Biostatistics in Medical Health Sciences
- Branches of Biostatistics
- Modes of Operation for Biostatistics
- Vital Health Statistics
- Sources of Vital Statistics and Demographic Data
- Vital Statistics: Rates, Ratios, and Proportions
- Important Vital Health Statistics
- Demographic Transition
- Life Expectancy

INTRODUCTION

Sir Francis Galton is known as the "Father of Biostatistics" (Fig. 17.1). He was the first to apply statistical methods to the study of human differences and inheritance of intelligence, and introduced the use of questionnaires and surveys for collecting data on human communities, which he needed for genealogical and biographical works and for his anthropometric studies.

Most people have heard the statistic that heart disease is the leading cause of death in America nowadays; moreover, the incidence of diabetes has also increased in India. But how do we know this fact to be true? Where did that information come from?

Figure 17.1: Sir Francis Galton

Framingham heart study: In 1948, a lot was unknown about the factors leading to heart disease and stroke. A health research study known as the Framingham Heart Study was done on 5,209 people living in the town of Framingham. These participants had not developed any known symptoms of cardiovascular disease and never had a stroke or heart attack. They agreed to be followed over a period of time to help researchers learn what factors lead to both conditions.

The study was a landmark in several ways. It showed that there was not one cause for getting a heart attack. Information about several risk factors had also helped to estimate the risk of someone getting the heart disease. Framingham study, which is still going on today, helped us to know the major risk factors that lead to cardiovascular disease. To reach these conclusions, researchers simply followed the numbers, which are biostatistics numbers.

ORIGIN AND DEVELOPMENT OF BIOSTATISTICS IN MEDICAL RESEARCH

- In 1929, a huge paper on application of statistics was published in physiology journal by Dunn.
- In 1937, 15 articles on statistical methods by Austin Bradford Hill, were published in book form.
- In 1948, a RCT of streptomycin for pulmonary TB, was published in which Bradford Hill has a key influence. The growth of statistics in Medicine from 1952 was eight-fold increase by 1982.

Statistics arose out of biological sciences, particularly from the fields of Medicine and Public health. The methods are used in dealing with statistics in the fields of medicine, biology and public health for planning, conducting and analyzing data which arise in investigations of these branches.

ROLE OF BIOSTATISTICS IN MEDICAL HEALTH SCIENCES

Biostatistics is the branch of statistics concerned with mathematical facts and data related to biological events. It is the science that helps in managing medical uncertainties. Biostatistics covers applications and contributions not only from health, medicines and, nutrition but also from fields such as genetics, biology, epidemiology, and many others.

It mainly consists of various steps like generation of hypothesis, collection of data, and application of statistical analysis. Any science needs precision for its development. Precision is very important when it comes to health sciences. For precision, the facts, observations or measurements have to be expressed in figures.

Sources of Uncertainties

- Intrinsic due to biological, environmental and sampling factors.
  - Biological due to age, gender, heredity, party, height, weight, etc. Also due to variation in anatomical, physiological and biomechanical parameters.
  - Environment due to nutrition, smoking, pollution, facilities of water and sanitation, road traffic, legislation, stress and strain, etc.
  - Sampling fluctuations because the entire world cannot be studied and at least future cases can never be included.
- Natural variation among methods, observers and instruments, etc.
- Errors in measurement or assessment or errors in knowledge.
- Incomplete knowledge.

Any science demands precision for its development, and so does the medical science. Biostatistics is the term used when tools of statistics are applied to the data that are derived from biological sciences such as medicine.

Role of Biostatisticians in Medical Health Sciences

The biostatistician plays role in medical health sciences as follows:
- Identifies and develop treatments for disease and estimate their effects.

- Identifies risk factors for diseases.
- Designs, monitors, analyzes, interprets, and reports results of clinical studies.
- Develop statistical methodologies to address questions arising from medical/public health data.
- Locates, defines and measures extent of disease is ultimate objective.
- Improves the health of individual and community.

Need of Biostatistics in Medical Field Health Sciences

- **To have precision:** For precision, facts, observations, or measurements have to be expressed in figures. Everything in medicine be it research, diagnosis or treatment, depends on counting or measurement. High or low blood pressure has no meaning, unless it is expressed in figures. Thus, medical statistics or biostatistics can be called quantitative medicine.
- **To know variability:** In nature, blood pressure, pulse rate, action of a drug or any other measurement or counting varies not only from person to person but also from group to group. The extent of this variability in an attribute or a character, whether it is by chance, i.e., biological or normal, is learnt by studying statistics as a science.
- **To have organized data:** Variation of more than natural limits may be pathological, i.e., abnormal due to the play of certain external factors. Hence, biostatistics may also be called as science of variation. The data after collection, lying in a haphazard mass are of no use, unless they are properly sorted, presented, compared, analyzed and interpreted.
- **To interpret the results:** For a study of figures, one has to apply certain mathematical techniques called statistical methods. Biostatistics is a science which deals with development and application of the most appropriate methods for the:
  - Collection of data
  - Presentation of the collected data
  - Analysis and interpretation of the results
  - Making decisions on the basis of such analysis

BRANCHES OF BIOSTATISTICS

Descriptive Biostatistics

- Methods of producing quantitative summaries of information in biological sciences.
- Tabulation and graphical presentation.

Inferential Biostatistics

- Methods of making generalizations about a larger group based on information about a sample of that group in biological sciences.
- Primarily performed in two ways: Estimation and testing of hypothesis.

MODES OF OPERATION FOR BIOSTATISTICS

Biostatistics works in two ways:
1. As a science
2. As figures

Unit IX Applications of Statistical Methods in Health

As a Science

In Physiology and Anatomy

- To define what is normal or healthy in a population.
- To find the difference between means and proportions of normal at two places or in different periods. For example, the mean height of boys in Section A is less than the mean height in Section B. Whether this difference is due to chance or a natural variation or because of some other factors such as better nutrition playing a part, has to be decided.
- To find the correlation between two variables X and Y such as height and weight. Whether weight increases or decreases proportionately with height and if so by how much, has to be found.
- To find the limits of normality in variables such as weight and pulse rate, etc., in a population.

In Pharmacology

- To find the relative potency of a new drug with respect to a standard drug.
- To find the action of drug, it is given to animals or humans to see whether the changes produced are due to the drug or by chance.
- To compare the action of two different drugs or two successive dosages of the same drug.

In Medicine

- **To find an association between two attributes** such as cancer and smoking or filariasis and social class—an appropriate test is applied for this purpose.
- **To compare the efficacy of a particular drug, operation or line of treatment** and for this, the percentage cured, relieved or died in the experiment and control groups, is compared and difference due to chance or otherwise is found by applying statistical techniques.
- **To identify signs and symptoms of a disease or syndrome**
  - The proportional incidence of one symptom or another indicates whether it is a characteristic feature of the disease or not.
  - Cough in typhoid is found by chance and fever is found in almost every case.
- **To test usefulness of sera and vaccines in the field**
  - Deficiency of iodine as an important cause of goiter in a community is confirmed only after comparing the incidence of goiter cases before and after giving iodized salt.
  - Percentage of attacks or deaths among the vaccinated subjects is compared with the unvaccinated ones to find whether the difference observed is statistically significant.
  - In epidemiological studies, the role of causative factors is statistically tested.

In Clinical Medicine

- Evaluating the merits of different procedures.
- Documentation of medical history of diseases.
- In providing methods for definition of 'normal' and 'abnormal'.
- Planning and conducting of clinical studies.

In Preventive Medicine

- To find out the basic factors underlying the ill health.
- To provide the magnitude of any health problem in the community.

- To introduce and promote health legislation.
- To evaluate the health programs which were introduced in the community (success/failure).

In Health Planning and Evaluation

The data is used to make health planning after evaluation on large scale by governments. Statistics arises out of biological sciences, mainly from the fields of medicine and public health like:

- In carrying out a valid and reliable health situation analysis, including in proper summarization and interpretation of data.
- The methods used in dealing with statistics in the fields of medicine, biology and public health for planning, conducting and analyzing data which arise in investigations of these branches.
- In proper evaluation of the achievements and failures of a health programs.

In Biotechnology

- Biotechnology focuses on a whole range of topics, from genetic modification of plants and animals to gene therapy, reproductive therapy, medicine and drug manufacturing, and even energy production.
- In all cases, research is carried out by developing something and testing whether or not it has the desired performance. Determining performance requires statistical analysis of results.

In Community Medicine and Public Health

- To test whether the difference between two populations is real or a chance occurrence.
- To evaluate achievements of public health programs.
- To evaluate the efficacy of sera and vaccines in the field.
- To fix priorities in public health programs.
- To study the correlation between attributes in the same population.
- To measure the morbidity and mortality.
- To help promote health legislation and create administrative standards for oral health.
- It helps in compilation of data, drawing conclusions and making recommendations.
- In epidemiological studies, the role of causative factors is statistically tested.

For Students of Medicine/Dentistry

By learning the methods in biostatistics, a student learns to critically evaluate articles published in journals or papers read in medical and dental conferences. One can understand the basic methods of observation in clinical practice and research.

In Genetics

Statistics and human genetics go hand in hand with each other, having grown together, and there are many connections between the two. Some fundamental aspects in particular the concept of Analysis of Variance, first arose in human genetics. The statistical and probabilistic methods are now central for many aspects of analysis of problems/questions in human genetics. The most common areas where one can find an extensive application of statistical methods in human genetics are:

- Human genome project
- Linkage analysis
- Sequencing

In Environmental Science

Environmental statistics covers different types of studies:

- Targeted studies to describe the likely impact of changes being planned or of accidental occurrences.
- Baseline studies to document the present state of an environment to provide background in case of unknown changes in the future.
- Regular monitoring to attempt to detect changes in the environment.

In Nutrition

Over the last two decades, there have been revolutionary developments in life science technologies that are characterized by high efficiency, high throughput, and rapid computation. Biostatistics, which can be defined as the process of making scientific inferences from data that contain variability, has historically played an integral role in advancing nutritional sciences.

Nutritionists now have advanced methodologies for the analysis of DNA, RNA, protein, low molecular weight metabolites, as well as access to bioinformatics databases. Currently, in the era of systems biostatistics has become an increasingly important tool to quantitatively analyze information about biological macromolecules.

Appropriate statistical analyzes are expected to make an important contribution for solving major nutrition associated problems among humans and animals including obesity, diabetes, cardiovascular disease, cancer, ageing, and intrauterine growth retardation.

As Figures

Incidence and Prevalence

Health and vital statistics are the essential tools in demography, public health, medical practice and community services. Recording of vital events in birth and death registers and diseases in hospitals is similar to book keeping of the community, describing the incidence or prevalence of diseases, defects or deaths in a defined population. Such events are properly recorded by the public health or medical administrator and help in pondering over the questions like:

- What are the leading causes of death?
- What are the important causes of sickness?
- Whether a particular disease is rising or falling in severity and prevalence? etc.

Incidence

Incidence rate is defined as the number of new cases occurring in a defined population during a specified period of time. It is calculated as:

$$\text{Incidence} = \frac{\text{Number of new cases due to a specific disease during given time period}}{\text{Population at risk during that period}} \times 1000$$

It can also refer new spells or episodes of disease arising in a given period of time, per 1000 population. For example, a person may suffer from common cold more than once a year. If he had suffered twice, he would contribute two spells of sickness in the year. The formula in this case would be:

$$\text{Incidence rate (spell)} = \frac{\text{Number of spells of illness starting in a defined period}}{\text{Number of f person exposed to risk in that period}} \times 1000$$

Prevalence

Disease prevalence indicates specifically to all current cases (old and new) existing at a given point of time, or over a period of time in a given population. It is defined as the total number of all individuals who have an attribute or disease at a particular time or during a particular period, divided by the population at risk of having the attribute or disease at this point of time or midway through the period. Prevalence is of two types:

1. **Point prevalence:** Point prevalence of a disease is defined as the number of all current cases (old and new) existing at a given point of time in relation to a defined population. The 'point' here for all practical purposes consists of a day, several days or even few weeks depending upon the time it takes to scrutinize the population sample. It is calculated as:

$$= \frac{\text{Number of all current cases (old and new) of a specified disease at a given point in time}}{\text{Estimated population at the same point in time}} \times 100$$

2. **Period prevalence:** A less commonly used measure of prevalence is called period prevalence. It measures the frequency of all current cases (old and new) existing during a defined period of time like annual prevalence, expressed in relation to a defined population. It includes cases arising before but extending into or through to the year as well as those cases arising during the year. It is calculated as:

$$= \frac{\text{Number of existing cases (new and old) of a specific disease during a given period of time interval}}{\text{Estimated mid interval population at risk}} \times 100$$

Uses of Prevalence

- Prevalence rates are especially useful for administrative and planning purpose, e.g., hospital beds, manpower needs, rehabilitation facilities, etc.
- It helps to estimate the magnitude of health/disease problems in the community and identifies potential high risk population. For example in dental science:
  - To determine success or failure of specific oral healthcare programs or to evaluate the program action.
  - To find the statistical difference between means of two groups for example, mean plaque scores of two groups.
  - To assess the state of oral health in the community and to determine the availability and utilization of dental care facilities.
  - To indicate the basic factors underlying the state of oral health by diagnosing the community and find solutions to such problems.
  - To promote oral health legislation and in creating administrative standards for oral healthcare delivery.

> **Must Know**
>
> **Relationship between Prevalence and Incidence**
>
> Prevalence depends upon two factors; the incidence and duration of illness. Given the assumption that the population is stable, and incidence and duration are unchanging, the relationship between incidence and prevalence can be expressed as:
>
> $P = I \times D$, or
> $= \text{Incidence} \times \text{Mean duration}$

VITAL HEALTH STATISTICS

Epidemiology, as a public health discipline, uses scientific principles in studying health problems. The world is not a big laboratory and public health practitioners cannot conduct scientific experiments like researchers can do in a laboratory. Therefore, public health practitioners use what is available first, then collect whatever additional data they need through mostly observational studies. There are many good sources of information available. The data generated is demographic and an important part of vital health statistics.

Demographic Data

Demographic data include those variables that describe the characteristics of a population that is population size and how it changes over time. It is important to keep in mind that population trends can have a great impact on society. For example, what will happen to health services when baby boomers (those born in 1946–1965) who currently constitute the largest population group in the European countries, reach their 60s, 70s and 80s? And, how will Generation X (those born after 1946–1965), who currently are the smallest population groups, feel about taking care of them? The demographic data and vital statistics are useful tools in:

- Determining a community's health status.
- Deciding what is the best way for providing health services.
- Planning a public health program.
- Evaluating a program's effectiveness.

The population composition depends on age, sex, income, occupation, health services use, geographic location, and geographic density. The population includes the incidences of births, deaths, marriages, and divorces. To calculate the vital statistics the data has to be collected.

> ### Must Know
>
> "Geodemographics" is a new field that postulates—we can be defined by where we live, what we eat and buy. Keep in mind that the epidemiology mantra of "Person, Place and Time" can be accounted for by the use of demographic data. Think of what John Snow was able to do with the cholera epidemic in England during the 1800s. He was able to systematically map out (without GIS) where people were dying, and from this was able to infer a possible cause for the epidemic, without knowledge of the organism, and provided a simple solution to the problem, without enacting legislation—"remove the handle of a water pump".

Uses of Vital Statistics

- **For an individual:** Vital statistics is useful for an individual. The birth certificate issued by the registering authority is an important document having records of the date, time and place of birth and parentage of the person. It establishes him/her identity as a citizen of the country. It is a legal document and is used for admission to any institution, for getting a passport and to migrate to another country, etc. Likewise, a marriage certificate records the marital status of a couple and legalizes the birth of children from that marriage. The death certificate gives rights to the heirs of the deceased person in order to claim his or her property or for any other legal issues.
- **Legal use:** Vital statistics is legally useful. Certificates that relate to birth, death, marriage, divorce, etc., have legal importance. For example, a death certificate is an important legal document to settle any property dispute of the deceased person, or to claim his/her insurance policy, etc.
- **Health and family planning programs:** Vital statistics relating to births and deaths is used in health and family planning programs of the government. The causes of deaths, mortality and morbidity rates help in assessing the health conditions of the people. Accordingly, the

government can formulate health programs like malaria eradication, polio immunization, eradication of tuberculosis, etc. According to the statistical results, the government can open hospitals, maternity and child welfare centers, etc.

- **Study of social conditions:** Vital statistics like birth and death rates, divorce rate, widowhood, widow remarriage, etc., throws light on the social conditions and its customs and traditions of a society. Major reforms can be made based on the vital statistical data.
- **For administrators and planners:** Vital statistics data that relates to trend and growth of population in the various age groups, help planners and administrators to plan and formulate policies for food supplies, education, housing, public health, transport and communications, etc.
- **For the nation:** Vital statistics is very important for the nation. It helps in analyzing the population trends at any given point of time. It tends to fill the gap between two censuses. Vital statistics relates to the composition, size, distribution and growth of population. It forms the basis of population projections. It helps in formulating policies for providing social security to the people. The rules for immigration and emigration are framed on the basis of population growth data. Vital statistics is also useful in updating electoral rolls and demarcation of constituencies.

SOURCES OF VITAL STATISTICS AND DEMOGRAPHIC DATA

- Census
- Registration of vital events
- Sample registration system
- National sample survey
- Community survey
- National population register
- Morbidity surveys
- Institutional records

The above-mentioned sources are usually provided for defined populations (i.e., cities, states, political entities).

Census

Definition: A census of population is the total process of collecting, compiling, evaluating, analyzing and publishing demographic, economic and social data at a specific time, to all persons in the country.

Census data are very good sources of information. The enumeration of the entire population of a country or a region at a particular time is known as census. However, it is not easy to count everyone. Extraordinary efforts are taken by governments to get everyone counted.

Characteristics of Census

- **Individual enumeration:** A census treats each individual separately, but only once for the purpose of enumeration. Some important characteristics of each person are separately recorded that include marital status, sex, age, social status, religion, educational status, economic status, occupation, etc.
- **Simultaneity:** Ideally, census is taken in a given day. To avoid omissions and duplications in census, it should be taken in a given day, but it is not possible particularly in case of de jure census.
- **Universality within a defined territory:** Ideally, a national census should cover the country's entire territory and all people resident places.

> **Must Know**
>
> - "A de jure census" tallies people according to their regular or legal residence, whereas
> - "A de facto census" allocates them to the places where enumerated—normally where they spend the night of the day is enumerated.

Unit IX Applications of Statistical Methods in Health

- **Defined periodicity:** "Census should be taken at regular intervals, so that comparable information is made available in a fixed sequence." A series of censuses makes it possible to:
    - Appraise the past accurately
    - Describe the present
    - Estimate the future

Uses of the Census

- Population census is the primary source of basic national population data.
- Required for administrative purpose for many aspects of economic and social planning and research.
- It provides us with information on:
    - Trends in population growth.
    - Change in the age and sex structure of the population.
    - The course of mortality and fertility, migration and urbanization, etc.

Drawbacks of Census

Current issues about census data involve the controversy over replacing enumerating with sampling (statistician favorite), and new definitions for race and ethnicity (for resource allocation purposes). Since counting can be done in so many ways, and interracial marriages are on the rise, issues will remain.

Registration of Vital Events

Birth, death, marriage, registration of death are all vital events. Vital event is a part of vital statistics. Census is an intermittent counting of population, whereas registration of vital events like births and deaths, keeps a continuous check on the demographic changes. If it is complete and accurate, it can serve a reliable source of health information (Fig. 17.2). In India, vital statistics are collected under the births, deaths, marriages, 'Registration Act of 1886' and 'State Act'. The vital events like births, deaths, marriages, divorce and migrations are collected under this.

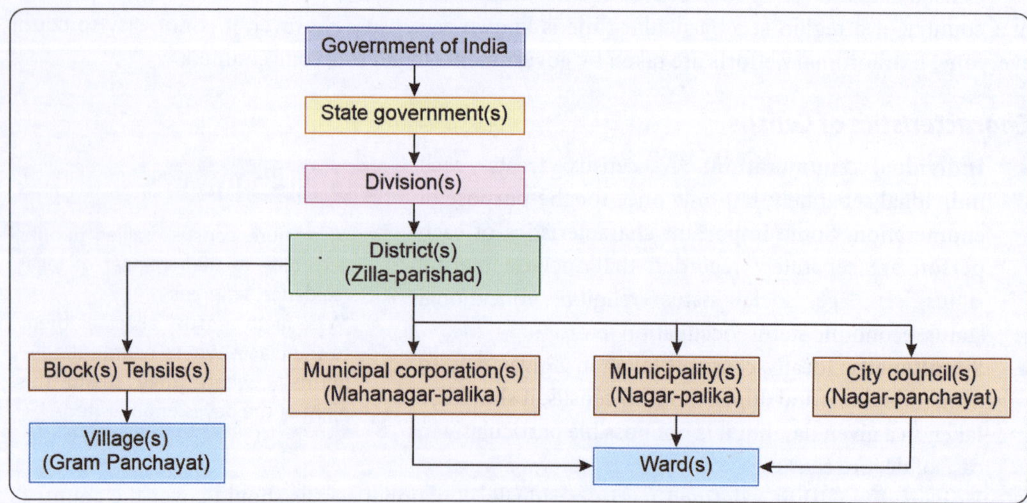

Figure 17.2: Administration involved in registration of vital events

Annual Registration of Vital Events

The laws require that all vital events must be registered.

- **Birth certificates:** These serve as proof of citizenship, age, birthplace and parentage. It requires following information to issue a birth certificate: Name; sex; date, time and place of birth; weight and length at birth; race and age of parents; father's occupation; mother's residence; physician or attendant's certification.

  The process for registering a child's birth differs from state to state. It is a process that most hospitals advise on. They issue the parents with proof of the birth, which has to be taken to the local government offices for it to be registered. The registration of births comes under the Act 1996.

- **Death certificates:** The death certificate is required as burial/cremation documents and in settlement of property and insurance claims. It requires following information to issue a death certificate: Name; date and time of death; race; age; parents' names; name and address of survivor (or informant); marital status; occupation; place of residence; cause(s) and place of death; If death occurred due to injury: accident, suicide or homicide then physician (or coroner)'s certification.

  The process for registering death takes place in Government hospitals/private hospitals/nursing homes/medical institutions. Such deaths are reported by the head of the institutions within 21 days of deaths to the concerned Registrars. The registration of deaths comes under the Act 1996.

- **Migrations:** The movement of people from one place to another in the world for the purpose of taking up permanent or semi permanent residence, usually across a political boundary is known as migration. It is of following types:
  - **Internal migration** that is moving to a new home within a state, country, or continent.
  - **External migration** that is moving to a new home in a different state, country, or continent.
  - **Emigration**, that is leaving one country to move to another.

- **Marriage:** A marriage which has already been solemnized can be registered either under the Hindu Marriage Act, 1955 or under the Special Marriage Act, 1954.

- **Divorce:** A divorce is a legal action between married people to terminate their marriage relationship. It can be referred to as dissolution of marriage and is basically, the legal action that ends the marriage before the death of either spouse. The registration of divorce in India differs, for Hindu Marriage Act, 1955 and for other religions, the Special Marriage Act, 1954 is applicable.

Uses of Vital Events

- **Analysis of demographic trends:** Vital statistics reflects on the changing pattern of the population pertaining to the years between two censuses.

- **Legal value:** The records regarding births, marriages, deaths, etc., are legal documents. They help to protect their rights in property, insurance, etc.

- **Help in planning of health services:** On the basis of vital statistics, governments decide about family planning, number of maternity homes and hospitals.

- **National health survey:** It includes the incidence or prevalence rates for many diseases, length of hospital stays, hospitalization by cause, number of days of disability, and patterns of ambulatory care. It is done with the help of interview survey, national health and nutrition survey, national hospital discharge survey, national ambulatory medical care survey and national nursing home survey.

- **Chronic disease registries:** Mostly cancer (tumor) oriented, but other diseases such as cardiovascular disease, TB, diabetes, and psychiatric disorders are also included. It can be population-based, or hospital-based.

Sample Registration System

Sample registration system (SRS) is a large-scale demographic survey for providing reliable annual estimates of infant mortality rate, birth rate, death rate and other fertility and mortality indicators at the national and subnational levels. The SRS began in 1964–65. It has over 6000 sampling units (for 10,000,000 population). It contains dual registration systems for births and deaths. It provides fertility and mortality estimates for every state and territory.

The registration of birth and death is an important source of demographic data although the data comes from voluntary registrations and there is no uniformity. In order to unify the civil registration, registration of Births and Deaths Act, 1969 was established. For generating reliable and continuous data, the Office of Registrar General of India, initiated the scheme of sample registration of birth and death, known as Sample Registration Survey (SRS) 1964–1965 which was on a pilot basis. This was implemented on full scale from1969 to 1970.

The SRS is a dual reporting system with continuous and retrospective recording of events by independent functions:

- The main objective of SRS is to provide reliable annual estimates of birth and death rates at the State and National level separately for rural and urban areas.
- Monitoring changes in vital indicators.
- Collection of additional data—proof of age, registration of birth, residential status.
- Integration of survey of causes of death in SRS.

The vital indicators like crude birth rate and crude death rate are tabulated as follows:

Crude birth rate (CBR)	Crude death rate (CDR)
Age-specific fertility rate (ASFR)	Age-specific mortality rate (ASMR)
General fertility rate (GFR)	Infant mortality rate (IMR)
Total fertility rate (TFR)	Neonatal mortality rate (NMR)
Age-specific marital fertility rate (ASMFR)	Early neonatal mortality rate
General marital fertility rate (GMFR)	Late neonatal mortality rate
Total marital fertility rate (TMFR)	Postneonatal mortality rate (PNMR)
Gross reproduction rate (GRR)	Perinatal mortality rate (PMR)
	Stillbirth rate

Structure of SRS

The structure of SRS is shown in Figure 17.3.

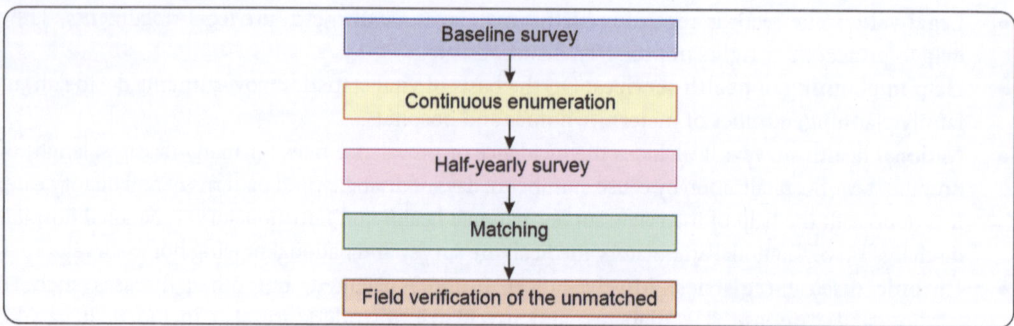

Figure 17.3: Structure of SRS

Requirements of SRS

- **Sample design (Fig. 17.4):** It is a single stage stratified simple random sampling:

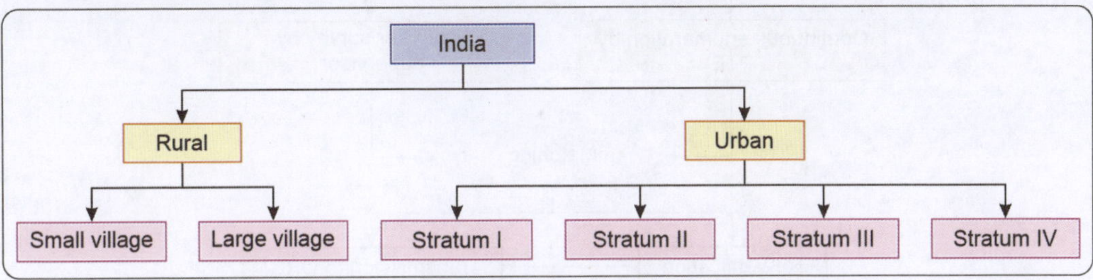

Figure 17.4: Sample design

- **Rural:**
  - Stratum I—Villages with <2000.
  - Stratum II—Villages with 2000 or more.
  - Villages with population <200 are excluded.
- **Urban:**
  - Stratum I—<1 Lakh
  - Stratum II—1 Lakh to <5
  - Stratum III—5 lakh or more
  - Stratum IV—4 metro cities
- **Sample size:** Sample size is estimated using IMR (infant mortality rate). The permissible level of error is 15% relative SE (standard error). Present sample consists of 8779 units (Table 17.1).

TABLE 17.1: Example of the sample units in a population covered

India/States/Union Territories	Number of sample units	Population covered
Bigger States/UTs	158–555	114,000–534,000
Smaller States	45–201	30,000–146,000
Union Territories	14–55	12,000–48,000

- **Types of SRS forms:**
  - Baseline survey forms
  - Continuous enumeration forms
  - Half-yearly survey forms
  - Compilation/tabulation forms

Baseline Survey

Mainly baseline survey and civil registration system are used to collect data for SRS.

Baseline survey, is a study that is done at the beginning of a project to get knowledge about current status of an item of study before a project starts (Fig. 17.5). The purpose of a baseline study is to provide an information base against which to monitor and assess an activity's progress and effectiveness during implementation and after the activity is completed. Therefore, it is important to find out what information is already available. It is continuous enumeration survey done half yearly by supervisor, matching verification and then transmission to Office of the Registrar General and Census Commissioner, India (ORGI).

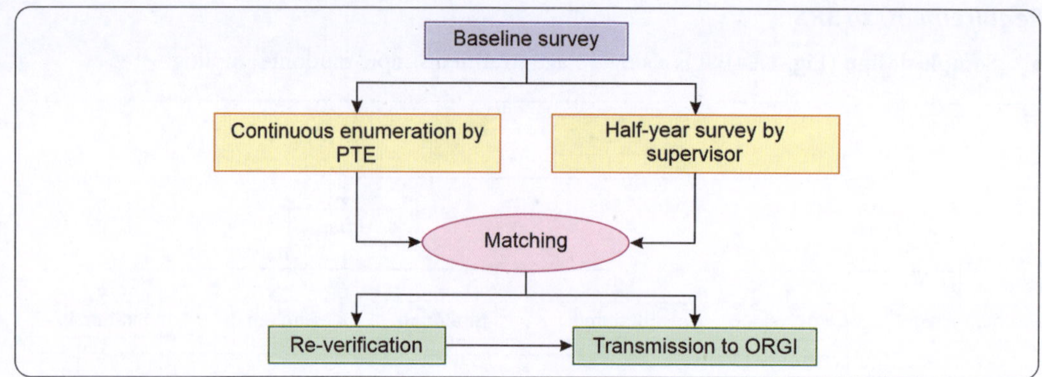

Figure 17.5: Baseline survey

- **Advantages of SRS**
  - Done every year.
  - Elimination of errors of duplication.
  - Self-evaluating technique.
  - Dual reporting system.
  - Sampling frame changes every 10 years, once.
  - Wider representation of population and overcoming previous limitations.
- **Disadvantage of SRS:** Only state level indicators are calculated.

Civil Registration System

Civil Registration System (CRS) is defined as the continuous permanent and compulsory recording of the occurrence of vital events, like, live births, deaths, fetal deaths, marriages, divorces, as well as annulments, judicial separation, adoption. Civil registration is performed under a law and regulation so as to provide legal basis to the records and certificate made from system.

National Sample Survey

The National Sample Survey (NSS) is one of the oldest continuing household sample surveys in the developing world. The survey is conducted on a regular basis by the National Sample Survey Organization (NSSO), which is India's premier data collection agency.

It carries out surveys on socioeconomic, demographic, agricultural and industrial subjects for collecting data from households and from enterprises that are located in villages and in the towns. It is a focal agency of the Government of India for collection of statistical data in the areas, which are vital for developmental planning. The National Sample Survey Directorate was started in the country, by the Ministry of Finance, Government of India, in 1950, at the instance of Prime Minister Pt. Nehru, to collect economic and social information from the whole country on the basis of random sampling. Later, it was transferred to the cabinet secretariat in 1957 and in 1970, it became a part of NSSO in the department of statistics under the ministry of planning. Since 1999 it is under the Ministry of Statistics and Program Implementation (MOSPI).

The NSSO has four divisions as:

1. Survey design and research (SDR)
2. Field operations division (FOD)
3. Data processing
4. Economic analysis

Objectives of NSSO

- To evolve statistical techniques for the analysis of statistical data, the solutions of administrative problems and estimation of future trends.
- To provide statistical and other information for the purpose of state or national planning and policy requirements.
- To provide and analyze information which are useful to research workers in socioeconomic fields.
- To collect and publish information which will be of use to those engaged in economic activities in the country.

Functions of NSSO

- NSSO conducts annual survey of industries (ASI) every year.
- It has the central responsibility of coordinating the results of the crop estimation surveys conducted by the states.
- To conduct large scale sample surveys on subjects like household consumer expenditure, employment and unemployment, health and medical services, etc.
- NSSO every year brings out reports on status of estimation of agricultural production in India.
- It decides the topics to be covered in a particular survey round.
- Agricultural wing FOD of NSSO has the overall responsibility of assisting the states by developing suitable survey techniques for obtaining reliable and timely estimates of crop yield.

Community Survey

Community survey is a term used by social epidemiologists for studies designed to measure health independently, by screening individuals living in their homes in the community, using special health measures (screening instruments).

- **Set objectives:** For this, set the objectives like
  - What do we want to learn?
  - How is this survey data going to help?
  - How do members feel about the community?
  - What do they love and what would they like to change?
  - How can we provide a better experience for the entire community and so on?
- Write survey questions carefully and keep unbiased approach.
- Test and retest are must before reaching to final point of survey.
  - First test internally with internal team to make sure everything is in line with the goals set for survey—we are always blind to our own mistakes.
  - Then, second round of testing involves piloting survey with a small number of people. This will make sure that the survey is going in right direction.
- Next, do the actual survey by using various online and offline methods. The results are collected and summarized.

National Population Register

The National Population Register (NPR) is a database of the identities of all Indian residents. The data of the NPR gets collected during the General Census. The database is maintained by the Registrar General and Census Commissioner of India. The National Register of Indian Citizens (NRIC) is a register of citizens of the country. It is prepared at the local—village level, sub-district—tehsil level, district, state and national level after verifying the details in the NPR and establishing the citizenship of each individual. The Indian government is creating a National Register of Indian Citizens which is a subset of the National Population Register.

Objectives of NPR

The goal of NPR is almost the same as for Unique Identification Authority of India (UIDAI), which issues Aadhaar cards. The objective of the NPR is to create a comprehensive identity database of every resident in the country. The database will contain demographic as well as biometric particulars. The goal is to improve implementation of the economic policies of the government and its various programs, in different segments of the population. NPR and UIDAI work closely together to create a database of Indian residents.

Morbidity Survey

Morbidity survey is the presence of disease or other adverse health events, including illness, injury or disability. Data on frequency and distribution of an illness can aid in controlling its spread and, may lead to the identification of its causes. The major methods for gathering morbidity data are through surveillance systems and sample surveys. These are both costly procedures and are used only selectively in developing country setting to gather data on health problems of major importance.

Sources of Morbidity Data

Morbidity data come from a variety of sources, including:
- **Healthcare sites:** Main source of data for surveillance and notifiable diseases (morbidity data) comes from hospital and clinic data, which means the populations of reference may not be easy to define. We must be aware that events like marriage and divorce are changing with impact on vital statistic data. Current cultural changes have resulted in the fewer people marrying. It also means that fewer people would be divorcing. Such changes can have an effect on how representative such statistics will be of the general population in the future.
- **Disease surveillance:** The systematic collection of pertinent information about events of interest. It is an orderly consolidation, analysis, and interpretation of these data. There is prompt dissemination of the results in a useful form. Timely and appropriate public health action are taken based on the findings. Initially, it was concerned with infectious diseases. Currently, it includes a wider range of health data including chronic diseases, environmental risk factors, healthcare practices and health behaviors.

Other sources are:
- Surveys
- Administrative data, e.g., insurance records
- Notifiable disease reporting systems
- Registries
- Clinic/hospital admissions–Laboratory specimens
- Sentinel surveillance
  - Administrative data systems
  - Other data sources—e.g., accident and injury reports

Institutional Records

Every organization generates records in the course of its everyday activities. These serve to document the activities, transactions, and functions of the organization. Following types of records are found:

Archival Institutional Records

A wealth of different types of archival record are found within family and estate collections, though because of the wide variety in geographical and chronological coverage, not every collection will contain every record type. Some of the most significant record types are:

- Legal papers
- Inventories
- Property records—title deeds and settlements
- Accounting papers—including rentals, vouchers, surveys and valuations
- Correspondence
- Enclosure papers
- Manorial papers—court rolls, terriers, surveys, etc.
- Personal and political papers
- Maps and plans

> **Must Know**
>
> **Record and Reports**
>
> A record is a permanent written communication that documents information relevant to a client's healthcare management. Reports are oral or written exchanges of information shared between caregivers and workers in a number of ways. A report is the summary of the services of person or personnel and of the agency. The reports must have:
>
> - Select relevant facts and the recording in neat, complete and uniform manner.
> - As these are valuable legal documents, these should be handled carefully, and accounted for.
> - Records are written immediately after an interview.

Hospital Records

Records are a practical and indispensable aid to the doctor, nurse and paramedical personnel in giving the best possible service to the clients. Report summarizes the services of the person or personnel and of the agency.

Characteristics of Hospital Records

- Records are confidential documents, accurately dated, timed and signed and not include abbreviations, jargon and meaningless phrases.
- A clinical, scientific, administrative and legal document relating to the healthcare given to the individual family or community.
- A practical and indispensable aid to doctor, nurse and paramedical personnel in giving the best possible service to their clients.
- Contain facts based on observation, conversation and action.
- Provide the practitioner with data required for the application of professional services.
- Tools of communication between health workers, the family and other development personnel.

Types of Hospital Health Records

- **Cumulative or continuing records:** Record is time-saving, economical and also helpful to review the total history of an individual and evaluate the progress over a long period.
- **Family folders:** All records, which relate to members of family, should be placed in a single-family folder. It gives the picture of the total services and helps to give effective, economic service to the family as a whole. Separate record forms may be needed for different types of service such as TB, maternity etc.

- **Records maintained in community settings:**
  - **Forms, case cards and registers:** Family record; Eligible couple and child register; Sterilization and IUD register; MCH Card/register; Child Card/ register; Birth and death register; Subcenters/PHC/clinic register; Stock and issue register; Reports of blood test of Malaria and Filaria; Malaria parasite positive case register and others.
  - **Diaries:** Diary of (males and females); and other diaries
  - **Return:** Monthly report; Complication report; PHC monthly report
  - In addition, each organization should maintain: Cumulative records and Family records
- **Records maintained in hospital:** The head nurse is responsible for safeguarding the patient's record from loss or destruction. No individual sheet is separated from the complete record unless, as with the doctor's order sheet, it is kept in a special place where its safety is guarded. The two parts of the record for which the nursing service is universally wholly responsible are the vital sign, graphic sheet and nurses' observation or nurses' notes. Various sources of a patient's clinical record are:
  - Records of nurses' observations
  - Nurses' notes
  - Records of orders carried out
  - Records of treatment
  - Records of admission and discharge
  - Records of equipment loss and replacement (inventory)
  - Records of personnel performance

Uses of Hospital Health Records

Effective health records show the health problem in the family and other factors that affect health. It indicates plans for future. It helps in the research for improvement in healthcare (Table 17.2).

TABLE 17.2: Uses of health records

For the individual and family	For the doctor	For the nurse	For authorities
Serve to document the history of the client	As guide for diagnosis, treatment, follow-up and evaluation of services	Provides with documentation of services rendered, i.e., shows health condition of the client	Provide the management with statistical information necessary for decision in regard to utilization of resources, planning for administrative control and future references
Assist in the continuity of care	Indicates progress and continuity of care	Provides data essential for planning and evaluation of services for further improvement.	Help the supervisor evaluate the services rendered, teaching done and a person's action and reactions.
Serve as evidence to support or to manage or face the legal questions that arise		Helps self-evaluation of medical practice	Serve as a guide for professional growth
Serve to recognize the health needs and can be used as a research and teaching tool		Records may be used for teaching and research	Enable to judge the quality and quantity of work done
Serve as communication tool between staff and other members involved in care			Indicate plans for the future

VITAL STATISTICS: RATES, RATIOS, AND PROPORTIONS

Vital statistics is a branch of biometry that deals with data and law of human mortality, morbidity and demography. Vital statistics is conventionally numerical records of marriage, births, sickness, and death by which the health and growth of community is studied.

Purpose of Collecting Vital Health Statistics

- **Community health:** To describe the level of community health, to diagnose community illness and to discover solutions to health problems.
- **Administrative purpose:** It provides clues for administrative action to create administrative standards of health activities.
- **Health programmed organization:** To determine success or failure of specific health programmed or undertake overall evaluation of public health work.
- **Legislation purpose:** To promote health legislation at local, state, and national level.
- **Government purpose:** To develop, policies, procedure at state and central level.

Uses of Vital Health Statistics

- To evaluate the impact of various National Health Programs.
- To plan for better future measures of disease control.
- To explain the hereditary nature of the disease.
- To plan and evaluate economic and social development.
- To determine the health status of individual.
- To compare the health status of individual one nation with others.
- It is a primary tool in research activities.

Along with the uses shown in Figure 17.6, vital health statistics is the only nationally representative source for:

- Mortality by cause of death.
- Risks of premature death by sex and age.
- Relative risks of death among subgroups.
- Cause-specific risk of dying trends.
- Small area data from vital statistics also help to identify localized health problems.

Mortality and morbidity are indicators of health status of a population:

Mortality

Mortality measures provide an indirect means to assess a community's health, underlying causes of death are necessarily useful in controlling many diseases and illnesses that exist within a given community. Mortality is the condition of being mortal, or susceptible to death. The opposite of mortality is immortality. It is an epidemiological transition. This refers to the change in disease patterns from mostly infectious diseases to mostly chronic and degenerative diseases. Death is a unique and universal event, and as a final event it is clearly defined. Age and cause at death provide an instant depiction of health status. In high mortality settings, information on trends of death (by causes) substantiates the progress of health programs survival rate improved with modernization. Population's age, mortality measures do not give an adequate picture of a population's health status Therefore, indicators of morbidity such as the prevalence of chronic diseases and disabilities become more important. This information is obtained from:

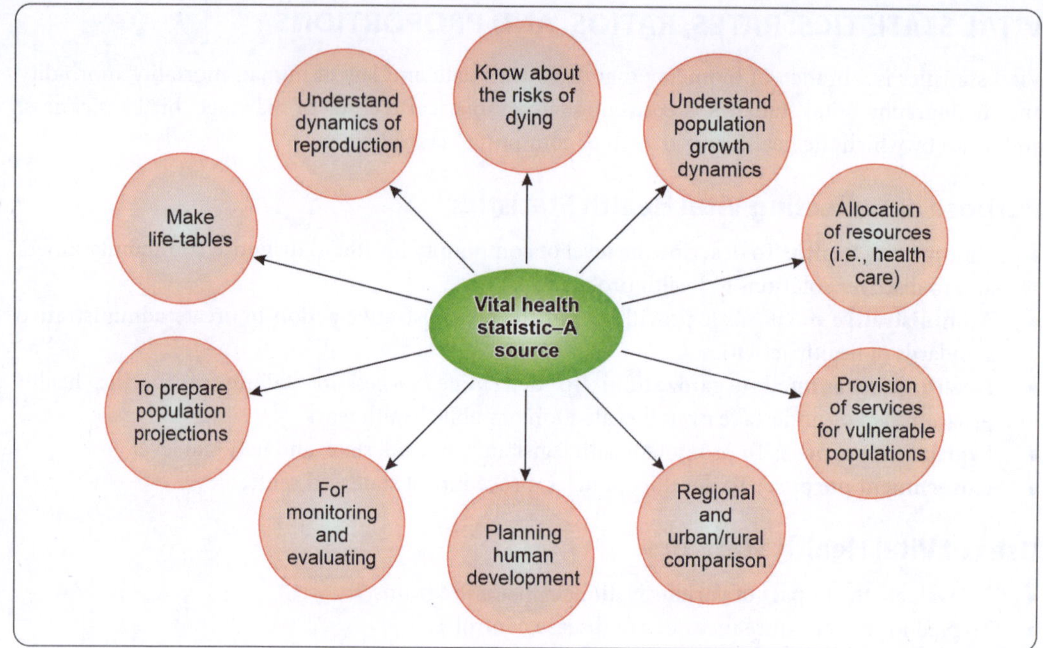

Figure 17.6: Uses of vital health statistics

- National vital registration systems—a major source in developed countries
- Sample registration systems (e.g., in China and India)
- Household surveys—to estimate infant and child mortality
- Special longitudinal investigations (e.g., maternal mortality studies)

Morbidity

The morbidity measures are useful for program planning and evaluation. Unfortunately, morbidity is not recorded as precisely as mortality, therefore difficult to analyze.

Methods to Collect Morbidity and Mortality Data

- **National sample survey:** The data collected from the census are not very reliable and available only once in 10 years. In absence of reliable data from the civil registration system (CRS), the need for reliable statistics at national and state levels is being met through sample surveys launched from time to time.
- **Sample registration system:** In this system, there is continuous enumeration of births and deaths in a sample of villages/urban blocks by a resident part-time enumerator, then an independent six-monthly retrospective survey by a full-time supervisor.
- **Health surveys:** A few important sources for demographic data are National Family Health Surveys (NFHS) and the District Levels Household Surveys (DLHS) conducted for evaluation of reproductive and child health programs. NFHS provides estimates of fertility, child mortality and a number of fertility, child mortality and a number of health parameters relating to infants and children at state level. The DLHS provides information at the district level on a number of indicators relating to child health, reproductive health problems and quality of services availability to them.

Sample Surveys for Morbidity

The sample surveys for morbidity are conducted for following reasons:
- The sample surveys are economical as low cost and less time are required as only limited units are examined and analyzed. Accuracy is high as enumeration and supervision are of good quality.
- This method is adaptable to many topics.
- Elaborate and in-depth information can be collected.

Principal Elements of Sample Surveys

- **Subjects of study:** Individual persons, records, etc.
- **Sample size:** Determined by the investigators considering precision required for estimates and resources available for the study.
- **Population to be sampled:** Dependent on study objectives.
- **Data collection procedures:** Unlimited, e.g., in depth interviews, physical, biological or cognitive measurements, direct observations, etc.
- **Frequency of enumeration:** Variable, i.e., single visit, or multiple rounds to the same individual or to different individuals.

Indicators of Morbidity

Incidence Rate

The number of persons contacting a disease during a given time period per 1000 population at risk, is known as incidence rate. It refers only to new cases during a defined period, for example, incidence for malaria will be given by:

$$= \frac{\text{Number of persons developing malaria during a given time period}}{\text{Population at risk}} \times k$$

Number of persons who have a particular disease/condition at a given point in time per 1,000 population is like a snapshot of an existing health situation. It includes all known cases of a disease that have not resulted in death, cure or remission.

Prevalence Rate

Prevalence of HIV/AIDS among adults at a given point in time will be:
Number of persons ages 15–49 with HIV/AIDS/ Total population ages 15–49 × k

Measures of Morbidity

Measures of morbidity is a frequency that is characterized by the number of persons in a population who become ill (incidence) or are ill at a given time (prevalence). Each rate is a measure of the relative frequency of deaths that occurred in a given population over a specific time period (time at risk). Population size is usually defined as the population at midyear.

These measures estimate the population at risk (a + b)/time (t) of one year. If this convention cannot be met, then the calculation should really be considered a "proportion" rather than a rate.

Morbidity rate is an assessment of the frequency of an event making itself known or occurring in a defined population. Morbidity rate is a broad statistic that relates to the likelihood of developing or contracting a certain illness or event. The topic can be better understood by looking at various subsets of the overall morbidity rate.

IMPORTANT VITAL HEALTH STATISTICS

Any attempts to generate vital statistics must meet the needs of statistical uses. The main motive of collecting and compiling vital statistics is to generate statistics. Continuity in the availability of vital statistics, their subsequent analysis and interpretation are essential for setting targets and evaluating social and economic plans, monitoring of health and population intervention programs, and measurement of important demographic indicators of levels of living and quality of life such as the expectation of life at birth and the infant mortality rate.

The vital health statistics used are as follows:

- **Rate:** Rate of the vital events is defined as the ratio of the total numbers of occurrences of the events to the total numbers of person exposed to the risk of occurrences of that event. Rate is an expression of the frequency with which an event occurs in a defined population.
    - Describes rapidity of occurrence during a stated period of time.
    - Example: Infant mortality rate

$$= \frac{\text{Number of deaths under 1 year during given calendar year}}{\text{Number of live births during same year}} \times 1,000$$

    - Two types of rates:
        1. Based on vital statistics only
        2. Based on vital statistics and population statistics
    - Rates used in vital statistics are:
        - **Crude rates:** Computed for an entire population
        - **Specific rates:** Consider differences among subgroups, computed by age, race, sex or other variables.
        - **Adjusted (standardized) rates:** To make valid summary comparisons between two or more groups with different age (or other) distributions.

- **Gross reproduction rate:** It is a measure of population which describes the rate of increase of population over a generation. It is defined as the average number of daughters among birth cohort of women, which they will bear in their life time, passing through the reproductive age and bearing children according to fixed schedule of fertility, if they survive to the end of child bearing period.

- **Net reproduction rate:** It is a measure of daughters which a cohort of girl infant will bear as grow to adulthood and pass through the child-period, provided that as they pass through each stage, they bear children at the rate indicated by a current schedule of age specific fertility rates and from birth till the end of the child bearing period, they are subjected to mortality as per life table.

- **Infant mortality rate:**

$$= \frac{\text{Number of deaths under 1 year during given calendar year}}{\text{Number of live births during the same year}} \times 1,000$$

- **Age-specific (infant) death rate:**

$$= \frac{\text{Number of deaths under 1 year during given calendar year}}{\text{Mid-period total population of children under 1 year}} \times 1,000$$

- **Crude birth rate:** Crude birth rate (CBR) is a basic measure of fertility. There are other fertility measures that are more population-at-risk specific and more comparable across time and geography (such as the general fertility rate and the total fertility rate). It is usually calculated for a calendar year.

- **Death rate:** It is a term used to define the number of deaths every year per 1000 people in a population. Natural increase in a population occurs where birth rate is greater than death rate.

  Death rate = Number of deaths per 1000 of the population (Deaths per 1000)

- **Cause-specific death rate:** Useful for analysis the death by cause. It is the number of deaths from a specified cause per 100,000 person-years at risk. For example:

  Population: 5,000,000; deaths: 4,000

$$\text{Cause-specific death rate} = \frac{4,000}{5,000,000} \times 100,000$$

$$= 80 \text{ accidental deaths/100,000 population/year}$$

- **Birth rate:** It is a term used to define the number of babies born every year per 1000 people in a population.

  Birth rate = Number of people born per 1000 of the population. (Birth per 1000)

  Birth rate is not the same as pregnancy rate, which is the total number of resident pregnancies including live births, induced abortions, and fetal deaths per 1,000 women aged 15–44 years for a specified geographical area (country, state/province, county etc.) during a specified time period.

  It is calculated as:

  - Number of resident live births for a specific area during a specified period
  - Divided by total population for that area (usually mid-year)
  - Multiplied by 1,000

$$\text{Birth rate} = \frac{\text{Total resident live births}}{\text{Total population}} \times 1,000$$

- **Natural population rate:** The natural population rate ignores any migration of people. It is always written as a percentage.

  Natural population increase = Birth rate – Death rate

- **Percentages**
  - Computing by hundreds.
  - Numerator must be part of denominator.
  - Example: % of premature babies.

$$= \frac{\text{Number of premature births}}{\text{Total number of births}} \times 100$$

  - Percentages are summary statistics.
    - Array of subcategories, using total as denominator.
    - Can obtain percentage distribution.
  - All percentages should add up to 100%.

- **General fertility rate:** The general fertility rate (GFR) is perhaps the most commonly used overall fertility measure because it matches often readily available numerator and denominator data in a broad age range that covers most of the female reproductive years, thus representing the population at greater likelihood of giving birth.

- **Total fertility rate (TFR):** This rate estimates the number of children a hypothetical cohort of 1,000 females in the specified population would bear, if they all went through their childbearing years experiencing the same age-specific birth rates for a specified time period. It is calculated as:

  - Sum the age-specific birth rates—ASBR (5 years age groups between 10 and 49) for female residents of a specific area during a specified period.
  - Multiply by 5.

> **Must Know**
> - If **birth rate > death rate**, population will **increase**
> - If **death rate > birth rate**, population will **decrease**

The total fertility rate is perhaps the most commonly used standardized fertility measure because it is ideal for comparative purposes and is a comprehensive summary measure readily understood. The sum of these ASBRs is multiplied by 5 because each ASBR represents a five-year cohort of women.

$$TFR = (\Sigma ASBR) \times 5$$

- **Infant mortality rate (IMR):** Infant mortality rate is deaths of babies under one year of age: Infant mortality rate is defined as the ratio of infant deaths registered in a given year to the total number of live births registered in the same year; usually expressed as per 1000 live births. It is calculated as:

$$\text{Infant mortality rate} = \frac{\text{Number of infant death in a year}}{\text{Number of live birth in the year}} \times 1000$$

It is a sensitive indicator and reflects the socioeconomic status of the country. It also reflects the medical and health facilities in a population.

- **Neonatal mortality rate:** (<28 days after birth):

$$\text{Neonatal mortality rate} = \frac{\text{Number of deaths under 28 days of age during a year}}{\text{Number of live births}} \times 1000$$

Low birth weight (<2.5 kg at birth) greatly increases the risk of infant mortality. It occurs basically due to the endogenous factors of death.

- **Postneonatal mortality rate:**

$$= \frac{\text{Death between 1st and 11th complete months}}{\text{Number of live birth}} \times 1000$$

It is affected by the exogenous factors (environments, sanitation, health facilities, etc.).

- **Case fatality rate:** It determines the killing power of a disease. It is simply the ratio of death to case. It is typically used in acute infectious diseases like food poisoning, cholera, etc. It is calculated as:

$$= \frac{\text{Total number of death due to a particular disease}}{\text{Total number of cases with same disease}} \times 100$$

$$= \frac{\text{Death due to the specific disease}}{\text{Total number of illness due to that disease}} \times 100$$

- **Ratio:** It is the value obtained by dividing one quantity by another. Used to indicate relative size of one number compared with another number.
    - Numerator does not have to be part of denominator.
    - Example:

$$\text{Sex ratio at birth} = \frac{\text{Number of male live births}}{\text{Number of female live births}} \times 100 \text{ (or 1,000)}$$

$$= \textit{number of male live births per 100 (or 1,000) female live births}$$

- **Sex ratio at birth:** It is an important demographic indicator used for determining the sex composition of a population. It also affects some critical demographic measures such as the number of years required for a population to double in size given a rate of population growth, which rises as the ratio of males to females at birth increases.

  It is calculated as:

  Number of resident male live births for a specific area during a specified period
    - Divided by number of resident female live births for that area and period
    - Multiplied by 100 or 1,000

$$= \frac{\text{Number of resident male live births}}{\text{Number of resident female live births}} \times 100 \text{ (or 1,000)}$$

- **Sex ratio and child women ratio:**

$$\text{Sex ratio} = \frac{\text{Male population}}{\text{Female population}} \times 100$$

$$\text{Child women ratio} = \frac{\text{Numbers of children} <5 \text{ years}}{\text{Total female population } 15\text{–}49 \text{ years}} \times 100$$

- **% Low (very low) birth weight:** Number of resident live births for a specific area during a specified period with a birth weight of <2,500 (1,500) grams is called low birth weight. It is calculated as:
    - Divided by number of resident live births for that area and period
    - Multiplied by 100 to get a %

$$= \frac{\text{Number of resident live births} <2,500 \text{ (1,500) grams}}{\text{Number of resident live births}} \times 100$$

- **% Preterm live births:**
    - Number of resident live births for a specific area during a specified period with a gestational age <37 completed weeks.
    - Divided by number of resident live births for that area and period.
    - Multiplied by 100 to get a %.

$$= \frac{\text{Number of resident preterm } (<37 \text{ weeks}) \text{ live births}}{\text{Number of resident live births}} \times 100$$

- **Proportion:** It is a type of ratio in which the numerator is included in the denominator. The ratio of a part to the whole, expressed as a "decimal fraction," (e.g., 0.2), as a fraction (1/5), or, loosely, as a percentage (20%).

- **Proportional mortality rate:** It is useful to know what proportion of total death is due to particular disease. The simplest measure of estimating the burden of a disease in the community is proportional mortality rate, i.e., the proportion of all deaths currently attributed to it.

- **Proportional mortality rate for a specific disease:**

$$= \frac{\text{No. of deaths from the specific disease in year}}{\text{Total deaths from all causes in that year}} \times 100$$

- **Perinatal mortality proportion:** Defined as the number of fetal plus neonatal deaths, divided by the number of live births plus fetal deaths, the quotient is multiplied by 1000. For example: Fetal deaths: 3,250; neonatal deaths: 5,750; live births: 475,000

$$\text{Perinatal mortality proportion} = \frac{3{,}250 + 5{,}750}{475{,}000 + 3{,}250} \times 1000$$

$$= 18.8 \text{ perinatal deaths/1000 fetal deaths plus live births}$$

- **Maternal mortality rate (MMR):** It is defined as the death of a woman apart from accident or incident, while pregnant or within 42 days of termination of pregnancy irrespective of the duration, from any cause related to or aggravated to by the pregnancy or its management.

$$\text{MMR} = \frac{\text{Number of female deaths from pregnancy, child birth, or puerperal causes in an year}}{\text{Number of live births in the same area during that year}} \times 1000$$

The problem with maternal mortality rate:

- Including maternal deaths in the numerator and only live births in the denominator. Fetal deaths are not represented. In total, this inflates the ratio.
- Multiple births—which inflate the denominator but has no effect on the numerator.

Proportional mortality ratio: Defined as the number of deaths assigned to a specific cause in a calendar year, divided by the total number of deaths in that year, the quotient is multiplied by 100.

For example:

Total deaths from all causes: 1,500,000; deaths from cancer: 675,000

$$\text{Proportional mortality ratio} = \frac{675{,}000}{1{,}500{,}000} \times 100$$

$$= 45\% \text{ of total deaths/year from cancer}$$

This is an easy measure to compute but is often misinterpreted. For example, the proportional mortality for accidental deaths may be greater for young people when compared to the elderly population, but death rates from accidents show higher values among the elderly population simply because of the mathematical impact of the large number of deaths from all causes among the elderly population.

Proportional mortality is very useful in occupational studies for measuring the relative importance of a specific cause of death. It is useful in making preliminary assessments when denominator data are unavailable.

- **Fetal death ratio:** It is defined as the number of fetal deaths in a calendar year, divided by the number of live deaths in that year, the quotient is multiplied by 1000. For example:
Fetal deaths: 2,450; live births: 525,000

$$\text{Fetal death ratio} = \frac{2,450}{525,000} \times 1000$$

$$= 4.7 \text{ fetal deaths per 1000 live births}$$

It is also defined as the delivery of a fetus that shows no evidence of life (no heart action, breathing, voluntary muscle movement) if the 20th week of gestation has been completed or if, the period of gestation was unstated.

This ratio is applied to fetal deaths occurring during the second half of pregnancy. No reporting is required for early miscarriages.

- **Neonatal mortality proportion:** It is defined as the number of deaths of neonates (infants <28 days of age) in a calendar year, divided by number of live births in that year, the quotient is multiplied by 1000. For example:

Deaths of neonates <28 days: 2,750; live births: 325,000

$$\text{Neonatal mortality proportion} = \frac{2,750}{325,000} \times 1000$$

$$= 8.5 \text{ neonatal deaths/1000 live births}$$

Neonatal mortality is an important indicator because the majority of infant deaths occur during the short time period following birth (first 28 days).

- **Prevalence proportion:** It is defined as the number of existing cases of a given disease at a given time, divided by the population at that time, the quotient is multiplied by 1000, 100,000, or 1,000,000 (whatever's convenient). For example:
Number of men alive with AIDS: 3,750; population: 15,000,000 men

$$\text{Prevalence proportion} = \frac{3,750}{15,000,000} \times 100,000$$

$$= 25 \text{ AIDS cases per 100,000 men}$$

- **Case-fatality proportion:** It is defined as the number of deaths assigned to a given cause in a certain period, divided by number of cases of the disease reported during the same period, the quotient is multiplied by 100. For example:

Report number of male AIDS cases: 45,000; deaths from the disease: 37,000.

$$\text{Case-fatality proportion} = \frac{37,000}{45,000} \times 100$$

$$= 82.2\% \text{ mortality among reported cases of AIDS}$$

Relative number of deaths as an indicator of the disease severity are used in case-fatality proportion. It is used as a means of showing the relative effectiveness of various methods of treatment.

Practical Tips

Adjustment of Rates (Rate Adjustment)

Adjusting or standardizing rates are used to make valid comparisons between populations that may differ in some significant way (i.e., age distribution). Standardized rates have no meaning in isolation, since adjusted rates are artificial. The numerical values of the adjusted rates depend on the choice of the standard population.

- Crude rates can only be used to make approximate comparisons between different populations. Such comparisons are invalid when populations are different in terms of such important characteristics as age, sex or race.
- Many diseases have different impacts on different groups. Adjusting rates make it possible to perform comparisons. Keep in mind, however, that adjusted rates are not real and are created solely for the purpose of performing comparisons that would otherwise not be possible to do.

Adjusted or standardized of age rates: When we want to compare the death rates of two populations with different age composition, we use 'age adjustment or age standardization.' There are two ways of standardizing death rates:

1. **Direct standardization (SDR_1):** It calculates a weighted average of the region's age-specific mortality rates.

   Direct Standardization $SDR_1 = [\sum$age groups $(M_{ar} P_{as})]/P_s \times 1000$, where:

   M_{ar} is the age-specific mortality rate for the region.

   P_{as} is the number of people in the age group in the standard population.

   P_s is the total standard population.

2. **Indirect standardization (SDR_2):** It uses age-specific mortality rates from the standard population to derive expected deaths in the region's population indirect standardization.

   $SDR_2 = D_r/[\sum$ age groups $(M_{as} P_{ar})] \times CDR_s$

   M_{as} is the age-specific mortality rate for the standard population.

   P_{ar} is the number of people in the age group in the region's population.

   D_r is the number of deaths in the region.

   CDR_s is the crude death rate for the standard population.

DEMOGRAPHIC TRANSITION

Demographic transition refers to the change from high rates (births and deaths) to low rates (births and deaths). Death rates drop before birth rates, therefore, there is a period of rapid population growth. This ends when birth rates finally drop.

Causes of Demographic Transition

Falling death rates are due to better nutrition and higher standards of living. Falling birth rates are due to social and economic changes:

- Women go for higher studies.
- More women work outside the home.
- More women marrying late.
- Women postpone childbearing.
- People choose to have less kids.

Factors Affecting Demographic Transition

Factors affecting the fertility rates are given in Table 17.3. These factors are different according to the socioeconomic backgrounds. The fertility rate has influence of government schemes, culture, technology and economics as again given in Table 17.3.

TABLE 17.3: Factors affecting fertility rates to cause demographic transition

Fertility rates	Fertility rates are affected by
Differ by religious group and contraception	Government policies, e.g., some governments pressure couples to have fewer kids, other governments encourage them to have more.
Differ by social class—ower classes tend to have higher fertility	Culture, e.g., religion and contraception
Differ by region—people in rural areas tend to have higher fertility	Technology, e.g., Are effective contraceptive methods available?
Differ by country—people in poor countries tend to have higher fertility	Economics, e.g., expense of having kids in industrial versus agricultural societies

Interrelationship of Fertility and Health to Bring Demographic Transitions

Examples are:

- Sex-selective abortion as in China and India, leading to imbalance in male female ratio.
- Female genital mutilation and maternal mortality.
- High fertility can increase maternal and child mortality.
- Illegal abortions and maternal mortality.
- Continuous child-bearing can have a negative impact on maternal health.
- Closely-spaced births (<18 months apart) and low birth weight babies (<2,500 g) are at higher risk.
- Problem of teenage pregnancies as in USA can lead to maternal and child mortality.
- STDs such as gonorrhea can lead to infertility in women.

Must Know

Uses and limitations of mortality data are tabulated as follows:

Uses of mortality data	Limitations in mortality data
In designing intervention program	Lack of uniformity
In explaining trends and differentials in overall mortality	Diseases with low vitality
Assessment and monitoring of public health problems and programs	Lack of accuracy
Gives clues for epidemiological research	Choosing a single cause of death
Indicating priorities for health action and allocation of resources	Incomplete reporting of death

LIFE EXPECTANCY

Life expectancy at birth is average number of years that will be lived by those who are born alive into a population, if the current age specific mortality rates persist. It is estimated for both sexes separately. Life expectancy is a good indicator of socioeconomic development in general. As an indicator of long-term survival, it can be considered a positive indicator. It helps to identify what is happening to overall standard of living for people in India. It is one of the broadest standards of living measure is the life expectancy.

The current life expectancy for India in 2024 is 70.62 years, a 0.29% increase from 2023. The life expectancy for India in 2023 was 70.42 years, a 0.33% increase from 2022.

STUDENT ASSIGNMENT

LONG ANSWER QUESTIONS

1. What are the vital statistics? Elaborate it.
2. What are the measures of health statistics? Discuss in detail.

SHORT ANSWER QUESTIONS

1. What is a mortality rate?
2. Define morbidity rate.
3. Write a short note on fertility rate.
4. What is death rate?
5. Write about the ratios and rates.

MULTIPLE CHOICE QUESTIONS

1. **Which of the following is an example for vital events?**
   a. Births
   b. Sickness
   c. Adoption
   d. All of these

2. **Which of the following methods can be used for obtaining vital statistics?**
   a. CBR
   b. CDR
   c. Registration method
   d. All of these

3. **Name the method in which vital events is continuously recorded:**
   a. Census enumeration method
   b. Registration method
   c. Life table
   d. None of these

4. **Which measure of fertility indicates the rate of growth of population due to live births?**
   a. CBR
   b. ASFR
   c. GFR
   d. All of these

5. **The capacity of women to bear children is known as:**
   a. Fertility
   b. Fecundity
   c. Mortality
   d. None of these

6. **The average number of live births occurring to one thousand women of childbearing age in a year is defined as:**
   a. ASFR
   b. GRR
   c. NRR
   d. GFR

7. **Name the fertility measure which considers only female population of childbearing age:**
   a. CBR
   b. GFR
   c. Both a and b
   d. None of these

Unit X

Use of Computers for Data Analysis

18

Computers in Data Analysis

"Information is the oil of the 21st century, and analytics is the combustion engine."
—Peter Sondergaard,
Senior Vice President and Global Head of Research for Gartner

LEARNING OBJECTIVES

After the completion of the chapter, the readers will be able to:
- Understand process of data analytics.
- Get familiar with use of various statistical packages.

CHAPTER OUTLINE

INTRODUCTION

Peter Sondergaard, Senior Vice President and Global Head of Research for the Worldwide Information Technology Research and Advisory Company Gartner, said "Information is the oil of the 21st century, and analytics is the combustion engine." So, what exactly is analytics and why is it so important to 21st century healthcare?

HEALTHCARE INDUSTRY—CLINICAL DATA WAREHOUSE

A hospital has an electronic health record system as well as specialized departmental systems like billing, diagnostic imaging, laboratory, pharmacy, nutrition services, anatomic pathology, etc. Each of these systems is designed and is intended for patient care, and captures specific data about the patient. Although, none of these systems have a complete set of data for any individual patient or for a group of patients.

Healthcare industry brings together data for a patient on a single, coordinated platform which can be used for analysis and reporting. This is done *via* a process known as Extraction-Transform-Load or ETL, which retrieves data from various clinical systems, synchronizes formats of data in a process called transformation, and cleans up the data, and then imports the data into the database of the clinical data warehouse (Fig.18.1).

The transformation process is very important because data can be stored in a variety of forms across systems. For example, a laboratory may use letters M, F, or U for patient gender (male, female, or unknown) while the radiology might use 1, 2, or 9 instead. Still, they must match the descriptions used in the clinical data warehouse and that process of converting them to match is called transformation.

Another important step is confirming that all records of a patient from various systems are linked together. This typically requires a master patient index (or a master person index) to link a patient's various identifiers across systems.

Characteristics of Clinical Data

The data should have certain qualities:

Interoperability

An ability to share and use data that begins with basic building blocks of what is shared—a data element. A data element is the basic unit of data that has a precise meaning. It is the level at which data is created and collected. This is the level which is essential to define clinical models and inputs for making clinical decisions. It is essential for computer understandability. It may be difficult to distinguish between data elements and terminology at times like:

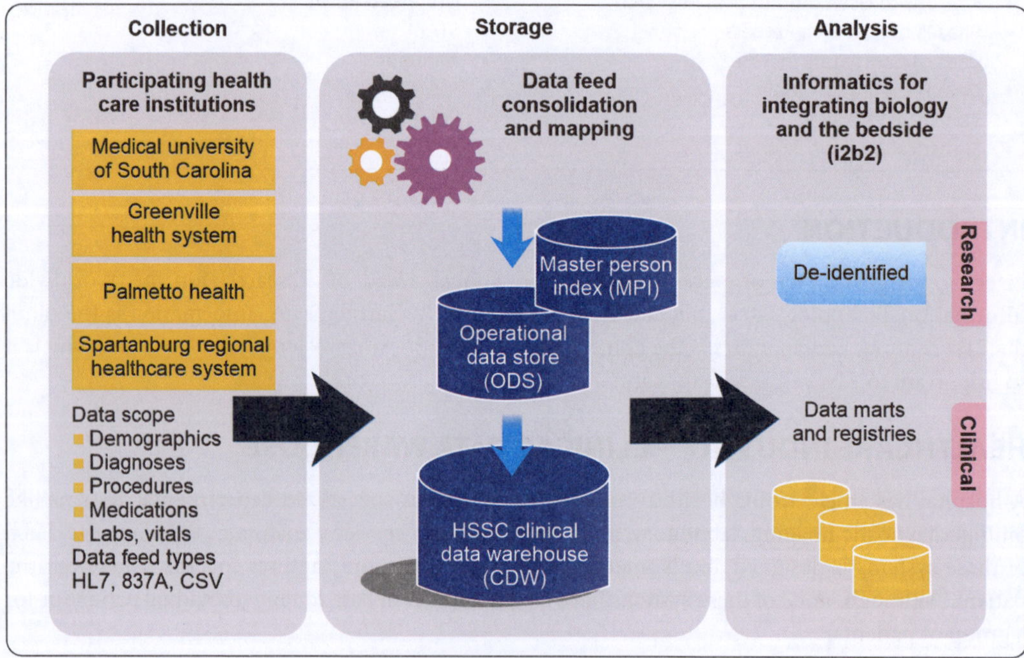

Figure 18.1: Clinical data warehouse

- Is a symptom a data element?
- Is hypertension a data element?
- Is a lab test a data element?
- Is atenolol a data element?

These all data elements are at different levels. Some are at the class level; others are at an item level. Some are generic and others are specific. One has to define every word that will be ultimately used to document healthcare and support secondary uses of the data.

A meta-dictionary is a collection or repository of data elements and their attributes.

Analytics

In words of Gartner "Analytics has emerged as a catch-all term for a variety of different business intelligence (BI) and application-related initiatives".

In 2015, the National Institute of Standards issued a formal definition of analytics, as follows:

"The term analytics refers to the discovery of meaningful patterns in data, and is one of the steps in the data life cycle of collection of raw data, preparation of information, analysis of patterns to synthesize knowledge, and action to produce value."

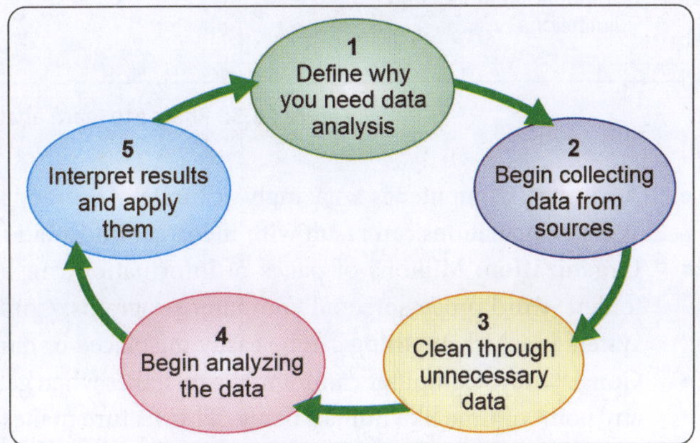

Figure 18.2: Process of analytics

Analytics is the entire process of data collection, extraction, transformation, analysis, interpretation, and reporting (Fig.18.2). It includes statistical analysis as one of the steps.

Analytics may be categorized into following types:

- **Descriptive:** Uses business intelligence and data mining. "What has happened?"
- **Predictive:** Uses statistical models and forecasts. "What could happen?"
- **Prescriptive:** Uses optimization and simulation. "What should we do?"
- **Diagnostic:** Gartner added a fourth type, of *diagnostic* analytics, which is defined as a form of advance analytics that examines data or content to answer the question "Why did it happen?".
- **Prescriptive analytics:** Gartner also added *prescriptive analytics* and defined it as "a form of advanced analytics which examines data or content to answer the question "What should be done?" and it is characterized by techniques like graph analysis, simulation, complex event processing, neural networks, recommendation engines, heuristics, and machine learning.
- **Statistical analysis system:** Main phases to learn any analytical tool (Fig. 18.3) are as follows:

REASONS TO USE COMPUTERS IN RESEARCH

The computers are extremely important in scientific research and the use of a computer helps in scientific research as an invaluable tool. Some of the main reasons are as follows:

- **Speed:** Computer processes numbers and information in a very short time. Therefore, researcher can process and analyze data quickly. The valuable saved time can be utilized in other useful works.

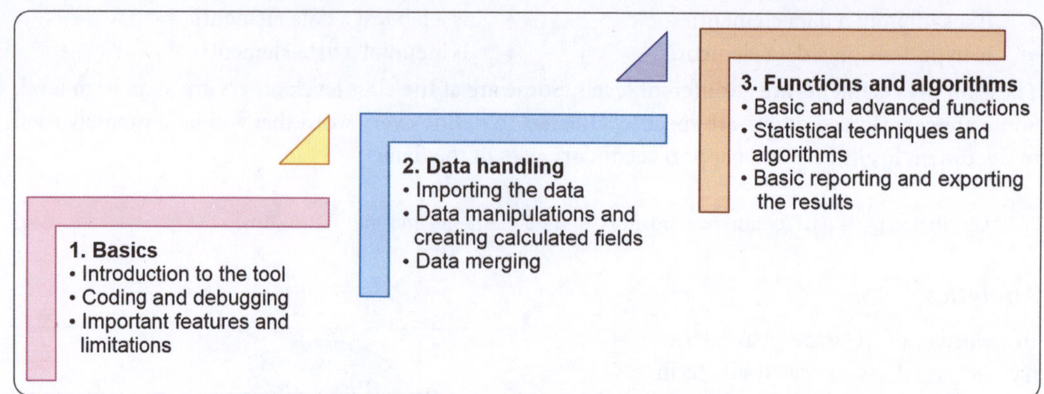

Figure 18.3: Phases to learn analytical tool

- **Accuracy:** Computer is amazingly accurate. Accuracy is very important in scientific research. Wrong calculations can result with incorrect information.
- **Organization:** Millions of pages of information can be stored in computer by using simple folders, word processors and computer programs. Computer is safer than using a paper filing system in which anything can be easily misplaced or damaged.
- **Consistency:** Computer cannot make mistakes when gets tired and do not lack concentration at any point of time like human being. This feature makes it exceptionally important in scientific research.

PHASES OF RESEARCH PROCESS

The major phases of the research process involve:

- **Conceptual phase:** The conceptual phase involves formulation of research problem, literature survey, theoretical frame work and developing hypothesis. Computers help in all steps of this phase. It may be review of literature or references stored by worldwide webs. Computer has advantage over searching the literatures in the form of books, journals and other newsletters at the libraries which consume considerable amount of time and effort.
- **Design and planning phase:** In planning phase to prepare and determine sample design computers are helpful. Design and planning phase involves population, research variables, sampling plan, reviewing research plan and pilot study. At all steps the computers are very useful for a researcher.
- **Data collection phase:** A huge data is collected during research and here computers play a major role for analysis. Collecting and preparing data for analysis is the most laborious and time-consuming aspect of the work. Initially the data is recorded on a questionnaire for later processing by computers. For this, the data is converted into Microsoft Word file or Excel spreadsheet or any other statistical software data file. These data can be directly opened with statistical software for analysis.
- **Preparing data for analysis:** The collecting and preparing data for analysis is the most laborious and time-consuming aspect of the work. Initially the data is recorded on a questionnaire for later processing by computers. For this, the data is converted into Microsoft word file or excel spreadsheet or any other statistical software data file. These data can be directly opened with statistical software's for analysis.

- **Data collection and storage:** Data can be stored easily in computes. Later on the necessary corrections or editing can be easily carried out whenever required. For example, the data editors like SPSS data editor, WordPad, word processors, UltraEdit, etc., can simplify the process of data analysis.

- **Exposition of data:** Mostly researcher wants to see the data in terms of such as—what they look like; how they are distributed, etc. One can also observe different dimensions of variables or plot them in various charts using a statistical application for data analysis.

- **Analysis of data:** Generalizations and interpretation of the data is required. There are softwares available to perform the mathematical part of the research like SPSS and spreadsheets. They can do various tasks like calculating the sample size for study, hypothesis testing and calculating the power of the study, etc.

- **Research publications:** The research article, research paper, research dissertation or research thesis are typed in word processing software and converted to portable data format (PDF) for further storage and publication. We can store/edit/access our documents by using online word processing software from anywhere using internet.

> **Practical Tips**
>
> To calculate the sample size required for a proposed study, standard deviation of the data from the pilot study is required for the sample size calculation. This can be easily done by doing calculations on computers.

USES OF COMPUTERS IN RESEARCH

Computers help in data entry, data editing, and data management including follow-up actions, etc. Computers allow greater flexibility in recording the data as well as greater ease for analysis of these data. For example, the data editors like SPSS data editor, WordPad, word processors, UltraEdit, etc., can simplify the process of data analysis.

For Exposition of Data

Mostly researcher wants to see the data in terms of: What they look like; how they are distributed, etc. One can also observe different dimensions of variables or plot them in various charts using a statistical application for data analysis.

To do analysis of data, generalizations and interpretation statistical analysis of the data are required. Many software are available to perform the mathematical part of the research such as SPSS and Spreadsheets. They can do various tasks like calculating the sample size for study, hypothesis testing and calculating the power of the study, etc. To be familiar with any one statistical package will be sufficient to carry out the most complex statistical analysis. Computers are useful not only for statistical analysis, but also to check the accuracy and completeness of the data as they are collected. These software help to display the results in graphical charts or diagrams.

In Research Publications

Preparation of the report or presentation of the results in the form of write ups are needed. The research article, research paper, research dissertation or research thesis are typed in word processing software and converted to portable data format (PDF) for further storage and publication. Online applications are available through which we can convert word files into any format like HTML, PDF, etc. We can store/edit/access our document by using online word processing software from anywhere using internet.

In Data Processing

Most important applications used in scientific research are data storage, data analysis, scientific simulations, instrumentation control and knowledge sharing.

- **Data storage** is the need of scientific research because every experiment generates a lot of data that has to be stored and analyzed to conclude, validate or disprove a set hypothesis. Generally, the computers are attached with experimental apparatuses and directly record data when generated. This data can be subjected to analysis with the help of specially designed software such as in SPSS data file, excel spreadsheet, lotus spreadsheet, ASCII/DOS text file, etc.

- The **data analysis** of statistical data is feasible using specially designed algorithms that are executed by computers. A tedious job of data analysis becomes a matter of a few minutes with the help of these algorithms. Without computers it could not have been possible to know the sequencing of the entire human genome. Data from different sources are stored and accessed through computer networks available in research labs making collaboration simpler.

- **Scientific simulation** is one of the major uses of computers in basic science and engineering projects such as a simulation, a mathematical demonstration of a problem or a virtual study of possible solutions. Problems that could not be experimented, can be studied using simulations with computers. Astrophysicists carry out simulations of structure formation, which are intended at studying large-scale structures like galaxies, space missions to the moon, satellite launches or other interplanetary missions.

Practical tips

Process of Data Analysis

Steps to be followed in data analysis are shown as follows:

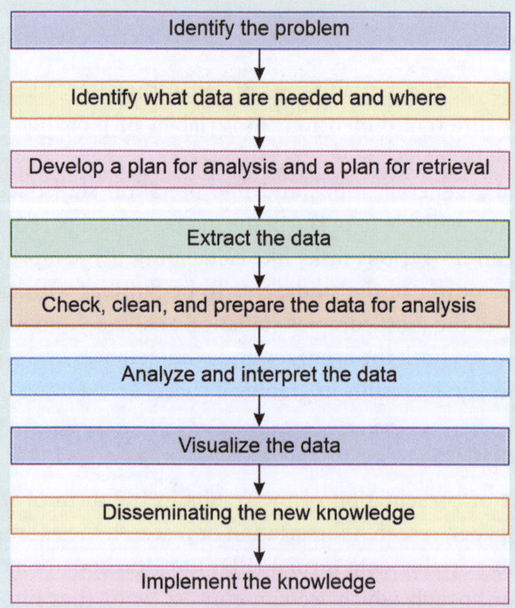

- **Instrumentation control** of most advanced scientific instruments always come with their specific on-board computers, which are programed to perform various functions. For example, the Hubble Space Craft has its own onboard computer system that can be remotely programed to investigate the unlimited space.
- **Knowledge sharing** in the form of internet is a new way to share knowledge. Nowadays, anyone can access the latest research papers, which are available for free on numerous websites. It has made international cooperation on scientific projects possible. Computers contribute to scientific research in every discipline, from biology to astrophysics providing new perceptions.

DATA PRESENTATION TOOLS

- **Spreadsheet package** is a data analysis tool. A spreadsheet is a computer application that is similar to a paper worksheet. It has multiple cells that together make up a grid of rows and columns. Each cell contains either numeric values or alphanumeric text. Microsoft Excel is most popular spreadsheet software. Other spreadsheet packages are Javelin Plus, Lotus 1-2-3 Quattro Pro, VisiCalc, Multiplan, SuperCalc, Plan Perfect, etc.
- **Word processor packages** or a word processor is known as document preparation system. It is a computer application used for the production (including composition, editing, formatting, and possibly printing) of any sort of printable material. The word processing packages are Microsoft Word, WordPerfect, Wordstar, Amipro, Softward, OpenOffice, Corel, Akshar (Gujarati), etc.
- **Presentation software** program is a computer software package used to display information, generally in the form of a slide show. It normally includes following major functions:
  - An editor that allows text to be inserted and formatted.
  - A method for inserting and manipulating graphic images.
  - A slideshow system to display the content.

  The presentation packages are Corel Presentations, Microsoft PowerPoint, Lotus Freelance Graphics, Apple Keynote, etc.
- **Database management packages:** Database is organized collection of information and DBMS is a software that is designed to manage a database. Various DBMS packages are Microsoft Access, Dbase or DbaseIII+, Paradox, FileMaker Pro FoxBase, Foxpro/Visual Foxpro, etc.

Must Know

- **Commercial database servers** that support multiusers are Oracle, Unify, MSQL Server, Sybase, Ingres, Informix, DB2 UDB (IBM), Integral, etc.
- **Open source database packages**: MySQL, PostgreSQL, Firebird, etc.
- **Browsers:** A web browser is a software application that allows a user to display and interact with text, images, videos, games, music, and other information located on a web page on a website on a local area network or the World Wide Web. Examples are: Microsoft Internet Explorer, Chrome (Google browser), Mozilla Firefox, Opera, Netscape Navigator and Safari.
- **Search engines:** Tools are required to search through internet in order to search the information. For example, Google (popular search engine), Internet Explorer, Yahoo, WebCrawler, Excite, AltaVista, etc.
- **Online data/documentation management:** In order to manage documents online the online data documentation search engines are: Dropbox, Google Drive, Google Docs, MS Sky Drive (free), Microsoft 365 (paid version), Office 2019, etc.
- **Online data collection:** To collect data, online from different users in the society and world. Online data collection tools are: Online forms, Online questionnaires, Online surveys, ChatGPT, etc.

Contd...

- **Collaboration tools:**
  - Skype: Voice and video conferencing
  - Google Hangouts: Voice and video conferencing
  - Zoom
- **Modern research tools:** Zotero, Evernote: Zotero and Evernote make collection of research data, and collaboration between colleagues possible, which was difficult, expensive or even impossible in the past. They save large amounts of time consumed for citing and creating bibliographies. Ever note allows the user to capture digital content, including PDF files or snippets of web pages or web pages; and organizes, interprets, shares, publishes and searches them.

STATISTICAL PACKAGES

The statistical packages are specialized computer programs for statistical analysis. They can be:
- Open-source statistical packages
- Public domain statistical packages
- Freeware statistical packages
- Proprietary statistical packages

Open-Source Statistical Packages

- **ADMB (Automatic Differentiation Model Builder):** A software for nonlinear statistical modeling based on C++.
- **DAP:** A free replacement for SAS
- **Fityk:** Nonlinear regression software
- **OpenEpi:** A web-based open source, operating for independent series of programs for use in epidemiology and statistics.
- **SciPy (stats models):** Regression, plotting. The example dataset is Generalized linear model (GLM) for Time series analysis, nonparametric statistics and ANOVA.
- **Public safety partnership project (PSPP):** A free software alternative to IBM SPSS statistics
- **R:** A free implementation of the S language.

Public Domain Statistical Packages

- **CSPro:** It was developed by US Census Bureau and ICF International. It is used for entering, editing, tabulating, mapping and dissemination of census and survey data.
- **Epi Info:** It is public domain statistical software for epidemiology. It was developed by Centers for Disease Control and Prevention (CDC) in Atlanta, Georgia (USA). It allows electronic survey creation, data entry and analysis. Within the analysis module, analytical routines include t-tests, ANOVA, nonparametric statistics, cross tabulations and stratification with estimates of odds ratios, risk factors, and risk differences, logistics regression (conditional and unconditional), survival analysis (Kaplan Meier and Cox proportional hazard), and analysis of complex survey data.
- **X-12-ARIMA:** It was developed by US Census Bureau software package for seasonal adjustments.

Freeware Statistical Packages

- **WinBUGS:** It helps in Bayesian analysis using Markov chain Monte Carlo methods.
- **WinPepi:** It has package of statistical programs for epidemiologists.

Proprietary Statistical Packages

- **GraphPad Instat:** Very simple with lots of guidance and explanations.
- **GraphPad Prism:** Facilitates biostatistics and nonlinear regression with clear explanations.
- **IBM SPSS Statistics:** Comprehensive statistical package.
- **IBM SPSS Modeler:** Comprehensive data mining and text analytics workbench.
- **MATLAB:** Programming language with statistical features.
- **SAS:** Comprehensive statistical package.
- **SPSS:** Statistical package for the social sciences.
- **StatsDirect:** Statistical package designed for biomedical, public health and general health science uses.
- **Microsoft Excel** has some add-ons for facilitating analysis, as follows:
    - **Analyse-it:** Add-on to Microsoft Excel for statistical analysis
    - **NumXL:** Add-on to Microsoft Excel for general statistics and econometrics
    - **RegressIt:** Add-on to Microsoft Excel for statistical and graphical analysis
    - **SPC XL:** Add-on to Microsoft Excel for general statistics
    - **Stats Helper:** Add-on to Microsoft Excel for descriptive statistics and Six Sigma.

> **Must Know**
>
> Most commonly used software in the field of research especially in pharmacy are:
> - SAS
> - SPSS
> - GraphPad InStat
> - GraphPad Prism
> - MATLAB

STATISTICAL ANALYSIS SYSTEM

Statistical analysis system (SAS) was developed by Jim Goodnight and John Shall in1966 at North Carolina State University. Initially it was developed for management and analysis of agricultural field experiments, now many companies use it. SAS institute was founded in 1976. It is a combination of a statistical package, a data—base management system, and a high-level programming language. It is a collection of modules and is used to process and analyze data.

The SAS is pronounced as "sass", and not spelled out as three letters. It provides a graphical point-and-click user interface for nontechnical users and more advanced options through the SAS programming language. The data step has two phases, compilation and execution. The SAS has >200 components, including:

- Base SAS—basic procedures and data management
- SAS/Stat—statistical analysis
- SAS/GRAPH—graphics and presentation
- SAS/OR—operations research
- SAS/ETS—econometrics and Time Series Analysis
- SAS/QC—quality control
- SAS/Insight—data mining
- SAS/PH—clinical trial analysis

The latest version of SAS is 9.4 M8/January 31, 2023 platform having high-performance analytics, ability to deploy in cloud environments, standardized data management, governance and control. One major disadvantage of SAS is the cost. Being in a closed environment, it is complete software in itself. A person cannot use its all applications without a proper license.

Features of SAS

The SAS is a tool which is a combination of three basic features:
1. It is a reporting tool.
2. It is an ETL (Extraction, Transformation, Load) tool.
3. It is also a forecasting tool.

The tools other than SAS have either of these features but not all, e.g., Business Objects, Cognos software has first feature.

Informatica has second feature and there is no other tool which has the power of forecasting feature. Therefore, SAS is used most widely in clinical trials and healthcare industry.

Advantages of SAS

- Has excellent data cleansing functions
- Can read and write almost any data format
- Has powerful data handling language
- Has countless options for output (print, HTML, excel, PDF, etc.)
- Can interact with multiple host system

Must Know

SAS is pronounced as "sass", and not spelled out as three letter.
A few terms to be known here are as follows:
- **Editor:** Where code is written or imported, and submitted?
- **Log:** What happened, including what went wrong?
- **Output:** Results of program procedures that produce output
- **Explorer:** Shows libraries (SAS and Windows), their files, and here data and graphs can be seen
- **Results:** Shows how the output is made up of tables, graphs, datasets, etc.
- **Notepad:** A useful place to keep bits of code

Basic Data-Driven Tasks

Basic data-driven tasks have two steps: Data step and Proc step (Fig. 18.4).

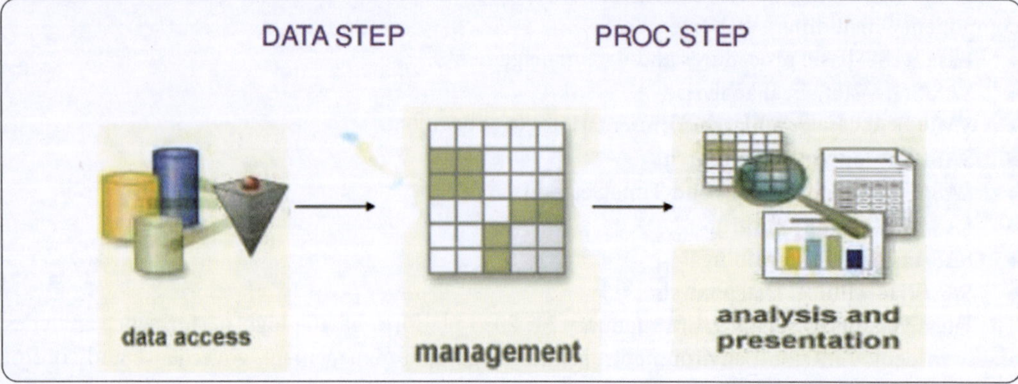

Figure 18.4: Basic steps in SAS

Accessing Data in SAS

- **Accessing data:** The data can be accessed that is stored anywhere, whether it is in a file on system, or data s stored in another data base system; and in almost any format, including raw data, SAS data sets (Fig. 18.5).
- **Managing of data:** It is easy with SAS, after accessing data. For this use the SAS programming language to manipulate it. Format the data, create variables (columns), and use operators to evaluate data values, use functions to create and recode data values, subset data and perform conditional processing (Fig. 18.5).

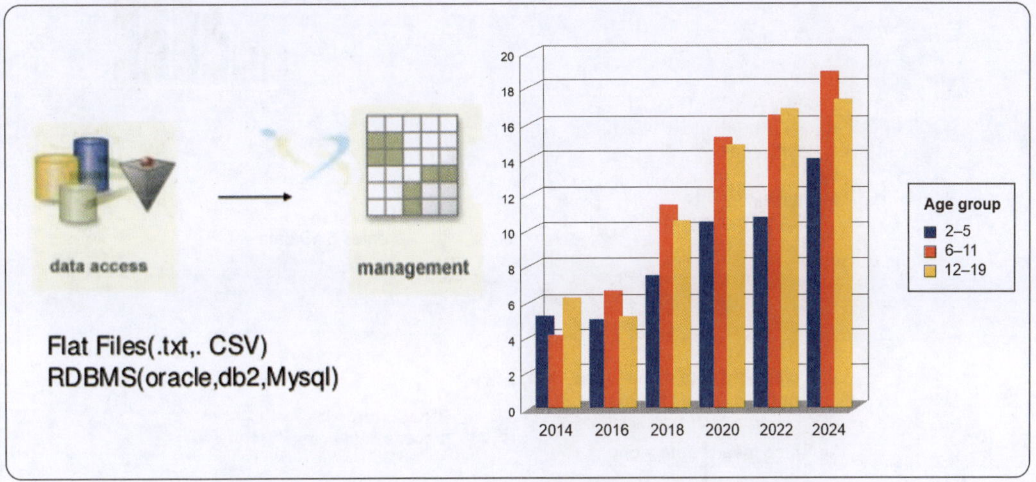

Figure 18.5: Accessing and creating the presentable data in SAS

The reporting procedures in sas are:
- PROC REPORT
- PROC PRINT
- PROC TABULATE

SAS Program Structure

SAS Program consists of two basic steps:

1. DATA statement
2. PROC statement

DATA steps: It creates and modifies SAS data sets. It begins with Data statement (Figs 18.6A and B). We can use data steps to:

- Enter data into SAS data sets
- Compute values
- Check or correct data
- Produce new data sets

PROC (Procedure) steps:
- Starts with PROC statement
- Performs specific analysis or functions
- Produce results and reports

Note: To execute SAS Statement—specify **Run** command

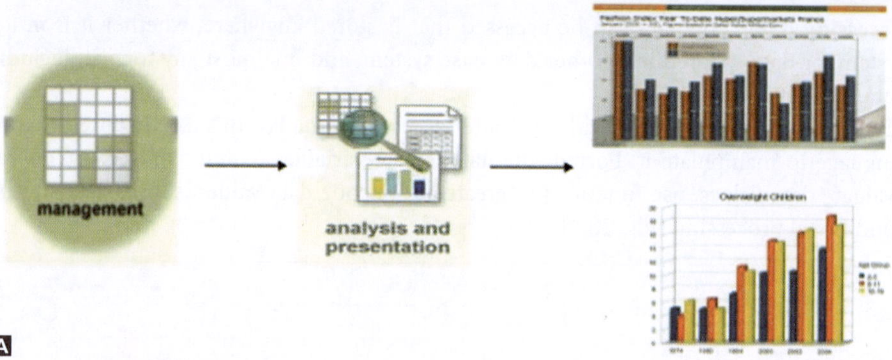

A

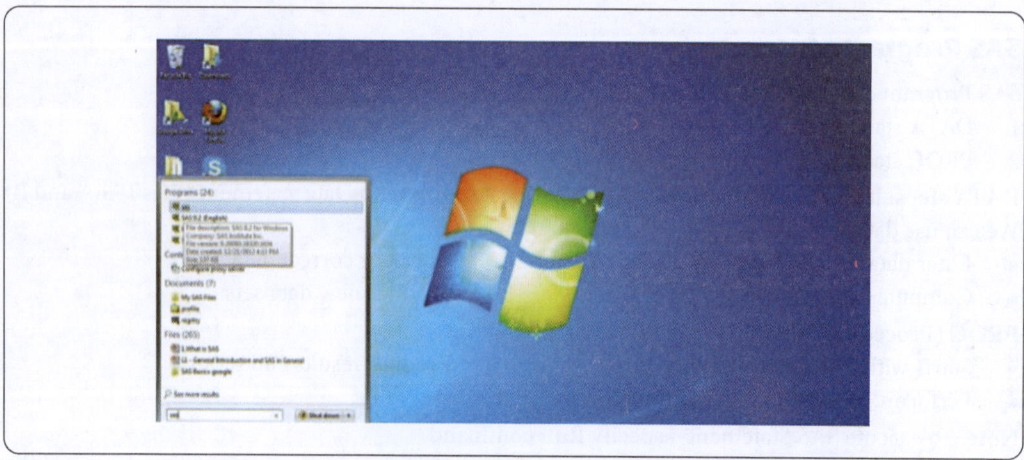

```
data   one;
         input   x  y;
datalines;
–3.2   0.0024
–3.1   0.0033
 .   .   .
;
run;

proc print data = one   (obs   =  5) ;
run;

proc means data = one ;
run;
```

DATA step
creates SAS data set

PROC step
process data in data set

B

Figures 18.6A and B: **A.** Formatting data; **B.** Data and PROC steps of SAS

Steps to Assess SAS

Step Boundaries of SAS

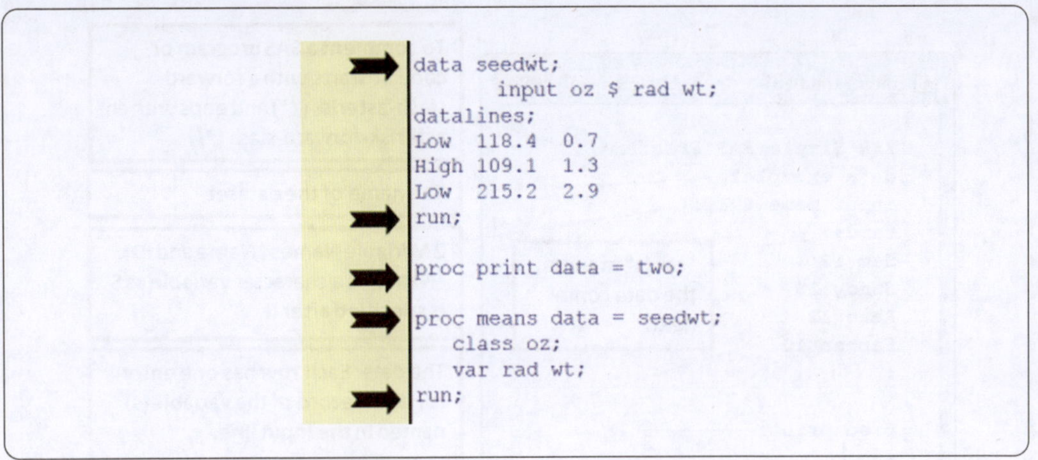

Submitting a SAS Program

When SAS program is executed, the output generated by SAS is divided into two major parts:

1. **SAS log:** It contains information about the processing of the SAS program, including any warning and error messages.
2. **SAS output:** It contains reports generated by SAS procedures and DATA steps.

SAS user interface:

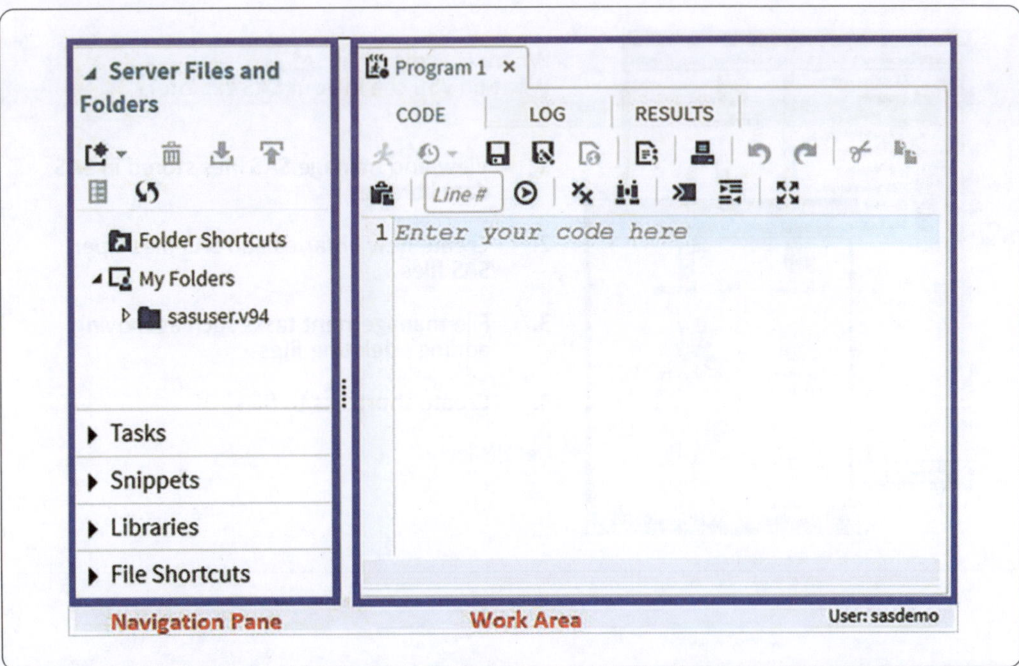

Window of SAS:

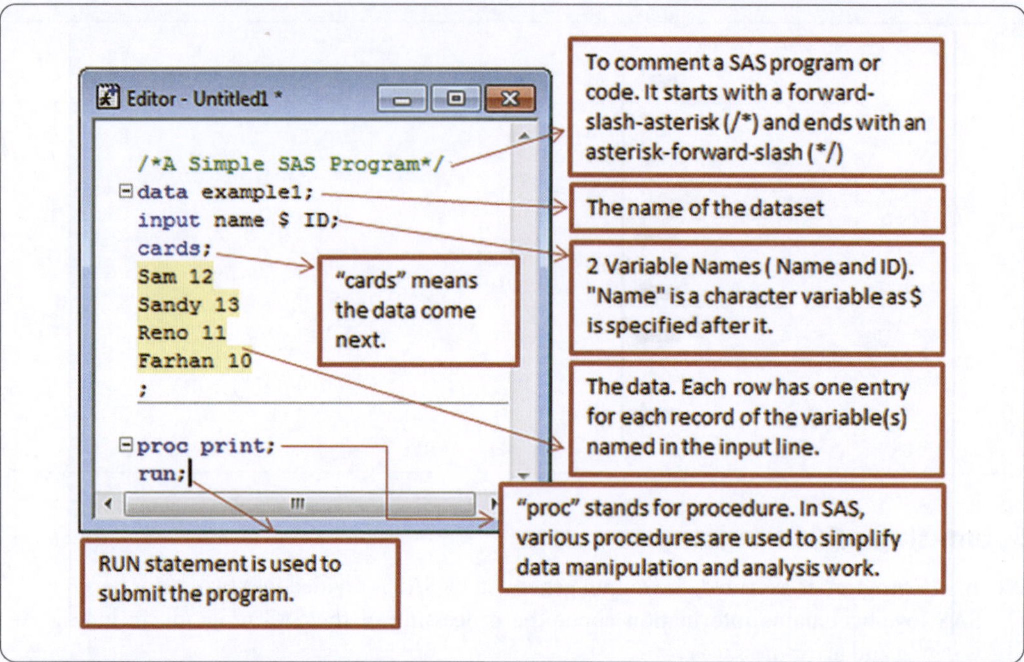

Explorer window of SAS:

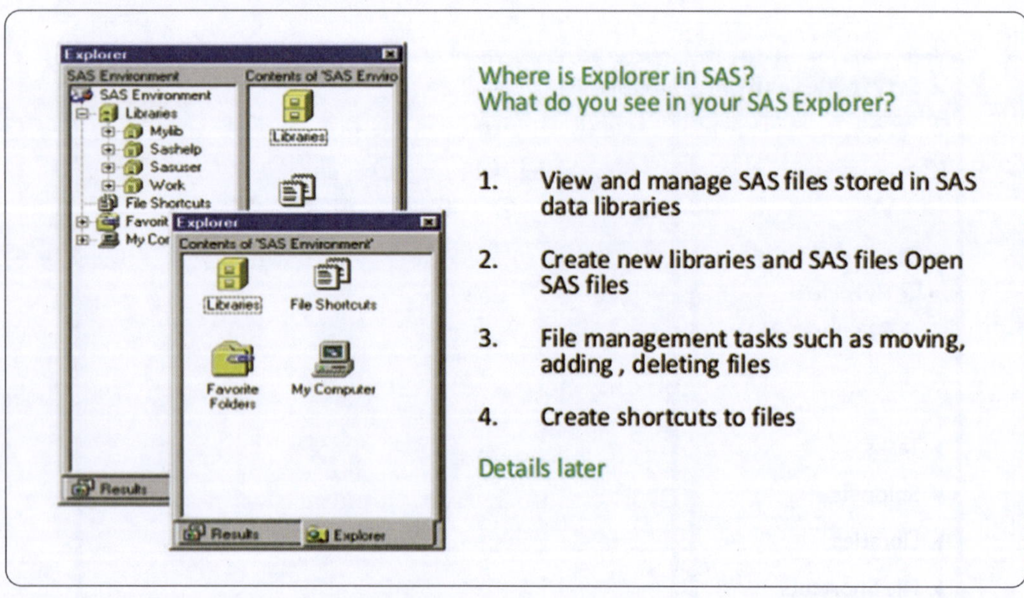

Editor Window: It contains SAS programs.

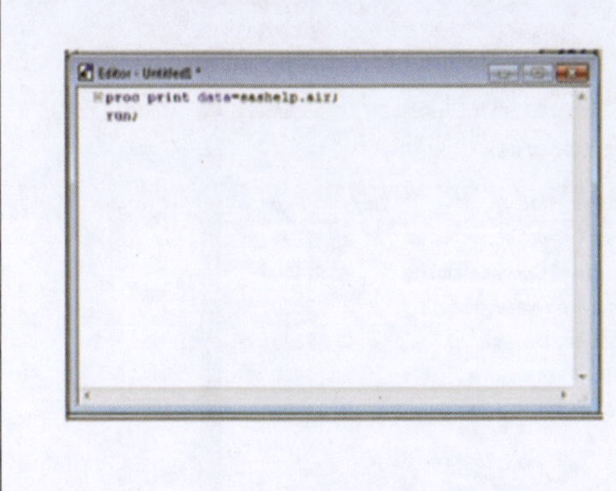

Where is editor in SAS?

1. Opening SAS program
2. Entering, editing and submitting SAS programs
3. Using the command line or menus
4. Clearing the contents
5. Support for keyboard shortcuts
6. Color coding and syntax checking of SAS language

Write this script in editor;

```
proc print data=sashelp.air;
run;
```

SAS log window: Contains a record of all commands submitted to SAS.

```
Log - (Untitled)
1      /*A Simple SAS Program*/
2      data example1;
3      input name $ ID;
4      cards;

NOTE: The data set WORK.EXAMPLE1 has 4 observations and 2 variables.
NOTE: DATA statement used (Total process time):
      real time               0.35 seconds
      cpu time                0.01 seconds


9      ;
10
11   proc print;
NOTE: Writing HTML Body file: sashtml.htm
12   run;

NOTE: There were 4 observations read from the data set WORK.EXAMPLE1.
NOTE: PROCEDURE PRINT used (Total process time):
      real time               1.65 seconds
      cpu time                0.28 seconds
```

Output window: Contains output based on SAS programs submitted in the Editor Window.

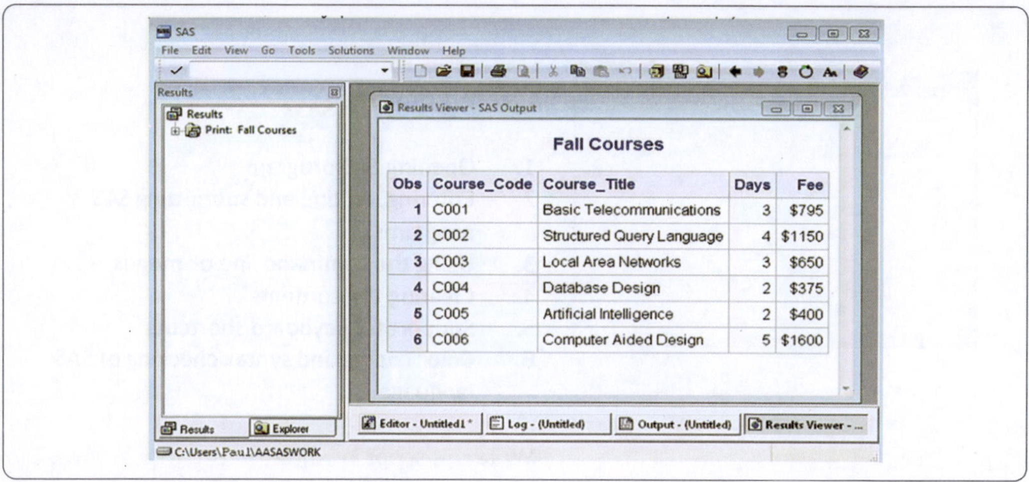

Results windows:

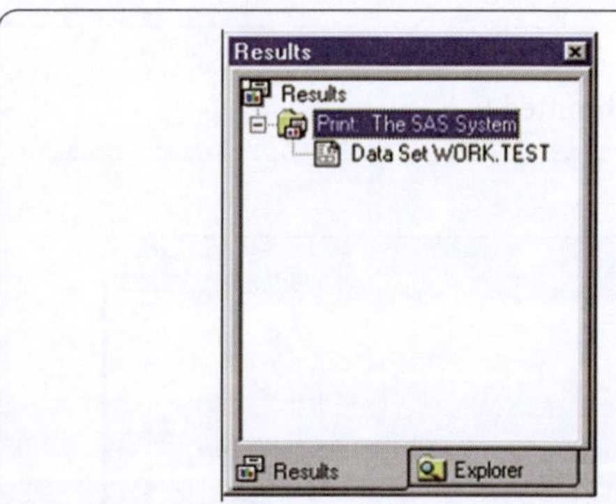

1. Helps navigate and manage output

2. View, save, and print individual items of output.

Comments and Help menu:

Two type of comments can be seen here.

1. One starts with an asterisk (*) and ends with a semicolon (;)
2. Other one starts with a slash asterisk (/*) and ends with an asterisk slash (*/).

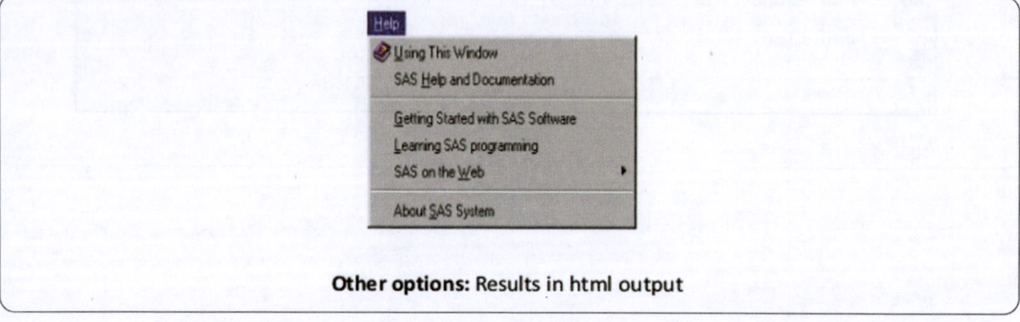

Other options: Results in html output

Note that SAS detects the end of a step when it encounters:

- a **RUN** statement (for most steps)
- a **QUIT** statement (for some procedures)
- the beginning of another step (DATA statement or PROC statement)
- Recommendation: use **RUN;** at end of each step

Libraries' folder in SAS: Data sets created in SAS are shown as library folder.

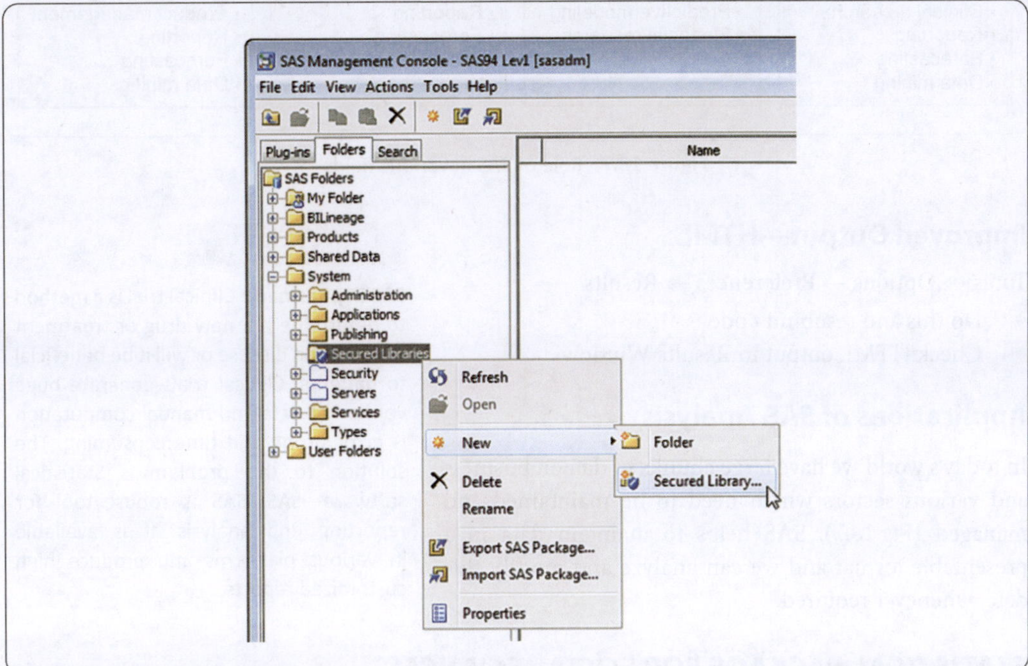

Steps to Access SAS

On Linux:

- **Type SAS:** This opens the SAS "display manager", which consists of three windows (program, log, and output). Some procedures must be run from the display manager.
- **Type SAS-nodms:** You will be prompted for each SAS statement, and output will scroll by on the screen.
- **Types SAS-studio:** SAS will act like a standard UNIX program, expecting input from standard input, sending the log to standard error, and the output to standard output.
- **Type SAS filename SAS:** This is the batch mode of SAS—your program is read from filename. SAS, the log goes to filename.log and the output goes to filename.1st

Problems with SAS

- Bad syntax
- **Missing**   ; at end of line
- **quote**   ' at end of title

Healthcare and pharmacy
- Clinical data integration
- Drug development
- Sales and marketing

SAS used for
- Statistical analysis
- Clinical research
- Reporting
- Forecasting
- Data mining

Financial services
- Banking
- Capital market
- Sales and marketing

SAS used for
- Reporting
- Forecasting
- Data mining
- Predictive modeling
- Financial research

Retail
- Customer intelligence
- Performance management
- Operations

SAS used for
- Market analysis
- Product management
- Reporting
- Forecasting
- Data mining

Telecom
- Network, services and IT resources
- Customer revenue

SAS used for
- Customer management
- Statistical analysis
- Product management
- Reporting
- Forecasting
- Data mining

Figure 18.7: Role of SAS in various fields

Improved Output—HTML

Tools → Options → Preferences → Results

- Do this and resubmit code
- Check HTML output in Results Window

Applications of SAS Analysis

In today's world we have large chunks of data in business and various sectors which need to be maintained and managed (Fig.18.7). SAS helps to maintain data in a presentable format and we can analyze and modify this data, whenever required.

> **Must Know**
>
> **SAS in pharmacy:** Clinical trial is a method to determine if a new drug or treatment will work on disease or will it be beneficial to patients. Clinical trials generate huge volume of data and manual computation is error prone and time consuming. The solution to this problem is Statistical software—SAS. SAS is robust tool for reporting and analysis. It is available in various platforms and produce high customized reports.

STATISTICAL PACKAGE FOR SOCIAL SCIENCES

The SPSS is the most popular tool for statisticians. SPSS stands for Statistical Package for Social Sciences. The current release of SPSS statistics is 9.4 MB. It is a comprehensive and flexible statistical analysis and data management solution. It is a computer program used for survey authoring, data mining, text analytics, statistical analysis, and collaboration and deployment. SPSS can take data from almost any type of file and use them to generate tabulated reports, charts, and plots of distributions and trends, descriptive statistics, and conduct complex statistical analyses. SPSS is among the most widely used programs for statistical analysis in social science.

It provides all analysis facilities like the following:

Uses of SPSS

This software helps in:

- **Descriptive statistics:** Cross tabulation, frequency distribution, measures of central tendency and dispersion, exploring and descriptive statistics like statistical inference, descriptive ratio statistics.
- **Bivariate statistics:** Mean, t-test, ANOVA, chi-square, z-test, correlation (partial, bivariate, distances), regression analysis, nonparametric tests.
- **Prediction for numerical outcomes:** Linear regression

- **Data exposition** by using various graphs like line, scatter, bar, ogive, histogram, pie chart.
- **Prediction for identifying groups:** Factor analysis, cluster analysis (two-step, K-means, hierarchical), discriminant.

Features of SPSS

- It is easy to learn and use.
- It includes a full range of data management system and editing tools.
- It provides in-depth statistical capabilities.
- It offers complete plotting, reporting and presentation features.
- **Effective design is guided by:**
  - A clear research question
  - Selecting an appropriate study design
  - Selecting the appropriate Statistics
- **Platforms for SPSS:** Linux, Mac OS, and Windows

Entering Data

- **Data editor:** The data editor offers a simple and efficient spreadsheet like facility for entering data and browsing the working data file. This window displays the content of the data file. One can create new data files or modify existing ones. One can have only one data file open at a time. This editor provides two views of the data:
  1. **Data view** that displays the actual data values or defined value labels.
  2. **Variable view** that displays variable definition information, including defined variable and value labels, data type, etc.
- **Pivot table editor:** Output can be modified in many ways with this editor, and it can create multidimensional tables. For example, we can edit text, swap data in rows and columns.
- **Text output editor:** Text output not displayed in pivot tables can be modified with the text output editor.
- **Chart editor:** High-resolution charts and plots can be modified in chart windows.

Saving Data

We need to save data and give it a name. The default extension name for **saving files is '.sav' and Ex. SSPS.sav.** It also enables to retrieve already saved file.

Interface of SPSS

The interface of SPSS is:
- **Data view**
  - The place to enter data
  - Columns: Variables
  - Rows: Records
- **Variable view**
  - The place to enter variables
  - List of all variables
  - Characteristics of all variables

Must Know

Variables

Variable is a user defined name of particular type of data to hold information (such as income or gender or temperature or dosage). Array of variable is a collection values of similar data types. The types of variables are as follows:

- Numeric
- Dot
- Date
- Comma
- Scientific notation
- Custom currency

Rules for naming variables

- Names must begin with a letter
- Names must not end with a period
- Names must be no longer than eight characters
- Names cannot contain blanks or special characters
- Names must be unique
- Names are not case sensitive

Note: It does not matter if you call your variable CLIENT, client, or CliENt. It is all client to SPSS.

- String

Basic Steps of Data Analysis in SPSS

Step 1: Get your data into SPSS: We can open a previously saved SPSS data file, read a spreadsheet, database, or text data file, or enter directly in the data editor.

Step 2: Enter data directly in SPSS

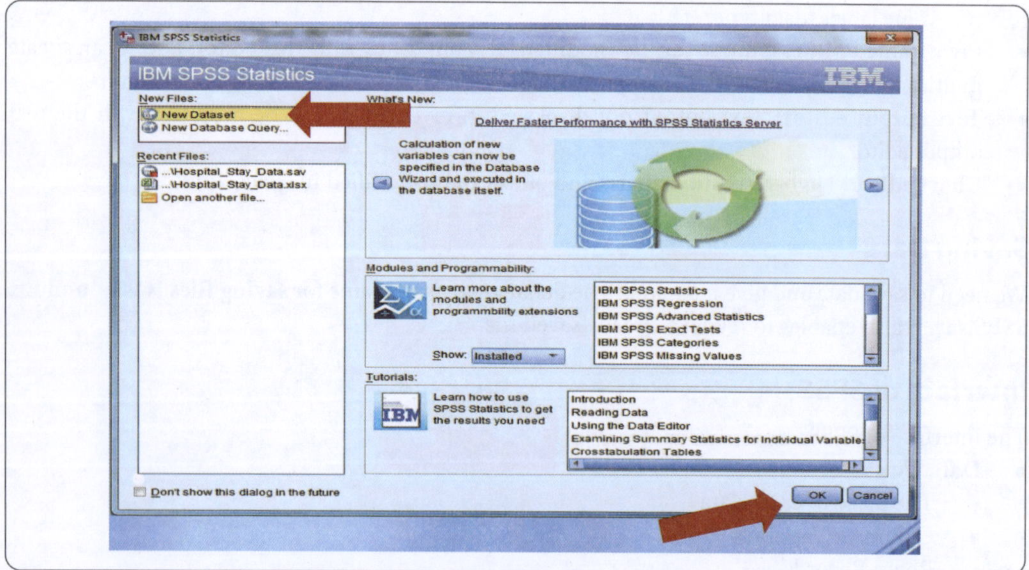

Step 3: Select a procedure: Select a procedure from the menus to calculate statistics or to create a chart.

Step 4: Select the variable for the analysis: Variables in the data file are displayed in a dialog box for the procedure.

Step 5: Run the procedure: Results are displayed in the viewer.

An example of SPSS: Hospital-stay Data

Data of patients staying in hospital is shown in Table 18.1.

TABLE 18.1: Data of patients staying in hospital

ID no.	Duration of hospital stay (days)	Age (years)	Sex 1 = M 2 = F	First temp. following admission in °F	First WBC (x 10⁹) following admission	Received antibiotic 1 = yes 2 = no	Received bacterial culture 1 = yes 2 = no	Service 1 = med. 2 = surg.
1	5	30	2	99.0	8	2	2	1
2	10	73	2	98.0	5	2	1	1
3	6	40	2	99.0	12	2	2	2
4	11	47	2	98.2	4	2	2	2
5	5	25	2	98.5	11	2	2	2
6	14	82	1	96.8	6	1	2	2
7	30	60	1	99.5	8	1	1	1
8	11	56	2	98.6	7	2	2	1
9	17	43	2	98.0	7	2	2	1
10	3	50	1	98.0	12	2	1	2
11	9	59	2	97.6	7	2	1	1
12	3	4	1	97.8	3	2	2	2
13	8	22	2	99.5	11	1	2	2
14	8	33	2	98.4	14	1	1	2
15	5	20	2	98.4	11	2	1	2
16	5	32	1	99.0	9	2	2	2
17	7	36	1	99.2	6	1	2	2
18	4	69	1	98.0	6	2	2	2
19	3	47	1	97.0	5	1	2	1
20	7	22	1	98.2	6	2	2	2
21	9	11	1	98.2	10	2	2	2
22	11	19	1	98.6	14	1	2	2
23	11	67	2	97.6	4	2	2	1
24	9	43	2	98.6	5	2	2	2
25	4	41	2	98.0	5	2	2	1

Step 1: Enter variables

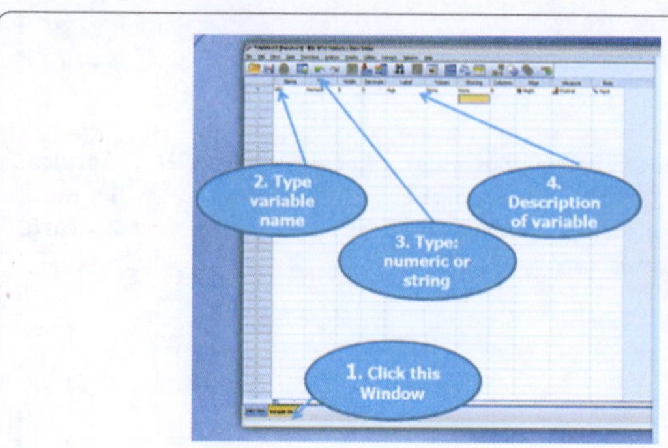

1. Click variable view

2. Type variable name under name column (**AGE**).

Note: Variable name can be 64 bytes long, and the first character must be a letter or one of the characters @, #, or $.

3. **Type:** Numeric, string, etc.

4. **Label:** Description of variables.

Step 2: Enter cases

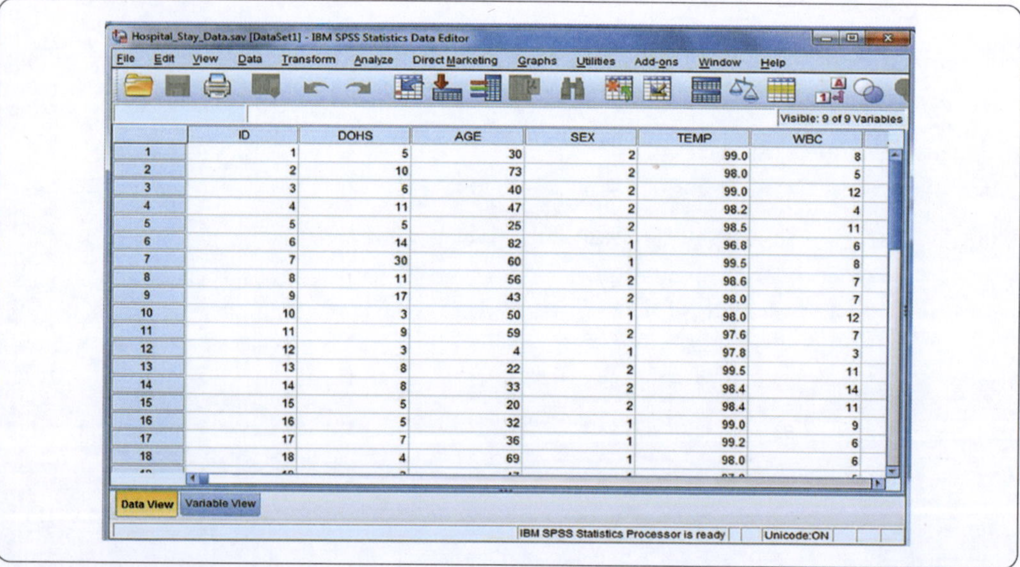

Step 3: Import Excel files in SPSS

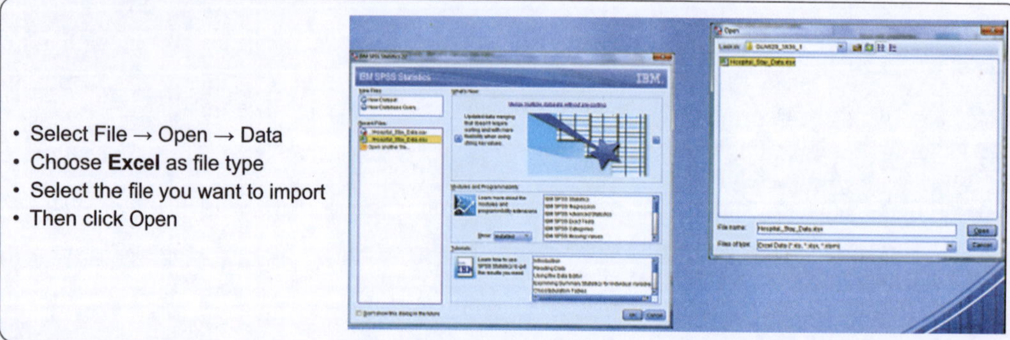

- Select File → Open → Data
- Choose **Excel** as file type
- Select the file you want to import
- Then click Open

STEP 4: Open Excel files in SPSS

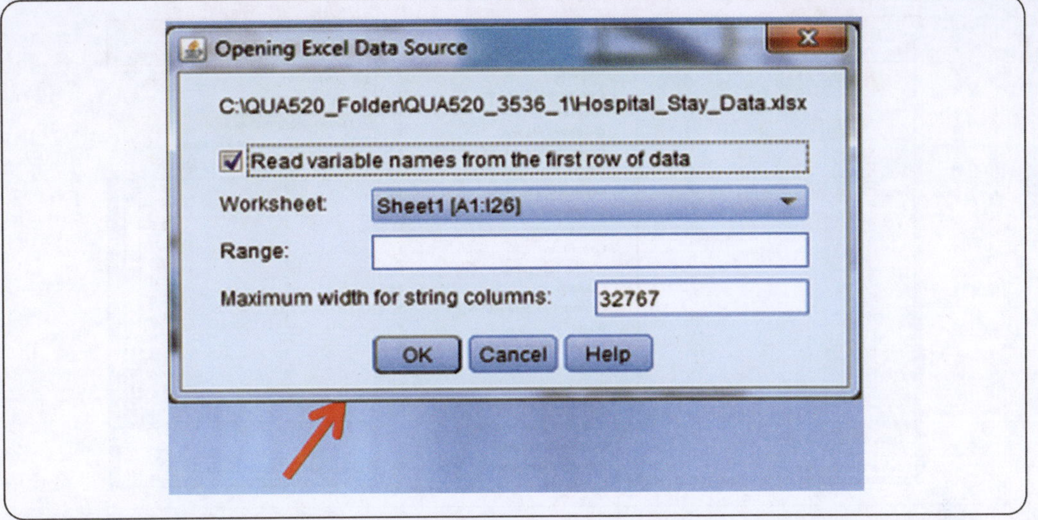

Step 5: Save file as SPSS data

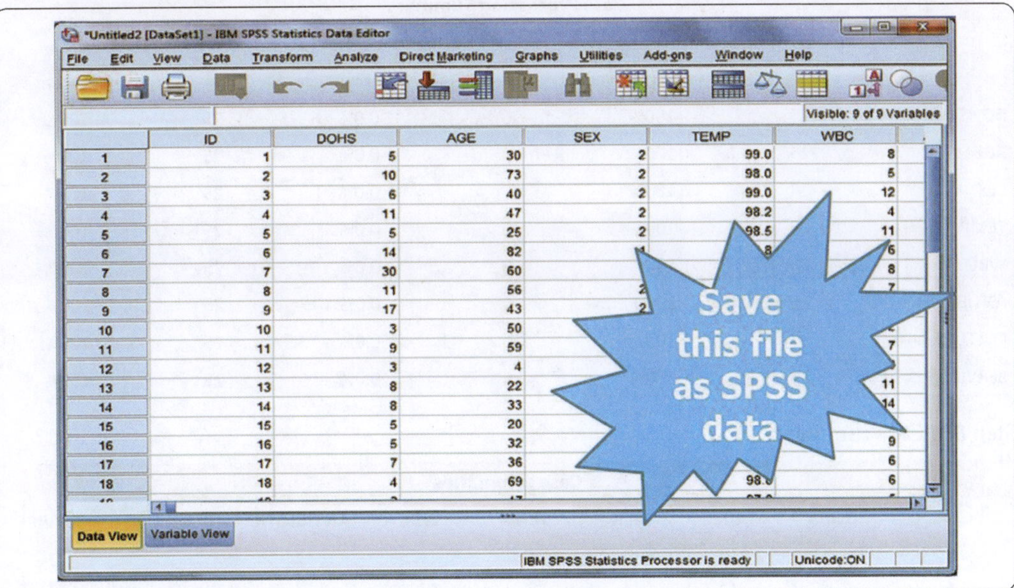

Step 6: Clean data after importing data files
- Run cases summaries for all variables.
- Run frequency for qualitative variables and description for quantitative variables.
- Check outputs to see if you have variables with wrong values.
- Check missing values if you have taken physical surveys.
- Sometimes, you need to recode string variables into numeric variables.

Step 7: Summaries of cases

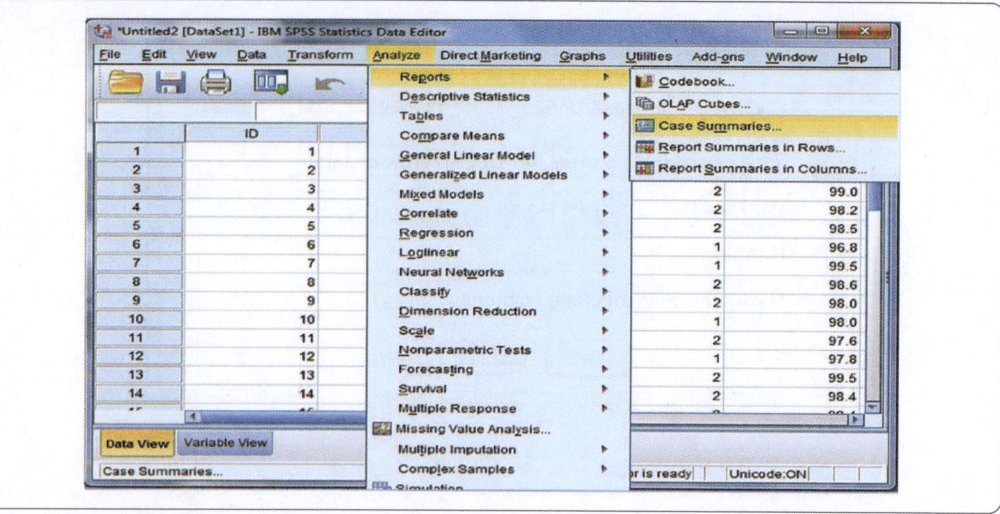

Step 8A: Case processing summary

	Case Processing Summary					
	Included		Excluded		Total	
	N	**Percent**	**N**	**Percent**	**N**	**Percent**
DOHS	25	100%	0	0.0%	25	100%
AGE	25	100%	0	0.0%	25	100%
SEX	25	100%	0	0.0%	25	100%
TEMP	25	100%	0	0.0%	25	100%
WBC	25	100%	0	0.0%	25	100%
ANTIBIOTIC	25	100%	0	0.0%	25	100%
CULTURE	25	100%	0	0.0%	25	100%
SERVICE	25	100%	0	0.0%	25	100%

Step 8B: Case summary

	Case summaries						
	DOHS	**AGE**	**SEX**	**TEMP**	**WBC**	**ANTIBIOTIC**	**BCULTURE**	**SERVICE**
1	5	30	2	99.0	8	2	2	1
2	10	73	2	98.0	5	2	1	1
3	6	40	2	99.0	12	2	2	2
4	11	47	2	98.2	4	2	2	2
5	6	26	2	98.6	11	2	2	1
6	14	82	1	98.8	6	1	2	1
7	30	60	1	99.6	8	1	1	12
8	11	56	2	98.6	87	2	2	1
9	17	43	2	98.0	7	2	2	2

Contd...

Case summaries							
10	3	50	1	98.0	12	2	1	2
11	9	59	2	97.6	7	2	1	2
12	3	4	1	97.8	3	2	2	2
13	8	22	2	99.6	11	1	2	2
14	8	33	2	95.4	14	1	1	2
15	6	20	2	98.4	11	2	1	2
16	5	22	1	99.0	2	2	2	2
17	7	36	1	99.2	6	1	2	2
18	4	69	1	98.0	6	2	2	2
19	3	47	1	97.0	5	1	2	1
20	7	22	1	98.2	6	2	2	2
21	9	11	1	98.2	10	2	2	2
22	11	19	1	98.6	14	1	2	2
23	11	67	2	97.6	4	2	2	1
24	9	43	2	98.6	5	2	2	2
25	4	41	2	98.0	6	2	2	1
Total N	25	25	15	25.0	25	25	25	25
Minimum	3	4	1	96.8	3	1	1	1
Maximum	30	82	2	99.5	14	2	2	2

Basic Statistical Analysis—SPSS

Descriptive statistics: It is useful for statistical analysis of qualitative variables. For this:

- Find wrong entries
- Have basic knowledge about the sample and targeted variables in a study
- Summarize data

Step 1A: Qualitative analysis:

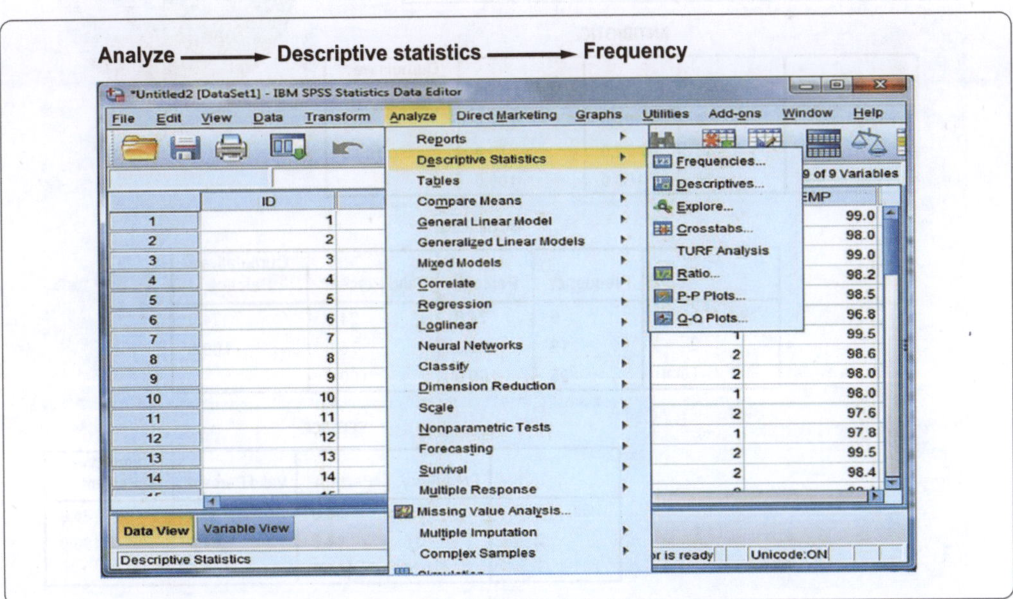

Step 1B: Qualitative analysis

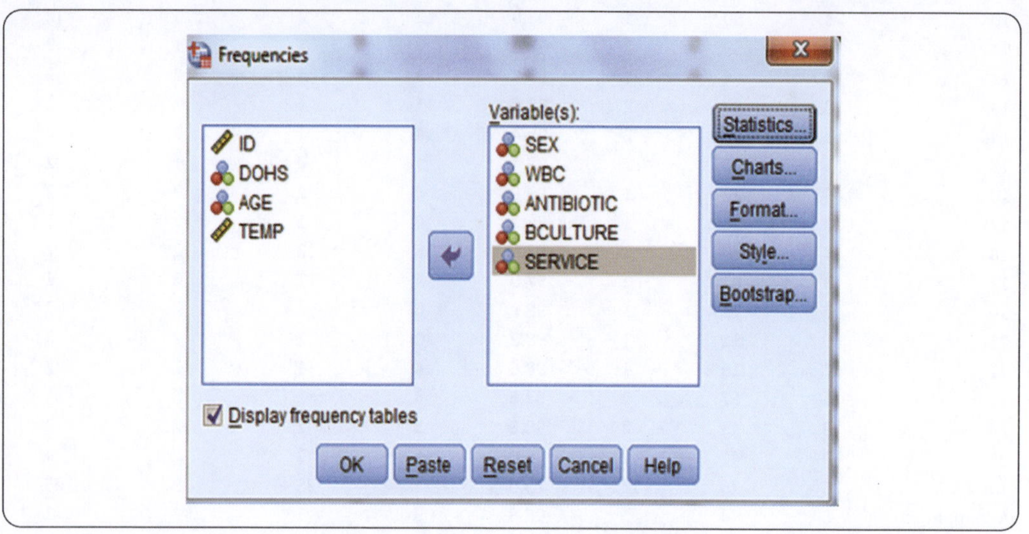

Step 1C: Qualitative analysis

SEX

		Frequency	Percent	Valid Percent	Cumulative Percent
Valid	1	11	44.0	44.0	44.0
	2	14	56.0	56.0	100.0
	Total	25	100.0	100.0	

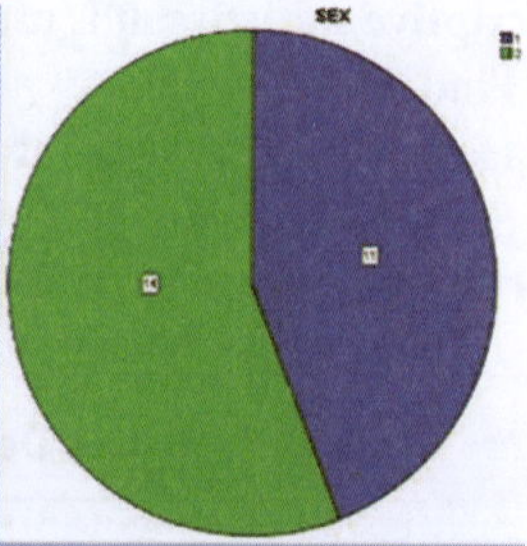

ANTIBIOTIC

		Frequency	Percent	Valid Percent	Cumulative Percent
Valid	1	7	28.0	28.0	28.0
	2	18	72.0	72.0	100.0
	Total	25	100.0	100.0	

BCULTURE

		Frequency	Percent	Valid Percent	Cumulative Percent
Valid	1	6	24.0	24.0	24.0
	2	19	76.0	76.0	100.0
	Total	25	100.0	100.0	

SERVICE

		Frequency	Percent	Valid Percent	Cumulative Percent
Valid	1	9	36.0	36.0	36.0
	2	16	64.0	64.0	100.0
	Total	25	100.0	100.0	

Step 1D: Quantitative analysis

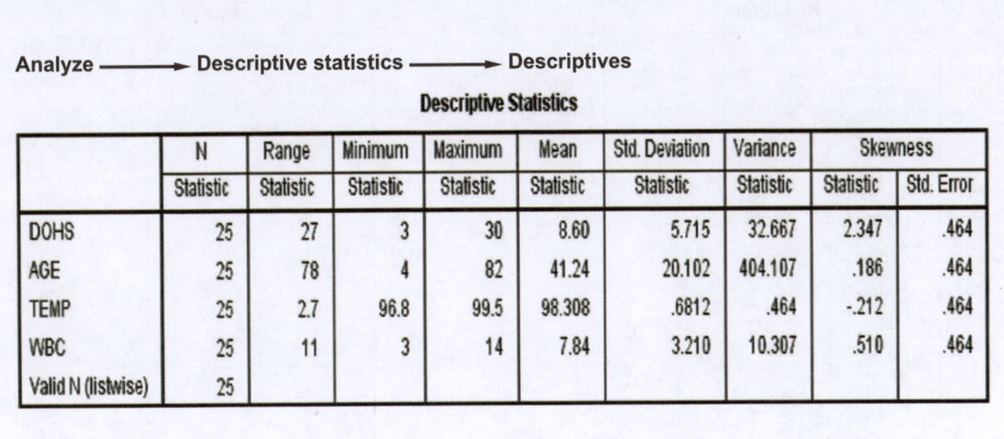

Analyze ⟶ Descriptive statistics ⟶ Descriptives

Descriptive Statistics

	N	Range	Minimum	Maximum	Mean	Std. Deviation	Variance	Skewness	
	Statistic	Statistic	Statistic	Statistic	Statistic	Statistic	Statistic	Statistic	Std. Error
DOHS	25	27	3	30	8.60	5.715	32.667	2.347	.464
AGE	25	78	4	82	41.24	20.102	404.107	.186	.464
TEMP	25	2.7	96.8	99.5	98.308	.6812	.464	-.212	.464
WBC	25	11	3	14	7.84	3.210	10.307	.510	.464
Valid N (listwise)	25								

Step 2A: Presenting data as histograms or Box plots

Age of patients that stayed in hospital is shown as histogram on left and box plot on right.

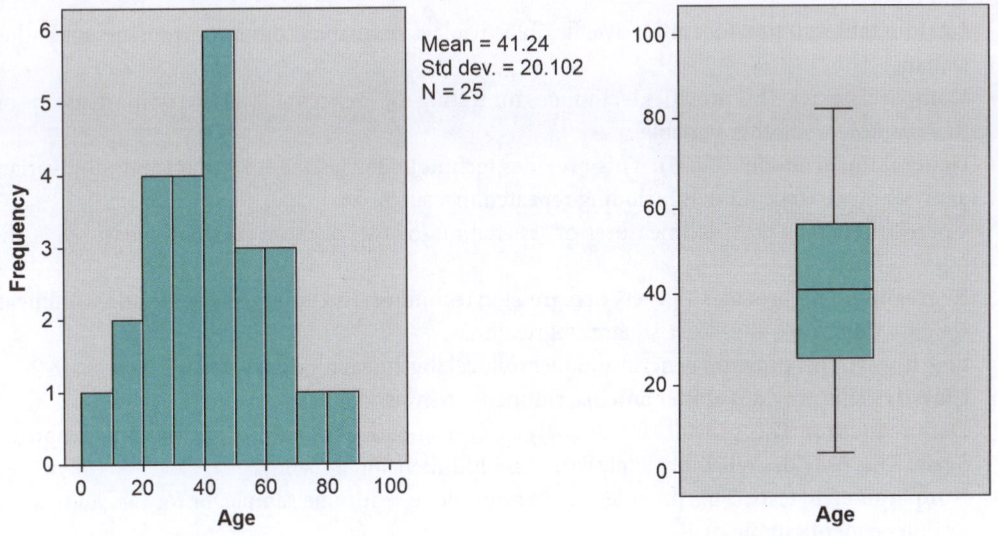

Step 2B: Duration of patients that stayed in hospital is shown as histogram on left and box plot on right.

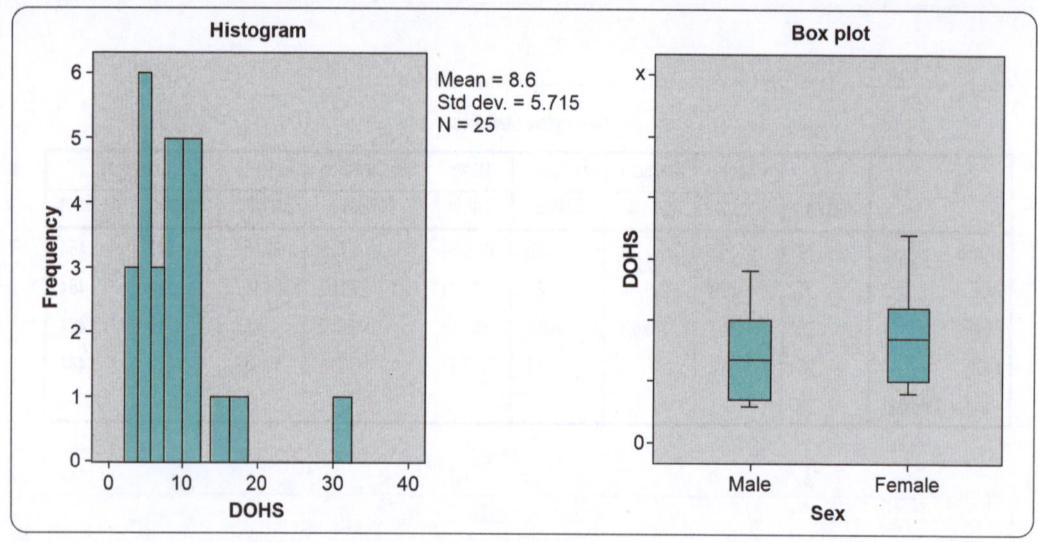

List of Statistical Procedures done by SPSS

- **Reports:** Report is a textual work made with the specific intention of relaying information or recounting certain events in a widely presentable form.
- **Descriptive statistics:** This provides techniques for summarizing data with statistics, charts, and reports.
- **Custom tables:** It provides attractive, flexible, displays frequency counts, percentages and other statistics.
- **Compare means:** This provides techniques for testing differences among two or more means on their values for another variable.
- **General linear model (GLM):** This provides technique for testing univariate and multivariate analysis-of-variance models including repeated measures.
- **Correlation:** This provides measures of association for two or more variables measured at the interval level.
- **Regression:** This provides a variety of regression techniques, including linear, logistic, nonlinear, weighted, and two-stage least-squares regression.
- **Log-linear:** This provides general and hierarchical log-linear analysis and logit analysis.
- **Classify:** This provides cluster and discriminant analysis
- **Data reduction:** This provides factor analysis, correspondence analysis, and optional scaling.
- **Scale:** This provides reliability analysis and multidimensional scaling.
- **Nonparametric tests:** This provides nonparametric tests for one sample, or for two and paired or independent sample.
- **Time series:** Provides exponential smoothing, auto-correlated regression, ARIMA, X11 ARIMA, seasonal decomposition, spectral analysis, and related techniques.
- **Survival:** This provides techniques for analyzing the time for some terminal event to occur, including Kaplan-Meier analysis and Cox regression.
- **Multiple response:** This provides facilities to define and analyze multiple-responses.

- **Graphs bar:** Generates a simple, clustered, or stacked bar chart of the data.
- **Area:** Generates a simple or stacked area chart of the data (Fig.18.8).

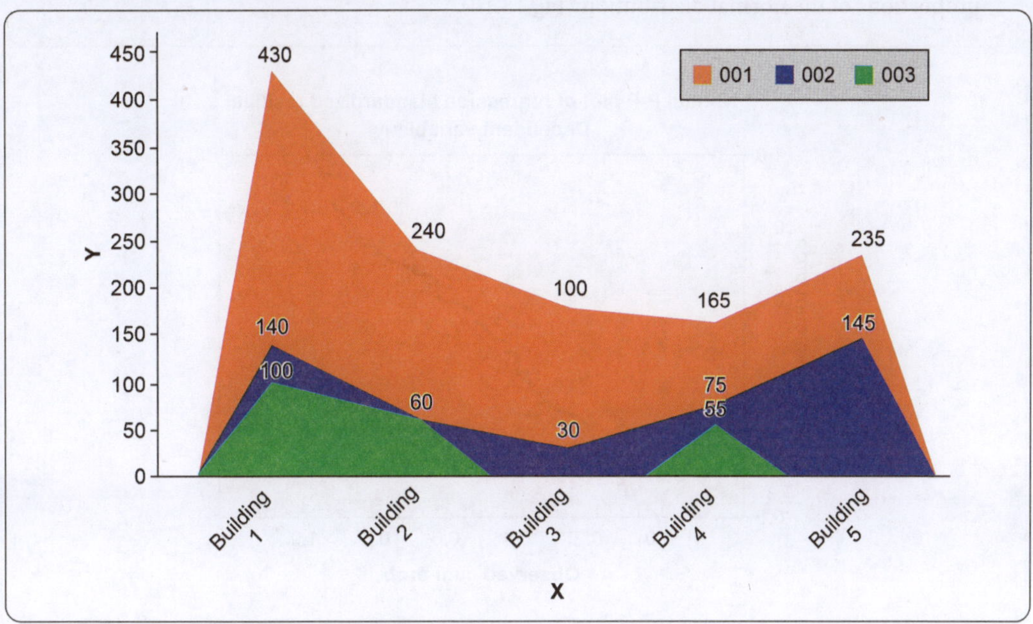

Figure 18.8: Area chart—SPSS

- **Pie:** Generates a simple pie chart or a composite bar chart from the data.
- **Box plot:** Generates box plot showing the median, outline, and extreme cases of individual variables.
- **Pareto:** Generates Pareto charts, bar charts with a line superimposed showing the cumulative sum (Fig. 18.9)

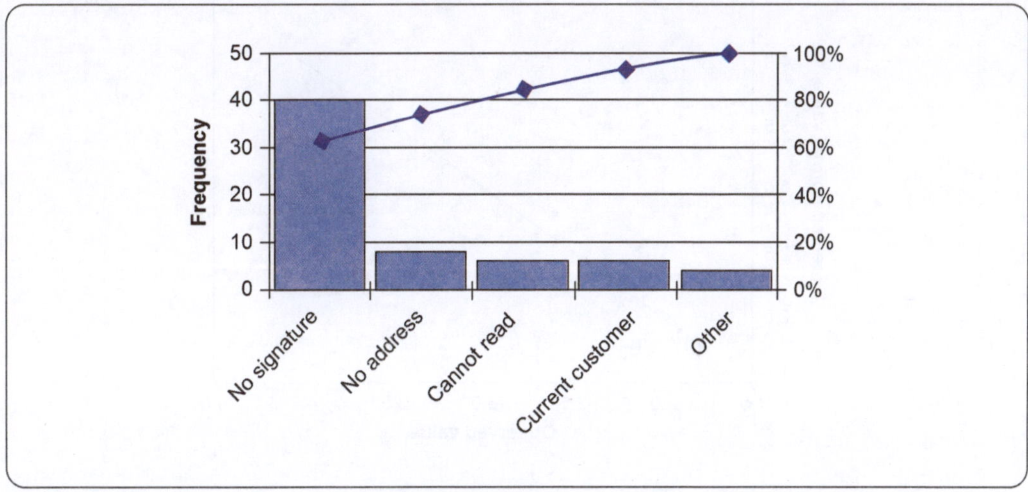

Figure 18.9: Pareto chart—SPSS

- **Control:** Produces the most commonly-used process-control charts.
- **Normal P-P Plots:** The cumulative proportions of variables' distribution against the cumulative proportions of the normal distribution (Fig.18.10).

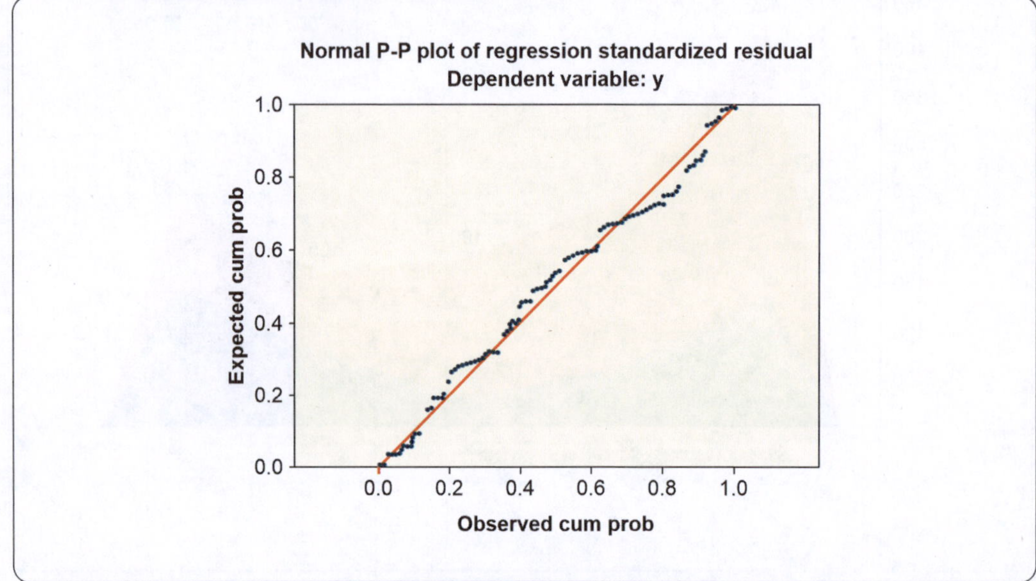

Figure 18.10: P-P plot—SPSS

- **Normal Q-Q Plots:** The quartiles of variables' distribution against the quartiles of the normal distribution (Fig.18.11).

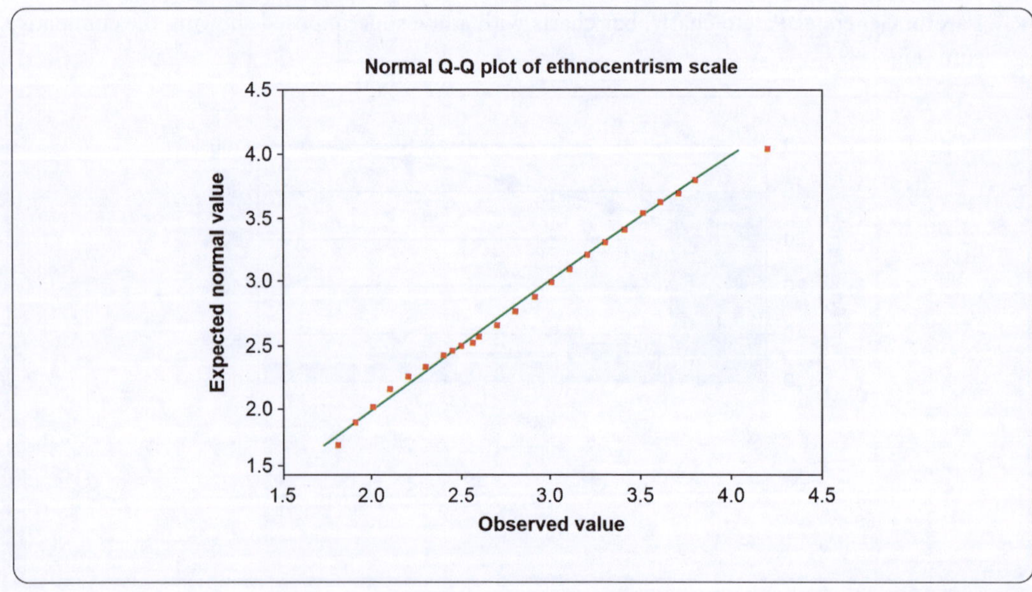

Figure 18.11: Q-Q plot—SPSS

- **Sequence:** Produces a plot of one or more variables by order in the file, suitable for examining time-series data.
- **Time series—autocorrelations:** It calculates and plots the autocorrelation function (ACF) and partial autocorrelation function of one or more series to any specified number of lags, displaying the Ljung-Box statistic at each lag to test the overall hypothesis that the ACF is zero at all lags (Fig.18.12).

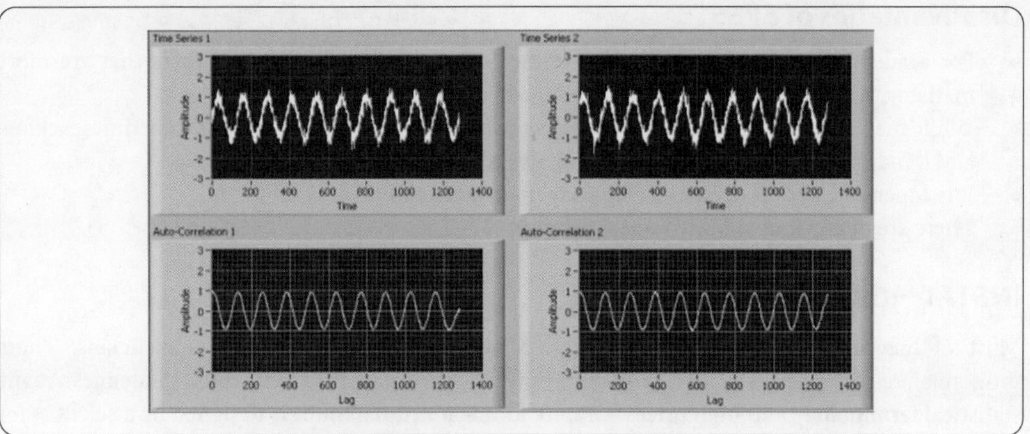

Figure 18.12: Time series—autocorrelation—SPSS

- **Time series—cross-correlations:** It calculates and plots the cross-correlation function of two or more series for positive, negative, and zero lags.
- **Time series—spectral:** It calculates and plots univariate or bivariate periodograms and spectral density functions, which express variation in a time series as the sum of a series of sinusoidal components. It can optionally save various components of the frequency analysis as new series (Fig.18.13).

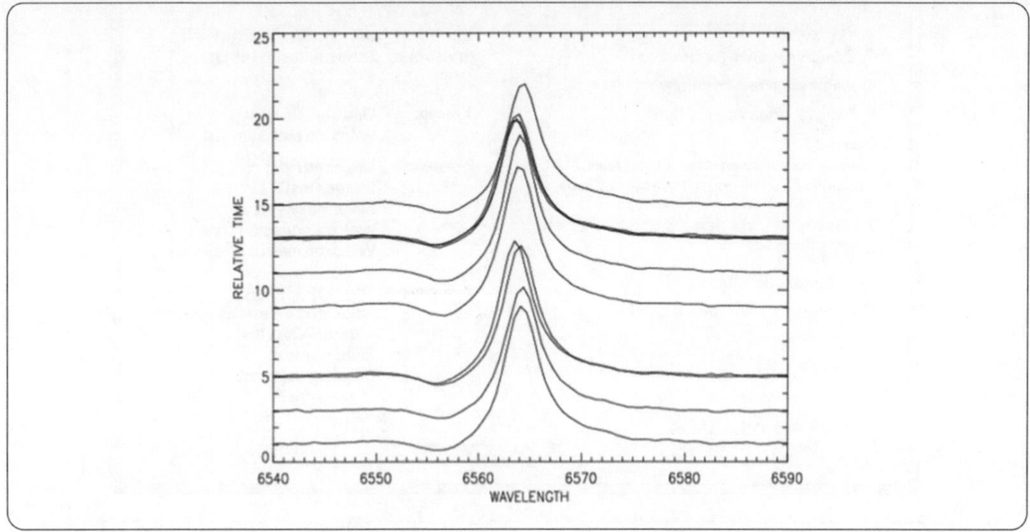

Figure 18.13: Time series—spectral SPSS

Advantages of SPSS

- It is user friendly.
- It is popular, and many data sets are easily loaded into it and other programs can easily import SPSS files.

Disadvantages of SPSS

- For academic use SPSS lags notably behind SAS, R and even perhaps others that are more mathematical rather than statistical for data analysis.
- While menu offerings of SPSS are typically the most basic data analysis and sometimes lacking, and it may produce inappropriate data analysis.
- It is expensive, and its license is definitely not user friendly.
- There are often compatibility issues with prior.

INSTAT—GRAPHPAD INSTAT

Most of the statistics programs are designed by statisticians, for use by statisticians. These programs are feature-packed and powerful, but can scare scientists with thick guidelines, vague statistical terminology and high prices. GraphPad InStat is different. It is designed by a scientist for scientists. With its help, even a person who is new to statistics can analyze data in just a few minutes (Figs 18.14 and 18.15).

Step 1 Enter data:

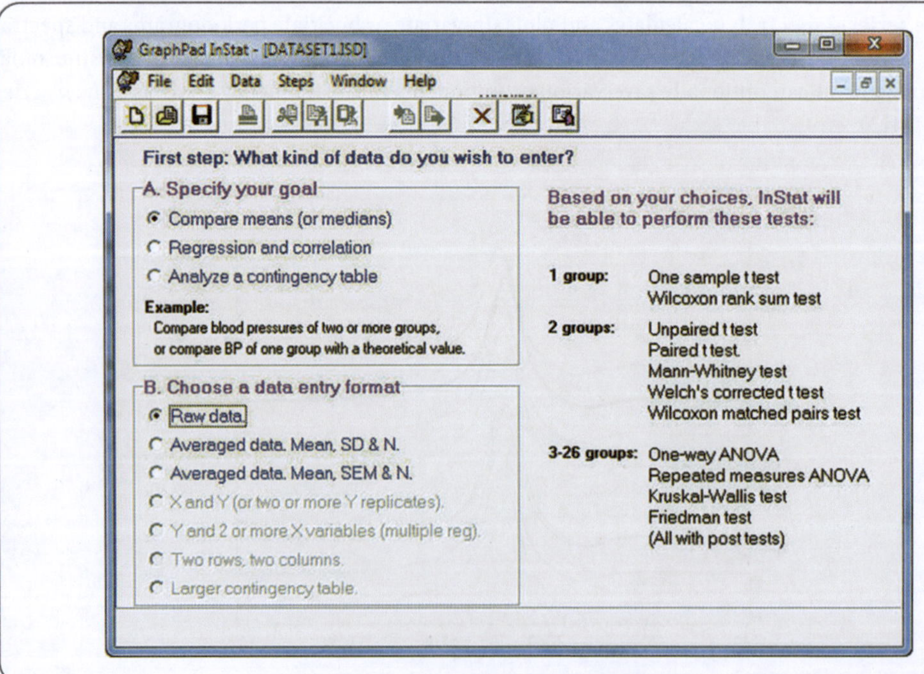

Figure 18.14: Using GraphPad InStat

Step 2 Results:

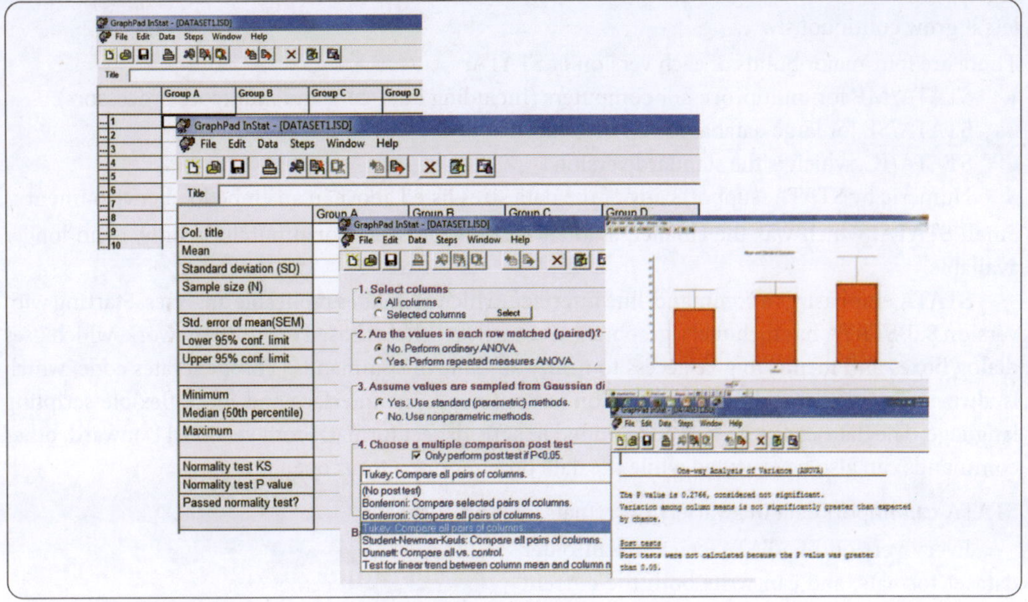

Figure 18.15: Using GraphPad InStat

GRAPHPAD PRISM

GraphPad Prism is built for analysis and graphing solution for scientific research. It saves time, makes appropriate analysis choices and presents graphical representation of data within minutes. The graph can be chosen, customized, styled, and labeled in chosen font and colors. The software allows to customize exports (transparency, file type, resolution, dimensions, color space RGB/CMYK) to meet the requirements of journals. With single click whole data can be shared in a single Prism file.

STATA

The name STATA is an abbreviation of words statistics and data. It is a multi-purpose statistical package that helps to explore, summarize and analyze datasets. It is extensively used in social science research. A dataset is a collection of several pieces of information called variables (usually arranged by columns). And a variable can have one or several values (information for one or several cases). STATA is the solution for data science needs. It helps to obtain and manipulate data. It can explore, visualize, model, and make inferences about data. Researcher can present the results in reproducible reports. STATA is a general-purpose statistical software package created in 1985 by STATA Corp. Most of its users work in research, especially in the fields of science, biomedicine, epidemiology, economics, political science and sociology.

Practical Tips

The software for parametric analysis:
- GraphPad InStat (not having analytical futures for analysis of Two-way ANOVA)
- GraphPad Prism
- IBM SPSS Statistics
- SAS
- StatsDirect
- MATLAB

The software for nonparametric analysis:
- GraphPad InStat
- GraphPad Prism
- IBM SPSS Statistics
- SAS
- StatXact
- SURVSOFT
- R Software

The capabilities of STATA include data management, statistical analysis, simulations, graphics, regression, and custom programming. It also has a system to disseminate user-written programs that lets it grow continuously.

There are four major builds of each version of STATA:

- STATA/MP for multiprocessor computers (including dual-core and multicore processors)
- STATA/SE for large databases
- STATA/IC, which is the standard version
- Numeric by STATA, supports any of the data sizes listed above in an embedded environment

Small STATA, which was the smaller, student version for educational purchase only, is no longer available.

STATA emphasizes a command-line interface, which facilitates replicable analyses. Starting with version 8.0, STATA has included a graphical user interface that is based on Qt framework, which uses dialog boxes and menus to give access to nearly all built-in commands. This generates code, which is always displayed, enabling the transition to command line interface and more flexible scripting language. The dataset can be viewed or edited in spreadsheet format. From version 11 onward, other commands can also be executed while the data browser or editor is open.

STATA can import data in a variety of formats like spreadsheets.

Every version of STATA can read all older dataset formats, and can write both the current and most recent previous dataset format, using the 'saveold' command, but older versions cannot read newer format datasets.

It can read and write SAS XPORT format datasets natively, using the 'fdause' and 'fdasave' commands.

> ### Must Know
>
> **Qt** is a cross-platform application development framework for desktop, embedded and mobile. Supported platforms include Linux, OS X, Windows, VxWorks, QNX, Android, iOS, BlackBerry, Sailfish OS and others. Qt is not a programming language on its own. It is a framework written in C++

Using STATA

STATA screen:

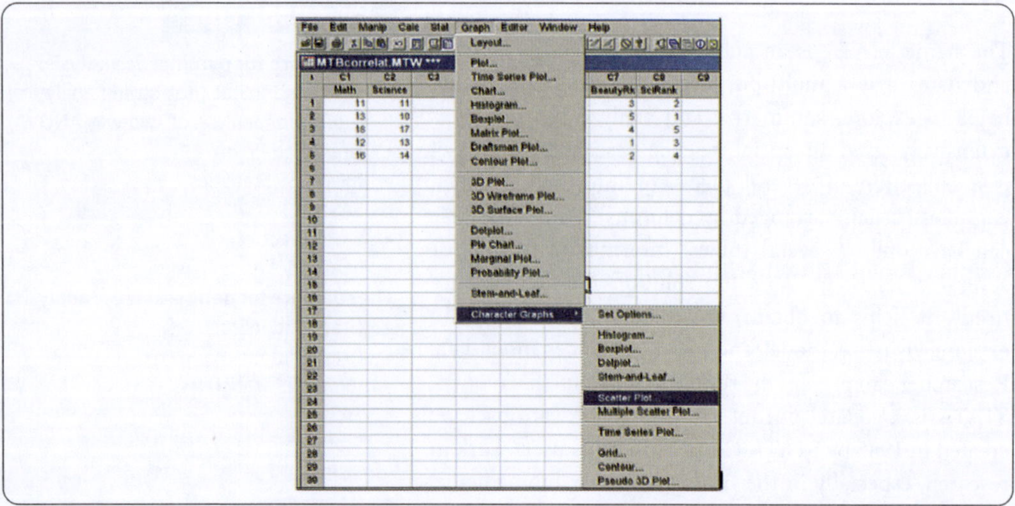

Commands on STATA: Frequently used commands on STATA are as follows:

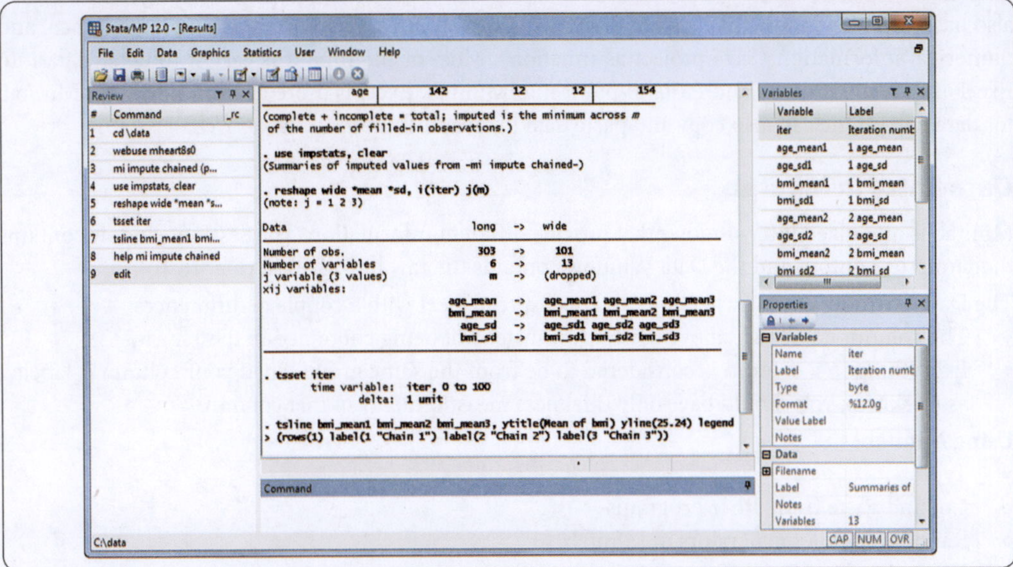

A few examples of commands are as follows:

- To perform a linear (OLS) regression of *y* on *x*:

```
regress y x [if]
```

The optional part *if* permits to limit the sample used in the command to a subset. For example, if the command should only be applied to the females in the sample, one could specify: If female = 1.

- To perform logistic regression of *y* on *x*:

```
logistic y x
```

- To display a scatter plot of *y* against *x* restricted to values of *x* below 10:

```
scatter y x if x <10
```

MINITAB

Minitab is a statistic package developed at the Pennsylvania State University by researchers Barbara F Ryan, Thomas A Ryan Jr., and Brian L Joiner in 1972. It began as a light version of OMNITAB 80, a statistical analysis program by NIST.

Comparison of Minitab with Excel:

Minitab	Excel
• Easier/Faster graphing	• Easier data entry
• Graphs and data analysis in 1-step	• No preset data formatting required for analysis
• Report writing tool within Minitab	• Need multiple tools and steps for data analysis and graphs
• Requires stacked data for most tools	

The main benefit of using Minitab is that one can get graphical and numerical analysis in one step instead of several as with Excel. Like Excel, Minitab can save multiple worksheets together. Minitab also has a report window (like a word document) so you can save your report(s) with graphical and numerical information (Save project as function). Most of the time it is easiest to enter data into Excel and then use Copy and Paste to put it into Minitab. Excel is more user friendly than Minitab for data entry. One can also copy and paste data from access into Minitab as well.

Data Entry in Minitab

Minitab is organized into windows that provide different information. The Session window contains the numerical output and the Data Window contains the raw information (Fig. 18.16).

The Data Window works basically as an Excel spreadsheet with a couple of differences:

- The column names are above the 1st row instead of being contained in the 1st row.
- Everything in a column is considered to be from the same group. So, if your column is labeled as thickness, you should have only thickness measurements in that column.

Using Minitab:

- Typing
- Cut and paste from other programs
- Random number generators in Minitab
- Importing from Excel, Text, ASCII, dBase files, etc.
- **Graph Manger** lists all created graphs. The Graph Manager is located at the top-middle of the screen and looks like stacked up graphs.
  - Click on the Graph Manager once to view a list of all your created graphs. It will display the last one selected on the right side of the screen.
  - To select a different graph, double click on any graph in the list.
  - To Rename Graph: Right click on any graph in the list, left click Rename, type in a new name and then hit **<enter>**.
  - To Delete Graph: Right click on any graph in the list, left click **Close**, left click on **No** and then hit **<enter>**.

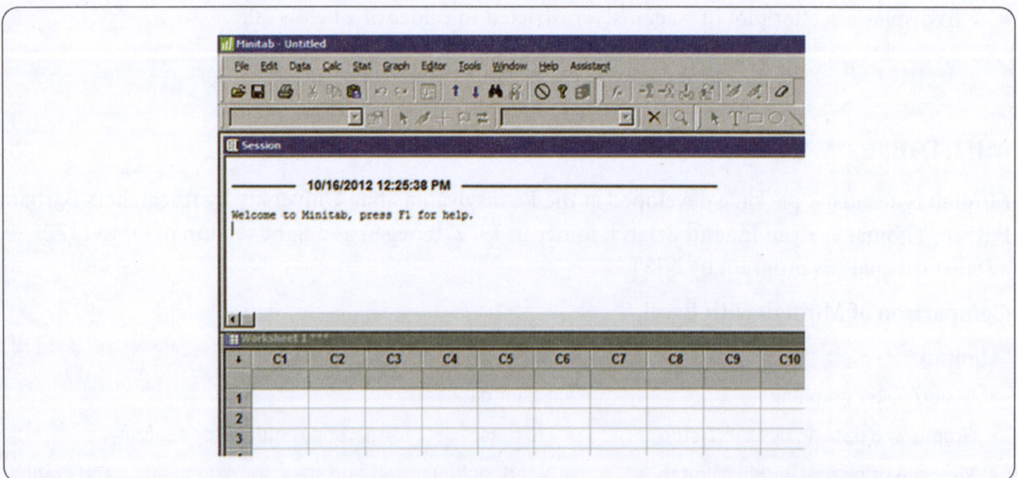

Figure 18.16: Minitab window

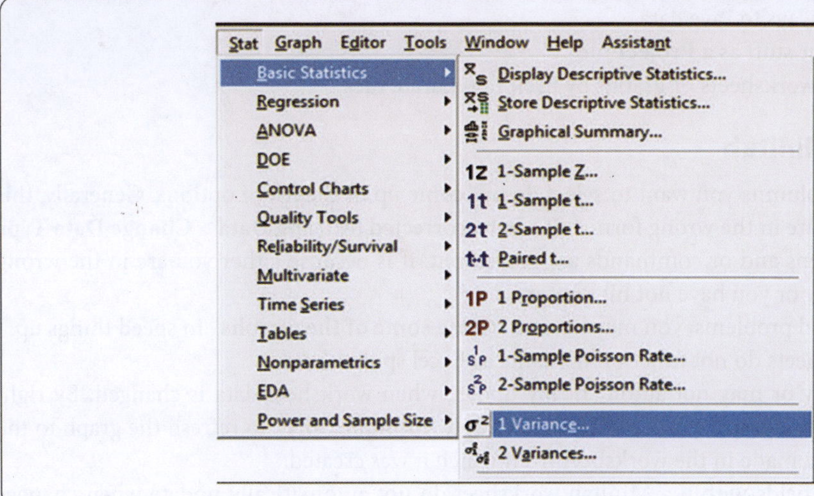

- **Worksheet manager** lists all created worksheets. The Worksheet Manager is located at the top-middle of the screen and looks like stacked up worksheets.
  - Click on the Worksheet Manager once to view a list of all your created worksheets. It will display the last one selected on the right side of the screen.
  - To select a different worksheet, double click on any worksheet in the list.
  - To Rename Worksheet: Right click on any worksheet in the list, left click **Rename**, type in a new name and then hit **<enter>**.
  - To Delete Worksheet: Right click on any worksheet in the list, left click **Close**, left click on **No** and then hit **<enter>**.

To create a new worksheet, **Click File > New > Minitab Worksheet**

Short Keys to Operate Minitab

Minitab has a set of training files. One can find them through the locations and it can also be accessed through Minitab's help feature. The data entry and manipulation short keys are shown as:

- **Minitab operating files**
  - Minitab has training files in its Data subdirectory
  - To find them go to:
    - C:/Program files/Minitab 14/English/ Sample Data
- **Minitab file extensions**
  - MPJ for project files
    - *Ex*: Data.mpj
  - MTW for Data files (Worksheets only)
    - *Ex*: Data.mtw
  - MFG for Graphs (Graphs only)
    - *Ex*: pareto I. mgf
- **Control C/Control V**
  - Copies data/Pastes data
- **Alt Tab**
  - Moves you from one windows application to another
  - Ex:
    - Minitab to PowerPoint for making presentations
    - Excel to Minitab for copying Data
- **Control E**
  - Pulls up previous menu
- **Control Tab**
  - Moves you from Data, Session, History, and Info Windows

Minitab has several ways to save data.

- Always save your stuff as a **Project** file.
- It can also save worksheets or graphs by itself in separate files.

Drawbacks of Minitab

- The expected columns you want to select do not come up in the list of options. Generally, this is because they are in the wrong format. It can be corrected by using **Data > Change Data Type**
- The menu screens and or commands are grayed out. It is because either you are in the wrong Minitab window or you have not hit **<enter>** yet.
- If you have speed problems, you may have to **"Close some of the Graphs"** to speed things up.
- Minitab Worksheets do not function the same as Excel spreadsheets
  - Graphs may or may not automatically update when worksheet data is changed. By right clicking over a graph, you can **"Update Graph Automatically"** to refresh the graph to the changes you made in the worksheet from which it was created.
  - Calculated fields within a Minitab worksheet do not automatically update when changes are made unless you have set the field with a formula. Note: Minitab does not recognize imbedded formulas imported from other applications
  - Use caution when closing worksheet or graph windows as they may be removed without warning. Use Tools > Options to reset these options

You can easily get graphs, line diagrams, etc., by loading data in Minitab. Statistical tests like chi-square, paired 't' test, 'F' test and many more can be easily done in Minitab.

MATLAB

MATLAB stands for MATrix LABoratory and is an interpreted language. It is liked by researchers for statistical analysis of their data. It has scientific programming environment. MATLAB is a good tool for the manipulation of matrices. It has great visualization capabilities. It has load of built-in functions. It is easy to learn and simple to use. The desktop view of MATLAB is as shown here:

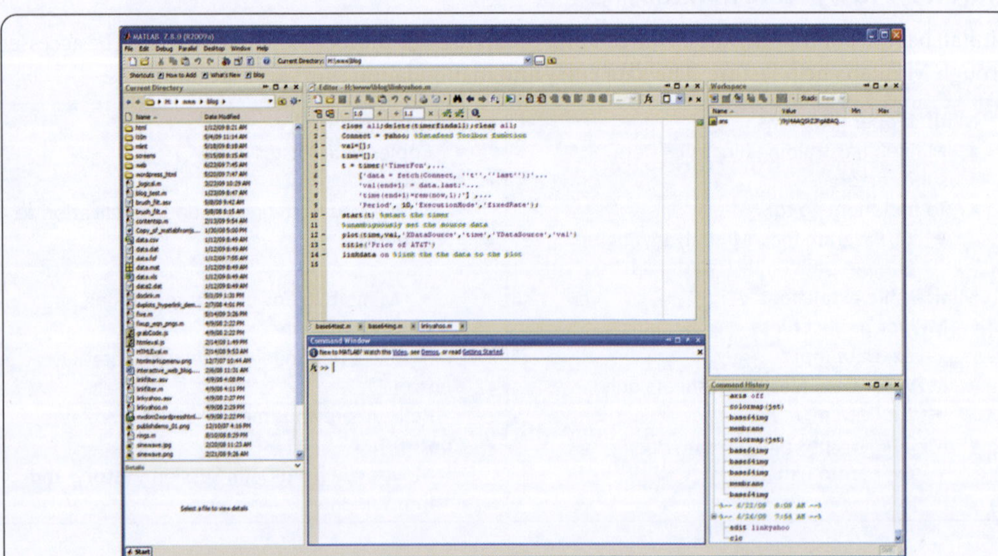

One does not have to declare type of variables or not even has to initialize it, just assign in command window:

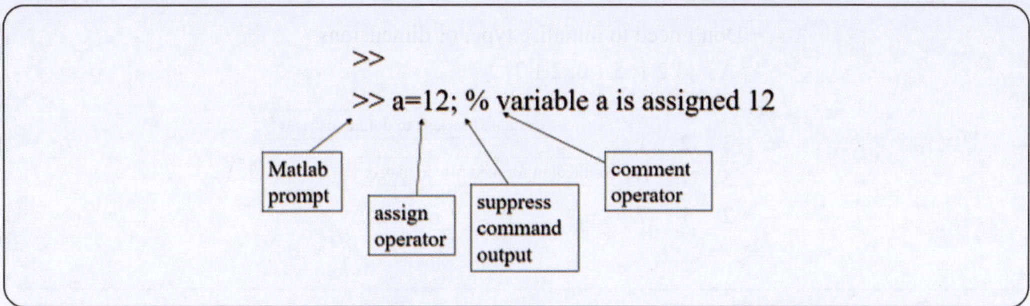

View the variable contents by simply typing the variable name at the command prompt:

```
>>a
a =    12
>>
>>a×2
a =    24
>>
```

The workspace is MATLAB's memory and it can manipulate variables stored in the workspace as shown here:

```
>>b = 10;
>>c = a–b
c=    12
>>
```

- **Display contents of workspace**
```
>>whos
Name        Size            Bytes class
a           1×1             8 double array
b           1×1             8 double array
c           1×1             8 double array
```
Grand total is 3 elements using 24 bytes
```
>>
```

- **Delete variable(s) from workspace**
```
>>clear a b; % delete a and b from workspace
>>whos
>>clear all; % delete all variables from workspace
>>whos
```

Help commands of MATLAB are as given here:
- help
```
>>help whos  % displays documentation for the function whos
>>lookfor convert  % displays functions with convert in the first help line
```
- Start MATLAB help documentation
```
>>helpdesk
```

Matrices in MATLAB

- Don't need to initialise type, or dimensions

>>A = [3 2 1; 5 1 0; 2 1 7] .

A =

   3   2   1

   5   1   0

   2   1   7

>>

square brackets to define matrices

semicolon for next row in matrix

Matrices are manipulated as:

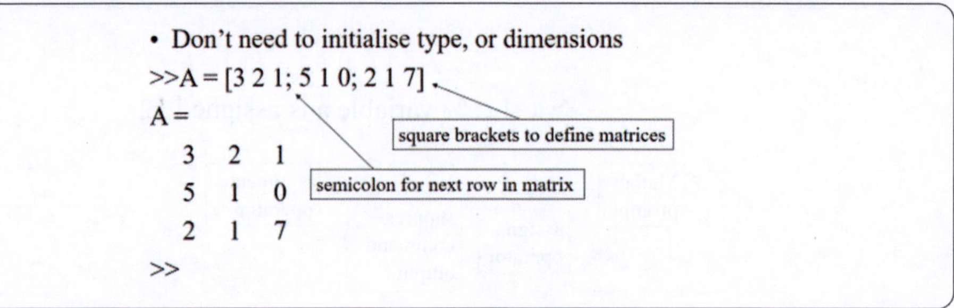

- Access elements of a matrix

>>A(1,2)

ans=

2

indices of matrix element(s)

- Remember Matrix(row,column)
- Naming convention Matrix variables start with a capital letter while vectors or scalar variables start with a simple letter

The: Operator: It is very important operator in MATLAB and means 'to'.

>> 1:10

ans =

   1   2   3   4   5   6   7   8   9   10

>> 1:2:10

ans =

   1   3   5   7   9

>>A(3,2:3)

ans =

   1   7

>>A(:,2)

ans =

   2

   1

   1

```
                                         A =
                                          3   2   1
                                          5   1   0
                                          2   1   7
>> A '        % transpose
>> B*A        % matrix multiplication    B =
>> B.*A       % element by element multiplication   1   3   1
>> B/A        % matrix division                      4   9   5
>> B./A       % element by element division          2   7   2
>> [B A]      % Join matrices (horizontally)
>> [B; A]     % Join matrices (vertically)
```

Scripts are used to execute a series of commands with the help of MATLAB editor.

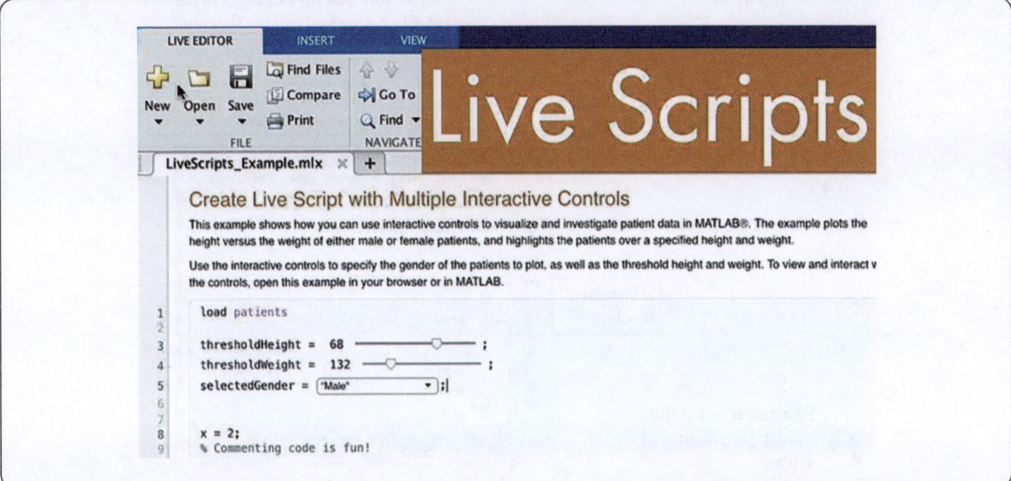

Scripts will manipulate and store variables and matrices in the MATLAB Workspace or memory. Scripts can also be obtained from the MATLAB command line by typing the – **'case sensitive!'** filename of the script file as >>**MyScript**

Scripts can be opened in the editor by the following >>**Open MyScript**.

Functions

- Users can write functions which can be called from the command line.
- Functions can accept input variable(s)/matrice(s) and will output variable(s)/matrice(s).
- Functions will **not** manipulate variable(s)/matrice(s) in the MATLAB Workspace.
- In MATLAB, functions closely resemble scripts and can be written in the MATLAB editor. MATLAB functions have the function keyword.
- Note that the file name of a function will be its calling function name.
- Do not overload any built-in functions by using the same filename for your functions or scripts.
- Functions can be opened for editing using the **Open** command. Many built-in MATLAB functions can also be viewed using this command.
- The functions have been shown as follows.

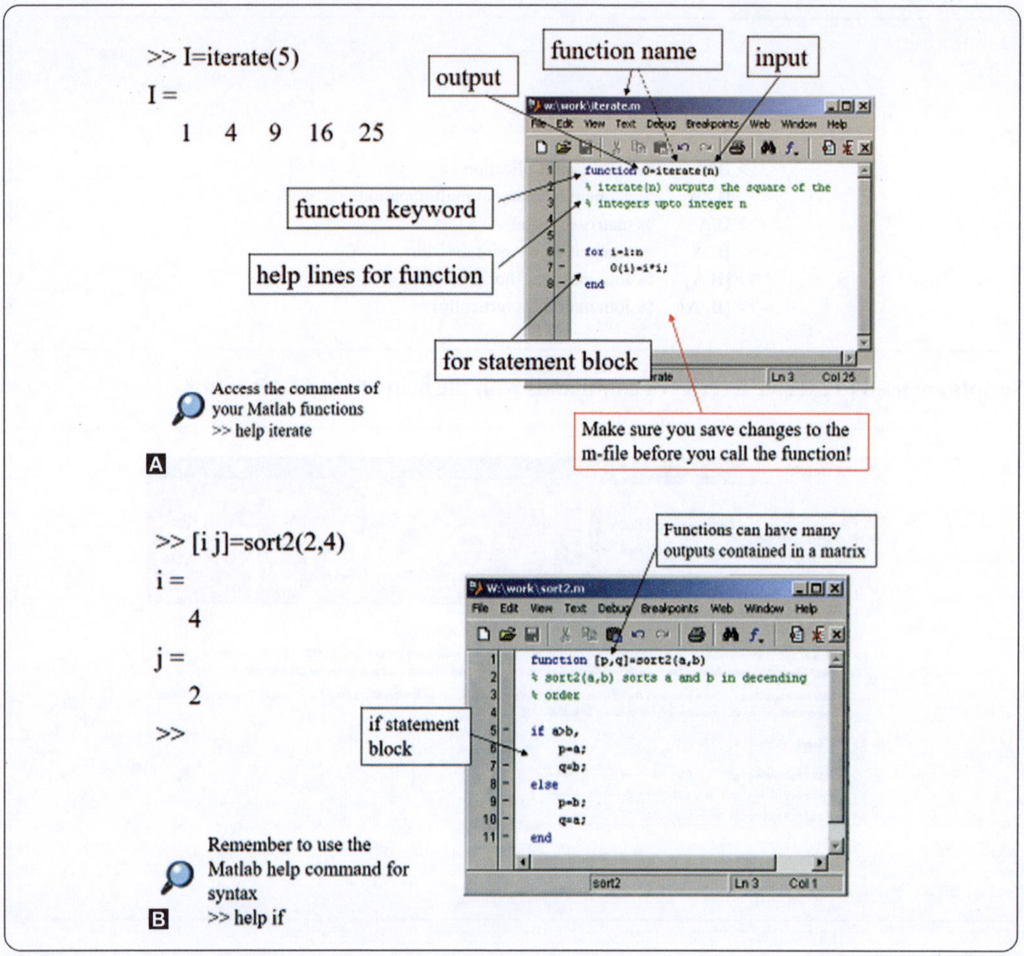

```
>> I=iterate(5)
I =
     1    4    9    16    25
```



```
>> [i j]=sort2(2,4)
i =
     4
j =
     2
>>
```


More Flow Controls on MATLAB are as follows:

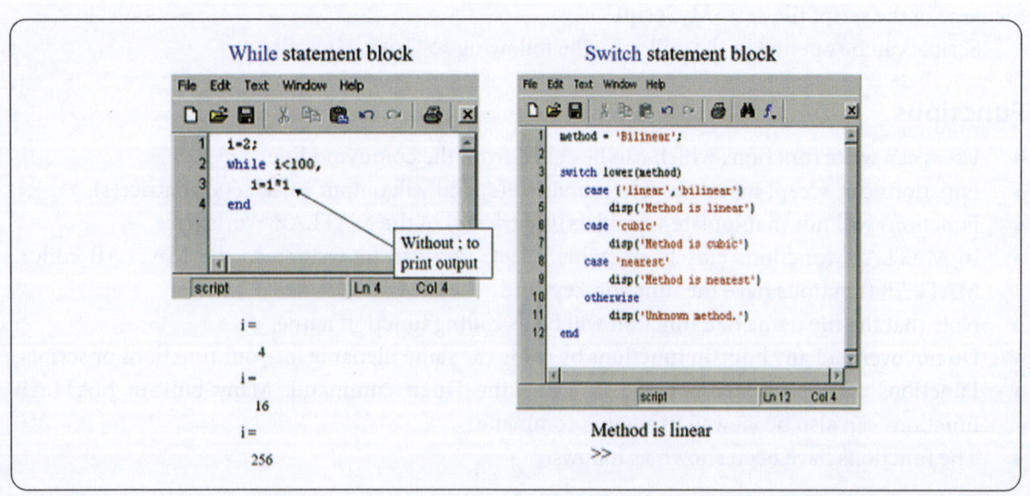

Debugging:

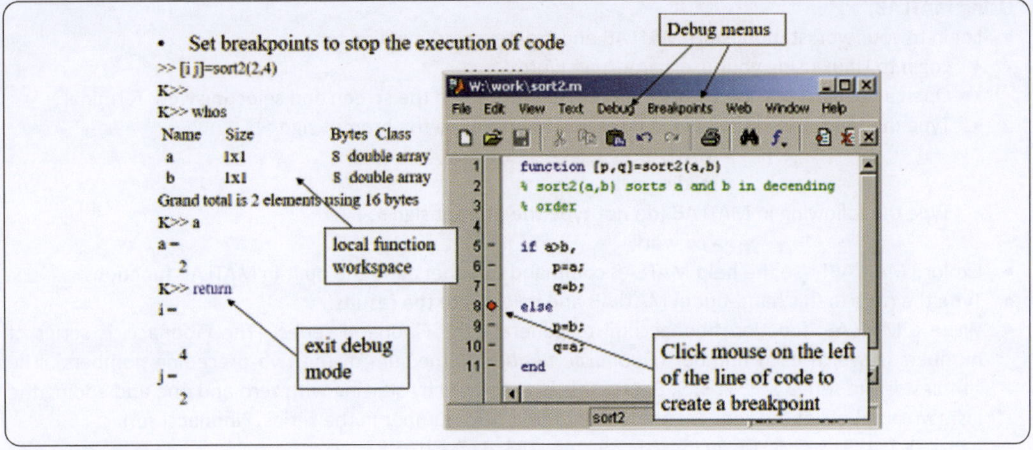

Plotting Data:

Investigate the function

>> y=A*cos(w*t+phi);

for different values of phi (e.g.: 0, pi/4, pi/3, pi/2), w (e.g.: 1, 2, 3, 4) and A (e.g.: 1, 0.5, 2). Use the **hold on** MATLAB command to display your plots in the same figure. Remember to type **hold off** to go back to normal plotting mode.

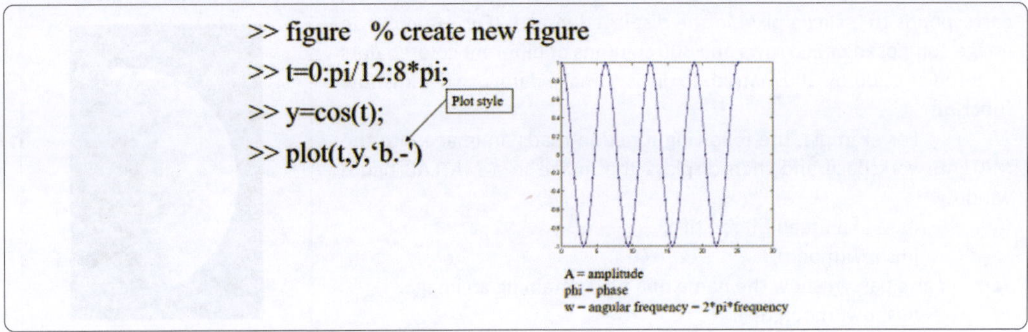

Useful operators and built-in functions

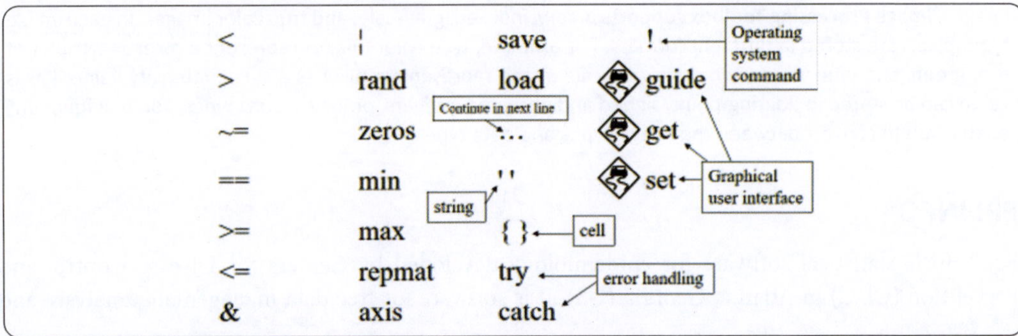

Practical Tips

Using MATLAB:

- Login to your workstation, start MATLAB and create a working directory
  - Login to Linux using your username/password
  - Open a terminal session by right clicking the mouse on the screen and selecting New Terminal
  - Type the following in the terminal session (do not type the prompt sign >)

    > MATLAB

    > mkdir work
  - Type the following in MATLAB (do not type the prompt sign >>)

    >> cd work
- Explore MATLAB! Use the **help** MATLAB command to understand the built-in MATLAB functions
- Type the code in this hand-out in MATLAB and investigate the results.
- Write a MATLAB 'function fibonacci.m' to generate the Fibonacci series. [The Fibonacci is series of numbers in which each number (*Fibonacci number*) is the sum of the two preceding numbers]. The simplest is the series 1, 1, 2, 3, 5, 8, etc. This is generated by starting with zero and one and adding the last two numbers of the sequence to generate the next number in the series. Fibonacci series:

    0, 1, 1, 2, 3, 5, 8, 13, 21, 34, 55, 89, 144, 233, 377, 610, 987, ...
- Create a graph of the Fibonacci series using the built-in **plot** MATLAB function.
- Plot the Fibonacci series in polar coordinates using the built-in MATLAB **polar** function. Eccentricity (rho) should be the Fibonacci number and angle (theta) should vary with the Fibonacci number's order in the sequence. Exit MATLAB by typing quit and logout of Linux.

    >> quit

Creating Images in MATLAB

In the MATLAB workspace, most images are represented as two-dimensional arrays (matrices), in which each element of the matrix corresponds to a single pixel in the displayed image. (For example, an image composed of 200 rows and 300 columns of different colored dots is stored as a 200-by-300 matrix). To display image data, use the **imshow function**.

For example, the following function reads an image into the MATLAB workspace and then displays the image in a MATLAB figure window.

    moon = imread('moon.tif');
    imshow(moon);

You can also pass imshow the name of a file containing an image.

    imshow('moon.tif');

The imshow function displays the image in a MATLAB figure window, as shown in the following figure.

This figure is enough to prove that MATLAB can create pictures which are very near to real life images. **Image Processing Toolbox** supports binary, indexed, grayscale, and true color images. In each image type, pixels are stored in different formats. For example, true color images represent a pixel as a triplet of red, green, and blue values, whereas grayscale image represents a pixel as a single intensity value. Pixels value can be stored in floating-point, signed and unsigned integers, or logical *data* types. Toolbox functions enable you to convert between the image types and data types.

EPI INFO

Epi Info is statistical software for epidemiology developed by Centers for Disease Control and Prevention (CDC) in Atlanta, Georgia (US). It is software for free data management, analysis, and visualization designed specifically for the public health community. This software is used extensively throughout CDC, domestically and internationally.

Features of Epi Info

- Rapid electronic form creation and data entry
- Statistical analysis
- Mapping and visualization
- Free and easy to use with 256 MB of RAM
- Flexible, lightweight and agile (when responding to emergencies)
- Robust (when performing large-scale, multi-user data collection)
- Standards based
- No IT expertise is needed in most cases

Requirements

Epi Info specifically requires:

- Microsoft Windows XP or above
- NET Framework 4.0 or above
- Recommended – 1 GHz processor
- Recommended – 256 MB RAM

Uses

- It is used to create electronic data entry forms. Templates can be utilized to facilitate form design. The data entry experience can be designed with intelligence, such as skip patterns, logical branching, and automatic calculations as shown here:

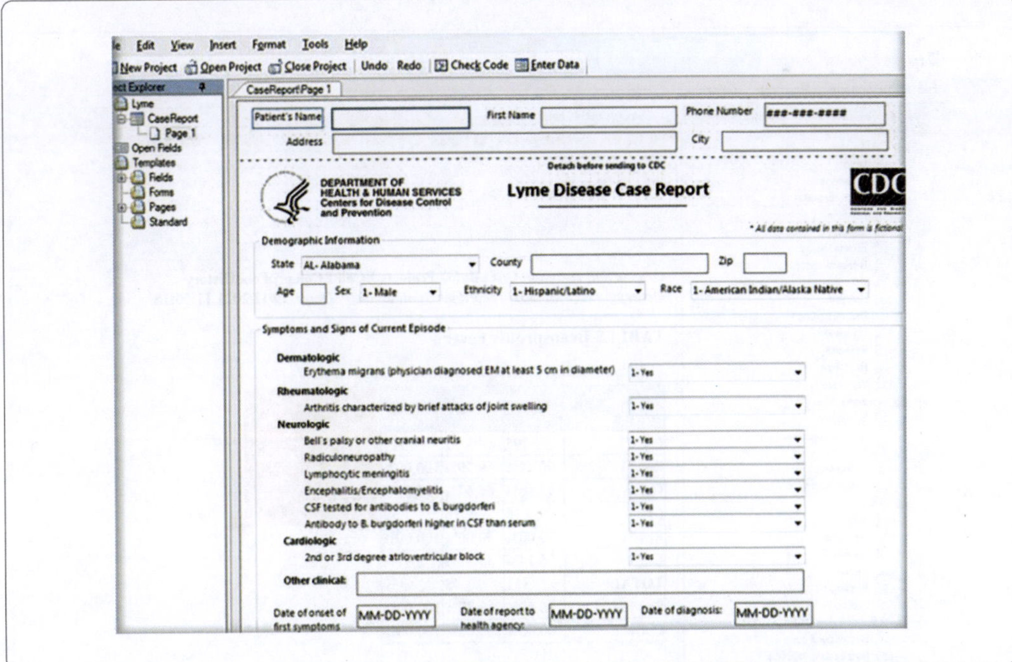

- Used to **collect data into the form**. Addresses can be geocoded into latitude and longitude. Data entry follows the intelligence rules tailored in the **Form Designer:**

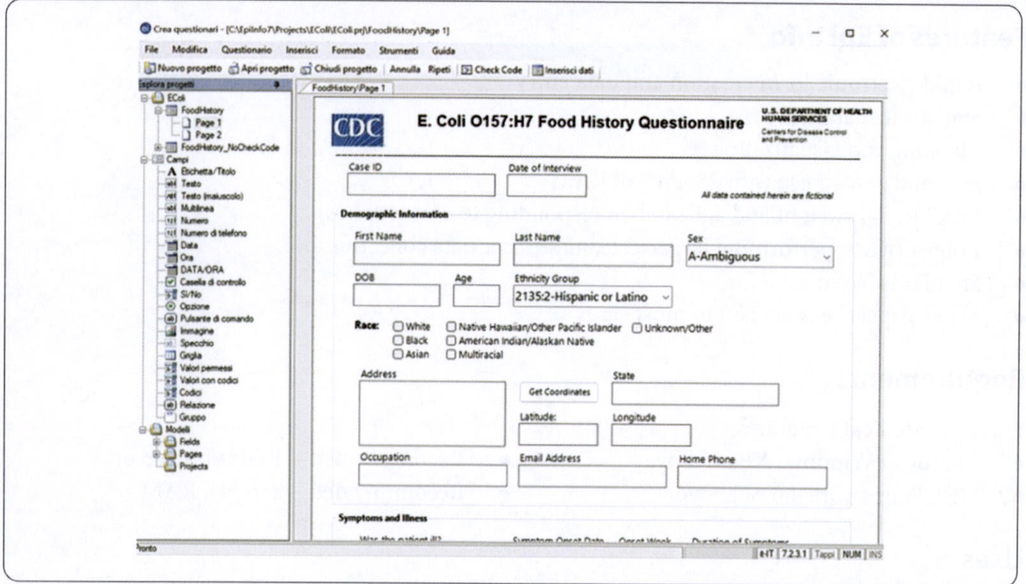

- **Data management and analysis**. Epi Info can read data, relate data tables, perform comparisons and run a wide variety of statistics. The supported data types include text files, Excel spreadsheets, Access databases, and MS SQL Server databases. Output is saved as HTML.

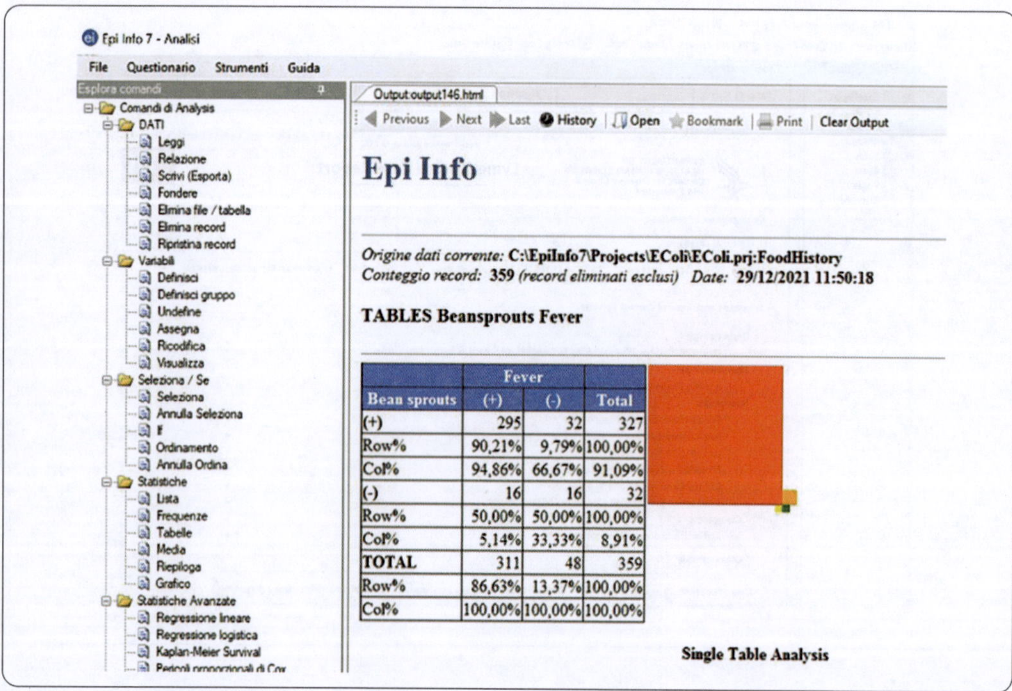

- Used as **Quick analysis** where only minimal data management is needed. Supports almost all of the statistics as **Classic analysis** and supports the same data types. Output is saved as HTML.

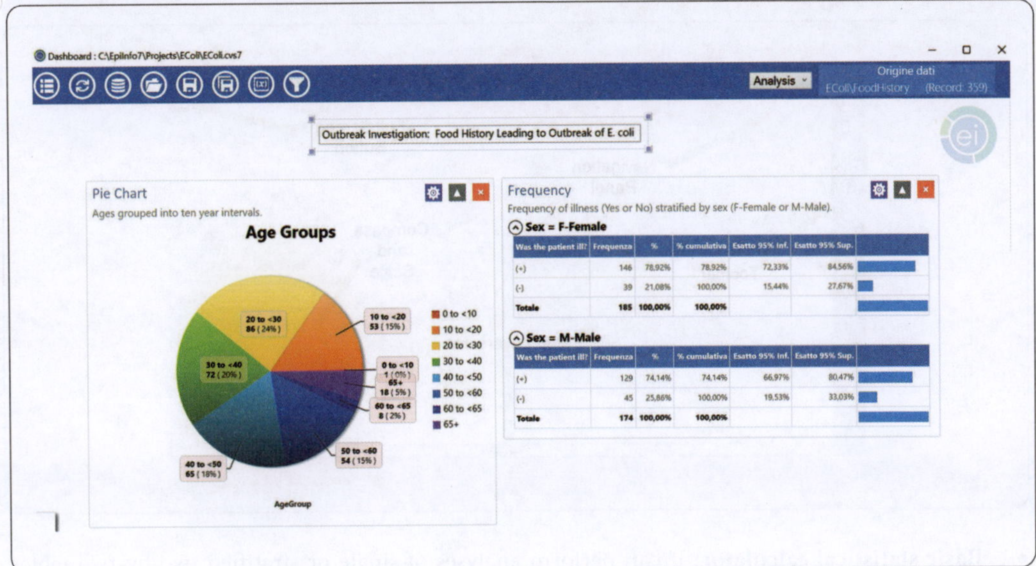

Dashboard : C:\EpiInfo7\Projects\EColi\EColi.cvs7
Analysis
Origine dati
EColi\FoodHistory (Record: 359)
Outbreak Investigation: Food History Leading to Outbreak of E. coli
Pie Chart
Ages grouped into ten year intervals.
Age Groups
20 to <30 86 (24%)
10 to <20 53 (15%)
30 to <40 72 (20%)
0 to <10 1 (0%)
65+ 18 (5%)
60 to <65 8 (2%)
50 to <60 54 (15%)
40 to <50 65 (18%)
0 to <10
10 to <20
20 to <30
30 to <40
40 to <50
50 to <60
60 to <65
65+
AgeGroup
Frequency
Frequency of illness (Yes or No) stratified by sex (F-Female or M-Male).
Sex = F-Female
Was the patient ill? | Frequenza | % | % cumulativa | Esatto 95% Inf. | Esatto 95% Sup.
(+) | 146 | 78,92% | 78,92% | 72,33% | 84,56%
(-) | 39 | 21,08% | 100,00% | 15,44% | 27,67%
Totale | 185 | 100,00% | 100,00%
Sex = M-Male
Was the patient ill? | Frequenza | % | % cumulativa | Esatto 95% Inf. | Esatto 95% Sup.
(+) | 129 | 74,14% | 74,14% | 66,97% | 80,47%
(-) | 45 | 25,86% | 100,00% | 19,53% | 33,03%
Totale | 174 | 100,00% | 100,00%

Epi Curve Chart
Epi Curve chart showing the count of cases by onset date.
E. Coli Outbreak
Case Count
Day
0
5
10
15
20
25
30
35
40

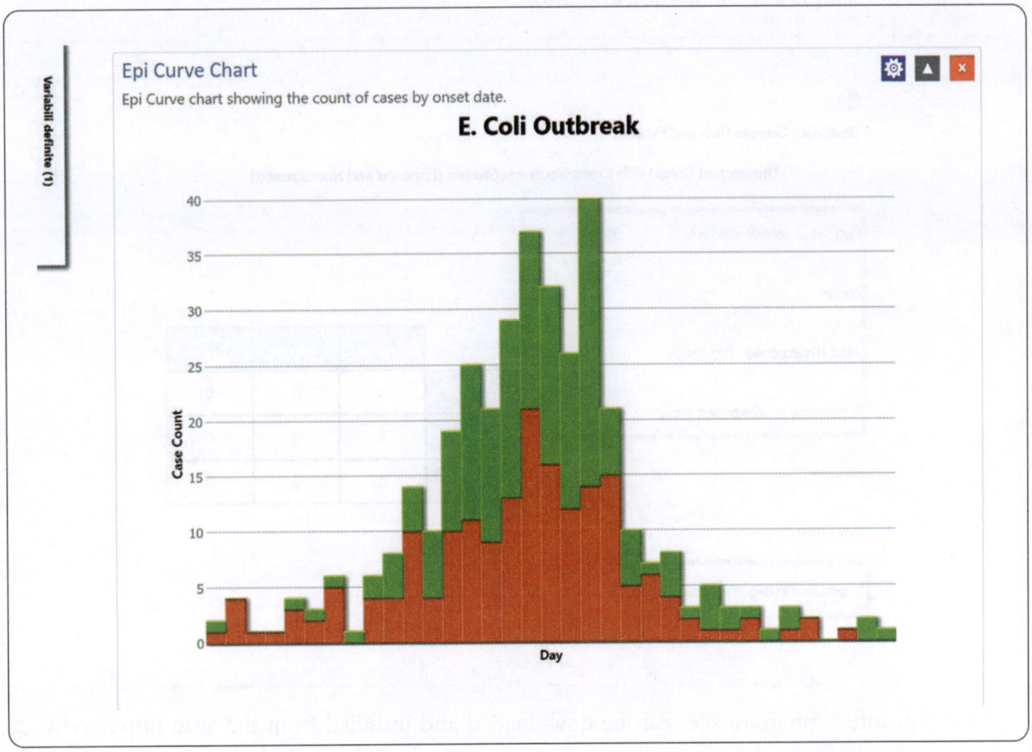

- **Create maps:** This is used to create case cluster or choropleth **maps**. Time lapse functionality is supported. Choropleth maps can be generated using shape files or from map servers such as nationalmaps.gov.

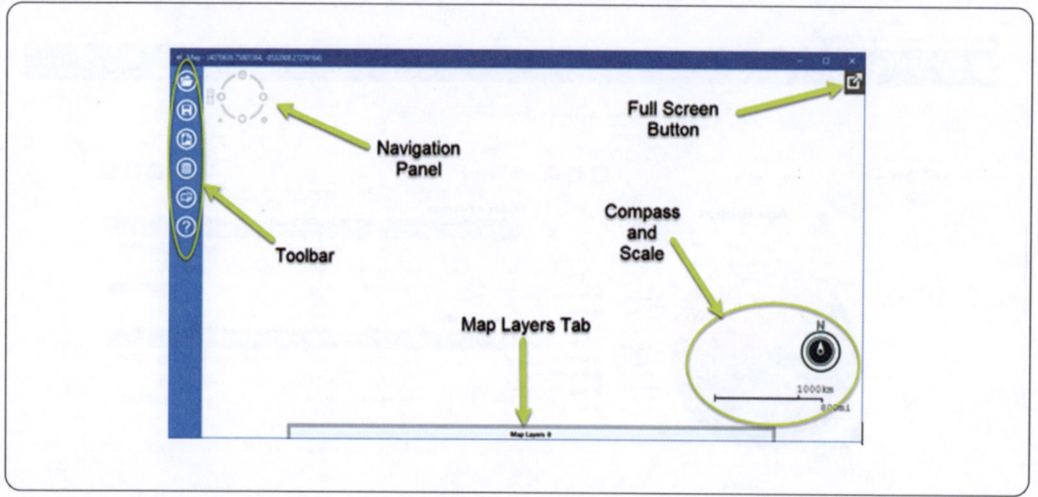

- **Basic statistical calculator:** It can perform analyses of single or stratified two-by-two tables, determine sample size for studies, and more.

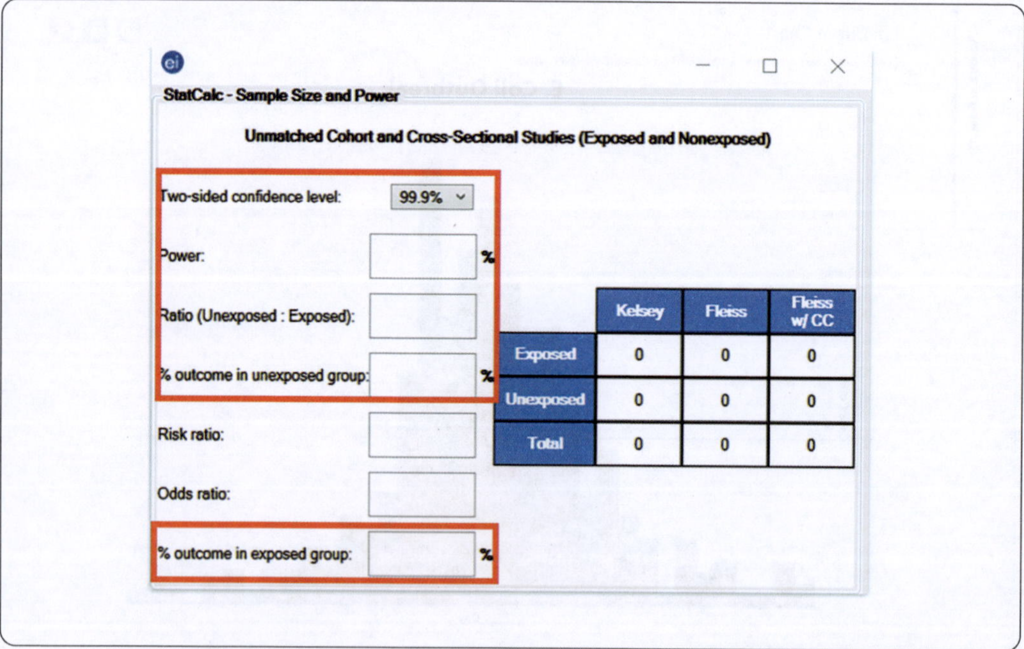

- Epi Info™ program files can be downloaded and installed from the Web http://www.cdc.gov/epiinfo

Practical Tips

Software to Calculate

Power and sample size

- PASS (screenshot)
- PS – power and sample size calculation
- nMaster

The software for parametric analysis:

- GraphPad InStat (not having analytical features for analysis of Two-way ANOVA)
- GraphPad Prism
- IBM SPSS Statistics
- SAS
- StatsDirect
- MATLAB

The software for nonparametric analysis:

- GraphPad InStat
- IBM SPSS Statistics
- StatXact
- R Software
- GraphPad Prism
- SAS
- SURVSOFT

For nonparametric analysis the methods used are as follows:

- Kruskal-Wallis one-way analysis of variance
- Siegel-Tukey test
- Wilcoxon signed-rank test
- Friedman's two-way analysis of variance
- Sign test
- Mann-Whitney U
- Spearman's rank correlation coefficient
- Kaplan-Meier
- McNemar's test

STUDENT ASSIGNMENT

LONG ANSWER QUESTIONS

1. What are statistical tools? How do these help to ease a research process?
2. Write in detail about MATLAB and its functions.

SHORT ANSWER QUESTION

1. Write notes on:
   a. SPSS
   b. SAS
   c. STATA

MULTIPLE CHOICE QUESTIONS

1. **What does SAS stand for?**
   a. Statistical Analysis System
   b. System Analysis Software
   c. Systematic Analysis System
   d. Statistical Analysis Software

2. **Which of the following SAS procedures is used for basic statistical analysis?**
   a. PROC SQL
   b. PROC MEANS
   c. PROC REPORT
   d. PROC FORMAT

3. **The "SPSS" is a package of programs for:**
   a. Manipulation
   b. Analyzing
   c. Presenting data
   d. All of these

4. **The "SPSS" is more widely use in:**
   a. Social and behavioral sciences
   b. Aerial science
   c. Both a and b
   d. None of these

5. **SPSS base provides method for:**
   a. Data description
   b. Linear regression
   c. Simple inference
   d. All of these

6. **In SPSS online help is provided from the:**
   a. Help menu
   b. Context menu
   c. Help button
   d. All of these

7. **SPSS also provides a toolbar for quick and easy access to _____ tasks.**
   a. Complex
   b. Simple
   c. Common
   d. None of these

ANSWER KEY

1. a   2. b   3. d   4. a   5. d   6. d   7. c

1. **The fundamental statistical indicators are:**
   - a. Mean
   - b. Median
   - c. Variance
   - d. Standard deviation

2. **The stages of a malignant disease (cancer) is recorded using the symbols 0, I, II, III, IV. The scale used is known as:**
   - a. Alphanumeric
   - b. Numerical
   - c. Ordinal
   - d. Nominal

3. **The average of a series of numerical values is:**
   - a. The sum of the values divided by their number
   - b. Lower than the minimum value in the series
   - c. Lower than the maximum value in the series
   - d. An indicator of central tendency for the values of the series

4. **Standard deviation:**
   - a. Is the square root of variance
   - b. Is measured using the unit of the variable
   - c. Is measured using the squared unit of the variable
   - d. Has values generally comparable with the average value

5. **Having two sets of data, we can compare their scattering as follows:**
   - a. For approximately equal average values, the one with a higher standard deviation is more scattered
   - b. For approximately equal standard deviation values, the one with a higher average is more scattered
   - c. For approximately equal standard deviation values, the one with a lower average is more scattered
   - d. If both the averages and standard deviations differ much between the series, we can compare scattering using the coefficient of variation

6. **The median of a series of numerical values is:**
   - a. A value for which half of the values are higher and half of the values are lower
   - b. The value located exactly midway between the minimum and maximum of the series
   - c. The most commonly encountered values among the series
   - d. A measure of the eccentricity of the series

7. **The median of a series of numerical values is:**
   - a. Equal to the average
   - b. A graph or chart
   - c. A number
   - d. A frequency table

8. **If a series of values consists of 21 numbers, then, for finding the median, we ordered the series ascending and we use:**
   a. The 11th value in the ordered series
   b. The mean between the 10th and 11th values
   c. The mean between the 11th and 12th values
   d. The 10th value in the ordered series

9. **The first quartile of a series of values is:**
   a. The value in the ordered series located at 25% of the number of values in the series
   b. The value of the ordered series located at 75% of the number of values in the series
   c. The numeric value for which a quarter of the series' values are lower
   d. The numeric value for which a quarter of the series' values are higher

10. **If in a group of 457 patients, for a risk factor we calculated an Odds Ratio OR = 12.74, the possibility of developing the disease being investigated is:**
    a. Very high when exposed to the factor
    b. Very small when exposed to the factor (protective factor)
    c. The same in the case of exposure in the case of nonexposure
    d. Lower in the exposed than in the unexposed, OR being <100

11. **Relative risk:**
    a. Shows the relationship between a factor assumed to influence the occurrence of disease, and the disease
    b. Is the ratio of the risk of disease for those exposed and those not exposed to that risk factor
    c. Cannot be greater than 1
    d. Is expressed as a percentage

12. **A clinical trial is more valuable when:**
    a. Sensitivity and specificity have higher values
    b. Sensitivity is higher than specificity
    c. Specificity is higher than sensitivity
    d. The sensitivity and specificity values are close, even equal, regardless of their values

13. **If in a group of 457 patients, for a risk factor we calculated a Relative Risk RR = 12.74, the possibility of developing the disease being investigated is:**
    a. Very high when exposed to the factor
    b. Very small when exposed to the factor
    c. The same in the case of exposure in the case of nonexposure
    d. Lower in the exposed than in the unexposed, RR being <100

14. **The sensitivity (SN) of a clinical trial:**
    a. Is the ratio of sick patients, diagnosed as positive, and the total number of sick patients.
    b. Is the ratio of healthy subjects, diagnosed as negative, and the total number of healthy subjects
    c. Is the ratio of sick patients, diagnosed as negative, and the total number of patients.
    d. Is the ratio of sick patients, diagnosed as negative, and the total number of healthy persons

15. **In a contingency table that shows data from a clinical trial is good to have high values for:**
    a. Sick subjects, diagnosed as negative
    b. Sick subjects, diagnosed as positive
    c. Healthy subjects, diagnosed as negative
    d. Healthy subjects, diagnosed as positive

16. **Pearson correlation coefficient, denoted by r, measures:**
    a. The scattering strength of data for a statistical series
    b. The strength of the correlation between the mean and median
    c. The strength of the correlation between two numerical parameters
    d. The tendency of simultaneous increase or decrease, or inverse evolution, for two numerical parameters

17. **For a clinical trial, the sensitivity is Sn = 0.562 and Specificity is Sp = 0.893. This means that:**
    a. The test is a valuable test because both indicators are >50%
    b. The test is a worthless test, since it gives errors when detecting both sick and healthy subjects
    c. The test is a worthless test, because the sensitivity is too low (lower than 75%)
    d. A perfect test

18. **A regression line is a straight line which:**
    a. Is located as close as possible to all the points of a scatter chart
    b. Is defined by an equation having 2 parameters—the slope and the intercept
    c. Provides an approximate relationship between the values of two parameters
    d. Is parallel to one of the coordinate axes

19. **The correlation coefficient computed for two parameters measured in 429 patients is r = 0.829. This means that:**
    a. The two parameters are directly correlated, and the link is weak—r is positive and close to 0
    b. The two parameters are inversely correlated, and the link is strong—r is negative and close to 1
    c. The two parameters are directly correlated, and the link is strong—r is positive and close to 1
    d. There are too few cases (under 30) and we do not trust this coefficient's value

20. **A frequency polygon is:**
    a. A statistical indicator that shows the scattering of a series of values
    b. A graph representing by a broken line the absolute frequencies of classes of a data series
    c. A graph that contains exactly the same information as the corresponding histogram
    d. A graph that contains less information than the corresponding histogram

21. **For a Histogram chart the following statements are true:**
    a. Each bar (class or column) is the same width
    b. The height of the bars is proportional to that class absolute frequency (number of individuals in the class)
    c. The width of the bars (classes) is obtained by dividing the difference between the maximum and the minimum values in the series we represent to the number of desired classes
    d. We do not lose any information of the original data series by making such a chart

22. **A Gaussian curve is a curve which is:**
    a. Symmetrical to the mean
    b. Symmetrical to the vertical axis, which passes through 0
    c. Has a maximum where the average of the series of values is located
    d. Tends to 0 toward plus infinity and minus infinity (i.e., very low and very high values)

23. **A Gaussian curve, the curve of a normal distribution, has which of the following features (where m = mean, s = standard deviation)?**
    a. In the interval [m – 1s; m + 1s] about 2/3 (~ 68%) of the series' values are located
    b. In the interval [m – 2s; m + 2s] about 95% of the series' values are located
    c. In the interval [m – 3s; m + 3s] about 99% of the series' values are located
    d. In the interval [m – 1s; m + 1s] about 50% of the series' values are located

24. **The result of a statistical test, denoted p, should be interpreted as:**
    a. The null hypothesis H0 is rejected if $p < 0.05$
    b. The null hypothesis H0 is rejected if $p > 0.05$
    c. The alternate hypothesis H1 is rejected if $p > 0.05$
    d. The null hypothesis H0 is accepted if $p < 0.05$

25. **The Student's t test is:**
    a. A parametric test
    b. A nonparametric test
    c. A test for comparing averages
    d. A test for comparing variances

26. **The Confidence Interval for the mean, calculated for a series of values, has the interpretation that:**
    a. The true mean, the one that approximates the population's mean, is almost certain inside the confidence interval
    b. The true variance is almost certain inside the confidence interval
    c. The true median is almost certain inside the confidence interval
    d. It is an interval that contains almost all the values of the series

27. **The null hypothesis (H0) when comparing two means should be interpreted as:**
    a. Data do not support the Hypothesis that the populations' means are different
    b. The compared values are different
    c. The two sampling averages do not differ significantly
    d. The two populations, from which the compared values were sampled, do not differ

28. **If, after performing a Student test for comparison of means, we obtain p = 0.0256, then:**
    a. We reject H0 and accept H1
    b. We accept H0
    c. We reject H1
    d. We cannot decide

29. **When you read scientific literature, do you know whether the statistical tests used are appropriate and why they are used?**
    a. Always
    b. Mostly
    c. Rarely
    d. Never

30. **Which of the following statements are true?**
    a. The p-value is the probability of the sample data arising by chance.
    b. The p-value is an arbitrary value, designated as the significance level.
    c. The p-value is the chance of getting an observed effect if the null hypothesis is false.
    d. The p-value is the chance of getting an observed effect if the null hypothesis is true.
    e. A very small p-value allows us to say that there is enough evidence to accept the null hypothesis.

31. **If the average of a series of values is 10 and their variance is 4, then the coefficient of variation (= the ratio standard deviation/average) is:**
    a. 40%
    b. 20%
    c. 80%
    d. 10%

32. **Answer true or false for the following statements:**
    a. The 95% confidence interval for the mean:
        i. Contains the sample mean with 95% certainty.
        ii. Is less likely to contain the population mean than the 99% confidence interval.
        iii. Contains 95% of the observations in the population.
        iv. Is approximately equal to the sample mean plus and minus two standard deviations
        v. Can be used to give an indication of whether the sample mean is a precise estimate of the population mean.

33. **Answer true or false for the following statements:**

    The paired t-test:
    i. Tests the null hypothesis that the two population means are equal
    ii. Must have equally sized numbers of observations in each group.
    iii. Assumes that the data in each group are normally distributed.
    iv. Is appropriate for comparing the means of independent groups of observations.
    v. When appropriately used, is more powerful when the sample size is large.

34. **Answer true or false for the following statements:**

    A correlation coefficient:
    i. Should not be calculated when there is an underlying relationship between the two variables but it is not linear.
    ii. Does not provide evidence of a causal relationship between two variables.
    iii. Should not be used to judge the biological importance of the relationship between two variables.
    iv. Should be performed only when certain assumptions are satisfied (e.g., variables measured on a random sample of individuals, both the variables are quantitative and at least one of the two variables need to be normally distributed).

35. **A study was conducted on the influence of spaying of bitches in their subsequent development of urinary incontinence. Young adult bitches presenting for spaying were randomly allocated to immediate ovariohysterectomy or to a deferred operation 6 months later. The bitches were followed over the 6 months.**
    a. What type of variable is 'development of urinary incontinence'?
        i. Qualitative variable
        ii. Quantitative variable
        iii. Categorical variable
        iv. Binary variable
        v. Continuous variable
    b. What statistical analysis would you use to answer the question in the given study?
        i. Two-sample t-test
        ii. Correlation
        iii. Chi-squared test
        iv. Paired t-test
        v. Linear regression

36. **Review the figures and answer the following questions.**

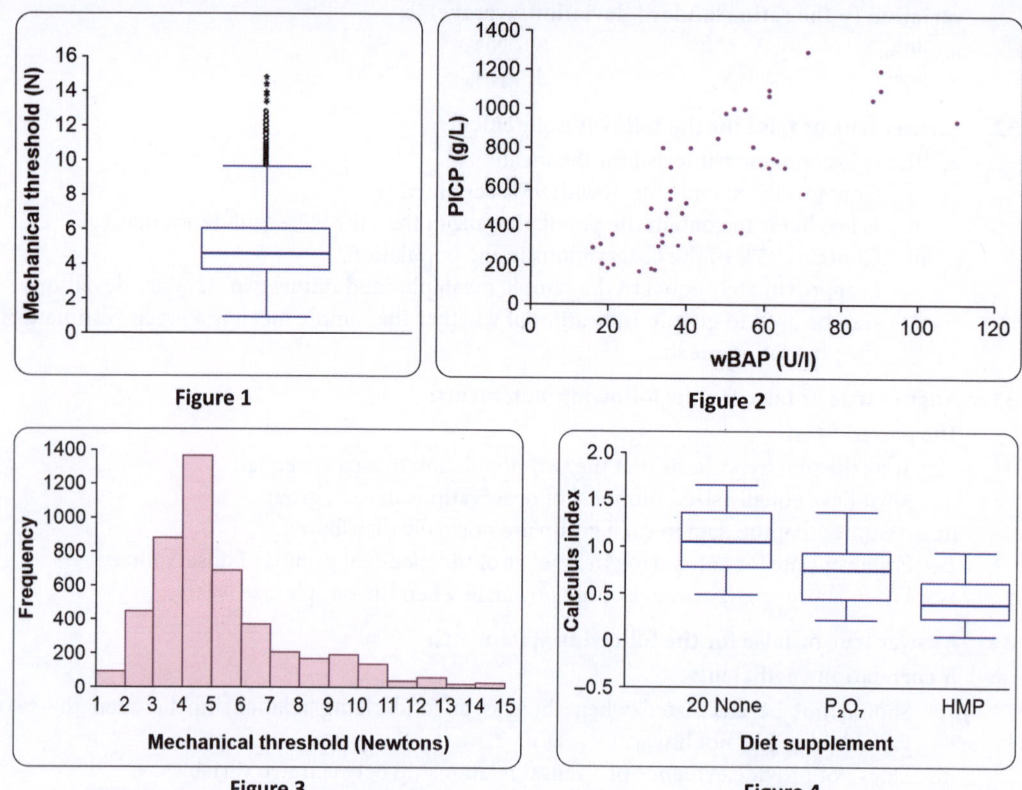

Figure 1

Figure 2

Figure 3

Figure 4

Now answer true or false for the following statements:

 i. The horizontal line within the box in a box-and-whisker plot in Figure 1 indicates the median value.

 ii. The scatter diagram in Figure 2 is useful to present data when we are interested in examining the relationship between two quantitative variables.

 iii. The histogram in Figure 3 is skewed to the right (or positively skewed) and can be transformed into a normal distribution using a logarithmic transformation of the data.

 iv. The box plots in Figure 4 demonstrate that the data for 3 groups of dogs are normally distributed.

 v. Figure 1 is an appropriate distribution for a continuous variable.

37. **A study was conducted to investigate the relationship between sheep live weight (kg) and its chest girth (cm). A random sample of 66 sheep was weighed and simultaneously had their chest girth measured. Answer true or false for the following statements:**

 i. Analysis of the data from this study could be performed using a two-sample t-test.

 ii. A scatter diagram should be used to present the data.

 iii. Chest girth measurement is a categorical variable.

 iv. Simple linear regression could be used to describe the straight line relationship between sheep live weight and chest girth.

 v. Sheep live weight can be predicted by measuring chest girth as long as the relationship between these variables is linear and chest girth is measured without error.

ANSWER KEY

1. a, d	2. c	3. a, c, d	4. a, b, d	5. a, c, d	6. a	7. c	8. a
9. a, c	10. b	11. a, b	12. a	13. a	14. a	15. b, c	16. c, d
17. c	18. a, b, c	19. c	20. b, c	21. b, c	22. a, c, d	23. a, b, c	24. a
25. a, c	26. a	27. a, c, d	28. a	29. b	30. b, d		

31. b (Standard deviation is square root of variance $\sqrt{4} = 2$, so the coefficient of variation is 2/10=0.2=20%)

32.
i. False: It contains the population mean with 95% certainty. It always contains the sample mean.
ii. True
iii. False: In repeated samples, around 95% of the confidence intervals (CI) contain the population mean. Another way to think about 95% CI is if the same study is repeated 100 times, then the mean of 95 of these 100 studies would lie somewhere within the 95% CI.
iv. False: It is approximately equal to ± two standard errors about the sample mean.
v. True (Narrow confidence intervals indicate the sample mean is a precise estimate.)

33.
i. False: Tests the null hypothesis that the mean of the differences in the population is zero.
ii. True (This is required in order to calculate the difference for each pair of observations.)
iii. False: The paired t-test makes the assumption that the differences between the pairs are normally distributed.
iv. False: The two-sample t-test should be used for comparing the means of independent groups of observations.
v. True

34. i, ii, iii, iv (All are true)

35. **a.** iii, iv; **b.** iii

36. i, ii, iii, iv, v (All are true)

37.
i. False: Simple linear regression or correlation analysis should be used to analyze the data.
ii. True
iii. False: This variable is a continuous variable.
iv. True
v. True

Note

Appendices

APPENDIX 1

HOW TO INVESTIGATE A CASE?

Many outbreak investigations are not straightforward; therefore, it is important to look for clues that will help you identifying factors that are associated with the illness in question.

For this, select an appropriate reference group and analyze the data for measures of association.

Steps followed will be:

1. **Selecting a reference group:** Selection of an appropriate reference or comparison group is critical to determining whether an association exists between the exposure and illness.
   - The reference group is the population of individuals that has had no exposure to the risk factor being analyzed.
   - The exposed and unexposed populations should be similar, with the exception of the exposure.
   - Therefore, if no direct association exists between the exposure and the illness, the attack rates will be relatively similar.

2. **Calculating rates and ratios:** To determine what factors are associated with the illness, we must analyze:
   - The data to measure the frequencies with which a potential exposure can be associated with the illness.
   - There are several ways to express measures of association in cohort studies.
   - **Attack rates** are calculated by dividing the number of new cases among the population during the limited time period (**X**) by the population at risk at the beginning of the period (**Y**). This number is then multiplied by (**100**) to express in a percentage. The formula can be expressed as:

$$AR = \frac{X}{Y} \times 100$$

   - **Risk ratios** compare the amount of risk associated with an event such as a disease or death in the exposed population to the amount of risk in the unexposed population. As a result, they are calculated by dividing the attack rate in the exposed population by the attack rate in the unexposed population. The formula can be expressed as:

$$\frac{AR\ (Exposed)}{AR\ (Unexposed)}$$

3. **Analyzing multiple risk factors:** When several risk factors are being considered simultaneously, it is often necessary to establish an experimental control, where there is an absence of exposure to all of the risk factors being analyzed. By establishing an experimental control, a uniform denominator is created and the resulting risk ratios can be compared. The following can assist with comparison of risk ratios.

- **RR = 1.0** indicates identical risk in both groups
- **RR >1.0** indicates an increased risk for the exposed group compared to the unexposed group
- **RR <1.0** indicates a decreased risk for the exposed group compared to the unexposed group

Remember:

- Identifying the correct association with the illness does not always occur on the first attempt; and knowing when to refocus and reanalyze often requires experience and judgment and might require advanced analysis.
- Generally, investigations are an iterative process in which a hypothesis is established, tested, and revised several times before association(s) can be established.
- It is essential to stay open and be alert to clues

TOOLS TO CONTROL INTERNAL AND EXTERNAL SOURCES OF VALIDITY

	Pretest/Post-test	Control group	Randomization	Additional groups
Internal sources				
History		X		
Maturation		X		
Pretesting				X
Measuring instrument		X		
Statistical regression		X	X	
Differential selection	X		X	
Experimental mortality	X			
Interaction of factors		X	X	
External sources				
Pretesting				X
Differential selection	X		X	
Procedures				X
Multiple treatment				

RULE OF CHOOSING CORRECT RESEARCH DESIGN

Choosing correct research design affects the research outcomes as shown in the following table:

Pre-experimental design: Loose in structure, could be biased

Aims of the research	Name of the design	Comments
To attempt to explain a consequent by an antecedent	One-shot experimental case study	An approach that prematurely links antecedents and consequences. The least reliable of all experimental approaches.
To evaluate the influence of a variable	One group pretest-post-test	An approach that provides a measure of change but can provide no conclusive results.
To determine the influence of a variable on one group and not on another	Static group comparison	Weakness lies in no examination of pre-experimental equivalence of groups. Conclusion is reached by comparing the performance of each group to determine the effect of a variable on one of them.

True experimental design: Greater control and refinement, greater control of validity

Aims of the research	Name of the design	Comments
To study the effect of an influence on a carefully controlled sample	Pretest-post-test control group	This design has been called "the old workhorse of traditional experimentation." If effectively carried out, this design controls for eight threats of internal validity. Data are analyzed by analysis of covariance on post-test scores with the pretest the covariate.
To minimize the effect of pretesting	Solomon four-group design	This is an extension of the pretest-post-test control group design and probably the most powerful experimental approach. Data are analyzed by analysis of variance on post-test scores.
To evaluate a situation that cannot be pretested	Post-test only control group	An adaptation of the last two groups in the Solomon four-group design. Randomness is critical. Probably, the simplest and best test for significance in this design is the t-test.

Quasi-experimental design: Not randomly selected

Aims of the research	Name of the design	Comments
To investigate a situation in which random selection and assignment are not possible	Nonrandomized control group pretest-posttest	One of the strongest and most widely used quasi-experimental designs. Differs from experimental designs because test and control groups are not equivalent. Comparing pretest results will indicate degree of equivalency between experimental and control groups.
To determine the influence of a variable introduced only after a series of initial observations and only where one group is available	Time series experiment	If substantial change follows introduction of the variable, then the variable can be suspect as to the cause of the change. To increase external validity, repeat the experiment in different places under different conditions.
To bolster the validity of the aforementioned design with the addition of a control group	Control group time series	A variant of the aforementioned design by accompanying it with a parallel set of observations without the introduction of the experimental variable.
To control history in time designs with a variant of the aforementioned design	Equivalent time-samples	An on-again, off-again design in which the experimental variable is sometimes present, sometimes absent.

Correlational and ex post facto design:

Aims of the research	Name of the design	Comments
To seek for cause-effect relationships between two sets of data	Causal-comparative correlational studies	A very deceptive procedure that requires much insight for its use. Causality cannot be inferred merely because a positive and close correlation ratio exists.
To search backward from consequent data for antecedent causes	Ex post facto studies	This approach is experimentation in reverse. Seldom is proof through data substantiation possible. Logic and inference are the principal tools of this design

APPENDIX 4

RESEARCH METHODOLOGY

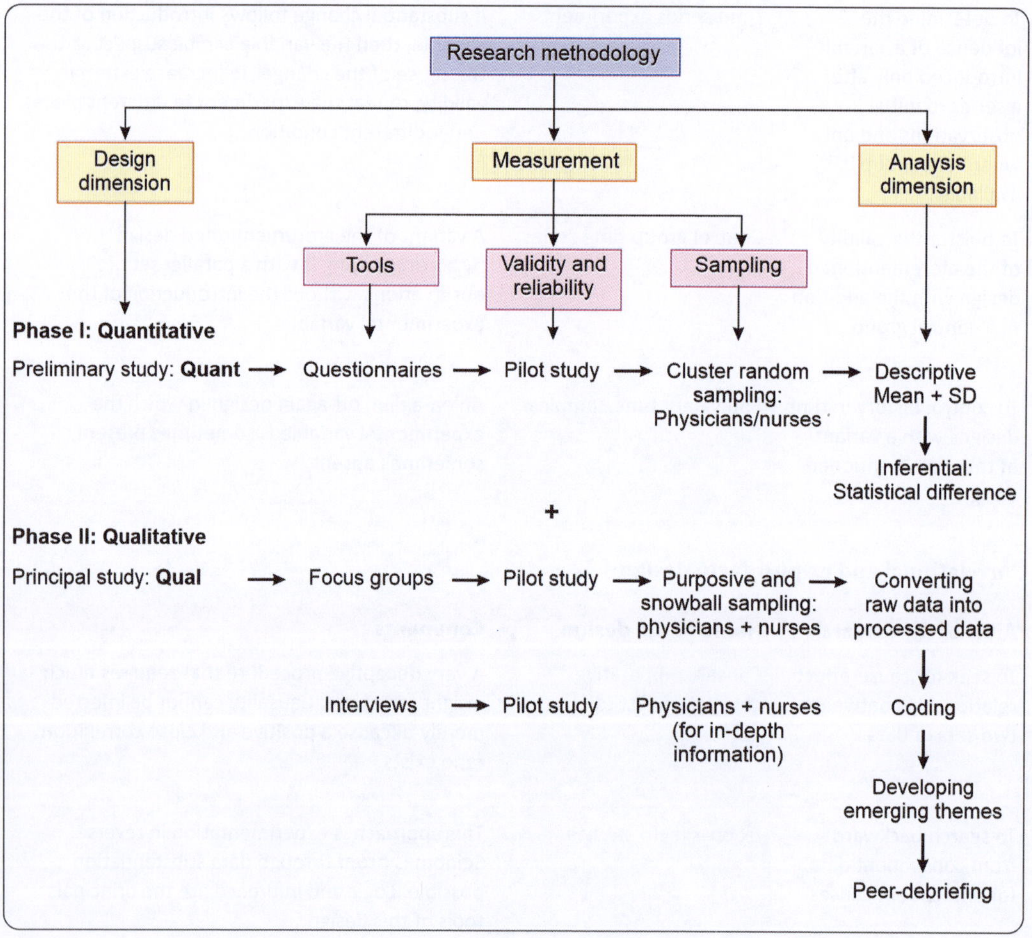

CHOOSING STATISTICAL TEST

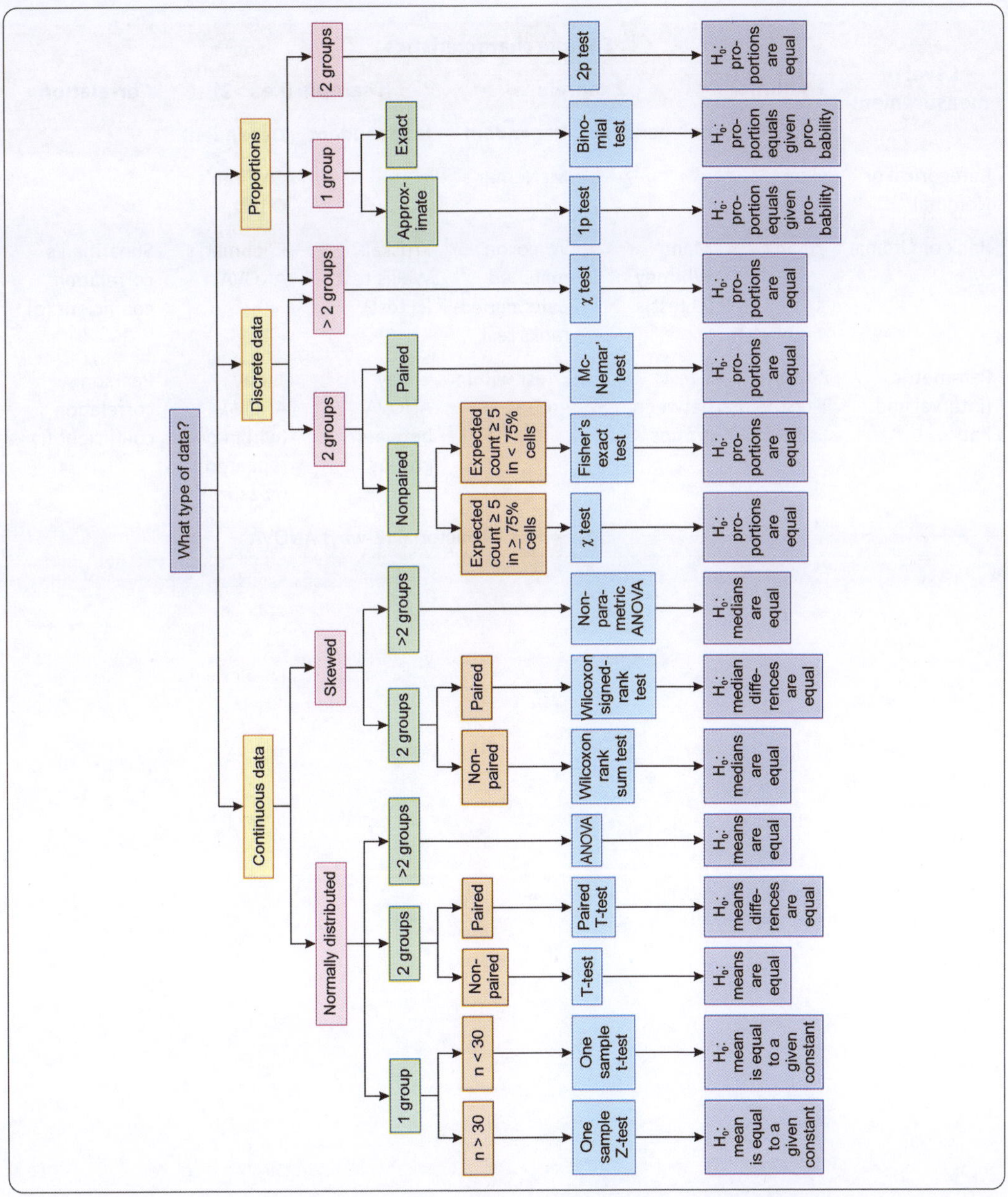

What type of data?

Discrete data → Proportions
- 2 groups → 2p test → H₀: proportions are equal
- 1 group → Exact → Binomial test → H₀: proportion equals given probability
- 1 group → Approximate → 1p test → H₀: proportion equals given probability

Discrete data
- > 2 groups → χ test → H₀: proportions are equal
- 2 groups → Paired → McNemar' test → H₀: proportions are equal
- 2 groups → Nonpaired → Expected count ≥ 5 in < 75% cells → Fisher's exact test → H₀: proportions are equal
- 2 groups → Nonpaired → Expected count ≥ 5 in ≥ 75% cells → χ test → H₀: proportions are equal

Continuous data → Skewed
- >2 groups → Non-parametric ANOVA → H₀: medians are equal
- 2 groups → Paired → Wilcoxon signed-rank test → H₀: median differences are equal
- 2 groups → Nonpaired → Wilcoxon rank sum test → H₀: medians are equal

Continuous data → Normally distributed
- >2 groups → ANOVA → H₀: means are equal
- 2 groups → Paired → Paired T-test → H₀: means differences are equal
- 2 groups → Nonpaired → T-test → H₀: means are equal
- 1 group → n < 30 → One sample t-test → H₀: mean is equal to a given constant
- 1 group → n > 30 → One sample Z-test → H₀: mean is equal to a given constant

APPENDIX 6

SELECTION OF STATISTICAL TEST

Based on sample characteristics:

- Level of measurement

Level of measurement	1 sample	Sample characteristics				Correlation
		2 sample		**K sample (i.e., >2)**		
		Independent	Dependent	Independent	Dependent	
Categorical or Nominal	χ^2 or nominal	χ^2	McNemar's χ^2	χ^2	Cochran's Q test	
Rank or Ordinal	χ^2	Mann-Whitney (U test)	Wilcoxon matched pairs signed-ranks test	Kruskal-Wallis test (H test)	Friedman's ANOVA	Spearman's correlation coefficient (ρ)
Parametric (Interval and Ratio)	Z-test or T-test	T-test between groups	T-test within groups	1-way ANOVA between groups	1-way ANOVA (within or repeated measure)	Pearson's correlation coefficient (r)
				Factorial (2-way) ANOVA		

APPENDIX 7

CALCULATING SAMPLE SIZE REQUIREMENT

Sample size for 1 sample z test is calculated as follows:

$$n = \frac{\sigma^2 \left(Z_{1-\beta} + Z_{1-\frac{\alpha}{2}} \right)^2}{\Delta^2}$$

Where

    $1 - \beta \equiv$ desired power

    $\alpha \equiv$ desired significance level (two-sided)

    $\sigma \equiv$ population standard deviation

    $\Delta = \mu_0 - \mu_a \equiv$ the difference worth detecting

Example: How large a sample is needed for a 1-sample z-test with 90% power and alpha = 0.05 (two tailed), when

$$\sigma = 40? \text{ Let } H_0 : \mu = 170 \text{ and } H_a : \mu = 190$$
$$(\text{thus, } \Delta = \mu_0 - \mu_a = 170 - 190 = -20)$$

Solution

$$n = \frac{\sigma^2 \left(Z_{1-\beta} + Z_{1-\frac{\alpha}{2}} \right)^2}{\Delta^2} = \frac{40^2 \, (1.28 + 1.96)^2}{-20^2} = 41.99$$

Round up to 42 to ensure adequate power.

Note

GLOSSARY

95% confidence interval: If the sampling distribution is relatively symmetric and bell-shaped, a 95% confidence interval can be estimated using statistic $\pm\ 2 \times SE$.

Age-specific mortality rate: A mortality rate limited to a particular age group. The numerator is the number of deaths in that age group; the denominator is the number of persons in that age group in the population.

Alternative hypothesis (H1): Proposes that the two variables are related in the population. If we assume that from two methods, method A is superior to method B, then this assumption is called alternative hypothesis.

Analytic study: A comparative study intended to identify and quantify associations, test hypotheses, and identify causes. Two common types are cohort study and case-control study.

Attack rate: A variant of an incident rate, applied to a narrowly defined population observed for a limited period of time, such as during an epidemic.

Attributable proportion: A measure of the public health impact of a causative factor; proportion of a disease in a group that is exposed to a particular factor which can be attributed to their exposure to that factor.

Bar chart: A visual display of the size of the different categories of a variable. Each category or value of the variable is represented by a bar.

Biostatistics: A branch of statistics, which is used to study biological phenomena. Here, statistics is used to infer a data obtained from health backgrounds.

Box plot: A visual display that summarizes data using a "box and whiskers" format to show the minimum and maximum values (ends of the whiskers), interquartile range (length of the box), and median (line through the box).

Case definition: A set of standard criteria for deciding whether a person has a particular disease or health-related condition, by specifying clinical criteria and limitations on time, place, and person.

Case: In epidemiology, a countable instance in the population or study group of a particular disease, health disorder, or condition under investigation. Sometimes, an individual with the particular disease.

Case-control study: A type of observational analytic study. Enrollment into the study is based on presence ("case") or absence ("control") of disease. Characteristics such as previous exposure are then compared between cases and controls.

Case-fatality rate: The proportion of persons with a particular condition (cases) who die from that condition. The denominator is the number of incident cases; the numerator is the number of cause-specific deaths among those cases.

Cause of disease: A factor (characteristic, behavior, event, etc.) that directly influences the occurrence of disease. A reduction of the factor in the population should lead to a reduction in the occurrence of disease.

Cause-specific mortality rate: The mortality rate from a specified cause for a population. The numerator is the number of deaths attributed to a specific cause during a specified time interval; the denominator is the size of the population at the midpoint of the time interval.

Class interval: A span of values of a continuous variable which are grouped into a single category for a frequency distribution of that variable.

Cohort study: A type of observational analytic study. Enrollment into the study is based on exposure characteristics or membership in a group. Disease, death, or other health-related outcomes are then ascertained and compared.

Cohort: A well-defined group of people who have had a common experience or exposure, who are then followed up for the incidence of new diseases or events, as in a cohort or prospective study. A group of people born during a particular period or year is called a birth cohort.

Confidence interval: A confidence interval for a parameter is an interval computed from sample data by a method that will capture the parameter for a specified proportion of all samples. The success rate of proportion of all samples whose intervals contain the parameter, is known as the confidence level. A 95% confidence interval will contain the true parameter for 95% of all samples.

Confidence limit: The minimum or maximum value of a confidence interval.

Contingency table: A two-variable table with cross-tabulated data. When the table is prepared by enumeration of qualitative data by entering the actual frequencies, and if that table represents occurrence of two sets of events, it is called the contingency table. (Latin, con – together, tangier – to touch). It is also called an association table.

Continuous random variable: Random variable that can take on any value within a specified interval or range of real numbers, and has an infinite number of possible values. Here, no gap is present when a character is measured in an experiment.

Control: A case-control study, which compares group of persons without disease.

Crude mortality rate: The mortality rate from all causes of death for a population.

Cumulative frequency curve: A plot of the cumulative frequency rather than the actual frequency for each class interval of a variable. This type of graph is useful for identifying medians, quartiles, and other percentiles.

Cumulative frequency: In a frequency distribution, the number or proportion of cases or events with a particular value or in a particular class interval, plus the total number or proportion of cases or events with smaller values of the variable.

Data: It is basic unit of any statistical analysis. It is raw material of statistics and is written as numbers. For example, noting patient's temperature, heartbeat or pulse rate.

Death-to-case ratio: The number of deaths attributed to a particular disease during a specified time period divided by the number of new cases of that disease identified during the same time period.

Degree of freedom: Denotes the extent of independence (freedom) enjoyed by a given set of observed frequencies.

Demographic information: The person's characteristics age, sex, race, and occupation of descriptive epidemiology used to characterize the populations at risk.

Denominator: The lower portion of a fraction used to calculate a rate or ratio. In a rate, the denominator is usually the population (or population experience, as in person-years, etc.) at risk.

Dependent variable: In a statistical analysis, the outcome variable(s) or the variable(s) whose values are the function of other variable(s) (called independent variable(s) in the relationship under study).

Descriptive epidemiology: The aspect of epidemiology concerned with organizing and summarizing health-related data according to time, place, and person.

Design of experiment: It means how to design an experiment that is how the observations or measurements should be obtained for a research problem to answer a research problem in an effective, well-organized and inexpensive way.

Determinant: Any factor, whether event, characteristic, or other definable entity, that brings about change in a health condition, or in other defined characteristics.

Discrete random variable: Characterized by intervals or gaps or interruptions in the values under observation—a small gap will remain in between two values.

Experiment: It is a way of getting an answer to a question that a researcher wants to know.

Experimental error: The unexplained random part of variation in any experiment is known as experimental error. An estimate of experimental error can be obtained by replication of the experiment.

Experimental study: A study in which the investigator specifies the exposure category for each individual (clinical trial) or community (community trial), then follows the individuals or community to detect the effects of the exposure.

Experimental unit: In order to do an experiment, the experimental material is divided into smaller parts called units which are randomly assigned to an experimental treatment.

Experiments: When first-hand information is important for a researcher the available data is not useful. For this, experiments help in collecting the useful information. A healthcare professional may like to know the effectiveness of one strategy that could motivate a patient's compliance among several others.

External sources: Someone in the world may have already worked on the same problem which is under observation of a researcher and a data must be there. Problem under observation can be solved by taking data from internet, journals, published reports, commercially available data banks, etc.

Factor: A factor is a variable that expresses a categorization. A factor can be fixed or random in nature.

Fixed factor: It is termed fixed factor if all the levels of interest are included in the experiment.

Frequency distribution: A complete summary of the frequencies of the values or categories of a variable; often displayed in a two column table: The left column lists the individual values or categories, the right column indicates the number of observations in each category.

Frequency polygon: A graph of a frequency distribution with values of the variable on the x-axis and the number of observations on the y-axis; data points are plotted at the midpoints of the intervals and are connected with a straight line.

Frequency: A hospital administrator may count the number of patients admitted on a particular day like 5, 9 and so on. This count is a number in which statistics is known as frequency.

Graph: A way to show quantitative data visually, using a system of coordinates.

Histogram: A graphic representation of the frequency distribution of a continuous variable. Rectangles are drawn in such a way that their bases lie on a linear scale representing different intervals, and their heights are proportional to the frequencies of the values within each of the intervals.

Independent variable: An exposure, risk factor, or other characteristic being observed or measured that is hypothesized to influence an event or manifestation (the dependent variable).

Individual data: Data that have not been put into a frequency distribution or rank ordered.

Inter-rater reliability: The extent to which the scores counted by coders correlate each other.

Interpreting 95% confidence interval: 95% of all samples yield intervals that contain the true parameter, so we can say, "95% sure" or "95% confident", that one interval contains the truth. For example, "We are 95% confident that the true proportion of all Indians that considered the economy as a 'top priority' in January 2024 is between 0.54 and 0.67."

Interquartile range: The central portion of a distribution, calculated as the difference between the third quartile and the first quartile; this range includes about one-half of the observations in the set, leaving one-quarter of the observations on each side.

Interval estimate: An interval estimate gives a range of plausible values for a population parameter.

Local control (error control): The replication is carried out with local control to reduce the experimental error. For example, if the experimental units are divided into different groups in a way that they are homogeneous within the blocks, then the variations among the blocks are eliminated. Ideally, the error component will enclose the variations because of the treatments only. This will further increase the efficiency of research design.

Margin of error: One common form of an interval estimate is statistic ± margin of error, where the margin of error reveals the precision of the sample statistic as a point estimate for the parameter. We use the spread of the sampling distribution to determine the margin of error for statistics.

Mean, arithmetic: The measure of central location commonly called the average. It is calculated by adding together all the individual values in a group of measurements and dividing by the number of values in the group.

Mean, geometric: The mean or average of a set of data measured on a logarithmic scale.

Measure of association: A quantified relationship between exposure and disease; includes relative risk, rate ratio, odds ratio.

Measure of central location: A central value that best represents a distribution of data. Measures of central location include the mean, median, and mode. Also called the measure of central tendency.

Measure of dispersion: A measure of the spread of a distribution out from its central value. Measures of dispersion used in epidemiology include the interquartile range, variance, and the standard deviation.

Median: The measure of central location which divides a set of data into two equal parts.

Medical surveillance: The monitoring of potentially exposed individuals to detect early symptoms of disease.

Midrange: The halfway point or midpoint in a set of observations. For most types of data, it is calculated as the sum of the smallest observation and the largest observation, divided by two. For age data, one is added to the numerator. The midrange is usually calculated as an intermediate step in determining other measures.

Mode: A measure of central location, the most frequently occurring value in a set of observations.

Morbidity: Any departure, subjective or objective, from a state of physiological or psychological well-being.

Mortality rate, infant: A ratio expressing the number of deaths among children less than one year of age reported during a given time period divided by the number of births reported during the same time period. The infant mortality rate is usually expressed per 1,000 live births.

Mortality rate, neonatal: A ratio expressing the number of deaths among children from birth up to but not including 28 days of age divided by the number of live births reported during the same time period. The neonatal mortality rate is usually expressed per 1,000 live births.

Mortality rate, postneonatal: A ratio expressing the number of deaths among children from 28 days up to but not including 1 year of age during a given time period divided by the number of lives births reported during the same time period. The postneonatal mortality rate is usually expressed per 1,000 live births.

Mortality rate: A measure of the frequency of occurrence of death in a defined population during a specified interval of time.

Nominal scale: Classification into unordered qualitative categories; e.g., race, religion, and country of birth as measurements of individual attributes are purely nominal scales, as there is no inherent order to their categories.

Normal curve: A bell-shaped curve that results when a normal distribution is graphed.

Normal distribution: The symmetrical clustering of values around a central location. The properties of a normal distribution include the following: (1) It is a continuous, symmetrical distribution; both tails extend to infinity; (2) The arithmetic mean, mode, and median are identical; and, (3) Its shape is completely determined by the mean and standard deviation.

Null hypothesis (H0): States that no association exists between the two cross-tabulated variables in the population, and therefore the variables are statistically independent, e.g., if we want to compare two methods like method A and method B for its superiority, and if the assumption is that both methods are equally good, then this assumption is called null hypothesis.

Numerator: The upper portion of a fraction.

Observational study: Epidemiological study in situations where nature is allowed to take its course. Changes or differences in one characteristic are studied in relation to changes or differences in others, without the intervention of the investigator.

Observations: The values obtained from measurement during a procedure are called observations.

Parameter: a characteristic of population, e.g., population mean μ; the variable of interest.

Percentile: The set of numbers from 0 to 100 that divide a distribution into 100 parts of equal area, or divide a set of ranked data into 100 class intervals with each interval containing 1/100 of the observations. A particular percentile, say the 5th percentile, is a cut point with 5% of the observations below it and the remaining 95% of the observations above it.

Pie chart: A circular chart in which the size of each "slice" is proportional to the frequency of each category of a variable.

Point estimate: They are our best guesses about a given data. We use the statistics from a sample as a point estimate for a population parameter. Point estimates will not match population parameters exactly.

Point prevalence: The amount of a particular disease presents in a population at a single point in time.

Population: The entire group of people of interest from whom the researcher needs to obtain information.

Prevalence rate: The proportion of persons in a population who have a particular disease or attribute at a specified point in time or over a specified period of time.

Prevalence: The number or proportion of cases or events or conditions in a given population.

Proportion: A type of ratio in which the numerator is included in the denominator. The ratio of a part to the whole, expressed as a "decimal fraction" (e.g., 0.2), as a fraction (1/5), or, loosely, as a percentage (20%).

Qualitative variables: Profession, ethnic group, etc., are variable that cannot be measured.

Quantitative variables: Characteristics like age, height and weight can be measured.

Random error: The extent to which a measured variable actually measures the conceptual variable (that is, the construct) that it is designed. These errors may cancel out as researcher collects large number of samples.

Random factor: A factor is known as random factor if all the levels of interest are not included in the experiment and those included are considered to be randomly chosen from all the levels of interest.

Random sampling: If we take random samples, the sampling distribution will be centered around the true population parameter. If sampling bias exists that is if random sample is not taken, the sampling distribution may give false information about the true parameter.

Random variables: A random variable is a variable whose value is unknown or a function that assigns different values to each experiment's outcomes. A random variable can be either discrete (having specific values) or continuous (any value in a continuous range). For example, variation in height according to age.

Range: In statistics, the difference between the largest and smallest values in a distribution. In common use, the span of values from smallest to largest.

Rate ratio: A comparison of two groups in terms of incidence rates, person-time rates, or mortality rates.

Rate: An expression of the frequency with which an event occurs in a defined population.

Ratio: The value obtained by dividing one quantity by another.

Reliability: The extent to which the variables are free from random error is usually determined by measuring the variables more than once.

Replication: It is the repetition of the experimental situation by replicating the experimental unit.

Research hypothesis: It is the conjecture or supposition that motivates the research.

Risk factor: An aspect of personal behavior or lifestyle, an environmental exposure, or an inborn or inherited characteristic that is associated with an increased occurrence of disease or other health-related event or condition.

Routine records: Every organization or healthcare setting keeps a record. In hospitals, records are kept and huge amount of information is recorded. These data from patients act as source to study a disease or prevalence statistics in the community. Such data can be subjected to statistical tests.

Sample population: It is a group of people/person, which have some characters in common for example, all neurons in human brain, all nurses/doctors in a hospital, etc.

Sample: It is part/portion of a population which is under study. It is difficult to assess population but a sample from a population of our own interest can give us similar results.

Sampling distribution: It is the distribution of sample statistics computed for different samples of the same size from the same population. A sampling distribution shows us how the sample statistic varies from sample to sample.

Sampling frame: Listing of population from which a sample is chosen. The sampling frame for any probability sample is a complete list of all cases in the population from which the sample will be drawn.

Sampling unit or elements: One unit from a population.

Sampling unit: The object of study which is measured during an experiment is called the sampling unit and it is not the experimental unit.

Sampling: The selection of a subset of population through various sampling techniques.

Scatter diagram: A graph in which each dot represents paired values for two continuous variables, with the x-axis representing one variable and the y-axis representing the other; used to display the relationship between the two variables; also called a scattergram.

Skewed: A distribution that is asymmetrical.

Specificity: The proportion of persons without disease who are correctly identified by a screening test or case definition as not having disease.

Standard deviation: The most widely used measure of dispersion of a frequency distribution, equal to the positive square root of the variance.

Standard error (of the mean): The standard deviation of a theoretical distribution of sample means about the true population mean.

Standard error (SE): The standard error of a statistic, i.e., SE is the standard deviation of the sample statistic. The standard error can be calculated as the standard deviation of the sampling distribution.

Statistic: The information obtained from the sample about the parameter. We measure the sample using statistics in order to draw inferences about the population and its parameters.

Statistical hypothesis: Hypothesis that are stated in such a way that they may be evaluated by appropriate statistical techniques.

Statistical inference: Generalizing from a sample to a population with calculated degree of certainty. Two forms of statistical inference are - **Hypothesis testing and Estimation**.

Statistics: It is a study of how to collect, organize, analyze and interpret a numerical data. In fact it is a branch of mathematics and deals with drawing inferences based on the probability.

Surveys: If a researcher wants to know an answer to currently introduced new drug of treatment in various hospitals, in a particular period of time, survey will be taken among patients. The survey is conducted on a sample of patients and is later generalized for population.

Systemic error: Sources of error including the style of measurement, tendency toward self-promotion, cooperative reporting, and other conceptual variables are being measured. So, we have to reduce these errors to prove scientific findings.

Table: A set of data arranged in rows and columns.

Treatment design: A treatment design is the way in which the levels of treatments are set in an experiment. For example, suppose a researcher has to investigate on some species of fishes for food. The food is placed in the water tanks containing the fishes. The response is observed as an increase in the weight of fish. The experimental unit is the tank, as the treatment is applied to the tank, not to the fish. Keep in mind that if the researcher had taken the fish in hand and placed the food in the mouth of fish, then the fish would have been the experimental unit because each of the fish would have received an independent scoop of food.

Treatment: These are different objects or procedures that are to be compared under an experiment.

Trend: A long-term movement or change in frequency, usually upward or downward.

Validity: The degree to which a measurement actually measures or detects what it is supposed to measure.

Variables: A characteristic when observed in different persons takes a different value and it is named as variable. For example, when diastolic blood pressure is measured in different people, the readings will be different.

Variance: A measure of the dispersion shown by a set of observations, defined by the sum of the squares of deviations from the mean, divided by the number of degrees of freedom in the set of observations.

Vital statistics: Systematically tabulated information about births, marriages, divorces, and deaths, based on registration of these vital events

STATISTICAL TABLES

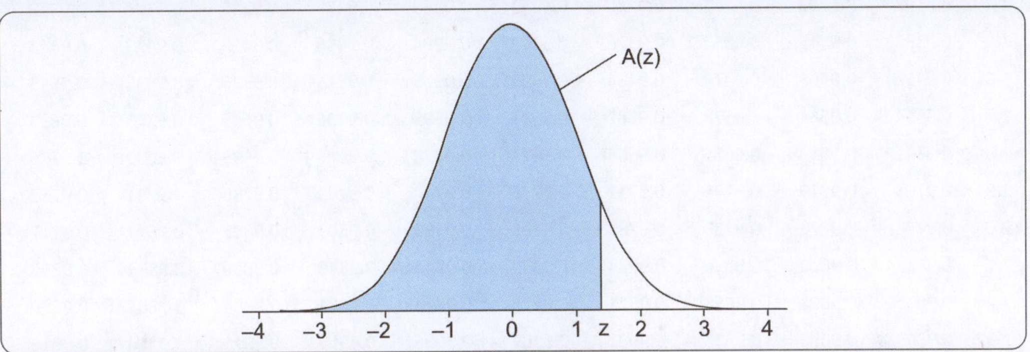

A(z) is the integral of the standardized normal distribution from — ∞ to z (in other words, the area under the curve to the left of z). It gives the probability of a normal random variable not being more than z standard deviations above its mean. Values of z of particular importance:

z	A(z)	
1.645	0.9500	Lower limit of right 5% tail
1.960	0.9750	Lower limit of right 2.5% tail
2.326	0.9900	Lower limit of right 1% tail
2.576	0.9950	Lower limit of right 0.5% tail
3.090	0.9990	Lower limit of right 0.1% tail
3.291	0.9995	Lower limit of right 0.05% tail

TABLE 1: Cumulative Standardized Normal Distribution

z	0.00	0.01	0.02	0.03	0.04	0.05	0.06	0.07	0.08	0.09
0.0	0.5000	0.5040	0.5080	0.5120	0.5160	0.5199	0.5239	0.5279	0.5319	0.5359
0.1	0.5398	0.5438	0.5478	0.5517	0.5557	0.5596	0.5636	0.5675	0.5714	0.5753
0.2	0.5793	0.5832	0.5871	0.5910	0.5948	0.5987	0.6026	0.6064	0.6103	0.6141
0.3	0.6179	0.6217	0.6255	0.6293	0.6331	0.6368	0.6406	0.6443	0.6480	0.6517
0.4	0.6554	0.6591	0.6628	0.6664	0.6700	0.6736	0.6772	0.6808	0.6844	0.6879
0.5	0.6915	0.6950	0.6985	0.7019	0.7054	0.7088	0.7123	0.7157	0.7190	0.7224
0.6	0.7257	0.7291	0.7324	0.7357	0.7389	0.7422	0.7454	0.7486	0.7517	0.7549
0.7	0.7580	0.7611	0.7642	0.7673	0.7704	0.7734	0.7764	0.7794	0.7823	0.7852
0.8	0.7881	0.7910	0.7939	0.7967	0.7995	0.8023	0.8051	0.8078	0.8106	0.8133
0.9	0.8159	0.8186	0.8212	0.8238	0.8264	0.8289	0.8315	0.8340	0.8365	0.8389

Contd...

z	0.00	0.01	0.02	0.03	0.04	0.05	0.06	0.07	0.08	0.09
1.0	0.8413	0.8438	0.8461	0.8485	0.8508	0.8531	0.8554	0.8577	0.8599	0.8621
1.1	0.8643	0.8665	0.8686	0.8708	0.8729	0.8749	0.8770	0.8790	0.8810	0.8830
1.2	0.8849	0.8869	0.8888	0.8907	0.8925	0.8944	0.8962	0.8980	0.8997	0.9015
1.3	0.9032	0.9049	0.9066	0.9082	0.9099	0.9115	0.9131	0.9147	0.9162	0.9177
1.4	0.9192	0.9207	0.9222	0.9236	0.9251	0.9265	0.9279	0.9292	0.9306	0.9319
1.5	0.9332	0.9345	0.9357	0.9370	0.9382	0.9394	0.9406	0.9418	0.9429	0.9441
1.6	0.9452	0.9463	0.9474	0.9484	0.9495	0.9505	0.9515	0.9525	0.9535	0.9545
1.7	0.9554	0.9564	0.9573	0.9582	0.9591	0.9599	0.9608	0.9616	0.9625	0.9633
1.8	0.9641	0.9649	0.9656	0.9664	0.9671	0.9678	0.9686	0.9693	0.9699	0.9706
1.9	0.9713	0.9719	0.9726	0.9732	0.9738	0.9744	0.9750	0.9756	0.9761	0.9767
2.0	0.9772	0.9778	0.9783	0.9788	0.9793	0.9798	0.9803	0.9808	0.9812	0.9817
2.1	0.9821	0.9826	0.9830	0.9834	0.9838	0.9842	0.9846	0.9850	0.9854	0.9857
2.2	0.9861	0.9864	0.9868	0.9871	0.9875	0.9878	0.9881	0.9884	0.9887	0.9890
2.3	0.9893	0.9896	0.9898	0.9901	0.9904	0.9906	0.9909	0.9911	0.9913	0.9916
2.4	0.9918	0.9920	0.9922	0.9925	0.9927	0.9929	0.9931	0.9932	0.9934	0.9936
2.5	0.9938	0.9940	0.9941	0.9943	0.9945	0.9946	0.9948	0.9949	0.9951	0.9952
2.6	0.9953	0.9955	0.9956	0.9957	0.9959	0.9960	0.9961	0.9962	0.9963	0.9964
2.7	0.9965	0.9966	0.9967	0.9968	0.9969	0.9970	0.9971	0.9972	0.9973	0.9974
2.8	0.9974	0.9975	0.9976	0.9977	0.9977	0.9978	0.9979	0.9979	0.9980	0.9981
2.9	0.9981	0.9982	0.9982	0.9983	0.9984	0.9984	0.9985	0.9985	0.9986	0.9986
3.0	0.9987	0.9987	0.9987	0.9988	0.9988	0.9989	0.9989	0.9989	0.9990	0.9990
3.1	0.9990	0.9991	0.9991	0.9991	0.9992	0.9992	0.9992	0.9992	0.9993	0.9993
3.2	0.9993	0.9993	0.9994	0.9994	0.9994	0.9994	0.9994	0.9995	0.9995	0.9995
3.3	0.9995	0.9995	0.9995	0.9996	0.9996	0.9996	0.9996	0.9996	0.9996	0.9997
3.4	0.9997	0.9997	0.9997	0.9997	0.9997	0.9997	0.9997	0.9997	0.9997	0.9998
3.5	0.9998	0.9998	0.9998	0.9998	0.9998	0.9998	0.9998	0.9998	0.9998	0.9998
3.6	0.9998	0.9998	0.9999							

TABLE 2: *t*-Distribution: Critical values of *t*

Degrees of freedom			Significance level					
	Two-tailed test:	10%	5%	2%	1%	0.2%	0.1%
	One-tailed test:	5%	2.5%	1%	0.5%	0.1%	0.05%
1		6.314	12.706	31.821	63.657	318.309	636.619
2		2.920	4.303	6.965	9.925	22.327	31.599
3		2.353	3.182	4.541	5.841	10.215	12.924
4		2.132	2.776	3.747	4.604	7.173	8.610
5		2.015	2.571	3.365	4.032	5.893	6.869
6		1.943	2.447	3.143	3.707	5.208	5.959

Contd...

Degrees of freedom		Significance level					
	Two-tailed test:	10%	5%	2%	1%	0.2%	0.1%
	One-tailed test:	5%	2.5%	1%	0.5%	0.1%	0.05%
7		1.894	2.365	2.998	3.499	4.785	5.408
8		1.860	2.306	2.896	3.355	4.501	5.041
9		1.833	2.262	2.821	3.250	4.297	4.781
10		1.812	2.228	2.764	3.169	4.144	4.587
11		1.796	2.201	2.718	3.106	4.025	4.437
12		1.782	2.179	2.681	3.055	3.930	4.318
13		1.771	2.160	2.650	3.012	3.852	4.221
14		1.761	2.145	2.624	2.977	3.787	4.140
15		1.753	2.131	2.602	2.947	3.733	4.073
16		1.746	2.120	2.583	2.921	3.686	4.015
17		1.740	2.110	2.567	2.898	3.646	3.965
18		1.734	2.101	2.552	2.878	3.610	3.922
19		1.729	2.093	2.539	2.861	3.579	3.883
20		1.725	2.086	2.528	2.845	3.552	3.850
21		1.721	2.080	2.518	2.831	3.527	3.819
22		1.717	2.074	2.508	2.819	3.505	3.792
23		1.714	2.069	2.500	2.807	3.485	3.768
24		1.711	2.064	2.492	2.797	3.467	3.745
25		1.708	2.060	2.485	2.787	3.450	3.725
26		1.706	2.056	2.479	2.779	3.435	3.707
27		1.703	2.052	2.473	2.771	3.421	3.690
28		1.701	2.048	2.467	2.763	3.408	3.674
29		1.699	2.045	2.462	2.756	3.396	3.659
30		1.697	2.042	2.457	2.750	3.385	3.646
32		1.694	2.037	2.449	2.738	3.365	3.622
34		1.691	2.032	2.441	2.728	3.348	3.601
36		1.688	2.028	2.434	2.719	3.333	3.582
38		1.686	2.024	2.429	2.712	3.319	3.566
40		1.684	2.021	2.423	2.704	3.307	3.551
42		1.682	2.018	2.418	2.698	3.296	3.538
44		1.680	2.015	2.414	2.692	3.286	3.526
46		1.679	2.013	2.410	2.687	3.277	3.515
48		1.677	2.011	2.407	2.682	3.269	3.505
50		1.676	2.009	2.403	2.678	3.261	3.496
60		1.671	2.000	2.390	2.660	3.232	3.460
70		1.667	1.994	2.381	2.648	3.211	3.435

Contd...

Degrees of freedom		Significance level					
	Two-tailed test:	10%	5%	2%	1%	0.2%	0.1%
	One-tailed test:	5%	2.5%	1%	0.5%	0.1%	0.05%
80		1.664	1.990	2.374	2.639	3.195	3.416
90		1.662	1.987	2.368	2.632	3.183	3.402
100		1.660	1.984	2.364	2.626	3.174	3.390
120		1.658	1.980	2.358	2.617	3.160	3.373
150		1.655	1.976	2.351	2.609	3.145	3.357
200		1.653	1.972	2.345	2.601	3.131	3.340
300		1.650	1.968	2.339	2.592	3.118	3.323
400		1.649	1.966	2.336	2.588	3.111	3.315
500		1.648	1.965	2.334	2.586	3.107	3.310
600		1.647	1.964	2.333	2.584	3.104	3.307
∞		1.645	1.960	2.326	2.576	3.090	3.291

TABLE 3: *F*-Distribution: Critical values of *F* (5% significance level)

v_2 \ v_1	1	2	3	4	5	6	7	8	9	10	12	14	16	18	20
1	161.45	199.50	215.71	224.58	230.16	233.99	236.77	238.88	240.54	241.88	243.91	245.36	246.46	247.32	248.01
2	18.51	19.00	19.16	19.25	19.30	19.33	19.35	19.37	19.38	19.40	19.41	19.42	19.43	19.44	19.45
3	10.13	9.55	9.28	9.12	9.01	8.94	8.89	8.85	8.81	8.79	8.74	8.71	8.69	8.67	8.66
4	7.71	6.94	6.59	6.39	6.26	6.16	6.09	6.04	6.00	5.96	5.91	5.87	5.84	5.82	5.80
5	6.61	5.79	5.41	5.19	5.05	4.95	4.88	4.82	4.77	4.74	4.68	4.64	4.60	4.58	4.56
6	5.99	5.14	4.76	4.53	4.39	4.28	4.21	4.15	4.10	4.06	4.00	3.96	3.92	3.90	3.87
7	5.59	4.74	4.35	4.12	3.97	3.87	3.79	3.73	3.68	3.64	3.57	3.53	3.49	3.47	3.44
8	5.32	4.46	4.07	3.84	3.69	3.58	3.50	3.44	3.39	3.35	3.28	3.24	3.20	3.17	3.15
9	5.12	4.26	3.86	3.63	3.48	3.37	3.29	3.23	3.18	3.14	3.07	3.03	2.99	2.96	2.94
10	4.96	4.10	3.71	3.48	3.33	3.22	3.14	3.07	3.02	2.98	2.91	2.86	2.83	2.80	2.77
11	4.84	3.98	3.59	3.36	3.20	3.09	3.01	2.95	2.90	2.85	2.79	2.74	2.70	2.67	2.65
12	4.75	3.89	3.49	3.26	3.11	3.00	2.91	2.85	2.80	2.75	2.69	2.64	2.60	2.57	2.54
13	4.67	3.81	3.41	3.18	3.03	2.92	2.83	2.77	2.71	2.67	2.60	2.55	2.51	2.48	2.46
14	4.60	3.74	3.34	3.11	2.96	2.85	2.76	2.70	2.65	2.60	2.53	2.48	2.44	2.41	2.39
15	4.54	3.68	3.29	3.06	2.90	2.79	2.71	2.64	2.59	2.54	2.48	2.42	2.38	2.35	2.33
16	4.49	3.63	3.24	3.01	2.85	2.74	2.66	2.59	2.54	2.49	2.42	2.37	2.33	2.30	2.28
17	4.45	3.59	3.20	2.96	2.81	2.70	2.61	2.55	2.49	2.45	2.38	2.33	2.29	2.26	2.23
18	4.41	3.55	3.16	2.93	2.77	2.66	2.58	2.51	2.46	2.41	2.34	2.29	2.25	2.22	2.19
19	4.38	3.52	3.13	2.90	2.74	2.63	2.54	2.48	2.42	2.38	2.31	2.26	2.21	2.18	2.16
20	4.35	3.49	3.10	2.87	2.71	2.60	2.51	2.45	2.39	2.35	2.28	2.22	2.18	2.15	2.12
21	4.32	3.47	3.07	2.84	2.68	2.57	2.49	2.42	2.37	2.32	2.25	2.20	2.16	2.12	2.10

Contd...

ν_1 / ν_2	1	2	3	4	5	6	7	8	9	10	12	14	16	18	20
22	4.30	3.44	3.05	2.82	2.66	2.55	2.46	2.40	2.34	2.30	2.23	2.17	2.13	2.10	2.07
23	4.28	3.42	3.03	2.80	2.64	2.53	2.44	2.37	2.32	2.27	2.20	2.15	2.11	2.08	2.05
24	4.26	3.40	3.01	2.78	2.62	2.51	2.42	2.36	2.30	2.25	2.18	2.13	2.09	2.05	2.03
25	4.24	3.39	2.99	2.76	2.60	2.49	2.40	2.34	2.28	2.24	2.16	2.11	2.07	2.04	2.01
26	4.22	3.37	2.98	2.74	2.59	2.47	2.39	2.32	2.27	2.22	2.15	2.09	2.05	2.02	1.99
27	4.21	3.35	2.96	2.73	2.57	2.46	2.37	2.31	2.25	2.20	2.13	2.08	2.04	2.00	1.97
28	4.20	3.34	2.95	2.71	2.56	2.45	2.36	2.29	2.24	2.19	2.12	2.06	2.02	1.99	1.96
29	4.18	3.33	2.93	2.70	2.55	2.43	2.35	2.28	2.22	2.18	2.10	2.05	2.01	1.97	1.94
30	4.17	3.32	2.92	2.69	2.53	2.42	2.33	2.27	2.21	2.16	2.09	2.04	1.99	1.96	1.93
35	4.12	3.27	2.87	2.64	2.49	2.37	2.29	2.22	2.16	2.11	2.04	1.99	1.94	1.91	1.88
40	4.08	3.23	2.84	2.61	2.45	2.34	2.25	2.18	2.12	2.08	2.00	1.95	1.90	1.87	1.84
50	4.03	3.18	2.79	2.56	2.40	2.29	2.20	2.13	2.07	2.03	1.95	1.89	1.85	1.81	1.78
60	4.00	3.15	2.76	2.53	2.37	2.25	2.17	2.10	2.04	1.99	1.92	1.86	1.82	1.78	1.75
70	3.98	3.13	2.74	2.50	2.35	2.23	2.14	2.07	2.02	1.97	1.89	1.84	1.79	1.75	1.72
80	3.96	3.11	2.72	2.49	2.33	2.21	2.13	2.06	2.00	1.95	1.88	1.82	1.77	1.73	1.70
90	3.95	3.10	2.71	2.47	2.32	2.20	2.11	2.04	1.99	1.94	1.86	1.80	1.76	1.72	1.69
100	3.94	3.09	2.70	2.46	2.31	2.19	2.10	2.03	1.97	1.93	1.85	1.79	1.75	1.71	1.68
120	3.92	3.07	2.68	2.45	2.29	2.18	2.09	2.02	1.96	1.91	1.83	1.78	1.73	1.69	1.66
150	3.90	3.06	2.66	2.43	2.27	2.16	2.07	2.00	1.94	1.89	1.82	1.76	1.71	1.67	1.64
200	3.89	3.04	2.65	2.42	2.26	2.14	2.06	1.98	1.93	1.88	1.80	1.74	1.69	1.66	1.62
250	3.88	3.03	2.64	2.41	2.25	2.13	2.05	1.98	1.92	1.87	1.79	1.73	1.68	1.65	1.61
300	3.87	3.03	2.63	2.40	2.24	2.13	2.04	1.97	1.91	1.86	1.78	1.72	1.68	1.64	1.61
400	3.86	3.02	2.63	2.39	2.24	2.12	2.03	1.96	1.90	1.85	1.78	1.72	1.67	1.63	1.60
500	3.86	3.01	2.62	2.39	2.23	2.12	2.03	1.96	1.90	1.85	1.77	1.71	1.66	1.62	1.59
600	3.86	3.01	2.62	2.39	2.23	2.11	2.02	1.95	1.90	1.85	1.77	1.71	1.66	1.62	1.59
750	3.85	3.01	2.62	2.38	2.23	2.11	2.02	1.95	1.89	1.84	1.77	1.70	1.66	1.62	1.58
1000	3.85	3.00	2.61	2.38	2.22	2.11	2.02	1.95	1.89	1.84	1.76	1.70	1.65	1.61	1.58

ν_1 / ν_2	25	30	35	40	50	60	75	100	150	200
1	249.26	250.10	250.69	251.14	251.77	252.20	252.62	253.04	253.46	253.68
2	19.46	19.46	19.47	19.47	19.48	19.48	19.48	19.49	19.49	19.49
3	8.63	8.62	8.60	8.59	8.58	8.57	8.56	8.55	8.54	8.54
4	5.77	5.75	5.73	5.72	5.70	5.69	5.68	5.66	5.65	5.65
5	4.52	4.50	4.48	4.46	4.44	4.43	4.42	4.41	4.39	4.39
6	3.83	3.81	3.79	3.77	3.75	3.74	3.73	3.71	3.70	3.69
7	3.40	3.38	3.36	3.34	3.32	3.30	3.29	3.27	3.26	3.25
8	3.11	3.08	3.06	3.04	3.02	3.01	2.99	2.97	2.96	2.95
9	2.89	2.86	2.84	2.83	2.80	2.79	2.77	2.76	2.74	2.73

Contd...

v_2 \ v_1	25	30	35	40	50	60	75	100	150	200
10	2.73	2.70	2.68	2.66	2.64	2.62	2.60	2.59	2.57	2.56
11	2.60	2.57	2.55	2.53	2.51	2.49	2.47	2.46	2.44	2.43
12	2.50	2.47	2.44	2.43	2.40	2.38	2.37	2.35	2.33	2.32
13	2.41	2.38	2.36	2.34	2.31	2.30	2.28	2.26	2.24	2.23
14	2.34	2.31	2.28	2.27	2.24	2.22	2.21	2.19	2.17	2.16
15	2.28	2.25	2.22	2.20	2.18	2.16	2.14	2.12	2.10	2.10
16	2.23	2.19	2.17	2.15	2.12	2.11	2.09	2.07	2.05	2.04
17	2.18	2.15	2.12	2.10	2.08	2.06	2.04	2.02	2.00	1.99
18	2.14	2.11	2.08	2.06	2.04	2.02	2.00	1.98	1.96	1.95
19	2.11	2.07	2.05	2.03	2.00	1.98	1.96	1.94	1.92	1.91
20	2.07	2.04	2.01	1.99	1.97	1.95	1.93	1.91	1.89	1.88
21	2.05	2.01	1.98	1.96	1.94	1.92	1.90	1.88	1.86	1.84
22	2.02	1.98	1.96	1.94	1.91	1.89	1.87	1.85	1.83	1.82
23	2.00	1.96	1.93	1.91	1.88	1.86	1.84	1.82	1.80	1.79
24	1.97	1.94	1.91	1.89	1.86	1.84	1.82	1.80	1.78	1.77
25	1.96	1.92	1.89	1.87	1.84	1.82	1.80	1.78	1.76	1.75
26	1.94	1.90	1.87	1.85	1.82	1.80	1.78	1.76	1.74	1.73
27	1.92	1.88	1.86	1.84	1.81	1.79	1.76	1.74	1.72	1.71
28	1.91	1.87	1.84	1.82	1.79	1.77	1.75	1.73	1.70	1.69
29	1.89	1.85	1.83	1.81	1.77	1.75	1.73	1.71	1.69	1.67
30	1.88	1.84	1.81	1.79	1.76	1.74	1.72	1.70	1.67	1.66
35	1.82	1.79	1.76	1.74	1.70	1.68	1.66	1.63	1.61	1.60
40	1.78	1.74	1.72	1.69	1.66	1.64	1.61	1.59	1.56	1.55
50	1.73	1.69	1.66	1.63	1.60	1.58	1.55	1.52	1.50	1.48
60	1.69	1.65	1.62	1.59	1.56	1.53	1.51	1.48	1.45	1.44
70	1.66	1.62	1.59	1.57	1.53	1.50	1.48	1.45	1.42	1.40
80	1.64	1.60	1.57	1.54	1.51	1.48	1.45	1.43	1.39	1.38
90	1.63	1.59	1.55	1.53	1.49	1.46	1.44	1.41	1.38	1.36
100	1.62	1.57	1.54	1.52	1.48	1.45	1.42	1.39	1.36	1.34
120	1.60	1.55	1.52	1.50	1.46	1.43	1.40	1.37	1.33	1.32
150	1.58	1.54	1.50	1.48	1.44	1.41	1.38	1.34	1.31	1.29
200	1.56	1.52	1.48	1.46	1.41	1.39	1.35	1.32	1.28	1.26
250	1.55	1.50	1.47	1.44	1.40	1.37	1.34	1.31	1.27	1.25
300	1.54	1.50	1.46	1.43	1.39	1.36	1.33	1.30	1.26	1.23
400	1.53	1.49	1.45	1.42	1.38	1.35	1.32	1.28	1.24	1.22
500	1.53	1.48	1.45	1.42	1.38	1.35	1.31	1.28	1.23	1.21
600	1.52	1.48	1.44	1.41	1.37	1.34	1.31	1.27	1.23	1.20
750	1.52	1.47	1.44	1.41	1.37	1.34	1.30	1.26	1.22	1.20
1000	1.52	1.47	1.43	1.41	1.36	1.33	1.30	1.26	1.22	1.19

TABLE 4: *F*-Distribution: Critical values of *F* (1% significance level)

ν_1 / ν_2	1	2	3	4	5	6	7	8	9	10	12	14	16	18	20
1	4052.18	4999.50	5403.35	5624.58	5763.65	5858.99	5928.36	5981.07	6022.47	6055.85	6106.32	6142.67	6170.10	6191.53	6208.73
2	98.50	99.00	99.17	99.25	99.30	99.33	99.36	99.37	99.39	99.40	99.42	99.43	99.44	99.44	99.45
3	34.12	30.82	29.46	28.71	28.24	27.91	27.67	27.49	27.35	27.23	27.05	26.92	26.83	26.75	26.69
4	21.20	18.00	16.69	15.98	15.52	15.21	14.98	14.80	14.66	14.55	14.37	14.25	14.15	14.08	14.02
5	16.26	13.27	12.06	11.39	10.97	10.67	10.46	10.29	10.16	10.05	9.89	9.77	9.68	9.61	9.55
6	13.75	10.92	9.78	9.15	8.75	8.47	8.26	8.10	7.98	7.87	7.72	7.60	7.52	7.45	7.40
7	12.25	9.55	8.45	7.85	7.46	7.19	6.99	6.84	6.72	6.62	6.47	6.36	6.28	6.21	6.16
8	11.26	8.65	7.59	7.01	6.63	6.37	6.18	6.03	5.91	5.81	5.67	5.56	5.48	5.41	5.36
9	10.56	8.02	6.99	6.42	6.06	5.80	5.61	5.47	5.35	5.26	5.11	5.01	4.92	4.86	4.81
10	10.04	7.56	6.55	5.99	5.64	5.39	5.20	5.06	4.94	4.85	4.71	4.60	4.52	4.46	4.41
11	9.65	7.21	6.22	5.67	5.32	5.07	4.89	4.74	4.63	4.54	4.40	4.29	4.21	4.15	4.10
12	9.33	6.93	5.95	5.41	5.06	4.82	4.64	4.50	4.39	4.30	4.16	4.05	3.97	3.91	3.86
13	9.07	6.70	5.74	5.21	4.86	4.62	4.44	4.30	4.19	4.10	3.96	3.86	3.78	3.72	3.66
14	8.86	6.51	5.56	5.04	4.69	4.46	4.28	4.14	4.03	3.94	3.80	3.70	3.62	3.56	3.51
15	8.68	6.36	5.42	4.89	4.56	4.32	4.14	4.00	3.89	3.80	3.67	3.56	3.49	3.42	3.37
16	8.53	6.23	5.29	4.77	4.44	4.20	4.03	3.89	3.78	3.69	3.55	3.45	3.37	3.31	3.26
17	8.40	6.11	5.18	4.67	4.34	4.10	3.93	3.79	3.68	3.59	3.46	3.35	3.27	3.21	3.16
18	8.29	6.01	5.09	4.58	4.25	4.01	3.84	3.71	3.60	3.51	3.37	3.27	3.19	3.13	3.08
19	8.18	5.93	5.01	4.50	4.17	3.94	3.77	3.63	3.52	3.43	3.30	3.19	3.12	3.05	3.00
20	8.10	5.85	4.94	4.43	4.10	3.87	3.70	3.56	3.46	3.37	3.23	3.13	3.05	2.99	2.94
21	8.02	5.78	4.87	4.37	4.04	3.81	3.64	3.51	3.40	3.31	3.17	3.07	2.99	2.93	2.88
22	7.95	5.72	4.82	4.31	3.99	3.76	3.59	3.45	3.35	3.26	3.12	3.02	2.94	2.88	2.83
23	7.88	5.66	4.76	4.26	3.94	3.71	3.54	3.41	3.30	3.21	3.07	2.97	2.89	2.83	2.78
24	7.82	5.61	4.72	4.22	3.90	3.67	3.50	3.36	3.26	3.17	3.03	2.93	2.85	2.79	2.74
25	7.77	5.57	4.68	4.18	3.85	3.63	3.46	3.32	3.22	3.13	2.99	2.89	2.81	2.75	2.70
26	7.72	5.53	4.64	4.14	3.82	3.59	3.42	3.29	3.18	3.09	2.96	2.86	2.78	2.72	2.66
27	7.68	5.49	4.60	4.11	3.78	3.56	3.39	3.26	3.15	3.06	2.93	2.82	2.75	2.68	2.63
28	7.64	5.45	4.57	4.07	3.75	3.53	3.36	3.23	3.12	3.03	2.90	2.79	2.72	2.65	2.60
29	7.60	5.42	4.54	4.04	3.73	3.50	3.33	3.20	3.09	3.00	2.87	2.77	2.69	2.63	2.57
30	7.56	5.39	4.51	4.02	3.70	3.47	3.30	3.17	3.07	2.98	2.84	2.74	2.66	2.60	2.55
35	7.42	5.27	4.40	3.91	3.59	3.37	3.20	3.07	2.96	2.88	2.74	2.64	2.56	2.50	2.44
40	7.31	5.18	4.31	3.83	3.51	3.29	3.12	2.99	2.89	2.80	2.66	2.56	2.48	2.42	2.37

Contd...

v_2 \ v_1	1	2	3	4	5	6	7	8	9	10	12	14	16	18	20
50	7.17	5.06	4.20	3.72	3.41	3.19	3.02	2.89	2.78	2.70	2.56	2.46	2.38	2.32	2.27
60	7.08	4.98	4.13	3.65	3.34	3.12	2.95	2.82	2.72	2.63	2.50	2.39	2.31	2.25	2.20
70	7.01	4.92	4.07	3.60	3.29	3.07	2.91	2.78	2.67	2.59	2.45	2.35	2.27	2.20	2.15
80	6.96	4.88	4.04	3.56	3.26	3.04	2.87	2.74	2.64	2.55	2.42	2.31	2.23	2.17	2.12
90	6.93	4.85	4.01	3.53	3.23	3.01	2.84	2.72	2.61	2.52	2.39	2.29	2.21	2.14	2.09
100	6.90	4.82	3.98	3.51	3.21	2.99	2.82	2.69	2.59	2.50	2.37	2.27	2.19	2.12	2.07
120	6.85	4.79	3.95	3.48	3.17	2.96	2.79	2.66	2.56	2.47	2.34	2.23	2.15	2.09	2.03
150	6.81	4.75	3.91	3.45	3.14	2.92	2.76	2.63	2.53	2.44	2.31	2.20	2.12	2.06	2.00
200	6.76	4.71	3.88	3.41	3.11	2.89	2.73	2.60	2.50	2.41	2.27	2.17	2.09	2.03	1.97
250	6.74	4.69	3.86	3.40	3.09	2.87	2.71	2.58	2.48	2.39	2.26	2.15	2.07	2.01	1.95
300	6.72	4.68	3.85	3.38	3.08	2.86	2.70	2.57	2.47	2.38	2.24	2.14	2.06	1.99	1.94
400	6.70	4.66	3.83	3.37	3.06	2.85	2.68	2.56	2.45	2.37	2.23	2.13	2.05	1.98	1.92
500	6.69	4.65	3.82	3.36	3.05	2.84	2.68	2.55	2.44	2.36	2.22	2.12	2.04	1.97	1.92
600	6.68	4.64	3.81	3.35	3.05	2.83	2.67	2.54	2.44	2.35	2.21	2.11	2.03	1.96	1.91
750	6.67	4.63	3.81	3.34	3.04	2.83	2.66	2.53	2.43	2.34	2.21	2.11	2.02	1.96	1.90
1000	6.66	4.63	3.80	3.34	3.04	2.82	2.66	2.53	2.43	2.34	2.20	2.10	2.02	1.95	1.90

v_2 \ v_1	25	30	35	40	50	60	75	100	150	200
1	6239.83	6260.65	6275.57	6286.78	6302.52	6313.03	6323.56	6334.11	6344.68	6349.97
2	99.46	99.47	99.47	99.47	99.48	99.48	99.49	99.49	99.49	99.49
3	26.58	26.50	26.45	26.41	26.35	26.32	26.28	26.24	26.20	26.18
4	13.91	13.84	13.79	13.75	13.69	13.65	13.61	13.58	13.54	13.52
5	9.45	9.38	9.33	9.29	9.24	9.20	9.17	9.13	9.09	9.08
6	7.30	7.23	7.18	7.14	7.09	7.06	7.02	6.99	6.95	6.93
7	6.06	5.99	5.94	5.91	5.86	5.82	5.79	5.75	5.72	5.70
8	5.26	5.20	5.15	5.12	5.07	5.03	5.00	4.96	4.93	4.91
9	4.71	4.65	4.60	4.57	4.52	4.48	4.45	4.41	4.38	4.36
10	4.31	4.25	4.20	4.17	4.12	4.08	4.05	4.01	3.98	3.96
11	4.01	3.94	3.89	3.86	3.81	3.78	3.74	3.71	3.67	3.66
12	3.76	3.70	3.65	3.62	3.57	3.54	3.50	3.47	3.43	3.41
13	3.57	3.51	3.46	3.43	3.38	3.34	3.31	3.27	3.24	3.22
14	3.41	3.35	3.30	3.27	3.22	3.18	3.15	3.11	3.08	3.06
15	3.28	3.21	3.17	3.13	3.08	3.05	3.01	2.98	2.94	2.92

Contd...

v_1 / v_2	25	30	35	40	50	60	75	100	150	200
16	3.16	3.10	3.05	3.02	2.97	2.93	2.90	2.86	2.83	2.81
17	3.07	3.00	2.96	2.92	2.87	2.83	2.80	2.76	2.73	2.71
18	2.98	2.92	2.87	2.84	2.78	2.75	2.71	2.68	2.64	2.62
19	2.91	2.84	2.80	2.76	2.71	2.67	2.64	2.60	2.57	2.55
20	2.84	2.78	2.73	2.69	2.64	2.61	2.57	2.54	2.50	2.48
21	2.79	2.72	2.67	2.64	2.58	2.55	2.51	2.48	2.44	2.42
22	2.73	2.67	2.62	2.58	2.53	2.50	2.46	2.42	2.38	2.36
23	2.69	2.62	2.57	2.54	2.48	2.45	2.41	2.37	2.34	2.32
24	2.64	2.58	2.53	2.49	2.44	2.40	2.37	2.33	2.29	2.27
25	2.60	2.54	2.49	2.45	2.40	2.36	2.33	2.29	2.25	2.23
26	2.57	2.50	2.45	2.42	2.36	2.33	2.29	2.25	2.21	2.19
27	2.54	2.47	2.42	2.38	2.33	2.29	2.26	2.22	2.18	2.16
28	2.51	2.44	2.39	2.35	2.30	2.26	2.23	2.19	2.15	2.13
29	2.48	2.41	2.36	2.33	2.27	2.23	2.20	2.16	2.12	2.10
30	2.45	2.39	2.34	2.30	2.25	2.21	2.17	2.13	2.09	2.07
35	2.35	2.28	2.23	2.19	2.14	2.10	2.06	2.02	1.98	1.96
40	2.27	2.20	2.15	2.11	2.06	2.02	1.98	1.94	1.90	1.87
50	2.17	2.10	2.05	2.01	1.95	1.91	1.87	1.82	1.78	1.76
60	2.10	2.03	1.98	1.94	1.88	1.84	1.79	1.75	1.70	1.68
70	2.05	1.98	1.93	1.89	1.83	1.78	1.74	1.70	1.65	1.62
80	2.01	1.94	1.89	1.85	1.79	1.75	1.70	1.65	1.61	1.58
90	1.99	1.92	1.86	1.82	1.76	1.72	1.67	1.62	1.57	1.55
100	1.97	1.89	1.84	1.80	1.74	1.69	1.65	1.60	1.55	1.52
120	1.93	1.86	1.81	1.76	1.70	1.66	1.61	1.56	1.51	1.48
150	1.90	1.83	1.77	1.73	1.66	1.62	1.57	1.52	1.46	1.43
200	1.87	1.79	1.74	1.69	1.63	1.58	1.53	1.48	1.42	1.39
250	1.85	1.77	1.72	1.67	1.61	1.56	1.51	1.46	1.40	1.36
300	1.84	1.76	1.70	1.66	1.59	1.55	1.50	1.44	1.38	1.35
400	1.82	1.75	1.69	1.64	1.58	1.53	1.48	1.42	1.36	1.32
500	1.81	1.74	1.68	1.63	1.57	1.52	1.47	1.41	1.34	1.31
600	1.80	1.73	1.67	1.63	1.56	1.51	1.46	1.40	1.34	1.30
750	1.80	1.72	1.66	1.62	1.55	1.50	1.45	1.39	1.33	1.29
1000	1.79	1.72	1.66	1.61	1.54	1.50	1.44	1.38	1.32	1.28

TABLE 5: *F*-Distribution: Critical values of *F* (0.1% significance level)

ν_2 \\ ν_1	1	2	3	4	5	6	7	8	9	10	12	14	16	18	20
1	4.05e05	5.00e05	5.40e05	5.62e05	5.76e05	5.86e05	5.93e05	5.98e05	6.02e05	6.06e05	6.11e05	6.14e05	6.17e05	6.19e05	6.21e05
2	998.50	999.00	999.17	999.25	999.30	999.33	999.36	999.37	999.39	999.40	999.42	999.43	999.44	999.44	999.45
3	167.03	148.50	141.11	137.10	134.58	132.85	131.58	130.62	129.86	129.25	128.32	127.64	127.14	126.74	126.42
4	74.14	61.25	56.18	53.44	51.71	50.53	49.66	49.00	48.47	48.05	47.41	46.95	46.60	46.32	46.10
5	47.18	37.12	33.20	31.09	29.75	28.83	28.16	27.65	27.24	26.92	26.42	26.06	25.78	25.57	25.39
6	35.51	27.00	23.70	21.92	20.80	20.03	19.46	19.03	18.69	18.41	17.99	17.68	17.45	17.27	17.12
7	29.25	21.69	18.77	17.20	16.21	15.52	15.02	14.63	14.33	14.08	13.71	13.43	13.23	13.06	12.93
8	25.41	18.49	15.83	14.39	13.48	12.86	12.40	12.05	11.77	11.54	11.19	10.94	10.75	10.60	10.48
9	22.86	16.39	13.90	12.56	11.71	11.13	10.70	10.37	10.11	9.89	9.57	9.33	9.15	9.01	8.90
10	21.04	14.91	12.55	11.28	10.48	9.93	9.52	9.20	8.96	8.75	8.45	8.22	8.05	7.91	7.80
11	19.69	13.81	11.56	10.35	9.58	9.05	8.66	8.35	8.12	7.92	7.63	7.41	7.24	7.11	7.01
12	18.64	12.97	10.80	9.63	8.89	8.38	8.00	7.71	7.48	7.29	7.00	6.79	6.63	6.51	6.40
13	17.82	12.31	10.21	9.07	8.35	7.86	7.49	7.21	6.98	6.80	6.52	6.31	6.16	6.03	5.93
14	17.14	11.78	9.73	8.62	7.92	7.44	7.08	6.80	6.58	6.40	6.13	5.93	5.78	5.66	5.56
15	16.59	11.34	9.34	8.25	7.57	7.09	6.74	6.47	6.26	6.08	5.81	5.62	5.46	5.35	5.25
16	16.12	10.97	9.01	7.94	7.27	6.80	6.46	6.19	5.98	5.81	5.55	5.35	5.20	5.09	4.99
17	15.72	10.66	8.73	7.68	7.02	6.56	6.22	5.96	5.75	5.58	5.32	5.13	4.99	4.87	4.78
18	15.38	10.39	8.49	7.46	6.81	6.35	6.02	5.76	5.56	5.39	5.13	4.94	4.80	4.68	4.59
19	15.08	10.16	8.28	7.27	6.62	6.18	5.85	5.59	5.39	5.22	4.97	4.78	4.64	4.52	4.43
20	14.82	9.95	8.10	7.10	6.46	6.02	5.69	5.44	5.24	5.08	4.82	4.64	4.49	4.38	4.29
21	14.59	9.77	7.94	6.95	6.32	5.88	5.56	5.31	5.11	4.95	4.70	4.51	4.37	4.26	4.17
22	14.38	9.61	7.80	6.81	6.19	5.76	5.44	5.19	4.99	4.83	4.58	4.40	4.26	4.15	4.06
23	14.20	9.47	7.67	6.70	6.08	5.65	5.33	5.09	4.89	4.73	4.48	4.30	4.16	4.05	3.96
24	14.03	9.34	7.55	6.59	5.98	5.55	5.23	4.99	4.80	4.64	4.39	4.21	4.07	3.96	3.87
25	13.88	9.22	7.45	6.49	5.89	5.46	5.15	4.91	4.71	4.56	4.31	4.13	3.99	3.88	3.79
26	13.74	9.12	7.36	6.41	5.80	5.38	5.07	4.83	4.64	4.48	4.24	4.06	3.92	3.81	3.72
27	13.61	9.02	7.27	6.33	5.73	5.31	5.00	4.76	4.57	4.41	4.17	3.99	3.86	3.75	3.66
28	13.50	8.93	7.19	6.25	5.66	5.24	4.93	4.69	4.50	4.35	4.11	3.93	3.80	3.69	3.60
29	13.39	8.85	7.12	6.19	5.59	5.18	4.87	4.64	4.45	4.29	4.05	3.88	3.74	3.63	3.54
30	13.29	8.77	7.05	6.12	5.53	5.12	4.82	4.58	4.39	4.24	4.00	3.82	3.69	3.58	3.49
35	12.90	8.47	6.79	5.88	5.30	4.89	4.59	4.36	4.18	4.03	3.79	3.62	3.48	3.38	3.29
40	12.61	8.25	6.59	5.70	5.13	4.73	4.44	4.21	4.02	3.87	3.64	3.47	3.34	3.23	3.14

Contd...

ν_1 / ν_2	1	2	3	4	5	6	7	8	9	10	12	14	16	18	20
50	12.22	7.96	6.34	5.46	4.90	4.51	4.22	4.00	3.82	3.67	3.44	3.27	3.41	3.04	2.95
60	11.97	7.77	6.17	5.31	4.76	4.37	4.09	3.86	3.69	3.54	3.32	3.15	3.02	2.91	2.83
70	11.80	7.64	6.06	5.20	4.66	4.28	3.99	3.77	3.60	3.45	3.23	3.06	2.93	2.83	2.74
80	11.67	7.54	5.97	5.12	4.58	4.20	3.92	3.70	3.53	3.39	3.16	3.00	2.87	2.76	2.68
90	11.57	7.47	5.91	5.06	4.53	4.15	3.87	3.65	3.48	3.34	3.11	2.95	2.82	2.71	2.63
100	11.50	7.41	5.86	5.02	4.48	4.11	3.83	3.61	3.44	3.30	3.07	2.91	2.78	2.68	2.59
120	11.38	7.32	5.78	4.95	4.42	4.04	3.77	3.55	3.38	3.24	3.02	2.85	2.72	2.62	2.53
150	11.27	7.24	5.71	4.88	4.35	3.98	3.71	3.49	3.32	3.18	2.96	2.80	2.67	2.56	2.48
200	11.15	7.15	5.63	4.81	4.29	3.92	3.65	3.43	3.26	3.12	2.90	2.74	2.61	2.51	2.42
250	11.09	7.10	5.59	4.77	4.25	3.88	3.61	3.40	3.23	3.09	2.87	2.71	2.58	2.48	2.39
300	11.04	7.07	5.56	4.75	4.22	3.86	3.59	3.38	3.21	3.07	2.85	2.69	2.56	2.46	2.37
400	10.99	7.03	5.53	4.71	4.19	3.83	3.56	3.35	3.18	3.04	2.82	2.66	2.53	2.43	2.34
500	10.96	7.00	5.51	4.69	4.18	3.81	3.54	3.33	3.16	3.02	2.81	2.64	2.52	2.41	2.33
600	10.94	6.99	5.49	4.68	4.16	3.80	3.53	3.32	3.15	3.01	2.80	2.63	2.51	2.40	2.32
750	10.91	6.97	5.48	4.67	4.15	3.79	3.52	3.31	3.14	3.00	2.78	2.62	2.49	2.39	2.31
1000	10.89	6.96	5.46	4.65	4.14	3.78	3.51	3.30	3.13	2.99	2.77	2.61	2.48	2.38	2.30

ν_1 / ν_2	25	30	35	40	50	60	75	100	150	200
1	6.24e05	6.26e05	6.28e05	6.29e05	6.30e05	6.31e05	6.32e05	6.33e05	6.35e0	6.35e05
2	999.46	999.47	999.47	999.47	999.48	999.48	999.49	999.49	999.49	999.49
3	125.84	125.45	125.17	124.96	124.66	124.47	124.27	124.07	123.87	123.77
4	45.70	45.43	45.23	45.09	44.88	44.75	44.61	44.47	44.33	44.26
5	25.08	24.87	24.72	24.60	24.44	24.33	24.22	24.12	24.01	23.95
6	16.85	16.67	16.54	16.44	16.31	16.21	16.12	16.03	15.93	15.89
7	12.69	12.53	12.41	12.33	12.20	12.12	12.04	11.95	11.87	11.82
8	10.26	10.11	10.00	9.92	9.80	9.73	9.65	9.57	9.49	9.45
9	8.69	8.55	8.46	8.37	8.26	8.19	8.11	8.04	7.96	7.93
10	7.60	7.47	7.37	7.30	7.19	7.12	7.05	6.98	6.91	6.87
11	6.81	6.68	6.59	6.52	6.42	6.35	6.28	6.21	6.14	6.10
12	6.22	6.09	6.00	5.93	5.83	5.76	5.70	5.63	5.56	5.52
13	5.75	5.63	5.54	5.47	5.37	5.30	5.24	5.17	5.10	5.07
14	5.38	5.25	5.17	5.10	5.00	4.94	4.87	4.81	4.74	4.71
15	5.07	4.95	4.86	4.80	4.70	4.64	4.57	4.51	4.44	4.41

Contd...

v_2 \ v_1	25	30	35	40	50	60	75	100	150	200
16	4.82	4.70	4.61	4.54	4.45	4.39	4.32	4.26	4.19	4.16
17	4.60	4.48	4.40	4.33	4.24	4.18	4.11	4.05	3.98	3.95
18	4.42	4.30	4.22	4.15	4.06	4.00	3.93	3.87	3.80	3.77
19	4.26	4.14	4.06	3.99	3.90	3.84	3.78	3.71	3.65	3.61
20	4.12	4.00	3.92	3.86	3.77	3.70	3.64	3.58	3.51	3.48
21	4.00	3.88	3.80	3.74	3.64	3.58	3.52	3.46	3.39	3.36
22	3.89	3.78	3.70	3.63	3.54	3.48	3.41	3.35	3.28	3.25
23	3.79	3.68	3.60	3.53	3.44	3.38	3.32	3.25	3.19	3.16
24	3.71	3.59	3.51	3.45	3.36	3.29	3.23	3.17	3.10	3.07
25	3.63	3.52	3.43	3.37	3.28	3.22	3.15	3.09	3.03	2.99
26	3.56	3.44	3.36	3.30	3.21	3.15	3.08	3.02	2.95	2.92
27	3.49	3.38	3.30	3.23	3.14	3.08	3.02	2.96	2.89	2.86
28	3.43	3.32	3.24	3.18	3.09	3.02	2.96	2.90	2.83	2.80
29	3.38	3.27	3.18	3.12	3.03	2.97	2.91	2.84	2.78	2.74
30	3.33	3.22	3.13	3.07	2.98	2.92	2.86	2.79	2.73	2.69
35	3.13	3.02	2.93	2.87	2.78	2.72	2.66	2.59	2.52	2.49
40	2.98	2.87	2.79	2.73	2.64	2.57	2.51	2.44	2.38	2.34
50	2.79	2.68	2.60	2.53	2.44	2.38	2.31	2.25	2.18	2.14
60	2.67	2.55	2.47	2.41	2.32	2.25	2.19	2.12	2.05	2.01
70	2.58	2.47	2.39	2.32	2.23	2.16	2.10	2.03	1.95	1.92
80	2.52	2.41	2.32	2.26	2.16	2.10	2.03	1.96	1.89	1.85
90	2.47	2.36	2.27	2.21	2.11	2.05	1.98	1.91	1.83	1.79
100	2.43	2.32	2.24	2.17	2.08	2.01	1.94	1.87	1.79	1.75
120	2.37	2.26	2.18	2.11	2.02	1.95	1.88	1.81	1.73	1.68
150	2.32	2.21	2.12	2.06	1.96	1.89	1.82	1.74	1.66	1.62
200	2.26	2.15	2.07	2.00	1.90	1.83	1.76	1.68	1.60	1.55
250	2.23	2.12	2.03	1.97	1.87	1.80	1.72	1.65	1.56	1.51
300	2.21	2.10	2.01	1.94	1.85	1.78	1.70	1.62	1.53	1.48
400	2.18	2.07	1.98	1.92	1.82	1.75	1.67	1.59	1.50	1.45
500	2.17	2.05	1.97	1.90	1.80	1.73	1.65	1.57	1.48	1.43
600	2.16	2.04	1.96	1.89	1.79	1.72	1.64	1.56	1.46	1.41
750	2.15	2.03	1.95	1.88	1.78	1.71	1.63	1.55	1.45	1.40
1000	2.14	2.02	1.94	1.87	1.77	1.69	1.62	1.53	1.44	1.38

TABLE 6: Critical Values of the Mann-Whitney U (Two-Tailed Testing)

n_2	α	\multicolumn{18}{c}{n_1}
---	---	3	4	5	6	7	8	9	10	11	12	13	14	15	16	17	18	19	20
3	.05	--	0	0	1	1	2	2	3	3	4	4	5	5	6	6	7	7	8
	.01	--	0	0	0	0	0	0	0	0	1	1	1	2	2	2	2	3	3
4	.05	--	0	1	2	3	4	4	5	6	7	8	9	10	11	11	12	13	14
	.01	--	--	0	0	0	1	1	2	2	3	3	4	5	5	6	6	7	8
5	.05	0	1	2	3	5	6	7	8	9	11	12	13	14	15	17	18	19	20
	.01	--	--	0	1	1	2	3	4	5	6	7	7	8	9	10	11	12	13
6	.05	1	2	3	5	6	8	10	11	13	14	16	17	19	21	22	24	25	27
	.01	--	0	1	2	3	4	5	6	7	9	10	11	12	13	15	16	17	18
7	.05	1	3	5	6	8	10	12	14	16	18	20	22	24	26	28	30	32	34
	.01	--	0	1	3	4	6	7	9	10	12	13	15	16	18	19	21	22	24
8	.05	2	4	6	8	10	13	15	17	19	22	24	26	29	31	34	36	38	41
	.01	--	1	2	4	6	7	9	11	13	15	17	18	20	22	24	26	28	30
9	.05	2	4	7	10	12	15	17	20	23	26	28	31	34	37	39	42	45	48
	.01	0	1	3	5	7	9	11	13	16	18	20	22	24	27	29	31	33	36
10	.05	3	5	8	11	14	17	20	23	26	29	33	36	39	42	45	48	52	55
	.01	0	2	4	6	9	11	13	16	18	21	24	26	29	31	34	37	39	42
11	.05	3	6	9	13	16	19	23	26	30	33	37	40	44	47	51	55	58	62
	.01	0	2	5	7	10	13	16	18	21	24	27	30	33	36	39	42	45	48
12	.05	4	7	11	14	18	22	26	29	33	37	41	45	49	53	57	61	65	69
	.01	1	3	6	9	12	15	18	21	24	27	31	34	37	41	44	47	51	54
13	.05	4	8	12	16	20	24	28	33	37	41	45	50	54	59	63	67	72	76
	.01	1	3	7	10	13	17	20	24	27	31	34	38	42	45	49	53	56	60
14	.05	5	9	13	17	22	26	31	36	40	45	50	55	59	64	67	74	78	83
	.01	1	4	7	11	15	18	22	26	30	34	38	42	46	50	54	58	63	67
15	.05	5	10	14	19	24	29	34	39	44	49	54	59	64	70	75	80	85	90
	.01	2	5	8	12	16	20	24	29	33	37	42	46	51	55	60	64	69	73
16	.05	6	11	15	21	26	31	37	42	47	53	59	64	70	75	81	86	92	98
	.01	2	5	9	13	18	22	27	31	36	41	45	50	55	60	65	70	74	79
17	.05	6	11	17	22	28	34	39	45	51	57	63	67	75	81	87	93	99	105
	.01	2	6	10	15	19	24	29	34	39	44	49	54	60	65	70	75	81	86
18	.05	7	12	18	24	30	36	42	48	55	61	67	74	80	86	93	99	106	112
	.01	2	6	11	16	21	26	31	37	42	47	53	58	64	70	75	81	87	92
19	.05	7	13	19	25	32	38	45	52	58	65	72	78	85	92	99	106	113	119
	.01	3	7	12	17	22	28	33	39	45	51	56	63	69	74	81	87	93	99
20	.05	8	14	20	27	34	41	48	55	62	69	76	83	90	98	105	112	119	127
	.01	3	8	13	18	24	30	36	42	48	54	60	67	73	79	86	92	99	105

TABLE 7: Critical Values of the Mann-Whitney U (One-Tailed Testing)

n_2	α	n_1																	
		3	4	5	6	7	8	9	10	11	12	13	14	15	16	17	18	19	20
3	.05	0	0	1	2	2	3	4	4	5	5	6	7	7	8	9	9	10	11
	.01	--	0	0	0	0	0	1	1	1	2	2	2	3	3	4	4	4	5
4	.05	0	1	2	3	4	5	6	7	8	9	10	11	12	14	15	16	17	18
	.01	--	--	0	1	1	2	3	3	4	5	5	6	7	7	8	9	9	10
5	.05	1	2	4	5	5	8	9	11	12	13	15	16	18	19	20	22	23	25
	.01	--	0	1	2	2	4	5	6	7	8	9	10	11	12	13	14	15	16
6	.05	2	3	5	7	8	10	12	14	16	17	19	21	23	25	26	28	30	32
	.01	--	1	2	3	4	6	7	8	9	11	12	13	15	16	18	19	20	22
7	.05	2	4	6	8	11	13	15	17	19	21	24	26	28	30	33	35	37	39
	.01	0	1	3	4	6	7	9	11	12	14	16	17	19	21	23	24	26	28
8	.05	3	5	8	10	13	15	18	20	23	26	28	31	33	36	39	41	44	47
	.01	0	2	4	6	7	9	11	13	15	17	20	22	24	26	28	30	32	34
9	.05	4	6	9	12	15	18	21	24	27	30	33	36	39	42	45	48	51	54
	.01	1	3	5	7	9	11	14	16	18	21	23	26	28	31	33	36	38	40
10	.05	4	7	11	14	17	20	24	27	31	34	37	41	44	48	51	55	58	62
	.01	1	3	6	8	11	13	16	19	22	24	27	30	33	36	38	41	44	47
11	.05	5	8	12	16	19	23	27	31	34	38	42	46	50	54	57	61	65	69
	.01	1	4	7	9	12	15	18	22	25	28	31	34	37	41	44	47	50	53
12	.05	5	9	13	17	21	26	30	34	38	42	47	51	55	60	64	68	72	77
	.01	2	5	8	11	14	17	21	24	28	31	35	38	42	46	49	53	56	60
13	.05	6	10	15	19	24	28	33	37	42	47	51	56	61	65	70	75	80	84
	.01	2	5	9	12	16	20	23	27	31	35	39	43	47	51	55	59	63	67
14	.05	7	11	16	21	26	31	36	41	46	51	56	61	66	71	77	82	87	92
	.01	2	6	10	13	17	22	26	30	34	38	43	47	51	56	60	65	69	73
15	.05	7	12	18	23	28	33	39	44	50	55	61	66	72	77	83	88	94	100
	.01	3	7	11	15	19	24	28	33	37	42	47	51	56	61	66	70	75	80
16	.05	8	14	19	25	30	36	42	48	54	60	65	71	77	83	89	95	101	107
	.01	3	7	12	16	21	26	31	36	41	46	51	56	61	66	71	76	82	87
17	.05	9	15	20	26	33	39	45	51	57	64	70	77	83	89	96	102	109	115
	.01	4	8	13	18	23	28	33	38	44	49	55	60	66	71	77	82	88	93
18	.05	9	16	22	28	35	41	48	55	61	68	75	82	88	95	102	109	116	123
	.01	4	9	14	19	24	30	36	41	47	53	59	65	70	76	82	88	94	100
19	.05	10	17	23	30	37	44	51	58	65	72	80	87	94	101	109	116	123	130
	.01	4	9	15	20	26	32	38	44	50	56	63	69	75	82	88	94	101	107
20	.05	11	18	25	32	39	47	54	62	69	77	84	92	100	107	115	123	130	138
	.01	5	10	16	22	28	34	40	47	53	60	67	73	80	87	93	100	107	114

TABLE 8: Critical Values of the Wilcoxon Signed-Rank Test

n	Two-Tailed Test		One-Tailed Test	
	$\alpha = .05$	$\alpha = .01$	$\alpha = .05$	$\alpha = .01$
5	--	--	0	--
6	0	--	2	--
7	2	--	3	0
8	3	0	5	1
9	5	1	8	3
10	8	3	10	5
11	10	5	13	7
12	13	7	17	9
13	17	9	21	12
14	21	12	25	15
15	25	15	30	19
16	29	19	35	23
17	34	23	41	27
18	40	27	47	32
19	46	32	53	37
20	52	37	60	43
21	58	42	67	49
22	65	48	75	55
23	73	54	83	62
24	81	61	91	69
25	89	68	100	76
26	98	75	110	84
27	107	83	119	92
28	116	91	130	101
29	126	100	140	110
30	137	109	151	120

TABLE 9: Chi-square distribution table

d.f.	.995	.99	.975	.95	.9	.1	.05	.025	.01
1	0.00	0.00	0.00	0.00	0.02	2.71	3.84	5.02	6.63
2	0.01	0.02	0.05	0.10	0.21	4.61	5.99	7.38	9.21
3	0.07	0.11	0.22	0.35	0.58	6.25	7.81	9.35	11.34
4	0.21	0.30	0.48	0.71	1.06	7.78	9.49	11.14	13.28
5	0.41	0.55	0.83	1.15	1.61	9.24	11.07	12.83	15.09
6	0.68	0.87	1.24	1.64	2.20	10.64	12.59	14.45	16.81

Contd...

d.f.	.995	.99	.975	.95	.9	.1	.05	.025	.01
7	0.99	1.24	1.69	2.17	2.83	12.02	14.07	16.01	18.48
8	1.34	1.65	2.18	2.73	3.49	13.36	15.51	17.53	20.09
9	1.73	2.09	2.70	3.33	4.17	14.68	16.92	19.02	21.67
10	2.16	2.56	3.25	3.94	4.87	15.99	18.31	20.48	23.21
11	2.60	3.05	3.82	4.57	5.58	17.28	19.68	21.92	24.72
12	3.07	3.57	4.40	5.23	6.30	18.55	21.03	23.34	26.22
13	3.57	4.11	5.01	5.89	7.04	19.81	22.36	24.74	27.69
14	4.07	4.66	5.63	6.57	7.79	21.06	23.68	26.12	29.14
15	4.60	5.23	6.26	7.26	8.55	22.31	25.00	27.49	30.58
16	5.14	5.81	6.91	7.96	9.31	23.54	26.30	28.85	32.00
17	5.70	6.41	7.56	8.67	10.09	24.77	27.59	30.19	33.41
18	6.26	7.01	8.23	9.39	10.86	25.99	28.87	31.53	34.81
19	6.84	7.63	8.91	10.12	11.65	27.20	30.14	32.85	36.19
20	7.43	8.26	9.59	10.85	12.44	28.41	31.41	34.17	37.57
22	8.64	9.54	10.98	12.34	14.04	30.81	33.92	36.78	40.29
24	9.89	10.86	12.40	13.85	15.66	33.20	36.42	39.36	42.98
26	11.16	12.20	13.84	15.38	17.29	35.56	38.89	41.92	45.64
28	12.46	13.56	15.31	16.93	18.94	37.92	41.34	44.46	48.28
30	13.79	14.95	16.79	18.49	20.60	40.26	43.77	46.98	50.89
32	15.13	16.36	18.29	20.07	22.27	42.58	46.19	49.48	53.49
34	16.50	17.79	19.81	21.66	23.95	44.90	48.60	51.97	56.06
38	19.29	20.69	22.88	24.88	27.34	49.51	53.38	56.90	61.16
42	22.14	23.65	26.00	28.14	30.77	54.09	58.12	61.78	66.21
46	25.04	26.66	29.16	31.44	34.22	58.64	62.83	66.62	71.20
50	27.99	29.71	32.36	34.76	37.69	63.17	67.50	71.42	76.15
55	31.73	33.57	36.40	38.96	42.06	68.80	73.31	77.38	82.29
60	35.53	37.48	40.48	43.19	46.46	74.40	79.08	83.30	88.38
65	39.38	41.44	44.60	47.45	50.88	79.97	84.82	89.18	94.42
70	43.28	45.44	48.76	51.74	55.33	85.53	90.53	95.02	100.43
75	47.21	49.48	52.94	56.05	59.79	91.06	96.22	100.84	106.39
80	51.17	53.54	57.15	60.39	64.28	96.58	101.88	106.63	112.33
85	55.17	57.63	61.39	64.75	68.78	102.08	107.52	112.39	118.24
90	59.20	61.75	65.65	69.13	73.29	107.57	113.15	118.14	124.12
95	63.25	65.90	69.92	73.52	77.82	113.04	118.75	123.86	129.97
100	67.33	70.06	74.22	77.93	82.36	118.50	124.34	129.56	135.81

These tables concern tests of the hypothesis that a population correlation coefficient (ρ) is 0. The values in the tables are the minimum values which need to be reached by a sample correlation coefficient in order to be significant at the level shown, on a one-tailed test.

TABLE 10: Critical values for correlation coefficients

Product moment coefficient					
Level					**Sample size, n**
0.10	**0.05**	**0.025**	**0.01**	**0.005**	
0.8000	0.9000	0.9500	0.9800	0.9900	4
0.6870	0.8054	0.8783	0.9343	0.9587	5
0.6084	0.7293	0.8114	0.8822	0.9172	6
0.5509	0.6694	0.7545	0.8329	0.8745	7
0.5067	0.6215	0.7067	0.7887	0.8343	8
0.4716	0.5822	0.6664	0.7498	0.7977	9
0.4428	0.5494	0.6319	0.7155	0.7646	10
0.4187	0.5214	0.6021	0.6851	0.7348	11
0.3981	0.4973	0.5760	0.6581	0.7079	12
0.3802	0.4762	0.5529	0.6339	0.6835	13
0.3646	0.4575	0.5324	0.6120	0.6614	14
0.3507	0.4409	0.5140	0.5923	0.6411	15
0.3383	0.4259	0.4973	0.5742	0.6226	16
0.3271	0.4124	0.4821	0.5577	0.6055	17
0.3170	0.4000	0.4683	0.5425	0.5897	18
0.3077	0.3887	0.4555	0.5285	0.5751	19
0.2992	0.3783	0.4438	0.5155	0.5614	20
0.2914	0.3687	0.4329	0.5034	0.5487	21
0.2841	0.3598	0.4227	0.4921	0.5368	22
0.2774	0.3515	0.4133	0.4815	0.5256	23
0.2711	0.3438	0.4044	0.4716	0.5151	24
0.2653	0.3365	0.3961	0.4622	0.5052	25
0.2598	0.3297	0.3882	0.4534	0.4958	26
0.2546	0.3233	0.3809	0.4451	0.4869	27
0.2497	0.3172	0.3739	0.4372	0.4785	28
0.2451	0.3115	0.3673	0.4297	0.4705	29
0.2407	0.3061	0.3610	0.4226	0.4629	30
0.2070	0.2638	0.3120	0.3665	0.4026	40
0.1843	0.2353	0.2787	0.3281	0.3610	50
0.1678	0.2144	0.2542	0.2997	0.3301	60
0.1550	0.1982	0.2352	0.2776	0.3060	70
0.1448	0.1852	0.2199	0.2597	0.2864	80
0.1364	0.1745	0.2072	0.2449	0.2702	90
0.1292	0.1654	0.1966	0.2324	0.2565	100

TABLE 11: Spearman correlation coefficient table

n	a				
	0.10	0.05	0.025	0.01	0.005
5	0.800	0.900	1.000	1.000	–
6	0.657	0.829	0.886	0.943	1.000
7	0.571	0.714	0.786	0.893	0.929
8	0.524	0.643	0.738	0.833	0.881
9	0.483	0.600	0.700	0.783	0.833
10	0.455	0.564	0.648	0.745	0.794
11	0.427	0.536	0.618	0.709	0.755
12	0.406	0.503	0.587	0.678	0.727
13	0.385	0.484	0.560	0.648	0.703
14	0.367	0.464	0.538	0.626	0.679
15	0.354	0.446	0.521	0.604	0.654
16	0.341	0.429	0.503	0.582	0.635
17	0.328	0.414	0.488	0.566	0.618
18	0.317	0.401	0.472	0.550	0.600
19	0.309	0.391	0.460	0.535	0.584
20	0.299	0.380	0.447	0.522	0.570
21	0.292	0.370	0.436	0.509	0.556
22	0.284	0.361	0.425	0.497	0.544
23	0.278	0.353	0.416	0.486	0.532
24	0.271	0.344	0.407	0.476	0.521
25	0.265	0.337	0.398	0.466	0.511
26	0.259	0.331	0.390	0.457	0.501
27	0.255	0.324	0.383	0.449	0.492
28	0.250	0.318	0.375	0.441	0.483
29	0.245	0.321	0.368	0.433	0.475
30	0.240	0.306	0.362	0.425	0.467

INDEX

Refer 'f' for figure and 't' for table respectively.

Note